The Java® Tutorial

Fifth Edition

The Java® Tutorial

A Short Course on the Basics

Fifth Edition

Sharon Biocca Zakhour
Sowmya Kannan
Raymond Gallardo

Addison-Wesley

Upper Saddle River, NJ • Boston • Indianapolis • San Francisco
New York • Toronto • Montreal • London • Munich • Paris • Madrid
Capetown • Sydney • Tokyo • Singapore • Mexico City

The publisher offers excellent discounts on this book when ordered in quantity for bulk purchases or special sales, which may include electronic versions and/or custom covers and content particular to your business, training goals, marketing focus, and branding interests. For more information, please contact

> U.S. Corporate and Government Sales
> (800) 382-3419
> corpsales@pearsontechgroup.com

For sales outside the United States, please contact:

> International Sales
> international@pearson.com

Visit us on the Web: informit.com/aw

Cataloging-in-Publication Data is on file with the Library of Congress.

ISBN-13: 978-0-13-276169-7
ISBN-10: 0-13-276169-6

Text printed in the United States on recycled paper at Edwards Brothers Malloy in Ann Arbor, Michigan
First printing, March 2013

Contents

Preface

Since the acquisition of Sun Microsystems by Oracle Corporation in early 2010, it has been an exciting time for the Java language. As evidenced by the activities of the Java Community Process program, the Java language continues to evolve. The publication of this fifth edition of *The Java® Tutorial* reflects release 7 of the Java Platform Standard Edition (Java SE) and references the Application Programming Interface (API) of that release.

This edition introduces new features added to the platform since the publication of the fourth edition (under release 6), such as a section on NIO.2, the new file I/O API, and information on migrating legacy code to the new API. The deployment coverage has been expanded with new chapters on "Doing More with Java Rich Internet Applications" (Chapter 18) and "Deployment in Depth" (Chapter 19). A section on the Fork/Join feature has been added to the "Concurrency" chapter (Chapter 12). Information reflecting Project Coin developments has been added where appropriate, including the new try-with-resources statement, the ability to catch more than one type of exception with a single exception handler, support for binary literals, and diamond syntax, which results in cleaner generics code.

In addition to coverage of new features, previous chapters have been rewritten to include new information. For example, "Generics" (Chapter 6), "Java Web Start" (Chapter 16), and "Applets" (Chapter 17) have been updated. The appendix for the Java Certification exam has also been completely replaced.

If you plan to take one of the Java SE 7 certification exams, this book can help. The appendix, "Preparing for Java Programming Language Certification," lists the three exams that are available, detailing the items covered on each exam, cross-referenced to places in the book where you can find more information about each topic. Note that this is one source, among others, that you will want to use to prepare for your exam.

All the material has been thoroughly reviewed by members of Oracle Java engineering to ensure that the information is accurate and up to date. This book is based on the online tutorial hosted on Oracle's web site at the following URL:

```
http://docs.oracle.com/javase/tutorial
```

The information in this book, often referred to as "the core tutorial," is essential for most beginning to intermediate programmers. Once you have mastered this material, you can explore the rest of the Java platform documentation on the web site. If you are interested in developing sophisticated Rich Internet Applications (RIAs), check out JavaFX, the new cutting-edge Java graphical user interface (GUI) toolkit. As of the release of Java SE 7 update 5, you automatically get the JavaFX Software Development Kit (SDK) when you download the JDK. To learn more, see the JavaFX documentation at the following URL:

```
http://docs.oracle.com/javafx
```

As always, our goal is to create an easy-to-read, practical programmers' guide to help you learn how to use the rich environment provided by Java to build applications, applets, and components. Go forth and program!

Who Should Read This Book?

This book is geared toward both novice and experienced programmers.

- *New programmers* can benefit most from reading the book from beginning to end, including the step-by-step instructions for compiling and running your first program in Chapter 1, "Getting Started."
- *Programmers experienced with procedural languages* such as C may want to start with the material on object-oriented concepts and features of the Java programming language.
- *Experienced programmers* may want to jump feet first into the more advanced topics, such as generics, concurrency, or deployment.

This book contains information to address the learning needs of programmers with various levels of experience.

How to Use This Book

This book is designed so you can read it straight through or skip around from topic to topic. The information is presented in a logical order, and forward references are avoided wherever possible.

The examples in this tutorial are compiled against the JDK 7 release. *You need to download this release (or later) in order to compile and run most examples.*

Some material referenced in this book is available online (e.g., the downloadable examples, the solutions to the questions and exercises, the JDK 7 guides, and the API specification). You will see footnotes like the following:

    7/docs/api/java/lang/Class.html

and

    tutorial/java/generics/examples/BoxDemo.java

The Java Tutorials are also available in two e-book formats:

- mobi e-book files for Kindle
- ePub e-book files for iPad, Nook, and other devices that support the ePub format

Each e-book contains a single trail, which is equivalent to several related chapters in this book. You can download the e-books via the link "In Book Form" on the home page for the Java Tutorials:

    http://docs.oracle.com/javase/tutorial/index.html

We welcome feedback on this edition. To contact us, please see the tutorial feedback page:

    http://docs.oracle.com/javase/feedback.html

This book would not be what it is without the Oracle Java engineering team who tirelessly reviews the technical content of our writing. For this edition of the book, we especially want to thank Alan Bateman, Alex Buckley, Calvin Cheung, Maurizio Cimadamore, Joe Darcy, Andy Herrick, Stuart Marks, Igor Nekrestyanov, Thomas Ng, Nam Nguyen, and Daniel Smith.

Illustrators Jordan Douglas and Dawn Tyler created our professional graphics, quickly and efficiently. Devika Gollapudi provided invaluable assistance by capturing our screenshots for publication.

Editors Deborah Owens and Susan Shepard provided careful and thorough copy edits of our JDK 7 work.

Thanks for the support of our team: Bhavesh Patel, Devika Gollapudi, and Santhosh La.

Last but not least, thanks for the support of our management: Alan Sommerer, who saw us through the acquisition and beyond; Barbara Ramsey; Sophia Mikulinsky; and Sowmya Kannan, recently elevated as manager of our team.

About the Authors

Sharon Biocca Zakhour is a principal technical writer on staff at Oracle Corporation and was formerly at Sun Microsystems. She has contributed to Java SE platform documentation for more than twelve years, including *The Java™ Tutorial, Fourth Edition* (Addison-Wesley, 2007), and *The JFC Swing Tutorial, Second Edition* (Addison-Wesley, 2004). She graduated from the University of California, Berkeley, with a B.A. in computer science and has worked as a programmer, developer support engineer, and technical writer for thirty years.

Sowmya Kannan was previously a principal technical writer at Oracle Corporation and Sun Microsystems. She is currently the manager of the Java SE documentation team and has more than fifteen years of experience in the design, development, and documentation of the Java platform, Java-based middleware, and web applications.

Raymond Gallardo is a technical writer for Oracle Corporation. His previous engagements include college instructor, technical writer for IBM, and bicycle courier. He obtained his B.Sc. in computer science and English from the University of Toronto and his M.A. in creative writing from the City College of New York.

1

Getting Started

Chapter Contents

This chapter provides everything you'll need to know about getting started with the Java programming language. The first section provides an overview of Java technology as a whole. It discusses both the Java programming language and platform, providing a broad overview of what this technology can do and how it will make your life easier. The second section provides information on the "Hello World!" application. This hands-on approach describes what to download, install, and type while creating a simple "Hello World!" application. It provides separate instructions for the NetBeans integrated development environment (NetBeans IDE), Microsoft Windows, Solaris, and Linux. The third section discusses the "Hello World!" application, describing each section of code in detail. It covers source code comments, the `HelloWorldApp` class definition block, and the `main` method. The fourth section presents common problems and solutions. This is the section to read if you have trouble compiling or running the programs presented in this chapter. The chapter ends with questions and exercises to test your understanding.

The Java Technology Phenomenon

Talk about Java technology seems to be everywhere, but what exactly is it? This section explains how Java technology is both a programming language and a platform and provides an overview of what this technology can do for you.

1

The Java Programming Language

The Java programming language is a high-level language that can be characterized by all of the following buzzwords:

- Simple
- Object oriented
- Distributed
- Multithreaded
- Dynamic
- Architecture neutral
- Portable
- High performance
- Robust
- Secure

Each of the preceding buzzwords is explained in *The Java Language Environment*, a white paper written by James Gosling and Henry McGilton.[1]

In the Java programming language, all source code is first written in plain text files ending with the `.java` extension. These source files are then compiled into `.class` files by the `javac` compiler. A `.class` file does not contain code that is native to your processor; it instead contains *bytecodes*—the machine language of the Java Virtual Machine (Java VM).[2] The `java` launcher tool then runs your application with an instance of the Java Virtual Machine.

Because the Java Virtual Machine is available on many different operating systems, the same `.class` files are capable of running on Microsoft Windows, Solaris, Linux, or Mac OS X. Some virtual machines, such as the Java HotSpot Virtual Machine, perform additional steps at runtime to give your application a performance boost.[3] This includes various tasks such as finding performance bottlenecks and recompiling (to native code) frequently used sections of code.

The Java Platform

A *platform* is the hardware or software environment in which a program runs. We've already mentioned some of the most popular platforms, like Microsoft Windows, Linux,

---

1. `http://www.oracle.com/technetwork/java/langenv-140151.html`
2. The terms *Java Virtual Machine* and *Java VM* indicate a Virtual Machine for the Java platform.
3. `http://www.oracle.com/technetwork/java/javase/tech/index-jsp-136373.html`

Solaris, and Mac. Most platforms can be described as a combination of the operating system and underlying hardware. The Java platform differs from most other platforms in that it's a software-only platform that runs on top of other hardware-based platforms.

The Java platform has two components:

- The Java Virtual Machine
- The Java Application Programming Interface (API)

You've already been introduced to the Java Virtual Machine; it's the basis for the Java platform and is ported onto various hardware-based platforms.

Figure 1.1 An Overview of the Software Development Process

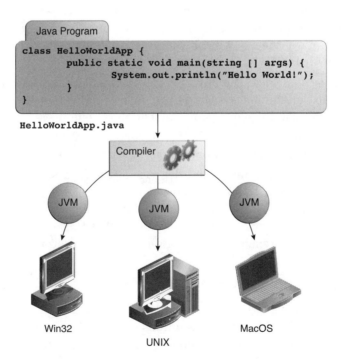

Figure 1.2 Through the Java Virtual Machine,
the Same Application Is Capable of Running on Multiple Platforms

1

The API is a large collection of ready-made software components that provide many useful capabilities. It is grouped into libraries of related classes and interfaces; these libraries are known as *packages*. The next section, "What Can Java Technology Do?," highlights some of the functionality provided by the API. As a platform-independent environment, the Java platform can be a bit slower than native code. However, advances in compiler and virtual machine technologies are bringing performance close to that of native code without threatening portability.

What Can Java Technology Do?

The general-purpose, high-level Java programming language is a powerful software platform. Every full implementation of the Java platform gives you the following features:

- *Development tools.* The development tools provide everything you'll need for compiling, running, monitoring, debugging, and documenting your applications. As a new developer, the main tools you'll be using are the `javac` compiler, the `java` launcher, and the `javadoc` documentation tool.
- *API.* The API provides the core functionality of the Java programming language. It offers a wide array of useful classes ready for use in your own applications. It spans everything from basic objects, to networking and security, to XML generation and database access, and more. The core API is very large; to get an overview of what it contains, consult the Java Platform Standard Edition (Java SE) 7 Documentation.[4]
- *Deployment technologies.* The Java SE Development Kit (JDK) software provides standard mechanisms such as the Java Web Start software and Java Plug-In software for deploying your applications to end users.
- *User interface toolkits.* The JavaFX, Swing, and Java 2D toolkits make it possible to create sophisticated graphical user interfaces (GUIs).
- *Integration libraries.* Integration libraries such as the Java Interactive Data Language (IDL) API, Java Database Connectivity (JDBC) API, Java Naming and Directory Interface (JNDI) API, Java Remote Method Invocation (RMI), and Java Remote Method Invocation over Internet Inter-ORB Protocol Technology (Java RMI-IIOP Technology) enable database access and manipulation of remote objects.

How Will Java Technology Change My Life?

We can't promise you fame, fortune, or even a job if you learn the Java programming language. Still, it is likely to make your programs better and requires less effort than other languages. We believe that Java technology will help you do the following:

---

4. `7/docs/index.html`

Figure 1.3 The API and Java Virtual Machine Insulate the Program
from the Underlying Hardware

- *Get started quickly.* Although the Java programming language is a powerful object-oriented language, it's easy to learn, especially for programmers already familiar with C or C++.
- *Write less code.* Comparisons of program metrics (class counts, method counts, and so on) suggest that a program written in the Java programming language can be four times smaller than the same program written in C++.
- *Write better code.* The Java programming language encourages good coding practices, and automatic garbage collection helps you avoid memory leaks. Its object orientation, its JavaBeans component architecture, and its wide-ranging, easily extendible API let you reuse existing, tested code and thus help you introduce fewer bugs.
- *Develop programs more quickly.* The Java programming language is simpler than C++, and as such, your development time could be up to twice as fast when writing in it. Your programs will also require fewer lines of code.
- *Avoid platform dependencies.* You can keep your program portable by avoiding the use of libraries written in other languages.
- *Write once and run anywhere.* Because applications written in the Java programming language are compiled into machine-independent bytecodes, they run consistently on any Java platform.
- *Distribute software more easily.* With Java Web Start software, users will be able to launch your applications with a single click of the mouse. An automatic version check at start-up ensures that users are always up to date with the latest version of your software. If an update is available, the Java Web Start software will automatically update their installation.

The "Hello World!" Application

This section provides detailed instructions for compiling and running a simple "Hello World!" application. It provides information on getting started with the NetBeans

1

IDE, an integrated development environment that greatly simplifies the software development process. The NetBeans IDE runs on all popular platforms; platform-specific instructions are provided for getting started without an IDE. First, we provide instructions for users of the NetBeans IDE. The NetBeans IDE runs on the Java platform, which means that you can use it with any operating system for which there is a JDK 7 available. We recommend using the NetBeans IDE instead of the command line whenever possible.

Next, we give command-line instructions for users of Microsoft Windows. We also provide these command-line instructions for users of Solaris and Linux. Finally, we list some common problems (and their solutions); consult the end of this section if you have problems compiling or running your application.

"Hello World!" for the NetBeans IDE

It's time to write your first application! These detailed instructions are for users of the NetBeans IDE. As mentioned previously, the NetBeans IDE runs on the Java platform; you can use it with any operating system for which there is a JDK 7 available.

A Checklist

To write your first program, you'll need the following:

1. *The Java SE Development Kit (JDK 7 has been selected in this example).* To obtain this for all platforms, consult the Java SE Downloads Index.[5]
2. *The NetBeans IDE.* To obtain this for all platforms, consult the NetBeans IDE Downloads Index.[6]

Creating Your First Application

Your first application, `HelloWorldApp`, will simply display the greeting "Hello World!" To create this program, do the following:

1. *Create an IDE project.* When you create an IDE project, you create an environment in which to build and run your applications. Using IDE projects eliminates configuration issues normally associated with developing on the command line. You can build or run your application by choosing a single menu item within the IDE.
2. *Add code to the generated source file.* A source file contains code, written in the Java programming language, that you and other programmers can understand.

---

5. http://www.oracle.com/technetwork/java/javase/downloads/index.html
6. http://netbeans.org/downloads/index.html

1

As part of creating an IDE project, a skeleton source file will be automatically generated. You will then modify the source file to add the "Hello World!" message.

3. *Compile the source file into a* `.class` *file.* The IDE invokes the Java programming language compiler (`javac`), which takes your source file and translates its text into instructions that the Java Virtual Machine can understand. The instructions contained within this file are known as *bytecodes*.

4. *Run the program.* The IDE invokes the Java application launcher tool (`java`), which uses the Java Virtual Machine to run your application.

Create an IDE Project

To create an IDE project, do the following:

1. Launch the NetBeans IDE.
   - On Microsoft Windows systems, use the NetBeans IDE item in the **Start** menu.
   - On Solaris and Linux systems, execute the IDE launcher script by navigating to the IDE's `bin` directory and typing `./netbeans`.
   - On Mac OS X systems, click the NetBeans IDE application icon.
2. In the NetBeans IDE, choose **File** and then select **New Project** (Figure 1.4).
3. In the New Project wizard, expand the Java category and select **Java Application** (Figure 1.5).
4. In the Name and Location page of the wizard, do the following (Figure 1.6):

Figure 1.4 The NetBeans IDE with the New Project Menu Item Selected

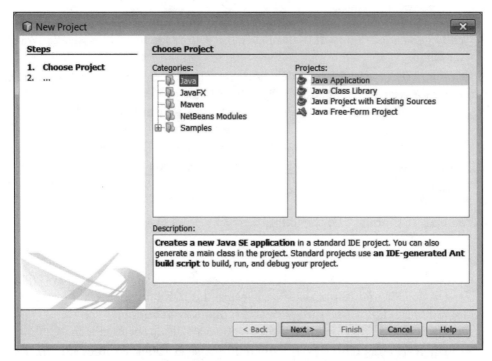

Figure 1.5 The NetBeans IDE, New Project Wizard, Choose Project Page

Figure 1.6 The NetBeans IDE, New Project Wizard, Name and Location Page

- In the Project Name field, type `Hello World App`.
- In the Create Main Class field, type `helloworldapp.HelloWorldApp`.
- Leave the Set as Main Project check box selected.

5. Click **Finish**.

The project is created and opened in the IDE (Figure 1.7). You should see the following components:

- The Projects window, which contains a tree view of the components of the project, including source files, libraries that your code depends on, and so on
- The Source Editor window, with a file called `HelloWorldApp` open
- The Navigator window, which you can use to quickly navigate between elements within the selected class

Add JDK 7 to the Platform List (If Necessary)

It may be necessary to add JDK 7 to the IDE's list of available platforms. To do this, choose **Tools** and then select **Java Platforms**, as shown in Figure 1.8.

If you don't see JDK 7 (which might appear as 1.7 or 1.7.0) in the list of installed platforms, click **Add Platform**, navigate to your JDK 7 install directory, and click **Finish**. You should now see the newly added platform depicted in Figure 1.9.

To set this JDK as the default for all projects, you can run the IDE with the `--jdkhome` switch on the command line. You can also do this by entering the path to the JDK in the `netbeans_j2sdkhome` property of your `INSTALLATION_DIRECTORY/ etc/netbeans.conf` file.

To specify this JDK for the current project only, select **Hello World App** in the Projects pane, choose **File** and then select **Project Properties** (Hello World App), click **Libraries**, and then select **JDK 7** under the Java Platform pull-down menu. You should see a screen similar to Figure 1.10. The IDE is now configured for JDK 7.

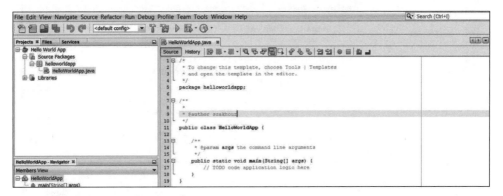

Figure 1.7 The NetBeans IDE with the HelloWorldApp Project Open

1

Add Code to the Generated Source File

When you created this project, you left the Create Main Class check box selected in the New Project wizard. The IDE has therefore created a skeleton class for you. You can add the "Hello World!" message to the skeleton code by replacing the line

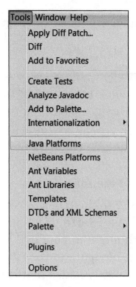

Figure 1.8 Selecting the Java Platform Manager from the Tools Menu

Figure 1.9 The Java Platform Manager

Figure 1.10 The Libraries Category in the Hello World App Project Properties

```
// TODO code application logic here
```

with the line

```
System.out.println("Hello World!"); // Display the string.
```

Optionally, you can replace these four lines of generated code

```
/**
 *
 * @author
 */
```

with these lines

```
/**
 * The HelloWorldApp class implements an application that
 * simply prints "Hello World!" to standard output.
 */
```

These four lines are a code comment and do not affect how the program runs. Later sections of this chapter explain the use and format of code comments.

> **Note**
>
> Type all code, commands, and file names exactly as shown. Both the compiler (javac) and launcher (java) are *case sensitive*, so you must capitalize consistently. For example, HelloWorldApp is *not* the same as helloworldapp.

Save your changes by selecting **File** and then **Save**. The file should look something like the following:

```
/*
 * To change this template, choose Tools | Templates
 * and open the template in the editor.
 */

package helloworldapp;

/**
 * The HelloWorldApp class implements an application that
 * simply prints "Hello World!" to standard output.
 */
public class HelloWorldApp {

    /**
     * @param args the command line arguments
     */
    public static void main(String[] args) {
        System.out.println("Hello World!"); // Display the string.
    }
}
```

Compile the Source File into a .class File

To compile your source file, from the IDE's main menu, select **Run** and then **Build Main Project**. The Output window opens and displays output similar to Figure 1.11.

If the build output concludes with the statement BUILD SUCCESSFUL, then congratulations! You have successfully compiled your program!

If the build output concludes with the statement BUILD FAILED, then you probably have a syntax error in your code. Errors are reported in the Output window as hyperlinked text. You can double click this hyperlinked text to navigate to the source of an error. You can then fix the error and once again by selecting **Run** and then **Build Main Project**.

When you build the project, the bytecode file HelloWorldApp.class is generated. You can see where the new file is generated by opening the Files window and expanding the Hello World App/build/classes/helloworldapp node, as shown in Figure 1.12. Now that you have built the project, you can run your program.

Run the Program

From the IDE's menu bar, select **Run** and then **Run Main Project**. Figure 1.13 shows what you should now see. Congratulations! Your program works!

Figure 1.11 Output Window Showing the Results of Building the HelloWorldApp Project

Figure 1.12 Files Window Showing the Generated .class File

Figure 1.13 The Program Prints "Hello World!" to the Output Window
(along with Other Output from the Build Script)

1

Continuing with the NetBeans IDE

The remainder of this chapter explains the code in this simple application. The chapters that follow go deeper into core language features and provide many more examples. Although the rest of this book does not give specific instructions about using the NetBeans IDE, you can easily use the IDE to write and run the sample code. The following are some tips on using the IDE and explanations of some IDE behavior that you are likely to see:

- Once you have created a project in the IDE, you can add files to the project using the New File wizard. Select **File** and then **New File**, and choose a template in the wizard, such as the Empty Java File template.

- You can compile and run an individual file (as opposed to a whole project) using the IDE's Compile File (**F9**) and Run File (**Shift+F6**) commands. If you use the Run Main Project command, the IDE will run the file that the IDE associates as the main class of the main project. Therefore, if you create an additional class in your HelloWorldApp project and then try to run that file with the Run Main Project command, the IDE will run the `HelloWorldApp` file instead.

- You might want to create separate IDE projects for sample applications that include more than one source file.

- As you are typing in the IDE, a code completion box might periodically appear. You can either ignore the code completion box and keep typing, or you can select one of the suggested expressions. If you would prefer not to have the code completion box automatically appear, you can turn off the feature. Select **Tools**, then **Options**, and then **Editor**. Click on the Code Completion tab, and clear the Auto Popup Completion Window check box.

- If you want to rename the node for a source file in the Projects window, select **Refactor** from IDE's main menu. The IDE prompts you with the Rename dialog box and leads you through the options of renaming the class and the updating of code that refers to that class. Make the changes and click **Refactor** to apply the changes. This sequence of clicks might seem unnecessary if you have just a single class in your project, but it is very useful when your changes affect other parts of your code in larger projects.

- For a more thorough guide to the features of the NetBeans IDE, see the NetBeans Documentation page.[7]

"Hello World!" for Microsoft Windows

It's time to write your first application! The following instructions are for users of Windows.

---

7. `http://www.netbeans.org/kb/index.html`

A Checklist

To write your first program, you'll need the following:

1. *JDK 7.* You can download the Windows version.[8] (Make sure to download the JDK, *not* the Java Runtime Environment, or JRE.) Consult the instructions.[9]
2. *A text editor.* In this example, we'll use Notepad, a simple editor included with the Windows platforms. You can easily adapt these instructions if you use a different text editor.

These two items are all you will need to write your first application.

Creating Your First Application

Your first application, `HelloWorldApp`, will simply display the greeting "Hello World!" To create this program, do the following:

1. *Create a source file.* A source file contains code, written in the Java programming language, that you and other programmers can understand. You can use any text editor to create and edit source files.
2. *Compile the source file into a* `.class` *file.* The Java programming language compiler (`javac`) takes your source file and translates its text into instructions that the Java Virtual Machine can understand. As mentioned previously, the instructions contained within this file are known as *bytecodes*.
3. *Run the program.* The Java application launcher tool (`java`) uses the Java Virtual Machine to run your application.

Create a Source File

To create a source file, you have two options: You can save the file `HelloWorldApp.java` on your computer and avoid a lot of typing, or you can use the following (longer) instructions.

First, start your editor, such as Notepad. In a new document, type in the following code:

```
/**
 * The HelloWorldApp class implements an application that
 * simply prints "Hello World!" to standard output.
 */
class HelloWorldApp {
    public static void main(String[] args) {
        System.out.println("Hello World!"); // Display the string.
    }
}
```

---

8. http://www.oracle.com/technetwork/java/javase/downloads/index.html
9. 7/docs/webnotes/install

1

> **Note**
>
> Type all code, commands, and file names exactly as shown. Both the compiler (`javac`)
> and launcher (`java`) are *case sensitive*, so you must capitalize consistently. For example,
> `HelloWorldApp` is *not* the same as `helloworldapp`.

Save the code in a file with the name `HelloWorldApp.java`. To do this in Notepad, in the menu bar, select **File** and then **Save As**. Then, in the **Save As** dialog box, do the following:

1. Using the Save in combo box, specify the folder (directory) where you'll save your file. In this example, the directory is `java` on the C drive.
2. In the File name text field, type `"HelloWorldApp.java"`, including the quotation marks.
3. From the Save as type combo box, choose Text Documents (*.txt).
4. In the Encoding combo box, leave the encoding as ANSI.

When you're finished, the dialog box should resemble Figure 1.14. Now click **Save**, and exit Notepad.

Compile the Source File into a .class File

Bring up a shell, or "command," window. You can do this from the **Start** menu by choosing **Command Prompt** or by choosing **Run ...** and then entering `cmd`. The shell window should look similar to Figure 1.15.

The prompt shows your *current directory*. When you bring up the prompt, your current directory is usually your home directory, as shown in Figure 1.15.

To compile your source file, change your current directory to the directory where your file is located. For example, if your source directory is `java` on the C drive, type the following command at the prompt and press **Enter**:

```
cd C:\java
```

Now the prompt should change to `C:\java>`.

> **Note**
>
> To change to a directory on a different drive, you must type an extra command: the name
> of the drive. For example, to change to the `java` directory on the D drive, you must enter
> `D:`, as shown in Figure 1.16.

Figure 1.14 The Save As Dialog Just Before You Click Save

Figure 1.15 A Shell Window

Figure 1.16 Changing the Directory on an Alternate Drive

If you enter dir at the prompt, you should see your source file, as Figure 1.17 shows. Now you are ready to compile. At the prompt, type the following command and press **Enter**:

```
javac HelloWorldApp.java
```

The compiler has generated a bytecode file, HelloWorldApp.class. At the prompt, type dir to see the new file that was generated, as shown in Figure 1.18. Now that you have a .class file, you can run your program.

Run the Program

In the same directory, enter the following command at the prompt:

```
java HelloWorldApp
```

Figure 1.19 shows what you should now see. Congratulations! Your program works! If you encounter problems with the instructions in this or any other steps in this section, consult the section "Common Problems (and Their Solutions)" at the end of this chapter.

"Hello World!" for Solaris and Linux

It's time to write your first application! These detailed instructions are for users of Solaris and Linux.

A Checklist

To write your first program, you'll need the following:

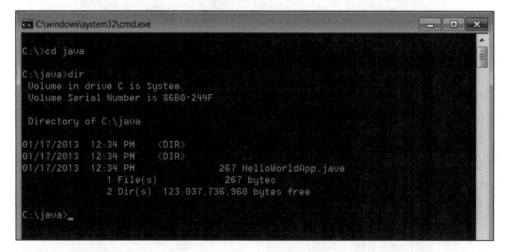

Figure 1.17 Directory Listing Showing the .java Source File

Figure 1.18 Directory Listing Showing the Generated .class File

```
C:\windows\system32\cmd.exe

C:\java>java HelloWorldApp
Hello World!

C:\java>_
```

Figure 1.19 The Program Prints "Hello World!" on the Screen

1. *JDK 7.* You can download the Solaris or Linux version.[10] (Make sure you download the JDK, *not* the JRE.) Consult the installation instructions.[11]

2. *A text editor.* In this example, we'll use pico, an editor available for many UNIX-based platforms. You can easily adapt these instructions if you use a different text editor, such as vi or emacs.

These two items are all you'll need to write your first application.

Creating Your First Application

Your first application, `HelloWorldApp`, will simply display the greeting "Hello World!" To create this program, do the following:

1. *Create a source file.* A source file contains code, written in the Java programming language, that you and other programmers can understand. You can use any text editor to create and edit source files.

---

10. `http://www.oracle.com/technetwork/java/javase/downloads/index.html`
11. `7/docs/webnotes/install`

1

2. *Compile the source file into a* `.class` *file.* The Java programming language compiler (`javac`) takes your source file and translates its text into instructions that the Java Virtual Machine can understand. As mentioned previously, the instructions contained within this `.class` file are known as *bytecodes*.

3. *Run the program.* The Java application *launcher tool* (`java`) uses the Java Virtual Machine to run your application.

Create a Source File

To create a source file, you have two options: You can save the file `HelloWorldApp.java` on your computer and avoid a lot of typing, or you can use the following (longer) instructions.

First, open a shell, or "terminal," window, as shown in Figure 1.20. When you first bring up the prompt, your *current directory* will usually be your *home directory*. You can change your current directory to your home directory at any time by typing `cd` at the prompt and then pressing **Return**.

The source files you create should be kept in a separate directory. You can create a directory by using the command `mkdir`. For example, to create the directory `examples/java` in the `/tmp` directory, use the following commands:

```
cd /tmp
mkdir examples
cd examples
mkdir java
```

To change your current directory to this new directory, enter the following:

```
cd /tmp/examples/java
```

Now you can start creating your source file. Start the `pico` editor by typing `pico` at the prompt and pressing **Return**. If the system responds with the message `pico: command not found`, then `pico` is most likely unavailable. Consult your system administrator for more information, or use another editor. When you start `pico`, it'll display a new, blank *buffer*. This is the area in which you will type your code.

Type the following code into the new buffer:

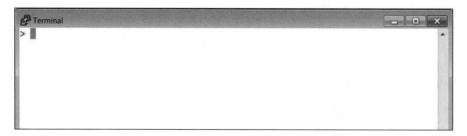

Figure 1.20 A New Terminal Window

```
/**
 * The HelloWorldApp class implements an application that
 * simply prints "Hello World!" to standard output.
 */
class HelloWorldApp {
    public static void main(String[] args) {
        System.out.println("Hello World!"); // Display the string.
    }
}
```

> **Note**
>
> Type all code, commands, and file names exactly as shown. Both the compiler (`javac`)
> and launcher (`java`) are *case sensitive*, so you must capitalize consistently. For example,
> `HelloWorldApp` is *not* the same as `helloworldapp`.

Save the code in a file with the name `HelloWorldApp.java`. In the `pico` editor, you do this by typing **Ctrl+O** and then, at the bottom where you see the prompt `File Name to Write:`, entering the directory in which you wish to create the file, followed by `HelloWorldApp.java`. For example, if you wish to save `HelloWorldApp.java` in the directory `/tmp/examples/java`, then you type `/tmp/examples/java/HelloWorldApp.java` and press **Return**. You can type **Ctrl+X** to exit `pico`.

Compile the Source File into a .class File

Open another shell window. To compile your source file, change your current directory to the directory where your file is located. For example, if your source directory is `/tmp/examples/java`, type the following command at the prompt and press **Return**:

```
cd /tmp/examples/java
```

If you enter `pwd` at the prompt, you should see the current directory, which in this example has been changed to `/tmp/examples/java`. If you enter `ls` at the prompt, you should see your file.

Now you are ready to compile the source file. At the prompt, type the following command and press **Return**:

```
javac HelloWorldApp.java
```

```
Terminal
> cd /tmp/examples/java
> pwd
/tmp/examples/java
> ls
HelloWorldApp.java
>
```

Figure 1.21 Results of the ls Command Showing the .java Source File

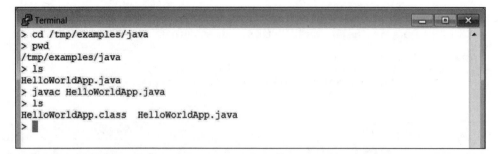

Figure 1.22 Results of the ls Command Showing the Generated .class File

```
Terminal                                              _  □  x
> cd /tmp/examples/java
> pwd
/tmp/examples/java
> ls
HelloWorldApp.java
> javac HelloWorldApp.java
> ls
HelloWorldApp.class  HelloWorldApp.java
> java HelloWorldApp
Hello World!
> █
```

Figure 1.23 The Output Prints "Hello World!" on the Screen

The compiler has generated a bytecode file, HelloWorldApp.class. At the prompt, type ls to see the new file that was generated, as shown in Figure 1.22. Now that you have a .class file, you can run your program.

Run the Program

In the same directory, enter the following command at the prompt:

```
java HelloWorldApp
```

Figure 1.23 shows what you should now see. Congratulations! Your program works!

A Closer Look at the "Hello World!" Application

Now that you've seen the "Hello World!" application (and perhaps even compiled and run it), you might be wondering how it works. Here again is its code:

```
class HelloWorldApp {
    public static void main(String[] args) {
        System.out.println("Hello World!"); // Display the string.
    }
```

```
    }
```

The "Hello World!" application consists of three primary components: source code comments, the `HelloWorldApp` class definition, and the main method. The following explanation will provide you with a basic understanding of the code, but the deeper implications will only be apparent after you've finished reading the rest of this book.

Source Code Comments

The following bold text defines the *comments* of the "Hello World!" application:

```
/**
 * The HelloWorldApp class implements an application that
 * simply prints "Hello World!" to standard output.
 */
class HelloWorldApp {
    public static void main(String[] args) {
        System.out.println("Hello World!"); // Display the string.
    }
}
```

Comments are ignored by the compiler but are useful to other programmers. The Java programming language supports three kinds of comments:

  `/* text */`   The compiler ignores everything from `/*` to `*/`.

  `/** documentation */`   This indicates a documentation comment (*doc comment*, for short). The compiler ignores this kind of comment, just like it ignores comments that use `/*` and `*/`. The Javadoc tool uses doc comments when preparing automatically generated documentation. For more information on Javadoc, see the Javadoc Tool Documentation.[12]

  `// text`   The compiler ignores everything from `//` to the end of the line.

The HelloWorldApp Class Definition

The following bold text begins the class definition block for the "Hello World!" application:

```
/**
 * The HelloWorldApp class implements an application that
 * simply displays "Hello World!" to the standard output.
 */
class HelloWorldApp {
    public static void main(String[] args) {
        System.out.println("Hello World!"); // Display the string.
    }
```

---

12. 7/docs/technotes/guides/javadoc/index.html

1

```
}
```

As shown previously, the most basic form of a class definition is as follows:

```
class name {
    . . .
}
```

The keyword `class` begins the class definition for a class named name, and the code for each class appears between the opening and closing curly braces marked in bold. Chapter 2 provides an overview of classes in general, and Chapter 4 discusses classes in detail. For now, it is enough to know that every application begins with a class definition.

The main Method

The following bold text begins the definition of the `main` method:

```
/**
 * The HelloWorldApp class implements an application that
 * simply displays "Hello World!" to the standard output.
 */
class HelloWorldApp {
    public static void main(String[] args) {
        System.out.println("Hello World!"); //Display the string.
    }
}
```

In the Java programming language, every application must contain a `main` method whose signature is as follows:

```
public static void main(String[] args)
```

The modifiers `public` and `static` can be written in either order (public static or static public), but the convention is to use `public  static`, as shown here. You can name the argument anything you want, but most programmers choose `args` or `argv`.

The `main` method is similar to the `main` function in C and C++; it's the entry point for your application and will subsequently invoke all the other methods required by your program. The `main` method accepts a single argument: an array of elements of type `String`.

```
public static void main(String[] args)
```

This array is the mechanism through which the runtime system passes information to your application. Here's an example:

```
java MyApp arg1 arg2
```

Each string in the array is called a *command-line argument*. Command-line arguments let users affect the operation of the application without recompiling it. For example, a sorting program might allow the user to specify that the data be sorted in descending order with this command-line argument:

```
-descending
```

The "Hello World!" application ignores its command-line arguments, but you should be aware of the fact that such arguments do exist. Finally, see the following line:

```
System.out.println("Hello World!");
```

This uses the System class from the core library to print the "Hello World!" message to standard output. Portions of this library (also known as the *Application Programming Interface*, or *API*) will be discussed in later chapters.

Common Problems (and Their Solutions)

Compiler Problems

Common Error Messages on Microsoft Windows Systems

'javac' is not recognized as an internal or external command, operable program or batch file
If you receive this error, Windows cannot find the compiler (javac). Here's one way to tell Windows where to find javac. Suppose you installed the JDK in C:\ jdk1.7.0. At the prompt, you would type the following command and press **Enter**:

```
C:\jdk1.7.0\bin\javac HelloWorldApp.java
```

If you choose this option, you'll have to begin your javac and java commands with C:\jdk1.7.0\bin\ each time you compile or run a program. To avoid this extra typing, consult the JDK 7 installation instructions.[13]

Class names, 'HelloWorldApp', are only accepted if annotation processing is explicitly requested
If you receive this error, you forgot to include the .java suffix when compiling the program; the command is javac HelloWorldApp.java, not javac HelloWorldApp.

---

13. 7/docs/webnotes/install/windows/jdk-installation-windows.html#path

1

Common Error Messages on UNIX Systems

`javac: Command not found`

If you receive this error, UNIX cannot find the compiler, `javac`. Here's one way to tell UNIX where to find `javac`. Suppose you installed the JDK in `/usr/local/jdk1.7.0`. At the prompt, you would type the following command and press **Enter**:

```
/usr/local/jdk1.7.0/javac HelloWorldApp.java
```

If you choose this option, each time you compile or run a program, you'll have to begin your `javac` and `java` commands with `/usr/local/jdk1.7.0/`. To avoid this extra typing, you could add this information to your PATH variable. The steps for doing so will vary depending on which shell you are currently running.

`Class names, 'HelloWorldApp', are only accepted if annotation processing is explicitly requested`

If you receive this error, you forgot to include the `.java` suffix when compiling the program. Remember, the command is `javac  HelloWorldApp.java`, not `javac HelloWorldApp`.

Syntax Errors (All Platforms)

If you mistype part of a program, the compiler may issue a syntax error. The message usually displays the type of error, the line number where the error was detected, the code on that line, and the position of the error within the code. Here's an error caused by omitting a semicolon at the end of a statement:

```
testing.java:14: ';' expected.
System.out.println("Input has " + count + " chars.")
                                                    ^
1 error
```

If you see any compiler errors, then your program did not successfully compile, and the compiler did not create a `.class` file. Carefully verify the program, fix any errors that you detect, and try again.

Semantic Errors

In addition to verifying that your program is syntactically correct, the compiler checks for other basic correctness. For example, the compiler warns you each time you use a variable that has not been initialized:

```
testing.java:13: Variable count may not have been initialized.
        count++;
        ^
```

1

```
testing.java:14: Variable count may not have been initialized.
    System.out.println("Input has " + count + " chars.");
                                       ^
2 errors
```

Again, your program did not successfully compile, and the compiler did not create a `.class` file. Fix the error and try again.

Runtime Problems

Error Messages on Microsoft Windows Systems

`Exception in thread "main" java.lang.NoClassDefFoundError: HelloWorldApp`

If you receive this error, java cannot find your bytecode file, `HelloWorldApp.class`. Note that java tries to find your `.class` file in your current directory (among other places). Thus if your `.class` file is in `C:\java`, you should change your current directory accordingly. To change your directory, type the following command at the prompt and press **Enter**:

```
cd c:\java
```

The prompt should change to `C:\java>`. If you enter `dir` at the prompt, you should see your `.java` and `.class` files. Now enter java `HelloWorldApp` again. If you still have problems, you might have to change your `CLASSPATH` variable. To see if this is necessary, try clobbering the `CLASSPATH` with the following command:

```
set CLASSPATH=
```

Now enter java `HelloWorldApp` again. If the program works now, you'll have to change your `CLASSPATH` variable. To set this variable, consult the JDK 7 installation instructions.[14] The `CLASSPATH` variable is set in the same manner.

`Exception in thread "main" java.lang.NoClassDefFoundError: HelloWorldApp/class`

A common mistake made by beginner programmers is to try and run the java launcher on the `.class` file that was created by the compiler. For example, you'll get this error if you try to run your program with java `HelloWorldApp.class` instead of java `HelloWorldApp`. Remember, the argument is the *name of the class* that you want to use, *not* the file name.

---

14. `7/docs/webnotes/install/windows/jdk-installation-windows.html#path`

1

`Exception in thread "main" java.lang.NoSuchMethodError: main`

The Java Virtual Machine requires that the class you execute with it has a `main` method at which to begin the execution of your application. The section "A Closer Look at the 'Hello World!' Application" discusses the `main` method in detail.

Error Messages on UNIX Systems

`Exception in thread "main" java.lang.NoClassDefFoundError:`
`HelloWorldApp`

If you receive this error, java cannot find your bytecode file, `HelloWorldApp.class`. Note that java tries to find your bytecode file in your current directory (among other places). Thus if your bytecode file is in `/home/jdoe/java`, you should change your current directory accordingly. To change your directory, type the following command at the prompt and press **Return**:

```
cd /home/jdoe/java
```

If you enter `pwd` at the prompt, you should see `/home/jdoe/java`. If you enter `ls` at the prompt, you should see your `.java` and `.class` files. Now enter java `HelloWorldApp` again.

If you still have problems, you might have to change your `CLASSPATH` environment variable. To see if this is necessary, try clobbering the `CLASSPATH` with the following command:

```
unset CLASSPATH
```

Now enter java `HelloWorldApp` again. If the program works now, you'll have to change your `CLASSPATH` variable in the same manner as the `PATH` variable given previously.

`Exception in thread "main" java.lang.NoClassDefFoundError:`
`HelloWorldApp/class`

A common mistake made by beginner programmers is to try and run the java launcher on the `.class` file that was created by the compiler. For example, you'll get this error if you try to run your program with java `HelloWorldApp.class` instead of java `HelloWorldApp`. Remember, the argument is the *name of the class* that you want to use, *not* the file name.

`Exception in thread "main" java.lang.NoSuchMethodError: main`

The Java Virtual Machine requires that the class you execute with it has a `main` method at which to begin the execution of your application. The section "A Closer Look at the 'Hello World!' Application" discusses the `main` method in detail.

Questions and Exercises: Getting Started

Questions

1. When you compile a program written in the Java programming language, the compiler converts the human-readable source file into platform-independent code that a Java Virtual Machine can understand. What is this platform-independent code called?

2. Which of the following is *not* a valid comment?

   a. `/** comment */`

   b. `/* comment */`

   c. `/* comment`

   d. `// comment`

3. What is the first thing you should check if you see the following error at runtime?

   ```
   Exception in thread "main" java.lang.NoClassDefFoundError:
   HelloWorldApp.java.
   ```

4. What is the correct signature of the `main` method?

5. When declaring the `main` method, which modifier must come first, `public` or `static`?

6. Which parameters does the `main` method define?

Exercises

1. Change the `HelloWorldApp.java` program so that it displays `Hola Mundo!` instead of `Hello World!`.

2. Here is a slightly modified version of the `HelloWorldApp`:

   ```
   // HelloWorldApp2.java
   // INTENTIONALLY UNCOMPILABLE!
   /**
    * The HelloWorldApp class implements an application that
    * simply prints "Hello World!" to standard output.
    */
   class HelloWorldApp2 {
     public static void main(String[] args) {
       System.out.println("Hello World!"); // Display the string.
     }
   }
   ```

   The program has an error. Define the error and fix it so that the program successfully compiles and runs.

Answers

You can find answers to these questions and exercises at `http://docs.oracle.com/`
`javase/tutorial/getStarted/QandE/answers.html`.

2

Object-Oriented Programming Concepts

If you've never used an object-oriented programming language before, you'll need to learn a few basic concepts before you can begin writing any code. This chapter will introduce you to objects, classes, inheritance, interfaces, and packages. Each section focuses on how these concepts relate to the real world, while simultaneously providing an introduction to the syntax of the Java programming language.

The first section focuses on objects. An object is a software bundle of related state and behavior. Software objects are often used to model the real-world objects that you find in everyday life. This section explains how state and behavior are represented within an object, introduces the concept of data encapsulation, and explains the benefits of designing your software in this manner.

The second section discusses classes. A class is a blueprint or prototype from which objects are created. This section defines a class that models the state and behavior of a real-world object. It intentionally focuses on the basics, showing how even a simple class can cleanly model state and behavior.

The third section focuses on inheritance. Inheritance provides a powerful and natural mechanism for organizing and structuring your software. This section explains how classes inherit state and behavior from their superclasses and explains how to derive one class from another using the simple syntax provided by the Java programming language.

The fourth section discusses interfaces. An interface is a contract between a class and the outside world. When a class implements an interface, it promises to provide the behavior published by that interface. This section defines a simple interface and explains the necessary changes for any class that implements it.

The last section describes packages. A package is a namespace for organizing classes and interfaces in a logical manner. Placing your code into packages makes large software projects easier to manage. This section explains why this is useful and introduces you to the Application Programming Interface (API) provided by the Java platform.

The chapter ends with questions and exercises to test your understanding of objects, classes, inheritance, interfaces, and packages.

What Is an Object?

Objects are key to understanding *object-oriented* technology. Look around right now and you'll find many examples of real-world objects: your dog, your desk, your television set, your bicycle, and so on.

Real-world objects share two characteristics: they all have *state* and *behavior*. Dogs have state (name, color, breed) and behavior (barking, fetching, wagging tail). Bicycles also have state (current gear, current pedal cadence, current speed) and behavior (changing gear, changing pedal cadence, applying brakes). Identifying the state and behavior for real-world objects is a great way to begin thinking in terms of object-oriented programming.

Take a minute right now to observe the real-world objects that are in your immediate area. For each object that you see, ask yourself two questions: "What possible states can this object be in?" and "What possible behaviors can this object show?" Make sure to write down your observations. As you do, you'll notice that real-world objects vary in complexity; your desktop lamp may have only two possible states (on and off) and two possible behaviors (turn on, turn off), but your desktop radio might have additional states (on, off, current volume, current station) and behavior (turn on, turn off, increase volume, decrease volume, seek, scan, tune). You may also notice that some objects, in turn, will also contain other objects. These real-world observations all translate into the world of object-oriented programming.

Software objects are conceptually similar to real-world objects: they too consist of state and related behavior. An object stores its state in *fields* (known as *variables* in some programming languages) and exposes its behavior through *methods* (known as *functions* in some programming languages). Methods operate on an object's internal state and serve as the primary mechanism for object-to-object communication. Hiding the internal state and requiring that all interaction be performed through

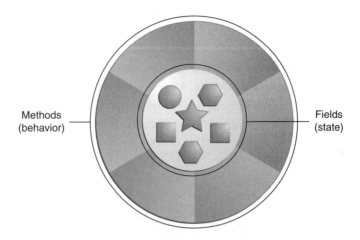

Figure 2.1 A Software Object

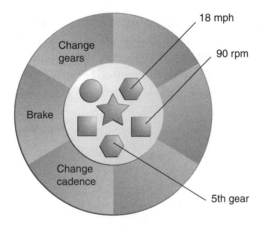

Figure 2.2 A Bicycle Modeled as a Software Object

an object's methods is known as *data encapsulation*—a fundamental principle of object-oriented programming.

For example, consider a bicycle. By attributing state (current gear, current pedal cadence, current speed) and providing methods for changing that state, the object remains in control of how the outside world is allowed to use it. For example, if the bicycle only has six gears, a method to change gears could reject any value that is less than one or greater than six.

Bundling code into individual software objects provides a number of benefits, including the following:

1. *Modularity.* The source code for an object can be written and maintained independently from the source code for other objects. Once created, an object can be easily passed around inside the system.

2. *Information hiding.* The user only interacts with an object's methods; thus the details of its internal implementation remain hidden from the outside world.

3. *Code reuse.* If an object already exists (perhaps written by another software developer), you can use that object in your program. This allows specialists to implement, test, and debug complex, task-specific objects, which you can then trust to run in your own code.

4. *Pluggability and easier debugging.* If a particular object turns out to be problematic, you can simply remove it from your application and plug in a different object as its replacement. This is analogous to fixing mechanical problems in the real world. If a bolt breaks, you replace it, not the entire machine.

What Is a Class?

In the real world, you'll often find many individual objects, all of the same kind. There may be thousands of other bicycles in existence, all of the same make and model. Each bicycle was built from the same set of blueprints and therefore contains the same components. In object-oriented terms, we say that your bicycle is an *instance* of the *class of objects* known as bicycles. A *class* is the blueprint from which individual objects are created.

The following `Bicycle` class illustrates one possible implementation of a bicycle:

```
class Bicycle {

    int cadence = 0;
    int speed = 0;
    int gear = 1;

    void changeCadence(int newValue) {
        cadence = newValue;
    }

    void changeGear(int newValue) {
        gear = newValue;
    }

    void speedUp(int increment) {
        speed = speed + increment;
    }

    void applyBrakes(int decrement) {
        speed = speed - decrement;
    }
```

```
    void printStates() {
        System.out.println("cadence:" +
            cadence + " speed:" +
            speed + " gear:" + gear);
    }
}
```

The syntax of the Java programming language will look new to you, but the design of this class is based on the previous discussion of bicycle objects. The fields cadence, speed, and gear represent the object's state, and the methods (changeCadence, changeGear, speedUp, etc.) define its interaction with the outside world.

You may have noticed that the Bicycle class does not contain a main method. That's because it is not a complete application; it's just the blueprint for bicycles that might be *used* in an application. The responsibility of creating and using new Bicycle objects belongs to some other class in your application.

Here's a BicycleDemo class that creates two separate Bicycle objects and invokes their methods:

```
class BicycleDemo {
    public static void main(String[] args) {

        // Create two different
        // Bicycle objects
        Bicycle bike1 = new Bicycle();
        Bicycle bike2 = new Bicycle();

        // Invoke methods on
        // those objects
        bike1.changeCadence(50);
        bike1.speedUp(10);
        bike1.changeGear(2);
        bike1.printStates();

        bike2.changeCadence(50);
        bike2.speedUp(10);
        bike2.changeGear(2);
        bike2.changeCadence(40);
        bike2.speedUp(10);
        bike2.changeGear(3);
        bike2.printStates();
    }
}
```

The output of this test prints the ending pedal cadence, speed, and gear for the two bicycles:

```
cadence:50 speed:10 gear:2
cadence:40 speed:20 gear:3
```

What Is Inheritance?

2

Different kinds of objects often have a certain amount in common with each other. Mountain bikes, road bikes, and tandem bikes, for example, all share the characteristics of bicycles (current speed, current pedal cadence, current gear). Yet each also has additional features that make it different: tandem bicycles have two seats and two sets of handlebars, road bikes have drop handlebars, and some mountain bikes have an additional chain ring, giving them a lower gear ratio.

Object-oriented programming allows classes to *inherit* commonly used state and behavior from other classes. In this example, `Bicycle` now becomes the *superclass* of `MountainBike`, `RoadBike`, and `TandemBike`. In the Java programming language, each class is allowed to have one direct superclass, and each superclass has the potential for an unlimited number of *subclasses* (Figure 2.3).

The syntax for creating a subclass is simple. At the beginning of your class declaration, use the `extends` keyword, followed by the name of the class to inherit from:

```
class MountainBike extends Bicycle {

    // new fields and methods defining
    // a mountain bike would go here

}
```

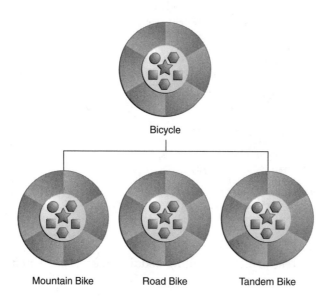

Bicycle

Mountain Bike   Road Bike   Tandem Bike

Figure 2.3 A Hierarchy of Bicycle Classes

This gives `MountainBike` all the same fields and methods as `Bicycle` yet allows its code to focus exclusively on the features that make it unique. This makes code for your subclasses easy to read. However, you must take care to properly document the state and behavior that each superclass defines, since that code will not appear in the source file of each subclass.

What Is an Interface?

As you've already learned, objects define their interaction with the outside world through the methods that they expose. Methods form the object's *interface* with the outside world; the buttons on the front of your television set, for example, are the interface between you and the electrical wiring on the other side of its plastic casing. You press the power button to turn the television on and off.

In its most common form, an interface is a group of related methods with empty bodies. A bicycle's behavior, if specified as an interface, might appear as follows:

```
interface Bicycle {

    //  wheel revolutions per minute
    void changeCadence(int newValue);

    void changeGear(int newValue);

    void speedUp(int increment);

    void applyBrakes(int decrement);
}
```

To implement this interface, the name of your class would change (e.g., to a particular brand of bicycle such as `ACMEBicycle`), and you'd use the `implements` keyword in the class declaration:

```
class ACMEBicycle implements Bicycle {

    // remainder of this class
    // implemented as before
}
```

Implementing an interface allows a class to become more formal about the behavior it promises to provide. Interfaces form a contract between the class and the outside world, and this contract is enforced at build time by the compiler. If your class claims to implement an interface, all methods defined by that interface must appear in the interface's source code before the class will successfully compile.

> **Note:** To actually compile the `ACMEBicycle` class, you'll need to add the `public` keyword to the beginning of the implemented interface methods. You'll learn the reasons for this later on in Chapters 4 and 5.

What Is a Package?

A package is a namespace that organizes a set of related classes and interfaces. Conceptually you can think of packages as being similar to different folders on your computer. You might keep HTML pages in one folder, images in another, and scripts or applications in yet another. Because software written in the Java programming language can be composed of hundreds or thousands of individual classes, it makes sense to keep things organized by placing related classes and interfaces into packages.

The Java platform provides an enormous class library (a set of packages) suitable for use in your own applications. This library is known as the *Application Programming Interface*, or *API*. Its packages represent the tasks most commonly associated with general-purpose programming. For example, a `String` object contains state and behavior for character strings; a `File` object allows a programmer to easily create, delete, inspect, compare, or modify a file on the file system; a `Socket` object allows for the creation and use of network sockets; and various graphical user interface (GUI) objects control buttons and check boxes and anything else related to GUIs. There are literally thousands of classes to choose from. This allows you, the programmer, to focus on the design of your particular application rather than the infrastructure required to make it work.

The Java Platform API Specification[1] contains the complete listing for all packages, interfaces, classes, fields, and methods supplied by the Java SE platform. Load the page in your browser and bookmark it. As a programmer, it will become your single most important piece of reference documentation.

Questions and Exercises: Object-Oriented Programming Concepts

Questions

1. Real-world objects contain ___ and ___.
2. A software object's state is stored in ___.
3. A software object's behavior is exposed through ___.

---

1. `7/docs/api/index.html`

2

4. Hiding internal data from the outside world and accessing it only through publicly exposed methods is known as data ___.

5. A blueprint for a software object is called a ___.

6. Common behavior can be defined in a ___ and inherited into a ___ using the ___ keyword.

7. A collection of methods with no implementation is called an ___.

8. A namespace that organizes classes and interfaces by functionality is called a ___.

9. The term *API* stands for ___?

Exercises

1. Create new classes for each real-world object that you observed at the beginning of the chapter. Refer to the `Bicycle` class if you forget the required syntax.

2. For each new class that you've created, create an interface that defines its behavior, and then require your class to implement it. Omit one or two methods and try compiling. What does the error look like?

Answers

You can find answers to these questions and exercises at `http://docs.oracle` `.com/javase/tutorial/java/concepts/QandE/answers.html`.

3

Language Basics

You've already learned that objects store their state in fields. However, the Java programming language also uses the term *variable* as well. The first section of this chapter discusses this relationship, plus variable naming rules and conventions, basic data types (primitive types, character strings, and arrays), default values, and literals.

The second section describes the operators of the Java programming language. It presents the most commonly used operators first and the less common operators last. Each discussion includes code samples that you can compile and run.

Operators may be used in building expressions, which compute values. Expressions are the core components of statements. Statements may be grouped into blocks. The third section discusses expressions, statements, and blocks using example code that you've already seen.

The final section describes the control flow statements supported by the Java programming language. It covers the decision-making, looping, and branching statements that enable your programs to conditionally execute particular blocks of code.

Note that each section contains its own questions and exercises to test your understanding.

Variables

As you learned in the previous chapter, an object stores its state in *fields*:

```
int cadence = 0;
int speed = 0;
int gear = 1;
```

In Chapter 2, the section "What Is an Object?" introduced you to fields, but you probably still have a few questions: What are the rules and conventions for naming a field? Besides `int`, what other data types are there? Do fields have to be initialized when they are declared? Are fields assigned a default value if they are not explicitly initialized? We'll explore the answers to such questions in this chapter, but before we do, there are a few technical distinctions you must first become aware of. In the Java programming language, the terms *field* and *variable* are both used; this is a common source of confusion among new developers, since both often seem to refer to the same thing.

The Java programming language defines the following kinds of variables:

- *Instance variables (nonstatic fields).* Technically speaking, objects store their individual states in nonstatic fields—that is, fields declared without the `static` keyword. Nonstatic fields are also known as *instance variables* because their values are unique to each *instance* of a class (i.e., each object); the `currentSpeed` of one bicycle is independent from the `currentSpeed` of another.

- *Class variables (static fields).* A *class variable* is any field declared with the `static` modifier; this tells the compiler that there is exactly one copy of this variable in existence, regardless of how many times the class has been instantiated. A field defining the number of gears for a particular kind of bicycle could be marked as `static` since conceptually the same number of gears will apply to all instances. The code `static int numGears = 6;` would create such a static field. Additionally, the keyword `final` could be added to indicate that the number of gears will never change.

- *Local variables.* Similar to how an object stores its state in fields, a method will often store its temporary state in *local variables*. The syntax for declaring a local variable is similar to declaring a field (e.g., `int count = 0;`). There is no special keyword to designate a variable as local; that determination comes entirely from the location in which the variable is declared—which is between the opening and closing braces of a method. As such, local variables are only visible to the methods in which they are declared; they are not accessible from the rest of the class.

- *Parameters.* You've already seen examples of parameters, both in the `Bicycle` class and in the `main` method of the "Hello World!" application. Recall that the signature for the `main` method is `public static void main(String[] args)`. Here, the `args` variable is the parameter to this method. The important thing to remember is that parameters are always classified as *variables*, not *fields*. This applies to other parameter-accepting constructs as well (such as constructors and exception handlers) that you'll learn about in later chapters.

This said, from this point forward, we use the following general guidelines when discussing fields and variables. If we are talking about *fields in general* (excluding local variables and parameters), we may simply use the term *fields*. If the discussion applies to *all of the above*, we may simply use *variables*. If the context calls for a distinction, we will use specific terms (static field, local variables, etc.), where appropriate. You may also occasionally see the term *member* used as well. A type's fields, methods, and nested types are collectively called its *members*.

Naming

Every programming language has its own set of rules and conventions for the kinds of names that you're allowed to use, and the Java programming language is no different. The rules and conventions for naming your variables can be summarized as follows:

- Variable names are case sensitive. A variable's name can be any legal identifier—an unlimited-length sequence of Unicode letters and digits, beginning with a letter, a dollar sign (`$`), or an underscore character (`_`). The convention, however, is to always begin your variable names with a letter, not a dollar sign or underscore. Additionally, the dollar sign, by convention, is never used at all. You may find some situations where autogenerated names will contain the dollar sign, but your variable names should always avoid using it. A similar convention exists for the underscore character; while it's technically legal to begin your variable's name with an underscore, this practice is discouraged. White space is not permitted.

- Subsequent characters may be letters, digits, dollar signs, or underscore characters. Conventions (and common sense) apply to this rule as well. When choosing a name for your variables, use full words instead of cryptic abbreviations. Doing so will make your code easier to read and understand. In many cases, it will also make your code self-documenting; fields named `cadence`, `speed`, and `gear`, for example, are much more intuitive than abbreviated versions, such as

3

s, c, and g. Also keep in mind that the name you choose must not be a keyword or reserved word.

- If the name you choose consists of only one word, spell that word in all lower-case letters. If it consists of more than one word, capitalize the first letter of each subsequent word. The names gearRatio and currentGear are prime examples of this convention. If your variable stores a constant value, such as static final int NUM_GEARS = 6, the convention changes slightly, capitalizing every letter and separating subsequent words with the underscore character. By convention, the underscore character is never used elsewhere.

Primitive Data Types

The Java programming language is statically typed, which means that all variables must first be declared before they can be used. This involves stating the variable's type and name, as you've already seen:

```
int gear = 1;
```

Doing so tells your program that a field named *gear* exists, holds numerical data, and has an initial value of 1. A variable's data type determines the values it may contain plus the operations that may be performed on it. In addition to int, the Java programming language supports seven other *primitive data types*. A primitive type is predefined by the language and named by a reserved keyword. Primitive values do not share state with other primitive values. The eight primitive data types supported by the Java programming language are as follows:

1. The **byte** data type is an 8-bit signed two's complement integer. It has a minimum value of –128 and a maximum value of 127 (inclusive). The byte data type can be useful for saving memory in large arrays, in situations where the memory savings actually matter. They can also be used in place of int, where their limits help to clarify your code; the fact that a variable's range is limited can serve as a form of documentation.

2. The **short** data type is a 16-bit signed two's complement integer. It has a minimum value of –32,768 and a maximum value of 32,767 (inclusive). As with byte, the same guidelines apply: you can use a short to save memory in large arrays, in situations where the memory savings actually matter.

3. The **int** data type is a 32-bit signed two's complement integer. It has a minimum value of –2,147,483,648 and a maximum value of 2,147,483,647 (inclusive). For integral values, this data type is generally the default choice unless there is a reason to choose something else. This data type will most likely be

large enough for the numbers your program will use, but if you need a wider range of values, use `long` instead.

4. The **long** data type is a 64-bit signed two's complement integer. It has a minimum value of −9,223,372,036,854,775,808 and a maximum value of 9,223,372,036,854,775,807 (inclusive). Use this data type when you need a range of values wider than those provided by `int`.

3

5. The **float** data type is a single-precision 32-bit IEEE 754 floating point. Its range of values is beyond the scope of this discussion but is specified in the Java Language Specification.[1] As with the recommendations for `byte` and `short`, use a `float` (instead of `double`) if you need to save memory in large arrays of floating-point numbers. This data type should never be used for precise values, such as currency. For that, you will need to use the `java.math.BigDecimal` class instead.[2] Chapter 8 (specifically the section "Numbers and Strings") covers `BigDecimal` and other useful classes provided by the Java platform.

6. The **double** data type is a double-precision 64-bit IEEE 754 floating point. Its range of values is beyond the scope of this discussion but is specified in the Java Language Specification.[3] For decimal values, this data type is generally the default choice. As mentioned previously, this data type should never be used for precise values, such as currency.

7. The **boolean** data type has only two possible values: `true` and `false`. Use this data type for simple flags that track true-or-false conditions. This data type represents one bit of information, but its "size" isn't something that's precisely defined.

8. The **char** data type is a single 16-bit Unicode character. It has a minimum value of `'\u0000'` (or 0) and a maximum value of `'\uffff'` (or 65,535, inclusive).

In addition to the eight primitive data types, the Java programming language also provides special support for character strings via the `java.lang.String`[4] class. Enclosing your character string within double quotes will automatically create a new `String` object; for example, `String s = "this is a string";`. `String` objects are *immutable*, which means that once created, their values cannot be changed. The `String` class is not technically a primitive data type, but considering the special support given to it by the language, you'll probably tend to think

1. `specs/jls/se7/html/jls-4.html#jls-4.2.3`
2. `7/docs/api/java/math/BigDecimal.html`
3. `specs/jls/se7/html/jls-4.html#jls-4.2.3`
4. `7/docs/api/java/lang/String.html`

of it as such. You'll learn more about the `String` class in Chapter 8, "Simple Data Objects."

Default Values

It's not always necessary to assign a value when a field is declared. Fields that are declared but not initialized will be set to a reasonable default by the compiler. Generally speaking, this default will be zero or `null`, depending on the data type. Relying on such default values, however, is generally considered bad programming style. Table 3.1 summarizes the default values for the previously given data types.

Local variables are slightly different; the compiler never assigns a default value to an uninitialized local variable. If you cannot initialize your local variable where it is declared, make sure to assign it a value before you attempt to use it. Accessing an uninitialized local variable will result in a compile-time error.

Literals

You may have noticed that the new keyword isn't used when initializing a variable of a primitive type. Primitive types are special data types built into the language; they are not objects created from a class. A *literal* is the source code representation of a fixed value; literals are represented directly in your code without requiring computation. As shown here, it's possible to assign a literal to a variable of a primitive type:

```
boolean result = true;
char capitalC = 'C';
byte b = 100;
short s = 10000;
int i = 100000;
```

Table 3.1 Default Values for Data Types

Data Type	Default Value (for Fields)
byte	0
short	0
int	0
long	0L
float	0.0f
double	0.0d
char	'\u0000'
String (or any object)	null
boolean	false

Integer Literals

An integer literal is of type `long` if it ends with the letter L or l; otherwise, it is of type `int`. It is recommended that you use the upper case letter L because the lower case letter l is hard to distinguish from the digit 1.

Values of the integral types `byte`, `short`, `int`, and `long` can be created from `int` literals. Values of type `long` that exceed the range of `int` can be created from `long` literals. Integer literals can be expressed by these number systems:

3

- *Decimal.* Base 10, whose digits consist of the numbers 0 through 9 (This is the number system you use every day.)
- *Hexadecimal.* Base 16, whose digits consist of the numbers 0 through 9 and the letters A through F
- *Binary.* Base 2, whose digits consists of the numbers 0 and 1 (You can create binary literals in Java SE 7 and later.)

For general-purpose programming, the decimal system is likely to be the only number system you'll ever use. However, if you need to use another number system, the following example shows the correct syntax. The prefix `0x` indicates hexadecimal and `0b` indicates binary:

```
// The number 26, in decimal
int decVal = 26;
// The number 26, in hexadecimal
int hexVal = 0x1a;
// The number 26, in binary
int binVal = 0b11010;
```

Floating-Point Literals

A floating-point literal is of type `float` if it ends with the letter F or f; otherwise, its type is `double` and it can optionally end with the letter D or d. The floating-point types (`faloat` and `double`) can also be expressed using E or e (for scientific notation), F or f (32-bit float literal), and D or d (64-bit double literal, which is the default and by convention is omitted):

```
double d1 = 123.4;
// same value as d1, but in scientific notation
double d2 = 1.234e2;
float f1 = 123.4f;
```

Character and String Literals

Literals of types `char` and `String` may contain any Unicode (UTF-16) characters. If your editor and file system allow it, you can use such characters directly in your

code. If not, you can use a "Unicode escape" such as `'\u0108'` (for a capital C with
a circumflex,Ĉ) or `"S\u00ED Se\u00F1or"` (for *Sí Señor* in Spanish). Always use
'single quotes' for `char` literals and "double quotes" for `String` literals. Unicode
escape sequences may be used elsewhere in a program (such as in field names, for
example), not just in `char` or `String` literals.

The Java programming language also supports a few special escape sequences for
`char` and `String` literals: `\b` (backspace), `\t` (tab), `\n` (line feed), `\f` (form feed), `\r`
(carriage return), `\"` (double quote), `\'` (single quote), and `\\` (backslash). There's
also a special `null` literal that can be used as a value for any reference type; `null`
may be assigned to any variable, except variables of primitive types. There's little
you can do with a `null` value beyond testing for its presence. Therefore, `null` is
often used in programs as a marker to indicate that some object is unavailable.

Finally, there's also a special kind of literal called a *class literal*, formed by taking
a type name and appending `.class` (e.g., `String.class`). This refers to the object
(of type `Class`) that represents the type itself.

Using Underscore Characters in Numeric Literals

In Java SE 7 and later, any number of underscore characters (_) can appear anywhere between digits in a numerical literal. This feature allows you to separate
groups of digits in numeric literals, which can improve the readability of your code.
For instance, if your code contains numbers with many digits, you can use an underscore to separate digits in groups of three, similar to how you would use a comma
or a space as a separator. The following example shows other ways you can use the
underscore in numeric literals:

```
long creditCardNumber = 1234_5678_9012_3456L;
long socialSecurityNumber = 999_99_9999L;
float pi = 3.14_15F;
long hexBytes = 0xFF_EC_DE_5E;
long hexWords = 0xCAFE_BABE;
long maxLong = 0x7fff_ffff_ffff_ffffL;
byte nybbles = 0b0010_0101;
long bytes = 0b11010010_01101001_10010100_10010010;
```

You can only place underscores between digits; you cannot place underscores in
the following places:

- At the beginning or end of a number
- Adjacent to a decimal point in a floating-point literal
- Prior to an F or L suffix
- In positions where a string of digits is expected

The following examples demonstrate valid and invalid underscore placements (which are bold) in numeric literals:

```
// Invalid: cannot put underscores
// adjacent to a decimal point
float pi1 = 3_.1415F;
// Invalid: cannot put underscores
// adjacent to a decimal point
float pi2 = 3._1415F;
// Invalid: cannot put underscores
// prior to an L suffix
long socialSecurityNumber1 = 999_99_9999_L;

// This is an identifier, not
// a numeric literal
int x1 = _52;
// OK (decimal literal)
int x2 = 5_2;
// Invalid: cannot put underscores
// At the end of a literal
int x3 = 52_;
// OK (decimal literal)
int x4 = 5_____2;

// Invalid: cannot put underscores
// in the 0x radix prefix
int x5 = 0_x52;
// Invalid: cannot put underscores
// at the beginning of a number
int x6 = 0x_52;
// OK (hexadecimal literal)
int x7 = 0x5_2;
// Invalid: cannot put underscores
// at the end of a number
int x8 = 0x52_;
```

Arrays

An *array* is a container object that holds a fixed number of values of a single type. The length of an array is established when the array is created. After creation, its length is fixed. You've seen an example of arrays already, in the main method of the "Hello World!" application (Chapter 1). This section discusses arrays in greater detail.

Each item in an array is called an *element*, and each element is accessed by its numerical *index*. As shown in Figure 3.1, numbering begins with 0. Therefore the ninth element, for example, would be accessed at index 8.

The following program, ArrayDemo, creates an array of integers, puts some values in it, and prints each value to standard output:

Figure 3.1 An Array of Ten Elements

```
class ArrayDemo {
    public static void main(String[] args) {
        // declares an array of integers
        int[] anArray;

        // allocates memory for 10 integers
        anArray = new int[10];

        // initialize first element
        anArray[0] = 100;
        // initialize second element
        anArray[1] = 200;
        // etc.
        anArray[2] = 300;
        anArray[3] = 400;
        anArray[4] = 500;
        anArray[5] = 600;
        anArray[6] = 700;
        anArray[7] = 800;
        anArray[8] = 900;
        anArray[9] = 1000;

        System.out.println("Element at index 0: " + anArray[0]);
        System.out.println("Element at index 1: " + anArray[1]);
        System.out.println("Element at index 2: " + anArray[2]);
        System.out.println("Element at index 3: " + anArray[3]);
        System.out.println("Element at index 4: " + anArray[4]);
        System.out.println("Element at index 5: " + anArray[5]);
        System.out.println("Element at index 6: " + anArray[6]);
        System.out.println("Element at index 7: " + anArray[7]);
        System.out.println("Element at index 8: " + anArray[8]);
        System.out.println("Element at index 9: " + anArray[9]);
    }
}
```

The output from this program is as follows:

```
Element at index 0: 100
Element at index 1: 200
Element at index 2: 300
Element at index 3: 400
Element at index 4: 500
```

```
Element at index 5: 600
Element at index 6: 700
Element at index 7: 800
Element at index 8: 900
Element at index 9: 1000
```

3

In a real-world programming situation, you'd probably use one of the supported *looping constructs* to iterate through each element of the array, rather than write each line individually as shown here. However, this example clearly illustrates the array syntax. You'll learn about the various looping constructs (`for`, `while`, and `do-while`) later on in the "Control Flow" section of this chapter.

Declaring a Variable to Refer to an Array

The program given previously declares `anArray` with the following line of code:

```
// declares an array of integers
int[] anArray;
```

Like declarations for variables of other types, an array declaration has two components: the array's type and the array's name. An array's type is written as `type[ ]`, where `type` is the data type of the contained elements. The square brackets are special symbols indicating that this variable holds an array. The size of the array is not part of its type (which is why the brackets are empty). An array's name can be anything you want, provided that it follows the rules and conventions, as previously discussed in the "Naming" section. As with variables of other types, the declaration does not actually create an array; it simply tells the compiler that this variable will hold an array of the specified type.

Similarly, you can declare arrays of other types:

```
byte[] anArrayOfBytes;
short[] anArrayOfShorts;
long[] anArrayOfLongs;
float[] anArrayOfFloats;
double[] anArrayOfDoubles;
boolean[] anArrayOfBooleans;
char[] anArrayOfChars;
String[] anArrayOfStrings;
```

You can also place the square brackets after the array's name:

```
// this form is discouraged
float anArrayOfFloats[];
```

However, convention discourages this form; the brackets identify the array type and should appear with the type designation.

Creating, Initializing, and Accessing an Array

One way to create an array is with the new operator. The next statement in the `ArrayDemo` program allocates an array with enough memory for ten integer elements and assigns the array to the `anArray` variable:

```
// create an array of integers
anArray = new int[10];
```

If this statement were missing, the compiler would print an error like the following, and compilation would fail:

```
ArrayDemo.java:4: Variable anArray may not have been initialized.
```

The next few lines assign values to each element of the array:

```
anArray[0] = 100; // initialize first element
anArray[1] = 200; // initialize second element
anArray[2] = 300; // etc.
```

Each array element is accessed by its numerical index:

```
System.out.println("Element 1 at index 0: " + anArray[0]);
System.out.println("Element 2 at index 1: " + anArray[1]);
System.out.println("Element 3 at index 2: " + anArray[2]);
```

Alternatively, you can use the shortcut syntax to create and initialize an array:

```
int[] anArray = {
    100, 200, 300,
    400, 500, 600,
    700, 800, 900, 1000
};
```

Here the length of the array is determined by the number of values provided between { and }.

You can also declare an array of arrays (also known as a *multidimensional* array) by using two or more sets of square brackets, such as `String[][]` names. Each element, therefore, must be accessed by a corresponding number of index values.

In the Java programming language, a multidimensional array is simply an array whose components are themselves arrays. This is unlike arrays in C or Fortran. Consequentially, the rows are allowed to vary in length, as shown in the following `MultiDimArrayDemo` program:

```
class MultiDimArrayDemo {
    public static void main(String[] args) {
        String[][] names = {
            {"Mr. ", "Mrs. ", "Ms. "},
            {"Smith", "Jones"}
        };
        // Mr. Smith
        System.out.println(names[0][0] + names[1][0]);
        // Ms. Jones
        System.out.println(names[0][2] + names[1][1]);
    }
}
```

The output from this program is as follows:

```
Mr. Smith
Ms. Jones
```

Finally, you can use the built-in `length` property to determine the size of any array. The code

```
System.out.println(anArray.length);
```

will print the array's size to standard output.

Copying Arrays

The `System` class has an `arraycopy` method that you can use to efficiently copy data from one array to another:

```
public static void arraycopy(Object src, int srcPos,
                             Object dest, int destPos, int length)
```

The two `Object` arguments specify the source array (i.e., the array to copy *from*) and the destination array (i.e., the array to copy *to*). The three `int` arguments specify the starting position in the source array, the starting position in the destination array, and the number of array elements to copy.

The following program, `ArrayCopyDemo`, declares an array of `char` elements, spelling the word *decaffeinated*. It uses `arraycopy` to copy a subsequence of array components into a second array:

```
class ArrayCopyDemo {
    public static void main(String[] args) {
        char[] copyFrom = { 'd', 'e', 'c', 'a', 'f', 'f', 'e',
                            'i', 'n', 'a', 't', 'e', 'd' };
        char[] copyTo = new char[7];

        System.arraycopy(copyFrom, 2, copyTo, 0, 7);
        System.out.println(new String(copyTo));
    }
}
```

The output from this program is the following:

```
caffein
```

Summary of Variables

The Java programming language uses the terms *fields* and *variables* as part of its terminology. Instance variables (nonstatic fields) are unique to each instance of a class. Class variables (static fields) are fields declared with the `static` modifier; there is exactly one copy of a class variable, regardless of how many times the class has been instantiated. Local variables represent temporary states inside a method. Parameters are variables that provide extra information to a method; both local variables and parameters are always classified as *variables* (not *fields*). When naming your fields or variables, there are rules and conventions that you should (or must) follow.

The eight primitive data types are `byte`, `short`, `int`, `long`, `float`, `double`, `boolean`, and `char`. The `java.lang.String`[5] class represents character strings. The compiler will assign a reasonable default value for these types of fields. For local variables, a default value is never assigned. A *literal* is the source code representation of a fixed value. An *array* is a container object that holds a fixed number of values of a single type. The length of an array is established when the array is created. After creation, its length is fixed.

Questions and Exercises: Variables

Questions

1. The term *instance variable* is another name for ___.
2. The term *class variable* is another name for ___.
3. A local variable stores temporary state; it is declared inside a ___.

---

5.   `7/docs/api/java/lang/String.html`

4. A variable declared within the opening and closing parenthesis of a method signature is called a ____.
5. What are the eight primitive data types supported by the Java programming language?
6. Character strings are represented by the class ____.
7. An ____ is a container object that holds a fixed number of values of a single type.

3

Exercises

1. Create a small program that defines some fields. Try creating some illegal field names and see what kind of error the compiler produces. Use the naming rules and conventions as a guide.
2. In the program you create, try leaving the fields uninitialized and print out their values. Try the same with a local variable and see what kind of compiler errors you can produce. Becoming familiar with common compiler errors will make it easier to recognize bugs in your code.

Answers

You can find answers to these questions and exercises at `http://docs.oracle.com/javase/tutorial/java/nutsandbolts/QandE/answers_variables.html`.

Operators

Now that you've learned how to declare and initialize variables, you probably want to know how to *do something* with them. Learning the operators of the Java programming language is a good place to start. Operators are special symbols that perform specific operations on one, two, or three *operands* and then return a result.

As we explore the operators of the Java programming language, it may be helpful for you to know ahead of time which operators have the highest precedence. The operators in Table 3.2 are listed according to precedence order. The closer to the top of the table an operator appears, the higher its precedence. Operators with higher precedence are evaluated before operators with relatively lower precedence. Operators on the same line have equal precedence. When operators of equal precedence appear in the same expression, a rule must govern which is evaluated first. All binary operators except for the assignment operators are evaluated from left to right; assignment operators are evaluated right to left.

In general-purpose programming, certain operators tend to appear more frequently than others; for example, the assignment operator (=) is far more common than the unsigned right shift operator (>>>). With this in mind, the following discussion first focuses on the operators that you're most likely to use on a regular basis

Table 3.2 Operator Precedence

Operators	Precedence
postfix	*expr++ expr--*
unary	*++expr --expr +expr -expr ~* !
multiplicative	* / %
additive	+ -
shift	<< >> >>>
relational	< > <= >= instanceof
equality	== !=
bitwise AND	&
bitwise exclusive OR	^
bitwise inclusive OR	|
logical AND	&&
logical OR	||
ternary	? :
assignment	= += -= *= /= %= &= ^= |= <<= >>= >>>=

and then focuses on those that are less common. Each discussion is accompanied by sample code that you can compile and run. Studying its output will help reinforce what you've just learned.

Assignment, Arithmetic, and Unary Operators

The Simple Assignment Operator

One of the most common operators that you'll encounter is the simple assignment operator, =. You saw this operator in the `Bicycle` class; it assigns the value on its right to the operand on its left:

```
int cadence = 0;
int speed = 0;
int gear = 1;
```

This operator can also be used on objects to assign *object references*, which will be discussed in more detail in Chapter 4, "Creating Objects."

The Arithmetic Operators

The Java programming language provides operators that perform addition, subtraction, multiplication, and division. There's a good chance you'll recognize them by their counterparts in basic mathematics. The only symbol that might look new to you is %, which divides one operand by another and returns the remainder as its result.

+	additive operator (also used for String concatenation)
–	subtraction operator
*	multiplication operator
/	division operator
%	remainder operator

The following program, `ArithmeticDemo`, tests the arithmetic operators:

```
class ArithmeticDemo {

    public static void main (String[] args){

        // result is now 3
        int result = 1 + 2;
        System.out.println(result);

        // result is now 2
        result = result - 1;
        System.out.println(result);

        // result is now 4
        result = result * 2;
        System.out.println(result);

        // result is now 2
        result = result / 2;
        System.out.println(result);

        // result is now 10
        result = result + 8;
        // result is now 3
        result = result % 7;
        System.out.println(result);
    }
}
```

You can also combine the arithmetic operators with the simple assignment operator to create *compound assignments*. For example, x+=1; and x=x+1; both increment the value of x by 1. The + operator can also be used for concatenating (joining) two strings together, as shown in the following `ConcatDemo` program:

```
class ConcatDemo {
    public static void main(String[] args){
        String firstString = "This is";
        String secondString =
            " a concatenated string.";
        String thirdString =
            firstString+secondString;
        System.out.println(thirdString);
    }
}
```

By the end of this program, the variable `thirdString` contains `"This is a concatenated string."`, which gets printed to standard output.

The Unary Operators

The unary operators require only one operand; they perform various operations, such as incrementing or decrementing a value by one, negating an expression, or inverting the value of a boolean:

```
+        Unary plus operator; indicates
         positive value (numbers are
         positive without this, however)
-        Unary minus operator; negates
         an expression
++       Increment operator; increments
         a value by 1
--       Decrement operator; decrements
         a value by 1
!        Logical complement operator;
         inverts the value of a boolean
```

The following program, `UnaryDemo`, tests the unary operators:

```
class UnaryDemo {

    public static void main(String[] args){
        // result is now 1
        int result = +1;
        System.out.println(result);
        // result is now 0
        result--;
        System.out.println(result);
        // result is now 1
        result++;
        System.out.println(result);
        // result is now -1
        result = -result;
        System.out.println(result);
        boolean success = false;
        // false
        System.out.println(success);
        // true
        System.out.println(!success);
    }
}
```

The increment/decrement operators can be applied before (prefix) or after (postfix) the operand. The code `result++;` and `++result;` will both end in `result` being incremented by one. The only difference is that the prefix version (`++result`) evaluates to the incremented value, whereas the postfix version (`result++`) evaluates to the original value. If you are just performing a simple increment/decrement, it doesn't really matter which version you choose. But if you use this operator in part of a larger expression, your choice may make a significant difference.

The following program, `PrePostDemo`, illustrates the prefix/postfix unary increment operator:

```
class PrePostDemo {
    public static void main(String[] args){
        int i = 3;
        i++;
        // prints 4
        System.out.println(i);
        ++i;
        // prints 5
        System.out.println(i);
        // prints 6
        System.out.println(++i);
        // prints 6
        System.out.println(i++);
        // prints 7
        System.out.println(i);
    }
}
```

Equality, Relational, and Conditional Operators

The Equality and Relational Operators

The equality and relational operators determine if one operand is greater than, less than, equal to, or not equal to another operand. The majority of these operators will probably look familiar to you as well. Keep in mind that you must use ==, not =, when testing if two primitive values are equal.

```
==        equal to
!=        not equal to
>         greater than
>=        greater than or equal to
<         less than
<=        less than or equal to
```

The following program, `ComparisonDemo`, tests the comparison operators:

```
class ComparisonDemo {

    public static void main(String[] args){
        int value1 = 1;
        int value2 = 2;
        if(value1 == value2)
            System.out.println("value1 == value2");
        if(value1 != value2)
            System.out.println("value1 != value2");
        if(value1 > value2)
            System.out.println("value1 > value2");
        if(value1 < value2)
```

```
                    System.out.println("value1 < value2");
                if(value1 <= value2)
                    System.out.println("value1 <= value2");
        }
    }
```

3

The output is as follows:

```
    value1 != value2
    value1 <  value2
    value1 <= value2
```

The Conditional Operators

The `&&` and `||` operators perform `Conditional-AND` and `Conditional-OR` operations on two boolean expressions. These operators exhibit "short-circuiting" behavior, which means that the second operand is evaluated only if needed.

```
    &&      Conditional-AND
    ||      Conditional-OR
```

The following program, `ConditionalDemo1`, tests these operators:

```
class ConditionalDemo1 {

    public static void main(String[] args){
        int value1 = 1;
        int value2 = 2;
        if((value1 == 1) && (value2 == 2))
            System.out.println("value1 is 1 AND value2 is 2");
        if((value1 == 1) || (value2 == 1))
            System.out.println("value1 is 1 OR value2 is 1");
    }
}
```

Another conditional operator is `?:`, which can be thought of as shorthand for an `if-then-else` statement (discussed in the "Control Flow Statements" section of this chapter). This operator is also known as the *ternary operator* because it uses three operands. In the next example, this operator should be read as follows: "If `someCondition` is `true`, assign the value of `value1` to `result`. Otherwise, assign the value of `value2` to `result`."

The following program, `ConditionalDemo2`, tests the `?:` operator:

```
class ConditionalDemo2 {

    public static void main(String[] args){
        int value1 = 1;
        int value2 = 2;
        int result;
        boolean someCondition = true;
        result = someCondition ? value1 : value2;
```

```
            System.out.println(result);
        }
    }
```

Because someCondition is true, the program prints 1 to the screen. Use the ?: operator instead of an if-then-else statement if it makes your code more readable (e.g., when the expressions are compact and without side effects, such as assignments).

The Type Comparison Operator instanceof

The instanceof operator compares an object to a specified type. You can use it to test if an object is an instance of a class, an instance of a subclass, or an instance of a class that implements a particular interface.

The following program, InstanceofDemo, defines a parent class (named Parent), a simple interface (named MyInterface), and a child class (named Child) that inherits from the parent and implements the interface.

```
class InstanceofDemo {
    public static void main(String[] args) {

        Parent obj1 = new Parent();
        Parent obj2 = new Child();

        System.out.println("obj1 instanceof Parent: "
            + (obj1 instanceof Parent));
        System.out.println("obj1 instanceof Child: "
            + (obj1 instanceof Child));
        System.out.println("obj1 instanceof MyInterface: "
            + (obj1 instanceof MyInterface));
        System.out.println("obj2 instanceof Parent: "
            + (obj2 instanceof Parent));
        System.out.println("obj2 instanceof Child: "
            + (obj2 instanceof Child));
        System.out.println("obj2 instanceof MyInterface: "
            + (obj2 instanceof MyInterface));
    }
}

class Parent {}
class Child extends Parent implements MyInterface {}
interface MyInterface {}
```

The output is as follows:

```
obj1 instanceof Parent: true
obj1 instanceof Child: false
obj1 instanceof MyInterface: false
obj2 instanceof Parent: true
obj2 instanceof Child: true
obj2 instanceof MyInterface: true
```

When using the `instanceof` operator, keep in mind that `null` is not an instance of anything.

Bitwise and Bit Shift Operators

The Java programming language also provides operators that perform bitwise and bit shift operations on integral types. The operators discussed in this section are less common. Therefore they are covered only briefly; the intent is to simply make you aware that these operators exist.

The unary bitwise complement operator (~) inverts a bit pattern; it can be applied to any of the integral types, making every 0 a 1 and every 1 a 0. For example, a `byte` contains 8 bits; applying this operator to a value whose bit pattern is 00000000 would change its pattern to 11111111.

The signed left shift operator (<<) shifts a bit pattern to the left, and the signed right shift operator (>>) shifts a bit pattern to the right. The bit pattern is given by the left-hand operand, and the number of positions to shift is given by the right-hand operand. The unsigned right shift operator (>>>) shifts a zero into the leftmost position, while the leftmost position after >> depends on sign extension.

The bitwise & operator performs a bitwise AND operation. The bitwise ^ operator performs a bitwise exclusive OR operation. The bitwise | operator performs a bitwise inclusive OR operation.

The following program, `BitDemo`, uses the bitwise AND operator to print the number 2 to standard output:

```
class BitDemo {
    public static void main(String[] args) {
        int bitmask = 0x000F;
        int val = 0x2222;
        // prints "2"
        System.out.println(val & bitmask);
    }
}
```

Summary of Operators

The following quick reference summarizes the operators supported by the Java programming language.

Simple Assignment Operator

=   Simple assignment operator

Arithmetic Operators

+   Additive operator (also used for `String` concatenation)

- Subtraction operator
* Multiplication operator
/ Division operator
% Remainder operator

Unary Operators

+ Unary plus operator; indicates a positive value, although numbers can be positive without this
- Unary minus operator; negates an expression
++ Increment operator; increments a value by 1
-- Decrement operator; decrements a value by 1
! Logical complement operator; inverts the value of a boolean

Equality and Relational Operators

== Equal to
!= Not equal to
> Greater than
>= Greater than or equal to
< Less than
<= Less than or equal to

Conditional Operators

&& Conditional AND
|| Conditional OR
?: Ternary (shorthand for if-then-else statement)

Type Comparison Operator

instanceof   Compares an object to a specified type

Bitwise and Bit Shift Operators

~ Unary bitwise complement
<< Signed left shift
>> Signed right shift
>>> Unsigned right shift
& Bitwise AND
^ Bitwise exclusive OR
| Bitwise inclusive OR

Questions and Exercises: Operators

Questions

1. Consider the following code snippet:

```
arrayOfInts[j] > arrayOfInts[j+1]
```

   Which operators does the code contain?

2. Consider the following code snippet:

```
int i = 10;
int n = i++%5;
```

   a. What are the values of i and n after the code is executed?

   b. What are the final values of i and n if instead of using the postfix increment operator (i++), you use the prefix version (++i)?

3. To invert the value of a boolean, which operator would you use?

4. Which operator is used to compare two values: = or ==?

5. Explain the following code sample: result = someCondition ? value1 : value2;

Exercises

1. Change the following program so that it uses compound assignments:

```
class ArithmeticDemo {

    public static void main (String[] args){

        int result = 1 + 2; // result is now 3
        System.out.println(result);

        result = result - 1; // result is now 2
        System.out.println(result);

        result = result * 2; // result is now 4
        System.out.println(result);

        result = result / 2; // result is now 2
        System.out.println(result);

        result = result + 8; // result is now 10
        result = result % 7; // result is now 3
        System.out.println(result);
    }
}
```

2. In the following program, explain why the value 6 is printed twice in a row:

```
class PrePostDemo {

    public static void main(String[] args){
        int i = 3;
        i++;
```

```
                        System.out.println(i);    // "4"
                        ++i;
                        System.out.println(i);    // "5"
                        System.out.println(++i);  // "6"
                        System.out.println(i++);  // "6"
                        System.out.println(i);    // "7"
                }
        }
```

Answers

You can find answers to these questions and exercises at http://docs.oracle.com/
javase/tutorial/java/nutsandbolts/QandE/answers_operators.html.

Expressions, Statements, and Blocks

Now that you understand variables and operators, it's time to learn about *expressions*, *statements*, and *blocks*. Operators can be used in building expressions, which compute values. Expressions are the core components of statements, and statements can be grouped into blocks.

Expressions

An *expression* is a construct made up of variables, operators, and method invocations (which are constructed according to the syntax of the language) that evaluates to a single value. You've already seen examples of expressions, illustrated here in bold:

```
int cadence = 0;
anArray[0] = 100;
System.out.println("Element 1 at index 0: " + anArray[0]);

int result = 1 + 2; // result is now 3
if (value1 == value2)
    System.out.println("value1 == value2");
```

The data type of the value returned by an expression depends on the elements used in the expression. The expression cadence = 0 returns an int because the assignment operator returns a value of the same data type as its left-hand operand; in this case, cadence is an int. As you can see from the other expressions, an expression can return other types of values as well, such as boolean or String.

The Java programming language allows you to construct compound expressions from various smaller expressions as long as the data type required by one part of the expression matches the data type of the other. Here's an example of a compound expression:

```
1 * 2 * 3
```

In this particular example, the order in which the expression is evaluated is unimportant because the result of the multiplication is independent of the order; the outcome is always the same, regardless of the order of the numbers being multiplied. However, this is not true for all expressions. For example, the following expression gives different results, depending on the order in which you perform the addition and the division operations:

```
x + y / 100     // ambiguous
```

You can specify exactly how an expression will be evaluated using parentheses. For example, to make the previous expression unambiguous, you could write the following:

```
(x + y) / 100  // unambiguous, recommended
```

If you don't explicitly indicate the order for the operations to be performed, the order is determined by the precedence assigned to the operators in use within the expression. Operators that have a higher precedence get evaluated first. For example, the division operator has a higher precedence than the addition operator. Therefore, the following two statements are equivalent:

```
x + y / 100

x + (y / 100)  // unambiguous, recommended
```

When writing compound expressions, be explicit and indicate with parentheses which operators should be evaluated first. This practice makes code easier to read and maintain.

Statements

Statements are roughly equivalent to sentences in natural languages. A statement forms a complete unit of execution. The following types of expressions can be made into a statement by terminating the expression with a semicolon:

- Assignment expressions
- Any use of ++ or --
- Method invocations
- Object-creation expressions

Such statements are called *expression statements*. Here are some examples of expression statements:

```
// assignment statement
aValue = 8933.234;
// increment statement
aValue++;
// method invocation statement
System.out.println("Hello World!");
// object creation statement
Bicycle myBike = new Bicycle();
```

In addition to expression statements, there are two other kinds of statements: *declaration statements* and *control flow statements*. A *declaration statement* declares a variable. You've seen many examples of declaration statements already:

```
// declaration statement
double aValue = 8933.234;
```

A *control flow statements* regulates the order in which statements get executed. You'll learn about control flow statements later on in this chapter.

Blocks

A *block* is a group of zero or more statements between braces and can be used anywhere a single statement is allowed. The following example, `BlockDemo`, illustrates the use of blocks:

```
class BlockDemo {
    public static void main(String[] args) {
        boolean condition = true;
        if (condition) { // begin block 1
            System.out.println("Condition is true.");
        } // end block one
        else { // begin block 2
            System.out.println("Condition is false.");
        } // end block 2
    }
}
```

Questions and Exercises: Expressions, Statements, and Blocks

Questions

1. Operators may be used in building ___, which compute values.
2. Expressions are the core components of ___.
3. Statements can be grouped into ___.
4. The following code snippet is an example of a ___ expression.

```
1 * 2 * 3
```

5. Statements are roughly equivalent to sentences in natural languages, but instead of ending with a period, a statement ends with a ___.

6. A block is a group of zero or more statements between balanced ___ and can be used anywhere a single statement is allowed.

Exercises

Identify the following kinds of expression statements:

- `aValue = 8933.234;`
- `aValue++;`
- `System.out.println("Hello World!");`
- `Bicycle myBike = new Bicycle();`

Answers

You can find answers to these questions and exercises at `http://docs.oracle.com/ javase/tutorial/java/nutsandbolts/QandE/answers_expressions.html`.

Control Flow Statements

The statements inside your source files are generally executed from top to bottom, in the order that they appear. *Control flow statements*, however, break up the flow of execution by employing decision making, looping, and branching, enabling your program to *conditionally* execute particular blocks of code. This section describes the decision-making statements (`if-then`, `if-then-else`, `switch`), looping statements (`for`, `while`, `do-while`), and branching statements (`break`, `continue`, `return`) supported by the Java programming language.

The if-then and if-then-else Statements

The if-then Statement

The `if-then` statement is the most basic of all the control flow statements. It tells your program to execute a certain section of code *only if* a particular test evaluates to `true`. Returning to our bike example, the `Bicycle` class could allow the brakes to decrease the bicycle's speed *only if* the bicycle is already in motion. One possible implementation of the `applyBrakes` method could be as follows:

```
void applyBrakes() {
    // the "if" clause: bicycle must be moving
    if (isMoving){
        // the "then" clause: decrease current speed
        currentSpeed--;
    }
}
```

If this test evaluates to `false` (meaning that the bicycle is not in motion), control jumps to the end of the `if-then` statement.

In addition, the opening and closing braces are optional, provided that the "then" clause contains only one statement:

```
void applyBrakes() {
    // same as above, but without braces
    if (isMoving)
        currentSpeed--;
}
```

Deciding when to omit the braces is a matter of personal taste. Omitting them can make the code more brittle. A common mistake is forgetting to add the newly required braces when adding a second statement to the *then* clause. The compiler cannot catch this sort of error; you'll just get the wrong results.

The if-then-else Statement

The `if-then-else` statement provides a secondary path of execution when an *if* clause evaluates to `false`. You could use an `if-then-else` statement in the `applyBrakes` method to take some action if the brakes are applied when the bicycle is not in motion. In this case, the action is to simply print an error message stating that the bicycle has already stopped:

```
void applyBrakes() {
    if (isMoving) {
        currentSpeed--;
    } else {
        System.err.println("The bicycle has " + "already stopped!");
    }
}
```

The following program, `IfElseDemo`, assigns a grade based on the value of a test score: an A for a score of 90% or above, a B for a score of 80% or above, and so on:

```
class IfElseDemo {
    public static void main(String[] args) {

        int testscore = 76;
        char grade;

        if (testscore >= 90) {
            grade = 'A';
        } else if (testscore >= 80) {
            grade = 'B';
        } else if (testscore >= 70) {
            grade = 'C';
        } else if (testscore >= 60) {
            grade = 'D';
```

```
            } else {
                grade = 'F';
            }
            System.out.println("Grade = " + grade);
        }
    }
```

The output from the program is as follows:

```
    Grade = C
```

You may have noticed that the value of `testscore` can satisfy more than one expression in the compound statement: `76 >= 70` and `76 >= 60`. However, once a condition is satisfied, the appropriate statements are executed (`grade = 'C';`) and the remaining conditions are not evaluated.

The switch Statement

Unlike `if-then` and `if-then-else` statements, `switch` statements can have a number of possible execution paths. A `switch` works with the `byte`, `short`, `char`, and `int` primitive data types. It also works with *enumerated types* (discussed in Chapter 4, "Enum Types"), the `String`[6] class, and a few special classes that wrap certain primitive types: `Character`,[7] `Byte`,[8] `Short`,[9] and `Integer`[10] (discussed in Chapter 8, "Numbers and Strings").

The following code example, `SwitchDemo`, declares an `int` named `month` whose value represents a month. The code displays the name of the month, based on the value of `month`, using the `switch` statement:

```
    public class SwitchDemo {
        public static void main(String[] args) {

            int month = 8;
            String monthString;
            switch (month) {
                case 1:  monthString = "January";
                         break;
                case 2:  monthString = "February";
                         break;
                case 3:  monthString = "March";
                         break;
```

---

6. 7/docs/api/java/lang/String.html

7. 7/docs/api/java/lang/Character.html

8. 7/docs/api/java/lang/Byte.html

9. 7/docs/api/java/lang/Short.html

10. 7/docs/api/java/lang/Integer.html

```
            case 4:   monthString = "April";
                      break;
            case 5:   monthString = "May";
                      break;
            case 6:   monthString = "June";
                      break;
            case 7:   monthString = "July";
                      break;
            case 8:   monthString = "August";
                      break;
            case 9:   monthString = "September";
                      break;
            case 10:  monthString = "October";
                      break;
            case 11:  monthString = "November";
                      break;
            case 12:  monthString = "December";
                      break;
            default:  monthString = "Invalid month";
                      break;
        }
        System.out.println(monthString);
    }
}
```

In this case, August is printed to standard output.

The body of a switch statement is known as a *switch block*. A statement in the switch block can be labeled with one or more case or default labels. The switch statement evaluates its expression and executes all statements that follow the matching case label.

You could also display the name of the month with if-then-else statements:

```
int month = 8;
if (month == 1) {
    System.out.println("January");
} else if (month == 2) {
    System.out.println("February");
}
    . . .   // and so on
```

The choice between if-then-else statements or a switch statement depends on readability and the expression that the statement is testing. An if-then-else statement can test expressions based on ranges of values or conditions, whereas a switch statement tests expressions based only on a single integer, enumerated value, or String object.

Another point of interest is the break statement. Each break statement terminates the enclosing switch statement. Control flow continues with the first statement following the switch block. The break statements are necessary because without them, statements in switch blocks *fall through*: all statements after the matching case label are executed in sequence, regardless of the expression of subsequent `case` labels, until a `break` statement is encountered. The program `SwitchDemoFallThrough` shows statements in a `switch` block that fall through. The program displays the month corresponding to the integer `month` and the months that follow in the year:

```java
public class SwitchDemoFallThrough {

    public static void main(String args[]) {
        java.util.ArrayList<String> futureMonths =
            new java.util.ArrayList<String>();

        int month = 8;

        switch (month) {
            case 1:  futureMonths.add("January");
            case 2:  futureMonths.add("February");
            case 3:  futureMonths.add("March");
            case 4:  futureMonths.add("April");
            case 5:  futureMonths.add("May");
            case 6:  futureMonths.add("June");
            case 7:  futureMonths.add("July");
            case 8:  futureMonths.add("August");
            case 9:  futureMonths.add("September");
            case 10: futureMonths.add("October");
            case 11: futureMonths.add("November");
            case 12: futureMonths.add("December");
                     break;
            default: break;
        }

        if (futureMonths.isEmpty()) {
            System.out.println("Invalid month number");
        } else {
            for (String monthName : futureMonths) {
                System.out.println(monthName);
            }
        }
    }
}
```

This is the output from the code:

```
August
September
October
November
December
```

Technically, the final `break` is not required because flow falls out of the `switch` statement. Using a `break` is recommended so that modifying the code is easier and less error prone. The `default` section handles all values that are not explicitly handled by one of the `case` sections.

The following code example, SwitchDemo2, shows how a statement can have multiple case labels. The code example calculates the number of days in a particular month:

```java
class SwitchDemo2 {
    public static void main(String[] args) {

        int month = 2;
        int year = 2000;
        int numDays = 0;

        switch (month) {
            case 1: case 3: case 5:
            case 7: case 8: case 10:
            case 12:
                numDays = 31;
                break;
            case 4: case 6:
            case 9: case 11:
                numDays = 30;
                break;
            case 2:
                if (((year % 4 == 0) &&
                        !(year % 100 == 0))
                        || (year % 400 == 0))
                    numDays = 29;
                else
                    numDays = 28;
                break;
            default:
                System.out.println("Invalid month.");
                break;
        }
        System.out.println("Number of Days = "
                            + numDays);
    }
}
```

This is the output from the code:

```
Number of Days = 29
```

Using Strings in switch Statements

In Java SE 7 and later, you can use a String object in the switch statement's expression. The following code example, StringSwitchDemo, displays the number of the month based on the value of the String named month:

```java
public class StringSwitchDemo {

    public static int getMonthNumber(String month) {

        int monthNumber = 0;
```

```java
    if (month == null) {
        return monthNumber;
    }

    switch (month.toLowerCase()) {
        case "january":
            monthNumber = 1;
            break;
        case "february":
            monthNumber = 2;
            break;
        case "march":
            monthNumber = 3;
            break;
        case "april":
            monthNumber = 4;
            break;
        case "may":
            monthNumber = 5;
            break;
        case "june":
            monthNumber = 6;
            break;
        case "july":
            monthNumber = 7;
            break;
        case "august":
            monthNumber = 8;
            break;
        case "september":
            monthNumber = 9;
            break;
        case "october":
            monthNumber = 10;
            break;
        case "november":
            monthNumber = 11;
            break;
        case "december":
            monthNumber = 12;
            break;
        default:
            monthNumber = 0;
            break;
    }

    return monthNumber;
}

public static void main(String[] args) {

    String month = "August";

    int returnedMonthNumber =
        StringSwitchDemo.getMonthNumber(month);

    if (returnedMonthNumber == 0) {
        System.out.println("Invalid month");
```

```
        } else {
            System.out.println(returnedMonthNumber);
        }
    }
}
```

The output from this code is 8.

The `String` in the `switch` expression is compared with the expressions associated with each `case` label, just as if the `String.equals`[11] method was being used. In order for the `StringSwitchDemo` example to accept any month regardless of case, `month` is converted to lowercase (with the `toLowerCase`[12] method), and all the strings associated with the `case` labels are in lowercase.

> **Note**
>
> This example checks if the expression in the `switch` statement is `null`. Ensure that the expression in any `switch` statement is not null to prevent a `NullPointerException` from being thrown.

The while and do-while Statements

The `while` statement continually executes a block of statements while a particular condition is `true`. Its syntax can be expressed as follows:

```
while (expression) {
    statement(s)
}
```

The `while` statement evaluates *expression*, which must return a `boolean` value. If the expression evaluates to `true`, the `while` statement executes the *statement*(s) in the `while` block. The `while` statement continues testing the expression and executing its block until the expression evaluates to `false`. Using the `while` statement to print values from 1 through 10 can be accomplished via the following `WhileDemo` program:

```
class WhileDemo {
    public static void main(String[] args){
        int count = 1;
        while (count < 11) {
            System.out.println("Count is: " + count);
```

---

11. 7/docs/api/java/lang/String.html#equals(java.lang.Object)

12. 7/docs/api/java/lang/String.html#toLowerCase()

```
            count++;
        }
    }
}
```

3

You can also implement an infinite loop using the `while` statement:

```
while (true){
    // your code goes here
}
```

The Java programming language also provides a `do-while` statement, which can be expressed as follows:

```
do {
    statement(s)
} while (expression);
```

The difference between `do-while` and `while` is that `do-while` evaluates its expression at the bottom of the loop instead of the top. Therefore, the statements within the do block are always executed at least once, as shown in the following `DoWhileDemo` program:

```
class DoWhileDemo {
    public static void main(String[] args){
        int count = 1;
        do {
            System.out.println("Count is: " + count);
            count++;
        } while (count < 11);
    }
}
```

The for Statement

The `for` statement provides a compact way to iterate over a range of values. Programmers often refer to it as the *for loop* because of the way in which it repeatedly loops until a particular condition is satisfied. The general form of the `for` statement can be expressed as follows:

```
for (initialization; termination;
    increment) {
    statement(s)
}
```

When using this version of the `for` statement, keep the following factors in mind:

- The *initialization* expression initializes the loop; it's executed once, as the loop begins.
- When the *termination* expression evaluates to `false`, the loop terminates.
- The *increment* expression is invoked after each iteration through the loop; it is perfectly acceptable for this expression to increment *or* decrement a value.

The following program, `ForDemo`, uses the general form of the `for` statement to print the numbers 1 through 10 to standard output:

```
class ForDemo {
    public static void main(String[] args){
        for(int i=1; i<11; i++){
            System.out.println("Count is: " + i);
        }
    }
}
```

Here is the output of this program:

```
Count is: 1
Count is: 2
Count is: 3
Count is: 4
Count is: 5
Count is: 6
Count is: 7
Count is: 8
Count is: 9
Count is: 10
```

Notice how the code declares a variable within the initialization expression. The scope of this variable extends from its declaration to the end of the block governed by the `for` statement, so it can be used in the termination and increment expressions as well. If the variable that controls a `for` statement is not needed outside of the loop, it's best to declare the variable in the initialization expression. The names i, j, and k are often used to control `for` loops; declaring them within the initialization expression limits their life span and reduces errors.

The three expressions of the `for` loop are optional; an infinite loop can be created as follows:

```
// infinite loop
for ( ; ; ) {

    // your code goes here
}
```

The `for` statement also has another form designed for iteration through collections and arrays. This form is sometimes referred to as the *enhanced for* statement and can be used to make your loops more compact and easy to read. To demonstrate, consider the following array, which holds the numbers 1 through 10:

```
int[] numbers = {1,2,3,4,5,6,7,8,9,10};
```

The following program, `EnhancedForDemo`, uses the enhanced `for` to loop through the array:

```
class EnhancedForDemo {
    public static void main(String[] args){
        int[] numbers =
            {1,2,3,4,5,6,7,8,9,10};
        for (int item : numbers) {
            System.out.println("Count is: " + item);
        }
    }
}
```

In this example, the variable `item` holds the current value from the numbers array. The output from this program is the same as before:

```
Count is: 1
Count is: 2
Count is: 3
Count is: 4
Count is: 5
Count is: 6
Count is: 7
Count is: 8
Count is: 9
Count is: 10
```

We recommend using this form of the `for` statement instead of the general form whenever possible.

Branching Statements

The break Statement

The `break` statement has two forms: labeled and unlabeled. You saw the unlabeled form in the previous discussion of the `switch` statement. You can also use an unlabeled `break` to terminate a `for`, `while`, or `do-while` loop, as shown in the following `BreakDemo` program:

```
class BreakDemo {
    public static void main(String[] args) {
```

```
            int[] arrayOfInts = { 32, 87, 3, 589,
                                  12, 1076, 2000,
                                  8, 622, 127 };
            int searchfor = 12;

            int i;
            boolean foundIt = false;

            for (i = 0; i < arrayOfInts.length; i++) {
                if (arrayOfInts[i] == searchfor) {
                    foundIt = true;
                    break;
                }
            }

            if (foundIt) {
                System.out.println("Found " + searchfor + " at index " + i);
            } else {
                System.out.println(searchfor + " not in the array");
            }
        }
    }
```

This program searches for the number 12 in an array. The break statement
(shown in bold) terminates the for loop when that value is found. Control flow then
transfers to the statement after the for loop. Here is the program's output:

```
Found 12 at index 4
```

An unlabeled break statement terminates the innermost switch, for, while,
or do-while statements, but a labeled break terminates an outer statement. The
following program, BreakWithLabelDemo, is similar to the previous program but
uses nested for loops to search for a value in a two-dimensional array. When the
value is found, a labeled break terminates the outer for loop (labeled *search*):

```
class BreakWithLabelDemo {
    public static void main(String[] args) {

        int[][] arrayOfInts = {
            { 32, 87, 3, 589 },
            { 12, 1076, 2000, 8 },
            { 622, 127, 77, 955 }
        };
        int searchfor = 12;

        int i;
        int j = 0;
        boolean foundIt = false;

search:
        for (i = 0; i < arrayOfInts.length; i++) {
            for (j = 0; j < arrayOfInts[i].length;
```

```
            j++) {
            if (arrayOfInts[i][j] == searchfor) {
                foundIt = true;
                break search;
            }
        }
    }

    if (foundIt) {
        System.out.println("Found " + searchfor + " at " + i + ", " + j);
    } else {
        System.out.println(searchfor + " not in the array");
    }
}
}
```

This is the output of the program:

```
Found 12 at 1, 0
```

The break statement terminates the labeled statement; it does not transfer the flow of control to the label. Control flow is transferred to the statement immediately following the labeled (terminated) statement.

The continue Statement

The continue statement skips the current iteration of a for, while, or do-while loop. The unlabeled form skips to the end of the innermost loop's body and evaluates the boolean expression that controls the loop. The following program, ContinueDemo, steps through a String, counting the occurrences of the letter *p*. If the current character is not a *p*, the continue statement skips the rest of the loop and proceeds to the next character. If it is a *p*, the program increments the letter count:

```
class ContinueDemo {
    public static void main(String[] args) {

        String searchMe
            = "peter piper picked a " + "peck of pickled peppers";
        int max = searchMe.length();
        int numPs = 0;

        for (int i = 0; i < max; i++) {
            // interested only in p's
            if (searchMe.charAt(i) != 'p')
                continue;

            // process p's
            numPs++;
        }
        System.out.println("Found " + numPs + " p's in the string.");
```

```
        }
    }
```

Here is the output of this program:

```
 Found 9 p's in the string.
```

To see this effect more clearly, try removing the continue statement and recompiling. When you run the program again, the count will be wrong, saying that it found 35 *p*'s instead of 9.

A labeled continue statement skips the current iteration of an outer loop marked with the given label. The following example program, ContinueWithLabelDemo, uses nested loops to search for a substring within another string. Two nested loops are required: one to iterate over the substring and the other to iterate over the string being searched. The following program, ContinueWithLabelDemo, uses the labeled form of the continue statement to skip an iteration in the outer loop:

```
class ContinueWithLabelDemo {
    public static void main(String[] args) {

        String searchMe = "Look for a substring in me";
        String substring = "sub";
        boolean foundIt = false;

        int max = searchMe.length() - substring.length();

    test:
        for (int i = 0; i <= max; i++) {
            int n = substring.length();
            int j = i;
            int k = 0;
            while (n-- != 0) {
                if (searchMe.charAt(j++) != substring.charAt(k++)) {
                    continue test;
                }
            }
            foundIt = true;
                break test;
        }
        System.out.println(foundIt ? "Found it" : "Didn't find it");
    }
}
```

Here is the output from this program:

```
Found it
```

The return Statement

The last of the branching statements is the `return` statement. The `return` statement exits from the current method, and control flow returns to where the method was invoked. The `return` statement has two forms: one that returns a value and another that doesn't. To return a value, simply put the value (or an expression that calculates the value) after the `return` keyword:

```
return ++count;
```

The data type of the returned value must match the type of the method's declared return value. When a method is declared `void`, use the form of `return` that doesn't return a value:

```
return;
```

Chapter 4 covers everything you need to know about writing methods.

Summary of Control Flow Statements

The `if-then` statement is the most basic of all the control flow statements. It tells your program to execute a certain section of code *only if* a particular test evaluates to `true`. The `if-then-else` statement provides a secondary path of execution when an `if` clause evaluates to `false`. Unlike `if-then` and `if-then-else`, the `switch` statement allows for any number of possible execution paths. The `while` and `do-while` statements continually execute a block of statements while a particular condition is `true`. The difference between `do-while` and `while` is that `do-while` evaluates its expression at the bottom of the loop instead of the top. Therefore, the statements within the `do` block are always executed at least once. The `for` statement provides a compact way to iterate over a range of values. It has two forms, one of which was designed for looping through collections and arrays.

Questions and Exercises: Control Flow Statements

Questions

1. The most basic control flow statement supported by the Java programming language is the ___ statement.
2. The ___ statement allows for any number of possible execution paths.
3. The ___ statement is similar to the `while` statement but evaluates its expression at the ___ of the loop.
4. How do you write an infinite loop using the `for` statement?
5. How do you write an infinite loop using the `while` statement?

Exercises

1. Consider the following code snippet:

   ```
   if (aNumber >= 0)
       if (aNumber == 0)
           System.out.println("first string");
   else System.out.println("second string");
   System.out.println("third string");
   ```

   a. What output do you think the code will produce if aNumber is 3?

   b. Write a test program containing the previous code snippet; make aNumber 3. What is the output of the program? Is it what you predicted? Explain why the output is what it is. In other words, what is the control flow for the code snippet?

   c. Using only spaces and line breaks, reformat the code snippet to make the control flow easier to understand.

   d. Use braces to further clarify the code.

Answers

You can find answers to these questions and exercises at http://docs.oracle.com/javase/tutorial/java/nutsandbolts/QandE/answers_flow.html.

4

Classes and Objects

With the knowledge you now have of the basics of the Java programming language, you can learn to write your own classes. In this chapter, you will find information about defining your own classes, including declaring member variables, methods, and constructors. You will learn to use your classes to create objects and how to use the objects you create. This chapter also covers nesting classes within other classes, enumerations, and annotations.

The first section shows you the anatomy of a class and how to declare fields, methods, and constructors. The second section covers creating and using objects. You will learn how to instantiate an object and, once instantiated, how to use the dot operator to access the object's instance variables and methods. The third section covers more aspects of classes that depend on object references and the dot operator: returning values from methods, the this keyword, class versus instance members, and access control. The fourth section discusses static nested classes, inner classes, anonymous inner classes, and local classes. The fifth section covers enumerations—specialized classes that allow you to define and use sets of constants. The final section describes three built-in annotations that you should know about. Annotations allow you to add information to your program that is not actually part of the program. Selected sections contain questions and exercises to test your understanding.

Classes

The introduction to object-oriented concepts in Chapter 2 used a `Bicycle` class as an example, with racing bikes, mountain bikes, and tandem bikes as subclasses. Here is sample code for a possible implementation of a `Bicycle` class, to give you an overview of a class declaration. Subsequent sections of this chapter will back up and explain class declarations step by step. For the moment, don't concern yourself with the details.

```
public class Bicycle {

    // the Bicycle class has
    // three fields
    public int cadence;
    public int gear;
    public int speed;

    // the Bicycle class has
    // one constructor
    public Bicycle(int startCadence, int startSpeed, int startGear) {
        gear = startGear;
        cadence = startCadence;
        speed = startSpeed;
    }

    // the Bicycle class has
    // four methods
    public void setCadence(int newValue) {
        cadence = newValue;
    }

    public void setGear(int newValue) {
        gear = newValue;
    }

    public void applyBrake(int decrement) {
        speed -= decrement;
    }

    public void speedUp(int increment) {
        speed += increment;
    }

}
```

A class declaration for a `MountainBike` class that is a subclass of `Bicycle` might look like this:

```
public class MountainBike extends Bicycle {

    // the MountainBike subclass has
    // one field
    public int seatHeight;

    // the MountainBike subclass has
    // one constructor
    public MountainBike(int startHeight, int startCadence,
                        int startSpeed, int startGear) {
        super(startCadence, startSpeed, startGear);
        seatHeight = startHeight;
    }

    // the MountainBike subclass has
    // one method
    public void setHeight(int newValue) {
        seatHeight = newValue;
    }

}
```

MountainBike inherits all the fields and methods of Bicycle and adds the field seatHeight and a method to set it. (Mountain bikes have seats that can be moved up and down as the terrain demands).

Declaring Classes

You've seen classes defined in the following way:

```
class MyClass {
    // field, constructor, and
    // method declarations
}
```

This is a *class declaration*. The *class body* (the area between the braces) contains all the code that provides for the life cycle of the objects created from the class: constructors for initializing new objects, declarations for the fields that provide the state of the class and its objects, and methods to implement the behavior of the class and its objects.

The preceding class declaration is a minimal one. It contains only those components of a class declaration that are required. You can provide more information about the class, such as the name of its superclass, whether it implements any interfaces, and so on, at the start of the class declaration. Here's an example:

```
class MyClass extends MySuperClass implements YourInterface {
    // field, constructor, and
    // method declarations
}
```

This means that `MyClass` is a subclass of `MySuperClass` and that it implements the `YourInterface` interface.

You can also add modifiers like *public* or *private* at the very beginning. Thus it's pretty clear that the opening line of a class declaration can become quite complicated. The modifiers *public* and *private*, which determine what other classes can access `MyClass`, are discussed later in this chapter. Chapter 5 will explain how and why you would use the *extends* and *implements* keywords in a class declaration. For the moment, you do not need to worry about these extra complications.

In general, class declarations can include these components, in order:

1. Modifiers such as *public*, *private*, and a number of others that you will encounter later

2. The class name, with the initial letter capitalized by convention

3. The name of the class's parent (superclass), if any, preceded by the keyword *extends* (Note that a class can only *extend* [subclass] one parent.)

4. A comma-separated list of interfaces implemented by the class, if any, preceded by the keyword *implements* (Note that a class can *implement* more than one interface.)

5. The class body, surrounded by braces: {}

Declaring Member Variables

There are several kinds of variables:

- *Member variables in a class.* These are called *fields.*
- *Variables in a method or block of code.* These are called *local variables.*
- *Variables in method declarations.* These are called *parameters.*

The `Bicycle` class uses the following lines of code to define its fields:

```
public int cadence;
public int gear;
public int speed;
```

Field declarations are composed of three components, in order:

1. Zero or more modifiers, such as `public` or `private`

2. The field's type

3. The field's name

The fields of `Bicycle` are named `cadence`, `gear`, and `speed` and are all of data type integer (`int`). The `public` keyword identifies these fields as public members, accessible by any object that can access the class.

Access Modifiers

The first (left-most) modifier used lets you control what other classes have access to a member field. For the moment, consider only `public` and `private`, defined as follows. Other access modifiers will be discussed later:

- *public modifier.* The field is accessible from all classes
- *private modifier.* The field is accessible only within its own class

In the spirit of encapsulation, it is common to make fields `private`. This means that they can only be *directly* accessed from the `Bicycle` class. We still need access to these values, however. This can be done *indirectly* by adding `public` methods that obtain the field values for us:

```
public class Bicycle {

    private int cadence;
    private int gear;
    private int speed;

    public Bicycle(int startCadence, int startSpeed, int startGear) {
        gear = startGear;
        cadence = startCadence;
        speed = startSpeed;
    }

    public int getCadence() {
        return cadence;
    }

    public void setCadence(int newValue) {
        cadence = newValue;
    }

    public int getGear() {
        return gear;
    }

    public void setGear(int newValue) {
        gear = newValue;
    }

    public int getSpeed() {
        return speed;
    }

    public void applyBrake(int decrement) {
```

4

```
            speed -= decrement;
        }

    public void speedUp(int increment) {
            speed += increment;
        }
    }
```

Types

All variables must have a type. You can use primitive types such as int, float, boolean, and so on, or you can use reference types, such as strings, arrays, or objects.

Variable Names

All variables, whether they are fields, local variables, or parameters, follow the same naming rules and conventions that were covered in Chapter 3. Be aware that the same naming rules and conventions are used for method and class names, with the following exceptions:

- The first letter of a class name should be capitalized.
- The first (or only) word in a method name should be a verb.

Defining Methods

Here is an example of a typical method declaration:

```
public double calculateAnswer(double wingSpan, int numberOfEngines,
                              double length, double grossTons) {
    //do the calculation here
}
```

The only required elements of a method declaration are the method's return type and name; a pair of parentheses, ( ); and a body between braces, { }. More generally, method declarations have six components (listed in order):

1. *Modifiers.* Some examples include public and private; you will learn some other examples later.
2. *The return type.* This is the data type of the value returned by the method (or void if the method does not return a value).
3. *The method name.* The rules for field names apply to method names as well, but the convention is a little different.
4. *The parameter list in parenthesis.* This is a comma-delimited list of input parameters, preceded by their data types, enclosed in parentheses. If there are no parameters, you must use empty parentheses.

5. *An exception list.* This will be discussed later.

6. *The method body, enclosed in braces.* The method's code, including the declaration of local variables, goes here.

Modifiers, return types, and parameters will be discussed later in this chapter. Exceptions are discussed in Chapter 9.

> **Definition**
>
> Two components of a method declaration compose the *method signature*—the method's name and the parameter types.

Here is the signature of the method declared previously:

```
calculateAnswer(double, int, double, double)
```

Naming a Method

Although a method name can be any legal identifier, code conventions restrict method names. By convention, method names should be a verb in lowercase or a multiword name that begins with a verb in lowercase followed by adjectives, nouns, and so on. In multiword names, the first letter of each of the second and following words should be capitalized. Here are some examples:

```
run
runFast
getBackground
getFinalData
compareTo
setX
isEmpty
```

Typically, a method has a unique name within its class. However, a method might have the same name as other methods due to *method overloading*.

Overloading Methods

The Java programming language supports *overloading* methods, and Java can distinguish between methods with different *method signatures*. This means that methods within a class can have the same name if they have different parameter lists. (Note there are some qualifications to this that will be discussed in Chapter 5.)

Suppose that you have a class that can use calligraphy to draw various types of data (strings, integers, etc.) and contains a method for drawing each data type. It is cumbersome to use a new name for each method (e.g., `drawString`, `drawInteger`, `drawFloat`). In the Java programming language, you can use the same name for all the drawing methods but pass a different argument list to each method. Thus the data-drawing class might declare four methods named `draw`, each of which has a different parameter list:

```
public class DataArtist {
    . . .
    public void draw(String s) {
        . . .
    }
    public void draw(int i) {
        . . .
    }
    public void draw(double f) {
        . . .
    }
    public void draw(int i, double f) {
        . . .
    }
}
```

Overloaded methods are differentiated by the number and the type of arguments passed into the method. In the code sample, `draw(String s)` and `draw(int i)` are distinct and unique methods because they require different argument types. You can't declare more than one method with the same name and the same number and type of arguments because the compiler won't be able to tell them apart.

The compiler does not consider return type when differentiating methods, so you cannot declare two methods with the same signature, even if they have a different return type.

Note

Overloaded methods should be used sparingly because they can make code much less readable.

Providing Constructors for Your Classes

A class contains constructors that are invoked to create objects from the class blueprint. Constructor declarations look like method declarations, but they use the name of the class and have no return type. For example, `Bicycle` has one constructor:

```
public Bicycle(int startCadence, int startSpeed, int startGear) {
    gear = startGear;
    cadence = startCadence;
    speed = startSpeed;
}
```

To create a new `Bicycle` object called `myBike`, a constructor is called by the new operator:

```
Bicycle myBike = new Bicycle(30, 0, 8);
```

`new Bicycle(30, 0, 8)` creates space in memory for the object and initializes its fields.

Although `Bicycle` only has one constructor, it could have others, including a no-argument constructor:

```
public Bicycle() {
    gear = 1;
    cadence = 10;
    speed = 0;
}
```

`Bicycle yourBike = new Bicycle();` invokes the no-argument constructor to create a new `Bicycle` object called `yourBike`.

Both constructors could have been declared in `Bicycle` because they have different argument lists. As with methods, the Java platform differentiates constructors on the basis of the number of arguments in the list and their types. You cannot write two constructors that have the same number and type of arguments for the same class because the platform would not be able to tell them apart. Doing so causes a compile-time error.

You don't necessarily need to provide any constructors for your class, but if you choose to provide the constructors, you must be careful. The compiler automatically provides a no-argument, default constructor for any class without constructors. This default constructor will call the no-argument constructor of the superclass. In this situation, the compiler will complain if the superclass doesn't have a no-argument constructor, so you must verify that it does. If your class has no explicit superclass, then it has an implicit superclass of `Object`, which *does* have a no-argument constructor.

You can use a superclass constructor yourself. The `MountainBike` class at the beginning of this chapter did just that. This will be discussed in Chapter 5. You can use access modifiers in a constructor's declaration to control which other classes can call the constructor.

Note

If another class cannot call a `MyClass` constructor, then it cannot directly create `MyClass` objects.

Passing Information to a Method or a Constructor

The declaration for a method or a constructor declares the number and the type of the arguments for that method or constructor. For example, the following is a method that computes the monthly payments for a home loan based on the amount of the loan, the interest rate, the length of the loan (the number of periods), and the future value of the loan:

```
public double computePayment(
                    double loanAmt,
                    double rate,
                    double futureValue,
                    int numPeriods) {
    double interest = rate / 100.0;
    double partial1 = Math.pow((1 + interest),
                    - numPeriods);
    double denominator = (1 - partial1) / interest;
    double answer = (-loanAmt / denominator)
                    - ((futureValue * partial1) / denominator);
    return answer;
}
```

This method has four parameters: the loan amount, the interest rate, the future value, and the number of periods. The first three are double-precision floating-point numbers, and the fourth is an integer. The parameters are used in the method body and will take on the values of the arguments that are passed in at runtime.

> **Note**
>
> *Parameters* refers to the list of variables in a method declaration. *Arguments* are the actual values that are passed in when the method is invoked. When you invoke a method, the arguments used must match the declaration's parameters in type and order.

Parameter Types

You can use any data type for a parameter of a method or a constructor. This includes primitive data types, such as doubles, floats, and integers (which you saw in the `computePayment` method) and reference data types, such as objects and arrays.

Here's an example of a method that accepts an array as an argument. In this example, the method creates a new `Polygon` object and initializes it from an array of `Point` objects. Assume that `Point` is a class that represents an x, y coordinate:

```
public Polygon polygonFrom(Point[] corners) {
    // method body goes here
}
```

Arbitrary Number of Arguments

4

You can use a construct called *varargs* to pass an arbitrary number of values to a method. You use varargs when you don't know how many of a particular type of argument will be passed to the method. It's a shortcut to creating an array manually. (Note that the previous method could have used varargs rather than an array.)

To use varargs, you follow the type of the last parameter with an ellipsis (...), then a space, and the parameter name. The method can then be called with any number of that parameter, including zero:

```
public Polygon polygonFrom(Point . . . corners) {
    int numberOfSides = corners.length;
    double squareOfSide1, lengthOfSide1;
    squareOfSide1 = (corners[1].x - corners[0].x)
                  * (corners[1].x - corners[0].x)
                  + (corners[1].y - corners[0].y)
                  * (corners[1].y - corners[0].y);
    lengthOfSide1 = Math.sqrt(squareOfSide1);

    // more method body code follows that creates and returns a
    // polygon connecting the Points
}
```

As you can see, inside the method, `corners` is treated like an array. The method can be called either with an array or with a sequence of arguments. The code in the method body will treat the parameter as an array in either case.

You will most commonly see varargs with the printing methods. Here is an example `printf` method:

```
public PrintStream printf(String format, Object . . . args)
```

This allows you to print an arbitrary number of objects. It can be called like this (or with yet a different number of arguments):

```
System.out.printf("%s: %d, %s%n", name, idnum, address);
```

It can also be called like this:

```
System.out.printf("%s: %d, %s, %s, %s%n", name, idnum, address, phone, email);
```

Parameter Names

When you declare a parameter to a method or a constructor, you provide a name for that parameter. This name is used within the method body to refer to the passed-in argument.

The name of a parameter must be unique in its scope. It cannot be the same as the name of another parameter for the same method or constructor, and it cannot be the name of a local variable within the method or constructor.

A parameter can have the same name as one of the class's fields. If this is the case, the parameter is said to *shadow* the field. Shadowing fields can make your code difficult to read, and shadowing is conventionally only used within constructors and methods that set a particular field. For example, consider the following Circle class and its setOrigin method:

```
public class Circle {
    private int x, y, radius;
    public void setOrigin(int x, int y) {
        . . .
    }
}
```

The Circle class has three fields: x, y, and radius. The setOrigin method has two parameters, each of which has the same name as one of the fields. Each method parameter shadows the field that shares its name. So using the simple names x or y within the body of the method refers to the parameter, *not* the field. To access the field, you must use a qualified name. This will be discussed later in this chapter, in the section titled "Using the this Keyword."

Passing Primitive Data Type Arguments

Primitive arguments, such as an int or a double, are passed into methods *by value*. This means that any changes to the values of the parameters exist only within the scope of the method. When the method returns, the parameters are gone and any changes to them are lost. Here is an example:

```
public class PassPrimitiveByValue {

    public static void main(String[] args) {

        int x = 3;

        // invoke passMethod() with
        // x as argument
        passMethod(x);

        // print x to see if its
```

```
            // value has changed
            System.out.println("After invoking passMethod, x = " + x);

    }

    // change parameter in passMethod()
    public static void passMethod(int p) {
        p = 10;
    }
}
```

When you run this program, the output is the following:

```
After invoking passMethod, x = 3
```

Passing Reference Data Type Arguments

Reference data type parameters, such as objects, are also passed into methods *by value*. This means that when the method returns, the passed-in reference still references the same object as before. *However*, the values of the object's fields *can* be changed in the method if they have the proper access level.

For example, consider a method in an arbitrary class that moves Circle objects:

```
public void moveCircle(Circle circle, int deltaX, int deltaY) {
    // code to move origin of
    // circle to x+deltaX, y+deltaY
    circle.setX(circle.getX() + deltaX);
    circle.setY(circle.getY() + deltaY);

    // code to assign a new
    // reference to circle
    circle = new Circle(0, 0);
}
```

Let the method be invoked with these arguments:

```
moveCircle(myCircle, 23, 56)
```

Inside the method, circle initially refers to myCircle. The method changes the x and y coordinates of the object that circle references (i.e., myCircle) by 23 and 56, respectively. These changes will persist when the method returns. Then circle is assigned a reference to a new Circle object with x = y = 0. This reassignment has no permanence, however, because the reference was passed in by value and cannot change. Within the method, the object pointed to by circle has changed, but when the method returns, myCircle still references the same Circle object as before the method was called.

Objects

A typical Java program creates many objects, which, as you know, interact by invoking methods. Through these object interactions, a program can carry out various tasks, such as implementing a graphical user interface (GUI), running an animation, or sending and receiving information over a network. Once an object has completed the work for which it was created, its resources are recycled for use by other objects.

Here's a small program, called CreateObjectDemo, that creates three objects: one Point object and two Rectangle objects. You will need all three source files to compile this program:

```java
public class CreateObjectDemo {

    public static void main(String[] args) {

        // Declare and create a point object
        // and two rectangle objects.
        Point originOne = new Point(23, 94);
        Rectangle rectOne = new
            Rectangle(originOne, 100, 200);
        Rectangle rectTwo =
            new Rectangle(50, 100);

        // display rectOne's width,
        // height, and area
        System.out.println("Width of rectOne: "
                        + rectOne.width);
        System.out.println("Height of rectOne: "
                        + rectOne.height);
        System.out.println("Area of rectOne: "
                        + rectOne.getArea());

        // set rectTwo's position
        rectTwo.origin = originOne;

        // display rectTwo's position
        System.out.println("X Position of rectTwo: "
                        + rectTwo.origin.x);
        System.out.println("Y Position of rectTwo: "
                        + rectTwo.origin.y);

        // move rectTwo and display
        // its new position
        rectTwo.move(40, 72);
        System.out.println("X Position of rectTwo: "
                        + rectTwo.origin.x);
        System.out.println("Y Position of rectTwo: "
                        + rectTwo.origin.y);
    }
}
```

This program creates, manipulates, and displays information about various objects. Here's the output:

```
Width of rectOne: 100
Height of rectOne: 200
Area of rectOne: 20000
X Position of rectTwo: 23
Y Position of rectTwo: 94
X Position of rectTwo: 40
Y Position of rectTwo: 72
```

The following three sections use this example to describe the life cycle of an object within a program. They will teach you how to write code that creates and uses objects in your own programs. You will also learn how the system cleans up after an object when its life has ended.

Creating Objects

As you know, a class provides the blueprint for objects; you create an object from a class. Each of the following statements taken from the `CreateObjectDemo` program creates an object and assigns it to a variable:

```
Point originOne = new Point(23, 94);
Rectangle rectOne = new Rectangle(originOne, 100, 200);
Rectangle rectTwo = new Rectangle(50, 100);
```

The first line creates an object of the `Point` class, and the second and third lines each create an object of the `Rectangle` class. Each of these statements has three parts:

1. *Declaration.* The codes set in **bold** are all variable declarations that associate a variable name with an object type.
2. *Instantiation.* The new keyword is a Java operator that creates the object.
3. *Initialization.* The new operator is followed by a call to a constructor, which initializes the new object.

Declaring a Variable to Refer to an Object

Previously, you learned that to declare a variable, you write the following:

```
type name;
```

This notifies the compiler that you will use *name* to refer to data whose type is *type*. With a primitive variable, this declaration also reserves the proper amount of memory for the variable. You can also declare a reference variable on its own line:

```
Point originOne;
```

If you declare `originOne` like this, its value will be undetermined until an object is actually created and assigned to it. Simply declaring a reference variable does originOne

Figure 4.1 When Declared as Point originOne, the Variable Has No Initial Value

not create an object. For that, you need to use the new operator, as described in the next section. You must assign an object to `originOne` before you use it in your code. Otherwise, you will get a compiler error. A variable in this state, which currently references no object, can be illustrated as shown in Figure 4.1 (the variable name, `originOne`, plus a reference pointing to nothing).

Instantiating a Class

The new operator instantiates a class by allocating memory for a new object and returning a reference to that memory. The new operator also invokes the object constructor.

> **Note**
>
> The phrase *instantiating a class* means the same thing as *creating an object*. When you create an object, you are creating an *instance* of a class, therefore *instantiating* a class.

The new operator requires a single, postfix argument: a call to a constructor. The name of the constructor provides the name of the class to instantiate.

The new operator returns a reference to the object it created. This reference is usually assigned to a variable of the appropriate type:

```
Point originOne = new Point(23, 94);
```

The reference returned by the new operator does not need to be assigned to a variable. It can also be used directly in an expression. Here's an example:

```
int height = new Rectangle().height;
```

This statement will be discussed in the next section.

Initializing an Object

Here's the code for the `Point` class:

```
public class Point {
    public int x = 0;
    public int y = 0;
    //constructor
    public Point(int a, int b) {
        x = a;
        y = b;
    }
}
```

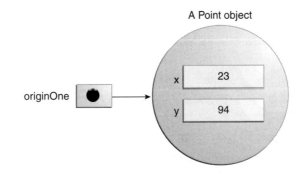

Figure 4.2 The originOne Variable Is Initialized

This class contains a single constructor. You can recognize a constructor because its declaration uses the same name as the class and it has no return type. The constructor in the Point class takes two integer arguments, as declared by the code (int a, int b). The following statement provides 23 and 94 as values for those arguments:

```
Point originOne = new Point(23, 94);
```

The result of executing this statement is illustrated in Figure 4.2.

Here's the code for the Rectangle class, which contains four constructors:

```
public class Rectangle {
    public int width = 0;
    public int height = 0;
    public Point origin;

    // four constructors
    public Rectangle() {
        origin = new Point(0, 0);
    }
    public Rectangle(Point p) {
        origin = p;
    }
    public Rectangle(int w, int h) {
        origin = new Point(0, 0);
        width = w;
        height = h;
    }
    public Rectangle(Point p, int w, int h) {
        origin = p;
        width = w;
        height = h;
    }

    // a method for moving the rectangle
    public void move(int x, int y) {
        origin.x = x;
```

```
        origin.y = y;
    }

    // a method for computing the area
    // of the rectangle
    public int getArea() {
        return width * height;
    }
}
```

Each constructor lets you provide initial values for the rectangle's size and width, using both primitive and reference types. If a class has multiple constructors, they must have different signatures. The Java compiler differentiates the constructors based on the number of arguments and argument type. When the Java compiler encounters the following code, it knows to call the constructor in the Rectangle class that requires a Point argument followed by two integer arguments:

```
Rectangle rectOne = new Rectangle(originOne, 100, 200);
```

This calls one of Rectangle's constructors that initializes origin to originOne. Also, the constructor sets width to 100 and height to 200. Now there are two references to the same Point object. An object can have multiple references to it, as shown in Figure 4.3.

The following line of code calls the Rectangle constructor, which requires two integer arguments to provide the initial values for width and height. If you inspect the code within the constructor, you will see that it creates a new Point object whose x and y values are initialized to zero:

```
Rectangle rectTwo = new Rectangle(50, 100);
```

The Rectangle constructor used in the following statement doesn't take any arguments, so it's called a *no-argument constructor*:

```
Rectangle rect = new Rectangle();
```

All classes have at least one constructor. If a class does not explicitly declare any, the Java compiler automatically provides a no-argument constructor, called the *default constructor*. This default constructor calls the class parent's no-argument constructor or the Object constructor (if the class has no other parent). If the parent has no constructor (and Object does have one), the compiler will reject the program.

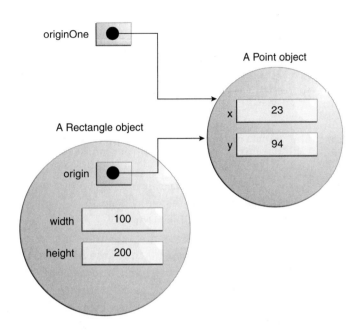

Figure 4.3 Two References to the Point Object

Using Objects

Once you've created an object, you probably want to use it for something. You may need to use the value of one of its fields, change one of its fields, or call one of its methods to perform an action.

Referencing an Object's Fields

Object fields are accessed by their name. You must use a name that is unambiguous. You may use a simple name for a field within its own class. For example, we can add a statement *within* the Rectangle class that prints the width and height:

```
System.out.println("Width and height are: " + width + ", " + height);
```

In this case, width and height are simple names.

Code that is outside the object's class must use an object reference or expression, followed by the dot operator (.), followed by a simple field name:

```
objectReference.fieldName
```

For example, the code in the `CreateObjectDemo` class is outside the code for the `Rectangle` class. So to refer to the `origin`, `width`, and `height` fields within the `Rectangle` object named `rectOne`, the `CreateObjectDemo` class must use the names `rectOne.origin`, `rectOne.width`, and `rectOne.height`, respectively. The program uses two of these names to display the `width` and the `height` of `rectOne`:

```
System.out.println("Width of rectOne: " + rectOne.width);
System.out.println("Height of rectOne: " + rectOne.height);
```

Attempting to use the simple names `width` and `height` from the code in the `CreateObjectDemo` class doesn't make sense. Those fields exist only within an object, and using them results in a compiler error.

Later, the program uses similar code to display information about `rectTwo`. Objects of the same type have their own copy of the same instance fields. Thus each `Rectangle` object has fields named `origin`, `width`, and `height`. When you access an instance field through an object reference, you reference that particular object's field. The two objects `rectOne` and `rectTwo` in the `CreateObjectDemo` program have different `origin`, `width`, and `height` fields.

To access a field, you can use a named reference to an object, as in the previous examples, or you can use any expression that returns an object reference. Recall that the new operator returns a reference to an object. So you could use the value returned from new to access a new object's fields:

```
int height = new Rectangle().height;
```

This statement creates a new `Rectangle` object and immediately gets its height. In essence, the statement calculates the default height of a `Rectangle`. Note that after this statement has been executed, the program no longer has a reference to the created `Rectangle` because the program never stored the reference anywhere. The object is unreferenced, and its resources are free to be recycled by the Java Virtual Machine.

Calling an Object's Methods

You should also use an object reference to invoke an object's method. You append the method's simple name to the object reference, with an intervening dot operator (.). You should also provide any arguments to the method in parentheses:

```
objectReference.methodName(argumentList);
```

If the method does not require any arguments, use empty parentheses:

```
objectReference.methodName();
```

The `Rectangle` class has two methods: `getArea()` to compute the rectangle's area and `move()` to change the rectangle's origin. Here's the `CreateObjectDemo` code that invokes these two methods:

```
System.out.println("Area of rectOne: " + rectOne.getArea());
    . . .
rectTwo.move(40, 72);
```

The first statement invokes `rectOne`'s `getArea()` method and displays the results. The second statement moves `rectTwo`, with the `move()` method assigning new values to the object's `origin.x` and `origin.y`.

As with instance fields, `objectReference` must be a reference to an object. You can use a variable name, but you also can use any expression that returns an object reference. The `new` operator returns an object reference, so you can use the value returned from `new` to invoke a new object's methods:

```
new Rectangle(100, 50).getArea()
```

The expression `new Rectangle(100, 50)` returns an object reference that refers to a `Rectangle` object. As shown, you can use the `dot` notation to invoke the new `Rectangle`'s `getArea()` method to compute the area of the new rectangle.

Some methods, such as `getArea()`, return a value. For methods that return a value, you can use the method invocation in expressions. You can assign the return value to a variable and use it to make decisions or control a loop. This code assigns the value returned by `getArea()` to the variable `areaOfRectangle`:

```
int areaOfRectangle = new Rectangle(100, 50).getArea();
```

Remember, invoking a method on a particular object is the same as sending a message to that object. In this case, the object that `getArea()` is invoked on is the rectangle returned by the constructor.

The Garbage Collector

Some object-oriented languages require that you keep track of all the objects you create and that you explicitly destroy them when they are no longer needed. Managing memory explicitly is tedious and error prone. The Java platform allows you to create as many objects as you want (limited, of course, by what your system can handle), and you don't have to worry about destroying them. The Java runtime environment deletes objects when it determines that they are no longer being used. This process is called *garbage collection*.

An object is eligible for garbage collection when there are no more references to that object. References that are held in a variable are usually dropped when the variable goes out of scope. You can also explicitly drop an object reference by setting the variable to the special value `null`. Remember that a program can have multiple references to the same object; all references to an object must be dropped before the object is eligible for garbage collection.

The Java runtime environment has a garbage collector that periodically frees the memory used by objects that are no longer referenced. The garbage collector does its job automatically when it determines that the time is right.

More on Classes

This section covers more aspects of classes that depend on object references and the `dot` operator.

Returning a Value from a Method

A method returns to the code that invoked it when it completes all the statements in the method, reaches a `return` statement, or throws an exception (discussed later)—whichever occurs first. You declare a method's return type in its method declaration. Within the body of the method, you use the `return` statement to return the value.

Any method declared `void` doesn't return a value. It does not need to contain a `return` statement, but it may do so. In such a case, a `return` statement can be used to branch out of a control flow block and exit the method. It is simply used like this:

```
return;
```

If you try to return a value from a method that is declared `void`, you will get a compiler error. Any method that is not declared `void` must contain a `return` statement with a corresponding return value:

```
return returnValue;
```

The data type of the return value must match the method's declared return type. For example, you can't return an integer (`int`) value from a method declared to return a `boolean`.

The `getArea()` method in the `RectangleRectangle` class discussed previously returns an integer:

```
// a method for computing the area of the rectangle
public int getArea() {
    return width * height;
}
```

This method returns the integer obtained from the expression width * height.

The getArea method returns a primitive type. A method can also return a reference type. For example, in a program to manipulate Bicycle objects, we might have a method like this:

```
public Bicycle seeWhosFastest(Bicycle myBike, Bicycle yourBike,
                              Environment env) {
    Bicycle fastest;
    // code to calculate which bike is
    // faster, given each bike's gear
    // and cadence and given the
    // environment (terrain and wind)
    return fastest;
}
```

Returning a Class or Interface

If this section confuses you, skip it and return to it after you have finished reading Chapter 5.

When a method uses a class name as its return type, such as whosFastest does, the class of the type of the returned object must be either a subclass or the exact class of the return type. Suppose you have a class hierarchy in which ImaginaryNumber is a subclass of java.lang.Number, which is in turn a subclass of Object, as illustrated in Figure 4.4.

Now suppose that you have a method declared to return a Number:

```
public Number returnANumber() {
    . . .
}
```

Figure 4.4 The Class Hierarchy for ImaginaryNumber

The `returnANumber` method can return an `ImaginaryNumber` but not an `Object`. `ImaginaryNumber` is a `Number` because it's a subclass of `Number`. However, an `Object` is not necessarily a `Number`—it could be a `String` or another type.

You can override a method and define it to return a subclass of the original method:

```
public ImaginaryNumber returnANumber() {
    . . .
}
```

This technique, called *covariant return type*, means that the return type is allowed to vary in the same direction as the subclass.

> **Note**
> You also can use interface names as return types. In this case, the object returned must implement the specified interface.

Using the this Keyword

Within an instance method or a constructor, `this` is a reference to the *current object*—the object whose method or constructor is being called. You can refer to any member of the current object from within an instance method or a constructor by using `this`.

Using this with a Field

The most common reason for using the `this` keyword is because a field is shadowed by a method or constructor parameter. For example, the `Point` class was written as follows:

```
public class Point {
    public int x = 0;
    public int y = 0;
    //constructor
    public Point(int a, int b) {
        x = a;
        y = b;
    }
}
```

However, it could have been written like this:

```
public class Point {
    public int x = 0;
    public int y = 0;
```

```
        //constructor
        public Point(int x, int y) {
            this.x = x;
            this.y = y;
        }
    }
```

Each argument to the constructor shadows one of the object's fields; inside the constructor **x** is a local copy of the constructor's first argument. To refer to the Point field **x**, the constructor must use **this.x**.

Using this with a Constructor

From within a constructor, you can also use the this keyword to call another constructor in the same class. Doing so is called an *explicit constructor invocation*. Here's another Rectangle class, with a different implementation than the one in the "Objects" section of this chapter:

```
public class Rectangle {
    private int x, y;
    private int width, height;

    public Rectangle() {
        this(0, 0, 0, 0);
    }
    public Rectangle(int width, int height) {
        this(0, 0, width, height);
    }
    public Rectangle(int x, int y, int width, int height) {
        this.x = x;
        this.y = y;
        this.width = width;
        this.height = height;
    }
        . . .
}
```

This class contains a set of constructors. Each constructor initializes some or all of the rectangle's member variables. The constructors provide a default value for any member variable whose initial value is not provided by an argument. For example, the no-argument constructor calls the four-argument constructor with four zero values, and the two-argument constructor calls the four-argument constructor with two zero values. As before, the compiler determines which constructor to call, based on the number and the type of arguments. If present, the invocation of another constructor must be the first line in the constructor.

Controlling Access to Members of a Class

Access level modifiers determine whether other classes can use a particular field or invoke a particular method. There are two levels of access control:

- *At the top level.* public or package-private (no explicit modifier)
- *At the member level.* public, private, protected, or package-private (no explicit modifier)

A class may be declared with the modifier public, in which case that class is visible to all classes everywhere. If a class has no modifier (the default, also known as *package-private*), it is visible only within its own package. (*Packages* are named groups of related classes—you will learn about them in Chapter 7.)

At the member level, you can also use the public modifier or no modifier (package-private), and both modifiers carry the same meaning as they would in the top-level classes. For members, there are two additional access modifiers: private and protected. The private modifier specifies that the member can only be accessed in its own class. The protected modifier specifies that the member can only be accessed within its own package (as with package-private) and, in addition, by a subclass of its class in another package.

Table 4.1 shows the access to members permitted by each modifier. The first data column indicates whether the class itself has access to the member defined by the access level. As you can see, a class always has access to its own members. The second column indicates whether classes in the same package as the class (regardless of their parentage) have access to the member. The third column indicates whether subclasses of the class declared outside this package have access to the member. The fourth column indicates whether all classes have access to the member.

Access levels affect you in two ways. First, when you use classes that come from another source, such as the classes in the Java platform, access levels determine which members of those classes your own classes can use. Second, when you write a class, you need to decide which access level every member variable and every method in your class should have.

Table 4.1 Access Levels

Modifier	Class	Package	Subclass	World
public	Y	Y	Y	Y
protected	Y	Y	Y	N
no modifier	Y	Y	N	N
private	Y	N	N	N

Let's look at a collection of classes and see how access levels affect visibility. Figure 4.5 shows the four classes in this example and how they are related. Table 4.2 shows where the members of the alpha class are visible for each of the access modifiers that can be applied to them.

> **Note**
>
> If other programmers use your class, you want to ensure that errors from misuse cannot happen. Access levels can help you do this:
> - Use the most restrictive access level that makes sense for a particular member. Use `private` unless you have a good reason not to.
> - Avoid `public` fields, except for constants; `public` fields tend to link you to a particular implementation and limit your flexibility in changing your code.

Understanding Instance and Class Members

In this section, we discuss the use of the `static` keyword to create fields and methods that belong to the class rather than to an instance of the class.

Class Variables

When a number of objects are created from the same class blueprint, they each have their own distinct copies of *instance variables*. In the case of the `Bicycle` class, the

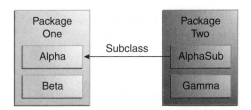

Figure 4.5 Classes and Packages of the Example Used to Illustrate Access Levels

Table 4.2 Visibility

Modifier	Alpha	Beta	Alphasub	Gamma
public	Y	Y	Y	Y
protected	Y	Y	Y	N
no modifier	Y	Y	N	N
private	Y	N	N	N

instance variables are `cadence`, `gear`, and `speed`. Each `Bicycle` object has its own values for these variables, stored in different memory locations.

Sometimes you want to have variables that are common to all objects. This is accomplished with the `static` modifier. Fields that have the `static` modifier in their declaration are called *static fields* or *class variables*. They are associated with the class rather than with any object. Every instance of the class shares a class variable, which is in one fixed location in memory. Any object can change the value of a class variable, but class variables can also be manipulated without creating an instance of the class.

For example, suppose you want to create a number of `Bicycle` objects and assign each a serial number, beginning with one for the first object. This ID number is unique to each object and is therefore an instance variable. At the same time, you need a field to keep track of how many `Bicycle` objects have been created so that you know which ID to assign to the next object. Such a field is not related to any individual object but to the class as a whole. For this, you need a class variable, number-OfBicycles, as follows:

```
public class Bicycle{

    private int cadence;
    private int gear;
    private int speed;

    // add an instance variable for
    // the object ID
    private int id;

    // add a class variable for the
    // number of Bicycle objects instantiated
    private static int numberOfBicycles = 0;
          . . .
}
```

Class variables are referenced by the class name itself:

```
Bicycle.numberOfBicycles
```

This makes it clear that they are class variables.

Note

You can also refer to static fields with an object reference like `myBike.numberOfBicycles`, but this is discouraged because it does not make it clear that they are class variables.

You can use the `Bicycle` constructor to set the `id` instance variable and increment the numberOfBicycles class variable:

```
public class Bicycle{

    private int cadence;
    private int gear;
    private int speed;
    private int id;
    private static int numberOfBicycles = 0;

    public Bicycle(int startCadence, int startSpeed, int startGear){
        gear = startGear;
        cadence = startCadence;
        speed = startSpeed;

        // increment number of Bicycles
        // and assign ID number
        id = ++numberOfBicycles;
    }

    // new method to return the ID instance variable
    public int getID() {
        return id;
    }
        . . .
}
```

Class Methods

The Java programming language supports static methods as well as static variables. Static methods, which have the `static` modifier in their declarations, should be invoked with the class name, without the need for creating an instance of the class:

```
ClassName.methodName(args)
```

> **Note**
> You can also refer to static methods with an object reference:
>
> ```
> instanceName.methodName(args)
> ```
>
> However, this is discouraged because it is unclear that these are class methods.

A common use for static methods is to access static fields. For example, we could add a static method to the `Bicycle` class to access the numberOfBicycles static field:

```
public static int getNumberOfBicycles() {
    return numberOfBicycles;
}
```

Not all combinations of instance and class variables and methods are allowed:

- Instance methods can access instance variables and instance methods directly.
- Instance methods can access class variables and class methods directly.
- Class methods can access class variables and class methods directly.
- Class methods *cannot* access instance variables or instance methods directly—they must use an object reference. Also, class methods cannot use the this keyword, as there is no instance for this to refer to.

Constants

The static modifier, in combination with the final modifier, is also used to define constants. The final modifier indicates that the value of this field cannot change.

For example, the following variable declaration defines a constant named PI, whose value is an approximation of pi (the ratio of the circumference of a circle to its diameter):

```
static final double PI = 3.141592653589793;
```

Constants defined in this way cannot be reassigned, and you will get a compile-time error if your program tries to do so. By convention, the names of constant values are spelled in uppercase letters. If the name is composed of more than one word, the words are separated by an underscore (_).

> **Note**
>
> If a primitive type or a string is defined as a constant and the value is known at the compile time, the compiler replaces the constant name everywhere in the code with its value. This is called a *compile-time constant*. If the value of the constant in the outside world changes (e.g., if it is legislated that pi actually should be 3.975), you will need to recompile any classes that use this constant to get the current value.

The Bicycle Class

After all the modifications made in this section, the Bicycle class is now as follows:

```
public class Bicycle{

    private int cadence;
    private int gear;
```

```
        private int speed;

        private int id;

        private static int numberOfBicycles = 0;

        public Bicycle(int startCadence,
                       int startSpeed,
                       int startGear){
            gear = startGear;
            cadence = startCadence;
            speed = startSpeed;

            id = ++numberOfBicycles;
        }
        public int getID() {
            return id;
        }
        public static int getNumberOfBicycles() {
            return numberOfBicycles;
        }
        public int getCadence(){
            return cadence;
        }
        public void setCadence(int newValue){
            cadence = newValue;
        }
        public int getGear(){
        return gear;
        }
        public void setGear(int newValue){
            gear = newValue;
        }
        public int getSpeed(){
            return speed;
        }
        public void applyBrake(int decrement){
            speed -= decrement;
        }
        public void speedUp(int increment){
            speed += increment;
        }
    }
```

Initializing Fields

As you have seen, you can often provide an initial value for a field in its declaration:

```
public class BedAndBreakfast {

    // initialize to 10
    public static int capacity = 10;

    // initialize to false
    private boolean full = false;
}
```

This works well when the initialization value is available and the initialization can be put on one line. However, this form of initialization has limitations because of its simplicity. If initialization requires some logic (e.g., error handling or a for loop to fill a complex array), simple assignment is inadequate. Instance variables can be initialized in constructors, where error handling or other logic can be used. To provide the same capability for class variables, the Java programming language includes *static initialization blocks*.

> **Note**
> It is not necessary to declare fields at the beginning of the class definition, although this is the most common practice. It is only necessary that they be declared and initialized before they are used.

Static Initialization Blocks

A *static initialization block* is a normal block of code enclosed in braces and preceded by the static keyword. Here is an example:

```
static {
    // whatever code is needed for initialization goes here
}
```

A class can have any number of static initialization blocks, and they can appear anywhere in the class body. The runtime system guarantees that static initialization blocks are called in the order that they appear in the source code.

There is an alternative to static blocks. You can write a private static method:

```
class Whatever {
    public static varType myVar = initializeClassVariable();

    private static varType initializeClassVariable() {

        // initialization code goes here
    }
}
```

The advantage of private static methods is that they can be reused later if you need to reinitialize the class variable.

Initializing Instance Members

Normally you would use code to initialize an instance variable in a constructor. There are two alternatives to using a constructor to initialize instance variables: initializer blocks and final methods.

Initializer blocks variables look just like static initializer blocks without the `static` keyword:

```
{
    // whatever code is needed for initialization goes here
}
```

The Java compiler copies initializer blocks into every constructor. Therefore, this approach can be used to share a block of code between multiple constructors.

A final method cannot be overridden in a subclass. This is discussed in Chapter 5. Here is an example final method for initializing an instance variable:

```
class Whatever {
    private varType myVar = initializeInstanceVariable();

    protected final varType initializeInstanceVariable() {

        // initialization code goes here
    }
}
```

This is especially useful if subclasses might want to reuse the initialization method. The method is final because calling nonfinal methods during instance initialization can cause problems.

Summary of Creating and Using Classes and Objects

A class declaration names the class and encloses the class body between braces. The class name can be preceded by modifiers. The class body contains fields, methods, and constructors for the class. A class uses fields to contain state information and uses methods to implement behavior. Constructors that initialize a new instance of a class use the name of the class and look like methods without a return type.

You control access to classes and members in the same way: by using an access modifier such as `public` in their declaration. You specify a class variable or a class method by using the `static` keyword in the member's declaration. A member that is not declared as `static` is implicitly an instance member. Class variables are shared by all instances of a class and can be accessed through the class name as well as an instance reference. Instances of a class get their own copy of each instance variable, which must be accessed through an instance reference.

You create an object from a class by using the new operator and a constructor. The new operator returns a reference to the object that was created. You can assign the reference to a variable or use it directly.

Instance variables and methods that are accessible to code outside of the class that they are declared in can be referred to by using a qualified name. A qualified name of an instance variable looks like this:

```
objectReference.variableName
```

A qualified name of a method looks like this:

```
objectReference.methodName(argumentList)
```

Alternately, a qualified name of a method can also look like this:

```
objectReference.methodName()
```

The garbage collector automatically cleans up unused objects. An object is unused if the program holds no more references to it. You can explicitly drop a reference by setting the variable holding the reference to null.

Questions and Exercises: Classes

Questions

1. Consider the following class:

   ```
   public class IdentifyMyParts {
       public static int x = 7;
       public int y = 3;
   }
   ```

   a. What are the class variables?

   b. What are the instance variables?

   c. What is the output from the following code?

   ```
   IdentifyMyParts a = new IdentifyMyParts();
   IdentifyMyParts b = new IdentifyMyParts();
   a.y = 5;
   b.y = 6;
   a.x = 1;
   b.x = 2;
   System.out.println("a.y = " + a.y);
   System.out.println("b.y = " + b.y);
   System.out.println("a.x = " + a.x);
   System.out.println("b.x = " + b.x);
   System.out.println("IdentifyMyParts.x = " + IdentifyMyParts.x);
   ```

Exercises

1. Write a class whose instances represent single playing cards from a deck of cards. Keep in mind that playing cards have two distinguishing properties: rank and suit. (Be sure to keep your solution, as you will be asked to rewrite it later on in this chapter, in the "Enum Types" section.)

> **Note**
>
> You can use the `assert` statement to check your assignments. Write the following:
>
> ```
> assert (boolean expression to test);
> ```
>
> If the `boolean` expression is false, you will get an error message. For example,
>
> ```
> assert toString(ACE) == "Ace";
> ```
>
> This statement should return `true`, so there will be no error message. If you use the `assert` statement, you must run your program with the ea flag:
>
> ```
> java -ea YourProgram.class
> ```

2. Write a class whose instances represent a *full* deck of cards. (You should also keep this solution for later use.)
3. Write a small program to test your deck and card classes. The program can be as simple as creating a deck and displaying the cards.

Answers

You can find answers to these questions and exercises at `http://docs.oracle.com/javase/tutorial/java/javaOO/QandE/creating-answers.html`.

Questions and Exercises: Objects

Questions

1. What's wrong with the following program?
   ```java
   public class SomethingIsWrong {
       public static void main(String[] args) {
           Rectangle myRect;
           myRect.width = 40;
           myRect.height = 50;
           System.out.println("myRect's area is " + myRect.area());
       }
   }
   ```

2. The following code creates one array and one string object. How many refer-
    ences to those objects exist after the code executes? Is either object eligible for
    garbage collection?

```
    . . .
String[] students = new String[10];
String studentName = "Peter Parker";
students[0] = studentName;
studentName = null;
    . . .
```

3. How does a program destroy an object that it creates?

Exercises

1. Fix the program called SomethingIsWrong from question 1.
2. Given the following class, called NumberHolder, write some code that creates
    an instance of the class, initializes its two member variables, and then displays
    the value of each member variable:

```
public class NumberHolder {
    public int anInt;
    public float aFloat;
}
```

Answers

You can find answers to these questions and exercises at http://docs.oracle.com/
javase/tutorial/java/javaOO/QandE/objects-answers.html.

Nested Classes

The Java programming language allows you to define a class within another class.
Such a class is called a *nested class* and is illustrated here:

```
class OuterClass {
    . . .
    class NestedClass {
        . . .
    }
}
```

Definition

Nested classes are divided into two categories: static and nonstatic. Nested classes that are declared *static* are simply called *static nested classes*. Nonstatic nested classes are called *inner classes*.

```
class OuterClass {
    . . .
```

```
    static class StaticNestedClass {
        . . .
    }
    class InnerClass {
        . . .
    }
}
```

A nested class is a member of its enclosing class. Nonstatic nested classes (inner classes) have access to other members of the enclosing class, even if they are declared private. Static nested classes do not have access to other members of the enclosing class. As a member of the `OuterClass`, a nested class can be declared private, public, protected, or package private. (Recall that outer classes can only be declared public or package private.)

Why Use Nested Classes?

There are several compelling reasons for using nested classes, including the following:

- *Logical grouping of classes.* If a class is useful to only one other class, then it is logical to embed it in that class and keep the two together. Nesting such "helper classes" makes their package more streamlined.
- *Increased encapsulation.* Consider two top-level classes, A and B, where B needs access to members of A that would otherwise be declared private. By hiding class B within class A, A's members can be declared private and B can access them. In addition, B itself can be hidden from the outside world.
- *More readable, maintainable code.* Nesting small classes within top-level classes places the code closer to where it is used.

Static Nested Classes

As with class methods and variables, a static nested class is associated with its outer class. And like static class methods, a static nested class cannot refer directly to instance variables or methods defined in its enclosing class—it can use them only through an object reference.

> **Note**
> A static nested class interacts with the instance members of its outer class (and other classes) just like any other top-level class. In effect, a static nested class is behaviorally a top-level class that has been nested in another top-level class for packaging convenience.

Static nested classes are accessed using the enclosing class name:

```
OuterClass.StaticNestedClass
```

For example, to create an object for the static nested class, use this syntax:

```
OuterClass.StaticNestedClass nestedObject =
    new OuterClass.StaticNestedClass();
```

Inner Classes

As with instance methods and variables, an inner class is associated with an instance of its enclosing class and has direct access to that object's methods and fields. Also, because an inner class is associated with an instance, it cannot define any static members itself.

Objects that are instances of an inner class exist *within* an instance of the outer class. Consider the following classes:

```
class OuterClass {
    . . .
    class InnerClass {
        . . .
    }
}
```

An instance of `InnerClass` can exist only within an instance of `OuterClass` and has direct access to the methods and fields of its enclosing instance. Figure 4.6 illustrates this idea.

To instantiate an inner class, you must first instantiate the outer class. Then create the inner object within the outer object with this syntax:

```
OuterClass.InnerClass innerObject = outerObject.new InnerClass();
```

Additionally, there are two special kinds of inner classes: local classes and anonymous classes (also called *anonymous inner classes*). Both of these will be discussed briefly in the next section.

> **Note**
>
> If you want more information on the taxonomy of the different kinds of classes in the Java programming language (which can be tricky to describe concisely, clearly, and correctly), consult Joseph Darcy's blog on "Nested, Inner, Member and Top-Level Classes."[1]

---

1.   `https://blogs.oracle.com/darcy/entry/nested_inner_member_and_top`

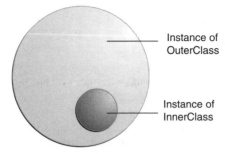

Figure 4.6 An Instance of InnerClass Exists within an Instance of OuterClass

Inner Class Example

To see an inner class in use, let's first consider an array. In the following example, we will create an array, fill it with integer values, and then output only values of even indices of the array, in ascending order. The DataStructure class given consists of the following:

- The DataStructure outer class includes methods to add an integer onto the array and print out values of even indices of the array.
- The InnerEvenIterator inner class is similar to a standard Java iterator. Iterators are used to step through a data structure and typically have methods to test for the last element, retrieve the current element, and move to the next element.
- A main method instantiates a DataStructure object (ds) and uses it to fill the arrayOfInts array with integer values (0, 1, 2, 3, etc.). It then calls a printEven method to print out values of even indices of arrayOfInts.

```
public class DataStructure {
    // create an array
    private final static int SIZE = 15;
    private int[] arrayOfInts = new int[SIZE];

    public DataStructure() {
        // fill the array with ascending integer values
        for (int i = 0; i < SIZE; i++) {
            arrayOfInts[i] = i;
        }
    }

    public void printEven() {
        // print out values of even indices of the array
        InnerEvenIterator iterator = this.new InnerEvenIterator();
        while (iterator.hasNext()) {
            System.out.println(iterator.getNext() + " ");
        }
    }
}
```

```
        // inner class implements the Iterator pattern
        private class InnerEvenIterator {
            // start stepping through the array from the beginning
            private int next = 0;

            public boolean hasNext() {
                // check if a current element is the last in the array
                return (next <= SIZE - 1);
            }

            public int getNext() {
                // record a value of an even index of the array
                int retValue = arrayOfInts[next];
                //get the next even element
                next += 2;
                return retValue;
            }
        }

        public static void main(String s[]) {
            // fill the array with integer values and print out only
            // values of even indices
            DataStructure ds = new DataStructure();
            ds.printEven();
        }
    }
```

Here is the output:

```
 0 2 4 6 8 10 12 14
```

Note that the `InnerEvenIterator` class refers directly to the `arrayOfInts` instance variable of the `DataStructure` object.

Inner classes can be used to implement helper classes like the one shown in the example. If you plan on handling user-interface events, you will need to know how to use inner classes because the event-handling mechanism makes extensive use of them.

Local and Anonymous Inner Classes

There are two additional types of inner classes. You can declare an inner class within the body of a method. Such a class is known as a *local inner class*. You can also declare an inner class within the body of a method without naming it. These classes are known as *anonymous inner classes*. You will encounter such classes in advanced Java programming.

Modifiers

You can use the same modifiers for inner classes that you use for other members of the outer class. For example, you can use the access specifiers—private,

Table 4.3 Types of Nested Classes

Type	Scope	Inner
Static nested class	Member	N
Inner (nonstatic) class	Member	Y
Local class	Local	Y
Anonymous class	Only the point where it is defined	Y

4

`public`, and `protected`—to restrict access to inner classes, just as you do with other class members.

Summary of Nested Classes

A class defined within another class is called a *nested class*. Like other members of a class, a nested class can be declared static or not. A nonstatic nested class is called an *inner class*. An instance of an inner class can exist only within an instance of its enclosing class and has access to its enclosing class's members even if they are declared private. Table 4.3 shows the types of nested classes.

Questions and Exercises: Nested Classes

Questions

1. The program `Problem.java`[2] doesn't compile. What do you need to do to make it compile? Why?

2. Use the Java API documentation for the `Box`[3] class (in the `javax.swing` package) to help you answer the following questions:

   a. What static nested class does `Box` define?

   b. What inner class does `Box` define?

   c. What is the superclass of `Box`'s inner class?

   d. Which of `Box`'s nested classes can you use from any class?

   e. How do you create an instance of `Box`'s `Filler` class?

Exercises

1. Get the file `Class1.java`.[4] Compile and run `Class1`. What is the output?

---

2. `tutorial/java/javaOO/QandE/Problem.java`
3. `7/docs/api/javax/swing/Box.html`
4. `tutorial/java/javaOO/QandE/Class1.java`

Answers

You can find answers to these questions and exercises at `http://docs.oracle.com/javase/tutorial/java/javaOO/QandE/nested-answers.html`.

Enum Types

An *enum type* is a type whose *fields* consist of a fixed set of constants. Common examples include compass directions (values of NORTH, SOUTH, EAST, and WEST) and the days of the week. Because they are constants, the names of an enum type's fields are in uppercase letters.

In the Java programming language, you define an enum type by using the enum keyword. For example, you would specify a days-of-the-week enum type as follows:

```
public enum Day {
    SUNDAY, MONDAY, TUESDAY, WEDNESDAY,
    THURSDAY, FRIDAY, SATURDAY
}
```

You should use enum types any time you need to represent a fixed set of constants. That includes natural enum types such as the planets in our solar system and data sets where you know all possible values at compile time (e.g., the choices on a menu, command line flags).

Here is some code that shows you how to use the Day enum defined previously:

```
public class EnumTest {
    Day day;

    public EnumTest(Day day) {
        this.day = day;
    }

    public void tellItLikeItIs() {
        switch (day) {
            case MONDAY:
                System.out.println("Mondays are bad.");
                break;

            case FRIDAY:
                System.out.println("Fridays are better.");
                break;

            case SATURDAY: case SUNDAY:
                System.out.println("Weekends are best.");
                break;

            default:
                System.out.println("Midweek days are so-so.");
                break;
        }
    }
}
```

```
        public static void main(String[] args) {
            EnumTest firstDay = new EnumTest(Day.MONDAY);
            firstDay.tellItLikeItIs();
            EnumTest thirdDay = new EnumTest(Day.WEDNESDAY);
            thirdDay.tellItLikeItIs();
            EnumTest fifthDay = new EnumTest(Day.FRIDAY);
            fifthDay.tellItLikeItIs();
            EnumTest sixthDay = new EnumTest(Day.SATURDAY);
            sixthDay.tellItLikeItIs();
            EnumTest seventhDay = new EnumTest(Day.SUNDAY);
            seventhDay.tellItLikeItIs();
        }
    }
```

Here is the output:

```
Mondays are bad.
Midweek days are so-so.
Fridays are better.
Weekends are best.
Weekends are best.
```

Java programming language enum types are much more powerful than their counterparts in other languages. The enum declaration defines a class (called an *enum type*).
The enum class body can include methods and other fields. The compiler automatically
adds some special methods when it creates an enum. For example, there is a static values method that returns an array containing all the values of the enum in the order
they are declared. This method is commonly used in combination with the for-each
construct to iterate over the values of an enum type. For example, this code from the
Planet class example iterates over all the planets in the solar system:

```
for (Planet p : Planet.values()) {
    System.out.printf("Your weight on %s is %f%n",
                      p, p.surfaceWeight(mass));
}
```

> **Note**
>
> *All* enums implicitly extend java.lang.Enum. Since Java does not support multiple
> inheritance, an enum cannot extend anything else.

In the following example, Planet is an enum type that represents the planets in
the solar system. They are defined with constant mass and radius properties. Each
enum constant is declared with values for the mass and radius parameters. These
values are passed to the constructor when the constant is created. Java requires
that the constants be defined first, prior to any fields or methods. Also, when there
are fields and methods, the list of enum constants must end with a semicolon.

> **Note**
>
> The constructor for an enum type must be package-private or private access. It automatically creates the constants that are defined at the beginning of the enum body. You cannot invoke an enum constructor yourself.

4

In addition to its properties and constructor, `Planet` has methods that allow you to retrieve the surface gravity and weight of an object on each planet. Here is a sample program that takes your weight on earth (in any unit) and calculates and prints your weight on all planets (in the same unit):

```java
public enum Planet {
    MERCURY (3.303e+23, 2.4397e6),
    VENUS   (4.869e+24, 6.0518e6),
    EARTH   (5.976e+24, 6.37814e6),
    MARS    (6.421e+23, 3.3972e6),
    JUPITER (1.9e+27,   7.1492e7),
    SATURN  (5.688e+26, 6.0268e7),
    URANUS  (8.686e+25, 2.5559e7),
    NEPTUNE (1.024e+26, 2.4746e7);

    private final double mass;   // in kilograms
    private final double radius; // in meters
    Planet(double mass, double radius) {
        this.mass = mass;
        this.radius = radius;
    }
    private double mass() { return mass; }
    private double radius() { return radius; }

    // universal gravitational constant  (m3 kg-1 s-2)
    public static final double G = 6.67300E-11;

    double surfaceGravity() {
        return G * mass / (radius * radius);
    }
    double surfaceWeight(double otherMass) {
        return otherMass * surfaceGravity();
    }
    public static void main(String[] args) {
        if (args.length != 1) {
            System.err.println("Usage: java Planet <earth_weight>");
            System.exit(-1);
        }
        double earthWeight = Double.parseDouble(args[0]);
        double mass = earthWeight/EARTH.surfaceGravity();
        for (Planet p : Planet.values())
            System.out.printf("Your weight on %s is %f%n",
                            p, p.surfaceWeight(mass));
    }
}
```

If you run `Planet.class` from the command line with an argument of 175, you get fhe following output:

```
$ java Planet 175
Your weight on MERCURY is 66.107583
Your weight on VENUS is 158.374842
Your weight on EARTH is 175.000000
Your weight on MARS is 66.279007
Your weight on JUPITER is 442.847567
Your weight on SATURN is 186.552719
Your weight on URANUS is 158.397260
Your weight on NEPTUNE is 199.207413
```

Question and Exercises: Enum Types

Question

1. True or false: An Enum type can be a subclass of `java.lang.String`.

Exercises

1. Rewrite the class `Card` from the exercise in the "Questions and Exercises: Classes" section so that it represents the rank and suit of a card with enum types.
2. Rewrite the `Deck` class in the same way.

Answers

You can find answers to these questions and exercises at `http://docs.oracle.com/javase/tutorial/java/javaOO/QandE/enum-answers.html`.

Annotations

Annotations provide data about a program that are not part of the program itself. They have no direct effect on the operation of the code they annotate. Annotations have a number of uses, including the following:

- *Information for the compiler.* Annotations can be used by the compiler to detect errors or suppress warnings.
- *Compiler-time and deployment-time processing.* Software tools can process annotation information to generate code, XML files, and so forth.
- *Runtime processing.* Some annotations are available to be examined at runtime.

Annotations can be applied to a program's declarations of classes, fields, methods, and other program elements. The annotation appears first, often (by convention) on its own line, and may include *elements* with named or unnamed values:

```
@Author(
    name = "Benjamin Franklin",
    date = "3/27/2003"
)
class MyClass() { }
```

Here is another example:

```
@SuppressWarnings(value = "unchecked")
void myMethod() { }
```

If there is just one element named `value`, then the name may be omitted:

```
@SuppressWarnings("unchecked")
void myMethod() { }
```

Also, if an annotation has no elements, the parentheses may be omitted:

```
@Override
void mySuperMethod() { }
```

Documentation

Many annotations replace what would otherwise have been comments in code. Suppose that a software group has traditionally begun the body of every class with comments providing important information:

```
public class Generation3List extends Generation2List {

    // Author: John Doe
    // Date: 3/17/2002
    // Current revision: 6
    // Last modified: 4/12/2004
    // By: Jane Doe
    // Reviewers: Alice, Bill, Cindy

    // class code goes here

}
```

To add this same metadata with an annotation, you must first define the annotation type. The syntax for doing this is as follows:

```
@interface ClassPreamble {
    String author();
    String date();
    int currentRevision() default 1;
```

```
        String lastModified() default "N/A";
        String lastModifiedBy() default "N/A";
        // Note use of array
        String[] reviewers();
    }
```

The annotation type definition looks somewhat like an interface definition, where the keyword `interface` is preceded by the @ character (@ = "AT," as in Annotation Type). Annotation types are, in fact, a form of interface, which will be covered in Chapter 5.

The body of this annotation definition contains annotation type element declarations, which look a lot like methods. Note that these can be used to define optional default values.

Once the annotation type has been defined, you can use annotations of that type, with the values filled in, like this:

```
@ClassPreamble (
    author = "John Doe",
    date = "3/17/2002",
    currentRevision = 6,
    lastModified = "4/12/2004",
    lastModifiedBy = "Jane Doe",
    // Note array notation
    reviewers = {"Alice", "Bob", "Cindy"}
)
public class Generation3List extends Generation2List {

// class code goes here

}
```

Note

To make the information in `@ClassPreamble` appear in Javadoc-generated documentation, you must annotate the `@ClassPreamble` definition itself with the `@Documented` annotation:

```
    // import this to use @Documented
    import java.lang.annotation.*;

    @Documented
    @interface ClassPreamble {

        // Annotation element definitions

    }
```

Annotations Used by the Compiler

There are three annotation types that are predefined by the language specification itself: @Deprecated, @Override, and @SuppressWarnings.

The @Deprecated[5] annotation indicates that the marked element is deprecated and should no longer be used. The compiler generates a warning whenever a program uses a method, class, or field with the @Deprecated annotation. When an element is deprecated, it should also be documented using the Javadoc @deprecated tag, as shown in the following example. The use of the @ symbol in both Javadoc comments and annotations is not coincidental—they are related conceptually. Also, note that the Javadoc tag starts with a lowercase d and the annotation starts with an uppercase D:

```
// Javadoc comment follows
/**
 * @deprecated
 * explanation of why it
 * was deprecated
 */
@Deprecated
static void deprecatedMethod() { }
}
```

The @Override[6] annotation informs the compiler that the element is meant to override an element declared in a superclass. (Overriding methods will be discussed in Chapter 5.)

```
// mark method as a superclass method
// that has been overridden
@Override
int overriddenMethod() { }
```

While it's not required to use this annotation when overriding a method, it helps prevent errors. If a method marked with @Override fails to correctly override a method in one of its superclasses, the compiler generates an error.

The @SuppressWarnings[7] annotation tells the compiler to suppress specific warnings that it would otherwise generate. In the following example, a deprecated method is used, which would normally cause the compiler to generate a warning. In this case, however, the annotation suppresses the warning:

---

5. 7/docs/api/java/lang/Deprecated.html

6. 7/docs/api/java/lang/Override.html

7. 7/docs/api/java/lang/SuppressWarnings.html

```
    // use a deprecated method and tell
    // compiler not to generate a warning
    @SuppressWarnings("deprecation")
    void useDeprecatedMethod() {
        // deprecation warning
        // - suppressed
        objectOne.deprecatedMethod();
    }
```

Every compiler warning belongs to a category. The Java Language Specification lists two warning categories: *deprecation* and *unchecked*. The unchecked warning can occur when interfacing with legacy code written before the advent of generics (Chapter 6). To suppress more than one category of warnings, use the following syntax:

```
@SuppressWarnings({"unchecked", "deprecation"})
```

Annotation Processing

The more advanced uses of annotations include writing annotation processors that can read Java programs and take actions based on annotations. An annotation processor might, for example, generate auxiliary source code, relieving the programmer of having to create boilerplate code that always follows predictable patterns. To facilitate this task, release 5.0 of the Java SE Development Kit (JDK) includes an annotation-processing tool called apt. As of release 6 of the JDK, the functionality of apt is a standard part of the Java compiler.

To make annotation information available at runtime, the annotation type itself must be annotated with @Retention(RetentionPolicy.RUNTIME), as follows:

```
import java.lang.annotation.*;

@Retention(RetentionPolicy.RUNTIME)
@interface AnnotationForRuntime {

    // Elements that give information
    // for runtime processing

}
```

Questions and Exercises: Annotations

Questions

1. What is wrong with the following interface?

    ```
    public interface House {
        @Deprecated
        void open();
    ```

```
            void openFrontDoor();
            void openBackDoor();
        }
```

2. Consider this implementation of the House interface shown in question 1:

```
    public class MyHouse implements House {
        public void open() {}
        public void openFrontDoor() {}
        public void openBackDoor() {}
    }
```

If you compile this program, the compiler complains that open has been deprecated (in the interface). What can you do to get rid of that warning?

Exercise

1. Define an annotation type for an enhancement request with elements id, synopsis, engineer, and date. Specify default values as *unassigned* for engineer and *unknown* for date.

Answers

You can find answers to these questions and exercises at http://docs.oracle.com/ javase/tutorial/java/javaOO/QandE/annotations-answers.html.

5

Interfaces and Inheritance

Chapter Contents

You saw an example of implementing an interface in Chapter 4. You can read more about interfaces in the first section of this chapter: what they are for, why you might want to write one, and how to write one. The second section of this chapter describes the way in which you can derive one class from another—that is, how a subclass can inherit fields and methods from a superclass. You will learn that all classes are derived from the Object class and also learn how to modify the methods that a subclass inherits from a superclass. This section also covers interface-like abstract classes. Each section ends with questions and exercises to test your understanding.

Interfaces

There are a number of situations in software engineering when it is important for disparate groups of programmers to agree to a "contract" that spells out how their software interacts. Each group should be able to write their code without any knowledge of how the other group's code is written. Generally speaking, *interfaces* are such contracts.

For example, imagine a futuristic society where computer-controlled robotic cars transport passengers through city streets without a human operator. Automobile manufacturers write software (Java, of course) that operates the automobile—stop, start, accelerate, turn left, and so forth. Another industrial group, electronic guidance instrument manufacturers, make computer systems that receive GPS data and wireless transmission of traffic conditions and use that information to drive the car.

The auto manufacturers must publish an industry-standard interface that spells out in detail what methods can be invoked to make the car move (any car, from any manufacturer). The guidance manufacturers can then write software that invokes the methods described in the interface to command the car. Neither industrial group needs to know *how* the other group's software is implemented. In fact, each group considers its software highly proprietary and reserves the right to modify it at any time, as long as it continues to adhere to the published interface.

Interfaces in Java

In the Java programming language, an *interface* is a reference type, similar to a class, that can *only* contain constants, method signatures, and nested types. There are no method bodies. Interfaces cannot be instantiated—they can only be *implemented* by classes or *extended* by other interfaces. Extension is discussed later in this chapter.

Defining an interface is similar to creating a new class:

```
public interface OperateCar {

    // constant declarations, if any

    // method signatures

    // An enum with values RIGHT, LEFT
    int turn(Direction direction,
            double radius,
            double startSpeed,
            double endSpeed);
    int changeLanes(Direction direction,
                    double startSpeed,
                    double endSpeed);
    int signalTurn(Direction direction,
                    boolean signalOn);
    int getRadarFront(double distanceToCar,
                    double speedOfCar);
    int getRadarRear(double distanceToCar,
                    double speedOfCar);
        . . . . . . .
    // more method signatures
}
```

Note that the method signatures have no braces and are terminated with a semicolon.

To use an interface, you write a class that *implements* the interface. When an instantiable class implements an interface, it provides a method body for each of the methods declared in the interface. Here is an example:

```
public class OperateBMW760i implements OperateCar {

    // the OperateCar method signatures, with implementation --
    // for example:
    int signalTurn(Direction direction, boolean signalOn) {
        // code to turn BMW's LEFT turn indicator lights on
        // code to turn BMW's LEFT turn indicator lights off
        // code to turn BMW's RIGHT turn indicator lights on
        // code to turn BMW's RIGHT turn indicator lights off
    }

    // other members, as needed -- for example, helper classes not
    // visible to clients of the interface
}
```

In this robotic car example, it is the automobile manufacturers who will implement the interface. Chevrolet's implementation will be substantially different from that of Toyota, of course, but both manufacturers will adhere to the same interface. The guidance manufacturers, who are the clients of the interface, will build systems that use GPS data on a car's location, digital street maps, and traffic data to drive the car. In doing so, the guidance systems will invoke the interface methods: turn, change lanes, brake, accelerate, and so forth.

Interfaces as APIs

The robotic car example shows an interface being used as an industry-standard Application Programming Interface (API). APIs are also common in commercial software products. Typically, a company sells a software package that contains complex methods that another company wants to use in its own software product. An example would be a package of digital image–processing methods that are sold to companies making end-user graphics programs. The image-processing company writes its classes to implement an interface, which it makes public to its customers. The graphics company then invokes the image-processing methods using the signatures and return types defined in the interface. While the image-processing company's API is made public (to its customers), its implementation of the API is kept as a closely guarded secret—in fact, the company could revise the implementation at a later date as long as it continues to implement the same, original interface that its customers rely on.

Interfaces and Multiple Inheritance

Interfaces have another very important role in the Java programming language. Interfaces are not part of the class hierarchy, although they work in combination with classes. The Java programming language does not permit multiple inheritance but provides an alternative. (Inheritance is discussed later in this chapter.)

In Java, a class can inherit from only one class but it can implement more than one interface. Therefore, objects can have multiple types: the type of their own class and the types of all the interfaces that they implement. This means that if a variable is declared to be the type of an interface, its value can reference any object that is instantiated from any class that implements the interface. This is discussed later in this chapter, in the section titled "Using an Interface as a Type."

Defining an Interface

An interface declaration consists of modifiers, the keyword `interface`, the interface name, a comma-separated list of parent interfaces (if any), and the interface body. Here is an example:

```
public interface GroupedInterface extends Interface1, Interface2, Interface3 {

    // constant declarations

    // base of natural logarithms
    double E = 2.718282;

    // method signatures
    void doSomething (int i, double x);
    int doSomethingElse(String s);
}
```

The `public` access specifier indicates that the interface can be used by any class in any package. If you do not specify that the interface is public, your interface will be accessible only to classes defined in the same package as the interface.

An interface can extend other interfaces, just as a class can extend or subclass another class. However, whereas a class can extend only one other class, an interface can extend any number of interfaces. The interface declaration includes a comma-separated list of all the interfaces that it extends.

The Interface Body

The interface body contains method declarations for all the methods included in the interface. A method declaration within an interface is followed by a semicolon but no braces because an interface does not provide implementations for the methods declared within it. All methods declared in an interface are implicitly `public`, so the public modifier can be omitted.

An interface can contain constant declarations in addition to method declarations. All constant values defined in an interface are implicitly `public`, `static`, and `final`. Once again, these modifiers can be omitted.

Implementing an Interface

To declare a class that implements an interface, include an `implements` clause in the class declaration. Your class can implement more than one interface, so the `implements` keyword is followed by a comma-separated list of the interfaces implemented by the class. By convention, the `implements` clause follows the `extends` clause, if there is one.

A Sample Interface: Relatable

Consider an interface that defines how to compare the size of objects:

```
public interface Relatable {

    // this (object calling isLargerThan)
    // and other must be instances of
    // the same class returns 1, 0, -1
    // if this is greater // than, equal
    // to, or less than other
    public int isLargerThan(Relatable other);
}
```

If you want to be able to compare the size of similar objects, no matter what they are, the class that instantiates them should implement `Relatable`.

Any class can implement `Relatable` if there is some way to compare the relative "size" of objects instantiated from the class. For strings, it could be number of characters; for books, it could be number of pages; for students, it could be weight; and so forth. For planar geometric objects, area would be a good choice (see the `RectanglePlus` class that follows), while volume would work for three-dimensional geometric objects. All such classes can implement the `isLargerThan()` method. If you know that a class implements `Relatable`, then you know that you can compare the size of the objects instantiated from that class.

Implementing the Relatable Interface

Here is the `Rectangle` class that was presented in Chapter 4, "Creating Objects," rewritten to implement `Relatable`:

```
public class RectanglePlus
    implements Relatable {
    public int width = 0;
    public int height = 0;
    public Point origin;

    // four constructors
    public RectanglePlus() {
        origin = new Point(0, 0);
    }
```

```
    public RectanglePlus(Point p) {
        origin = p;
    }
    public RectanglePlus(int w, int h) {
        origin = new Point(0, 0);
        width = w;
        height = h;
    }
    public RectanglePlus(Point p, int w, int h) {
        origin = p;
        width = w;
        height = h;
    }

    // a method for moving the rectangle
    public void move(int x, int y) {
        origin.x = x;
        origin.y = y;
    }

    // a method for computing
    // the area of the rectangle
    public int getArea() {
        return width * height;
    }

    // a method required to implement
    // the Relatable interface
    public int isLargerThan(Relatable other) {
        RectanglePlus otherRect
            = (RectanglePlus)other;
        if (this.getArea() < otherRect.getArea())
            return -1;
        else if (this.getArea() > otherRect.getArea())
            return 1;
        else
            return 0;
    }
}
```

Because `RectanglePlus` implements `Relatable`, the size of any two `RectanglePlus` objects can be compared.

Note

The `isLargerThan` method, as defined in the `Relatable` interface, takes an object of type `Relatable`. The bold lines of code cast `other` to a `RectanglePlus` instance. Type casting tells the compiler what the object really is. Invoking `getArea` directly on the `other` instance (`other.getArea()`) would fail to compile because the compiler does not understand that `other` is actually an instance of `RectanglePlus`.

Using an Interface as a Type

When you define a new interface, you are defining a new reference data type. You can use interface names anywhere you can use any other data type name. If you define a reference variable whose type is an interface, any object you assign to it *must* be an instance of a class that implements the interface.

As an example, here is a method for finding the largest object in a pair of objects, for *any* objects that are instantiated from a class that implements `Relatable`:

```
public Object findLargest(Object object1, Object object2) {
    Relatable obj1 = (Relatable)object1;
    Relatable obj2 = (Relatable)object2;
    if ((obj1).isLargerThan(obj2) > 0)
        return object1;
    else
        return object2;
}
```

Because `object1` has been cast to a `Relatable` type, it can now invoke the `isLargerThan` method.

If you make a point of implementing `Relatable` in a wide variety of classes, the objects instantiated from *any* of those classes can be compared with the findLargest() method, provided that both objects are of the same class. Similarly, they can all be compared with the following methods:

```
public Object findSmallest(Object object1, Object object2) {
    Relatable obj1 = (Relatable)object1;
    Relatable obj2 = (Relatable)object2;
    if ((obj1).isLargerThan(obj2) < 0)
        return object1;
    else
        return object2;
}

public boolean isEqual(Object object1, Object object2) {
    Relatable obj1 = (Relatable)object1;
    Relatable obj2 = (Relatable)object2;
    if ( (obj1).isLargerThan(obj2) == 0)
        return true;
    else
        return false;
}
```

These methods work for any "relatable" objects, no matter what their class inheritance is. When they implement `Relatable`, they can be of both their own class (or superclass) type and a `Relatable` type. This gives them some of the advantages of multiple inheritance, where they can have behavior from both a superclass and an interface.

Rewriting Interfaces

Consider an interface that you have developed called `DoIt`:

```
public interface DoIt {
   void doSomething(int i, double x);
   int doSomethingElse(String s);
}
```

Suppose that, at a later time, you want to add a third method to `DoIt`, changing the interface in the following way:

```
public interface DoIt {
   void doSomething(int i, double x);
   int doSomethingElse(String s);
   boolean didItWork(int i, double x, String s);
}
```

If you make this change, all classes that implement the old `DoIt` interface will break because they don't implement the interface anymore. Programmers relying on this interface will protest loudly.

Try to anticipate all uses for your interface and specify it completely from the beginning. Given that this is often impossible, you may need to create more interfaces later. For example, you could create a `DoItPlus` interface that extends `DoIt`:

```
public interface DoItPlus extends DoIt {
   boolean didItWork(int i, double x, String s);
}
```

Now users of your code can choose to continue to use the old interface or upgrade to the new interface.

Summary of Interfaces

An interface defines a protocol of communication between two objects. An interface declaration contains signatures but no implementations for a set of methods and may also contain constant definitions. A class that implements an interface must implement all methods declared in the interface. An interface name can be used anywhere a type can be used.

Questions and Exercises: Interfaces

Questions

1. What methods would a class that implements the `java.lang.CharSequence` interface need to implement?

2. What is wrong with the following interface?

```java
public interface SomethingIsWrong {
    void aMethod(int aValue){
        System.out.println("Hi Mom");
    }
}
```

3. Fix the interface in question 2.

4. Is the following interface valid?

```java
public interface Marker {
}
```

5

Exercises

1. Write a class that implements the `CharSequence` interface found in the `java.lang` package. Your implementation should return the string backward. Select one of the sentences from this book to use as the data. Write a small `main` method to test your class; make sure to call all four methods.

2. Suppose you have written a time server that periodically notifies its clients of the current date and time. Write an interface that the server could use to enforce a particular protocol for its clients.

Answers

You can find answers to these questions and exercises at `http://docs.oracle.com/javase/tutorial/java/IandI/QandE/interfaces-answers.html`.

Inheritance

You have seen *inheritance* mentioned several times in previous sections and chapters. In the Java language, classes can be *derived* from other classes, thereby *inheriting* fields and methods from those classes.

> **Definition**
>
> A class that is derived from another class is called a *subclass* (and also a *derived class*, *extended class*, or *child class*). The class from which the subclass is derived is called a *superclass* (and also a *base class* or *parent class*).
>
> Aside from `Object`, which has no superclass, every class has one and only one direct superclass (single inheritance). In the absence of any other explicit superclass, every class is implicitly a subclass of `Object`.
>
> Classes can be derived from classes that are derived from classes that are derived from classes and so on, and these are all ultimately derived from the topmost class, `Object`. Classes of this nature are said to be *descended* from all the classes in the inheritance chain, stretching all the way back to `Object`.

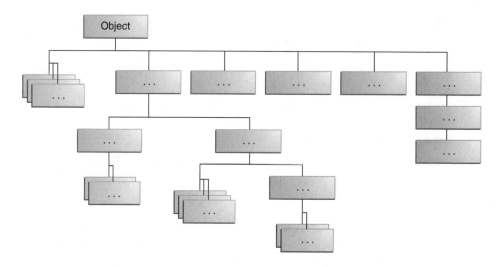

Figure 5.1 All Classes in the Java Platform Are Descendants of Object

The idea of inheritance is simple but powerful: When you want to create a new class and there is already a class that includes some of the code you want, you can derive your new class from the existing class. In doing this, you can reuse the fields and methods of the existing class without having to write (and debug!) them yourself.

A subclass inherits all the *members* (fields, methods, and nested classes) from its superclass. Constructors are not members, so they are not inherited by subclasses, but the constructor of the superclass can be invoked from the subclass.

The Java Platform Class Hierarchy

The Object[1] class, defined in the java.lang package, defines and implements behavior common to all classes—including the ones that you write. In the Java platform, many classes derive directly from Object, other classes derive from some of those classes, and so on, forming a hierarchy of classes (Figure 5.1). At the top of the hierarchy, Object is the most general of all classes. Classes near the bottom of the hierarchy provide more specialized behavior.

An Example of Inheritance

Here is the sample code for a possible implementation of a Bicycle class that was presented in Chapter 4:

```
public class Bicycle {

    // the Bicycle class has
```

---

1.   7/docs/api/java/lang/Object.html

```
// three fields
public int cadence;
public int gear;
public int speed;

// the Bicycle class has
// one constructor
public Bicycle(int startCadence, int startSpeed, int startGear) {
    gear = startGear;
    cadence = startCadence;
    speed = startSpeed;
}

// the Bicycle class has
// four methods
public void setCadence(int newValue) {
    cadence = newValue;
}

public void setGear(int newValue) {
    gear = newValue;
}

public void applyBrake(int decrement) {
    speed -= decrement;
}

public void speedUp(int increment) {
    speed += increment;
}

}
```

A class declaration for a `MountainBike` class that is a subclass of `Bicycle` might look like this:

```
public class MountainBike extends Bicycle {

    // the MountainBike subclass adds
    // one field
    public int seatHeight;

    // the MountainBike subclass has one
    // constructor
    public MountainBike(int startHeight,
                        int startCadence,
                        int startSpeed,
                        int startGear) {
        super(startCadence, startSpeed, startGear);
        seatHeight = startHeight;
    }

    // the MountainBike subclass adds
    // one method
    public void setHeight(int newValue) {
        seatHeight = newValue;
    }
}
```

MountainBike inherits all the fields and methods of Bicycle and adds the field seatHeight and a method to set it. Aside from the constructor, it is as if you had written a new MountainBike class entirely from scratch, with four fields and five methods. However, you didn't have to do all the work. This would be especially valuable if the methods in the Bicycle class were complex and had taken substantial time to debug.

What You Can Do in a Subclass

A subclass inherits all the *public* and *protected* members of its parent, no matter what package the subclass is in. If the subclass is in the same package as its parent, it also inherits the *package-private* members of the parent. You can use the inherited members as is, replace them, hide them, or supplement them with new members:

- You can use the inherited fields directly, just like any other fields.
- You can declare a field in the subclass with the same name as the one in the superclass, thus *hiding* it (not recommended).
- You can declare new fields in the subclass that are not in the superclass.
- You can use the inherited methods directly, as they are.
- You can write a new *instance* method in the subclass that has the same signature as the one in the superclass, thus *overriding* it.
- You can write a new *static* method in the subclass that has the same signature as the one in the superclass, thus *hiding* it.
- You can declare new methods in the subclass that are not in the superclass.
- You can write a subclass constructor that invokes the constructor of the superclass, either implicitly or by using the keyword super.

The following sections in this chapter will expand on these topics.

Private Members in a Superclass

A subclass does not inherit the private members of its parent class. However, if the superclass has public or protected methods for accessing its private fields, these can also be used by the subclass.

A nested class has access to all the private members of its enclosing class—both fields and methods. Therefore, a public or protected nested class inherited by a subclass has indirect access to all the private members of the superclass.

Casting Objects

We have seen that a given object is of the data type of the class from which it was instantiated. Here is an example:

```
public MountainBike myBike = new MountainBike();
```

In this case, myBike is of type MountainBike. MountainBike is descended from Bicycle and Object. Therefore, a MountainBike is both a Bicycle and an Object, and it can be used wherever Bicycle or Object objects are called for. The reverse is not necessarily true: a Bicycle *may* be a MountainBike, but it isn't necessarily. Similarly, an Object *may* be a Bicycle or a MountainBike, but it isn't necessarily.

Casting shows the use of an object of one type in place of another type among the objects permitted by inheritance and implementations. Here is an example:

```
Object obj = new MountainBike();
```

In this case, obj is both an Object and a MountainBike (until such time as obj is assigned another object that is *not* a MountainBike). This is called *implicit casting*.

On the other hand, we can write the following:

```
MountainBike myBike = obj;
```

Here we would get a compile-time error because obj is not known to the compiler to be a MountainBike. However, we can *tell* the compiler that we promise to assign a MountainBike to obj by *explicit casting*:

```
MountainBike myBike = (MountainBike)obj;
```

This cast inserts a runtime check where obj is assigned a MountainBike so that the compiler can safely assume that obj is a MountainBike. If obj is not a MountainBike at runtime, an exception will be thrown.

> **Note**
>
> You can make a logical test to determine the type of a particular object by using the instanceof operator. This can save you from a runtime error due to an improper cast. Here is an example:
>
> ```
> if (obj instanceof MountainBike) {
>     MountainBike myBike = (MountainBike)obj;
> }
> ```
>
> The instanceof operator verifies that obj refers to a MountainBike so that we can make the cast with confidence that there will be no runtime errors.

Overriding and Hiding Methods

Instance Methods

An instance method in a subclass with the same signature (name, plus the number and the type of its parameters) and return type as an instance method in the superclass *overrides* the superclass's method. The ability of a subclass to override a method allows a class to inherit from a superclass whose behavior is "close enough" and then modify this behavior as needed. The overriding method has the same name, number, type of parameters, and return type as the method it overrides. An overriding method can also return a subtype of the type returned by the overridden method. This is called a *covariant return type.*

When overriding a method, you might want to use the @Override annotation, which instructs the compiler that you intend to override a method in the superclass. If, for some reason, the compiler detects that the method does not exist in one of the superclasses, it will generate an error. For more information on @Override, see Chapter 4, "Annotations."

Class Methods

If a subclass defines a class method with the same signature as a class method in the superclass, the method in the subclass *hides* the one in the superclass. The distinction between hiding and overriding has important implications. The version of the overridden method that gets invoked is the one in the subclass. The version of the hidden method that gets invoked depends on whether it is invoked from the superclass or the subclass. Let's look at an example that contains two classes. The first is Animal, which contains one instance method and one class method:

```
public class Animal {
    public static void testClassMethod() {
        System.out.println("The class" + " method in Animal.");
    }
    public void testInstanceMethod() {
        System.out.println("The instance " + " method in Animal.");
    }
}
```

The second class, a subclass of Animal, is called Cat:

```
public class Cat extends Animal {
    public static void testClassMethod() {
        System.out.println("The class method" + " in Cat.");
    }
    public void testInstanceMethod() {
        System.out.println("The instance method" + " in Cat.");
    }

    public static void main(String[] args) {
```

```
            Cat myCat = new Cat();
            Animal myAnimal = myCat;
            Animal.testClassMethod();
            myAnimal.testInstanceMethod();
        }
    }
```

The `Cat` class overrides the instance method in `Animal` and hides the class method in `Animal`. The `main` method in this class creates an instance of `Cat` and calls `testClassMethod()` on the class and `testInstanceMethod()` on the instance. The output from this program is as follows:

```
The class method in Animal.
The instance method in Cat.
```

As promised, the version of the hidden method that gets invoked is the one in the superclass, and the version of the overridden method that gets invoked is the one in the subclass.

Modifiers

The access specifier for an overriding method can allow more (but not less) access than the overridden method. For example, a protected instance method in the super-class can be made public but not private in the subclass. You will get a compile-time error if you attempt to change an instance method in the superclass to a class method in the subclass, and vice versa.

Summary

Table 5.1 summarizes what happens when you define a method with the same signature as a method in a superclass.

> **Note**
> In a subclass, you can overload the methods inherited from the superclass. Such overload-ed methods neither hide nor override the superclass methods—they are new methods, unique to the subclass.

Table 5.1 Defining a Method with the Same Signature as a Superclass's Method

	Superclass instance method	Superclass static method
Subclass instance method	Overrides	Generates a compile-time error
Subclass static method	Generates a compile-time error	Hides

Polymorphism

The dictionary definition of *polymorphism* refers to a principle in biology in which an organism or species can have many different forms or stages. This principle can also be applied to object-oriented programming and languages like the Java language. Subclasses of a class can define their own unique behaviors and yet share some of the same functionality of the parent class.

Polymorphism can be demonstrated with a minor modification to the `Bicycle` class. For example, a `printDescription` method could be added to the class that displays all the data currently stored in an instance:

```
public void printDescription(){
    System.out.println("\nBike is " + "in gear " + this.gear
        + " with a cadence of " + this.cadence +
        " and traveling at a speed of " + this.speed + ". ");
}
```

To demonstrate polymorphic features in the Java language, extend the `Bicycle` class with a `MountainBike` and a `RoadBike` class. For `MountainBike`, add a field for `suspension`, which is a `String` value that indicates if the bike has a front shock absorber (`Front`) or a front and back shock absorber (`Dual`).

Here is the updated class:

```
public class MountainBike extends Bicycle {
    private String suspension;

    public MountainBike(
                int startCadence,
                int startSpeed,
                int startGear,
                String suspensionType){
        super(startCadence,
            startSpeed,
            startGear);
        this.setSuspension(suspensionType);
    }

    public String getSuspension(){
      return this.suspension;
    }

    public void setSuspension(String suspensionType) {
        this.suspension = suspensionType;
    }

    public void printDescription() {
        super.printDescription();
        System.out.println("The " + "MountainBike has a" +
            getSuspension() + " suspension.");
    }
}
```

Note the overridden `printDescription` method. In addition to the information provided previously, additional data about the suspension is included to the output.

Next, create the `RoadBike` class. Because road or racing bikes have skinny tires, add an attribute to track the tire width (`tireWidth`). Here is the `RoadBike` class:

```
public class RoadBike extends Bicycle{
    // In millimeters (mm)
    private int tireWidth;

    public RoadBike(int startCadence,
                    int startSpeed,
                    int startGear,
                    int newTireWidth){
        super(startCadence,
              startSpeed,
              startGear);
        this.setTireWidth(newTireWidth);
    }

    public int getTireWidth(){
      return this.tireWidth;
    }

    public void setTireWidth(int newTireWidth){
        this.tireWidth = newTireWidth;
    }

    public void printDescription(){
        super.printDescription();
        System.out.println("The RoadBike" + " has " + getTireWidth() +
            " MM tires.");
    }
}
```

Note that, once again, the `printDescription` method has been overridden. This time, information about the tire width is displayed.

To summarize, there are three classes: `Bicycle`, `MountainBike`, and `RoadBike`. The two subclasses override the `printDescription` method and print unique information.

Here is a test program that creates three `Bicycle` variables. Each variable is assigned to one of the three bicycle classes. Each variable is then printed:

```
public class TestBikes {
  public static void main(String[] args){
    Bicycle bike01, bike02, bike03;

    bike01 = new Bicycle(20, 10, 1);
    bike02 = new MountainBike(20, 10, 5, "Dual");
    bike03 = new RoadBike(40, 20, 8, 23);

    bike01.printDescription();
    bike02.printDescription();
```

```
      bike03.printDescription();
   }
}
```

The following is the output from the test program:

```
Bike is in gear 1 with a cadence of 20 and traveling at a speed of 10.

Bike is in gear 5 with a cadence of 20 and traveling at a speed of 10.
The MountainBike has a Dual suspension.

Bike is in gear 8 with a cadence of 40 and traveling at a speed of 20.
The RoadBike has 23 MM tires.
```

The Java Virtual Machine calls the appropriate method for the object that is referenced by each variable. It does not call the method that is defined by the variable's type. This behavior is referred to as *virtual method invocation* and demonstrates an aspect of the important polymorphism features in the Java language.

Hiding Fields

Within a class, a field that has the same name as a field in the superclass hides the superclass's field, even if their types are different. Within the subclass, the field in the superclass cannot be referenced by its simple name. Instead, the field must be accessed through super, which is covered in the next section. Generally speaking, we don't recommend hiding fields because it makes code difficult to read.

Using the Keyword super

Accessing Superclass Members

If your method overrides one of its superclass's methods, you can invoke the overridden method through the use of the keyword super. You can also use super to refer to a hidden field (although, as mentioned previously, hiding fields is discouraged). Consider this class, Superclass:

```
public class Superclass {

    public void printMethod() {
        System.out.println("Printed in Superclass.");
    }
}
```

Here is a subclass, called Subclass, that overrides printMethod():

```
public class Subclass extends Superclass {

    // overrides printMethod in Superclass
    public void printMethod() {
        super.printMethod();
        System.out.println("Printed in Subclass.");
    }
    public static void main(String[] args) {
        Subclass s = new Subclass();
        s.printMethod();
    }
}
```

5

Within `Subclass`, the simple name `printMethod()` refers to the one declared in `Subclass`, which overrides the one in `Superclass`. So to refer to `printMethod()` inherited from `Superclass`, `Subclass` must use a qualified name, using `super` as shown. Compiling and executing `Subclass` prints the following:

```
Printed in Superclass.
Printed in Subclass.
```

Subclass Constructors

The following example illustrates how to use the `super` keyword to invoke a super-class's constructor. Recall from the `Bicycle` example that `MountainBike` is a sub-class of `Bicycle`. Here is the `MountainBike` (subclass) constructor that calls the superclass constructor and then adds initialization code of its own:

```
public MountainBike(int startHeight,
                    int startCadence,
                    int startSpeed,
                    int startGear) {
    super(startCadence, startSpeed, startGear);
    seatHeight = startHeight;
}
```

Invocation of a superclass constructor must be the first line in the subclass constructor. The syntax for calling a superclass constructor is as follows:

```
super();
```

Here is an alternative:

```
super(parameter list);
```

In `super()`, the superclass no-argument constructor is called. In `super(parameter list)`, the superclass constructor with a matching parameter list is called.

> **Note**
>
> If a constructor does not explicitly invoke a superclass constructor, the Java compiler automatically inserts a call to the no-argument constructor of the superclass. If the super class does not have a no-argument constructor, you will get a compile-time error. `Object` *does* have such a constructor, so if `Object` is the only superclass, there is no problem.

5

If a subclass constructor invokes a constructor of its superclass, either explicitly or implicitly, you might think that there will be a whole chain of constructors called, all the way back to the constructor of `Object`. In fact, this is the case. It is called *constructor chaining*, and you need to be aware of it when there is a long line of class descent.

Object as a Superclass

In the `java.lang` package, the `Object`[2] class sits at the top of the class hierarchy tree. Every class descends directly or indirectly from the `Object` class. Every class you use or write inherits the instance methods of `Object`. You need not use any of these methods, but if you choose to do so, you may need to override them with code that is specific to your class. The following are the methods inherited from `Object` that are discussed in this section:

- `protected Object clone() throws CloneNotSupportedException`— Creates and returns a copy of this object
- `public boolean equals(Object obj)`—Indicates whether some other object is "equal to" this one
- `protected void finalize() throws Throwable`—Called by the garbage collector on an object when garbage collection determines that there are no more references to the object
- `public final Class getClass()`—Returns the runtime class of an object
- `public int hashCode()`—Returns a hash code value for the object
- `public String toString()`—Returns a string representation of the object

The `notify`, `notifyAll`, and `wait` methods of `Object` all play a part in synchronizing the activities of independently running threads in a program and will be discussed in more detail in later chapters. There are five of these methods:

---

2. `7/docs/api/java/lang/Object.html`

- `public final void notify()`
- `public final void notifyAll()`
- `public final void wait()`
- `public final void wait(long timeout)`
- `public final void wait(long timeout, int nanos)`

Note
There are some subtle aspects to a number of these methods, especially the `clone` method.

5

The clone() Method

If a class, or one of its superclasses, implements the `Cloneable` interface, you can use the `clone()` method to create a copy from an existing object. Use the following to create a clone:

```
aCloneableObject.clone();
```

Object's implementation of this method checks to see whether the object on which `clone()` was invoked implements the `Cloneable` interface. If the object does not, the method throws a `CloneNotSupportedException` exception. Exception handling will be covered in Chapter 9. For the moment, you need to know that `clone()` must be declared as follows if you are going to write a `clone()` method to override the one in `Object`:

```
protected Object clone() throws CloneNotSupportedException
```

Here is an alternative:

```
public Object clone() throws CloneNotSupportedException
```

If the object on which `clone()` was invoked does implement the `Cloneable` interface, Object's implementation of the `clone()` method creates an object of the same class as the original object and initializes the new object's member variables to have the same values as the original object's corresponding member variables. The simplest way to make your class cloneable is to add `implements Cloneable` to your class's declaration. Then your objects can invoke the `clone()` method.

For some classes, the default behavior of Object's `clone()` method works just fine. If, however, an object contains a reference to an external object, say `ObjExternal`, you may need to override `clone()` to get correct behavior. Otherwise, a change in

ObjExternal made by one object will be visible in its clone also. This means that the original object and its clone are not independent—to decouple them, you must override clone() so that it clones the object *and* ObjExternal. Then the original object references ObjExternal and the clone references a clone of ObjExternal, so that the object and its clone are truly independent.

The equals() Method

The equals() method compares two objects for equality and returns true if they are equal. The equals() method provided in the Object class uses the identity operator (==) to determine whether two objects are equal. For primitive data types, this gives the correct result. For objects, however, it does not. The equals() method provided by Object tests whether the object *references* are equal—that is, if the objects compared are the exact same object.

To test whether two objects are equal in the sense of *equivalency* (containing the same information), you must override the equals() method. Here is an example of a Book class that overrides equals():

```java
public class Book {
    . . .
    public boolean equals(Object obj) {
        if (obj instanceof Book)
            return ISBN.equals((Book)obj.getISBN());
        else
            return false;
    }
}
```

Consider this code that tests two instances of the Book class for equality:

```java
// Swing Tutorial, 5th edition
Book firstBook  = new Book("0132761696");
Book secondBook = new Book("0132761696");
if (firstBook.equals(secondBook)) {
    System.out.println("objects are equal");
} else {
    System.out.println("objects are not equal");
}
```

This program displays objects are equal even though firstBook and secondBook reference two distinct objects. They are considered equal because the objects compared contain the same ISBN number. You should always override the equals() method if the identity operator is not appropriate for your class.

Note
If you override equals(), you must override hashCode() as well.

The finalize() Method

The `Object` class provides a callback method, `finalize()`, that *may be* invoked on an object when it becomes garbage. `Object`'s implementation of `finalize()` does nothing—you can override `finalize()` to do cleanup, which includes freeing resources.

The `finalize()` method *may be* called automatically by the system, but it is uncertain when and if it will even be called. Therefore, you should not rely on this method to do your cleanup for you. For example, if you don't close file descriptors in your code after performing I/O and you expect `finalize()` to close them for you, you may run out of file descriptors.

The getClass() Method

You cannot override `getClass`. The `getClass()` method returns a `Class` object, which has methods you can use to get information about the class, such as its name (`getSimpleName()`), its superclass (`getSuperclass()`), and the interfaces it implements (`getInterfaces()`). For example, the following method gets and displays the class name of an object:

```java
void printClassName(Object obj) {
    System.out.println("The object's" + " class is " +
        obj.getClass().getSimpleName());
}
```

The `Class`[3] class, in the `java.lang` package, has a large number of methods (more than fifty). For example, you can test to see if the class is an annotation (`isAnnotation()`), an interface (`isInterface()`), or an enumeration (`isEnum()`). You can see what the object's fields are (`getFields()`) or what its methods are (`getMethods()`), and so on.

The hashCode() Method

The value returned by `hashCode()` is the object's hash code, which is the object's memory address in hexadecimal. By definition, if two objects are equal, their hash code must also be equal. If you override the `equals()` method, you change the way two objects are equated and `Object`'s implementation of `hashCode()` is no longer valid. Therefore, if you override the `equals()` method, you must also override the `hashCode()` method.

The toString() Method

You should always consider overriding the `toString()` method in your classes. The `Object`'s `toString()` method returns a `String` representation of the object, which is very useful for debugging. The `String` representation for an object

---

3. `7/docs/api/java/lang/Class.html`

depends entirely on the object, which is why you need to override `toString()` in your classes.

You can use `toString()` along with `System.out.println()` to display a text representation of an object, such as an instance of `Book`:

```
System.out.println(firstBook.toString());
```

For a properly overridden `toString()` method, this would print something useful, like the following message:

```
ISBN: 0132761696; The Swing Tutorial; A Guide to Constructing GUIs, 5th Edition
```

Writing Final Classes and Methods

You can declare some or all of a class's methods *final*. You use the `final` keyword in a method declaration to indicate that the method cannot be overridden by subclasses. The `Object` class does this—a number of its methods are `final`.

You might wish to make a method final if it has an implementation that should not be changed and it is critical to the consistent state of the object. For example, you might want to make the `getFirstPlayer` method in this `ChessAlgorithm` class final:

```
class ChessAlgorithm {
    enum ChessPlayer { WHITE, BLACK }
        . . .
    final ChessPlayer getFirstPlayer() {
        return ChessPlayer.WHITE;
    }
        . . .
}
```

Methods called from constructors should generally be declared final. If a constructor calls a nonfinal method, a subclass may redefine that method with surprising or undesirable results.

Note that you can also declare an entire class final. A class that is declared final cannot be subclassed. This is particularly useful, for example, when creating an immutable class like the `String` class.

Abstract Methods and Classes

An *abstract class* is a class that is declared `abstract`—it may or may not include abstract methods. Abstract classes can't be instantiated, but they can be subclassed.

An *abstract method* is a method that is declared without an implementation (i.e., without braces and followed by a semicolon). Here is an example:

```
abstract void moveTo(double deltaX, double deltaY);
```

If a class includes abstract methods, the class itself must be declared `abstract`:

```
public abstract class GraphicObject {
    // declare fields
    // declare non-abstract methods
    abstract void draw();
}
```

When an abstract class is subclassed, the subclass usually provides implementations for all the abstract methods in its parent class. However, if it does not, the subclass must also be declared `abstract`.

> **Note**
>
> All the methods in an *interface* are *implicitly* abstract, so the `abstract` modifier is not used with interface methods. (It could be—it's just not necessary.)

Abstract Classes versus Interfaces

Unlike interfaces, abstract classes can contain fields that are not `static` and `final`, and they can contain implemented methods. Such abstract classes are similar to interfaces, but they provide a partial implementation, leaving it to subclasses to complete the implementation. If an abstract class contains *only* abstract method declarations, it should be declared as an interface instead.

Multiple interfaces can be implemented by classes anywhere in the class hierarchy, whether or not they are related to one another in any way. Think of `Comparable` or `Cloneable`, for example.

By comparison, abstract classes are most commonly subclassed to share pieces of implementation. A single abstract class is subclassed by similar classes that have a lot in common (the implemented parts of the abstract class) but also have some differences (the abstract methods).

An Abstract Class Example

In an object-oriented drawing application, you can draw circles, rectangles, lines, Bezier curves, and many other graphic objects. These objects all have certain states (e.g., position, orientation, line color, fill color) and behaviors (e.g. move to, rotate, resize, draw) in common. Some of these states and behaviors are the same for all graphic objects (e.g., position, fill color, move to). Others require different implementations (e.g., resize, draw). All `GraphicObject` objects must know how to draw or resize themselves; they just differ in how they do it. This is a perfect situation for an

Figure 5.2 Classes Rectangle, Line, Bezier, and Circle Inherit from GraphicObject

abstract superclass. You can take advantage of the similarities and declare that all the graphic objects inherit from the same abstract parent object (Figure 5.2).

First you declare an abstract class, `GraphicObject`, to provide member variables and methods that are wholly shared by all subclasses, such as the current position and the `moveTo` method. `GraphicObject` also declares abstract methods for methods, such as `draw` or `resize`, that need to be implemented by all subclasses but must be implemented in different ways. The `GraphicObject` class can look something like this:

```
abstract class GraphicObject {
    int x, y;
      . . .
    void moveTo(int newX, int newY) {
          . . .
    }
    abstract void draw();
    abstract void resize();
}
```

Each nonabstract subclass of `GraphicObject`, such as `Circle` and `Rectangle`, must provide implementations for the `draw` and `resize` methods:

```
class Circle extends GraphicObject {
    void draw() {
          . . .
    }
    void resize() {
          . . .
    }
}
class Rectangle extends GraphicObject {
    void draw() {
          . . .
    }
    void resize() {
          . . .
    }
}
```

When an Abstract Class Implements an Interface

In the previous section, it was noted that a class that implements an interface must implement *all* the interface's methods. It is possible, however, to define a class that does not implement all the interface methods, provided that the class is declared abstract. Here is an example:

```
abstract class X implements Y {
   // implements all but one method of Y
}

class XX extends X {
   // implements the remaining method in Y
}
```

In this case, class X must be `abstract` because it does not fully implement Y, but class XX does in fact implement Y.

Class Members

An abstract class may have `static` fields and `static` methods. You can use these static members with a class reference (e.g., `AbstractClass.staticMethod()`) as you would with any other class.

Summary of Inheritance

Except for the `Object` class, a class has exactly one direct superclass. A class inherits fields and methods from all its superclasses, whether direct or indirect. A subclass can override methods that it inherits, or it can hide fields or methods that it inherits. (Note that, as mentioned previously, hiding fields is generally bad programming practice.) Table 5.1 shows the effect of declaring a method with the same signature as a method in the superclass.

The `Object` class is the top of the class hierarchy. All classes are descendants from this class and inherit methods from it. Useful methods inherited from `Object` include `toString()`, `equals()`, `clone()`, and `getClass()`.

You can prevent a class from being subclassed by using the final keyword in the class's declaration. Similarly, you can prevent a method from being overridden by subclasses by declaring it as a final method.

An abstract class can only be subclassed; it cannot be instantiated. An abstract class can contain abstract methods—methods that are declared but not implemented. Subclasses then provide the implementations for the abstract methods.

Questions and Exercises: Inheritance

Questions

1. Consider the following two classes:

```
public class ClassA {
    public void methodOne(int i) {
    }
    public void methodTwo(int i) {
    }
    public static void methodThree(int i) {
    }
    public static void methodFour(int i) {
    }
}

public class ClassB extends ClassA {
    public static void methodOne(int i) {
    }
    public void methodTwo(int i) {
    }
    public void methodThree(int i) {
    }
    public static void methodFour(int i) {
    }
}
```

a. Which method overrides a method in the superclass?

b. Which method hides a method in the superclass?

c. What do the other methods do?

2. Consider the Card, Deck, and DisplayDeck classes you wrote in Chapter 4, "Questions and Exercises: Classes." What Object methods should each of these classes override?

Exercise

1. Write the implementations for the methods from your answer to question 2.

Answers

You can find answers to these questions and exercises at http://docs.oracle.com/javase/tutorial/java/IandI/QandE/inherit-answers.html.

6

Generics

Chapter Contents

In any nontrivial software project, bugs are simply a fact of life. Careful planning, programming, and testing can help reduce their pervasiveness, but somehow, somewhere, they'll always find a way to creep into your code. This becomes especially apparent as new features are introduced and your code base grows in size and complexity.

Fortunately, some bugs are easier to detect than others. Compile-time bugs, for example, can be detected early on; you can use the compiler's error messages to figure out what the problem is and fix it right then and there. Runtime bugs, however, can be much more problematic; they don't always surface immediately, and when they do, it may be at a point in the program that is far removed from the actual cause of the problem. Generics, introduced in Java SE 5.0, add stability to your code by making more of your bugs detectable at compile time.

Why Use Generics?

In a nutshell, generics enable *types* (classes and interfaces) to be parameters when defining classes, interfaces, and methods. Much like the more familiar *formal parameters* used in method declarations, type parameters provide a way for you to reuse the same code with different inputs. The difference is that the inputs to formal parameters are values, while the inputs to type parameters are types.

Code that uses generics has many benefits over nongeneric code:

- *Stronger type checks at compile time.* A Java compiler applies strong type checking to generic code and issues errors if the code violates type safety. Fixing compile-time errors is easier than fixing runtime errors, which can be difficult to find.
- *Elimination of casts.* The following nongeneric code snippet requires casting:

```
List list = new ArrayList();
list.add("hello");
String s = (String) list.get(0);
```

  When rewritten using generics, the code does not require casting:

```
List<String> list = new ArrayList<String>();
list.add("hello");
String s = list.get(0);    // no cast
```

- *The ability to implement generic algorithms.* By using generics, programmers can implement generic algorithms that work on collections of different types, can be customized, and are type safe and easier to read.

Generic Types

A *generic type* is a generic class or interface that is parameterized over types. The following Box class will be modified to demonstrate the concept.

A Simple Box Class

Begin by examining a nongeneric Box class that operates on objects of any type. It only needs to provide two methods: set, which adds an object to the box, and get, which retrieves it:

```
public class Box {
    private Object object;

    public void set(Object object) { this.object = object; }
    public Object get() { return object; }
}
```

Since its methods accept or return an `Object`, you are free to pass in whatever you want, provided that it is not one of the primitive types. At compile time, there is no way to verify how the class is used. One part of the code may place an `Integer` in the box and expect to get `Integers` out of it, while another part of the code may mistakenly pass in a `String`, resulting in a runtime error.

A Generic Version of the Box Class

A *generic class* is defined with the following format:

```
class name<T1, T2, . . . , Tn> { /* . . . */ }
```

The type parameter section, delimited by angle brackets (<>), follows the class name. It specifies the *type parameters* (also called *type variables*) `T1`, `T2`, . . . , and `Tn`.

To update the `Box` class to use generics, you create a *generic type declaration* by changing the code `public class Box` to `public class Box<T>`. This introduces the type variable `T`, which can be used anywhere inside the class.

With this change, the `Box` class becomes the following:

```java
/**
 * Generic version of the Box class.
 * @param <T> the type of the value being boxed
 */
public class Box<T> {
    // T stands for "Type"
    private T t;

    public void set(T t) { this.t = t; }
    public T get() { return t; }
}
```

As you can see, all occurrences of `Object` are replaced by `T`. A type variable can be any nonprimitive type you specify: any class type, interface type, array type, or even another type variable. This same technique can be applied to create generic interfaces.

Type Parameter Naming Conventions

By convention, type parameter names are single, uppercase letters. This stands in sharp contrast to the variable naming conventions that you already know about, with good reason: without this convention, it would be difficult to tell the difference between a type variable and an ordinary class or interface name.

The most commonly used type parameter names are as follows:

- E—Element (used extensively by the Java Collections Framework)
- K—Key
- N—Number
- T—Type
- V—Value
- S, U, V, and so on—Second, third, and fourth types

You'll see these names used throughout the Java SE Application Programming Interface (API) and the rest of this chapter.

Invoking and Instantiating a Generic Type

To reference the generic Box class from within your code, you must perform a *generic type invocation*, which replaces T with some concrete value, such as Integer:

```
Box<Integer> integerBox;
```

You can think of a generic type invocation as being similar to an ordinary method invocation, but instead of passing an argument to a method, you are passing a *type argument* (Integer in this case) to the Box class itself.

> **Note**
>
> Many developers use the terms *type parameter* and *type argument* interchangeably, but these terms are not the same. In code, one provides type arguments in order to create a parameterized type. Therefore, the T in Foo<T> is a type parameter and the String in Foo<String> f is a type argument. This chapter observes this definition when using these terms.

Like any other variable declaration, this code does not actually create a new Box object. It simply declares that integerBox will hold a reference to a "Box of Integer," which is how Box<Integer> is read.

An invocation of a generic type is generally known as a *parameterized type*. To instantiate this class, use the new keyword, as usual, but place <Integer> between the class name and the parentheses:

```
Box<Integer> integerBox = new Box<Integer>();
```

The Diamond

In Java SE 7 and later, you can replace the type arguments required to invoke the constructor of a generic class with an empty set of type arguments (<>) as long as the compiler can determine, or infer, the type arguments from the context. This pair of angle brackets (<>) is informally called *the diamond*. For example, you can create an instance of Box<Integer> with the following statement:

```
Box<Integer> integerBox = new Box<>();
```

For more information on diamond notation and type inference, see the "Type Inference" section later on in this chapter.

Multiple Type Parameters

As mentioned previously, a generic class can have multiple type parameters. One example is the generic OrderedPair class, which implements the generic Pair interface:

```
public interface Pair<K, V> {
    public K getKey();
    public V getValue();
}

public class OrderedPair<K, V> implements Pair<K, V> {

    private K key;
    private V value;

    public OrderedPair(K key, V value) {
        this.key = key;
        this.value = value;
    }

    public K getKey()   { return key; }
    public V getValue() { return value; }
}
```

The following statements create two instantiations of the OrderedPair class:

```
Pair<String, Integer> p1 = new OrderedPair<String, Integer>("Even", 8);
Pair<String, String>  p2 = new OrderedPair<String, String>("hello", "world");
```

The code, new OrderedPair<String, Integer>, instantiates K as a String and V as an Integer. Therefore, the parameter types of OrderedPair's constructor are String and Integer, respectively. Due to autoboxing, it is valid to pass a String and an int to the class.

As mentioned previously, because a Java compiler can infer the K and V types from the declaration OrderedPair<String, Integer>, these statements can be shortened using diamond notation:

```
OrderedPair<String, Integer> p1 = new OrderedPair<>("Even", 8);
OrderedPair<String, String>  p2 = new OrderedPair<>("hello", "world");
```

To create a generic interface, follow the same conventions as you would to create a generic class.

Parameterized Types

You can also substitute a type parameter (e.g., K or V) with a parameterized type (e.g., List<String>). Here is an example, using OrderedPair<V, K>:

```
OrderedPair<String, Box<Integer>> p = new OrderedPair<>("primes", new
    Box<Integer>( . . . ));
```

Raw Types

A *raw type* is the name of a generic class or interface without any type arguments. Here is an example, given the generic Box class:

```
public class Box<T> {
    public void set(T t) { /* . . . */ }
    // . . .
}
```

To create a parameterized type of Box<T>, you supply an actual type argument for the formal type parameter T:

```
Box<Integer> intBox = new Box<>();
```

If the actual type argument is omitted, you create a raw type of Box<T>:

```
Box rawBox = new Box();
```

Therefore, Box is the raw type of the generic type Box<T>. However, a nongeneric class or interface type is *not* a raw type.

Raw types show up in legacy code because lots of API classes (such as the Collections classes) were not generic prior to the Java SE Development Kit (JDK) 5.0. When using raw types, you essentially get pregenerics behavior: a Box gives you Objects. For backward compatibility, assigning a parameterized type to its raw type is allowed:

```
Box<String> stringBox = new Box<>();
Box rawBox = stringBox;              // OK
```

However, if you assign a raw type to a parameterized type, you get a warning:

```
Box rawBox = new Box();            // rawBox is a raw type of Box<T>
Box<Integer> intBox = rawBox;      // warning: unchecked conversion
```

You also get a warning if you use a raw type to invoke generic methods defined in the corresponding generic type:

```
Box<String> stringBox = new Box<>();
Box rawBox = stringBox;
rawBox.set(8);  // warning: unchecked invocation to set(T)
```

The warning shows that raw types bypass generic type checks, deferring the catch of unsafe code to runtime. Therefore, you should avoid using raw types.

The "Type Erasure" section later on in this chapter has more information on how the Java compiler uses raw types.

Unchecked Error Messages

As mentioned previously, when mixing legacy code with generic code, you may encounter warning messages similar to the following:

```
Note: Example.java uses unchecked or unsafe operations.
Note: Recompile with -Xlint:unchecked for details.
```

This can happen when using an older API that operates on raw types, as shown in the following example:

```
public class WarningDemo {
    public static void main(String[] args){
        Box<Integer> bi;
        bi = createBox();
    }

    static Box createBox(){
        return new Box();
    }
}
```

The term *unchecked* means that the compiler does not have enough type information to perform all type checks necessary to ensure type safety. The unchecked warning is disabled, by default, though the compiler gives a hint. To see all unchecked warnings, recompile with –Xlint:unchecked.

Recompiling the previous example with –Xlint:unchecked reveals the following additional information:

```
WarningDemo.java:4: warning: [unchecked] unchecked conversion
found   : Box
required: Box<java.lang.Integer>
        bi = createBox();
                      ^
1 warning
```

To completely disable unchecked warnings, use the -Xlint:-unchecked flag. The @SuppressWarnings("unchecked") annotation suppresses unchecked warnings. If you are unfamiliar with the @SuppressWarnings syntax, see Chapter 4, "Annotations."

Generic Methods

Generic methods are methods that introduce their own type parameters. This is similar to declaring a generic type, but the type parameter's scope is limited to the method where it is declared. Static and nonstatic generic methods are allowed, as are generic class constructors.

The syntax for a generic method includes a type parameter, inside angle brackets, that appears before the method's return type. For static generic methods, the type parameter section must appear before the method's return type.

The Util class includes a generic method, compare, which compares two Pair objects:

```java
public class Util {
    // Generic static method
    public static <K, V> boolean compare(Pair<K, V> p1, Pair<K, V> p2) {
        return p1.getKey().equals(p2.getKey()) &&
                p1.getValue().equals(p2.getValue());
    }
}

public class Pair<K, V> {

    private K key;
    private V value;

    // Generic constructor
    public Pair(K key, V value) {
        this.key = key;
        this.value = value;
    }

    // Generic methods
    public void setKey(K key) { this.key = key; }
    public void setValue(V value) { this.value = value; }
    public K getKey()   { return key; }
    public V getValue() { return value; }
}
```

The complete syntax for invoking this method is as follows:

```java
Pair<Integer, String> p1 = new Pair<>(1, "apple");
Pair<Integer, String> p2 = new Pair<>(2, "pear");
boolean same = Util.<Integer, String>compare(p1, p2);
```

The type has been explicitly provided, as shown in bold. Generally, this can be left out and the compiler will infer the type that is needed:

```
Pair<Integer, String> p1 = new Pair<>(1, "apple");
Pair<Integer, String> p2 = new Pair<>(2, "pear");
boolean same = Util.compare(p1, p2);
```

This feature, known as *type inference*, allows you to invoke a generic method as an ordinary method, without specifying a type between angle brackets. This topic is further discussed later on, in "Type Inference."

Bounded Type Parameters

There may be times when you want to restrict the types that can be used as type arguments in a parameterized type. For example, a method that operates on numbers might only want to accept instances of Number or its subclasses. This is what *bounded type parameters* are for.

To declare a bounded type parameter, list the type parameter's name, followed by the extends keyword, followed by its *upper bound*, which in this example is Number. Note that, in this context, extends is used in a general sense to mean either *extends* (as in classes) or *implements* (as in interfaces):

```
public class Box<T> {

    private T t;

    public void set(T t) {
        this.t = t;
    }

    public T get() {
        return t;
    }

    public <U extends Number> void inspect(U u){
        System.out.println("T: " + t.getClass().getName());
        System.out.println("U: " + u.getClass().getName());
    }

    public static void main(String[] args) {
        Box<Integer> integerBox = new Box<Integer>();
        integerBox.set(new Integer(10));
        integerBox.inspect("some text"); // error: this is still String!
    }
}
```

If we modify our generic method to include this bounded type parameter, compilation will now fail, since our invocation of inspect still includes a String:

```
Box.java:21: <U>inspect(U) in Box<java.lang.Integer> cannot
   be applied to (java.lang.String)
                        integerBox.inspect("10");
                        ^
1 error
```

In addition to limiting the types you can use to instantiate a generic type, bounded type parameters allow you to invoke methods defined in the bounds:

```
public class NaturalNumber<T extends Integer> {

    private T n;

    public NaturalNumber(T n)  { this.n = n; }

    public boolean isEven() {
        return n.intValue() % 2 == 0;
    }

    // . . .
}
```

The isEven method invokes the intValue method defined in the Integer class through n.

Multiple Bounds

The previous example illustrates the use of a type parameter with a single bound, but a type parameter can have *multiple bounds*:

```
<T extends B1 & B2 & B3>
```

A type variable with multiple bounds is a subtype of all the types listed in the bound. If one of the bounds is a class, it must be specified first, as follows:

```
Class A { /* . . . */ }
interface B { /* . . . */ }
interface C { /* . . . */ }

class D <T extends A & B & C> { /* . . . */ }
```

If bound A is not specified first, you get a compile-time error:

```
class D <T extends B & A & C> { /* . . . */ }  // compile-time error
```

Generic Methods and Bounded Type Parameters

Bounded type parameters are key to the implementation of generic algorithms. Consider the following method, which counts the number of elements in an array T[ ] that are greater than a specified element elem:

```
public static <T> int countGreaterThan(T[] anArray, T elem) {
    int count = 0;
    for (T e : anArray)
        if (e > elem)   // compiler error
            ++count;
    return count;
}
```

The implementation of the method is straightforward, but it does not compile because the greater than operator (>) applies only to primitive types such as short, int, double, long, float, byte, and char. You cannot use the greater than operator to compare objects. To fix the problem, use a type parameter bounded by the Comparable<T> interface:

```
public interface Comparable<T> {
    public int compareTo(T o);
}
```

The resulting code is as follows:

```
public static <T extends Comparable<T>> int countGreaterThan(T[] anArray, T elem) {
    int count = 0;
    for (T e : anArray)
        if (e.compareTo(elem) > 0)
            ++count;
    return count;
}
```

Generics, Inheritance, and Subtypes

As you already know, it is possible to assign an object of one type to an object of another type, provided that the types are compatible. For example, you can assign an Integer to an Object, since Object is one of Integer's supertypes:

```
Object someObject = new Object();
Integer someInteger = new Integer(10);
someObject = someInteger;   // OK
```

In object-oriented terminology, this is called an *is a* relationship. Since an `Integer` *is a* kind of `Object`, the assignment is allowed. But `Integer` is also a kind of `Number`, so the following code is valid as well:

```
public void someMethod(Number n) { /* . . . */ }

someMethod(new Integer(10));    // OK
someMethod(new Double(10.1);    // OK
```

The same is also true with generics. You can perform a generic type invocation, passing `Number` as its type argument, and any subsequent invocation of `add` will be allowed if the argument is compatible with `Number`:

```
Box<Number> box = new Box<Number>();
box.add(new Integer(10));    // OK
box.add(new Double(10.1));   // OK
```

Now consider the following method:

```
public void boxTest(Box<Number> n) { /* . . . */ }
```

What type of argument does it accept? By looking at its signature, you can see that it accepts a single argument whose type is `Box<Number>`. But what does that mean? Are you allowed to pass in `Box<Integer>` or `Box<Double>`, as you might expect? The answer is *no* because, as shown in Figure 6.1, `Box<Integer>` and `Box<Double>` are not subtypes of `Box<Number>`. This is a common misunderstanding when it comes to programming with generics and is an important concept to learn.

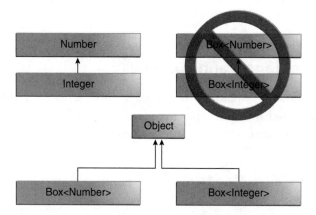

Figure 6.1 Box<Integer> Is Not a Subtype of Box<Number>
Even Though Integer Is a Subtype of Number

Note

Given two concrete types A and B (e.g., Number and Integer), MyClass has no relationship to MyClass<B>, regardless of whether or not A and B are related. The common parent of MyClass and MyClass<B> is Object.

For information on how to create a subtype-like relationship between two generic classes when the type parameters are related, see the section on "Wildcards and Subtyping" later on in this chapter.

Generic Classes and Subtyping

You can subtype a generic class or interface by extending or implementing it. The relationship between the type parameters of one class or interface and the type parameters of another are determined by the extends and implements clauses.

Using the Collections classes as an example, as shown in Figure 6.2, ArrayList<E> implements List<E>, and List<E> extends Collection<E>. So ArrayList<String> is a subtype of List<String>, which is a subtype of Collection<String>. So long as you do not vary the type argument, the subtyping relationship is preserved between the types.

Now imagine we want to define our own list interface, PayloadList (Figure 6.3), which associates an optional value of generic type P with each element. Its declaration might resemble the following:

Figure 6.2 A Sample Collections Hierarchy

Figure 6.3 A Sample PayloadList Hierarchy

```
interface PayloadList<E,P> extends List<E> {
  void setPayload(int index, P val);
    . . .
}
```

The following parameterizations of `PayloadList` are subtypes of `List<String>`:

- `PayloadList<String,String>`
- `PayloadList<String,Integer>`
- `PayloadList<String,Exception>`

Type Inference

Type inference is a Java compiler's ability to look at each method invocation and corresponding declaration to determine the type argument (or arguments) that makes the invocation applicable. The inference algorithm determines the types of the arguments and, if available, the type that the result is being assigned or returned. Finally, the inference algorithm tries to find the *most specific* type that works with all the arguments.

To illustrate this last point, in the following example, inference determines that the second argument being passed to the `pick` method is of type `Serializable`:

```
static <T> T pick(T a1, T a2) { return a2; }
Serializable s = pick("d", new ArrayList<String>());
```

Type Inference and Generic Methods

The previous discussion of generic methods introduced you to type inference, which enables you to invoke a generic method as you would an ordinary method, without specifying a type between angle brackets. Consider the following example, Box-Demo, which requires the `Box` class:

```
public class BoxDemo {

  public static <U> void addBox(U u,
      java.util.List<Box<U>> boxes) {
    Box<U> box = new Box<>();
    box.set(u);
    boxes.add(box);
  }

  public static <U> void outputBoxes(java.util.List<Box<U>> boxes) {
    int counter = 0;
    for (Box<U> box: boxes) {
      U boxContents = box.get();
      System.out.println("Box #" + counter + " contains [" +
```

```
                      boxContents.toString() + "]");
            counter++;
         }
      }

      public static void main(String[] args) {
         java.util.ArrayList<Box<Integer>> listOfIntegerBoxes =
            new java.util.ArrayList<>();
         BoxDemo.<Integer>addBox(Integer.valueOf(10), listOfIntegerBoxes);
         BoxDemo.addBox(Integer.valueOf(20), listOfIntegerBoxes);
         BoxDemo.addBox(Integer.valueOf(30), listOfIntegerBoxes);
         BoxDemo.outputBoxes(listOfIntegerBoxes);
      }
   }
```

The following is the output from this example:

```
Box #0 contains [10]
Box #1 contains [20]
Box #2 contains [30]
```

The generic method `addBox` defines one type parameter, named U. Generally, a Java compiler can infer the type parameters of a generic method call. Consequently, in most cases, you do not need to specify them. For example, to invoke the generic method `addBox`, you can specify the type parameter as follows:

```
BoxDemo.<Integer>addBox(Integer.valueOf(10), listOfIntegerBoxes);
```

Alternatively, if you omit the type parameters, a Java compiler automatically infers (from the method's arguments) that the type parameter is `Integer`:

```
BoxDemo.addBox(Integer.valueOf(20), listOfIntegerBoxes);
```

Type Inference and Instantiation of Generic Classes

You can replace the type arguments required to invoke the constructor of a generic class with an empty set of type parameters (<>; informally known as *the diamond*) as long as the compiler can infer the type arguments from the context.

For example, consider the following variable declaration:

```
Map<String, List<String>> myMap = new HashMap<String, List<String>>();
```

You can substitute the parameterized type of the constructor with an empty set of type parameters (<>):

```
Map<String, List<String>> my Map = new HashMap<>();
```

In order to take advantage of type inference during generic class instantiation, you must place notation inside the diamond. In the following example, the compiler generates an unchecked conversion warning because the `HashMap()` constructor refers to the `HashMap` raw type, not the `Map<String, List<String>>` type:

```
Map<String, List<String>> myMap = new HashMap(); // unchecked conversion warning
```

Java supports limited type inference for generic instance creation; you can only use type inference if the parameterized type of the constructor is obvious from the context. For example, the following code does not compile:

```
List<String> list = new ArrayList<>();
list.add("A");

// The following statement should fail since addAll expects
// Collection<? extends String>
list.addAll(new ArrayList<>());
```

Note that the diamond often works in method calls; however, for greater clarity, it is suggested that you use the diamond primarily to initialize a variable where it is declared. Note that the following example can successfully compile:

```
List<? extends String> list2 = new ArrayList<>();
list.addAll(list2);
```

Type Inference and Generic Constructors of Generic and Nongeneric Classes

Note that constructors can be generic (i.e., declare their own formal type parameters) in both generic and nongeneric classes. Consider the following example:

```
class MyClass<X> {
  <T> MyClass(T t) {
    // . . .
  }
}
```

Now consider the following instantiation of the class `MyClass`:

```
new MyClass<Integer>("")
```

This statement creates an instance of the parameterized type `MyClass<Integer>`; the statement explicitly specifies the type `Integer` for the formal type parameter, X, of the generic class `MyClass<X>`. Note that the constructor for this generic class contains a formal type parameter, T. The compiler infers the type String for the formal type parameter, T, of the constructor of this generic class (because the actual parameter of this constructor is a String object).

Compilers from releases prior to Java SE 7 are able to infer the actual type parameters of generic constructors, similar to generic methods. However, compilers in Java SE 7 and later can infer the actual type parameters of the generic class being instantiated if you use the diamond (<>). Consider the following example:

```
MyClass<Integer> myObject = new MyClass<>("");
```

In this example, the compiler infers the type Integer for the formal type parameter, X, of the generic class MyClass<X>. It infers the type String for the formal type parameter, T, of the constructor of this generic class.

> **Note**
> It is important to note that the inference algorithm uses only invocation arguments and, possibly, an obvious expected return type to infer types. The inference algorithm does not use results from later in the program.

Wildcards

In generic code, the question mark (?), called the *wildcard*, represents an unknown type. The wildcard can be used in a variety of situations: as the type of a parameter, field, or local variable, or sometimes as a return type (though it is better programming practice to be more specific). The wildcard is never used as a type argument for a generic method invocation, a generic class instance creation, or a supertype.

The following sections discuss wildcards in more detail, including upper-bounded wildcards, lower-bounded wildcards, and wildcard capture.

Upper-Bounded Wildcards

You can use an upper-bounded wildcard to relax the restrictions on a variable. For example, say you want to write a method that works on List<Integer>, List<Double>, *and* List<Number>; you can achieve this by using an upper-bounded wildcard.

To declare an upper-bounded wildcard, use the wildcard character (?), followed by the extends keyword, followed by its *upper bound*. Note that, in this context, extends is used in a general sense to mean either *extends* (as in classes) or *implements* (as in interfaces).

To write the method that works on lists of `Number` and the subtypes of `Number`, such as `Integer`, `Double`, and `Float`, you would specify `List<? extends Number>`. The term `List<Number>` is more restrictive than `List<? extends Number>` because the former matches a list of type `Number` only, whereas the latter matches a list of type `Number` or any of its subclasses.

Consider the following `process` method:

```
public static void process(List<? extends Foo> list) { /* . . . */ }
```

The upper-bounded wildcard, `<? extends Foo>`, where `Foo` is any type, matches `Foo` and any subtype of `Foo`. The `process` method can access the list elements as type `Foo`:

```
public static void process(List<? extends Foo> list) {
    for (Foo elem : list) {
        // . . .
    }
}
```

In the `foreach` clause, the `elem` variable iterates over each element in the list. Any method defined in the `Foo` class can now be used on `elem`.

The `sumOfList` method returns the sum of the numbers in a list:

```
public static double sumOfList(List<? extends Number> list) {
    double s = 0.0;
    for (Number n : list)
        s += n.doubleValue();
    return s;
}
```

The following code, using a list of `Integer` objects, prints `sum = 6.0`:

```
List<Integer> li = Arrays.asList(1, 2, 3);
System.out.println("sum = " + sumOfList(li));
```

A list of `Double` values can use the same `sumOfList` method. The following code prints `sum = 7.0`:

```
List<Double> ld = Arrays.asList(1.2, 2.3, 3.5);
System.out.println("sum = " + sumOfList(ld));
```

Unbounded Wildcards

The unbounded wildcard type is specified using the wildcard character (`?`)—for example, `List<?>`. This is called a *list of unknown type*. There are two scenarios where an unbounded wildcard is a useful approach:

- It is useful if you are writing a method that can be implemented using functionality provided in the `Object` class.
- It is useful when the code is using methods in the generic class that don't depend on the type parameter (e.g., `List.size` or `List.clear`). In fact, `Class<?>` is often used because most of the methods in `Class<T>` do not depend on T.

Consider the following method, `printList`:

```
public static void printList(List<Object> list) {
    for (Object elem : list)
        System.out.println(elem + " ");
    System.out.println();
}
```

The goal of `printList` is to print a list of any type, but it fails to achieve that goal: It prints only a list of `Object` instances. It cannot print `List<Integer>`, `List<String>`, `List<Double>`, and so on. This is because they are not subtypes of `List<Object>`. To write a generic `printList` method, use `List<?>`:

```
public static void printList(List<?> list) {
    for (Object elem: list)
        System.out.print(elem + " ");
    System.out.println();
}
```

For any concrete type A, `List` is a subtype of `List<?>`. Thus you can use `printList` to print a list of any type:

```
List<Integer> li = Arrays.asList(1, 2, 3);
List<String> ls = Arrays.asList("one", "two", "three");
printList(li);
printList(ls);
```

It's important to note that `List<Object>` and `List<?>` are not the same. You can insert an `Object`, or any subtype of `Object`, into a `List<Object>`. But you can only insert `null` into a `List<?>`. The "Guidelines for Wildcard Use" section has more information on how to determine what kind of wildcard, if any, should be used in a given situation.

Note

The `Arrays.asList`[1] method is used in examples throughout this chapter. This static factory method converts the specified array and returns a fixed-size list.

---

1. 7/docs/api/java/util/Arrays.html#asList(T...)

Lower-Bounded Wildcards

The "Upper-Bounded Wildcards" section shows that an upper-bounded wildcard restricts the unknown type to be a specific type or a subtype of that type and is represented using the extends keyword. In a similar way, a lower-bounded wildcard restricts the unknown type to be a specific type or a supertype of that type. A lower-bounded wildcard is expressed using the wildcard character (?), followed by the super keyword, followed by its *lower bound*: <? super A>.

> **Note**
>
> You can specify either an upper bound or a lower bound for a wildcard; you cannot specify both.

Say you want to write a method that puts Integer objects into a list. To maximize flexibility, you would like the method to work on List<Integer>, List<Number>, and List<Object>—anything that can hold Integer values.

To write the method that works on lists of Integer and the supertypes of Integer, such as Integer, Number, and Object, you would specify List<? super Integer>. The term List<Integer> is more restrictive than List<? super Integer> because the former matches a list of type Integer only, whereas the latter matches a list of any type that is a supertype of Integer.

The following code adds the numbers 1 through 10 to the end of a list:

```
public static void addNumbers(List<? super Integer> list) {
    for (int i = 1; i <= 10; i++) {
        list.add(i);
    }
}
```

The "Guidelines for Wildcard Use" section in this chapter provides guidance on when to use upper-bounded wildcards and when to use lower-bounded wildcards.

Wildcards and Subtyping

As described previously in "Generics, Inheritance, and Subtypes," generic classes or interfaces are not related merely because there is a relationship between their types. However, you can use wildcards to create a relationship between generic classes or interfaces.

Consider the following two regular (nongeneric) classes:

```
class A { /* . . . */ }
```

```
class B extends A { /* . . . */ }
```

For these classes, it would be reasonable to write the following code:

```
B b = new B();
A a = b;
```

This example shows that inheritance of regular classes follows the rule of subtyping: class B is a subtype of class A if B extends A. This rule does not apply to generic types:

```
List<B> lb = new ArrayList<>();
List la = lb;    // compile-time error
```

Given that Integer is a subtype of Number, what is the relationship between List<Integer> and List<Number>? Although Integer is a subtype of Number, List<Integer> is not a subtype of List<Number> and, in fact, these two types are not related. The common parent of List<Number> and List<Integer> is List<?> (Figure 6.4).

In order to create a relationship between these classes so that the code can access Number's methods through List<Integer>'s elements, use an upper-bounded wildcard:

```
List<? extends Integer> intList = new ArrayList<>();
// OK. List<? extends Integer> is a subtype of List<? extends Number>
List<? extends Number>  numList = intList;
```

Because Integer is a subtype of Number, and numList is a list of Number objects, a relationship now exists between intList (a list of Integer objects) and numList. Figure 6.5 shows the relationships between several List classes declared with both upper- and lower-bounded wildcards.

The "Guidelines for Wildcard Use" section later on in this chapter has more information about the ramifications of using upper- and lower-bounded wildcards.

Figure 6.4 The Common Parent Is List<?>

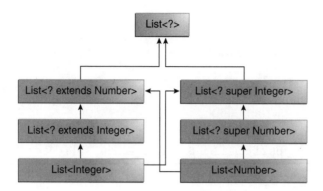

Figure 6.5 A Hierarchy of Several Generic List Class Declarations

Wildcard Capture and Helper Methods

In some cases, the compiler infers the type of a wildcard. For example, a list may be defined as `List<?>`, but when evaluating an expression, the compiler infers a particular type from the code. This scenario is known as *wildcard capture*. For the most part, you don't need to worry about wildcard capture, except when you see an error message that contains the phrase `capture of`.

The `WildcardError` example produces a capture error when compiled:

```
import java.util.List;

public class WildcardError {

    void foo(List<?> i) {
        i.set(0, i.get(0));
    }
}
```

In this example, the compiler processes the `i` input parameter as being of type `Object`. When the `foo` method invokes `List.set(int, E)`[2], the compiler is not able to confirm the type of object that is being inserted into the list and an error is produced. When this type of error occurs, it typically means that the compiler believes that you are assigning the wrong type to a variable. Generics were added to the Java language for this reason—to enforce type safety at compile time.

The `WildcardError` example generates the following error when compiled by Oracle's JDK 7 `javac` implementation:

```
WildcardError.java:6: error: method set in interface List<E> cannot
    be applied to given types;
```

---

2. `7/docs/api/java/util/List.html#set(int,E)`

```
     i.set(0, i.get(0));
       ^
  required: int,CAP#1
  found: int,Object
  reason: actual argument Object cannot be converted to CAP#1 by method
     invocation conversion
  where E is a type-variable:
     E extends Object declared in interface List
  where CAP#1 is a fresh type-variable:
     CAP#1 extends Object from capture of ?
1 error
```

In this example, the code is attempting to perform a safe operation, so how can you work around the compiler error? You can fix it by writing a *private helper method*, which captures the wildcard. In this case, you can work around the problem by creating the private helper method, `fooHelper`, as shown in `WildcardFixed`:

```java
public class WildcardFixed {

    void foo(List<?> i) {
        fooHelper(i);
    }

    // Helper method created so that the wildcard can be captured
    // through type inference.
    private <T> void fooHelper(List<T> l) {
        l.set(0, l.get(0));
    }
}
```

Thanks to the helper method, the compiler uses inference to determine that `T` is `CAP#1`, the capture variable, in the invocation. The example now compiles successfully.

By convention, helper methods are generally named *originalMethodName-Helper*. Now consider a more complex example, `WildcardErrorBad`:

```java
import java.util.List;

public class WildcardErrorBad {

    void swapFirst(List<? extends Number> l1, List<? extends Number> l2) {
        Number temp = l1.get(0);
        l1.set(0, l2.get(0)); // expected a CAP#1 extends Number,
                              // got a CAP#2 extends Number;
                              // same bound, but different types
        l2.set(0, temp);      // expected a CAP#1 extends Number,
                              // got a Number
    }
}
```

In this example, the code is attempting an unsafe operation. For example, consider the following invocation of the swapFirst method:

```
List<Integer> li = Arrays.asList(1, 2, 3);
List<Double>  ld = Arrays.asList(10.10, 20.20, 30.30);
swapFirst(li, ld);
```

While List<Integer> and List<Double> both fulfill the criteria of List<? extends Number>, it is clearly incorrect to take an item from a list of Integer values and attempt to place it into a list of Double values.

Compiling the code with Oracle's JDK javac compiler produces the following error:

```
WildcardErrorBad.java:7: error: method set in interface List<E> cannot be
    applied to given types;
        l1.set(0, l2.get(0)); // expected a CAP#1 extends Number,
          ^
    required: int,CAP#1
    found: int,Number
    reason: actual argument Number cannot be converted to CAP#1 by method
        invocation conversion
    where E is a type-variable:
      E extends Object declared in interface List
    where CAP#1 is a fresh type-variable:
      CAP#1 extends Number from capture of ? extends Number
WildcardErrorBad.java:10: error: method set in interface List<E> cannot
    be applied to given types;
        l2.set(0, temp);      // expected a CAP#1 extends Number,
          ^
    required: int,CAP#1
    found: int,Number
    reason: actual argument Number cannot be converted to CAP#1 by method
        invocation conversion
    where E is a type-variable:
      E extends Object declared in interface List
    where CAP#1 is a fresh type-variable:
      CAP#1 extends Number from capture of ? extends Number
WildcardErrorBad.java:15: error: method set in interface List<E> cannot
    be applied to given types;
        i.set(0, i.get(0));
         ^
    required: int,CAP#1
    found: int,Object
    reason: actual argument Object cannot be converted to CAP#1 by method
        invocation conversion
    where E is a type-variable:
      E extends Object declared in interface List
    where CAP#1 is a fresh type-variable:
      CAP#1 extends Object from capture of ?
3 errors
```

There is no helper method to work around the problem because the code is fundamentally wrong.

Guidelines for Wildcard Use

One of the more confusing aspects when learning to program with generics is determining when to use an upper-bounded wildcard and when to use a lower-bounded wildcard. This section provides some guidelines to follow when designing your code.

For purposes of this discussion, it is helpful to think of variables as serving one of two functions:

- An *in* variable serves up data to the code. Imagine a copy method with two arguments: copy(src, dest). The src argument provides the data to be copied, so it is the *in* parameter.
- An *out* variable holds data for use elsewhere. In the copy example, copy(src, dest), the dest argument accepts data, so it is the *out* parameter.

Of course, some variables are used for both in and out purposes, as discussed later. You can use the in and out principles when deciding whether to use a wildcard and what type of wildcard is appropriate. The following list provides the guidelines that you should follow:

- An invariable is defined with an upper-bounded wildcard, using the extends keyword.
- An out variable is defined with a lower-bounded wildcard, using the super keyword.
- In the case where the in variable can be accessed using methods defined in the Object class, use an unbounded wildcard.
- In the case where the code needs to access the variable as both an in and an out variable, do not use a wildcard.

These guidelines do not apply to a method's return type. Using a wildcard as a return type should be avoided because it forces programmers using the code to deal with wildcards.

A list defined by List<? extends . . . > can be informally thought of as read only, but that is not a strict guarantee. Suppose you have the following two classes:

```
class NaturalNumber {

    private int i;

    public NaturalNumber(int i) { this.i = i; }
    // . . .
}

class EvenNumber extends NaturalNumber {
```

```
      public EvenNumber(int i) { super(i); }
      // . . .
 }
```

Consider the following code:

```
List<EvenNumber> le = new ArrayList<>();
List<? extends NaturalNumber> ln = le;
ln.add(new NaturalNumber(35));  // compile-time error
```

Because `List<EvenNumber>` is a subtype of `List<? extends NaturalNumber>`, you can assign `le` to `ln`. But you cannot use `ln` to add a natural number to a list of even numbers. The following operations on the list are possible:

- You can add `null`.
- You can invoke `clear`.
- You can get the iterator and invoke `remove`.
- You can capture the wildcard and write elements that you've read from the list.

You can see that the list defined by `List<? extends NaturalNumber>` is not read only in the strictest sense of the word, but you might think of it that way because you cannot store a new element or change an existing element in the list.

Type Erasure

Generics were introduced to the Java language to provide tighter type checks at compile time and to support generic programming. To implement generics, the Java compiler applies type erasure to achieve the following:

- Replace all type parameters in generic types with their bounds or `Object` if the type parameters are unbounded. The produced bytecode, therefore, contains only ordinary classes, interfaces, and methods.
- Insert type casts if necessary to preserve type safety.
- Generate bridge methods to preserve polymorphism in extended generic types.

Type erasure ensures that no new classes are created for parameterized types; consequently, generics incur no runtime overhead.

Erasure of Generic Types

During the type erasure process, the Java compiler erases all type parameters and replaces each with its first bound if the type parameter is bounded or `Object` if the type parameter is unbounded.

Consider the following generic class that represents a node in a singly linked list:

```
public class Node<T> {

    private T data;
    private Node<T> next;

    public Node(T data, Node<T> next) }
        this.data = data;
        this.next = next;
    }

    public T getData() { return data; }
    // . . .
}
```

Because the type parameter `T` is unbounded, the Java compiler replaces it with `Object`:

```
public class Node {

    private Object data;
    private Node next;

    public Node(Object data, Node next) {
        this.data = data;
        this.next = next;
    }

    public Object getData() { return data; }
    // . . .
}
```

In the following example, the generic `Node` class uses a bounded type parameter:

```
public class Node<T extends Comparable<T>> {

    private T data;
    private Node<T> next;

    public Node(T data, Node<T> next) {
        this.data = data;
        this.next = next;
    }

    public T getData() { return data; }
    // . . .
}
```

The Java compiler replaces the bounded type parameter `T` with the first bound class, `Comparable`:

```
public class Node {
```

```
    private Comparable data;
    private Node next;

    public Node(Comparable data, Node next) {
        this.data = data;
        this.next = next;
    }

    public Comparable getData() { return data; }
    // . . .
}
```

Erasure of Generic Methods

The Java compiler also erases type parameters in generic method arguments. Consider the following generic method:

```
// Counts the number of occurrences of elem in anArray.

public static <T> int count(T[] anArray, T elem) {
    int cnt = 0;
    for (T e : anArray)
        if (e.equals(elem))
            ++cnt
        return cnt;
}
```

Because T is unbounded, the Java compiler replaces it with Object:

```
public static int count(Object[] anArray, Object elem) {
    int cnt = 0;
    for (Object e : anArray)
        if (e.equals(elem))
            ++cnt;
        return cnt;
}
```

Suppose the following classes are defined:

```
class Shape { /* . . . */ }
class Circle extends Shape { /* . . . */ }
class Rectangle extends Shape { /* . . . */ }
```

You can write a generic method to draw different shapes:

```
public static <T extends Shape> void draw(T shape) { /* . . . */ }
```

The Java compiler replaces T with Shape:

```
public static void draw(Shape shape) { /* . . . */ }
```

Effects of Type Erasure and Bridge Methods

Sometimes type erasure causes a situation that you may not have anticipated. The following example shows how this can occur. The example shows how a compiler sometimes creates a synthetic method, called a bridge method, as part of the type erasure process.

Consider the following two classes:

```java
public class Node<T> {

    private T data;

    public Node(T data) { this.data = data; }

    public void setData(T data) {
        System.out.println("Node.setData");
        this.data = data;
    }
}
public class MyNode extends Node<Integer> {
    public MyNode(Integer data) { super(data); }

    public void setData(Integer data) {
        System.out.println("MyNode.setData");
        super.setData(data);
    }
}
```

Now, consider the following code:

```java
MyNode mn = new MyNode(5);
Node n = mn;              // A raw type - compiler throws an unchecked warning
n.setData("Hello");      // Causes a ClassCastException to be thrown.
Integer x = mn.data;
```

After type erasure, this code changes as follows:

```java
MyNode mn = new MyNode(5);
Node n = (MyNode)mn;        // A raw type - compiler throws an unchecked warning
n.setData("Hello");
Integer x = (String)mn.data; // Causes a ClassCastException to be thrown.
```

Here is what happens as the code is executed:

- `n.setData("Hello");` causes the method `setData(Object)` to be executed on the object of class `MyNode`. (The `MyNode` class inherited `setData(Object)` from `Node`.)
- In the body of `setData(Object)`, the data field of the object referenced by n is assigned to a `String`.

- The data field of that same object, referenced via mn, can be accessed and is expected to be an integer (since mn is a `MyNode`, which is a `Node<Integer>`).
- Trying to assign a `String` to an `Integer` causes a `ClassCastException` from a cast inserted at the assignment by a Java compiler.

Bridge Methods

When compiling a class or interface that extends a parameterized class or implements a parameterized interface, the compiler may need to create a synthetic method, called a *bridge method*, as part of the type erasure process. You normally don't need to worry about bridge methods, but you might be puzzled if one appears in a stack trace.

After type erasure, the `Node` and `MyNode` classes are as follows:

```
public class Node {

    private Object data;

    public Node(Object data) { this.data = data; }

    public void setData(Object data) {
        System.out.println("Node.setData");
        this.data = data;
    }
}

public class MyNode extends Node {

    public MyNode(Integer data) { super(data); }

    public void setData(Integer data) {
        System.out.println(Integer data);
        super.setData(data);
    }
}
```

After type erasure, the method signatures do not match. The `Node` method becomes `setData(Object)` and the `MyNode` method becomes `setData(Integer)`. Therefore, the `MyNode setData` method does not override the `Node setData` method.

To solve this problem and preserve the polymorphism of generic types after type erasure, a Java compiler generates a bridge method to ensure that subtyping works as expected. For the `MyNode` class, the compiler generates the following bridge method for `setData`:

```
class MyNode extends Node {
    // Bridge method generated by the compiler

    public void setData(Object data) {
        setData((Integer) data);
    }
}
```

```
        public void setData(Integer data) {
            System.out.println("MyNode.setData");
            super.setData(data);
        }

        // . . .
    }
```

As you can see, the bridge method, which has the same method signature as the
Node class's setData method after type erasure, delegates to the original setData
method.

Nonreifiable Types

The "Type Erasure" section discusses the process where the compiler removes information related to type parameters and type arguments. Type erasure has consequences
related to variable arguments (also known as *varargs*), methods where a vararg formal parameters contains nonreifiable type. See Chapter 4, "Passing Information to a
Method or a Constructor," for more information about varargs methods.

Nonreifiable Types Defined

A *reifiable type* is a type whose type information is fully available at runtime. This
includes primitives, nongeneric types, raw types, and invocations of unbound wildcards.

Nonreifiable types are types whose information has been removed at compile time
by type erasure—invocations of generic types that are not defined as unbounded
wildcards. A nonreifiable type does not have all its information available at runtime.
Examples of nonreifiable types are List<String> and List<Number>; the Java
Virtual Machine (Java VM) cannot tell the difference between these types at runtime. As shown in the section "Restrictions on Generics" later in this chapter, there
are certain situations where nonreifiable types cannot be used (e.g., in an instanceof
expression or as an element in an array).

Heap Pollution

Heap pollution occurs when a variable of a parameterized type refers to an object
that is not of that parameterized type. This situation occurs if the program performed some operation that gives rise to an unchecked warning at compile time.
An *unchecked warning* is generated if, either at compile time (within the limits of
the compile-time type checking rules) or at runtime, the correctness of an operation
involving a parameterized type (e.g., a cast or method call) cannot be verified. For
example, heap pollution occurs when mixing raw types and parameterized types or
when performing unchecked casts.

In normal situations, when all code is compiled at the same time, the compiler
issues an unchecked warning to draw your attention to potential heap pollution. If

you compile sections of your code separately, it is difficult to detect the potential risk of heap pollution. If you ensure that your code compiles without warnings, then no heap pollution can occur.

Potential Vulnerabilities of Varargs Methods with Nonreifiable Formal Parameters

Generic methods that include vararg input parameters can cause heap pollution. Consider the following `ArrayBuilder` class:

```
public class ArrayBuilder {

  public static <T> void addToList (List<T> listArg, T . . . elements)
  {
    for (T x : elements) {
      listArg.add(x);
    }
  }

  public static void faultyMethod(List<String> . . . l) {
    Object[] objectArray = l;      // Valid
    objectArray[0] = Arrays.asList(42);
    String s = l[0].get(0);        // ClassCastException thrown here
  }

}
```

The following example, `HeapPollutionExample`, uses the `ArrayBuiler` class:

```
public class HeapPollutionExample {

  public static void main(String[] args) {

    List<String> stringListA = new ArrayList<String>();
    List<String> stringListB = new ArrayList<String>();

    ArrayBuilder.addToList(stringListA, "Seven", "Eight", "Nine");
    ArrayBuilder.addToList(stringListA, "Ten", "Eleven", "Twelve");
    List<List<String>> listOfStringLists =
      new ArrayList<List<String>>();
    ArrayBuilder.addToList(listOfStringLists,
      stringListA, stringListB);

    ArrayBuilder.faultyMethod(Arrays.asList("Hello!"),
            Arrays.asList("World!"));
  }
}
```

When this is compiled, the following warning is produced by the definition of the `ArrayBuilder.addToList` method:

```
warning: [varargs] Possible heap pollution from parameterized vararg type T
```

When the compiler encounters a varargs method, it translates the varargs formal parameter into an array. However, the Java programming language does not permit the creation of arrays of parameterized types. In the method `ArrayBuilder.addToList`, the compiler translates the varargs formal parameter `T . . . elements` to the formal parameter `T[] elements`, an array. However, because of type erasure, the compiler converts the varargs formal parameter to `Object[] elements`. Consequently, there is a possibility of heap pollution.

The following statement assigns the varargs formal parameter `l` to the `Object` array `objectArgs`:

```
Object[] objectArray = l;
```

This statement can potentially introduce heap pollution. A value that does match the parameterized type of the varargs formal parameter `l` can be assigned to the variable `objectArray` and thus can be assigned to `l`. However, the compiler does not generate an unchecked warning at this statement. The compiler has already generated a warning when it translated the varargs formal parameter `List<String> . . . l` to the formal parameter `List[] l`. This statement is valid; the variable `l` has the type `List[]`, which is a subtype of `Object[]`.

Consequently, the compiler does not issue a warning or error if you assign a `List` object of any type to any array component of the `objectArray` array as shown by this statement:

```
objectArray[0] = Arrays.asList(42);
```

The first array component of the `objectArray` array is assigned with a `List` object that contains one object of type `Integer`.

Suppose you invoke `ArrayBuilder.faultyArray` with the following statement:

```
ArrayBuilder.faultyMethod(Arrays.asList("Hello!"), Arrays.asList("World!"));
```

At runtime, the Java VM throws a `ClassCastException` at the following statement:

```
// ClassCastException thrown here
String s = l[0].get(0);
```

The object stored in the first array component of the variable `l` has the type `List<Integer>`, but this statement is expecting an object of type `List<String>`.

Prevent Warnings from Varargs Methods with Nonreifiable Formal Parameters

If you declare a varargs method that has parameters of a parameterized type and you ensure that the body of the method does not throw a `ClassCastException` or other similar exception due to improper handling of the varargs formal parameter, you can prevent the warning that the compiler generates for these kinds of varargs methods by adding the following annotation to static and nonconstructor method declarations:

```
@SafeVarargs
```

The `@SafeVarargs` annotation is a documented part of the method's contract; this annotation asserts that the implementation of the method will not improperly handle the varargs formal parameter.

It is also possible, though less desirable, to suppress such warnings by adding the following to the method declaration:

```
@SuppressWarnings({"unchecked", "varargs"})
```

However, this approach does not suppress warnings generated from the method's call site. If you are unfamiliar with the `@SuppressWarnings` syntax, see Chapter 4, "Annotations."

Restrictions on Generics

To use Java generics effectively, you must consider the following restrictions.

Cannot Instantiate Generic Types with Primitive Types

Consider the following parameterized type:

```
class Pair<K, V> {

    private K key;
    private V value;

    public Pair(K key, V value) {
        this.key = key;
        this.value = value;
    }

    // . . .
}
```

When creating a `Pair` object, you cannot substitute a primitive type for the type parameter K or V:

```
Pair<int, char> p = new Pair<>(8, 'a');  // compile-time error
```

You can only substitute nonprimitive types for the type parameters K and V:

```
Pair<Integer, Character> p = new Pair<>(8, 'a');
```

Note that the Java compiler autoboxes 8 to Integer.valueOf(8) and 'a' to
Character('a'):

```
Pair<Integer, Character> p = new Pair<>(Integer.valueOf(8), new Character('a'));
```

For more information on autoboxing, see Chapter 8.

Cannot Create Instances of Type Parameters

You cannot create an instance of a type parameter. For example, the following code
causes a compile-time error:

```
public static <E> void append(List<E> list) {
    E elem = new E();  // compile-time error
    list.add(elem);
}
```

As a workaround, you can create an object of a type parameter through reflection:

```
public static <E> void append(List<E> list, Class<E> cls) throws Exception
{
    E elem = cls.newInstance();   // OK
    list.add(elem);
}
```

You can invoke the append method as follows:

```
List<String> ls = new ArrayList<>();
append(ls, String.class);
```

Cannot Declare Static Fields Whose Types Are Type Parameters

A class's static field is a class-level variable shared by all nonstatic objects of the class.
Hence, static fields of type parameters are not allowed. Consider the following class:

```
public class MobileDevice<T> {
    private static T os;

    // . . .
}
```

If static fields of type parameters were allowed, then the following code would be confused:

```
MobileDevice<Smartphone> phone = new MobileDevice<>();
MobileDevice<Pager> pager = new MobileDevice<>();
MobileDevice<TabletPC> pc = new MobileDevice<>();
```

Because the static field os is shared by phone, pager, and pc, what is the actual type of os? It cannot be Smartphone, Pager, and TabletPC at the same time. You cannot, therefore, create static fields of type parameters.

Cannot Use Casts or instanceof with Parameterized Types

Because the Java compiler erases all type parameters in generic code, you cannot verify which parameterized type for a generic type is being used at runtime:

```
public static <E> void rtti(List<E> list) {
    if (list instanceof ArrayList<Integer>) {  // compile-time error
        // . . .
    }
}
```

The set of parameterized types passed to the rtti method is as follows:

```
S = { ArrayList<Integer>, ArrayList<String> LinkedList<Character>, . . . }
```

The runtime does not keep track of type parameters, so it cannot tell the difference between an ArrayList<Integer> and an ArrayList<String>. The most you can do is to use an unbounded wildcard to verify that the list is an ArrayList:

```
public static void rtti(List<?> list) {
    if (list instanceof ArrayList<?>) {  // OK; instanceof requires a
                                         // reifiable type
        // . . .
    }
}
```

Typically, you cannot cast to a parameterized type unless it is parameterized by unbounded wildcards. Here is an example:

```
List<Integer> li = new ArrayList<>();
List<Number> ln = (List<Number>) li;  // compile-time error
```

However, in some cases, the compiler knows that a type parameter is always valid and allows the cast. Here's an example:

```
List<String> l1 = . . . ;
ArrayList<String> l2 = (ArrayList<String>)l1;   // OK
```

Cannot Create Arrays of Parameterized Types

You cannot create arrays of parameterized types. For example, the following code does not compile:

```
List<Integer>[] arrayOfLists = new List<Integer>[2];   // compile-time error
```

The following code illustrates what happens when different types are inserted into an array:

```
Object[] strings = new String[2];
strings[0] = "hi";    // OK
strings[1] = 100;     // An ArrayStoreException is thrown.
```

If you try the same thing with a generic list, there would be a problem:

```
Object[] stringLists = new List<String>[];   // compiler error, but pretend
                                              // it's allowed
stringLists[0] = new ArrayList<String>();     // OK
stringLists[1] = new ArrayList<Integer>();    // An ArrayStoreException
                                              // should be thrown,
                                              // but the runtime can't detect it.
```

If arrays of parameterized lists were allowed, the previous code would fail to throw the desired `ArrayStoreException`.

Cannot Create, Catch, or Throw Objects of Parameterized Types

A generic class cannot extend the `Throwable` class directly or indirectly. For example, the following classes will not compile:

```
// Extends Throwable indirectly
class MathException<T> extends Exception { /* . . . */ }     // compile-time error

// Extends Throwable directly
class QueueFullException<T> extends Throwable { /* . . . */ } // compile-time error
```

A method cannot catch an instance of a type parameter:

```
public static <T extends Exception, J> void execute(List<J> jobs) {
    try {
        for (J job : jobs)
            // . . .
    } catch (T e) {   // compile-time error
        // . . .
```

```
        }
    }
```

You can, however, use a type parameter in a `throws` clause:

```
class Parser<T extends Exception> {
    public void parse(File file) throws T {      // OK
        // . . .
    }
}
```

Cannot Overload a Method Where the Formal Parameter Types of Each Overload Erase to the Same Raw Type

A class cannot have two overloaded methods that will have the same signature after type erasure:

```
public class Example {
    public void print(Set<String> strSet) { }
    public void print(Set<Integer> intSet) { }
}
```

The overloads would all share the same `classfile` representation, which will generate a compile-time error.

Questions and Exercises: Generics

Questions

1. Will the following class compile? If not, why?

```
public final class Algorithm {
    public static T max(T x, T y) {
        return x > y ? x : y;
    }
}
```

2. If the compiler erases all type parameters at compile time, why should you use generics?

3. What is the following class converted to after type erasure?

```
public class Pair<K, V> {

    public Pair(K key, V value) {
        this.key = key;
        this.value = value;
    }

    public K getKey(); { return key; }
```

```
        public V getValue(); { return value; }

        public void setKey(K key)     { this.key = key; }
        public void setValue(V value) { this.value = value; }

        private K key;
        private V value;
    }
```

4. What is the following method converted to after type erasure?

```
    public static <T extends Comparable<T>>
        int findFirstGreaterThan(T[] at, T elem) {
        // . . .
    }
```

5. Will the following method compile? If not, why?

```
    public static void print(List<? extends Number> list) {
        for (Number n : list)
            System.out.print(n + " ");
        System.out.println();
    }
```

6. Will the following class compile? If not, why?

```
    public class Singleton<T> {

        public static T getInstance() {
            if (instance == null)
                instance = new Singleton<T>();

            return instance;
        }

        private static T instance = null;
    }
```

7. Review the following classes:

```
    class Shape { /* . . . */ }
    class Circle extends Shape { /* . . . */ }
    class Rectangle extends Shape { /* . . . */ }

    class Node<T> { /* . . . */ }
```

Will the following code compile? If not, why?

```
    Node<Circle> nc = new Node<>();
    Node<Shape>  ns = nc;
```

8. Consider this class:

```
    class Node<T> implements Comparable<T> {
        public int compareTo(T obj) { /* . . . */ }
        // . . .
    }
```

Will the following code compile? If not, why?

```
Node<String> node = new Node<>();
Comparable<String> comp = node;
```

Exercises

1. Write a generic method to count the number of elements in a collection that have a specific property (e.g., odd integers, prime numbers, palindromes).
2. Write a generic method to exchange the positions of two different elements in an array.
3. Write a generic method to find the maximal element in the range `[begin, end]` of a list.

Answers

You can find answers to these questions and exercises at `http://docs.oracle.com/ javase/tutorial/java/generics/QandE/generics-answers.html`.

7

Packages

This chapter explains how to bundle classes and interfaces into packages, use classes that are in packages, and arrange your file system so that the compiler can find your source files.

To make types easier to find and use, avoid naming conflicts, and control access, programmers bundle groups of related types into packages.

> **Definition**
>
> A *package* is a grouping of related types providing access protection and namespace management. Note that *types* refers to classes, interfaces, enumerations, and annotation types. Enumerations and annotation types are special kinds of classes and interfaces, respectively, so *types* are often referred to as *classes* and *interfaces* in this chapter.

The types that are part of the Java platform are members of various packages that bundle classes by function: fundamental classes are in `java.lang`, classes for reading and writing (input and output) are in `java.io`, and so on. You can put your types in packages, too.

Suppose you write a group of classes that represent graphic objects, such as circles, rectangles, lines, and points. You also write an interface, `Draggable`, which classes implement if they can be dragged with the mouse.

```
//in the Draggable.java file
public interface Draggable {
    . . .
}

//in the Graphic.java file
public abstract class Graphic {
    . . .
}

//in the Circle.java file
public class Circle extends Graphic
    implements Draggable {
    . . .
}

//in the Rectangle.java file
public class Rectangle extends Graphic
    implements Draggable {
    . . .
}

//in the Point.java file
public class Point extends Graphic
    implements Draggable {
    . . .
}

//in the Line.java file
public class Line extends Graphic
    implements Draggable {
    . . .
}
```

You should bundle these classes and the interface in a package for several reasons, including the following:

- You and other programmers can easily determine that these types are related.
- You and other programmers know where to find types that can provide graphics-related functions.
- The names of your types won't conflict with the type names in other packages because the package creates a new namespace.
- You can allow types within the package to have unrestricted access to one another yet still restrict access for types outside the package.

Creating a Package

To create a package, you choose a name for the package. (Naming conventions are discussed in the next section, "Naming a Package.") You then put a `package` statement with that name at the top of *every source file* containing the types (classes, interfaces, enumerations, and annotation types) that you want to include in the package.

The package statement (e.g., `package graphics;`) must be the first line in the source file. There can only be one package statement in each source file, and it applies to all types in the file.

> **Note**
> If you put multiple types in a single source file, only one can be `public`, and it must have the same name as the source file. For example, you can define `public class Circle` in the file `Circle.java`, define `public interface Draggable` in the file `Draggable.java`, define `public enum Day` in the file `Day.java`, and so forth.
>
> You can include nonpublic types in the same file as a public type, but this is strongly discouraged, unless the nonpublic types are small and closely related to the public type. Either way, only the public type will be accessible from outside the package. All the top-level, nonpublic types will be *package private*.

If you put the graphics interface and classes listed in the preceding section in a package called `graphics`, you would need six source files:

```
//in the Draggable.java file
package graphics;
public interface Draggable {
    . . .
}

//in the Graphic.java file
package graphics;
public abstract class Graphic {
    . . .
}

//in the Circle.java file
package graphics;
public class Circle extends Graphic
    implements Draggable {
    . . .
}

//in the Rectangle.java file
package graphics;
public class Rectangle extends Graphic
    implements Draggable {
```

```
        . . .
    }

    //in the Point.java file
    package graphics;
    public class Point extends Graphic
        implements Draggable {
            . . .
    }

    //in the Line.java file
    package graphics;
    public class Line extends Graphic
        implements Draggable {
            . . .
    }
```

7

If you do not use a `package` statement, your type ends up in an unnamed package. Generally speaking, an unnamed package is only for small or temporary applications or when you are just beginning the development process. Otherwise, classes and interfaces belong in named packages.

Naming a Package

With programmers worldwide writing classes and interfaces using the Java programming language, it is likely that many programmers will use the same name for different types. In fact, the previous example does just that: it defines a `Rectangle` class when there is already a `Rectangle` class in the `java.awt` package. Still, the compiler allows both classes to have the same name if they are in different packages. The fully qualified name of each `Rectangle` class includes the package name. That is, the fully qualified name of the `Rectangle` class in the `graphics` package is `graphics.Rectangle`, and the fully qualified name of the `Rectangle` class in the `java.awt` package is `java.awt.Rectangle`.

This works well unless two independent programmers use the same name for their packages. What prevents this problem? Convention.

Naming Conventions

Package names are written in all lowercase to avoid conflict with the names of classes or interfaces. Companies use their reversed Internet domain name to begin their package names (e.g., `com.example.mypackage` for a package named `mypackage` created by a programmer at `example.com`).

Name collisions that occur within a single company need to be handled by convention within that company, perhaps by including the region or the project name

Table 7.1 Legalizing Package Names

Domain name	Package name prefix
hyphenated-name.example.org	org.example.hyphenated_name
example.int	int_.example
123name.example.com	com.example._123name

after the company name (e.g., com.example.region.mypackage). Packages in the Java language itself begin with java. or javax.

In some cases, the Internet domain name may not be a valid package name. This can occur if the domain name contains a hyphen or other special character, the package name begins with a digit or other character that is illegal to use at the beginning of a Java name, or the package name contains a reserved Java keyword, such as *int*. In this event, the suggested convention is to add an underscore (Table 7.1).

Using Package Members

The types that compose a package are known as the *package members*. To use a public package member from outside its package, you must do one of the following:

- Refer to the member by its fully qualified name.
- Import the package member.
- Import the member's entire package.

Each is appropriate for different situations, as explained in the sections that follow.

Referring to a Package Member by Its Qualified Name

So far, most of the examples in this book have referred to types by their simple names, such as Rectangle and StackOfInts. You can use a package member's simple name if the code you are writing is in the same package as that member or if that member has been imported.

However, if you are trying to use a member from a different package and that package has not been imported, you must use the member's fully qualified name, which includes the package name. Here is the fully qualified name for the Rectangle class declared in the graphics package in the previous example:

```
graphics.Rectangle
```

You could use this qualified name to create an instance of graphics.Rectangle:

```
graphics.Rectangle myRect = new graphics.Rectangle();
```

Qualified names are all right for infrequent use. When a name is used repetitively, however, typing the name repeatedly becomes tedious and the code becomes difficult to read. As an alternative, you can *import* the member or its package and then use its simple name.

Importing a Package Member

To import a specific member into the current file, put an `import` statement at the beginning of the file before any type definitions but after the `package` statement, if there is one. Here's how you would import the `Rectangle` class from the `graphics` package created in the previous section:

```
import graphics.Rectangle;
```

Now you can refer to the `Rectangle` class by its simple name:

```
Rectangle myRectangle = new Rectangle();
```

This approach works well if you use just a few members from the `graphics` package. But if you use many types from a package, you should import the entire package.

Importing an Entire Package

To import all the types contained in a particular package, use the `import` statement with the asterisk (*) wildcard character:

```
import graphics.*;
```

Now you can refer to any class or interface in the `graphics` package by its simple name:

```
Circle myCircle = new Circle();
Rectangle myRectangle = new Rectangle();
```

The asterisk in the `import` statement can be used only to specify all the classes within a package, as shown here. It cannot be used to match a subset of the classes in a package. For example, the following does not match all the classes in the `graphics` package that begin with A:

```
// does not work
import graphics.A*;
```

Instead, it generates a compiler error. With the `import` statement, you generally import only a single package member or an entire package. For convenience, the Java compiler automatically imports two entire packages for each source file: (1) the `java.lang` package and (2) the current package (the package for the current file).

> **Note**
>
> Another, less-common form of `import` allows you to import the public nested classes of an enclosing class. For example, if the `graphics.Rectangle` class contained useful nested classes, such as `Rectangle.DoubleWide` and `Rectangle.Square`, you could import `Rectangle` and its nested classes by using the following *two* statements:
>
> ```
> import graphics.Rectangle;
> import graphics.Rectangle.*;
> ```
>
> Be aware that the second import statement will *not* import `Rectangle`.
>
> Another less common form of `import`, the *static import statement*, will be discussed later on in this chapter.

Apparent Hierarchies of Packages

At first, packages appear to be hierarchical, but they are not. For example, the Java Application Programming Interface (API) includes a `java.awt` package, a `java.awt.color` package, a `java.awt.font` package, and many others that begin with `java.awt`. However, the `java.awt.color` package, the `java.awt.font` package, and other `java.awt.xxxx` packages are *not included* in the `java.awt` package. The prefix `java.awt` (the Java Abstract Window Toolkit) is used for a number of related packages to make the relationship evident, but it is not meant to show inclusion.

Importing `java.awt.*` imports all the types in the `java.awt` package, but it does not import `java.awt.color`, `java.awt.font` or any other `java.awt` packages. If you plan to use the classes and other types in `java.awt.color` as well as those in `java.awt`, you must import both packages with all their files:

```
import java.awt.*;
import java.awt.color.*;
```

Name Ambiguities

If a member in one package shares its name with a member in another package and both packages are imported, you must refer to each member by its qualified name. For example, the `graphics` package defined a class named `Rectangle`.

The `java.awt` package also contains a `Rectangle` class. If both `graphics` and `java.awt` have been imported, the following is ambiguous:

```
Rectangle rect;
```

In such a situation, you have to use the member's fully qualified name to indicate exactly which `Rectangle` class you want. Here is an example:

```
graphics.Rectangle rect;
```

The Static Import Statement

There are situations where you need frequent access to static final fields (constants) and static methods from one or two classes. Prefixing the name of these classes over and over can result in cluttered code. The *static import* statement gives you a way to import the constants and static methods that you want to use so that you do not need to prefix the name of their class.

The `java.lang.Math` class defines the `PI` constant and many static methods, including methods for calculating sines, cosines, tangents, square roots, maxima, minima, exponents, and many more. Here's an example:

```
public static final double PI = 3.141592653589793;
public static double cos(double a)
{
    . . .
}
```

Ordinarily, to use these objects from another class, you prefix the class name, as follows:

```
double r = Math.cos(Math.PI * theta);
```

You can use the static import statement to import the static members of `java.lang.Math` so that you don't need to prefix the class name, `Math`. The static members of `Math` can be imported individually:

```
import static java.lang.Math.PI;
```

They can also be imported as a group:

```
import static java.lang.Math.*;
```

Once they have been imported, the static members can be used without qualification. For example, here is a revised version of the previous code snippet:

```
double r = cos(PI * theta);
```

You can write your own classes that contain constants and static methods that you use frequently and then use the static import statement. Here's an example:

```
import static mypackage.MyConstants.*;
```

> **Note**
> Use static import very sparingly. Overusing static import can result in code that is difficult to read and maintain because readers of the code won't know which class defines a particular static object. Used properly, static import makes code more readable by removing class name repetition.

Managing Source and Class Files

Many implementations of the Java platform rely on hierarchical file systems to manage source and class files, although the Java Language Specification does not require this. The strategy is as follows.

Put the source code for a class, interface, enumeration, or annotation type in a text file whose name is the simple name of the type and whose extension is .java. Here's an example:

```
//in the Rectangle.java file
package graphics;
public class Rectangle {
    . . .
}
```

Then, put the source file in a directory whose name reflects the name of the package to which the type belongs:

```
. . . . . .\graphics\Rectangle.java
```

The qualified name of the package member (graphics.Rectangle) and the path name to the file (graphics\Rectangle.java) are parallel, assuming the Microsoft Windows file name separator backslash. (For Unix, use the forward slash.)

Recall that by convention a company uses its reversed Internet domain name for its package names. Thus a company whose Internet domain name is example.com would precede all its package names with com.example. Each component of the package name corresponds to a subdirectory. So if this company had a `com.exam-ple.graphics` package that contained a `Rectangle.java` source file, it would be contained in a series of subdirectories, like this:

```
 . . . . \com\example\graphics\Rectangle.java
```

When you compile a source file, the compiler creates a different output file for each type defined in it. The base name of the output file is the name of the type, and its extension is `.class`. Here is an example source file:

```
//in the Rectangle.java file
package com.example.graphics;
public class Rectangle {
        . . .
}

class Helper{
        . . .
}
```

The compiled files from this source will be located as follows:

```
<path to parent directory of output files>\com\example\graphics\Rectangle.class
<path to parent directory of output files>\com\example\graphics\Helper.class
```

Like the `.java` source files, the compiled `.class` files should be in a series of directories that reflect the package name. However, the path to the `.class` files does not have to be the same as the path to the `.java` source files. You can arrange your source and class directories separately:

```
<path_one>\sources\com\example\graphics\Rectangle.java
<path_two>\classes\com\example\graphics\Rectangle.class
```

By doing this, you can give the `classes` directory to other programmers without revealing your sources. You also need to manage source and class files in this manner so that the compiler and the Java Virtual Machine (Java VM) can find all the types your program uses.

The full path to the `classes` directory is called the *class path*: `<path_two>\classes`.

This is set with the `CLASSPATH` system variable. Both the compiler and the Java VM construct the path to your `.class` files by adding the package name to the class path. For example, say this is your class path:

```
<path_two>\classes
```

And this is the package name:

```
com.example.graphics
```

The compiler and Java VM look for `.class` files here:

```
<path_two>\classes\com\example\graphics
```

A class path may include several paths, separated by a semicolon (Windows) or colon (Unix). By default, the compiler and the Java VM search the current directory and the JAR file containing the Java platform classes so that these directories are automatically in your class path.

Setting the CLASSPATH System Variable

To display the current `CLASSPATH` variable, use these commands in Windows and Unix (Bourne shell):

```
In Windows:   C:\> set CLASSPATH
In Unix:      % echo $CLASSPATH
```

To delete the current contents of the `CLASSPATH` variable, use these commands:

```
In Windows:   C:\> set CLASSPATH=
In Unix:      % unset CLASSPATH; export CLASSPATH
```

To set the `CLASSPATH` variable, use these commands (for example):

```
In Windows:   C:\> set CLASSPATH=C:\users\george\java\classes
In Unix:      % CLASSPATH=/home/george/java/classes; export CLASSPATH
```

Summary of Packages

To create a package for a type, put a `package` statement as the first statement in the source file that contains the type (class, interface, enumeration, or annotation type).

To use a public type that's in a different package, you have three choices: (1) use the fully qualified name of the type, (2) import the type, or (3) import the entire package of which the type is a member.

The path names for a package's source and class files mirror the name of the package.

You might have to set your `CLASSPATH` so that the compiler and the Java VM can find the `.class` files for your types.

Table 7.2 Destination Packages

Package name	Class name
mygame.server	Server
mygame.shared	Utilities
mygame.client	Client

Questions and Exercises: Creating and Using Packages

Questions

Assume you have written some classes. Belatedly, you decide they should be split into three packages, as listed in Table 7.2. Furthermore, assume the classes are currently in the default package (i.e., they have no package statements).

1. Which line of code will you need to add to each source file to put each class in the right package?

2. To adhere to the directory structure, you will need to create some subdirectories in the development directory and put source files in the correct subdirectories. What subdirectories must you create? Which subdirectory does each source file go in?

3. Do you think you'll need to make any other changes to the source files to make them compile correctly? If so, what?

Exercises

Download the source files listed here:

- Client.java[1]
- Server.java[2]
- Utilities.java[3]

1. Implement the changes you proposed in questions 1 through 3 using the source files you just downloaded.

---

1. tutorial/java/package/QandE/question/Client.java
2. tutorial/java/package/QandE/question/Server.java
3. tutorial/java/package/QandE/question/Utilities.java

2. Compile the revised source files. *Hint:* If you're invoking the compiler from the command line (as opposed to using a builder), invoke the compiler from the directory that contains the `mygame` directory you just created.

Answers

You can find answers to these questions and exercises at `http://docs.oracle.com/javase/tutorial/java/package/QandE/packages-answers.html`.

7

8

Numbers and Strings

Chapter Contents

This chapter begins with a discussion of the Number class (in the java.lang package) and its subclasses. In particular, the first section talks about the situations where you would use instantiations of these classes rather than the primitive data types. Additionally, this section talks about other classes you might need to use while working with numbers, such as formatting or using mathematical functions to complement the operators built into the language. Finally, this section discusses autoboxing and unboxing, compiler features that can simplify your code.

The second section discusses characters, and the third section discusses strings. Strings are widely used in Java programming and are a sequence of characters. In the Java programming language, strings are objects. This section describes using the String class to create and manipulate strings. It also compares the String and StringBuilder classes. There are questions and exercises throughout the chapter to test your knowledge.

Numbers

This section begins with a discussion of the Number[1] class in the java.lang package, its subclasses, and the situations where you would use instantiations of these

---

1. 7/docs/api/java/lang/Number.html

classes rather than the primitive number types. This section also presents the PrintStream[2] and DecimalFormat[3] classes, which provide methods for writing formatted numerical output. Finally, the Math[4] class in java.lang is discussed. It contains mathematical functions to complement the operators built into the language. This class has methods for the trigonometric functions, exponential functions, and so forth.

The Numbers Classes

When working with numbers, most of the time you use the primitive types in your code. Here is an example:

```
int i = 500;
float gpa = 3.65f;
byte mask = 0xff;
```

There are, however, reasons to use objects in place of primitives, and the Java platform provides *wrapper* classes for each of the primitive data types. These classes "wrap" the primitive in an object. Often, the compiler does the wrapping—if you use a primitive where an object is expected, the compiler *boxes* the primitive in its wrapper class for you. Similarly, if you use a number object when a primitive is expected, the compiler *unboxes* the object for you. For more information, see the section "Autoboxing and Unboxing" later in this chapter.

> **Note**
> There are four other subclasses of Number that are not discussed here. BigDecimal and BigInteger are used for high-precision calculations. AtomicInteger and AtomicLong are used for multithreaded applications.

All the numeric wrapper classes are subclasses of the abstract class Number (Figure 8.1). There are three reasons that you might use a Number object rather than a primitive:

1. As an argument of a method that expects an object (often used when manipulating collections of numbers)

---

2. 7/docs/api/java/io/PrintStream.html

3. 7/docs/api/java/text/DecimalFormat.html

4. 7/docs/api/java/lang/Math.html

2. To use constants defined by the class, such as MIN_VALUE and MAX_VALUE, that provide the upper and lower bounds of the data type

3. To use class methods for converting values to and from other primitive types, for converting to and from strings, and for converting between number systems (decimal, octal, hexadecimal, binary)

Table 8.1 lists the instance methods that all the subclasses of the Number class implement.

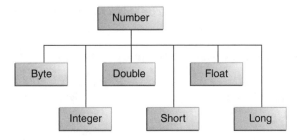

Figure 8.1 Subclasses of the Number Class

Table 8.1 Methods Implemented by All Subclasses of the Number Class

Method	Description
byte byteValue() short shortValue() int intValue() long longValue() float floatValue() double doubleValue()	These methods convert the value of the Number object to the primitive data type returned.
int compareTo(Byte anotherByte) int compareTo(Double anotherDouble) int compareTo(Float anotherFloat) int compareTo(Integer anotherInteger) int compareTo(Long anotherLong) int compareTo(Short anotherShort)	These methods compare the Number object to the argument.
boolean equals(Object obj)	This method determines whether the number object is equal to the argument. The methods return true if the argument is not null and is an object of the same type and with the same numeric value. There are some extra requirements for Double and Float objects that are described in the Java Application Programming Interface (API) documentation.

Each `Number` class contains other methods that are useful for converting numbers to and from strings and for converting between number systems. Table 8.2 lists these methods in the `Integer` class. Methods for the other `Number` subclasses are similar.

Formatting Numeric Print Output

Earlier you saw the use of the `print` and `println` methods for printing strings to standard output (`System.out`). Since all numbers can be converted to strings (as you will see later in this chapter), you can use these methods to print out an arbitrary mixture of strings and numbers. The Java programming language has other

Table 8.2 Conversion Methods in the Integer Class

Method	Description
`static Integer decode(String s)`	Decodes a string into an integer and can accept string representations of decimal, octal, or hexadecimal numbers as input
`static int parseInt(String s)`	Returns an integer (decimal only)
`static int parseInt(String s, int radix)`	Returns an integer, given a string representation of decimal, binary, octal, or hexadecimal (`radix` equals 10, 2, 8, or 16, respectively) numbers as input
`String toString()`	Returns a `String` object representing the value of this `Integer`
`static String toString(int i)`	Returns a `String` object representing the specified integer
`static Integer valueOf(int i)`	Returns an `Integer` object holding the value of the specified primitive
`static Integer valueOf(String s)`	Returns an `Integer` object holding the value of the specified string representation
`static Integer valueOf(String s, int radix)`	Returns an `Integer` object holding the integer value of the specified string representation, parsed with the value of radix (e.g., if s equals 333 and `radix` equals 8, the method returns the base-ten integer equivalent of the octal number 333)

methods, however, that allow you to exercise much more control over your print output when numbers are included.

The printf and format Methods

The `java.io` package includes a `PrintStream` class that has two formatting methods that you can use to replace `print` and `println`. These methods, `format` and `printf`, are equivalent to one another. The familiar `System.out` that you have been using happens to be a `PrintStream` object, so you can invoke `PrintStream` methods on `System.out`. Thus you can use `format` or `printf` anywhere in your code where you have previously been using `print` or `println`. Here's an example:

```
System.out.format(. . . . .);
```

The syntax for these two `java.io.PrintStream`[5] methods is the same:

```
public PrintStream format(String format, Object . . . args)
```

Here, `format` is a string that specifies the formatting to be used and `args` is a list of the variables to be printed using that formatting. A simple example would be the following:

```
System.out.format("The value of " + "the float variable is " +
    "%f, while the value of the " + "integer variable is %d, " +
    "and the string is %s", floatVar, intVar, stringVar);
```

The first parameter, `format`, is a format string specifying how the objects in the second parameter, `args`, are to be formatted. The format string contains plain text as well as *format specifiers*, which are special characters that format the arguments of `Object . . . args`. (The notation `Object . . . args` is called *varargs*, which means that the number of arguments may vary.)

Format specifiers begin with a percent sign and end with a *converter*. The converter is a character indicating the type of argument to be formatted. In between the percent sign and the converter, you can have optional flags and specifiers. There are many converters, flags, and specifiers, which are documented in `java.util.Formatter`.[6]

Here is a basic example:

```
int i = 461012;
System.out.format("The value of i is: %d%n", i);
```

---

5. 7/docs/api/java/io/PrintStream.html
6. 7/docs/api/java/util/Formatter.html

The `%d` specifies that the single variable is a decimal integer. The `%n` is a platform-independent new line character. The output is as follows:

```
The value of i is: 461012
```

The `printf` and `format` methods are overloaded. Each has a version with the following syntax:

```
public PrintStream format(Locale l, String format, Object . . . args)
```

To print numbers in the French system (where a comma is used in place of a decimal point), for example, you would use the following:

```
System.out.format(Locale.FRANCE,
    "The value of the float " + "variable is %f, while the " +
    "value of the integer variable " + "is %d, and the string is %s%n",
    floatVar, intVar, stringVar);
```

An Example

The following program, `TestFormat.java`, shows some of the formatting that you can accomplish using the `format` method. (Note that Table 8.3 lists some of the converters and flags that are used in this sample program.) The output is shown within double quotes in the embedded comment:

```
import java.util.Calendar;
import java.util.Locale;

public class TestFormat {

    public static void main(String[] args) {
        long n = 461012;
        System.out.format("%d%n", n);      //  -->  "461012"
        System.out.format("%08d%n", n);    //  -->  "00461012"
        System.out.format("%+8d%n", n);    //  -->  " +461012"
        System.out.format("%,8d%n", n);    //  -->  " 461,012"
        System.out.format("%+,8d%n%n", n); //  -->  "+461,012"

        double pi = Math.PI;

        System.out.format("%f%n", pi);      // -->  "3.141593"
        System.out.format("%.3f%n", pi);    // -->  "3.142"
        System.out.format("%10.3f%n", pi);  // -->  "     3.142"
        System.out.format("%-10.3f%n", pi); // -->  "3.142"
        System.out.format(Locale.FRANCE,
                    "%-10.4f%n%n", pi); // -->  "3,1416"

        Calendar c = Calendar.getInstance();
        System.out.format("%tB %te, %tY%n", c, c, c); // -->  "May 29, 2006"
```

```
        System.out.format("%tl:%tM %tp%n", c, c, c);  // --> "2:34 am"

        System.out.format("%tD%n", c);     // --> "05/29/06"
    }
}
```

Note

The discussion in this section covers just the basics of the `format` and `printf` methods. Further detail can be found in Chapter 10. Also, using `String.format` to create strings is covered in the "Strings" section.

Table 8.3 Converters and Flags Used in TestFormat.java

Converter	Flag	Explanation
d		A decimal integer
f		A float
n		A new line character appropriate to the platform running the application—always use `%n`, rather than `\n`
tB		A date and time conversion—locale-specific full name of month
td, te		A date and time conversion—two-digit day of month, with `td` having leading zeroes as needed (whereas `te` does not)
ty, tY		A date and time conversion—`ty` = two-digit year, `tY` = four-digit year
tl		A date and time conversion—hour in twelve-hour clock
tM		A date and time conversion—minutes in two digits, with leading zeroes as necessary
tp		A date and time conversion—locale-specific, am/pm (lowercase)
tm		A date and time conversion—months in two digits, with leading zeroes as necessary
tD		A date and time conversion—date as `%tm%td%ty`
	08	Eight characters in width, with leading zeroes as necessary
	+	Includes sign, whether positive or negative
	,	Includes locale-specific grouping characters
	-	Left justified
	.3	Three places after decimal point
	10.3	Ten characters in width, right justified, with three places after decimal point

The DecimalFormat Class

You can use the `java.text.DecimalFormat`[7] class to control the display of leading and trailing zeroes, prefixes and suffixes, grouping (thousands) separators, and the decimal separator. `DecimalFormat` offers a great deal of flexibility in the formatting of numbers, but it can make your code more complex.

The example that follows creates a `DecimalFormat` object, `myFormatter`, by passing a pattern string to the `DecimalFormat` constructor. The `format()` method, which `DecimalFormat` inherits from `NumberFormat`, is then invoked by `myFormatter`—it accepts a `double` value as an argument and returns the formatted number in a string. Here is a sample program that illustrates the use of `DecimalFormat`:

```
import java.text.*;

public class DecimalFormatDemo {

    static public void customFormat(String pattern, double value ) {
        DecimalFormat myFormatter = new DecimalFormat(pattern);
        String output = myFormatter.format(value);
        System.out.println(value + "  " + pattern + "  " + output);
    }

    static public void main(String[] args) {

        customFormat("###,###.###", 123456.789);
        customFormat("###.##", 123456.789);
        customFormat("000000.000", 123.78);
        customFormat("$###,###.###", 12345.67);
    }
}
```

The output is as follows:

```
123456.789   ###,###.###   123,456.789
123456.789   ###.##   123456.79
123.78   000000.000   000123.780
12345.67   $###,###.###   $12,345.67
```

Table 8.4 explains each line of output.

Beyond Basic Arithmetic

The Java programming language supports basic arithmetic with its arithmetic operators: +, −, *, /, and %. The Math[8] class in the `java.lang` package provides methods

---

7. 7/docs/api/java/text/DecimalFormat.html

8. 7/docs/api/java/lang/Math.html

Table 8.4 DecimalFormat.java Output

Value	Pattern	Output	Explanation
123456.789	###,###.###	123,456.789	The pound sign (#) denotes a digit, the comma is a placeholder for the grouping separator, and the period is a placeholder for the decimal separator.
123456.789	###.##	123456.79	The value has three digits to the right of the decimal point, but the pattern has only two. The format method handles this by rounding up.
123.78	000000.000	000123.780	The pattern specifies leading and trailing zeroes because the 0 character is used instead of the pound sign (#).
12345.67	$###,###.###	$12,345.67	The first character in the pattern is the dollar sign ($). Note that it immediately precedes the leftmost digit in the formatted output.

8

and constants for doing more advanced mathematical computation. The methods in the Math class are all static, so you call them directly from the class, as follows:

```
Math.cos(angle);
```

> **Note**
> Using the static import language feature, you don't have to write Math in front of every math function:
>
> ```
> import static java.lang.Math.*;
> ```
>
> This allows you to invoke the Math class methods by their simple names:
>
> ```
> cos(angle);
> ```

Constants and Basic Methods

The Math class includes two constants:

- Math.E, which is the base of natural logarithms
- Math.PI, which is the ratio of the circumference of a circle to its diameter

The Math class also includes more than 40 static methods. Table 8.5 lists a number of the basic methods. The following program, BasicMathDemo, illustrates how to use some of these methods:

Table 8.5 Basic Math Methods

Method	Description

`double abs(double d)`
`float abs(float f)`
`int abs(int i)`
`long abs(long lng)`
	Returns the absolute value of the argument

`double ceil(double d)`	Returns the smallest integer that is greater than or equal to the argument as a `double`
`double floor(double d)`	Returns the largest integer that is less than or equal to the argument as a `double`
`double rint(double d)`	Returns the integer that is closest in value to the argument as a `double`
`long round(double d)` `int round(float f)`	Returns the closest `long` or `int`, as indicated by the method's return type, to the argument

`double min(double arg1, double arg2)`
`float min(float arg1, float arg2)`
`int min(int arg1, int arg2)`
`long min(long arg1, long arg2)`
	Returns the smaller of the two arguments

`double max(double arg1, double arg2)`
`float max(float arg1, float arg2)`
`int max(int arg1, int arg2)`
`long max(long arg1, long arg2)`
	Returns the larger of the two arguments

```
public class BasicMathDemo {
    public static void main(String[] args) {
        double a = -191.635;
        double b = 43.74;
        int c = 16, d = 45;

        System.out.printf("The absolute value " + "of %.3f is %.3f%n",
                a, Math.abs(a));

        System.out.printf("The ceiling of " + "%.2f is %.0f%n",
                b, Math.ceil(b));

        System.out.printf("The floor of " + "%.2f is %.0f%n",
                b, Math.floor(b));

        System.out.printf("The rint of %.2f " + "is %.0f%n",
                b, Math.rint(b));
```

```
        System.out.printf("The max of %d and " + "%d is %d%n",
                          c, d, Math.max(c, d));

        System.out.printf("The min of of %d " + "and %d is %d%n",
                          c, d, Math.min(c, d));
    }
}
```

Here's the output from this program:

```
The absolute value of -191.635 is 191.635
The ceiling of 43.74 is 44
The floor of 43.74 is 43
The rint of 43.74 is 44
The max of 16 and 45 is 45
The min of 16 and 45 is 16
```

Exponential and Logarithmic Methods

8

Table 8.6 lists exponential and logarithmic methods of the Math class. The following program, ExponentialDemo, displays the value of e, then calls each of the methods listed in Table 8.6 on arbitrarily chosen numbers:

```
public class ExponentialDemo {
    public static void main(String[] args) {
        double x = 11.635;
        double y = 2.76;

        System.out.printf("The value of " + "e is %.4f%n", Math.E);

        System.out.printf("exp(%.3f) " + "is %.3f%n", x, Math.exp(x));

        System.out.printf("log(%.3f) is " + "%.3f%n", x, Math.log(x));

        System.out.printf("pow(%.3f, %.3f) " + "is %.3f%n", x, y, Math.pow(x, y));

        System.out.printf("sqrt(%.3f) is " + "%.3f%n", x, Math.sqrt(x));
    }
}
```

Here's the output you'll see when you run ExponentialDemo:

```
The value of e is 2.7183
exp(11.635) is 112983.831
log(11.635) is 2.454
pow(11.635, 2.760) is 874.008
sqrt(11.635) is 3.411
```

Trigonometric Methods

The Math class also provides a collection of trigonometric functions, which are summarized in Table 8.7. The value passed into each of these methods is an angle expressed in radians. You can use the toRadians method to convert from degrees to radians.

Table 8.6 Exponential and Logarithmic Methods

Method	Description
double exp(double d)	Returns the base of the natural logarithms, e, to the power of the argument
double log(double d)	Returns the natural logarithm of the argument
double pow(double base, double exponent)	Returns the value of the first argument raised to the power of the second argument
double sqrt(double d)	Returns the square root of the argument

Table 8.7 Trigonometric Methods

Method	Description
double sin(double d)	Returns the sine of the specified double value
double cos(double d)	Returns the cosine of the specified double value
double tan(double d)	Returns the tangent of the specified double value
double asin(double d)	Returns the arcsine of the specified double value
double acos(double d)	Returns the arccosine of the specified double value
double atan(double d)	Returns the arctangent of the specified double value
double atan2(double y, double x)	Converts rectangular coordinates (x, y) to polar coordinate (r, theta) and returns theta
double toDegrees(double d) double toRadians(double d)	Converts the argument to degrees or radians

Here's a program, `TrigonometricDemo`, that uses each of the methods listed in Table 8.7 to compute various trigonometric values for a 45-degree angle:

```
public class TrigonometricDemo {
    public static void main(String[] args) {
        double degrees = 45.0;
        double radians = Math.toRadians(degrees);

        System.out.format("The value of pi " + "is %.4f%n", Math.PI);

        System.out.format("The sine of %.1f " + "degrees is %.4f%n", degrees,
                        Math.sin(radians));

        System.out.format("The cosine of %.1f " + "degrees is %.4f%n", degrees,
                        Math.cos(radians));

        System.out.format("The tangent of %.1f " + "degrees is %.4f%n", degrees,
                        Math.tan(radians));

        System.out.format("The arcsine of %.4f " + "is %.4f degrees %n",
                        Math.sin(radians),
                        Math.toDegrees(Math.asin(Math.sin(radians))));

        System.out.format("The arccosine of %.4f " + "is %.4f degrees %n",
                        Math.cos(radians),
                        Math.toDegrees(Math.acos(Math.cos(radians))));

        System.out.format("The arctangent of %.4f " + "is %.4f degrees %n",
                        Math.tan(radians),
                        Math.toDegrees(Math.atan(Math.tan(radians))));
    }
}
```

The output of this program is as follows:

```
The value of pi is 3.1416
The sine of 45.0 degrees is 0.7071
The cosine of 45.0 degrees is 0.7071
The tangent of 45.0 degrees is 1.0000
The arcsine of 0.7071 is 45.0000 degrees
The arccosine of 0.7071 is 45.0000 degrees
The arctangent of 1.0000 is 45.0000 degrees
```

Random Numbers

The `random()` method returns a pseudo-randomly-selected number between 0.0 and 1.0. The range includes 0.0 but not 1.0. In other words, `0.0 <= Math.random() < 1.0`. To get a number in a different range, you can perform arithmetic on the value returned by the random method. For example, to generate an integer between 0 and 9, you would write the following:

```
int number = (int)(Math.random() * 10);
```

By multiplying the value by 10, the range of possible values becomes `0.0 <= number < 10.0`.

Using `Math.random` works well when you need to generate a single random number. If you need to generate a series of random numbers, you should create an instance of `java.util.Random` and invoke methods on that object to generate numbers.

Autoboxing and Unboxing

Autoboxing is the automatic conversion that the Java compiler makes between the primitive types and their corresponding object wrapper classes. For example, converting an `int` to an `Integer`, a `double` to a `Double`, and so on. If the conversion goes the other way, this is called *unboxing*.

Here is the simplest example of autoboxing:

```
Character ch = 'a';
```

The rest of the examples in this section use generics. If you are not yet familiar with the syntax of generics, see Chapter 6. Consider the following code:

```
List<Integer> li = new ArrayList<>();
for (int i = 1; i < 50; i += 2)
    li.add(i);
```

Although you add the `int` values as primitive types, rather than `Integer` objects, to `li`, the code compiles. Because `li` is a list of `Integer` objects, not a list of `int` values, you may wonder why the Java compiler does not issue a compile-time error. The compiler does not generate an error because it creates an `Integer` object from `i` and adds the object to `li`. Thus the compiler converts the previous code to the following at runtime:

```
List<Integer> li = new ArrayList<>();
for (int i = 1; i < 50; i += 2)
    li.add(Integer.valueOf(i));
```

Converting a primitive value (an `int`, for example) into an object of the corresponding wrapper class (`Integer`) is called *autoboxing*. The Java compiler applies autoboxing when a primitive value is (1) passed as a parameter to a method that expects an object of the corresponding wrapper class or (2) assigned to a variable of the corresponding wrapper class.

Consider the following method:

```java
public static int sumEven(List<Integer> li) {
    int sum = 0;
    for (Integer i: li)
        if (i % 2 == 0)
            sum += i;
        return sum;
}
```

Because the remainder (%) and unary plus (+=) operators do not apply to `Integer` objects, you may wonder why the Java compiler compiles the method without issuing any errors. The compiler does not generate an error because it invokes the `intValue` method to convert an `Integer` to an `int` at runtime:

```java
public static int sumEven(List<Integer> li) {
    int sum = 0;
    for (Integer i : li)
        if (i.intValue() % 2 == 0)
            sum += i.intValue();
        return sum;
}
```

Converting an object of a wrapper type (`Integer`) to its corresponding primitive (`int`) value is called *unboxing*. The Java compiler applies unboxing when an object of a wrapper class is (1) passed as a parameter to a method that expects a value of the corresponding primitive type or (2) assigned to a variable of the corresponding primitive type.

The following example shows how this works:

```java
import java.util.ArrayList;
import java.util.List;

public class Unboxing {

    public static void main(String[] args) {
        Integer i = new Integer(-8);

        // 1. Unboxing through method invocation
        int absVal = absoluteValue(i);
        System.out.println("absolute value of " + i + " = " + absVal);

        List<Double> ld = new ArrayList<>();
        ld.add(3.1416);    // Π is autoboxed through method invocation.
```

```
        // 2. Unboxing through assignment
        double phi = ld.get(0);
        System.out.println("phi = " + phi);
    }

    public static int absoluteValue(int i) {
        return (i < 0) ? -i : i;
    }
}
```

The program prints the following:

```
absolute value of -8 = 8
phi = 3.1416
```

Autoboxing and unboxing allow developers write cleaner code, making it easier to read. Table 8.8 lists the primitive types and their corresponding wrapper classes, which are used by the Java compiler for autoboxing and unboxing.

Summary of Numbers

You use one of the wrapper classes—Byte, Double, Float, Integer, Long, or Short—to wrap a number of primitive types in an object. The Java compiler automatically wraps (boxes) primitives for you when necessary and unboxes them again when necessary.

The Number classes include constants and useful class methods. The MIN_VALUE and MAX_VALUE constants contain the smallest and largest values that can be contained by an object of that type. The byteValue, shortValue, and similar methods convert one numeric type to another. The valueOf method converts a string to a number, and the toString method converts a number to a string.

To format a string containing numbers for output, you can use the printf() or format() methods in the PrintStream class. Alternatively, you can use the NumberFormat class to customize numerical formats using patterns.

Table 8.8 Primitive Type and Equivalent Wrapper Class

Primitive type	Wrapper class
boolean	Boolean
byte	Byte
char	Character
float	Float
int	Integer
long	Long
short	Short

The Math class contains a variety of class methods for performing mathematical functions, including exponential, logarithmic, and trigonometric methods. Math also includes basic arithmetic functions, such as absolute value and rounding, and a method, `random()`, for generating random numbers.

Questions and Exercises: Numbers

Questions

1. Use the API documentation to find the answers to the following questions:

   a. What `Integer` method can you use to convert an int into a string that expresses the number in hexadecimal? For example, what method converts the integer 65 into the string 41?

   b. What `Integer` method would you use to convert a string expressed in base 5 into the equivalent int? For example, how would you convert the string 230 into the integer value 65? Show the code you would use to accomplish this task.

   c. What `double` method can you use to detect whether a floating-point number has the special value `Not a Number` (NaN)?

2. What is the value of the following expression and why?

   ```
   Integer.valueOf(1).equals(Long.valueOf(1))
   ```

Exercises

1. Change `MaxVariablesDemo` to show minimum values instead of maximum values. You can delete all code related to the variables `aChar` and `aBoolean`. What is the output?

2. Create a program that reads an unspecified number of integer arguments from the command line and adds them together. For example, suppose that you enter the following:

   ```
   java Adder 1 3 2 10
   ```

   The program should display 16 and then exit. The program should also display an error message if the user enters only one argument. You can base your program on `ValueOfDemo`.

3. Create a program that is similar to the previous one but has the following differences:

   - Instead of reading integer arguments, it reads floating-point arguments.
   - It displays the sum of the arguments, using exactly two digits to the right of the decimal point.

   For example, suppose that you enter the following:

```
java FPAdder 1 1e2 3.0 4.754
```

The program would display 108.75. Depending on your locale, the decimal point might be a comma instead of a period.

Answers

You can find answers to these questions and exercises at http://docs.oracle.com/javase/tutorial/java/data/QandE/numbers-answers.html.

Characters

Most of the time, if you are using a single character value, you will use the primitive char type. Here's an example:

```
char ch = 'a';
// Unicode for uppercase Greek omega character
char uniChar = '\u039A';
// an array of chars
char[] charArray = { 'a', 'b', 'c', 'd', 'e' };
```

There are times, however, when you need to use a char as an object (e.g., as a method argument where an object is expected). The Java programming language provides a *wrapper* class that "wraps" the char in a Character object for this purpose. An object of type Character contains a single field, whose type is char. This Character class also offers a number of useful class (i.e., static) methods for manipulating characters.

You can create a Character object with the Character constructor:

```
Character ch = new Character('a');
```

The Java compiler will also create a Character object for you under some circumstances. For example, if you pass a primitive char into a method that expects an object, the compiler automatically converts the char to a Character for you. As described previously, this feature is called *autoboxing*—or *unboxing*, if the conversion goes the other way.

> **Note**
> The Character class is immutable, so that once it is created, a Character object cannot be changed.

Table 8.9 Useful Methods in the Character Class

Method	Description
boolean isLetter(char ch) boolean isDigit(char ch)	Determines whether the specified char value is a letter or digit, respectively
boolean isWhitespace(char ch)	Determines whether the specified char value is white space
boolean isUpperCase(char ch) boolean isLowerCase(char ch)	Determines whether the specified char value is uppercase or lowercase, respectively
char toUpperCase(char ch) char toLowerCase(char ch)	Returns the uppercase or lowercase form of the specified char value
toString(char ch)	Returns a String object representing the specified character value (i.e., a one-character string)

Table 8.10 Escape Sequences

Escape sequence	Description
\t	Insert a tab in the text at this point
\b	Insert a backspace in the text at this point
\n	Insert a new line in the text at this point
\r	Insert a carriage return in the text at this point
\f	Insert a form feed in the text at this point
\'	Insert a single quote character in the text at this point
\"	Insert a double quote character in the text at this point
\\	Insert a backslash character in the text at this point

Table 8.9 lists some of the most useful methods in the Character class but is not exhaustive. For a complete listing of all methods in this class (there are more than 50), refer to the java.lang.Character API specification.[9]

Escape Sequences

A character preceded by a backslash (\) is an *escape sequence* and has special meaning to the compiler. Table 8.10 shows the Java escape sequences.

When an escape sequence is encountered in a print statement, the compiler interprets it accordingly. For example, if you want to put quotes within quotes, you

9. 7/docs/api/java/lang/Character.html

must use the escape sequence \" on the interior quotes. Consider the following the sentence:

```
She said "Hello!" to me.
```

To print this, you would write the following:

```
System.out.println("She said \"Hello!\" to me.");
```

Strings

Strings, which are widely used in Java programming, are a sequence of characters. In the Java programming language, strings are objects. The Java platform provides the String[10] class to create and manipulate strings.

Creating Strings

The most direct way to create a string is to write the following:

```
String greeting = "Hello world!";
```

In this case, "Hello world!" is a *string literal*—a series of characters in your code that is enclosed in double quotes. Whenever the compiler encounters a string literal in your code, it creates a String object with its value—in this case, Hello world!.

As with any other object, you can create String objects by using the new keyword and a constructor. The String class has thirteen constructors that allow you to provide the initial value of the string using different sources, such as an array of characters:

```
char[] helloArray = { 'h', 'e', 'l', 'l', 'o', '.' };
String helloString = new String(helloArray);
System.out.println(helloString);
```

The last line of this code snippet displays hello.

> **Note**
>
> The String class is immutable, so once a String object is created, it cannot be changed. The String class has a number of methods that appear to modify strings, as will be discussed later. Since strings are immutable, what these methods really do is create and return a new string that contains the result of the operation.

---

10. 7/docs/api/java/lang/String.html

String Length

Methods used to obtain information about an object are known as *accessor methods*. One accessor method that you can use with strings is the length() method, which returns the number of characters contained in the string object. Consider the following two lines of code:

```
String palindrome = "Dot saw I was Tod";
int len = palindrome.length();
```

When these lines are executed, len equals 17.

A *palindrome* is a word or sentence that is symmetric—it is spelled the same forward and backward, ignoring case and punctuation. Here is a short but (as we will soon see) inefficient program to reverse a palindrome string. It invokes the String method charAt(i), which returns the ith character in the string, counting from zero:

```
public class StringDemo {
    public static void main(String[] args) {
        String palindrome = "Dot saw I was Tod";
        int len = palindrome.length();
        char[] tempCharArray = new char[len];
        char[] charArray = new char[len];

        // put original string in an
        // array of chars
        for (int i = 0; i < len; i++) {
            tempCharArray[i] =
                palindrome.charAt(i);
        }

        // reverse array of chars
        for (int j = 0; j < len; j++) {
            charArray[j] =
                tempCharArray[len - 1 - j];
        }

        String reversePalindrome =
            new String(charArray);
        System.out.println(reversePalindrome);
    }
}
```

Running the program produces this output:

```
doT saw I was toD
```

To accomplish the string reversal, the program had to convert the string to an array of characters (first for loop), reverse the array into a second array (second for loop), and then convert back to a string. The `String`[11] class includes a method, `getChars()`, to convert a string or portion of a string into an array of characters so we could replace the first `for` loop in the program with the following:

```
palindrome.getChars(0, len, tempCharArray, 0);
```

Concatenating Strings

The `String` class includes a method for concatenating two strings:

```
string1.concat(string2);
```

This returns a new string that is `string1` with `string2` added to it at the end. You can also use the `concat()` method with string literals:

```
"My name is ".concat("Rumplestiltskin");
```

However, strings are more commonly concatenated with the + operator:

```
"Hello," + " world" + "!"
```

The results of this are as follows:

```
"Hello, world!"
```

The + operator is widely used in `print` statements. Consider the following example:

```
String string1 = "saw I was ";
System.out.println("Dot " + string1 + "Tod");
```

This produces the following result:

```
Dot saw I was Tod
```

Such a concatenation can be a mixture of any objects. For each object that is not a `String`, its `toString()` method is called to convert it to a `String`.

---

11. 7/docs/api/java/lang/String.html

Creating Format Strings

You have seen the use of the printf() and format() methods to print output with formatted numbers. The String class has an equivalent class method, format(), that returns a String object rather than a PrintStream object.

Using String's static format() method allows you to create a formatted string that you can reuse, as opposed to a one-time print statement. Consider the following example:

```
System.out.printf("The value of the float " +
                  "variable is %f, while " +
                  "the value of the " +
                  "integer variable is %d, " +
                  "and the string is %s",
                  floatVar, intVar, stringVar);
```

Instead of this, you can write the following:

```
String fs;
fs = String.format("The value of the float " +
                   "variable is %f, while " +
                   "the value of the " +
                   "integer variable is %d, " +
                   " and the string is %s",
                   floatVar, intVar, stringVar);
System.out.println(fs);
```

Converting between Numbers and Strings

Converting Strings to Numbers

Frequently, a program ends up with numeric data in a string object—a value entered by the user, for example. The Number subclasses that wrap primitive numeric types (Byte[12], Integer[13], Double[14], Float[15], Long[16], and Short[17]) all provide a class method named valueOf that converts a string to an object of that type. The following example, ValueOfDemo, gets two strings from the command line, converts them to numbers, and performs arithmetic operations on the values:

```java
public class ValueOfDemo {
    public static void main(String[] args) {

        // this program requires two
        // arguments on the command line
        if (args.length == 2) {
            // convert strings to numbers
            float a = (Float.valueOf(args[0])).floatValue();
            float b = (Float.valueOf(args[1])).floatValue();

            // do some arithmetic
            System.out.println("a + b = " +
                               (a + b));
            System.out.println("a - b = " +
                               (a - b));
            System.out.println("a * b = " +
                               (a * b));
            System.out.println("a / b = " +
                               (a / b));
            System.out.println("a % b = " +
                               (a % b));
        } else {
            System.out.println("This program " +
                "requires two command-line arguments.");
        }
    }
}
```

The following is the output from the program when you use 4.5 and 87.2 for the command-line arguments:

12. 7/docs/api/java/lang/Byte.html

13. 7/docs/api/java/lang/Integer.html

14. 7/docs/api/java/lang/Double.html

15. 7/docs/api/java/lang/Float.html

16. 7/docs/api/java/lang/Long.html

17. 7/docs/api/java/lang/Short.html

```
a + b = 91.7
a - b = -82.7
a * b = 392.4
a / b = 0.0516055
a % b = 4.5
```

Note

Each of the Number subclasses that wrap primitive numeric types also provides a par-seXXXX() method (e.g., parseFloat()) that can be used to convert strings to primitive numbers. Since a primitive type is returned instead of an object, the parseFloat() method is more direct than the valueOf() method. For example, in the ValueOfDemo program, we could use the following:

```
float a = Float.parseFloat(args[0]);
float b = Float.parseFloat(args[1]);
```

8

Converting Numbers to Strings

Sometimes you need to convert a number to a string because you need to operate on the value in its string form. There are several easy ways to convert a number to a string:

```
int i;
// Concatenate "i" with an empty string; conversion is handled for you.
String s1 = "" + i;
```

Here is another method:

```
// The valueOf class method.
String s2 = String.valueOf(i);
```

Each of the Number subclasses includes a class method, toString(), that will convert its primitive type to a string. Here is an example:

```
int i;
double d;
String s3 = Integer.toString(i);
String s4 = Double.toString(d);
```

The ToStringDemo example uses the toString method to convert a number to a string. The program then uses some string methods to compute the number of digits before and after the decimal point:

```
public class ToStringDemo {

    public static void main(String[] args) {
```

```
        double d = 858.48;
        String s = Double.toString(d);

        int dot = s.indexOf('.');

        System.out.println(dot + " digits " +
            "before decimal point.");
        System.out.println( (s.length() - dot - 1) +
            " digits after decimal point.");
    }
}
```

The output of this program is as follows:

```
3 digits before decimal point.
2 digits after decimal point.
```

Manipulating Characters in a String

The `String` class has a number of methods for examining the contents of strings, finding characters or substrings within strings, changing the case of strings, and other tasks.

Getting Characters and Substrings by Index

You can get the character at a particular index within a string by invoking the `charAt()` accessor method. The index of the first character is the letter O, while the index of the last character is `length()-1`. For example, the following code obtains the character at index 9 in a string:

```
String anotherPalindrome = "Niagara. O roar again!";
char aChar = anotherPalindrome.charAt(9);
```

Indices begin at zero, so the character at index 9 is the letter O, as illustrated in Figure 8.2. If you want to get more than one consecutive character from a string, you can use the `substring` method. The `substring` method has two versions, as shown in Table 8.11.

Returning to the Niagara palindrome, the following code obtains the substring that extends from index 11 up to but not including index 15, which is the word "roar" (Figure 8.3):

```
String anotherPalindrome = "Niagara. O roar again!";
String roar = anotherPalindrome.substring(11, 15);
```

Other Methods for Manipulating Strings

Table 8.12 shows several other `String` class methods for manipulating strings.

Figure 8.2 The Character at Index 9

Table 8.11 The substring Methods in the String Class

Method	Description
`String substring(int beginIndex, int endIndex)`	This method returns a new string that is a substring of this string. The first integer argument specifies the index of the first character. The second integer argument is the index of the last character minus one.
`String substring(int beginIndex)`	This method returns a new string that is a substring of this string. The integer argument specifies the index of the first character. Here, the returned substring extends to the end of the original string.

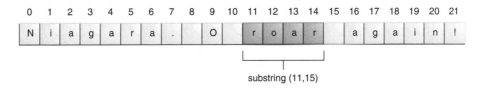

Figure 8.3 Substring from Index 11 to 15

Table 8.12 Other Methods in the String Class for Manipulating Strings

Method	Description
`String[] split(String regex)` `String[] split(String regex, int limit)`	These methods search for a match as specified by the string argument (which contains a regular expression) and splits this string into an array of strings accordingly. The optional integer argument specifies the maximum size of the returned array. Regular expressions are covered in Chapter 13.
`CharSequence subSequence(int beginIndex, int endIndex)`	This method returns a new character sequence constructed from `beginIndex` index up until `endIndex` minus one.
`String trim()`	This method returns a copy of this string with leading and trailing white space removed.
`String toLowerCase()` `String toUpperCase()`	These methods return a copy of the string converted to lowercase or uppercase. If no conversions are necessary, they return the original string.

Searching for Characters and Substrings in a String

Here are some other `String` methods for finding characters or substrings within a string. The `String` class provides accessor methods that return the position within the string of a specific character or substring: `indexOf()` and `lastIndexOf()`. The `indexOf()` methods search forward from the beginning of the string, and the `lastIndexOf()` methods search backward from the end of the string. If a character or substring is not found, `indexOf()` and `lastIndexOf()` return −1.

The `String` class also provides a search method, `contains`, which returns `true` if the string contains a particular character sequence. Use this method when you only need to know that the string contains a character sequence and the precise location isn't important. Table 8.13 describes the various string search methods.

> **Note**
>
> `CharSequence` is an interface that is implemented by the `String` class. Therefore, you can use a string as an argument for the `contains()` method.

Replacing Characters and Substrings into a String

The `String` class has very few methods for inserting characters or substrings into a string. In general, they are not needed: you can create a new string by concatenation of substrings you have *removed* from a string with the substring that you want to insert. However, the `String` class does have four methods for *replacing* found characters or substrings, as shown in Table 8.14.

Table 8.13 The Search Methods in the String Class

Method	Description
`int indexOf(int ch)` `int lastIndexOf(int ch)`	Returns the index of the first (last) occurrence of the specified character
`int indexOf(int ch, int fromIndex)` `int lastIndexOf(int ch, int fromIndex)`	Returns the index of the first (last) occurrence of the specified character, searching forward (backward) from the specified index
`int indexOf(String str)` `int lastIndexOf(String str)`	Returns the index of the first (last) occurrence of the specified substring
`int indexOf(String str, int fromIndex)` `int lastIndexOf(String str, int fromIndex)`	Returns the index of the first (last) occurrence of the specified substring, searching forward (backward) from the specified index
`boolean contains(CharSequence s)`	Returns true if the string contains the specified character sequence

Table 8.14 Methods in the String Class for Manipulating Strings

Method	Description
`String replace(char oldChar, char newChar)`	Returns a new string by replacing all occurrences of `oldChar` in the string with `newChar`
`String replace(CharSequence target, CharSequence replacement)`	Replaces each substring that matches the literal target sequence with the specified literal replacement sequence
`String replaceAll(String regex, String replacement)`	Replaces each substring that matches the given regular expression with the given replacement
`String replaceFirst(String regex, String replacement)`	Replaces the first substring that matches the given regular expression with the given replacement

An Example

The following class, `Filename`, illustrates the use of `lastIndexOf()` and `substring()` to isolate different parts of a file name:

> **Note**
>
> The methods in the following `Filename` class don't do any error checking and assume that their argument contains a full directory path and a file name with an extension. If these methods were production code, they would verify that their arguments were properly constructed.

```
public class Filename {
    private String fullPath;
    private char pathSeparator,
                extensionSeparator;

    public Filename(String str, char sep, char ext) {
        fullPath = str;
        pathSeparator = sep;
        extensionSeparator = ext;
    }

    public String extension() {
        int dot = fullPath.lastIndexOf(extensionSeparator);
        return fullPath.substring(dot + 1);
    }

    // gets filename without extension
    public String filename() {
        int dot = fullPath.lastIndexOf(extensionSeparator);
        int sep = fullPath.lastIndexOf(pathSeparator);
        return fullPath.substring(sep + 1, dot);
    }
```

```
    public String path() {
        int sep = fullPath.lastIndexOf(pathSeparator);
        return fullPath.substring(0, sep);
    }
}
```

Here is a program, `FilenameDemo`, that constructs a `Filename` object and calls all of its methods:

```
public class FilenameDemo {
    public static void main(String[] args) {
        final String FPATH = "/home/user/index.html";
        Filename myHomePage = new Filename(FPATH, '/', '.');
        System.out.println("Extension = " + myHomePage.extension());
        System.out.println("Filename = " + myHomePage.filename());
        System.out.println("Path = " + myHomePage.path());
    }
}
```

Here's the output from the program:

```
Extension = html
Filename = index
Path = /home/user
```

As shown in Figure 8.4, our `extension` method uses `lastIndexOf` to locate the last occurrence of the period (`.`) in the file name. Then `substring` uses the return value of `lastIndexOf` to extract the file name extension—that is, the substring from the period to the end of the string. This code assumes that the file name has a period in it; if the file name does not have a period, `lastIndexOf` returns −1, and the substring method throws a `StringIndexOutOfBoundsException`.

Notice that the `extension` method uses `dot + 1` as the argument to substring. If the period character (`.`) is the last character of the string, `dot + 1` is equal to the length of the string, which is one larger than the largest index into the string (because indices start at zero). This is a legal argument to `substring`

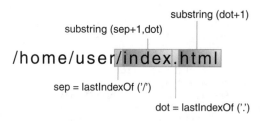

Figure 8.4 Isolating Different Parts of a File Name

because that method accepts an index equal to but not greater than the length of the string and interprets it to mean "the end of the string."

Comparing Strings and Portions of Strings

The String class has a number of methods for comparing strings and portions of strings. Table 8.15 lists these methods.

The following program, RegionMatchesDemo, uses the regionMatches method to search for a string within another string:

```
public class RegionMatchesDemo {
    public static void main(String[] args) {
        String searchMe = "Green Eggs and Ham";
        String findMe = "Eggs";
        int searchMeLength = searchMe.length();
        int findMeLength = findMe.length();
        boolean foundIt = false;
        for (int i = 0;
             i <= (searchMeLength - findMeLength);
             i++) {
            if (searchMe.regionMatches(i, findMe, 0, findMeLength)) {
                foundIt = true;
                System.out.println(searchMe.substring(i, i + findMeLength));
                break;
            }
        }
        if (!foundIt)
            System.out.println("No match found.");
    }
}
```

The output from this program is Eggs.

The program steps through the string referred to by searchMe one character at a time. For each character, the program calls the regionMatches method to determine whether the substring beginning with the current character matches the string the program is looking for.

The StringBuilder Class

StringBuilder[18] objects are like String[19] objects, except that they can be modified. Internally, these objects are treated like variable-length arrays that contain a sequence of characters. At any point, the length and content of the sequence can be changed through method invocations.

18. 7/docs/api/java/lang/StringBuilder.html

19. 7/docs/api/java/lang/String.html

Table 8.15 Methods for Comparing Strings

Method	Description
`boolean endsWith(String suffix)` `boolean startsWith(String prefix)`	These methods return `true` if this string ends with or begins with the substring specified as an argument to the method.
`boolean startsWith(String prefix, int offset)`	This method considers the string beginning at the index `offset` and returns `true` if it begins with the substring specified as an argument.
`int compareTo(String anotherString)`	This method compares two strings lexicographically. It returns an integer indicating whether this string is greater than (> 0), equal to (= 0), or less than (< 0) the argument.
`int compareToIgnoreCase (String str)`	This method compares two strings lexicographically, ignoring differences in case. It returns an integer indicating whether this string is greater than (> 0), equal to (= 0), or less than (< 0) the argument.
`boolean equals(Object anObject)`	This method returns `true` if and only if the argument is a `String` object that represents the same sequence of characters as this object.
`boolean equalsIgnoreCase(String anotherString)`	This method returns `true` if and only if the argument is a `String` object that represents the same sequence of characters as this object, ignoring differences in case.
`boolean regionMatches(int toffset, String other, int ooffset, int len)`	This method tests whether the specified region of this string matches the specified region of the `String` argument. The region is of length `len` and begins at the index `toffset` for this string and `ooffset` for the other string.
`boolean regionMatches(boolean ignoreCase, int toffset, String other, int ooffset, int len)`	This method tests whether the specified region of this string matches the specified region of the `String` argument. The region is of length `len` and begins at the index `toffset` for this string and `ooffset` for the other string. The boolean argument indicates whether case should be ignored; if `true`, case is ignored when comparing characters.
`boolean matches(String regex)`	This method tests whether this string matches the specified regular expression. Regular expressions are discussed in Chapter 13.

Strings should always be used unless string builders offer an advantage in terms of better performance or simpler code. (Consult the sample program at the end of this section.) For example, if you need to concatenate a large number of strings, appending to a `StringBuilder` object is more efficient.

Length and Capacity

The `StringBuilder` class, like the `String` class, has a `length()` method that returns the length of the character sequence in the builder. Unlike strings, every string builder also has a *capacity*—the number of character spaces that have been allocated. The capacity, which is returned by the `capacity()` method, is always greater than or equal to the length (usually greater than) and will automatically expand as necessary to accommodate additions to the string builder. For example, the following code will produce a string builder with a length of 9 and a capacity of 16 (Figure 8.5):

```
// creates empty builder, capacity 16
StringBuilder sb = new StringBuilder();
// adds 9 character string at beginning
sb.append("Greetings");
```

Table 8.16 StringBuilder Constructors

Constructor	Description
`StringBuilder()`	Creates an empty string builder with a capacity of 16 (16 empty elements)
`StringBuilder(CharSequence cs)`	Constructs a string builder containing the same characters as the specified `CharSequence`, plus an extra 16 empty elements trailing the `CharSequence`
`StringBuilder(int initCapacity)`	Creates an empty string builder with the specified initial capacity
`StringBuilder(String s)`	Creates a string builder whose value is initialized by the specified string, plus an extra 16 empty elements trailing the string

Figure 8.5 Creating a StringBuilder

The `StringBuilder` class has some methods related to length and capacity that the `String` class does not have (Table 8.17). A number of operations (e.g., `append()`, `insert()`, or `setLength()`) can increase the length of the character sequence in the string builder so that the resultant `length()` is greater than the current `capacity()`. When this happens, the capacity is automatically increased.

StringBuilder Operations

The principal operations of a `StringBuilder` that are not available in `String` are the `append()` and `insert()` methods, which are overloaded so that they can accept data of any type. Each converts its argument to a string and then appends or inserts the characters of that string to the character sequence in the string builder. The append method always adds these characters at the end of the existing character sequence, while the insert method adds the characters at a specified point. Table 8.18 shows a number of the methods of the `StringBuilder` class.

> **Note**
> You can use any `String` method on a `StringBuilder` object by first converting the string builder to a string with the `toString()` method of the `StringBuilder` class. Then convert the string back into a string builder using the `StringBuilder(String str)` constructor.

An Example

The `StringDemo` program that was listed in the section titled "Strings" is an example of a program that would be more efficient if a `StringBuilder` were used instead of a `String`. `StringDemo` reversed a palindrome. Here, once again, is its listing:

```java
public class StringDemo {
    public static void main(String[] args) {
        String palindrome = "Dot saw I was Tod";
        int len = palindrome.length();
        char[] tempCharArray = new char[len];
        char[] charArray = new char[len];

        // put original string in an
        // array of chars
        for (int i = 0; i < len; i++) {
            tempCharArray[i] =
                palindrome.charAt(i);
        }

        // reverse array of chars
        for (int j = 0; j < len; j++) {
            charArray[j] =
                tempCharArray[len - 1 - j];
```

```
        }
        String reversePalindrome =
            new String(charArray);
        System.out.println(reversePalindrome);
    }
]
```

Running the program produces this output:

```
doT saw I was toD
```

To accomplish the string reversal, the program converts the string to an array of characters (first `for` loop), reverses the array into a second array (second `for` loop), and then converts back to a string. If you convert the `palindrome` string to a string builder, you can use the `reverse()` method in the `StringBuilder` class. It makes the code simpler and easier to read:

```
public class StringBuilderDemo {
    public static void main(String[] args) {
        String palindrome = "Dot saw I was Tod";

        StringBuilder sb = new StringBuilder(palindrome);

        sb.reverse();  // reverse it

        System.out.println(sb);
    }
}
```

Running this program produces the same output:

```
doT saw I was toD
```

Note that `println()` prints a string builder:

Table 8.17 Length and Capacity Methods

Method	Description
void setLength(int newLength)	This method sets the length of the character sequence. If newLength is less than length(), the last characters in the character sequence are truncated. If newLength is greater than length(), null characters are added at the end of the character sequence.
void ensureCapacity(int minCapacity)	This method ensures that the capacity is at least equal to the specified minimum.

```
System.out.println(sb);
```

This is because `sb.toString()` is called implicitly, as it is with any other object in a `println()` invocation.

Table 8.18 Various StringBuilder Methods

Method	Description
StringBuilder append(boolean b) StringBuilder append(char c) StringBuilder append(char[] str) StringBuilder append(char[] str, int offset, int len) StringBuilder append(double d) StringBuilder append(float f) StringBuilder append(int i) StringBuilder append(long lng) StringBuilder append(Object obj) StringBuilder append(String s)	These methods append the argument to the string builder. The data are converted to a string before the append operation takes place.
StringBuilder delete(int start, int end) StringBuilder deleteCharAt(int index)	The first method deletes the subsequence from start to end−1 (inclusive) in the StringBuilder's char sequence. The second method deletes the character located at index.

StringBuilder insert(int offset, boolean b)
StringBuilder insert(int offset, char c)
StringBuilder insert(int offset, char[]
  str)
StringBuilder insert(int index, char[] str,
  int offset, int len)
StringBuilder insert(int offset, double d)
StringBuilder insert(int offset, float f)
StringBuilder insert(int offset, int i)
StringBuilder insert(int offset, long lng)
StringBuilder insert(int offset, Object
  obj)
StringBuilder insert(int offset, String s)
	These methods insert the second argument into the string builder. The first integer argument indicates the index before which the data are to be inserted. The data are converted to a string before the insert operation takes place.

StringBuilder replace(int start, int end, String s) void setCharAt(int index, char c)	These methods replace the specified character(s) in this string builder.
StringBuilder reverse()	This method reverses the sequence of characters in the string builder.
String toString()	This method returns a string that contains the character sequence in the builder.

> **Note**
>
> There is also a `StringBuffer` class that is *exactly* the same as the `StringBuilder` class, except that it is thread safe by virtue of having its methods synchronized. Threads will be discussed in Chapter 12.

Summary of Characters and Strings

Most of the time, if you are using a single character value, you will use the primitive `char` type. There are times, however, when you need to use a `char` as an object (e.g., as a method argument where an object is expected). The Java programming language provides a *wrapper* class that "wraps" the `char` in a `Character` object for this purpose. An object of type `Character` contains a single field whose type is `char`. This `Character` class also offers a number of useful class (i.e., static) methods for manipulating characters.

Strings are a sequence of characters and are widely used in Java programming. In the Java programming language, strings are objects. The `String`[20] class has over 60 methods and 13 constructors.

It is common to create a string with a variant of the following statement (rather than using one of the `String` constructors):

```
String s = "Hello world!";
```

The `String` class has many methods to find and retrieve substrings; these can then be easily reassembled into new strings using the + concatenation operator.

The `String` class also includes a number of utility methods, including `split()`, `toLowerCase()`, `toUpperCase()`, and `valueOf()`. The `valueOf()` method is indispensable for converting user input strings to numbers. The `Number` subclasses also have methods for converting strings to numbers and vice versa.

In addition to the `String` class, there is also a `StringBuilder`[21] class. Working with `StringBuilder` objects can sometimes be more efficient than working with strings. The `StringBuilder` class offers a few methods that can be useful for strings, including `reverse()`. In general, however, the `String` class has a wider variety of methods.

A string can be converted to a string builder using a `StringBuilder` constructor. A string builder can be converted to a string with the `toString()` method.

---

20. 7/docs/api/java/lang/String.html
21. 7/docs/api/java/lang/StringBuilder.html

Questions and Exercises: Characters and Strings

Questions

1. What is the initial capacity of the following string builder?

```
StringBuilder sb = new StringBuilder("Able was I ere I saw Elba.");
```

2. Consider the following string:

```
String hannah = "Did Hannah see bees? Hannah did.";
```

   a. What is the value displayed by the expression hannah.length()?

   b. What is the value returned by the method call hannah.charAt(12)?

   c. Write an expression that refers to the letter b in the string referred to by hannah.

3. How long is the string returned by the following expression? What is the string?

```
"Was it a car or a cat I saw?".substring(9, 12)
```

4. In the following program, called ComputeResult, what is the value of result after each numbered line executes?

```
public class ComputeResult {
    public static void main(String[] args) {
        String original = "software";
        StringBuilder result = new StringBuilder("hi");
        int index = original.indexOf('a');

/*1*/    result.setCharAt(0, original.charAt(0));
/*2*/    result.setCharAt(1, original.charAt(original.length()-1));
/*3*/    result.insert(1, original.charAt(4));
/*4*/    result.append(original.substring(1,4));
/*5*/    result.insert(3, (original.substring(index, index+2) + " "));

        System.out.println(result);
    }
}
```

Exercises

1. Show two ways to concatenate the following two strings together to get the string "Hi, mom.":

```
String hi = "Hi, ";
String mom = "mom.";
```

2. Write a program that computes your initials from your full name and displays them.

3. An anagram is a word or a phrase made by transposing the letters of another word or phrase; for example, *parliament* is an anagram of *partial men* and

software is an anagram of *swear oft*. Write a program that figures out whether one string is an anagram of another string. The program should ignore white space and punctuation.

Answers

You can find answers to these questions and exercises at `http://docs.oracle.com/javase/tutorial/java/data/QandE/characters-answers.html`.

8

9

Exceptions

Chapter Contents

The Java programming language uses *exceptions* to handle errors and other exceptional events. This chapter describes when and how to use exceptions.

The first section defines an *exception*. An exception is an event that occurs during the execution of a program that disrupts the normal flow of instructions. The second section discusses the *catch or specify requirement* and describes the three kinds of exceptions. The third section covers how to catch and handle exceptions. The discussion includes the `try`, `catch`, and `finally` blocks, as well as chained exceptions and logging. It also includes information on the `try`-with-resources statement. The fourth section covers how to specify the exceptions thrown by a method. The fifth section covers how to throw exceptions, chain exceptions, and create an exception class. The sixth section explains the correct and incorrect use of the unchecked exceptions indicated by subclasses of `RuntimeException`. The final section discusses the use of exceptions to manage errors, which has some advantages over

257

traditional error-management techniques. The chapter ends with a summary and questions and exercises to test your knowledge.

What Is an Exception?

The term *exception* is shorthand for the phrase *exceptional event*.

> **Definition**
>
> An *exception* is an event that occurs during the execution of a program and disrupts the normal flow of the program's instructions.

When an error occurs within a method, the method creates an object and hands it off to the runtime system. The object, called an *exception object*, contains information about the error, including its type and the state of the program when the error occurred. Creating an exception object and handing it to the runtime system is called *throwing an exception*.

After a method throws an exception, the runtime system attempts to find a way to handle it. An ordered list of methods for handling the exception is called. This list of methods is known as the *call stack* (Figure 9.1).

The runtime system searches the call stack for a method that contains a block of code that can handle the exception. This block of code is called an *exception handler*. The search begins with the method in which the error occurred and proceeds through the call stack in the reverse order in which the methods were called. When an appropriate handler is found, the runtime system passes the exception to the handler. An exception handler is considered appropriate if the type of the exception object thrown matches the type that can be handled by the handler.

The exception handler chosen is said to *catch the exception*. If the runtime system exhaustively searches all the methods in the call stack without finding an appropriate exception handler, as shown in Figure 9.2, the runtime system (and consequently the program) terminates.

Using exceptions to manage errors has some advantages over traditional error-management techniques. You can learn more in the "Advantages of Exceptions" section later in this chapter.

The Catch or Specify Requirement

Valid Java programming language code must honor the *catch or specify requirement*. This means that code that might throw certain exceptions must be enclosed by either of the following:

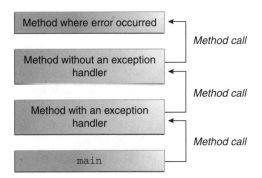

Figure 9.1 The Call Stack

Figure 9.2 Searching the Call Stack for the Exception Handler

- *A try statement that catches the exception.* The `try` statement must provide a handler for the exception, as described in the section "Catching and Handling Exceptions" later in this chapter.
- *A method that specifies that it can throw the exception.* The method must provide a `throws` clause that lists the exception, as described in the section "Specifying the Exceptions Thrown by a Method" later in this chapter.

Code that fails to honor the catch or specify requirement will not compile. However, not all exceptions are subject to the catch or specify requirement. To understand why, we need to look at the three basic categories of exceptions, only one of which is subject to the requirement.

The Three Kinds of Exceptions

The first kind of exception is the *checked exception*. These are exceptional conditions that a well-written application should anticipate and recover from. For example, suppose an application prompts a user for an input file name and then opens the file by passing the name to the constructor for `java.io.FileReader`. Normally, the user provides the name of an existing, readable file, so the construction of the `FileReader` object succeeds and the execution of the application proceeds normally. But sometimes the user supplies the name of a nonexistent file, and the constructor throws `java.io.FileNotFoundException`. A well-written program will catch this exception and notify the user of the mistake, possibly prompting for a corrected file name.

Checked exceptions are subject to the catch or specify requirement. All exceptions are checked exceptions, except for those indicated by `Error`, `RuntimeException`, and their subclasses.

The second kind of exception is the *error*. These are exceptional conditions that are external to the application, which the application usually cannot anticipate or recover from. For example, suppose that an application successfully opens a file for input but is unable to read the file because of a hardware or system malfunction. The unsuccessful read will throw `java.io.IOError`. An application might choose to catch this exception in order to notify the user of the problem, but it also might make sense for the program to print a stack trace and exit.

Errors are not subject to the catch or specify requirement. Errors are those exceptions indicated by `Error` and its subclasses.

The third kind of exception is the *runtime exception*. These are exceptional conditions that are internal to the application, which the application usually cannot anticipate or recover from. These usually indicate programming bugs, such as logic errors or improper use of an Application Programming Interface (API). For example, consider the application described previously that passes a file name to the constructor for `FileReader`. If a logic error causes a `null` to be passed to the constructor, the constructor will throw `NullPointerException`. The application can catch this exception, but it probably makes more sense to eliminate the bug that caused the exception to occur.

Runtime exceptions are not subject to the catch or specify requirement. Runtime exceptions are those indicated by `RuntimeException` and its subclasses.

> **Definition**
> Errors and runtime exceptions are collectively known as *unchecked exceptions*.

Bypassing Catch or Specify

Some programmers consider the catch or specify requirement a serious flaw in the exception mechanism and bypass it by using unchecked exceptions in place of checked exceptions. In general, this is not recommended. Later in this chapter, the section "Unchecked Exceptions: The Controversy" talks about when it is appropriate to use unchecked exceptions.

Catching and Handling Exceptions

This section describes how to use the three exception handler components—the try, catch, and finally blocks—to write an exception handler. Then, the try-with-resources statement, introduced in Java SE 7, is explained. The try-with-resources statement is particularly suited to situations that use Closeable resources, such as streams. The last part of this section walks through an example and analyzes what occurs during various scenarios.

The following example defines and implements a class named ListOfNumbers. When constructed, ListOfNumbers creates an ArrayList that contains 10 Integer elements with sequential values 0 through 9. The ListOfNumbers class also defines a method named writeList, which writes the list of numbers into a text file called OutFile.txt. This example uses output classes defined in java.io, which are covered in Chapter 10.

```java
// Note: This class won't compile by design!
import java.io.*;
import java.util.List;
import java.util.ArrayList;

public class ListOfNumbers {

    private List<Integer> list;
    private static final int SIZE = 10;

    public ListOfNumbers () {
        list = new ArrayList<Integer>(SIZE);
        for (int i = 0; i < SIZE; i++) {
            list.add(new Integer(i));
        }
    }

    public void writeList() {
        PrintWriter out = new PrintWriter(new FileWriter("OutFile.txt"));

        for (int i = 0; i < SIZE; i++) {
            out.println("Value at: " + i + " = " + list.get(i));
        }
        out.close();
    }
}
```

The first line in boldface is a call to a constructor. The constructor initializes an output stream on a file. If the file cannot be opened, the constructor throws an IOException. The second boldface line is a call to the ArrayList class's get method, which throws an IndexOutOfBoundsException if the value of its argument is too small (less than 0) or too large (more than the number of elements currently contained by the ArrayList).

If you try to compile the ListOfNumbers class, the compiler prints an error message about the exception thrown by the FileWriter constructor. However, it does not display an error message about the exception thrown by get. The reason is that the exception thrown by the constructor, IOException, is a checked exception and the one thrown by the get method, IndexOutOfBoundsException, is an unchecked exception.

Now that you're familiar with the ListOfNumbers class and where the exceptions can be thrown within it, you're ready to write exception handlers to catch and handle those exceptions.

The try Block

The first step in constructing an exception handler is to enclose the code that might throw an exception within a try block. In general, a try block looks like the following:

```
try {
    code
}
catch and finally blocks . . .
```

The segment in the example labeled *code* contains one or more legal lines of code that could throw an exception. (The catch and finally blocks are explained in the next two subsections.)

To construct an exception handler for the writeList method from the ListOf-Numbers class, enclose the exception-throwing statements of the writeList method within a try block. There is more than one way to do this: You could put each line of code that might throw an exception within its own try block and provide separate exception handlers for each. You could also put the writeList code within a single try block and associate multiple handlers with it. The following listing uses one try block for the entire method because the code in question is very short:

```
private List<Integer> list;
private static final int SIZE = 10;

PrintWriter out = null;

try {
    System.out.println("Entered try statement");
    out = new PrintWriter(new FileWriter("OutFile.txt"));
    for (int i = 0; i < SIZE; i++) {
        out.println("Value at: " + i + " = " + list.get(i));
    }
}
catch and finally statements . . .
```

If an exception occurs within the `try` block, an exception handler associated with the exception handles it. To associate an exception handler with a `try` block, you must put a `catch` block after it; the next section shows you how.

The catch Blocks

You associate exception handlers with a `try` block by providing one or more `catch` blocks directly after the `try` block. No code can be between the end of the `try` block and the beginning of the first `catch` block:

```
try {

} catch (ExceptionType name) {

} catch (ExceptionType name) {

}
```

Each `catch` block is an exception handler and handles the type of exception indicated by its argument. The argument type, *ExceptionType*, declares the type of exception that the handler can handle and must be the name of a class that inherits from the `Throwable` class. The handler can refer to the exception with *name*.

The `catch` block contains code that is executed if and when the exception handler is invoked. The runtime system invokes the exception handler when the handler is the first one in the call stack whose *ExceptionType* matches the type of the exception thrown. The system considers it a match if the thrown object can legally be assigned to the exception handler's argument.

The following are two exception handlers for the `writeList` method—one for each of the two types of checked exceptions that can be thrown within the `try` statement:

```
try {

} catch (FileNotFoundException e) {
    System.err.println("FileNotFoundException: " + e.getMessage());
    throw new SampleException(e);

} catch (IOException e) {
    System.err.println("Caught IOException: " + e.getMessage());
}
```

Both handlers print an error message. The second handler does nothing else. By catching any `IOException` that is not caught by the first handler, it allows the program to continue executing.

The first handler, in addition to printing a message, throws a user-defined exception. (Throwing exceptions is covered in detail later in this chapter in the "How to Throw Exceptions" section.)

In this example, when the `FileNotFoundException` is caught, it throws a user-defined exception called `SampleException`. You might want to do this if you want your program to handle an exception in this situation in a specific way.

Exception handlers can do more than just print error messages or halt the program. They can also perform error recovery, prompt the user to make a decision, or propagate the error up to a higher-level handler using chained exceptions, as described in the "Chained Exceptions" section later in this chapter.

Catching More Than One Type of Exception with One Exception Handler

In Java SE 7 and later, a single `catch` block can handle more than one type of exception. This feature can reduce code duplication and lessen the temptation to catch an overly broad exception.

In the `catch` clause, specify the types of exceptions that block can handle, and separate each exception type with a pipe character (|):

```
catch (IOException|SQLException ex) {
    logger.log(ex);
    throw ex;
}
```

> **Note**
> If a `catch` block handles more than one exception type, then the `catch` parameter is implicitly `final`. In this example, the `catch` parameter `ex` is `final`, and therefore you cannot assign any values to it within the `catch` block.

The finally Block

The `finally` block *always* executes when the `try` block exits. This ensures that the `finally` block is executed even if an unexpected exception occurs. But `finally` is useful for more than just exception handling—it allows the programmer to avoid having cleanup code accidentally bypassed by a `return`, `continue`, or `break`. Putting cleanup code in a `finally` block is always a good practice, even when no exceptions are anticipated.

> **Note**
> If the Java Virtual Machine (Java VM) exits while the `try` or `catch` code is being executed, then the `finally` block may not execute. Likewise, if the thread executing the `try` or `catch` code is interrupted or killed, the `finally` block may not execute even though the application as a whole continues.

The `try` block of the `writeList` method that you've been working with here opens a `PrintWriter`. The program should close that stream before exiting the `writeList` method. This poses a somewhat complicated problem because `writeList`'s `try` block can exit in one of three ways:

1. The new `FileWriter` statement fails and throws an `IOException`.
2. The `vector.elementAt(i)` statement fails and throws an `ArrayIndexOutOfBoundsException`.
3. Everything succeeds and the `try` block exits normally.

The runtime system always executes the statements within the `finally` block regardless of what happens within the `try` block. So it's the perfect place to perform cleanup.

The following `finally` block for the `writeList` method cleans up and then closes the `PrintWriter`:

```
finally {
    if (out != null) {
        System.out.println("Closing PrintWriter");
        out.close();
    } else {
        System.out.println("PrintWriter not open");
    }
}
```

In the `writeList` example, you could provide for cleanup without the intervention of a `finally` block. For example, you could place the code to close the `PrintWriter` at the end of the `try` block and again within the exception handler for `ArrayIndexOutOfBoundsException`, as follows:

```
try {

    // Don't do this; it duplicates code.
    out.close();

} catch (FileNotFoundException e) {
    // Don't do this; it duplicates code.
    out.close();

    System.err.println("Caught FileNotFoundException: " + e.getMessage());
    throw new RuntimeException(e);

} catch (IOException e) {
    System.err.println("Caught IOException: " + e.getMessage());
}
```

However, this duplicates code, thus making the code difficult to read and error prone, should you modify it later. For example, if you add code that can throw a new type of exception to the `try` block, you have to remember to close the `PrintWriter` within the new exception handler.

> **Note**
>
> The `finally` block is a key tool for preventing resource leaks. When closing a file or otherwise recovering resources, place the code in a `finally` block to ensure that resource is *always* recovered.
>
> If you are using Java SE 7 or later, consider using the `try`-with-resources statement in these situations, which automatically releases system resources when no longer needed.

The try-with-resources Statement

The `try`-with-resources statement is a `try` statement that declares one or more resources. A *resource* is an object that must be closed after the program is finished with it. The `try`-with-resources statement ensures that each resource is closed at the end of the statement. Any object that implements `java.lang.AutoCloseable`, which includes all objects that implement `java.io.Closeable`, can be used as a resource.

The following example reads the first line from a file. It uses an instance of `BufferedReader` to read data from the file. `BufferedReader` is a resource that must be closed after the program is finished with it:

```
static String readFirstLineFromFile(String path) throws IOException {
    try (BufferedReader br =
                    new BufferedReader(new FileReader(path))) {
        return br.readLine();
    }
}
```

In this example, the resource declared in the `try`-with-resources statement is a `BufferedReader`. The declaration statement appears within parentheses immediately after the `try` keyword. The class `BufferedReader`, in Java SE 7 and later, implements the interface `java.lang.AutoCloseable`. Because the `BufferedReader` instance is declared in a `try`-with-resource statement, it will be closed regardless of whether the `try` statement completes normally or abruptly (as a result of the method `BufferedReader.readLine` throwing an `IOException`).

Prior to Java SE 7, you could use a `finally` block to ensure that a resource is closed, regardless of whether the `try` statement completes normally or abruptly. The following example uses a `finally` block instead of a `try`-with-resources statement:

```
static String readFirstLineFromFileWithFinallyBlock(String path)
                                                throws IOException {
    BufferedReader br = new BufferedReader(new FileReader(path));
```

```
        try {
            return br.readLine();
        } finally {
            if (br != null) br.close();
        }
    }
```

However, in this example, if the methods `readLine` and `close` both throw exceptions, then the method `readFirstLineFromFileWithFinallyBlock` throws the exception thrown from the finally block; the exception thrown from the `try` block is suppressed. In contrast, in the example `readFirstLineFromFile`, if exceptions are thrown from both the `try` block and the `try-with-resources` statement, then the method `readFirstLineFromFile` throws the exception thrown from the `try` block; the exception thrown from the `try-with-resources` block is suppressed. In Java SE 7 and later, you can retrieve suppressed exceptions; see the "Suppressed Exceptions" section later in this chapter for more information.

You may declare one or more resources in a `try-with-resources` statement. The following example retrieves the names of the files packaged in the zip file `zipFileName` and creates a text file that contains the names of these files:

```
public static void writeToFileZipFileContents(String zipFileName,
                                              String outputFileName)
    throws java.io.IOException {

    java.nio.charset.Charset charset =
        java.nio.charset.StandardCharsets.US_ASCII;
    java.nio.file.Path outputFilePath =
        java.nio.file.Paths.get(outputFileName);

    // Open zip file and create output file with
    // try-with-resources statement

    try (
        java.util.zip.ZipFile zf =
            new java.util.zip.ZipFile(zipFileName);
        java.io.BufferedWriter writer =
            java.nio.file.Files.newBufferedWriter(outputFilePath, charset)
    ) {
        // Enumerate each entry
        for (java.util.Enumeration entries =
                            zf.entries(); entries.hasMoreElements();) {
            // Get the entry name and write it to the output file
            String newLine = System.getProperty("line.separator");
            String zipEntryName =
                ((java.util.zip.ZipEntry)entries.nextElement()).getName() +
                newLine;
            writer.write(zipEntryName, 0, zipEntryName.length());
        }
    }
}
```

In this example, the `try-with-resources` statement contains two declarations that are separated by a semicolon: `ZipFile` and `BufferedWriter`. When the block of code that directly follows it terminates, either normally or because of an exception, the `close` methods of the `BufferedWriter` and `ZipFile` objects are automatically called in this order. Note that the `close` methods of resources are called in the *reverse* order of their creation.

The following example uses a `try-with-resources` statement to automatically close a `java.sql.Statement` object:

```
public static void viewTable(Connection con) throws SQLException {

    String query = "select COF_NAME, SUP_ID, PRICE, SALES, TOTAL from
        COFFEES";

    try (Statement stmt = con.createStatement()) {
        ResultSet rs = stmt.executeQuery(query);

        while (rs.next()) {
            String coffeeName = rs.getString("COF_NAME");
            int supplierID = rs.getInt("SUP_ID");
            float price = rs.getFloat("PRICE");
            int sales = rs.getInt("SALES");
            int total = rs.getInt("TOTAL");

            System.out.println(coffeeName + ", " + supplierID + ", " +
                            price + ", " + sales + ", " + total);
        }
    } catch (SQLException e) {
        JDBCTutorialUtilities.printSQLException(e);
    }
}
```

The resource `java.sql.Statement` used in this example is part of Java Database Connectivity 4.1 and later API.

Note

A `try-with-resources` statement can have `catch` and `finally` blocks just like an ordinary `try` statement. In a `try-with-resources` statement, any `catch` or `finally` block is run after the resources declared have been closed.

Suppressed Exceptions

An exception can be thrown from the block of code associated with the `try-with-resources` statement. In the example `writeToFileZipFileContents`, an exception can be thrown from the `try` block, and up to two exceptions can be thrown from the `try-with-resources` statement when it tries to close the `ZipFile` and `BufferedWriter` objects. If an exception is thrown from the `try` block and one or more exceptions are thrown from the try-with-resources statement, then those exceptions thrown from the try-with-resources statement are suppressed, and the exception thrown by the block is the one that is thrown by the writeToFileZipFileContents method. You can retrieve these suppressed exceptions by calling the Throwable.getSuppressed method from the exception thrown by the try block.

Classes That Implement the AutoCloseable or Closeable Interface

See the Javadoc of the AutoCloseable[1] and Closeable[2] interfaces for a list of classes that implement either of these interfaces. The Closeable interface extends the AutoCloseable interface. The close method of the Closeable interface throws exceptions of type IOException, while the close method of the AutoCloseable interface throws exceptions of type Exception. Consequently, subclasses of the AutoCloseable interface can override this behavior of the close method to throw specialized exceptions, such as IOException, or no exception at all.

Putting It All Together

The previous sections described how to construct the try, catch, and finally code blocks for the writeList method in the ListOfNumbers class. Now let's walk through the code and investigate what can happen.

When all the components are put together, the writeList method resembles the following:

```
public void writeList() {
    PrintWriter out = null;

    try {
        System.out.println("Entering" + " try statement");

        out = new PrintWriter(new FileWriter("OutFile.txt"));
        for (int i = 0; i < SIZE; i++)
            out.println("Value at: " + i + " = " + vector.elementAt(i));

    } catch (ArrayIndexOutOfBoundsException e) {
        System.err.println("Caught ArrayIndexOutOfBoundsException: "
                            + e.getMessage());

    } catch (IOException e) {
        System.err.println("Caught IOException: " + e.getMessage());

    } finally {
        if (out != null) {
```

---

1. 7/docs/api/java/lang/AutoCloseable.html

2. 7/docs/api/java/io/Closeable.html

```
                System.out.println("Closing PrintWriter");
                out.close();
        }
        else {
            System.out.println("PrintWriter not open");
        }
    }
}
```

As mentioned previously, this method's `try` block has three different exit possibilities. Here are two of them:

1. Code in the `try` statement fails and throws an exception. This could be an `IOException` caused by the new `FileWriter` statement or an `ArrayIndexOutOfBoundsException` caused by a wrong index value in the `for` loop.
2. Everything succeeds and the `try` statement exits normally.

Let's look at what happens in the `writeList` method during these two exit possibilities.

Scenario 1: An Exception Occurs

The statement that creates a `FileWriter` can fail for a number of reasons. For example, the constructor for the `FileWriter` throws an `IOException` if the program cannot create or write to the file indicated.

When `FileWriter` throws an `IOException`, the runtime system immediately stops executing the `try` block; method calls being executed are not completed. The runtime system then starts searching at the top of the method call stack for an appropriate exception handler. In this example, when the `IOException` occurs, the `FileWriter` constructor is at the top of the call stack. However, the `FileWriter` constructor doesn't have an appropriate exception handler, so the runtime system checks the next method—the `writeList` method—in the method call stack. The `writeList` method has two exception handlers: one for `IOException` and one for `ArrayIndexOutOfBoundsException`.

The runtime system checks `writeList`'s handlers in the order in which they appear after the `try` statement. The argument to the first exception handler is `ArrayIndexOutOfBoundsException`. This does not match the type of exception thrown, so the runtime system checks the next exception handler—`IOException`. This matches the type of exception that was thrown, so the runtime system ends its search for an appropriate exception handler. Now that the runtime has found an appropriate handler, the code in that `catch` block is executed.

After the exception handler executes, the runtime system passes control to the `finally` block. Code in the `finally` block executes regardless of the exception caught above it. In this scenario, the `FileWriter` was never opened and doesn't need to be closed. After the `finally` block finishes executing, the program continues with the first statement after the `finally` block.

Here's the complete output from the `ListOfNumbers` program that appears when an `IOException` is thrown:

```
Entering try statement
Caught IOException: OutFile.txt
PrintWriter not open
```

The boldface code in the following listing shows the statements that get executed during this scenario:

```
public void writeList() {
    PrintWriter out = null;

    try {
        System.out.println("Entering try statement");
        out = new PrintWriter(new FileWriter("OutFile.txt"));
        for (int i = 0; i < SIZE; i++)
            out.println("Value at: " + i + " = " + vector.elementAt(i));

    } catch (ArrayIndexOutOfBoundsException e) {
        System.err.println("Caught ArrayIndexOutOfBoundsException: "
                            + e.getMessage());

    } catch (IOException e) {
        System.err.println("Caught IOException: " + e.getMessage());
    } finally {
        if (out != null) {
            System.out.println("Closing PrintWriter");
            out.close();
        }
        else {
            System.out.println("PrintWriter not open");
        }
    }
}
```

Scenario 2: The try Block Exits Normally

In this scenario, all the statements within the scope of the `try` block execute successfully and throw no exceptions. Execution falls off the end of the `try` block, and the runtime system passes control to the `finally` block. Because everything was successful, the `PrintWriter` is open when control reaches the `finally` block, which closes the `PrintWriter`. Again, after the `finally` block finishes executing, the program continues with the first statement after the `finally` block.

Here is the output from the `ListOfNumbers` program when no exceptions are thrown:

```
Entering try statement
Closing PrintWriter
```

The boldface code in the following sample shows the statements that get executed during this scenario:

```
public void writeList() {
    PrintWriter out = null;
    try {
        System.out.println("Entering try statement");
        out = new PrintWriter(new FileWriter("OutFile.txt"));
        for (int i = 0; i < SIZE; i++)
            out.println("Value at: " + i + " = " + vector.elementAt(i));

    } catch (ArrayIndexOutOfBoundsException e) {
        System.err.println("Caught ArrayIndexOutOfBoundsException: "
                            + e.getMessage());

    } catch (IOException e) {
        System.err.println("Caught IOException: " + e.getMessage());

    } finally {
        if (out != null) {
            System.out.println("Closing PrintWriter");
            out.close();
        }
        else {
            System.out.println("PrintWriter not open");
        }
    }
}
```

Specifying the Exceptions Thrown by a Method

The previous section showed how to write an exception handler for the writeList method in the ListOfNumbers class. Sometimes it's appropriate for code to catch exceptions that can occur within it. In other cases, however, it's better to let a method further up the call stack handle the exception. For example, if you were providing the ListOfNumbers class as part of a package of classes, you probably couldn't anticipate the needs of all the users of your package. In this case, it's better to *not* catch the exception and allow a method further up the call stack to handle it.

If the writeList method doesn't catch the checked exceptions that can occur within it, the writeList method must specify that it can throw these exceptions. Let's modify the original writeList method to specify the exceptions it can throw instead of catching them. As a reminder, here's the original version of the writeList method that won't compile:

```
// Note: This method won't compile by design!
public void writeList() {
```

```
        PrintWriter out = new PrintWriter(new FileWriter("OutFile.txt"));
        for (int i = 0; i < SIZE; i++) {
            out.println("Value at: " + i + " = " + vector.elementAt(i));
        }
        out.close();
    }
```

To specify that `writeList` can throw two exceptions, add a `throws` clause to the method declaration for the `writeList` method. The `throws` clause comprises the `throws` keyword followed by a comma-separated list of all the exceptions thrown by that method. The clause goes after the method name and argument list and before the brace that defines the scope of the method. Here's an example:

```
public void writeList() throws IOException, ArrayIndexOutOfBoundsException {
```

Remember that `ArrayIndexOutOfBoundsException` is an unchecked exception; including it in the `throws` clause is not mandatory. You could just write the following:

```
public void writeList() throws IOException {
```

How to Throw Exceptions

Before you can catch an exception, some code somewhere must throw one. Any code can throw an exception: your code, code from a package written by someone else (e.g., the packages that come with the Java platform), or the Java runtime environment. Regardless of what throws the exception, it's always thrown with the `throw` statement.

As you have probably noticed, the Java platform provides numerous exception classes. All the classes are descendants of the `Throwable`[3] class, and they all allow programs to differentiate between the various types of exceptions that can occur during the execution of a program.

You can also create your own exception classes to represent problems that can occur within the classes you write. In fact, if you are a package developer, you might need to create your own set of exception classes to allow users to differentiate between errors that can occur in your package and errors that can occur in the Java platform or other packages.

You can also create *chained* exceptions. For more information, see the "Chained Exceptions" section.

3. `7/docs/api/java/lang/Throwable.html`

The throw Statement

All methods use the `throw` statement to throw an exception. The `throw` statement requires a single argument: a throwable object. *Throwable objects* are instances of any subclass of the `Throwable` class. Here's an example of a `throw` statement:

```
throw someThrowableObject;
```

Let's look at the `throw` statement in context. The following pop method is taken from a class that implements a common stack object. The method removes the top element from the stack and returns the object:

```
public Object pop() {
    Object obj;

    if (size == 0) {
        throw new EmptyStackException();
    }

    obj = objectAt(size - 1);
    setObjectAt(size - 1, null);
    size--;
    return obj;
}
```

The pop method checks to see whether any elements are on the stack. If the stack is empty (i.e., its size equals zero), pop instantiates a new `EmptyStackException` object (a member of `java.util`) and throws it. The "Creating Exception Classes" section in this chapter explains how to create your own exception classes. For now, all you need to remember is that you can throw only objects that inherit from the `java.lang.Throwable` class.

Note that the declaration of the pop method does not contain a `throws` clause. `EmptyStackException` is not a checked exception, so pop is not required to state that it might occur.

Throwable Class and Its Subclasses

The objects that inherit from the `Throwable` class include direct descendants (objects that inherit directly from the `Throwable` class) and indirect descendants (objects that inherit from children or grandchildren of the `Throwable` class). Figure 9.3 illustrates the class hierarchy of the `Throwable` class and its most significant

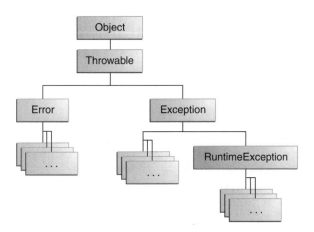

Figure 9.3 The Throwable Class

subclasses. As you can see, `Throwable` has two direct descendants: `Error`[4] and `Exception`.[5]

Error Class

When a dynamic linking failure or other hard failure in the Java VM occurs, the virtual machine throws an error. Simple programs typically do *not* catch or throw errors.

Exception Class

Most programs throw and catch objects that derive from the `Exception` class. An exception indicates that a problem occurred, but it is not a serious system problem. Most programs you write will throw and catch exceptions as opposed to errors.

The Java platform defines the many descendants of the `Exception` class. These descendants indicate various types of exceptions that can occur. For example, `IllegalAccessException` signals that a particular method could not be found, and `NegativeArraySizeException` indicates that a program attempted to create an array with a negative size.

One `Exception` subclass, `RuntimeException`, is reserved for exceptions that indicate incorrect use of an API. An example of a runtime exception is

---

4. 7/docs/api/java/lang/Error.html
5. 7/docs/api/java/lang/Exception.html

NullPointerException, which occurs when a method tries to access a member of an object through a null reference. The "Unchecked Exceptions: The Controversy" section later in this chapter discusses why most applications shouldn't throw runtime exceptions or subclass RuntimeException.

Chained Exceptions

An application often responds to an exception by throwing another exception. In effect, the first exception *causes* the second exception. It can be very helpful to know when one exception causes another. *Chained exceptions* help the programmer do this.

The following are the methods and constructors in Throwable that support chained exceptions:

```
Throwable getCause()
Throwable initCause(Throwable)
Throwable(String, Throwable)
Throwable(Throwable)
```

The Throwable argument to initCause and the Throwable constructors is the exception that caused the current exception; getCause returns the exception that caused the current exception, and initCause sets the current exception's cause.

The following example shows how to use a chained exception:

```
try {

} catch (IOException e) {
    throw new SampleException("Other IOException", e);
}
```

In this example, when an IOException is caught, a new SampleException exception is created with the original cause attached, and the chain of exceptions is thrown up to the next higher level exception handler.

Accessing Stack Trace Information

Now suppose that the higher-level exception handler wants to dump the stack trace in its own format.

Definition

A *stack trace* provides information on the execution history of the current thread and lists the names of the classes and methods that were called at the point when the exception occurred. A stack trace is a useful debugging tool that you'll normally take advantage of when an exception has been thrown.

The following code shows how to call the `getStackTrace` method on the exception object:

```
catch (Exception cause) {
    StackTraceElement elements[] = cause.getStackTrace();
    for (int i = 0, n = elements.length; i < n; i++) {
        System.err.println(elements[i].getFileName()
            + ":" + elements[i].getLineNumber()
            + ">> "
            + elements[i].getMethodName() + "()");
    }
}
```

Logging API

The next code snippet logs where an exception occurred from within the `catch` block. However, rather than manually parsing the stack trace and sending the output to `System.err()`, it sends the output to a file using the logging facility in the `java.util.logging`[6] package:

```
try {
    Handler handler = new FileHandler("OutFile.log");
    Logger.getLogger("").addHandler(handler);

} catch (IOException e) {
    Logger logger = Logger.getLogger("package.name");
    StackTraceElement elements[] = e.getStackTrace();
    for (int i = 0, n = elements.length; i < n; i++) {
        logger.log(Level.WARNING, elements[i].getMethodName());
    }
}
```

Creating Exception Classes

When faced with choosing the type of exception to throw, you can either use one written by someone else or you can write one of your own. The Java platform provides a lot of exception classes you can use, but you should write your own exception classes if you answer *yes* to any of the following questions:

- Do you need an exception type that isn't represented in the Java platform?
- Would it help users if they could differentiate your exceptions from those thrown by classes written by other vendors?
- Does your code throw more than one related exception?
- If you use someone else's exceptions, will users have access to those exceptions?
- Should your package be independent and self-contained?

---

6. `7/docs/api/java/util/logging/package-summary.html`

An Example

Suppose you are writing a linked list class. The class supports the following methods, among others:

- `objectAt(int n)`—Returns the object in the nth position in the list and throws an exception if the argument is less than zero or more than the number of objects currently in the list
- `firstObject()`—Returns the first object in the list and throws an exception if the list contains no objects
- `indexOf(Object o)`—Searches the list for the specified `Object`, returns its position in the list, and throws an exception if the object passed into the method is not in the list

The linked list class can throw multiple exceptions, and it would be convenient to be able to catch all exceptions thrown by the linked list with one exception handler. Also, if you plan to distribute your linked list in a package, all related code should be packaged together. Thus the linked list should provide its own set of exception classes. Figure 9.4 illustrates one possible class hierarchy for the exceptions thrown by the linked list.

Choosing a Superclass

Any `Exception` subclass can be used as the parent class of `LinkedListException`. However, a quick perusal of those subclasses shows that they are inappropriate because they are either too specialized or completely unrelated to `LinkedListException`. Therefore, the parent class of `LinkedListException` should be `Exception`.

Most applets and applications you write will throw objects that are exceptions. Errors are normally used for serious, hard errors in the system, such as those that prevent the Java VM from running.

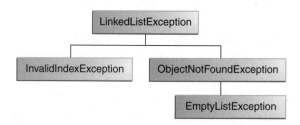

Figure 9.4 Example Exception Class Hierarchy

> **Note**
> For readable code, it's good practice to append the string `Exception` to the names of all classes that inherit (directly or indirectly) from the `Exception` class.

Unchecked Exceptions: The Controversy

Because the Java programming language does not require methods to catch or specify unchecked exceptions (`RuntimeException`, `Error`, and their subclasses), programmers may be tempted to write code that throws only unchecked exceptions or to make all their exception subclasses inherit from `RuntimeException`. Both of these shortcuts allow programmers to write code without bothering with compiler errors and without bothering to specify or to catch any exceptions. Although this may seem convenient to the programmer, it sidesteps the intent of the catch or specify requirement and can cause problems for others using your classes.

Why did the designers of the Java programming language decide to force a method to specify all uncaught checked exceptions that can be thrown within its scope? Any exception that can be thrown by a method is part of the method's public programming interface. Those who call a method must know about the exceptions that a method can throw so that they can decide what to do about them. These exceptions are as much a part of that method's programming interface as its parameters and `return` value.

This leads us to another question: if it's so good to document a method's API, including the exceptions it can throw, why not specify runtime exceptions too? Runtime exceptions represent problems that are the result of a programming problem, and as such, the API client code cannot reasonably be expected to recover from them or handle them in any way. Such problems include arithmetic exceptions, such as dividing by zero; pointer exceptions, such as trying to access an object through a null reference; and indexing exceptions, such as attempting to access an array element through an index that is too large or too small.

Runtime exceptions can occur anywhere in a program, and in a typical one, they can be very numerous. Having to add runtime exceptions in every method declaration would reduce a program's clarity. Thus the compiler does not require that you catch or specify runtime exceptions (although you can).

One case where it is common practice to throw a `RuntimeException` is when the user calls a method incorrectly. For example, a method can check if one of its arguments is incorrectly `null`. If an argument is `null`, the method might throw a `NullPointerException`, which is an unchecked exception.

Generally speaking, do not throw a `RuntimeException` or create a subclass of `RuntimeException` simply because you don't want to be bothered with specifying the exceptions your methods can throw. Here's the bottom line: If a client can reasonably be expected to recover from an exception, make it a checked exception. If a client cannot do anything to recover from the exception, make it an unchecked exception.

Advantages of Exceptions

Now that you know what exceptions are and how to use them, it's time to learn the advantages of using exceptions in your programs.

Advantage 1: Separating Error-Handling Code from "Regular" Code

Exceptions provide programmers with the means to sort out the details of what to do when something out of the ordinary happens in the main logic of a program. In traditional programming, error detection, reporting, and handling often lead to confusing spaghetti code. For example, consider the pseudocode method here that reads an entire file into memory:

```
readFile {
    open the file;
    determine its size;
    allocate that much memory;
    read the file into memory;
    close the file;
}
```

At first glance, this function seems simple enough, but it ignores all the following potential errors:

- What happens if the file can't be opened?
- What happens if the length of the file can't be determined?
- What happens if enough memory can't be allocated?
- What happens if the read fails?
- What happens if the file can't be closed?

To handle such cases, the `readFile` function must have more code for error detection, reporting, and handling. Here is an example of what the function might look like:

```
errorCodeType readFile {
    initialize errorCode = 0;

    open the file;
```

```
    if (theFileIsOpen) {
        determine the length of the file;
        if (gotTheFileLength) {
            allocate that much memory;
            if (gotEnoughMemory) {
                read the file into memory;
                if (readFailed) {
                    errorCode = -1;
                }
            } else {
                errorCode = -2;
            }
        } else {
            errorCode = -3;
        }
        close the file;
        if (theFileDidntClose && errorCode == 0) {
            errorCode = -4;
        } else {
            errorCode = errorCode and -4;
        }
    } else {
        errorCode = -5;
    }
    return errorCode;
}
```

There's so much error detection, reporting, and returning here that the original seven lines of code are lost in the clutter. Worse yet, the logical flow of the code has also been lost, thus making it difficult to tell whether the code is doing the right thing. Is the file really being closed if the function fails to allocate enough memory? It's even more difficult to ensure that the code continues to do the right thing when you modify the method three months after writing it. Many programmers solve this problem by simply ignoring it: errors are reported when their programs crash.

Exceptions enable you to write the main flow of your code and to deal with the exceptional cases elsewhere. If the readFile function used exceptions instead of traditional error-management techniques, it would look more like the following:

```
readFile {
    try {
        open the file;
        determine its size;
        allocate that much memory;
        read the file into memory;
        close the file;
    } catch (fileOpenFailed) {
        doSomething;
    } catch (sizeDeterminationFailed) {
        doSomething;
    } catch (memoryAllocationFailed) {
        doSomething;
    } catch (readFailed) {
        doSomething;
```

```
        } catch (fileCloseFailed) {
            doSomething;
        }
}
```

Note that exceptions don't spare you the effort of doing the work of detecting, reporting, and handling errors, but they do help you organize the work more effectively.

Advantage 2: Propagating Errors Up the Call Stack

A second advantage of exceptions is the ability to propagate error reporting up the call stack of methods. Suppose that the readFile method is the fourth method in a series of nested method calls made by the main program: method1 calls method2, which calls method3, which finally calls readFile:

```
method1 {
    call method2;
}

method2 {
    call method3;
}

method3 {
    call readFile;
}
```

Also suppose that method1 is the only method interested in the errors that might occur within readFile. Traditional error-notification techniques force method2 and method3 to propagate the error codes returned by readFile up the call stack until the error codes finally reach method1—the only method that is interested in them:

```
method1 {
    errorCodeType error;
    error = call method2;
    if (error)
        doErrorProcessing;
    else
        proceed;
}

errorCodeType method2 {
    errorCodeType error;
    error = call method3;
    if (error)
        return error;
    else
        proceed;
```

```
    }

errorCodeType method3 {
    errorCodeType error;
    error = call readFile;
    if (error)
        return error;
    else
        proceed;
}
```

Recall that the Java runtime environment searches backward through the call stack to find any methods that are interested in handling a particular exception. A method can duck any exceptions thrown within it, thereby allowing a method further up the call stack to catch it. Hence only the methods that care about errors have to worry about detecting errors:

```
method1 {
    try {
        call method2;
    } catch (exception e) {
        doErrorProcessing;
    }
}

method2 throws exception {
    call method3;
}

method3 throws exception {
    call readFile;
}
```

However, as the pseudocode shows, ducking an exception requires some effort on the part of the middleman methods. Any checked exceptions that can be thrown within a method must be specified in its throws clause.

Advantage 3: Grouping and Differentiating Error Types

Because all exceptions thrown within a program are objects, the grouping or categorizing of exceptions is a natural outcome of the class hierarchy. An example of a group of related exception classes in the Java platform are those defined in java.io—IOException and its descendants. IOException is the most general and represents any type of error that can occur when performing I/O. Its descendants represent more specific errors. For example, FileNotFoundException means that a file could not be located on disk.

A method can write specific handlers that can handle a very specific exception. The `FileNotFoundException` class has no descendants, so the following handler can handle only one type of exception:

```
catch (FileNotFoundException e) {
    . . .
}
```

A method can catch an exception based on its group or general type by specifying any of the exception's superclasses in the `catch` statement. For example, to catch all I/O exceptions, regardless of their specific type, an exception handler specifies an `IOException` argument:

```
catch (IOException e) {
    . . .
}
```

This handler will be able to catch all I/O exceptions, including `FileNotFound-Exception`, `EOFException`, and so on. You can find details about what occurred by querying the argument passed to the exception handler. For example, use the following to print the stack trace:

```
catch (IOException e) {
    // Output goes to System.err.
    e.printStackTrace();
    // Send trace to stdout.
    e.printStackTrace(System.out);
}
```

You could even set up an exception handler that handles any exception with the following handler:

```
// A (too) general exception handler
catch (Exception e) {
    . . .
}
```

The `Exception` class is close to the top of the `Throwable` class hierarchy. Therefore, this handler will catch many other exceptions in addition to those that the handler is intended to catch. You may want to handle exceptions this way if all you want your program to do, for example, is print out an error message for the user and then exit.

In most situations, however, you want exception handlers to be as specific as possible. The reason is that the first thing a handler must do is determine which type of exception occurred before it can decide on the best recovery strategy. In effect, by not catching specific errors, the handler must accommodate any possibility. Exception handlers that are too general can make code more error prone by catching and handling exceptions that weren't anticipated by the programmer and for which the handler was not intended.

As noted, you can create groups of exceptions and handle exceptions in a general fashion, or you can use the specific exception type to differentiate exceptions and handle exceptions in an exact fashion.

Summary of Exceptions

A program can use exceptions to indicate that an error occurred. To throw an exception, use the `throw` statement and provide it with an exception object—a descendant of `Throwable`—to provide information about the specific error that occurred. A method that throws an uncaught, checked exception must include a `throws` clause in its declaration.

A program can catch exceptions by using a combination of the `try`, `catch`, and `finally` blocks:

- The `try` block identifies a block of code in which an exception can occur.
- The `catch` block identifies a block of code, known as an *exception handler*, that can handle a particular type of exception.
- The `finally` block identifies a block of code that is guaranteed to execute and is the right place to close files, recover resources, and otherwise clean up after the code enclosed in the `try` block.

The `try` statement should contain at least one `catch` block or a `finally` block and may have multiple `catch` blocks.

The class of the exception object indicates the type of exception thrown. The exception object can contain further information about the error, including an error message. With exception chaining, an exception can point to the exception that caused it, which can in turn point to the exception that caused it, and so on.

Questions and Exercises: Exceptions

Questions

1. Is the following code legal?

```
try {

} finally {

}
```

2. What exception types can be caught by the following handler?

```
catch (Exception e) {

}
```

What is wrong with using this type of exception handler?

3. Is there anything wrong with the following exception handler as written? Will this code compile?

```
try {

} catch (Exception e) {

} catch (ArithmeticException a) {

}
```

4. Match each situation in the first list with an item in the second list.

a. `int[] A;`
   `A[0] = 0;`

b. The Java VM starts running your program, but it can't find the Java platform classes. (The Java platform classes reside in `classes.zip` or `rt.jar`.)

c. A program is reading a stream and reaches the end of stream marker.

d. Before closing the stream and after reaching the end of stream marker, a program tries to read the stream again.

___ error

___ checked exception

___ compile error

___ no exception

Exercises

1. Add a `readList` method to `ListOfNumbers.java`. This method should read in `int` values from a file, print each value, and append them to the end of the vector. You should catch all appropriate errors. You will also need a text file containing numbers to read in.

2. Modify the following `cat` method so that it will compile:

```
public static void cat(File file) {
    RandomAccessFile input = null;
    String line = null;

    try {
        input = new RandomAccessFile(file, "r");
        while ((line = input.readLine()) != null) {
```

```
                System.out.println(line);
            }
            return;
        } finally {
            if (input != null) {
                input.close();
            }
        }
    }
}
```

Answers

You can find answers to these questions and exercises at `http://docs.oracle.com/ javase/tutorial/essential/exceptions/QandE/answers.html`.

9

Chapter Contents

This chapter covers the Java platform classes used for basic I/O. It first focuses on I/O streams, a powerful concept that greatly simplifies I/O operations. The chapter also looks at serialization, which lets a program write whole objects out to streams and read them back again. Then the chapter looks at file I/O and file system operations, including random access files.

Most of the classes covered in the section "I/O Streams" are in the `java.io` package. Most of the classes covered in the section "File I/O" are in the `java.nio.file` package.

I/O Streams

An *I/O stream* represents an input source or an output destination. A stream can represent many different kinds of sources and destinations, including disk files, devices, other programs, and memory arrays.

Streams support many different kinds of data, including simple bytes, primitive data types, localized characters, and objects. Some streams simply pass on data; others manipulate and transform the data in useful ways.

No matter how they work internally, all streams present the same simple model to programs that use them: a stream is a sequence of data. A program uses an *input stream* to read data from a source, one item at a time, as indicated in Figure 10.1. A program uses an *output stream* to write data to a destination, one item at time, as indicated in Figure 10.2. In this chapter, we'll see streams that can handle all kinds of data, from primitive values to advanced objects.

The data source and data destination depicted in the figures can be anything that holds, generates, or consumes data. Obviously this includes disk files, but a source or destination can also be another program, a peripheral device, a network socket, or an array.

In the next section, we'll use the most basic kind of streams, *byte streams*, to demonstrate the common operations of I/O stream. For sample input, we'll use the example file xanadu.txt, which contains the following verse:

```
In Xanadu did Kubla Khan
A stately pleasure-dome decree:
Where Alph, the sacred river, ran
Through caverns measureless to man
Down to a sunless sea.
```

10

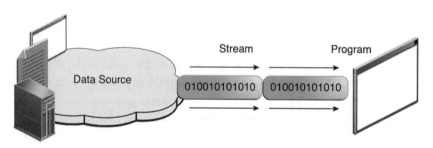

Figure 10.1 Reading Information into a Program

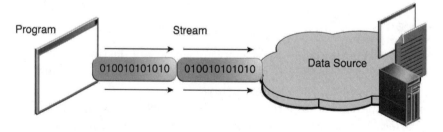

Figure 10.2 Writing Information from a Program

Byte Streams

Programs use byte streams to perform the input and output of 8-bit bytes. All byte stream classes are descended from InputStream[1] and OutputStream.[2]

There are many byte stream classes. To demonstrate how byte streams work, we'll focus on the file I/O byte streams, FileInputStream[3] and FileOutputStream.[4] Other kinds of byte streams are used in pretty much the same way; they differ mainly in the way they are constructed.

Using Byte Streams

We'll explore FileInputStream and FileOutputStream by examining an example program named CopyBytes, which uses byte streams to copy xanadu.txt, one byte at a time:

```java
import java.io.FileInputStream;
import java.io.FileOutputStream;
import java.io.IOException;

public class CopyBytes {
    public static void main(String[] args) throws IOException {

        FileInputStream in = null;
        FileOutputStream out = null;

        try {
            in = new FileInputStream("xanadu.txt");
            out = new FileOutputStream("outagain.txt");
            int c;

            while ((c = in.read()) != -1) {
                out.write(c);
            }
        } finally {
            if (in != null) {
                in.close();
            }
            if (out != null) {
                out.close();
            }
        }
    }
}
```

10

1. 7/docs/api/java/io/InputStream.html
2. 7/docs/api/java/io/OutputStream.html
3. 7/docs/api/java/io/FileInputStream.html
4. 7/docs/api/java/io/FileOutputStream.html

CopyBytes spends most of its time in a simple loop that reads the input stream and writes the output stream, one byte at a time, as shown in Figure 10.3. Notice that read() returns an int value. If the input is a stream of bytes, why doesn't read() return a byte value? Using an int variable as a return type allows read() to use −1 to indicate that it has reached the end of the stream.

Always Close Streams

Closing a stream when it's no longer needed is very important—so important that CopyBytes uses a finally block to guarantee that both streams will be closed even if an error occurs. This practice helps avoid serious resource leaks.

One possible error is that CopyBytes was unable to open one or both files. When that happens, the stream variable corresponding to the file never changes from its initial null value. That's why CopyBytes makes sure that each stream variable contains an object reference before invoking close.

When Not to Use Byte Streams

CopyBytes seems like a normal program, but it actually represents a kind of low-level I/O that you should avoid. Since xanadu.txt contains character data, the best approach is to use character streams, as discussed in the next section. There are also streams for more complicated data types. Byte streams should only be used for the most primitive I/O.

So why talk about byte streams? Because all other stream types are built on byte streams.

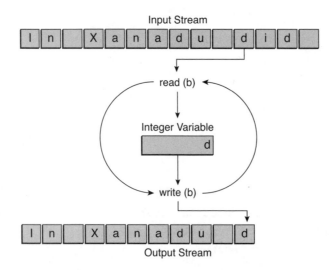

Figure 10.3 Simple Byte Stream Input and Output

Character Streams

The Java platform stores character values using Unicode conventions. Character stream I/O automatically translates this internal format to and from the local character set. In Western locales, the local character set is usually an 8-bit superset of ASCII.

For most applications, I/O with character streams is no more complicated than I/O with byte streams. Input and output done with stream classes automatically translates to and from the local character set. A program that uses character streams in place of byte streams automatically adapts to the local character set and is ready for internationalization—all without extra effort by the programmer.

If internationalization isn't a priority, you can simply use the character stream classes without paying much attention to character set issues. Later, if internationalization becomes a priority, your program can be adapted without extensive recoding.

Using Character Streams

All character stream classes are descended from Reader[5] and Writer.[6] As with byte streams, there are character stream classes that specialize in file I/O: FileReader[7] and FileWriter.[8] The CopyCharacters example illustrates these classes:

```java
import java.io.FileReader;
import java.io.FileWriter;
import java.io.IOException;

public class CopyCharacters {
    public static void main(String[] args) throws IOException {

        FileReader inputStream = null;
        FileWriter outputStream = null;

        try {
            inputStream = new FileReader("xanadu.txt");
            outputStream = new FileWriter("characteroutput.txt");

            int c;
            while ((c = inputStream.read()) != -1) {
                outputStream.write(c);
            }
        } finally {
            if (inputStream != null) {
                inputStream.close();
            }
```

---

5. 7/docs/api/java/io/Reader.html

6. 7/docs/api/java/io/Writer.html

7. 7/docs/api/java/io/FileReader.html

8. 7/docs/api/java/io/FileWriter.html

```
                    if (outputStream != null) {
                        outputStream.close();
                    }
                }
            }
        }
```

CopyCharacters is very similar to CopyBytes. The most important difference is that CopyCharacters uses FileReader and FileWriter for input and output in place of FileInputStream and FileOutputStream. Notice that both Copy-Bytes and CopyCharacters use an int variable to read to and write from. However, in CopyCharacters, the int variable holds a character value in its last 16 bits; in CopyBytes, the int variable holds a byte value in its last 8 bits.

Character Streams That Use Byte Streams

Character streams are often "wrappers" for byte streams. The character stream uses the byte stream to perform the physical I/O, while the character stream handles translation between characters and bytes. FileReader, for example, uses FileInputStream, while FileWriter uses FileOutputStream.

There are two general-purpose byte-to-character "bridge" streams: Input-StreamReader[9] and OutputStreamWriter.[10] Use them to create character streams when no prepackaged character stream classes meet your needs.

Line-Oriented I/O

Character I/O usually occurs in bigger units rather than single characters. One common unit is the line: a string of characters with a line terminator at the end. A line terminator can be a carriage-return/line-feed sequence (\r\n), a single carriage return (\r), or a single line feed ("\n"). Supporting all possible line terminators allows programs to read text files created on any of the widely used operating systems.

Let's modify the CopyCharacters example to use line-oriented I/O. To do this, we have to use two classes we haven't seen before, BufferedReader[11] and Print-Writer.[12] We'll explore these classes in greater depth in the "Buffered I/O Methods for Text Files" and "Formatting" sections later in the chapter. Right now, we're just interested in their support for line-oriented I/O.

---

9.   7/docs/api/java/io/InputStreamReader.html

10. 7/docs/api/java/io/OutputStreamWriter.html

11. 7/docs/api/java/io/BufferedReader.html

12. 7/docs/api/java/io/PrintWriter.html

The `CopyLines` example invokes `BufferedReader.readLine` and `Print-Writer.println` to do input and output one line at a time:

```java
import java.io.FileReader;
import java.io.FileWriter;
import java.io.BufferedReader;
import java.io.PrintWriter;
import java.io.IOException;

public class CopyLines {
    public static void main(String[] args) throws IOException {

        BufferedReader inputStream = null;
        PrintWriter outputStream = null;

        try {
            inputStream = new BufferedReader(new FileReader("xanadu.txt"));
            outputStream = new PrintWriter(new FileWriter("characteroutput.txt"));

            String l;
            while ((l = inputStream.readLine()) != null) {
                outputStream.println(l);
            }
        } finally {
            if (inputStream != null) {
                inputStream.close();
            }
            if (outputStream != null) {
                outputStream.close();
            }
        }
    }
}
```

Invoking `readLine` returns a line of text with the line. `CopyLines` outputs each line using `println`, which appends the line terminator for the current operating system. This might not be the same line terminator that was used in the input file.

There are many ways to structure text input and output beyond characters and lines. For more information, see the "Scanning and Formatting" section later in this chapter.

Buffered Streams

Most of the examples we've seen so far use *unbuffered* I/O. This means each read or write request is handled directly by the underlying operating system. This can make a program much less efficient, since each such request often triggers disk access, network activity, or some other operation that is relatively expensive.

To reduce this kind of overhead, the Java platform implements *buffered* I/O streams. Buffered input streams read data from a memory area known as a *buffer*;

the native input Application Programming Interface (API) is called only when the buffer is empty. Similarly, buffered output streams write data to a buffer, and the native output API is called only when the buffer is full.

A program can convert an unbuffered stream into a buffered stream using the wrapping idiom we've used several times now, where the unbuffered stream object is passed to the constructor for a buffered stream class. Here's how you might modify the constructor invocations in the `CopyCharacters` example to use buffered I/O:

```
inputStream = new BufferedReader(new FileReader("xanadu.txt"));
outputStream = new BufferedWriter(new FileWriter("characteroutput.txt"));
```

There are four buffered stream classes used to wrap unbuffered streams: `Buff-eredInputStream`[13] and `BufferedOutputStream`[14] create buffered byte streams, while `BufferedReader`[15] and `BufferedWriter`[16] create buffered character streams.

Flushing Buffered Streams

It often makes sense to write out a buffer at critical points, without waiting for it to fill. This is known as *flushing* the buffer.

Some buffered output classes support *autoflush*, specified by an optional constructor argument. When autoflush is enabled, certain key events cause the buffer to be flushed. For example, an autoflush `PrintWriter` object flushes the buffer on every invocation of `println` or `format`. See the section "Formatting" later in this chapter for more on these methods.

To flush a stream manually, invoke its flush method. The flush method is valid on any output stream but has no effect unless the stream is buffered.

Scanning and Formatting

Programming I/O often involves translating to and from the neatly formatted data humans like to work with. To assist you with these chores, the Java platform provides two APIs: The scanner API breaks input into individual tokens associated with bits of data. The formatting API assembles data into nicely formatted, user-friendly form.

---

13. 7/docs/api/java/io/BufferedInputStream.html
14. 7/docs/api/java/io/BufferedOutputStream.html
15. 7/docs/api/java/io/BufferedReader.html
16. 7/docs/api/java/io/BufferedWriter.html

Scanning

Objects of type Scanner[17] are useful for breaking down formatted input into tokens and translating individual tokens according to their data type.

Breaking Input into Tokens

By default, a scanner uses white space to separate tokens. (White space characters include blanks, tabs, and line terminators. For the full list, refer to the documentation for Character.isWhitespace.) To see how scanning works, let's look at ScanXan, a program that reads the individual words in xanadu.txt and prints them out, one per line:

```
import java.io.*;
import java.util.Scanner;

public class ScanXan {
    public static void main(String[] args) throws IOException {

        Scanner s = null;

        try {
            s = new Scanner(new BufferedReader
                        (new FileReader ("xanadu.txt")));

            while (s.hasNext()) {
                System.out.println(s.next());
            }
        } finally {
            if (s != null) {
                s.close();
            }
        }
    }
}
```

10

Notice that ScanXan invokes Scanner's close method when it is done with the scanner object. Even though a scanner is not a stream, you need to close it to indicate that you're done with its underlying stream.

The output of ScanXan looks like this:

```
In
Xanadu
did
Kubla
Khan
A
stately
pleasure-dome
   . . .
```

17. 7/docs/api/java/util/Scanner.html

To use a different token separator, invoke `useDelimiter()`, specifying a regular expression. For example, suppose you wanted the token separator to be a comma, optionally followed by white space. You would invoke the following:

```
s.useDelimiter(",\\s*");
```

Translating Individual Tokens

The `ScanXan` example treats all input tokens as simple `String` values. `Scanner` also supports tokens for all the Java language's primitive types (except for `char`), as well as `BigInteger` and `BigDecimal`. Also, numeric values can use thousands separators. Thus, in a US locale, `Scanner` correctly reads the string `32,767` as representing an integer value.

We have to mention the locale because thousands separators and decimal symbols are locale specific. The following example would not work correctly in all locales if we didn't specify that the scanner should use the US locale. That's not something you usually have to worry about because your input data usually comes from sources that use the same locale as you do.

The `ScanSum` example reads a list of `double` values and adds them up. Here's the source:

```java
import java.io.FileReader;
import java.io.BufferedReader;
import java.io.IOException;
import java.util.Scanner;
import java.util.Locale;

public class ScanSum {
    public static void main(String[] args) throws IOException {

        Scanner s = null;
        double sum = 0;

        try {
            s = new Scanner(new BufferedReader
                        (new FileReader ("usnumbers.txt")));
            s.useLocale(Locale.US);

            while (s.hasNext()) {
                if (s.hasNextDouble()) {
                    sum += s.nextDouble();
                } else {
                    s.next();
                }
            }
        } finally {
            s.close();
        }

        System.out.println(sum);
    }
}
```

And here's the sample input file, `usnumbers.txt`:

```
8.5
32,767
3.14159
1,000,000.1
```

The output string is `1032778.74159`. The period will be a different character in some locales because `System.out` is a `PrintStream` object and that class doesn't provide a way to override the default locale. We could override the locale for the whole program—or we could just use formatting, as described in the next section.

Formatting

Stream objects that implement formatting are instances of either `PrintWriter`, a character stream class, or `PrintStream`,[18] a byte stream class.

> **Note**
>
> The only `PrintStream` objects you are likely to need are `System.out` and `System.err`. (See the section "I/O from the Command Line" for more on these objects.) When you need to create a formatted output stream, instantiate `PrintWriter`, not `PrintStream`.

10

Like all byte and character stream objects, instances of `PrintStream` and `PrintWriter` implement a standard set of `write` methods for simple byte and character output. In addition, both `PrintStream` and `PrintWriter` implement the same set of methods for converting internal data into formatted output. Two levels of formatting are provided:

- The `print` and `println` methods format individual values in a standard way.
- The `format` method formats almost any number of values based on a format string, with many options for precise formatting.

The print and println Methods

Invoking `print` or `println` outputs a single value after converting the value using the appropriate `toString` method. We can see this in the `Root` example:

```
public class Root {
    public static void main(String[] args) {
        int i = 2;
        double r = Math.sqrt(i);
```

---

18. `7/docs/api/java/io/PrintStream.html`

```
            System.out.print("The square root of ");
            System.out.print(i);
            System.out.print(" is ");
            System.out.print(r);
            System.out.println(".");

            i = 5;
            r = Math.sqrt(i);
            System.out.println("The square root of " + i + " is " + r + ".");
        }
    }
```

Here is the output of Root:

```
The square root of 2 is 1.4142135623730951.
The square root of 5 is 2.23606797749979.
```

The i and r variables are formatted twice: the first time using code in an overload of print, the second time by conversion code automatically generated by the Java compiler, which also utilizes toString. You can format any value this way, but you don't have much control over the results.

The format Method

The format method formats multiple arguments based on a *format string*. The format string consists of static text embedded with *format specifiers*; except for the format specifiers, the format string is output unchanged.

Format strings support many features. In this book, we'll just cover some basics. For a complete description, consult the Java API specification.

The Root2 example formats two values with a single format invocation:

```
public class Root2 {
    public static void main(String[] args) {
        int i = 2;
        double r = Math.sqrt(i);

        System.out.format("The square root of %d is %f.%n", i, r);
    }
}
```

Here is the output:

```
The square root of 2 is 1.414214.
```

All format specifiers (like the three used in this example) begin with a percent symbol (%) and end with a one- or two-character *conversion* that specifies the kind of formatted output being generated. The three conversions used here are as follows:

- d formats an integer value as a decimal value.
- f formats a floating point value as a decimal value.
- n outputs a platform-specific line terminator.

Here are some other conversions:

- x formats an integer as a hexadecimal value.
- s formats any value as a string.
- tB formats an integer as a locale-specific month name.

In addition, there are also many other conversions.

> **Note**
>
> Except for %% and %n, all format specifiers must match an argument. If they don't, an exception is thrown.
>
> In the Java programming language, the \n escape always generates the line-feed character (\u000A). Don't use \n unless you specifically want a line-feed character. To get the correct line separator for the local platform, use %n.

In addition to the conversion, a format specifier can contain several additional elements that further customize the formatted output. Here's an example, Format, which uses every possible kind of element:

```
public class Format {
    public static void main(String[] args) {
        System.out.format("%f, %1$+020.10f %n", Math.PI);
    }
}
```

Here's the output:

```
3.141593, +00000003.1415926536
```

The additional elements are all optional. Figure 10.4 shows how the longer specifier breaks down into elements.

The elements must appear in the order shown. Working from the right, the optional elements are as follows:

- *Precision.* For floating point values, this is the mathematical precision of the formatted value. For s and other general conversions, this is the maximum width of the formatted value; the value is right truncated if necessary.

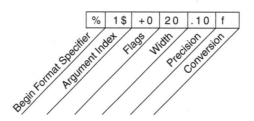

Figure 10.4 Elements of a Format Specifier

- *Width*. This is the minimum width of the formatted value; the value is padded if necessary. By default, the value is left padded with blanks.
- *Flags*. These specify additional formatting options. In the Format example, the + flag specifies that the number should always be formatted with a sign, and the 0 flag specifies that 0 is the padding character. Other flags can specify the use of padding on the right (-) and or locale-specific thousands separators in digits (,). Note that some flags cannot be used with certain other flags or with certain conversions.
- *The argument index*. This allows you to explicitly match a designated argument. You can also specify < to match the same argument as the previous specifier. Thus the example could have said System.out.format("%f, %<+020.10f %n", Math.PI);.

I/O from the Command Line

A program is often run from the command line and interacts with the user in the command-line environment. The Java platform supports this kind of interaction in two ways: through the *standard streams* and the *console*.

Standard Streams

Standard streams are a feature of many operating systems. By default, they read input from the keyboard and write output to the display. They also support I/O on files and between programs, but this feature is controlled by the command-line interpreter, not the program.

The Java platform supports three standard streams: *standard input*, accessed through System.in; *standard output*, accessed through System.out; and *standard error*, accessed through System.err. These objects are defined automatically and do not need to be opened. Standard output and standard error are both for output; having errors output separately allows the user to divert regular output to a file and still be able to read error messages. For more information, refer to the documentation for your command-line interpreter.

You might expect the standard streams to be character streams, but for histori-cal reasons, they are byte streams. `System.out` and `System.err` are defined as `PrintStream`[19] objects. Although it is technically a byte stream, `PrintStream` uti-lizes an internal character stream object to emulate many of the features of char-acter streams.

By contrast, `System.in` is a byte stream with no character-stream features. To use standard input as a character stream, wrap `System.in` in `InputStreamReader`:

```
InputStreamReader cin = new InputStreamReader(System.in);
```

The Console

A more advanced alternative to the standard streams is the console. This is a single, predefined object of type `Console`[20] that has most of the features provided by the standard streams and more. The console is particularly useful for secure password entry. The console object also provides input and output streams that are true char-acter streams through its `reader` and `writer` methods.

Before a program can use the console, it must attempt to retrieve the console object by invoking `System.console()`. If the console object is available, this method returns it. If `System.console` returns `NULL`, then console operations are not permitted, either because the operating system doesn't support them or because the program was launched in a noninteractive environment.

The console object supports secure password entry through its `readPassword` method. This method helps secure password entry in two ways: First, it suppresses echoing, so the password is not visible on the user's screen. Second, `readPassword` returns a character array, not a `String`, so the password can be overwritten, remov-ing it from memory as soon as it is no longer needed.

The `Password` example is a prototype program for changing a user's password. It demonstrates several `Console` methods:

```java
import java.io.Console;
import java.util.Arrays;
import java.io.IOException;

public class Password {

    public static void main (String args[]) throws IOException {

        Console c = System.console();
        if (c == null) {
            System.err.println("No console.");
            System.exit(1);
```

10

---

19. 7/docs/api/java/io/PrintStream.html

20. 7/docs/api/java/io/Console.html

```
        }

        String login = c.readLine("Enter your login: ");
        char [] oldPassword = c.readPassword("Enter your old password: ");

        if (verify(login, oldPassword)) {
            boolean noMatch;
            do {
                char [] newPassword1 = c.readPassword("Enter your new
                    password: ");
                char [] newPassword2 = c.readPassword("Enter new password
                    again: ");
                noMatch = ! Arrays.equals(newPassword1, newPassword2);
                if (noMatch) {
                    c.format("Passwords don't match. Try again.%n");
                } else {
                    change(login, newPassword1);
                    c.format("Password for %s changed.%n", login);
                }
                Arrays.fill(newPassword1, ' ');
                Arrays.fill(newPassword2, ' ');
            } while (noMatch);
        }

        Arrays.fill(oldPassword, ' ');
    }

    // Dummy change method.
    static boolean verify(String login, char[] password) {
        // This method always returns
        // true in this example.
        // Modify this method to verify
        // password according to your rules.
        return true;
    }

    // Dummy change method.
    static void change(String login, char[] password) {
        // Modify this method to change
        // password according to your rules.
    }
}
```

The Password class follows these steps:

1. Attempt to retrieve the console object. If the object is not available, abort.

2. Invoke Console.readLine to prompt for and read the user's login name.

3. Invoke Console.readPassword to prompt for and read the user's existing password.

4. Invoke verify to confirm that the user is authorized to change the password. (In this example, verify is a dummy method that always returns true.)

5. Repeat the following steps until the user enters the same password twice:

   a. Invoke Console.readPassword twice to prompt for and read a new password.

> b. If the user entered the same password both times, invoke change to change it. (Again, change is a dummy method.)
>
> c. Overwrite both passwords with blanks.

6. Overwrite the old password with blanks.

Data Streams

Data streams support binary I/O of primitive data type values (boolean, char, byte, short, int, long, float, and double) as well as String values. All data streams implement either the DataInput[21] interface or the DataOutput[22] interface. This section focuses on the most widely used implementations of these interfaces, DataInputStream[23] and DataOutputStream.[24]

The DataStreams example demonstrates data streams by writing out a set of data records and then reading them in again. Each record consists of three values related to an item on an invoice, as shown in Table 10.1.

Let's examine crucial code in DataStreams. First the program defines some constants containing the name of the data file and the data that will be written to it:

```
static final String dataFile = "invoicedata";

static final double[] prices = { 19.99, 9.99, 15.99, 3.99, 4.99 };
static final int[] units = { 12, 8, 13, 29, 50 };
static final String[] descs = {
    "Java T-shirt",
    "Java Mug",
    "Duke Juggling Dolls",
    "Java Pin",
    "Java Key Chain"
};
```

Table 10.1 Data Used for the DataStreams Example

Order in record	Data type	Data description	Output method	Input method	Sample value
1	double	Item price	DataOutputStream. writeDouble	DataInputStream. readDouble	19.99
2	int	Unit count	DataOutputStream. writeInt	DataInputStream. readInt	12
3	String	Item description	DataOutputStream. writeUTF	DataInputStream. readUTF	"Java T-Shirt"

---

21. 7/docs/api/java/io/DataInput.html

22. 7/docs/api/java/io/DataOutput.html

23. 7/docs/api/java/io/DataInputStream.html

24. 7/docs/api/java/io/DataOutputStream.html

Then `DataStreams` opens an output stream. Since a `DataOutputStream` can only
be created as a wrapper for an existing byte stream object, `DataStreams` provides
a buffered file output byte stream:

```
out = new DataOutputStream(new BufferedOutputStream(
            new FileOutputStream(dataFile)));
```

`DataStreams` writes out the records and closes the output stream:

```
for (int i = 0; i < prices.length; i ++) {
    out.writeDouble(prices[i]);
    out.writeInt(units[i]);
    out.writeUTF(descs[i]);
}
```

The `writeUTF` method writes out `String` values in a modified form of UTF-8. This
is a variable-width character encoding that only needs a single byte for common
Western characters.

Now `DataStreams` reads the data back in again. First it must provide an input
stream and variables to hold the input data. Like `DataOutputStream`, `DataIn-
putStream` must be constructed as a wrapper for a byte stream:

```
in = new DataInputStream(new
            BufferedInputStream(new FileInputStream(dataFile)));

double price;
int unit;
String desc;
double total = 0.0;
```

Now `DataStreams` can read each record in the stream, reporting on the data it
encounters:

```
try {
    while (true) {
        price = in.readDouble();
        unit = in.readInt();
        desc = in.readUTF();
        System.out.format("You ordered %d" + " units of %s at $%.2f%n",
            unit, desc, price);
        total += unit * price;
    }
} catch (EOFException e) {
}
```

Notice that `DataStreams` detects an end-of-file condition by catching `EOFException`[25] instead of testing for an invalid return value. All implementations of `DataInput` methods use `EOFException` instead of return values.

Also notice that each specialized `write` in `DataStreams` exactly matches the corresponding specialized `read`. It is up to the programmer to make sure that output types and input types are matched in this way: the input stream consists of simple binary data, with nothing to indicate the type of individual values or where they begin in the stream.

`DataStreams` uses one very bad programming technique: it uses floating-point numbers to represent monetary values. In general, floating point is bad for precise values. It's particularly bad for decimal fractions, because common values (such as `0.1`) do not have a binary representation.

The correct type to use for currency values is `java.math.BigDecimal`. Unfortunately, `BigDecimal` is an object type, so it won't work with data streams. However, `BigDecimal` *will* work with object streams, which are covered in the next section.

Object Streams

Just as data streams support I/O of primitive data types, object streams support I/O of objects. Most, but not all, standard classes support serialization of their objects. Those that do implement the marker interface `Serializable`.[26]

The object stream classes are `ObjectInputStream`[27] and `ObjectOutputStream`.[28] These classes implement `ObjectInput` and `ObjectOutput`, which are subinterfaces of `DataInput` and `DataOutput`. This means that all the primitive data I/O methods covered in the section "Data Streams" are also implemented in object streams. So an object stream can contain a mixture of primitive and object values. The `ObjectStreams` example illustrates this. `ObjectStreams` creates the same application as `DataStreams`, with a couple of changes. First, prices are now `BigDecimal` objects, to better represent fractional values. Second, a `Calendar`[29] object is written to the data file, indicating an invoice date.

If `readObject()` doesn't return the object type expected, attempting to cast it to the correct type may throw a `ClassNotFoundException`.[30] In this simple example, that can't happen, so we don't try to catch the exception. Instead, we notify the

---

25. 7/docs/api/java/io/EOFException.html
26. 7/docs/api/java/io/Serializable.html
27. 7/docs/api/java/io/ObjectInputStream.html
28. 7/docs/api/java/io/ObjectOutputStream.html
29. 7/docs/api/java/util/Calendar.html
30. 7/docs/api/java/lang/ClassNotFoundException.html

compiler that we're aware of the issue by adding `ClassNotFoundException` to the `main` method's `throws` clause.

Output and Input of Complex Objects

The `writeObject` and `readObject` methods are simple to use, but they contain some very sophisticated object management logic. This isn't important for a class like `Calendar`, which just encapsulates primitive values. But many objects contain references to other objects. If `readObject` is to reconstitute an object from a stream, it has to be able to reconstitute all the objects that the original object references. These additional objects might have their own references and so on. In this situation, `writeObject` traverses the entire web of object references and writes all objects in that web onto the stream. Thus a single invocation of `writeObject` can cause a large number of objects to be written to the stream.

This is demonstrated in Figure 10.5, where `writeObject` is invoked to write a single object named *a*. This object contains references to objects *b* and *c*, while *b* contains references to *d* and *e*. Invoking `writeobject(a)` writes not just *a* but all the objects necessary to reconstitute *a*, so the other four objects in this web are written also. When *a* is read back by `readObject`, the other four objects are read back as well, and all the original object references are preserved.

You might wonder what happens if two objects on the same stream both contain references to a single object. Will they both refer to a single object when they're read back? The answer is *yes*. A stream can only contain one copy of an object, though it can contain any number of references to it. Thus if you explicitly write an object to a stream twice, you're really writing only the reference twice. For example, consider the following code, which attempts to write an object ob twice to a stream:

```
Object ob = new Object();
out.writeObject(ob);
out.writeObject(ob);
```

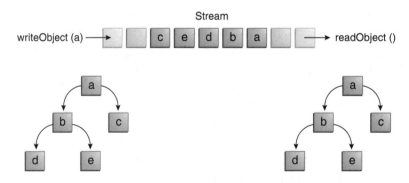

Figure 10.5 I/O of Multiple Referenced Objects

Each `writeObject` has to be matched by a `readObject`, so the code that reads the stream back will look something like this:

```
Object ob1 = in.readObject();
Object ob2 = in.readObject();
```

This results in two variables, `ob1` and `ob2`, which both refer to the same single object.

However, if a single object is written to two different streams, it is effectively duplicated—a single program reading both streams back will see two distinct objects.

File I/O (Featuring NIO.2)

The `java.nio.file` package and its related package, `java.nio.file.attribute`, provide comprehensive support for file I/O and for accessing the default file system. Though the API has many classes, you need to focus on only a few entry points. You will see that this API is very intuitive and easy to use. We begin this section by asking, what is a path? The `Path` class, the primary entry point for the package, is then introduced. Methods in the `Path` class relating to syntactic operations are explained. We then move on to the other primary class in the package, the `Files` class, which contains methods that deal with file operations. First, some concepts common to many file operations are introduced. We then cover methods for checking, deleting, copying, and moving files. This section then shows how metadata is managed before moving on to file I/O and directory I/O. Random access files are explained, and issues specific to symbolic and hard links are examined.

Next, some of the very powerful, but more advanced, topics are covered. First, the capability to recursively walk the file tree is demonstrated, followed by information about how to search for files using wildcards. Next, we explain and demonstrate how to watch a directory for changes. Then methods that didn't fit elsewhere are given some attention.

Finally, if you have file I/O code written prior to the Java SE 7 release, there is a map from the old API to the new API, as well as important information about the `File.toPath` method for developers who would like to leverage the new API without rewriting existing code.

What Is a Path? (And Other File System Facts)

A file system stores and organizes files on some form of media, generally one or more hard drives, in such a way that they can be easily retrieved. Most file systems in use today store the files in a tree (or *hierarchical*) structure. At the top of the tree is one (or more) root nodes. Under the root node, there are files and directories (*folders* in Microsoft Windows). Each directory can contain files and subdirectories, which in turn can contain files and subdirectories, and so on, potentially to an almost limitless depth.

What Is a Path?

Figure 10.6 shows a sample directory tree containing a single root node. Microsoft Windows supports multiple root nodes. Each root node maps to a volume, such as C:\ or D:\. Solaris supports a single root node, which is denoted by the slash character (/).

A file is identified by its path through the file system, beginning from the root node. For example, the statusReport file in Figure 10.6 is described by the following notation in Solaris:

```
/home/sally/statusReport
```

In Microsoft Windows, statusReport is described by the following notation:

```
C:\home\sally\statusReport
```

The character used to separate the directory names (also called the *delimiter*) is specific to the file system: Solaris uses the forward slash (/), and Microsoft Windows uses the backslash slash (\).

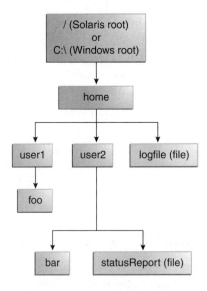

Figure 10.6 Sample Directory Structure

Relative or Absolute?

A path is either *relative* or *absolute*. An absolute path always contains the root element and the complete directory list required to locate the file. For example, `/home/sally/statusReport` is an absolute path. All the information needed to locate the file is contained in the path string.

A relative path needs to be combined with another path in order to access a file. For example, `joe/foo` is a relative path. Without more information, a program cannot reliably locate the `joe/foo` directory in the file system.

Symbolic Links

File system objects are typically directories or files. Everyone is familiar with these objects. But some file systems also support the notion of symbolic links. A symbolic link is also referred to as a *symlink* or a *soft link*.

A *symbolic link* is a special file that serves as a reference to another file. For the most part, symbolic links are transparent to applications, and operations on symbolic links are automatically redirected to the target of the link. (The file or directory being pointed to is called the *target* of the link.) Exceptions apply when a symbolic link is deleted or renamed, in which case the link itself is deleted or renamed—not the target of the link.

In Figure 10.7, `logFile` appears to be a regular file to the user, but it is actually a symbolic link to `dir/logs/HomeLogFile`. `HomeLogFile` is the target of the link.

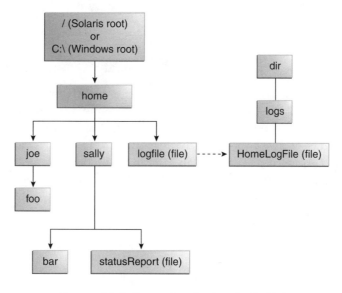

Figure 10.7 Example of a Symbolic Link

A symbolic link is usually transparent to the user. Reading or writing to a symbolic link is the same as reading or writing to any other file or directory.

The phrase *resolving a link* means substituting the actual location in the file system for the symbolic link. In the example, resolving `logFile` yields `dir/logs/HomeLogFile`.

In real-world scenarios, most file systems make liberal use of symbolic links. Occasionally, a carelessly created symbolic link can cause a circular reference. A circular reference occurs when the target of a link points back to the original link. The circular reference might be indirect: directory *a* points to directory *b*, which points to directory *c*, which contains a subdirectory pointing back to directory *a*. Circular references can cause havoc when a program is recursively walking a directory structure. However, this scenario has been accounted for and will not cause your program to loop infinitely.

The next section discusses the heart of file I/O support in the Java programming language: the `Path` class.

The Path Class

The `Path`[31] class, introduced in the Java SE 7 release, is one of the primary entry points of the `java.nio.file` package. If your application uses file I/O, you will want to learn about the powerful features of this class.

> **Note**
>
> If you have code created prior to Java SE 7 that uses `java.io.File`, you can still take advantage of the `Path` class functionality by using the `File.toPath` method. Consult the section "Legacy File I/O Code" at the end of this chapter for more information.

As its name implies, the `Path` class is a programmatic representation of a path in the file system. A `Path` object contains the file name and directory list used to construct the path and is used to examine, locate, and manipulate files.

A `Path` instance reflects the underlying platform. In Solaris, a `Path` uses the Solaris syntax (`/home/joe/foo`) and in Microsoft Windows, a `Path` uses the Windows syntax (`C:\home\joe\foo`). A `Path` is not system independent. You cannot compare a `Path` from a Solaris file system and expect it to match a `Path` from a Windows file system, even if the directory structure is identical and both instances locate the same relative file.

---

31. 7/docs/api/java/nio/file/Path.html

The file or directory corresponding to the `Path` might not exist. You can create a `Path` instance and manipulate it in various ways: you can append to it, extract pieces of it, and compare it to another path. At the appropriate time, you can use the methods in the `Files`[32] class to check the existence of the file corresponding to the `Path`, create the file, open it, delete it, change its permissions, and so on.

The next section examines the `Path` class in detail.

Path Operations

The `Path`[33] class includes various methods that can be used to obtain information about the path, access elements of the path, convert the path to other forms, or extract portions of a path. There are also methods for matching the path string and methods for removing redundancies in a path. This section addresses these `Path` methods, sometimes called *syntactic* operations, because they operate on the path itself and don't access the file system.

Creating a Path

A `Path` instance contains the information used to specify the location of a file or directory. At the time it is defined, a `Path` is provided with a series of one or more names. A root element or a file name might be included, but neither is required. A `Path` might consist of just a single directory or file name.

You can easily create a `Path` object by using one of the following `get` methods from the `Paths`[34] (note the plural) helper class:

```
Path p1 = Paths.get("/tmp/foo");
Path p2 = Paths.get(args[0]);
Path p3 = Paths.get(URI.create("file:///Users/joe/FileTest.java"));
```

The `Paths.get` method is shorthand for the following code:

```
Path p4 = FileSystems.getDefault().getPath("/users/sally");
```

The following example creates `/u/joe/logs/foo.log`, assuming your home directory is `/u/joe` (Solaris) or `C:\joe\logs\foo.log` (Microsoft Windows):

```
Path p5 = Paths.get(System.getProperty("user.home"),"logs", "foo.log");
```

32. 7/docs/api/java/nio/file/Files.html
33. 7/docs/api/java/nio/file/Path.html
34. 7/docs/api/java/nio/file/Paths.html

Retrieving Information about a Path

You can think of the Path as storing these name elements as a sequence. The highest element in the directory structure would be located at index zero. The lowest element in the directory structure would be located at index [n-1], where n is the number of name elements in the Path. Methods are available for retrieving individual elements or a subsequence of the Path using these indexes. The examples in this section use the structure shown in Figure 10.6.

The following code snippet defines a Path instance and then invokes several methods to obtain information about the path:

```
// None of these methods requires that the file corresponding
// to the Path exists.
// Microsoft Windows syntax
Path path = Paths.get("C:\\home\\joe\\foo");

// Solaris syntax
Path path = Paths.get("/home/joe/foo");

System.out.format("toString: %s%n", path.toString());
System.out.format("getFileName: %s%n", path.getFileName());
System.out.format("getName(0): %s%n", path.getName(0));
System.out.format("getNameCount: %d%n", path.getNameCount());
System.out.format("subpath(0,2): %s%n", path.subpath(0,2));
System.out.format("getParent: %s%n", path.getParent());
System.out.format("getRoot: %s%n", path.getRoot());
```

Table 10.2 shows the output for both Microsoft Windows and Solaris.

The previous example shows the output for an absolute path. In the following example, a relative path is specified:

```
// Solaris syntax
Path path = Paths.get("sally/bar");
or
// Microsoft Windows syntax
Path path = Paths.get("sally\\bar");
```

Table 10.3 shows the output for Windows and Solaris.

Removing Redundancies from a Path

Many file systems use a period (.) to denote the current directory and two periods (..) to denote the parent directory. You might have a situation where a Path contains redundant directory information. Perhaps a server is configured to save its log files in the /dir/logs/. directory, and you want to delete the trailing /. notation from the path.

The following examples both include redundancies:

```
/home/./joe/foo
/home/sally/../joe/foo
```

The `normalize` method removes any redundant elements, which includes any period (.) or double period (*directory/*..) occurrences. Both of the preceding examples normalize to /home/joe/foo.

It is important to note that `normalize` doesn't check at the file system when it cleans up a path. It is a purely syntactic operation. In the second example, if `sally`

Table 10.2 Output for Sample Code Using Absolute Path

Method invoked	Returns in Solaris	Returns in Microsoft Windows	Comment
toString	/home/joe/foo	C:\home\joe\foo	This method returns the string representation of the `Path`. If the path was created using `Filesystems.getDe-fault().getPath(String)` or `Paths.get` (the latter being a convenience method for `getPath`), the method performs minor syntactic cleanup. For example, in a UNIX operating system, it will correct the input string //home/joe/foo to /home/joe/foo.
getFileName	foo	foo	This method returns the file name or the last element of the sequence of name elements.
getName(0)	home	home	This method returns the path element corresponding to the specified index. The element at zero is the path element closest to the root.
getNameCount	3	3	This method returns the number of elements in the path.
subpath(0,2)	home/joe	home\joe	This method returns the subsequence of the `Path` (not including a root element) as specified by the beginning and ending indexes.
getParent	/home/joe	\home\joe	This method returns the path of the parent directory.
getRoot	/	C:\	This method returns the root of the path.

Table 10.3 Output for Sample Code Using Relative Path

Method invoked	Returns in Solaris	Returns in Microsoft Windows
`toString`	`sally/bar`	`sally\bar`
`getFileName`	`bar`	`bar`
`getName(0)`	`sally`	`sally`
`getNameCount`	2	2
`subpath(0,1)`	`sally`	`sally`
`getParent`	`sally`	`sally`
`getRoot`	`null`	`null`

were a symbolic link, removing `sally/..` might result in a `Path` that no longer locates the intended file.

To clean up a path while ensuring that the result locates the correct file, you can use the `toRealPath` method. This method is described in the next section.

Converting a Path

You can use three methods to convert the `Path`. If you need to convert the path to a string that can be opened from a browser, you can use `toUri`. Here is an example:

```
Path p1 = Paths.get("/home/logfile");
// Result is file:///home/logfile
System.out.format("%s%n", p1.toUri());
```

The `toAbsolutePath` method converts a path to an absolute path. If the passed-in path is already absolute, it returns the same `Path` object. The `toAbsolutePath` method can be very helpful when processing user-entered file names. Here is an example:

```
public class FileTest {
    public static void main(String[] args) {

        if (args.length < 1) {
            System.out.println("usage: FileTest file");
            System.exit(-1);
        }

        // Converts the input string to a Path object.
        Path inputPath = Paths.get(args[0]);

        // Converts the input Path
        // to an absolute path.
        // Generally, this means prepending
        // the current working
        // directory.  If this example
```

```
                    // were called like this:
                    //     java FileTest foo
                    // the getRoot and getParent methods
                    // would return null
                    // on the original "inputPath"
                    // instance. Invoking getRoot and
                    // getParent on the "fullPath"
                    // instance returns expected values.
                    Path fullPath = inputPath.toAbsolutePath();
            }
    }
```

The `toAbsolutePath` method converts the user input and returns a `Path` that returns useful values when queried. The file does not need to exist for this method to work.

The `toRealPath` method returns the *real* path of an existing file. This method performs several operations in one:

- If `true` is passed to this method and the file system supports symbolic links, this method resolves any symbolic links in the path.
- If the `Path` is relative, it returns an absolute path.
- If the `Path` contains any redundant elements, it returns a path with those elements removed.

This method throws an exception if the file does not exist or cannot be accessed. You can catch the exception when you want to handle any of these cases. Here is an example:

```
try {
    Path fp = path.toRealPath(true);
} catch (NoSuchFileException x) {
    System.err.format("%s: no such" + " file or directory%n", path);
    // Logic for case when file doesn't exist.
} catch (IOException x) {
    System.err.format("%s%n", x);
    // Logic for other sort of file error.
}
```

Joining Two Paths

You can combine paths by using the `resolve` method. You pass in a *partial path*, which is a path that does not include a root element, and that partial path is appended to the original path.

For example, consider the following code snippet (for Solaris):

```
// Solaris
Path p1 = Paths.get("/home/joe/foo");
// Result is /home/joe/foo/bar
```

```
System.out.format("%s%n", p1.resolve("bar"));
```

Alternately, consider the following code snippet (for Microsoft Windows):

```
// Microsoft Windows
Path p1 = Paths.get("C:\\home\\joe\\foo");
// Result is C:\home\joe\foo\bar
System.out.format("%s%n", p1.resolve("bar"));
```

Passing an absolute path to the `resolve` method returns the passed-in path for both instances:

```
// Result is /home/joe
Paths.get("foo").resolve("/home/joe");
```

Creating a Path between Two Paths

A common requirement when you are writing file I/O code is the capacity to construct a path from one location in the file system to another location. You can meet this using the `relativize` method. This method constructs a path originating from the original path and ending at the location specified by the passed-in path. The new path is *relative* to the original path.

For example, consider two relative paths defined as `joe` and `sally`:

```
Path p1 = Paths.get("joe");
Path p2 = Paths.get("sally");
```

In the absence of any other information, it is assumed that `joe` and `sally` are siblings—meaning nodes that reside at the same level in the tree structure. To navigate from `joe` to `sally`, you would expect to first navigate one level up to the parent node and then down to `sally`:

```
// Result is ../sally
Path p1_to_p2 = p1.relativize(p2);
// Result is ../joe
Path p2_to_p1 = p2.relativize(p1);
```

Consider a slightly more complicated example:

```
Path p1 = Paths.get("home");
Path p3 = Paths.get("home/sally/bar");
// Result is sally/bar
Path p1_to_p3 = p1.relativize(p3);
// Result is ../..
Path p3_to_p1 = p3.relativize(p1);
```

In this example, the two paths share the same node, home. To navigate from home to bar, you first navigate one level down to sally and then one more level down to bar. Navigating from bar to home requires moving up two levels.

A relative path cannot be constructed if only one of the paths includes a root element. If both paths include a root element, the capability to construct a relative path is system dependent. The recursive Copy example uses the relativize and resolve methods.

Comparing Two Paths

The Path class supports equals, enabling you to test two paths for equality. The startsWith and endsWith methods enable you to test whether a path begins or ends with a particular string. These methods are easy to use. Here's an example:

```
Path path = . . . ;
Path otherPath = . . . ;
Path beginning = Paths.get("/home");
Path ending = Paths.get("foo");

if (path.equals(otherPath)) {
    // equality logic here
} else if (path.startsWith(beginning)) {
    // path begins with "/home"
} else if (path.endsWith(ending)) {
    // path ends with "foo"
}
```

The Path class implements the Iterable[35] interface. The iterator method returns an object that enables you to iterate over the name elements in the path. The first element returned is that closest to the root in the directory tree. The following code snippet iterates over a path, printing each name element:

```
Path path = . . . ;
for (Path name: path) {
    System.out.println(name);
}
```

The Path class also implements the Comparable[36] interface. You can compare Path objects by using compareTo, which is useful for sorting.

You can also put Path objects into a Collection. See Chapter 11 for more information about this powerful feature.

---

35. 7/docs/api/java/lang/Iterable.html

36. 7/docs/api/java/lang/Comparable.html

When you want to verify that two `Path` objects locate the same file, you can use the `isSameFile` method, as described in the section "Checking Whether Two Paths Locate the Same File" later in this chapter.

File Operations

The `Files`[37] class is the other primary entry point of the `java.nio.file` package. This class offers a rich set of static methods for reading, writing, and manipulating files and directories. The `Files` methods work on instances of `Path` objects.

Releasing System Resources

Many of the resources that are used in this API, such as streams or channels, implement or extend the `java.io.Closeable`[38] interface. A requirement of a `Closeable` resource is that the `close` method must be invoked to release the resource when no longer required. Neglecting to close a resource can have a negative implication on an application's performance. The `try-with-resources` statement handles this step for you.

Catching Exceptions

With file I/O, unexpected conditions are a fact of life: a file doesn't exist when expected, the program doesn't have access to the file system, the default file system implementation does not support a particular function, and so on. Numerous errors can be encountered.

All methods that access the file system can throw an `IOException`. It is best practice to catch these exceptions by embedding these methods into a `try-with-resources` statement, introduced in the Java SE 7 release. With the `try-with-resources` statement, the compiler automatically generates the code to close the resource(s) when no longer required. The following code shows how this might look:

```
Charset charset = Charset.forName("US-ASCII");
String s = . . . ;
try (BufferedWriter writer = Files.newBufferedWriter(file, charset)) {
    writer.write(s, 0, s.length());
} catch (IOException x) {
    System.err.format("IOException: %s%n", x);
}
```

For more information, see "The try-with-resources Statement" section in Chapter 9.

---

37. 7/docs/api/java/nio/file/Files.html

38. 7/docs/api/java/io/Closeable.html

Alternatively, you can embed the file I/O methods in a `try` block and then catch any exceptions in a `catch` block. If your code has opened any streams or channels, you should close them in a `finally` block. The previous example would look something like the following using the `try-catch-finally` approach:

```
Charset charset = Charset.forName("US-ASCII");
String s = . . . ;
BufferedWriter writer = null;
try {
    writer = Files.newBufferedWriter(file, charset);
    writer.write(s, 0, s.length());
} catch (IOException x) {
    System.err.format("IOException: %s%n", x);
} finally {
    if (writer != null) writer.close();
}
```

For more information, see "Catching and Handling Exceptions" in Chapter 9.

In addition to `IOException`, many specific exceptions extend `FileSystemException`.[39] This class has some useful methods that return the file involved (`getFile`), the detailed message string (`getMessage`), the reason why the file system operation failed (`getReason`), and the "other" file involved, if any (`getOtherFile`).

The following code snippet shows how the `getFile` method might be used:

```
try ( . . . ) {
    . . .
} catch (NoSuchFileException x) {
    System.err.format("%s does not exist\n", x.getFile());
}
```

For purposes of clarity, the file I/O examples in this chapter may not show exception handling, but your code should always include it.

Varargs

Several `Files` methods accept an arbitrary number of arguments when flags are specified. For example, in the following method signature, the ellipses notation after the `CopyOption` argument indicates that the method accepts a variable number of arguments, or *varargs*, as they are typically called:

```
Path Files.move(Path, Path, CopyOption . . . )
```

When a method accepts a varargs argument, you can pass it a comma-separated list of values or an array (`CopyOption[ ]`) of values.

---

39. 7/docs/api/java/nio/file/FileSystemException.html

In the `move` example, the method can be invoked as follows:

```
import static java.nio.file.StandardCopyOption.*;

Path source = . . . ;
Path target = . . . ;
Files.move(source, target, REPLACE_EXISTING, ATOMIC_MOVE);
```

For more information about varargs syntax, see the section "Arbitrary Number of Arguments" in Chapter 4.

Atomic Operations

Several `Files` methods, such as `move`, can perform certain operations atomically in some file systems. An *atomic file operation* is an operation that cannot be interrupted or "partially" performed. Either the entire operation is performed or the operation fails. This is important when you have multiple processes operating on the same area of the file system and you need to guarantee that each process accesses a complete file.

Method Chaining

Many of the file I/O methods support the concept of *method chaining*. You first invoke a method that returns an object. You then immediately invoke a method on *that* object, which returns yet another object, and so on. Many of the I/O examples use the following technique:

```
String value = Charset.defaultCharset().decode(buf).toString();
UserPrincipal group =
    file.getFileSystem().getUserPrincipalLookupService().
        lookupPrincipalByName("me");
```

This technique produces compact code and enables you to avoid declaring temporary variables that you don't need.

What Is a Glob?

Two methods in the `Files` class accept a glob argument, but what is a *glob*? You can use glob syntax to specify pattern-matching behavior. A glob pattern is specified as a string and is matched against other strings, such as directory or file names. Glob syntax follows several simple rules:

- An asterisk (*) matches any number of characters (including none).
- Two asterisks (**) work like one (*) but cross directory boundaries. This syntax is generally used for matching complete paths.
- A question mark (?) matches exactly one character.

- Braces specify a collection of subpatterns. Here are some examples:
  - `{sun,moon,stars}` matches `sun`, `moon`, or `stars`.
  - `{temp*,tmp*}` matches all strings beginning with `temp` or `tmp`.
- Square brackets convey a set of single characters or, when the hyphen character (–) is used, a range of characters. Here are some examples:
  - `[aeiou]` matches any lowercase vowel.
  - `[0-9]` matches any digit.
  - `[A-Z]` matches any uppercase letter.
  - `[a-z,A-Z]` matches any uppercase or lowercase letter.
- Within the square brackets, `*`, `?`, and `\` match themselves. All other characters match themselves.
- To match `*`, `?`, or the other special characters, you can escape them by using the backslash character (`\`). Here are some examples:
  - `\\` matches a single backslash.
  - `\?` matches a question mark.

Here are some examples of glob syntax:

- `*.html`—Matches all strings that end in `.html`
- `???`—Matches all strings with exactly three letters or digits
- `*[0-9]*`—Matches all strings containing a numeric value
- `*.{htm,html,pdf}`—Matches any string ending with `.htm`, `.html`, or `.pdf`
- `a?*.java`—Matches any string beginning with `a`, followed by at least one letter or digit, and ending with `.java`
- `{foo*,*[0-9]*}`—Matches any string beginning with `foo` or any string containing a numeric value

> **Note**
>
> If you are typing the glob pattern and it contains one of the special characters, you must put the pattern in quotes (`"*"`), use the backslash (`\*`), or use whatever escape mechanism is supported at the command line.

The glob syntax is powerful and easy to use. However, if it is not sufficient for your needs, you can also use a regular expression. For more information, see Chapter 13.

For more information about the glob syntax, see the API specification for the `getPathMatcher` method in the `FileSystem` class.

Link Awareness

The `Files` class is "link aware." Every `Files` method either detects what to do when a symbolic link is encountered or provides an option enabling you to configure the behavior when a symbolic link is encountered.

Checking a File or Directory

Say you have a `Path` instance representing a file or directory. Does that file actually exist on the file system? Is it readable? Writable? Executable?

Verifying the Existence of a File or Directory

The methods in the `Path` class are syntactic, meaning that they operate on the `Path` instance, but eventually you must access the file system to verify that a particular `Path` exists or does not exist. You can do so with the `exists(Path, LinkOption . . . )` and the `notExists(Path, LinkOption . . . )` methods. Note that `!Files.exists(path)` is not equivalent to `Files.notExists(path)`. When you are testing a file's existence, three results are possible:

- The file is verified to exist.
- The file is verified to not exist.
- The file's status is unknown. This result can occur when the program does not have access to the file.

If both `exists` and `notExists` return `false`, the existence of the file cannot be verified.

Checking File Accessibility

To verify that the program can access a file as needed, you can use the `isReadable(Path)`, `isWritable(Path)`, and `isExecutable(Path)` methods.

The following code snippet verifies that a particular file exists and that the program has the ability to execute the file:

```
Path file = . . . ;
boolean isRegularExecutableFile = Files.isRegularFile(file) &
        Files.isReadable(file) & Files.isExecutable(file);
```

> **Note**
>
> Once any of these methods completes, there is no guarantee that the file can be accessed. A common security flaw in many applications is to perform a check and then access the file. For more information, use your favorite search engine to look up TOCTTOU (pronounced *TOCK-too*).

Checking Whether Two Paths Locate the Same File

When you have a file system that uses symbolic links, it is possible to have two different paths that locate the same file. The `isSameFile(Path, Path)` method compares two paths to determine if they locate the same file on the file system. Here is an example:

```
Path p1 = . . . ;
Path p2 = . . . ;

if (Files.isSameFile(p1, p2)) {
    // Logic when the paths locate the same file
}
```

Deleting a File or Directory

You can delete files, directories, or links. With symbolic links, the link itself is deleted—not the target of the link. With directories, the directory must be empty or the deletion fails.

The `Files` class provides two deletion methods: The `delete(Path)` method deletes the file or throws an exception if the deletion fails. For example, if the file does not exist, a `NoSuchFileException` is thrown. You can catch the exception to determine why the delete failed as follows:

```
try {
    Files.delete(path);
} catch (NoSuchFileException x) {
    System.err.format("%s: no such" + " file or directory%n", path);
} catch (DirectoryNotEmptyException x) {
    System.err.format("%s not empty%n", path);
} catch (IOException x) {
    // File permission problems are caught here.
    System.err.println(x);
}
```

The `deleteIfExists(Path)` method also deletes the file, but if the file does not exist, no exception is thrown. Failing silently is useful when you have multiple threads deleting files and you don't want to throw an exception just because one thread did so first.

Copying a File or Directory

You can copy a file or directory by using the `copy(Path, Path, CopyOption . . . )` method. The copy fails if the target file exists, unless the `REPLACE_EXISTING` option is specified.

Directories can be copied. However, files inside the directory are not copied, so the new directory is empty even when the original directory contains files.

When copying a symbolic link, the target of the link is copied. If you want to copy the link itself, and not the contents of the link, specify either the NOFOLLOW_LINKS or REPLACE_EXISTING option.

This method takes a varargs argument. The following StandardCopyOption and LinkOption enums are supported:

- REPLACE_EXISTING—This performs the copy even when the target file already exists. If the target is a symbolic link, the link itself is copied (and not the target of the link). If the target is a nonempty directory, the copy fails with the FileAlreadyExistsException exception.

- COPY_ATTRIBUTES—This copies the file attributes associated with the file to the target file. The exact file attributes supported are file-system and platform dependent, but last-modified-time is supported across platforms and is copied to the target file.

- NOFOLLOW_LINKS—This indicates that symbolic links should not be followed. If the file to be copied is a symbolic link, the link is copied (and not the target of the link).

If you are not familiar with enums, see Chapter 4, "Enum Types." The following shows how to use the copy method:

```
import static java.nio.file.StandardCopyOption.*;
. . .
Files.copy(source, target, REPLACE_EXISTING);
```

In addition to file copy, the Files class also defines methods that may be used to copy between a file and a stream. The copy(InputStream, Path, CopyOptions . . .) method may be used to copy all bytes from an input stream to a file. The copy(Path, OutputStream) method may be used to copy all bytes from a file to an output stream.

The Copy example uses the copy and Files.walkFileTree methods to support a recursive copy. See the section "Walking the File Tree" later in the chapter for more information.

Moving a File or Directory

You can move a file or directory by using the move(Path, Path, CopyOption . . .) method. The move fails if the target file exists, unless the REPLACE_EXISTING option is specified.

Empty directories can be moved. If the directory is not empty, the move is only allowed when the directory can be moved without moving the contents of that directory. On UNIX systems, moving a directory within the same partition generally consists of renaming the directory. In that situation, this method works even when the directory contains files.

This method requires a varargs argument. The following StandardCopyOption enums are supported:

- REPLACE_EXISTING—This performs the move even when the target file already exists. If the target is a symbolic link, the symbolic link is replaced but what it points to is not affected.
- ATOMIC_MOVE—This performs the move as an atomic file operation. If the file system does not support an atomic move, an exception is thrown. With an ATOMIC_MOVE, you can move a file into a directory and be guaranteed that any process watching the directory accesses a complete file.

The following shows how to use the move method:

```
import static java.nio.file.StandardCopyOption.*;
. . .
Files.move(source, target, REPLACE_EXISTING);
```

10

Though you can implement the move method on a single directory as shown, the method is most often used with the file tree recursion mechanism. For more information, see the section "Walking the File Tree" later in this chapter.

Managing Metadata (File and File Store Attributes)

The definition of *metadata* is *data about other data*. With a file system, the data is contained in its files and directories, and the metadata tracks information about each of these objects: Is it a regular file, a directory, or a link? What is its size, creation date, last modified date, file owner, group owner, and access permissions?

A file system's metadata is typically referred to as its *file attributes*. The Files class includes methods that can be used to obtain a single attribute of a file or to set an attribute (Table 10.4).

If a program needs multiple file attributes around the same time, it can be inefficient to use methods that retrieve a single attribute. Repeatedly accessing the file system to retrieve a single attribute can adversely affect performance. For this reason, the Files class provides two readAttributes methods to fetch a file's attributes in one bulk operation (Table 10.5).

Before showing examples of the readAttributes methods, it should be mentioned that different file systems have different notions about which attributes should be tracked. For this reason, related file attributes are grouped together into views. A *view* maps to a particular file system implementation, such as POSIX or DOS, or to a common functionality, such as file ownership.

The supported views are as follows:

Table 10.4 BasicFileAttributes Methods

Method	Comment
`size(Path)`	Returns the size of the specified file in bytes
`isDirectory(Path, LinkOption)`	Returns `true` if the specified `Path` locates a file that is a directory
`isRegularFile(Path,` `    LinkOption . . . )`	Returns `true` if the specified `Path` locates a file that is a regular file
`isSymbolicLink(Path)`	Returns `true` if the specified `Path` locates a file that is a symbolic link
`isHidden(Path)`	Returns `true` if the specified `Path` locates a file that is considered hidden by the file system

`getLastModifiedTime(Path,`
`    LinkOption . . . )`
`setLastModifiedTime(Path, FileTime)`
	Returns or sets the specified file's last modified time

`getOwner(Path, LinkOption . . . )` `setOwner(Path, UserPrincipal)`	Returns or sets the owner of the file

`getPosixFilePermissions(Path,`
`    LinkOption . . . )`
`setPosixFilePermissions(Path,`
`    Set<PosixFilePermission>)`
	Returns or sets a file's POSIX (Portable Operating System Interface) file permissions

`getAttribute(Path, String,`
`    LinkOption . . .`
`setAttribute (Path, String,`
`    Object, LinkOption . . . )`
	Returns or sets the value of a file attribute

Table 10.5 Methods in Files Class for Reading Attributes

Method	Comment
`readAttributes(Path, String,` `    LinkOption . . . )`	This reads a file's attributes as a bulk operation. The `String` parameter identifies the attributes to be read.
`readAttributes(Path, Class<A>,` `    LinkOption . . . )`	This reads a file's attributes as a bulk operation. The `Class<A>` parameter is the type of attributes requested and the method returns an object of that class.

- `BasicFileAttributeView`[40]—This provides a view of basic attributes that are required to be supported by all file system implementations.

- `DosFileAttributeView`[41]—This extends the basic attribute view with the standard 4 bits supported on file systems that support the DOS attributes.

- `PosixFileAttributeView`[42]—This extends the basic attribute view with attributes supported on file systems that support the POSIX family of standards, such as UNIX. These attributes include file owner, group owner, and the nine related access permissions.

- `FileOwnerAttributeView`[43]—This is supported by any file system implementation that supports the concept of a file owner.

- `AclFileAttributeView`[44]—This supports reading or updating a file's access control list (ACL). The NFSv4 ACL model is supported. Any ACL model that has a well-defined mapping to the NFSv4 model (e.g., Windows ACL) might also be supported.

- `UserDefinedFileAttributeView`[45]—This enables the support of metadata that is user defined. This view can be mapped to any extension mechanisms that a system supports. In Solaris, for example, you can use this view to store the MIME type of a file.

A specific file system implementation might support only the basic file attribute view, or it may support several of these file attribute views. A file system implementation might support other attribute views not included in this API.

In most instances, you should not have to deal directly with any of the `FileAttributeView` interfaces. (If you do need to work directly with the `FileAttributeView`, you can access it via the `getFileAttributeView(Path, Class<V>, LinkOption . . . )` method.)

The `readAttributes` methods use generics and can be used to read the attributes for any of the file attributes views. The examples in the rest of the sections that follow use the `readAttributes` methods.

---

40. `7/docs/api/java/nio/file/attribute/BasicFileAttributeView.html`

41. `7/docs/api/java/nio/file/attribute/DosFileAttributeView.html`

42. `7/docs/api/java/nio/file/attribute/PosixFileAttributeView.html`

43. `7/docs/api/java/nio/file/attribute/FileOwnerAttributeView.html`

44. `7/docs/api/java/nio/file/attribute/AclFileAttributeView.html`

45. `7/docs/api/java/nio/file/attribute/UserDefinedFileAttributeView.html`

Basic File Attributes

As mentioned previously, to read the basic attributes of a file, you can use one of the
`Files.readAttributes` methods, which reads all the basic attributes in one bulk
operation. This is far more efficient than accessing the file system separately to
read each individual attribute. The varargs argument currently supports the
`LinkOption`[46] enum, `NOFOLLOW_LINKS`. Use this option when you do not want
symbolic links to be followed.

> **Note**
>
> The set of basic attributes includes three time stamps: `creationTime`, `lastModifiedTime`,
> and `lastAccessTime`. Any of these time stamps might not be supported in a particular im-
> plementation, in which case the corresponding accessor method returns an implementation-
> specific value. When supported, the time stamp is returned as a `FileTime`[47] object.

The following code snippet reads and prints the basic file attributes for a given
file and uses the methods in the `BasicFileAttributes`[48] class:

```
Path file = . . . ;
BasicFileAttributes attr = Files.readAttributes(file,
    BasicFileAttributes.class);

System.out.println("creationTime: " + attr.creationTime());
System.out.println("lastAccessTime: " + attr.lastAccessTime());
System.out.println("lastModifiedTime: " + attr.lastModifiedTime());

System.out.println("isDirectory: " + attr.isDirectory());
System.out.println("isOther: " + attr.isOther());
System.out.println("isRegularFile: " + attr.isRegularFile());
System.out.println("isSymbolicLink: " + attr.isSymbolicLink());
System.out.println("size: " + attr.size());
```

In addition to the accessor methods shown in this example, there is a `fileKey`
method that returns either an object that uniquely identifies the file or `null` if no
file key is available.

Setting Time Stamps

The following code snippet sets the last modified time in milliseconds:

---

46. 7/docs/api/java/nio/file/LinkOption.html

47. 7/docs/api/java/nio/file/attribute/FileTime.html

48. 7/docs/api/java/nio/file/attribute/BasicFileAttributes.html

```
Path file = . . . ;
BasicFileAttributes attr =
    Files.readAttributes(file, BasicFileAttributes.class);
long currentTime = System.currentTimeMillis();
FileTime ft = FileTime.fromMillis(currentTime);
Files.setLastModifiedTime(file, ft);
}
```

DOS File Attributes

DOS file attributes are also supported on file systems other than DOS, such as Samba. The following snippet uses the methods of the `DosFileAttributes`[49] class:

```
Path file = . . . ;
try {
    DosFileAttributes attr =
        Files.readAttributes(file, DosFileAttributes.class);
    System.out.println("isReadOnly is " + attr.isReadOnly());
    System.out.println("isHidden is " + attr.isHidden());
    System.out.println("isArchive is " + attr.isArchive());
    System.out.println("isSystem is " + attr.isSystem());
} catch (UnsupportedOperationException x) {
    System.err.println("DOS file" +
        " attributes not supported:" + x);
}
```

However, you can set a DOS attribute using the `setAttribute(Path, String, Object, LinkOption . . . )` method, as follows:

```
Path file = . . . ;
Files.setAttribute(file, "dos:hidden", true);
```

POSIX File Permissions

POSIX is an acronym for *Portable Operating System Interface* for UNIX and is a set of IEEE and ISO standards designed to ensure interoperability among different flavors of UNIX. If a program conforms to these POSIX standards, it should be easily ported to other POSIX-compliant operating systems.

Besides file owner and group owner, POSIX supports nine file permissions: read, write, and execute permissions for the file owner, members of the same group, and "everyone else."

The following code snippet reads the POSIX file attributes for a given file and prints them to standard output. The code uses the methods in the `PosixFileAttributes`[50] class:

49. 7/docs/api/java/nio/file/attribute/DosFileAttributes.html

50. 7/docs/api/java/nio/file/attribute/PosixFileAttributes.html

```
Path file = . . . ;
PosixFileAttributes attr =
    Files.readAttributes(file, PosixFileAttributes.class);
System.out.format("%s %s %s%n",
    attr.owner().getName,
    attr.group().getName(),
    PosixFilePermissions.toString(attr.permissions()));
```

The PosixFilePermissions[51] helper class provides several useful methods, as follows:

- The toString method, used in the previous code snippet, converts the file permissions to a string (e.g., rw-r--r--).
- The fromString method accepts a string representing the file permissions and constructs a Set of file permissions.
- The asFileAttribute method accepts a Set of file permissions and constructs a file attribute that can be passed to the Path.createFile or Path.createDirectory method.

The following code snippet reads the attributes from one file and creates a new file, assigning the attributes from the original file to the new file:

```
Path sourceFile = . . . ;
Path newFile = . . . ;
PosixFileAttributes attrs =
    Files.readAttributes(sourceFile, PosixFileAttributes.class);
FileAttribute<Set<PosixFilePermission>> attr =
    PosixFilePermissions.asFileAttribute(attrs.permissions());
Files.createFile(file, attr);
```

The asFileAttribute method wraps the permissions as a FileAttribute. The code then attempts to create a new file with those permissions. Note that the umask also applies, so the new file might be more secure than the permissions that were requested.

To set a file's permissions to values represented as a hard-coded string, you can use the following code:

```
Path file = . . . ;
Set<PosixFilePermission> perms =
    PosixFilePermissions.fromString("rw-------");
FileAttribute<Set<PosixFilePermission>> attr =
    PosixFilePermissions.asFileAttribute(perms);
Files.setPosixFilePermissions(file, perms);
```

---

51. 7/docs/api/java/nio/file/attribute/PosixFilePermissions.html

The Chmod example recursively changes the permissions of files in a manner similar to the chmod Unix utility, which is used to set file permissions.

Setting a File or Group Owner

To translate a name into an object that you can store as a file owner or a group owner, you can use the UserPrincipalLookupService[52] service. This service looks up a name or group name as a string and returns a UserPrincipal object representing that string. You can obtain the user principal look-up service for the default file system by using the FileSystem.getUserPrincipalLookupService method.

The following code snippet shows how to set the file owner by using the setOwner method:

```
Path file = . . . ;
UserPrincipal owner = file.GetFileSystem().getUserPrincipalLookupService()
        .lookupPrincipalByName("sally");
Files.setOwner(file, owner);
```

There is no special-purpose method in the Files class for setting a group owner. However, a safe way to do so directly is through the POSIX file attribute view, as follows:

```
Path file = . . . ;
GroupPrincipal group =
    file.getFileSystem().getUserPrincipalLookupService()
        .lookupPrincipalByGroupName("green");
Files.getFileAttributeView(file, PosixFileAttributeView.class)
    .setGroup(group);
```

User-Defined File Attributes

If the file attributes supported by your file system implementation aren't sufficient for your needs, you can use the UserDefinedAttributeView to create and track your own file attributes.

Some implementations map this concept to features like NTFS alternative data streams and extended attributes on file systems such as ext3 and ZFS. Most implementations impose restrictions on the file size. For example, ext3 limits the size to 4 kilobytes.

A file's MIME type can be stored as a user-defined attribute by using this code snippet:

```
Path file = . . . ;
UserDefinedFileAttributeView view = Files
    .getFileAttributeView(file, UserDefinedFileAttributeView.class);
```

---

52. 7/docs/api/java/nio/file/attribute/UserPrincipalLookupService.html

```
view.write("user.mimetype",
           Charset.defaultCharset().encode("text/html"));
```

To read the MIME type attribute, you would use this code snippet:

```
Path file = . . . ;
UserDefinedFileAttributeView view = file
    .getFileAttributeView(UserDefinedFileAttributeView.class);
String name = "user.mimetype";
ByteBuffer buf = ByteBuffer.allocate(view.size(name));
view.read(name, buf);
buf.flip();
String value = Charset.defaultCharset().decode(buf).toString();
```

The Xdd example shows how to get, set, and delete a user-defined attribute.

> **Note**
>
> In Linux, you might need to enable extended attributes in order for user-defined attributes to work. If you receive an UnsupportedOperationException when trying to access the user-defined attribute view, you need to remount the file system. The following command remounts the root partition with extended attributes for the ext3 file system. If this command does not work for your flavor of Linux, consult the documentation:
>
> ```
> $ sudo mount -o remount,user_xattr /
> ```
>
> If you want to make the change permanent, add an entry to /etc/fstab.

File Store Attributes

You can use the FileStore[53] class to learn about a file store (e.g., how much space is available). The getFileStore(Path) method fetches the file store for the specified file.

The following code snippet from the DiskUsage example prints the space usage for the file store where a particular file resides:

```
Path file = . . . ;
FileStore store = Files.getFileStore(file);

long total = store.getTotalSpace() / 1024;
long used = (store.getTotalSpace() -
             store.getUnallocatedSpace()) / 1024;
long avail = store.getUsableSpace() / 1024;
```

---

53. 7/docs/api/java/nio/file/FileStore.html

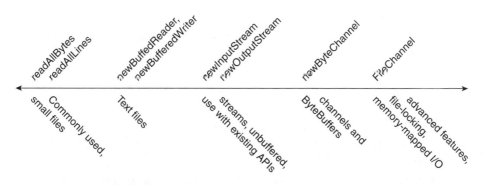

Figure 10.8 File I/O Methods Arranged from Less Complex to More Complex

The DiskUsage example[54] uses this API to print disk space information for all the stores in the default file system. This example uses the getFileStores method in the FileSystem class to fetch all the file stores for the file system.

Reading, Writing, and Creating Files

This section discusses the details of reading, writing, creating, and opening files. There is a wide array of file I/O methods to choose from. To help make sense of the API, Figure 10.8 arranges the file I/O methods by level of complexity.

On the far left of the diagram are the utility methods, readAllBytes and readAllLines, and the write methods designed for simple, common cases. To the right of those are the methods used to iterate over a stream or lines of text, such as newBufferedReader and newBufferedWriter, newInputStream and newOutputStream. These methods are interoperable with the java.io package. To the right of those are the methods for dealing with ByteChannels, Seekable-ByteChannels, and ByteBuffers, such as the newByteChannel method. Finally, on the far right are the methods that use FileChannel for advanced applications needing file locking or memory-mapped I/O.

> **Note**
> The methods for creating a new file enable you to specify an optional set of initial attributes for the file. For example, on a file system that supports the POSIX set of standards (such as UNIX), you can specify a file owner, group owner, or file permissions at the time the file is created. The section "Managing Metadata (File and File Store Attributes)" explains file attributes and how to access and set them.

54. `tutorial/essential/io/examples/DiskUsage.java`

The OpenOptions Parameter

Several of the methods in this section take an optional `OpenOptions` parameter. This parameter is optional and the API tells you the default behavior for the method when none is specified.

The following `StandardOpenOptions` enums are supported:

- `WRITE`—This option opens the file for write access.
- `APPEND`—This option appends the new data to the end of the file. It is used with the `WRITE` or `CREATE` options.
- `TRUNCATE_EXISTING`—This option truncates the file to zero bytes. It is used with the `WRITE` option.
- `CREATE_NEW`—This option creates a new file and throws an exception if the file already exists.
- `CREATE`—This option opens the file if it exists or creates a new file if it does not.
- `DELETE_ON_CLOSE`—This option deletes the file when the stream is closed. It is useful for temporary files.
- `SPARSE`—This advanced option hints that a newly created file will be sparse. It is honored on some file systems, such as NTFS, where large files with data "gaps" can be stored in a more efficient manner where those empty gaps do not consume disk space.
- `SYNC`—This keeps the file (both content and metadata) synchronized with the underlying storage device.
- `DSYNC`—This keeps the file content synchronized with the underlying storage device.

Commonly Used Methods for Small Files

Reading All Bytes or Lines from a File

If you have a smaller file and you would like to read its entire contents in one pass, you can use the `readAllBytes(Path)` or `readAllLines(Path, Charset)` method. These methods take care of most of the work for you, such as opening and closing the stream, but are not intended for handling large files. The following code shows how to use the `readAllBytes` method:

```
Path file = . . . ;
byte[] fileArray;
fileArray = Files.readAllBytes(file);
```

Writing All Bytes or Lines to a File

You can use one of the write methods to write bytes, or lines, to a file:

- `write(Path, byte[], OpenOption . . . )`
- `write(Path, Iterable< extends CharSequence>, Charset, OpenOption . . . )`

The following code snippet shows how to use a `write` method:

```
Path file = . . . ;
byte[] buf = . . . ;
Files.write(file, buf);
```

Buffered I/O Methods for Text Files

The `java.nio.file` package supports channel I/O, which moves data in buffers, bypassing some of the layers that can bottleneck stream I/O.

Reading a File by Using Buffered Stream I/O

The `newBufferedReader(Path, Charset)` method opens a file for reading, returning a `BufferedReader` that can be used to read text from a file in an efficient manner.

The following code snippet shows how to use the `newBufferedReader` method to read from a file. The file is encoded in US-ASCII:

```
Charset charset = Charset.forName("US-ASCII");
try (BufferedReader reader = Files.newBufferedReader(file, charset)) {
    String line = null;
    while ((line = reader.readLine()) != null) {
        System.out.println(line);
    }
} catch (IOException x) {
    System.err.format("IOException: %s%n", x);
}
```

Writing a File by Using Buffered Stream I/O

You can use the `newBufferedWriter(Path, Charset, OpenOption . . . )` method to write to a file using a `BufferedWriter`. The following code snippet shows how to create a file encoded in US-ASCII using this method:

```
Charset charset = Charset.forName("US-ASCII");
String s = . . . ;
try (BufferedWriter writer = Files.newBufferedWriter(file, charset)) {
    writer.write(s, 0, s.length());
} catch (IOException x) {
    System.err.format("IOException: %s%n", x);
}
```

10

Methods for Unbuffered Streams and Interoperable with java.io APIs

Reading a File by Using Stream I/O

To open a file for reading, use the `newInputStream(Path, OpenOption . . . )` method. This method returns an unbuffered input stream for reading bytes from the file:

```
Path file = . . . ;
try (InputStream in = Files.newInputStream(file);
    BufferedReader reader =
      new BufferedReader(new InputStreamReader(in))) {
    String line = null;
    while ((line = reader.readLine()) != null) {
        System.out.println(line);
    }
} catch (IOException x) {
    System.err.println(x);
}
```

Creating and Writing a File by Using Stream I/O

You can create a file, append to a file, or write to a file by using the `newOutputStream(Path, OpenOption . . . )` method. This method opens or creates a file for writing bytes and returns an unbuffered output stream.

The method takes an optional `OpenOption` parameter. If no open options are specified and the file does not exist, a new file is created. If the file exists, it is truncated. This option is equivalent to invoking the method with the `CREATE` and `TRUNCATE_EXISTING` options.

The following code snippet opens a log file. If the file does not exist, it is created. If the file exists, it is opened for appending:

```
import static java.nio.file.StandardOpenOption.*;

Path logfile = . . . ;

// Convert the string to a
// byte array.
String s = . . . ;
byte data[] = s.getBytes();

try (OutputStream out = new BufferedOutputStream(
                logfile.newOutputStream(CREATE, APPEND))) {
    . . .
    out.write(data, 0, data.length);
} catch (IOException x) {
    System.err.println(x);
}
```

Methods for Channels and ByteBuffers

Reading and Writing Files by Using Channel I/O

While stream I/O reads one character at a time, channel I/O reads one buffer at a time. The `ByteChannel`[55] interface provides basic read and write functionality. A `SeekableByteChannel`[56] is a `ByteChannel` that is capable of maintaining a position in the channel and changing that position. A `SeekableByteChannel` is also capable of truncating the file associated with the channel and querying the file for its size.

The ability to move to different points in the file and then read from or write to that location makes random access of a file possible. See the "Random Access Files" section later in this chapter for more information.

There are two methods for reading and writing channel I/O:

- `newByteChannel(Path, OpenOption . . . )`
- `newByteChannel(Path, Set<? extends OpenOption>, FileAttribute <?> . . . )`

> **Note**
>
> The `newByteChannel` methods return an instance of a `SeekableByteChannel`. With a default file system, you can cast this seekable byte channel to a `FileChannel`,[57] providing access to more advanced features such as mapping a region of the file directly into memory for faster access, locking a region of the file so other processes cannot access it, or reading and writing bytes from an absolute position without affecting the channel's current position.

Both `newByteChannel` methods enable you to specify a list of `OpenOption` options. The same open options used by the `newOutputStream` methods are supported, in addition to one more option: the indicator `READ` is required because the `SeekableByteChannel` supports both reading and writing.

Specifying `READ` opens the channel for reading. Specifying `WRITE` or `APPEND` opens the channel for writing. If none of these options is specified, the channel is opened for reading.

The following code snippet reads a file and prints it to standard output:

```
// Defaults to READ
```

---

55. 7/docs/api/java/nio/channels/ByteChannel.html

56. 7/docs/api/java/nio/channels/SeekableByteChannel.html

57. 7/docs/api/java/nio/channels/FileChannel.html

```
try (SeekableByteChannel sbc = Files.newByteChannel(file)) {
    ByteBuffer buf = ByteBuffer.allocate(10);

    // Read the bytes with the proper encoding for this platform.  If
    // you skip this step, you might see something that looks like
    // Chinese characters when you expect Latin-style characters.
    String encoding = System.getProperty("file.encoding");
    while (sbc.read(buf) > 0) {
        buf.rewind();
        System.out.print(Charset.forName(encoding).decode(buf));
        buf.flip();
    }
} catch (IOException x) {
    System.out.println("caught exception: " + x);
}
```

The following code snippet, written for UNIX and other POSIX file systems, creates a log file with a specific set of file permissions. This code creates a log file or appends to the log file if it already exists. The log file is created with read/write permissions for owner and read-only permissions for group:

```
import static java.nio.file.StandardCopyOption.*;

// Create the set of options for appending to the file.
Set<OpenOptions> options = new HashSet<OpenOption>();
options.add(APPEND);
options.add(CREATE);

// Create the custom permissions attribute.
Set<PosixFilePermission> perms =
    PosixFilePermissions.fromString("rw-r------");
FileAttribute<Set<PosixFilePermission>> attr =
    PosixFilePermissions.asFileAttribute(perms);

// Convert the string to a ByteBuffer.
String s = . . . ;
byte data[] = s.getBytes();
ByteBuffer bb = ByteBuffer.wrap(data);

try (SeekableByteChannel sbc = Files.newByteChannel(file, options, attr)) {
    sbc.write(bb);
} catch (IOException x) {
    System.out.println("exception thrown: " + x);
}
```

Methods for Creating Regular and Temporary Files

Creating Files

You can create an empty file with an initial set of attributes by using the createFile(Path, FileAttribute<?>) method. For example, if at the time of creation you want a file to have a particular set of file permissions, use the create-File method to do so. If you do not specify any attributes, the file is created with default attributes. If the file already exists, createFile throws an exception.

In a single atomic operation, the `createFile` method checks for the existence of the file and creates that file with the specified attributes, which makes the process more secure against malicious code.

The following code snippet creates a file with default attributes:

```
Path file = . . . ;
try {
    // Create the empty file with default permissions, etc.
    Files.createFile(file);
} catch (FileAlreadyExistsException x) {
    System.err.format("file named %s" +
        " already exists%n", file);
} catch (IOException x) {
    // Some other sort of failure, such as permissions.
    System.err.format("createFile error: %s%n", x);
}
```

Recall that the section "POSIX File Permissions" provided an example that used `createFile(Path, FileAttribute<?>)` to create a file with preset permissions.

You can also create a new file by using the `newOutputStream` methods described in the section "Creating and Writing a File by Using Stream I/O." If you open a new output stream and close it immediately, an empty file is created.

Creating Temporary Files

You can create a temporary file using one of the following `createTempFile` methods:

- `createTempFile(Path, String, String, FileAttribute<?>)`
- `createTempFile(String, String, FileAttribute<?>)`

The first method allows the code to specify a directory for the temporary file, and the second method creates a new file in the default temporary-file directory. Both methods allow you to specify a suffix for the file name, and the first method also allows you to specify a prefix. The following code snippet gives an example of the second method:

```
try {
    Path tempFile = Files.createTempFile(null, ".myapp");
    System.out.format("The temporary file" +
        " has been created: %s%n", tempFile)
    ;
} catch (IOException x) {
    System.err.format("IOException: %s%n", x);
}
```

The result of running this file would be something like this:

```
The temporary file has been created: /tmp/509668702974537184.myapp
```

The specific format of the temporary file name is platform specific.

Random Access Files

Random access files permit nonsequential, or random, access to a file's contents. To access a file randomly, you open the file, seek a particular location, and read from or write to that file.

This functionality is possible with the `SeekableByteChannel` interface. The `SeekableByteChannel` interface extends channel I/O with the notion of a current position. Methods enable you to set or query the position, and you can then read the the data from or write data to that location. The API consists of a few easy-to-use methods:

- `position`—Returns the channel's current position
- `position(long)`—Sets the channel's position
- `read(ByteBuffer)`—Reads bytes into the buffer from the channel
- `write(ByteBuffer)`—Writes bytes from the buffer to the channel
- `truncate(long)`—Truncates the file (or other entity) connected to the channel

The previous section, "Reading and Writing Files by Using Channel I/O," shows that the `Path.newByteChannel` methods return an instance of a `SeekableByteChannel`. On the default file system, you can use that channel as is, or you can cast it to a `FileChannel`,[58] giving you access to more advanced features, such as mapping a region of the file directly into memory for faster access, locking a region of the file, or reading and writing bytes from an absolute location without affecting the channel's current position.

The following code snippet opens a file for both reading and writing by using one of the `newByteChannel` methods. The `SeekableByteChannel` that is returned is cast to a `FileChannel`. Then, 12 bytes are read from the beginning of the file, and the string `"I was here!"` is written at that location. The current position in the file is moved to the end, and the 12 bytes from the beginning are appended. Finally, the string `"I was here!"` is appended, and the channel on the file is closed.

```
String s = "I was here!\n";
byte data[] = s.getBytes();
ByteBuffer out = ByteBuffer.wrap(data);

ByteBuffer copy = ByteBuffer.allocate(12);
```

58. 7/docs/api/java/nio/channels/FileChannel.html

```
try (FileChannel fc = (FileChannel.open(file, READ, WRITE))) {
    // Read the first 12
    // bytes of the file.
    int nread;
    do {
        nread = fc.read(copy);
    } while (nread != -1 && copy.hasRemaining());

    // Write "I was here!" at the beginning of the file.
    fc.position(0);
    while (out.hasRemaining())
        fc.write(out);
    out.rewind();

    // Move to the end of the file.  Copy the first 12 bytes to
    // the end of the file.  Then write "I was here!" again.
    long length = fc.size();
    fc.position(length-1);
    copy.flip();
    while (copy.hasRemaining())
        fc.write(copy);
    while (out.hasRemaining())
        fc.write(out);
} catch (IOException x) {
    System.out.println("I/O Exception: " + x);
}
```

10

Creating and Reading Directories

Some of the methods previously discussed, such as `delete`, work on files, links, *and* directories. But how do you list all the directories at the top of a file system? How do you list the contents of a directory or create a directory?

Listing a File System's Root Directories

You can list all the root directories for a file system by using the `FileSystem.get-RootDirectories` method. This method returns an `Iterable`, which enables you to use the *enhanced for* statement to iterate over all the root directories.

The following code snippet prints the root directories for the default file system:

```
Iterable<Path> dirs = FileSystems.getDefault().getRootDirectories();
for (Path name: dirs) {
    System.err.println(name);
}
```

Creating a Directory

You can create a new directory by using the `createDirectory(Path, FileAttribute<?>)` method. If you don't specify any `FileAttributes`, the new directory will have default attributes. Here is an example:

```
Path dir = . . . ;
Files.createDirectory(path);
```

The following code snippet creates a new directory on a POSIX file system that has specific permissions:

```
Set<PosixFilePermission> perms =
    PosixFilePermissions.fromString("rwxr-x---");
FileAttribute<Set<PosixFilePermission>> attr =
    PosixFilePermissions.asFileAttribute(perms);
Files.createDirectory(file, attr);
```

To create a directory several levels deep when one or more of the parent directories might not yet exist, you can use the convenience method, `createDirectories` `(Path, FileAttribute<?>)`. As with the `createDirectory(Path, FileAttribute<?>)` method, you can specify an optional set of initial file attributes. The following code snippet uses default attributes:

```
Files.createDirectories(Paths.get("foo/bar/test"));
```

The directories are created, as needed, from the top down. In the `foo/bar/test` example, if the `foo` directory does not exist, it is created. Next, the `bar` directory is created, if needed, and finally the `test` directory is created. Note that it is possible for this method to fail after creating some, but not all, of the parent directories.

Creating a Temporary Directory

You can create a temporary directory using one of `createTempDirectory` methods:

- `createTempDirectory(Path, String, FileAttribute<?> . . . )`
- `createTempDirectory(String, FileAttribute<?> . . . )`

The first method allows the code to specify a location for the temporary directory and the second method creates a new directory in the default temporary file directory.

Listing a Directory's Contents

You can list all the contents of a directory by using the `newDirectoryStream(Path)` method. This method returns an object that implements the `DirectoryStream`[59] interface. The class that implements the `DirectoryStream` interface also implements `Iterable`, so you can iterate through the directory stream, reading all of the objects. This approach scales well to very large directories.

---

59. `7/docs/api/java/nio/file/DirectoryStream.html`

The following code snippet shows how to print the contents of a directory:

```
Path dir = . . . ;
try (DirectoryStream<Path> stream = Files.newDirectoryStream(dir)) {
    for (Path file: stream) {
        System.out.println(file.getFileName());
    }
} catch (IOException | DirectoryIteratorException x) {
    // IOException can never be thrown by the iteration.
    // In this snippet, it can only be thrown by newDirectoryStream.
    System.err.println(x);
}
```

The `Path` objects returned by the iterator are the names of the entries resolved against the directory. Thus, if you are listing the contents of the `/tmp` directory, the entries are returned with the form `/tmp/a`, `/tmp/b`, and so on.

This method returns the entire contents of a directory: files, links, subdirectories, and hidden files. If you want to be more selective about the contents that are retrieved, you can use one of the other `newDirectoryStream` methods, as described later in this chapter.

Note that if there is an exception during directory iteration, then `DirectoryIteratorException` is thrown with the `IOException` as the cause. Iterator methods cannot throw exceptions to exceptions.

Filtering a Directory Listing Using Globbing

If you only want to fetch files and subdirectories where each name matches a particular pattern, you can do so by using the `newDirectoryStream(Path, String)` method, which provides a built-in glob filter. If you are not familiar with glob syntax, see the previous section, "What Is a Glob?"

For example, the following code snippet lists files relating to Java: `.class`, `.java`, and `.jar` files:

```
Path dir = . . . ;
try (DirectoryStream<Path> stream =
    Files.newDirectoryStream(dir, "*.{java,class,jar}")) {
    for (Path entry: stream) {
```

```
            System.out.println(entry.getFileName());
        }
    } catch (IOException x) {
        // IOException can never be thrown by the iteration.
        // In this snippet, it can // only be thrown by newDirectoryStream.
        System.err.println(x);
    }
```

Writing Your Own Directory Filter

Perhaps you want to filter the contents of a directory based on some condition
other than pattern matching. You can create your own filter by implementing the
DirectoryStream.Filter<T>[60] interface. This interface consists of one method,
accept, which determines whether a file fulfills the search requirement.

For example, the following code snippet implements a filter that only retrieves
directories:

```
DirectoryStream.Filter<Path> filter =
    newDirectoryStream.Filter<Path>() {
    public boolean accept(Path file) throws IOException {
        try {
            return (Files.isDirectory(path));
        } catch (IOException x) {
            // Failed to determine if it's a directory.
            System.err.println(x);
            return false;
        }
    }
};
```

Once the filter has been created, it can be invoked by using the new-
DirectoryStream(Path, DirectoryStream.Filter<? super Path>) method.
The following code snippet uses the isDirectory filter to print only the directory's
subdirectories to standard output:

```
Path dir = . . . ;
try (DirectoryStream<Path>
                    stream = Files.newDirectoryStream(dir, filter)) {
    for (Path entry: stream) {
        System.out.println(entry.getFileName());
    }
} catch (IOException x) {
    System.err.println(x);
}
```

This method is used to filter a single directory only. However, if you want to find
all the subdirectories in a file tree, you would use the mechanism described in the
"Walking the File Tree" section later in this chapter.

---

60. 7/docs/api/java/nio/file/DirectoryStream.Filter.html

Links, Symbolic or Otherwise

As mentioned previously, the `java.nio.file` package, and the `Path` class in particular, is "link aware." Every `Path` method either detects what to do when a symbolic link is encountered or it provides an option enabling you to configure the behavior when a symbolic link is encountered.

The discussion so far has been about symbolic or soft links, but some file systems also support *hard links*. Hard links are more restrictive than symbolic links, as follows:

- The target of the link must exist.
- Hard links are generally not allowed on directories.
- Hard links are not allowed to cross partitions or volumes. Therefore, they cannot exist across file systems.
- A hard link looks and behaves like a regular file, so they can be hard to find.
- A hard link is, for all intents and purposes, the same entity as the original file. They have the same file permissions, time stamps, and so on. All attributes are identical.

Because of these restrictions, hard links are not used as often as symbolic links, but the `Path` methods work seamlessly with hard links.

Creating a Symbolic Link

If your file system supports it, you can create a symbolic link by using the `createSymbolicLink(Path, Path, FileAttribute<?>)` method. The second `Path` argument represents the target file or directory (which may or may not exist). The following code snippet creates a symbolic link with default permissions:

```
Path newLink = . . . ;
Path target = . . . ;
try {
    Files.createSymbolicLink(newLink, target);
} catch (IOException x) {
    System.err.println(x);
} catch (UnsupportedOperationException x) {
    // Some file systems do not support symbolic links.
    System.err.println(x);
}
```

The `FileAttributes` vararg enables you to specify initial file attributes that are set atomically when the link is created. However, this argument is intended for future use and is not currently implemented.

Creating a Hard Link

You can create a hard (or *regular*) link to an existing file by using the createLink(Path, Path) method. The second Path argument locates the existing file, and it must exist or a NoSuchFileException is thrown. The following code snippet shows how to create a link:

```
Path newLink = . . . ;
Path existingFile = . . . ;
try {
    Files.createLink(newLink, existingFile);
} catch (IOException x) {
    System.err.println(x);
} catch (UnsupportedOperationException x) {
    // Some file systems do not
    // support adding an existing
    // file to a directory.
    System.err.println(x);
}
```

Detecting a Symbolic Link

To determine whether a Path instance is a symbolic link, you can use the isSymbolicLink(Path) method. The following code snippet shows how:

```
Path file = . . . ;
boolean isSymbolicLink =
    Files.isSymbolicLink(file);
```

For more information, see the "Managing Metadata (File and File Store Attributes)" section in this chapter.

Finding the Target of a Link

You can obtain the target of a symbolic link by using the readSymbolicLink(Path) method, as follows:

```
Path link = . . . ;
try {
    System.out.format("Target of link" +
        " '%s' is '%s'%n", link,
            Files.readSymbolicLink(link));
} catch (IOException x) {
    System.err.println(x);
}
```

If the Path is not a symbolic link, this method throws a NotLinkException.

Walking the File Tree

Do you need to create an application that will recursively visit all the files in a file tree? Perhaps you need to delete every `.class` file in a tree or find every file that hasn't been accessed in the last year. You can do so with the `FileVisitor`[61] interface.

The FileVisitor Interface

To walk a file tree, you first need to implement a `FileVisitor`. A `FileVisitor` specifies the required behavior at key points in the traversal process: when a file is visited, before a directory is accessed, after a directory is accessed, or when a failure occurs. The interface has four methods that correspond to these situations:

- `preVisitDirectory`—This is invoked before a directory's entries are visited.
- `postVisitDirectory`—This is invoked after all the entries in a directory are visited. If any errors are encountered, the specific exception is passed to the method.
- `visitFile`—This is invoked on the file being visited. The file's `BasicFileAttributes` package is passed to the method, or you can use the file attributes package to read a specific set of attributes. For example, you can choose to read the file's `DosFileAttributeView` to determine if the file has the "hidden" bit set.
- `visitFileFailed`—This is invoked when the file cannot be accessed. The specific exception is passed to the method. You can choose to throw the exception, print it to the console or a log file, and so on.

If you don't need to implement all four of the `FileVisitor` methods, instead of implementing the `FileVisitor` interface, you can extend the `SimpleFileVisitor`[62] class. This class, which implements the `FileVisitor` interface, visits all files in a tree and throws an `IOError` when an error is encountered. You can extend this class and override only the methods that you require.

Here is an example that extends `SimpleFileVisitor` to print all entries in a file tree. It prints the entry whether the entry is a regular file, a symbolic link, a directory, or some other "unspecified" type of file. It also prints the size, in bytes, of each file. Any exception that is encountered is printed to the console.

The `FileVisitor` methods are shown in bold:

---

61. `7/docs/api/java/nio/file/FileVisitor.html`
62. `7/docs/api/java/nio/file/SimpleFileVisitor.html`

```
import static java.nio.file.FileVisitResult.*;

public static class PrintFiles
    extends SimpleFileVisitor<Path> {

    // Print information about
    // each type of file.
    @Override
    public FileVisitResult visitFile(Path file,
                                BasicFileAttributes attr) {
        if (attr.isSymbolicLink()) {
            System.out.format("Symbolic link: %s ", file);
        } else if (attr.isRegularFile()) {
            System.out.format("Regular file: %s ", file);
        } else {
            System.out.format("Other: %s ", file);
        }
        System.out.println("(" + attr.size() + "bytes)");
        return CONTINUE;
    }

    // Print each directory visited.
    @Override
    public FileVisitResult postVisitDirectory(Path dir,
                                       IOException exc) {
        System.out.format("Directory: %s%n", dir);
        return CONTINUE;
    }

    // If there is some error accessing
    // the file, let the user know.
    // If you don't override this method
    // and an error occurs, an IOException
    // is thrown.
    @Override
    public FileVisitResult visitFileFailed(Path file,
                                    IOException exc) {
        System.err.println(exc);
        return CONTINUE;
    }
}
```

Kickstarting the Process

Once you have implemented your `FileVisitor`, how do you initiate the file walk? There are two `walkFileTree` methods in the `Files` class:

- `walkFileTree(Path, FileVisitor)`
- `walkFileTree(Path, Set<FileVisitOption>, int, FileVisitor)`

The first method requires only a starting point and an instance of your `FileVisitor`. You can invoke the `PrintFiles` file visitor as follows:

```
Path startingDir = . . . ;
PrintFiles pf = new PrintFiles();
Files.walkFileTree(startingDir, pf);
```

The second `walkFileTree` method enables you to additionally specify a limit on the number of levels visited and a set of `FileVisitOption`[63] enums. If you want to ensure that this method walks the entire file tree, you can specify `Integer. MAX_VALUE` for the maximum depth argument.

You can specify the `FileVisitOption` enum, `FOLLOW_LINKS`, which indicates that symbolic links should be followed.

This code snippet shows how the four-argument method can be invoked:

```
import static java.nio.file.FileVisitResult.*;

Path startingDir = . . . ;

EnumSet<FileVisitOption> opts = EnumSet.of(FOLLOW_LINKS);

Finder finder = new Finder(pattern);
Files.walkFileTree(startingDir, opts, Integer.MAX_VALUE, finder);
```

Considerations When Creating a FileVisitor

A file tree is walked depth first, but you cannot make any assumptions about the iteration order in which subdirectories are visited. If your program will be changing the file system, you need to carefully consider how you implement your `FileVisitor`. For example, if you are writing a recursive delete, you must first delete the files in a directory before deleting the directory itself. In this case, you delete the directory in `postVisitDirectory`.

If you are writing a recursive copy, you create the new directory in `preVisit-Directory` before attempting to copy the files to it (in `visitFiles`). If you want to preserve the attributes of the source directory (similar to the UNIX `cp -p` command), you need to do that *after* the files have been copied, in `postVisitDirectory`. The `Copy` example shows how to do this.

If you are writing a file search, you perform the comparison in the `visitFile` method. This method finds all the files that match your criteria, but it does not find the directories. If you want to find both files and directories, you must also perform the comparison in either the `preVisitDirectory` or `postVisitDirectory` method. The `Find` example shows how to do this.

You need to decide whether you want symbolic links to be followed. If you are deleting files, for example, following symbolic links might not be advisable. If you

---

63. `7/docs/api/java/nio/file/FileVisitOption.html`

are copying a file tree, you might want to allow it. By default, `walkFileTree` does not follow symbolic links.

The `visitFile` method is invoked for files. If you have specified the `FOLLOW_LINKS` option and your file tree has a circular link to a parent directory, the looping directory is reported in the `visitFileFailed` method with the `FileSystemLoopException`. The following code snippet shows how to catch a circular link and is from the `Copy` example:

```
@Override
public FileVisitResult
    visitFileFailed(Path file,
        IOException exc) {
    if (exc instanceof FileSystemLoopException) {
        System.err.println("cycle detected: " + file);
    } else {
        System.err.format("Unable to copy:" + " %s: %s%n", file, exc);
    }
    return CONTINUE;
}
```

This case can occur only when the program is following symbolic links.

Controlling the Flow

Perhaps you want to walk the file tree looking for a particular directory and, when found, you want the process to terminate. Perhaps you want to skip specific directories.

The `FileVisitor` methods return a `FileVisitResult`[64] value. You can abort the file-walking process or control whether a directory is visited by the values you return in the `FileVisitor` methods:

- `CONTINUE`—This indicates that the file walking should continue. If the `preVisitDirectory` method returns `CONTINUE`, the directory is visited.

- `TERMINATE`—This immediately aborts the file walking. No further file-walking methods are invoked after this value is returned.

- `SKIP_SUBTREE`—When `preVisitDirectory` returns this value, the specified directory and its subdirectories are skipped. This branch is "pruned out" of the tree.

- `SKIP_SIBLINGS`—When `preVisitDirectory` returns this value, the specified directory is not visited, `postVisitDirectory` is not invoked, and no further unvisited siblings are visited. If returned from the `postVisitDirectory`

---

64. 7/docs/api/java/nio/file/FileVisitResult.html

method, no further siblings are visited. Essentially, nothing further happens in the specified directory.

In this code snippet, any directory named SCCS is skipped:

```
import static java.nio.file.FileVisitResult.*;

public FileVisitResult
    preVisitDirectory(Path dir,
        BasicFileAttributes attrs) {
    (if (dir.getFileName().toString().equals("SCCS")) {
        return SKIP_SUBTREE;
    }
    return CONTINUE;
}
```

In this code snippet, as soon as a particular file is located, the file name is printed to standard output and the file walking terminates:

```
import static java.nio.file.FileVisitResult.*;

// The file we are looking for.
Path lookingFor = . . . ;

public FileVisitResult
    visitFile(Path file,
        BasicFileAttributes attr) {
    if (file.getFileName().equals(lookingFor)) {
        System.out.println("Located file: " + file);
        return TERMINATE;
    }
    return CONTINUE;
}
```

Examples

The following examples demonstrate the file-walking mechanism:

- Find—This recurses a file tree looking for files and directories that match a particular glob pattern. An example is discussed in the next section, "Finding Files."
- Chmod—This recursively changes permissions on a file tree (for POSIX systems only).
- Copy—This recursively copies a file tree.
- WatchDir—This demonstrates the mechanism that watches a directory for files that have been created, deleted, or modified. Calling this program with the -r option watches an entire tree for changes. For more information about the file notification service, see the section "Watching a Directory for Changes" later in this chapter.

Finding Files

If you have ever used a shell script, you have most likely used pattern matching to locate files. In fact, you have probably used it extensively. If you haven't used it, pattern matching uses special characters to create a pattern and then file names can be compared against that pattern. For example, in most shell scripts, an asterisk (*) matches any number of characters. For example, the following command lists all the files in the current directory that end in `.html`:

```
% ls *.html
```

The `java.nio.file` package provides programmatic support for this useful feature. Each file system implementation provides a `PathMatcher`.[65] You can retrieve a file system's `PathMatcher` by using the `getPathMatcher(String)` method in the `FileSystem` class. The following code snippet fetches the path matcher for the default file system:

```
String pattern = . . . ;
PathMatcher matcher =
    FileSystems.getDefault().getPathMatcher("glob:" + pattern);
```

The string argument passed to `getPathMatcher` specifies the syntax flavor and the pattern to be matched. This example specifies glob syntax. (For a refresher on glob syntax, consult the previous section, "What Is a Glob?")

Glob syntax is easy to use and flexible, but if you prefer, you can also use regular expressions, or *regex*, syntax. For further information about regex, see Chapter 13. Some file system implementations might support additional syntaxes.

If you want to use some other form of string-based pattern matching, you can create your own `PathMatcher` class. The examples in this section use glob syntax.

Once you have created your `PathMatcher` instance, you are ready to match files against it. The `PathMatcher` interface has a single method, `matches`, which takes a `Path` argument and returns a boolean: it either matches the pattern or doesn't. The following code snippet looks for files that end in `.java` or `.class` and prints those files to standard output:

```
PathMatcher matcher =
    FileSystems.getDefault().getPathMatcher("glob:*.{java,class}");

Path filename = . . . ;
if (matcher.matches(filename)) {
    System.out.println(filename);
}
```

65. 7/docs/api/java/nio/file/PathMatcher.html

Recursive Pattern Matching

Searching for files that match a particular pattern goes hand-in-hand with walking a file tree. How many times do you know a file is *somewhere* on the file system but can't find the exact location? Or perhaps you need to find all files in a file tree that have a particular file extension.

The Find example does precisely that. Find is similar to the UNIX find utility but is pared down functionally. You can extend this example to include other functionalities. For example, the find utility supports the –prune flag to exclude an entire subtree from the search. You could implement that functionality by returning SKIP_SUBTREE in the preVisitDirectory method. To implement the –L option, which follows symbolic links, you could use the four-argument walkFileTree method and pass in the FOLLOW_LINKS enum (but make sure that you test for circular links in the visitFile method).

To run the Find application, use the following format:

```
% java Find <path> -name "<glob_pattern>"
```

The pattern is placed inside quotation marks, so any wildcards are not interpreted by the shell:

```
% java Find . -name "*.html"
```

Here is the source code for the Find example:

```
/**
 * Sample code that finds files that match the specified glob pattern.
 * For more information on what constitutes a glob pattern, see
 * http://docs.oracle.com/javase/tutorial/essential/io/fileOps.html#glob
 *
 * The file or directories that match the pattern are printed to
 * standard out.  The number of matches is also printed.
 *
 * When executing this application, you must put the glob pattern
 * in quotes, so the shell will not expand any wild cards:
 *              java Find . -name "*.java"
 */

import java.io.*;
import java.nio.file.*;
import java.nio.file.attribute.*;
import static java.nio.file.FileVisitResult.*;
import static java.nio.file.FileVisitOption.*;
import java.util.*;

public class Find {

    public static class Finder
        extends SimpleFileVisitor<Path> {

        private final PathMatcher matcher;
```

10

```
        private int numMatches = 0;

        Finder(String pattern) {
            matcher = FileSystems.getDefault()
                    .getPathMatcher("glob:" + pattern);
        }

        // Compares the glob pattern against
        // the file or directory name.
        void find(Path file) {
            Path name = file.getFileName();
            if (name != null && matcher.matches(name)) {
                numMatches++;
                System.out.println(file);
            }
        }

        // Prints the total number of
        // matches to standard out.
        void done() {
            System.out.println("Matched: " + numMatches);
        }

        // Invoke the pattern matching
        // method on each file.
        @Override
        public FileVisitResult visitFile(Path file,
                BasicFileAttributes attrs) {
            find(file);
            return CONTINUE;
        }

        // Invoke the pattern matching
        // method on each directory.
        @Override
        public FileVisitResult preVisitDirectory(Path dir,
                BasicFileAttributes attrs) {
            find(dir);
            return CONTINUE;
        }

        @Override
        public FileVisitResult visitFileFailed(Path file,
                IOException exc) {
            System.err.println(exc);
            return CONTINUE;
        }
    }

    static void usage() {
        System.err.println("java Find <path>" +
            " -name \"<glob_pattern>\"");
        System.exit(-1);
    }

    public static void main(String[] args)
        throws IOException {

        if (args.length < 3 || !args[1].equals("-name"))
            usage();
```

```
        Path startingDir = Paths.get(args[0]);
        String pattern = args[2];

        Finder finder = new Finder(pattern);
        Files.walkFileTree(startingDir, finder);
        finder.done();
    }
}
```

Recursively walking a file tree is covered in the previous section, "Walking the File Tree."

Watching a Directory for Changes

Have you ever found yourself editing a file, using an integrated development environment (IDE) or another editor, and a dialog box appears to inform you that one of the open files has changed on the file system and needs to be reloaded? Or perhaps, like the NetBeans IDE, the application just quietly updates the file without notifying you. Figure 10.9 shows how this notification looks with the free editor, jEdit.[66]

To implement this functionality, called *file change notification*, a program must be able to detect what is happening to the relevant directory on the file system. One way to do so is to poll the file system looking for changes, but this approach is inefficient. It does not scale to applications that have hundreds of open files or directories to monitor.

10

Figure 10.9 jEdit Dialog Box Showing That a Modified File Is Detected

---

66. http://sourceforge.net/projects/jedit

The `java.nio.file` package provides a file change notification API, called the `WatchService` API. This API enables you to register a directory (or directories) with the watch service. When registering, you tell the service which types of events you are interested in: file creation, file deletion, or file modification. When the service detects an event of interest, it is forwarded to the registered process. The registered process has a thread (or a pool of threads) dedicated to watching for any pertinent events. When an event comes in, it is handled as needed.

Watch Service Overview

The WatchService API is fairly low level, allowing you to customize it. You can use it as is, or you can choose to create a high-level API on top of this mechanism so that it is suited to your particular needs.

Here are the basic steps required to implement a watch service:

- Create a `WatchService` "watcher" for the file system.
- Register each directory that you want monitored with the watcher. When registering a directory, you specify the types of events for which you want notification. You receive a `WatchKey` instance for each directory that you register.
- Implement an infinite loop to wait for incoming events. When an event occurs, the key is signaled and placed into the watcher's queue.
- Retrieve the key from the watcher's queue. You can obtain the file name from the key.
- Retrieve each pending event for the key. (There might be multiple events.) Process as needed.
- Reset the key, and resume waiting for events.
- Close the service. The watch service exits when the thread exits or when it is closed (by invoking its `closed` method).

`WatchKeys` are thread safe and can be used with the `java.nio.concurrent` package. You can dedicate a thread pool to this effort, which is described in Chapter 12.

Try It Out

Because this API is more advanced, try it out before proceeding. Save the `Watch-Dir` example to your computer, and compile it. Create a `test` directory that will be passed to the example. `WatchDir` uses a single thread to process all events, so it blocks keyboard input while waiting for events. Run the program in a separate window or in the background, as follows:

```
java WatchDir test &
```

Play with creating, deleting, and editing files in the `test` directory. When any of these events occurs, a message is printed to the console. When you have finished, delete the `test` directory and `WatchDir` will exit. Or, if you prefer, you can manually kill the process.

You can also watch an entire file tree by specifying the `-r` option. When you specify `-r`, `WatchDir` walks the file tree, registering each directory with the watch service.

Creating a Watch Service and Registering for Events

The first step is to create a new `WatchService`[67] by using the `newWatchService` method in the `FileSystem` class, as follows:

```
WatchService watcher = FileSystems.getDefault().newWatchService();
```

Next, register one or more objects with the watch service. Any object that implements the `Watchable`[68] interface can be registered. The `Path` class implements the `Watchable` interface, so each directory to be monitored is registered as a `Path` object.

As with any `Watchable` interface, the `Path` class implements two `register` methods. Our example uses the two-argument version, `register(WatchService, WatchEvent.Kind<?> . . . )`. (The three-argument version takes a `WatchEvent.Modifier`, which is not currently implemented.)

When registering an object with the watch service, you specify the types of events that you want to monitor. The supported `StandardWatchEventKinds`[69] event types are the following:

- `ENTRY_CREATE`—A directory entry is created.
- `ENTRY_DELETE`—A directory entry is deleted.
- `ENTRY_MODIFY`—A directory entry is modified.
- `OVERFLOW`—This indicates that events might have been lost or discarded. You do not have to register for the `OVERFLOW` event to receive it.

The following code snippet shows how to register a `Path` instance for all three event types:

---

67. 7/docs/api/java/nio/file/WatchService.html
68. 7/docs/api/java/nio/file/Watchable.html
69. 7/docs/api/java/nio/file/StandardWatchEventKinds.html

```
import static java.nio.file.StandardWatchEventKinds.*;

Path dir = . . . ;
try {
    WatchKey key = dir.register(watcher,
                            ENTRY_CREATE,
                            ENTRY_DELETE,
                            ENTRY_MODIFY);
} catch (IOException x) {
    System.err.println(x);
}
```

Processing Events

Here is a chronological breakdown of the events in an event-processing loop:

1. Get a watch key. Three methods are provided:

   - poll—This returns a queued key, if available, or returns immediately with a null value, if unavailable.

   - poll(long, TimeUnit)—This returns a queued key, if available. If a queued key is not immediately available, the program waits until the specified time. The TimeUnit argument determines whether the specified time is nanoseconds, milliseconds, or some other unit of time.

   - take—This returns a queued key, if available. If no queued key is available, this method waits.

2. Process the pending events for the key. You fetch the List of WatchEvents[70] from the pollEvents method.

3. Retrieve the type of event by using the kind method. No matter what events the key has registered for, it is possible to receive an OVERFLOW event. You can choose to handle the overflow or ignore it, but you should test for it.

4. Retrieve the file name associated with the event. The file name is stored as the context of the event, so the context method is used to retrieve it.

5. After the events for the key have been processed, you need to put the key back into a ready state by invoking reset. If this method returns false, the key is no longer valid and the loop can exit. *This step is very important.* If you fail to invoke reset, this key will not receive any further events.

A watch key has a state. At any given time, its state might be one of the following:

- Ready indicates that the key is ready to accept events. When first created, a key is in the ready state.

---

70. 7/docs/api/java/nio/file/WatchEvent.html

- `Signaled` indicates that one or more events are queued. Once the key has been signaled, it is no longer in the ready state until the `reset` method is invoked.

- `Invalid` indicates that the key is no longer active. This state happens when one of the following events occurs:

  ◌ The process explicitly cancels the key by using the `cancel` method.

  ◌ The directory becomes inaccessible.

  ◌ The watch service is closed.

Here is an example of an event-processing loop. It is taken from an email program that watches a directory, waiting for new files to appear. When a new file becomes available, it is examined to determine if it is a `text/plain` file via the `probeContentType(Path)` method. The intention is that `text/plain` files will be emailed to an alias, but that implementation detail is left to the reader.

The methods specific to the `WatchService` API are shown in bold:

```
for (;;) {

    // wait for key to be signaled
    WatchKey key;
    try {
        key = watcher.take();
    } catch (InterruptedException x) {
        return;
    }

    for (WatchEvent<?> event: key.pollEvents()) {
        WatchEvent.Kind<?> kind = event.kind();

        // This key is registered only
        // for ENTRY_CREATE events,
        // but an OVERFLOW event can
        // occur regardless if events
        // are lost or discarded.
        if (kind == OVERFLOW) {
            continue;
        }

        // The filename is the
        // context of the event.
        WatchEvent<Path> ev = (WatchEvent<Path>)event;
        Path filename = ev.context();

        // Verify that the new
        //   file is a text file.
        try {
            // Resolve the filename against the directory.
            // If the filename is "test" and the directory is "foo",
            // the resolved name is "test/foo".
            Path child = dir.resolve(filename);
```

10

```
                    if (!Files.probeContentType(child).equals("text/plain")) {
                        System.err.format("New file '%s'" +
                            " is not a plain text file.%n", filename);
                        continue;
                    }
                } catch (IOException x) {
                    System.err.println(x);
                    continue;
                }

                // Email the file to the
                //   specified email alias.
                System.out.format("Emailing file %s%n", filename);
                //Details left to reader. . . .
            }

            // Reset the key -- this step is critical if you want to
            // receive further watch events.  If the key is no longer valid,
            // the directory is inaccessible so exit the loop.
            boolean valid = key.reset();
            if (!valid) {
                break;
            }
        }
    }
```

Retrieving the File Name

The file name is retrieved from the event context. The `Email` example retrieves the file name with this code:

```
WatchEvent<Path> ev = (WatchEvent<Path>)event;
Path filename = ev.context();
```

When you compile the `Email` example, it generates the following error:

```
Note: Email.java uses unchecked or unsafe operations.
Note: Recompile with -Xlint:unchecked for details.
```

This error is a result of the line of code that casts the `WatchEvent<T>` to a `WatchEvent<Path>`. The `WatchDir` example avoids this error by creating a utility cast method that suppresses the unchecked warning, as follows:

```
@SuppressWarnings("unchecked")
static <T> WatchEvent<T> cast(WatchEvent<?> event) {
    return (WatchEvent<Path>)event;
}
```

If you are unfamiliar with the `@SuppressWarnings` syntax, see the section "Annotations" in Chapter 4.

When to Use and Not Use This API

The WatchService API is designed for applications that need to be notified about file change events. It is well suited for any application, like an editor or IDE, that potentially has many open files and needs to ensure that the files are synchronized with the file system. It is also well suited for an application server that watches a directory, perhaps waiting for .jsp or .jar files to drop in order to deploy them.

This API is *not* designed for indexing a hard drive. Most file system implementations have native support for file change notification. The WatchService API takes advantage of this support where available. However, when a file system does not support this mechanism, the watch service will poll the file system, waiting for events.

Other Useful Methods

A few useful methods did not fit elsewhere in this chapter and are covered in this section.

Determining MIME Type

To determine the MIME type of a file, you might find the probeContentType (Path) method useful. Here is an example:

```
try {
    String type = Files.probeContentType(filename);
    if (type == null) {
        System.err.format("'%s' has an" + " unknown filetype.%n",
                          filename);
    } else if (!type.equals("text/plain")) {
        System.err.format("'%s' is not" + " a plain text file.%n",
                          filename);
        continue;
    }
} catch (IOException x) {
    System.err.println(x);
}
```

Note that probeContentType returns null if the content type cannot be determined.

The implementation of this method is highly platform specific and is fallible. The content type is determined by the platform's default file type detector. For example, if the detector determines a file's content type to be application/x-java based on the .class extension, it might be fooled.

You can provide a custom FileTypeDetector[71] if the default is not sufficient for your needs. For example, the Email example uses the probeContentType method.

---

71. 7/docs/api/java/nio/file/spi/FileTypeDetector.html

Default File System

To retrieve the default file system, use the `getDefault` method. Typically, this `FileSystems` method (note the plural) is chained to one of the `FileSystem` methods (note the singular), as follows:

```
PathMatcher matcher =
    FileSystems.getDefault().getPathMatcher("glob:*.*");
```

Path String Separator

The path separator for POSIX file systems is the forward slash (/) for POSIX file systems and the backslash (\) for Microsoft Windows. Other file systems might use other delimiters. To retrieve the path separator for the default file system, you can use one of the following approaches:

```
String separator = File.separator;
String separator = FileSystems.getDefault().getSeparator();
```

The `getSeparator` method is also used to retrieve the path separator for any available file system.

File System's File Stores

A file system has one or more file stores to hold its files and directories. The *file store* represents the underlying storage device. In UNIX operating systems, each mounted file system is represented by a file store. In Microsoft Windows, each volume is represented by a file store: `C:`, `D:`, and so on.

To retrieve a list of all the file stores for the file system, you can use the `get-FileStores` method. This method returns an `Iterable`, which allows you to use the enhanced `for` statement described in Chapter 3 to iterate over all the root directories:

```
for (FileStore store: FileSystems.getDefault().getFileStores()) {
    . . .
}
```

If you want to retrieve the file store where a particular file is located, use the `getFileStore` method in the `Files` class, as follows:

```
Path file = . . . ;
FileStore store= Files.getFileStore(file);
```

The `DiskUsage` example uses the `getFileStores` method.

Legacy File I/O Code

Interoperability with Legacy Code

Prior to the Java SE 7 release, the `java.io.File` class was the mechanism used for file I/O, but it had several drawbacks:

- Many methods didn't throw exceptions when they failed, so it was impossible to obtain a useful error message. For example, if a file deletion failed, the program would receive a `delete fail` but wouldn't know if it was because the file didn't exist, the user didn't have permissions, or some other problem.
- The `rename` method didn't work consistently across platforms.
- There was no real support for symbolic links.
- More support for metadata was desired, such as file permissions, file owner, and other security attributes.
- Accessing file metadata was inefficient.
- Many of the `File` methods didn't scale. Requesting a large directory listing over a server could result in a hang. Large directories could also cause memory resource problems, resulting in a denial of service.
- It was not possible to write reliable code that could recursively walk a file tree and respond appropriately if there were circular symbolic links.

Perhaps you have legacy code that uses `java.io.File` and would like to take advantage of the `java.nio.file.Path` functionality with minimal impact to your code. The `java.io.File` class provides the `toPath` method, which converts an old style `File` instance to a `java.nio.file.Path` instance, as follows:

```
Path input = file.toPath();
```

You can then take advantage of the rich feature set available to the `Path` class. For example, assume you had some code that deleted a file:

```
file.delete();
```

You could modify this code to use the `Files.delete` method, as follows:

```
Path fp = file.toPath();
Files.delete(fp);
```

Conversely, the `Path.toFile` method constructs a `java.io.File` object for a `Path` object.

Mapping java.io.File Functionality to java.nio.file

Because the Java implementation of file I/O has been completely redesigned in the Java SE 7 release, you cannot swap one method for another. If you want to use the rich functionality offered by the `java.nio.file` package, your easiest solution is to use the `File.toPath` method as suggested in the previous section. However, if you don't want to use that approach or it is not sufficient for your needs, you must rewrite your file I/O code.

There is no one-to-one correspondence between the two APIs, but Table 10.6 gives you a general idea of what functionality in the `java.io.File` API maps to in the `java.nio.file` API and tells you where you can obtain more information.

Summary of Basic I/O and NIO.2

The `java.io` package contains many classes that your programs can use to read and write data. Most of the classes implement sequential access streams. The sequential access streams can be divided into two groups: those that read and write bytes and those that read and write Unicode characters. Each sequential access stream has a specialty, such as reading from or writing to a file, filtering data being read or written, or serializing an object.

The `java.nio.file` package provides extensive support for file and file system I/O. This is a very comprehensive API, but the key entry points are as follows:

- The `Path` class has methods for manipulating a path.
- The `Files` class has methods for file operations, such as moving, copying, and deleting, and methods for retrieving and setting file attributes.
- The `FileSystem` class has a variety of methods for obtaining information about the file system.

More information on NIO.2 can be found on the OpenJDK: NIO[72] project web site on `java.net`. This site includes resources for features provided by NIO.2 that are beyond the scope of this chapter, such as multicasting, asynchronous I/O, and creating your own file system implementation.

---

72. `http://openjdk.java.net/projects/nio`

Table 10.6. Mapping from Legacy File I/O to NIO.2

java.io.File functionality	java.nio.file functionality	Sections with more information
`java.io.File`	`java.nio.file.Path`	The Path Class
`java.io.RandomAccessFile`	The `SeekableByteChannel` functionality	Random Access Files
`File.canRead, canWrite, canExecute`	`Files.isReadable,` `Files.isWritable,` and `Files.isExecutable`	Checking a File or Directory Managing Metadata (File and File Store Attributes). Note that for UNIX file systems, "Managing Metadata (File and File Store Attributes)" describes the package used to check the nine file permissions.
`File.isDirectory(),` `File.isFile(),` and `File.length()`	`Files.isDirectory(Path,` `LinkOption . . . ),` `Files.isRegularFile(Path,` `LinkOption . . . ),` and `Files.size(Path)`	Managing Metadata (File and File Store Attributes)
`File.lastModified()` and `File.setLastModified(long)`	`Files.getLastModifiedTime(Path,` `LinkOption . . . )` and `Files.setLastMOdifiedTime(Path,` `FileTime)`	Managing Metadata (File and File Store Attributes)
The `File` methods that set various attributes (`setExecutable,` `setReadable,` `setReadOnly,` `setWritable`)	These methods are replaced by the `Files` method `setAttribute(Path,` `String, Object,` `LinkOption . . . ).`	Managing Metadata (File and File Store Attributes)
`new File(parent,` `"newfile")`	`parent.resolve("newfile")`	Path Operations
`File.renameTo`	`Files.move`	Moving a File or Directory
`File.delete`	`Files.delete`	Deleting a File or Directory
`File.createNewFile`	`Files.createFile`	Creating Files
`File.deleteOnExit`	Replaced by the `DELETE_ON_CLOSE` option specified in the `createFile` method	Creating Files

(continued on next page)

Table 10.6. Mapping from Legacy File I/O to NIO.2 (continued)

java.io.File functionality	java.nio.file functionality	Sections with more information
`File.createTempFile`	`Files.createTempFile(Path, String, FileAttributes<?>)`,`Files.createTempFile(Path, String, String, FileAttributes<?>)`	Creating Files Creating and Writing a File by Using Stream I/O Reading and Writing Files by Using Channel I/O
`File.exists`	`Files.exists` and `Files.notExists`	Checking a File or Directory
`File.compareTo` and `equals`	`Path.compareTo` and `equals`	Comparing Two Paths
`File.getAbsolutePath` and `getAbsoluteFile`	`Path.toAbsolutePath`	Converting a Path
`File.getCanonicalPath` and `getCanonicalFile`	`Path.toRealPath` or `normalize`	Converting a Path Removing Redundancies from a Path
`File.toURI`	`Path.toURI`	Converting a Path
`File.isHidden`	`Files.isHidden`	Retrieving Information about a Path
`File.list` and `list-Files`	`Path.newDirectoryStream`	Listing a Directory's Contents
`File.mkdir` and `mkdirs`	`Path.createDirectory`	Creating a Directory
`File.listRoots`	`FileSystem.getRootDirectories`	Listing a File System's Root Directories
`File.getTotalSpace`, `File.getFreeSpace`, and `File.getUsableSpace`	`FileStore.getTotalSpace`, `FileStore.getUnallocatedSpace`, `FileStore.getUsableSpace`, `FileStore.getTotalSpace`	File Store Attributes

Questions and Exercises: Basic I/O and NIO.2

Questions

1. What class and method would you use to read a few pieces of data that are at known positions near the end of a large file?

2. When invoking `format`, what is the best way to indicate a new line?

3. How would you determine the MIME type of a file?

4. What method(s) would you use to determine whether a file is a symbolic link?

Exercises

1. Write an example that counts the number of times a particular character, such as e, appears in a file. The character can be specified at the command line. You can use `xanadu.txt` as the input file.

2. The file `datafile` begins with a single `long` that tells you the offset of a single `int` piece of data within the same file. Write a program that gets the `int` piece of data. What is the `int` data?

Answers

You can find answers to these questions and exercises at `http://docs.oracle.com/ javase/tutorial/essential/io/QandE/answers.html`.

10

11

Collections

This chapter describes the Java Collections Framework. Here you will learn what collections are and how they can make your job easier and programs better. You'll learn about the core elements—interfaces, implementations, and algorithms—that compose the Java Collections Framework.

The first section tells you what collections are and how they'll make your job easier and increase the efficiency of your programs. This section also describes the core elements (interfaces, implementations, and algorithms).

The second section describes the core collection interfaces, which are the heart and soul of the Java Collections Framework. You'll learn general guidelines for effective use of these interfaces, including when to use which interface. You'll also learn idioms for each interface that will help you get the most out of the interfaces.

The third section describes the Java SE Development Kit's (JDK) general-purpose collection implementations and tells you when to use which implementation. You'll also learn about the wrapper implementations, which add functionality to general-purpose implementations.

The fourth section describes the polymorphic algorithms provided by the JDK to operate on collections. With any luck, you'll never have to write your own sort routine again!

The fifth section tells you why you might want to write your own collection implementation (instead of using one of the general-purpose implementations provided by the JDK) and how to go about it. It's easy with the JDK's abstract collection implementations!

The sixth section tells you how the collections framework interoperates with older Application Programming Interfaces (APIs) that predate the addition of collections to Java. It also tells you how to design new APIs so that they'll interoperate seamlessly with other new APIs.

There are questions and exercises throughout the chapter to test your knowledge.

Introduction to Collections

A *collection*—sometimes called a *container*—is simply an object that groups multiple elements into a single unit. Collections are used to store, retrieve, manipulate, and convey aggregate data. Typically, they represent data items that form a natural group, such as a poker hand (a collection of cards), a mail folder (a collection of letters), or a telephone directory (a mapping of names to phone numbers).

What Is a Collections Framework?

If you've used the Java programming language—or just about any other programming language—you're already familiar with collections. A *collections framework* is a unified architecture for representing and manipulating collections. All collections frameworks contain the following:

- *Interfaces*. These are abstract data types that represent collections. Interfaces allow collections to be manipulated independently of the details of their representation. In object-oriented languages, interfaces generally form a hierarchy.

- *Implementations*. These are the concrete implementations of the collection interfaces. In essence, they are reusable data structures.

- *Algorithms*. These are the methods that perform useful computations, such as searching and sorting, on objects that implement collection interfaces. The algorithms are said to be *polymorphic*—that is, the same method can be used on many different implementations of the appropriate collection interface. In essence, algorithms are reusable functionality.

Apart from the Java Collections Framework, the best-known examples of collections frameworks are the C++ Standard Template Library (STL) and Smalltalk's collection hierarchy. Historically, collections frameworks have been quite complex, which gave them a reputation for having a steep learning curve. We believe that the Java Collections Framework breaks with this tradition, as you will learn in this chapter.

Benefits of the Java Collections Framework

The Java Collections Framework provides the following benefits:

- *Reduced programming effort.* By providing useful data structures and algorithms, the collections framework frees you to concentrate on the important parts of your program rather than on the low-level "plumbing" required to make it work. By facilitating interoperability among unrelated APIs, the Java Collections Framework frees you from writing adapter objects or conversion code to connect APIs.

- *Increased program speed and quality.* This collections framework provides high-performance, high-quality implementations of useful data structures and algorithms. The various implementations of each interface are interchangeable, so programs can be easily tuned by switching collection implementations. Because you're free from the drudgery of writing your own data structures, you'll have more time to devote to improving programs' quality and performance.

- *Interoperability among unrelated APIs.* The collection interfaces are the vernacular by which APIs pass collections back and forth. If a preexisting network administration API furnishes a collection of node names and your graphical user interface (GUI) toolkit expects a collection of column headings, the two APIs will interoperate seamlessly, even though they were written independently.

- *Reduced effort to learn and to use new APIs.* Many APIs naturally take collections on input and furnish them as output. In the past, each such API had a small sub-API devoted to manipulating its collections. There was little consistency among these ad hoc collection sub-APIs, so you had to learn each one from scratch, and it was easy to make mistakes when using them. With the advent of standard collection interfaces, the problem went away.

- *Reduced effort to design new APIs.* This is the flip side of the previous advantage. Designers and implementers don't have to reinvent the wheel each time they create an API that relies on collections; instead, they can use standard collection interfaces.

11

- *Increased software reuse.* New data structures that conform to the standard collection interfaces are by nature reusable. The same goes for new algorithms that operate on objects that implement these interfaces.

Interfaces

The *core collection interfaces* encapsulate different types of collections, which are shown in Figure 11.1. These interfaces allow collections to be manipulated independently of the details of their representation. Core collection interfaces are the foundation of the Java Collections Framework. As you can see in Figure 11.1, the core collection interfaces form a hierarchy.

A `Set` is a special kind of `Collection`, a `SortedSet` is a special kind of `Set`, and so on. Note that the hierarchy consists of two distinct trees—a `Map` is not a true `Collection`. Also, note that all the core collection interfaces are generic. For example, here is the declaration of the `Collection` interface:

```
public interface Collection<E> . . .
```

The `<E>` syntax tells you that the interface is generic. When you declare a `Collection` instance, you can *and should* specify the type of object contained in the collection. Specifying the type allows the compiler to verify that the type of object you put into the collection is correct (at compile time), thus reducing errors at runtime. For information on generic types, see Chapter 6.

When you understand how to use these interfaces, you will know most of what there is to know about the Java Collections Framework. This chapter provides general guidelines for effective use of the interfaces, including when to use which interface. You'll also learn programming idioms for each interface to help you get the most out of it.

To keep the number of core collection interfaces manageable, the Java platform doesn't provide separate interfaces for each variant of each collection type (e.g., immutable, fixed size, and append only). Instead, the modification operations in

Figure 11.1 The Core Collection Interfaces

each interface are designated *optional*—a given implementation may elect not to support all operations. If an unsupported operation is invoked, a collection throws an `UnsupportedOperationException`.[1] Implementations are responsible for documenting which optional operations they support. All Java general-purpose implementations support all optional operations.

The following list describes the core collection interfaces:

- `Collection`—This is the root of the collection hierarchy. A collection represents a group of objects known as its *elements*. The `Collection` interface is the least common denominator that all collections implement and is used to pass collections around and manipulate them when maximum generality is desired. Some collections allow duplicate elements, and others do not. Some are ordered, and others are unordered. The Java platform doesn't provide any direct implementations of this interface but provides implementations of more specific subinterfaces, such as `Set` and `List`.

- `Set`—This is a collection that cannot contain duplicate elements. It models the mathematical set abstraction and is used to represent sets, such as the cards composing a poker hand, the courses making up a student's schedule, or the processes running on a machine.

- `List`—This is an ordered collection (sometimes called a *sequence*). A `List` can contain duplicate elements. The user of a `List` generally has precise control over where each element is inserted and can access elements by their integer index (position). If you've used `Vector`, you're familiar with the general flavor of `List`.

- `Queue`—This is a collection used to hold multiple elements prior to processing. Besides basic `Collection` operations, a `Queue` provides additional insertion, extraction, and inspection operations. A `Queue` typically (but not necessarily) orders elements in a FIFO (first-in, first-out) manner. Among the exceptions are priority queues, which order elements according to a supplied comparator or the elements' natural ordering. Whatever the ordering used, the head of the queue is the element that would be removed by a call to `remove` or `poll`. In a FIFO queue, all new elements are inserted at the tail of the queue. Other kinds of queues may use different placement rules. Every `Queue` implementation must specify its ordering properties.

- `Map`—This is an object that maps keys to values. A `Map` cannot contain duplicate keys; each key can map to at most one value. If you've used `Hashtable`, you're already familiar with the basics of `Map`.

---

1. 7/docs/api/java/lang/UnsupportedOperationException.html

The last two core collection interfaces are merely sorted versions of `Set` and `Map`:

- `SortedSet`—This is a `Set` that maintains its elements in ascending order. Several additional operations are provided to take advantage of the ordering. Sorted sets are used for naturally ordered sets, such as word lists and membership rolls.
- `SortedMap`—This is a `Map` that maintains its mappings in ascending key order. This is the `Map` analog of `SortedSet`. Sorted maps are used for naturally ordered collections of key/value pairs, such as dictionaries and phone directories.

The Collection Interface

A `Collection`[2] represents a group of objects known as *elements*. The `Collection` interface is used to pass around collections of objects where maximum generality is desired. For example, by convention, all general-purpose collection implementations have a constructor that takes a `Collection` argument. This constructor, known as a *conversion constructor*, initializes the new collection to contain all the elements in the specified collection, whatever the given collection's subinterface or implementation type. In other words, it allows you to *convert* the collection's type.

Suppose, for example, you have a `Collection<String>` c, which may be a `List`, a `Set`, or another kind of `Collection`. This idiom creates a new `ArrayList` (an implementation of the `List` interface), initially containing all the elements in c:

```
List<String> list = new ArrayList<String>(c);
```

Here is the `Collection` interface:

```
public interface Collection<E> extends Iterable<E> {
    // Basic operations
    int size();
    boolean isEmpty();
    boolean contains(Object element);
    // optional
    boolean add(E element);
    // optional
    boolean remove(Object element);
    Iterator<E> iterator();

    // Bulk operations
    boolean containsAll(Collection<?> c);
    // optional
    boolean addAll(Collection<? extends E> c);
    // optional
```

---

2. 7/docs/api/java/util/Collection.html

```
            boolean removeAll(Collection<?> c);
            // optional
            boolean retainAll(Collection<?> c);
            // optional
            void clear();

            // Array operations
            Object[] toArray();
            <T> T[] toArray(T[] a);
        }
```

The interface does what you'd expect, given that a `Collection` represents a group of objects. The interface has methods to tell you how many elements are in the collection (`size`, `isEmpty`), check whether a given object is in the collection (`contains`), add and remove an element from the collection (`add`, `remove`), and provide an iterator over the collection (`iterator`).

The `add` method is defined generally enough so that it makes sense for collections that allow duplicates as well as those that don't. It guarantees that the `Collection` will contain the specified element after the call completes and returns `true` if the `Collection` changes as a result of the call. Similarly, the `remove` method is designed to remove a single instance of the specified element from the `Collection`, assuming that it contains the element to start with, and to return `true` if the `Collection` was modified as a result.

Traversing Collections

There are two ways to traverse collections: (1) with the `for-each` construct and (2) by using an `Iterator`.

The for-each Construct

The `for-each` construct allows you to concisely traverse a collection or array using a `for` loop. See Chapter 3, "The for Statement." The following code uses the `for-each` construct to print out each element of a collection on a separate line:

```
        for (Object o : collection)
            System.out.println(o);
```

The Iterator

An `Iterator`[3] is an object that enables you to traverse through a collection and remove elements from the collection selectively, if desired. You get an `Iterator` for a collection by calling its `iterator` method. The following is the `Iterator` interface:

---

3. 7/docs/api/java/util/Iterator.html

```
public interface Iterator<E> {
    boolean hasNext();
    E next();
    void remove(); //optional
}
```

The `hasNext` method returns `true` if the iteration has more elements, and the `next` method returns the next element in the iteration. The `remove` method removes the last element that was returned by `next` from the underlying `Collection`. The `remove` method may be called only once per call to `next` and throws an exception if this rule is violated.

Note that `Iterator.remove` is the *only* safe way to modify a collection during iteration; the behavior is unspecified if the underlying collection is modified in any other way while the iteration is in progress. Use `Iterator` instead of the `for-each` construct when you need to do the following:

- Iterate over multiple collections in parallel
- Remove the current element

Note that the `for-each` construct hides the iterator, so you cannot call `remove`. Therefore, the `for-each` construct is not usable for filtering.

The following method shows you how to use an `Iterator` to filter an arbitrary `Collection` (i.e., traverse the collection removing specific elements):

```
static void filter(Collection<?> c) {
    for (Iterator<?> it = c.iterator(); it.hasNext(); )
        if (!cond(it.next()))
            it.remove();
}
```

This simple piece of code is polymorphic, which means that it works for *any* `Collection` regardless of implementation. This example demonstrates how easy it is to write a polymorphic algorithm using the Java Collections Framework.

Collection Interface Bulk Operations

Bulk operations perform an operation on an entire `Collection`. You could implement these shorthand operations using the basic operations, though in most cases such implementations would be less efficient. The following are the bulk operations:

- `containsAll`—Returns true if the target `Collection` contains all the elements in the specified `Collection`

- addAll—Adds all the elements in the specified `Collection` to the target `Collection`
- removeAll—Removes all the elements from the target `Collection` that are also contained in the specified `Collection`
- retainAll—Removes all the elements from the target `Collection` that are *not* also contained in the specified `Collection` (i.e., retains only those elements in the target `Collection` that are also contained in the specified `Collection`)
- clear—Removes all elements from the `Collection`

The `addAll`, `removeAll`, and `retainAll` methods all return `true` if the target `Collection` was modified in the process of executing the operation.

As a simple example of the power of bulk operations, consider the following idiom to remove *all* instances of a specified element, e, from a `Collection`, c:

```
c.removeAll(Collections.singleton(e));
```

More specifically, suppose you want to remove all the `null` elements from a `Collection`:

```
c.removeAll(Collections.singleton(null));
```

This idiom uses `Collections.singleton`, which is a static factory method that returns an immutable `Set` containing only the specified element.

Collection Interface Array Operations

The `toArray` methods are provided as a bridge between collections and older APIs that expect arrays on input. The array operations allow the contents of a `Collection` to be translated into an array. The simple form with no arguments creates a new array of `Object`. The more complex form allows the caller to provide an array or choose the runtime type of the output array.

For example, suppose that c is a `Collection`. The following snippet dumps the contents of c into a newly allocated array of `Object` whose length is identical to the number of elements in c:

```
Object[] a = c.toArray();
```

Suppose that c is known to contain only strings (perhaps because c is of type `Collection<String>`). The following snippet dumps the contents of c into a newly allocated array of `String` whose length is identical to the number of elements in c:

```
String[] a = c.toArray(new String[0]);
```

The Set Interface

A Set[4] is a Collection that cannot contain duplicate elements. It models the mathematical set abstraction. The Set interface contains *only* methods inherited from Collection and adds the restriction that duplicate elements are prohibited. Set also adds a stronger contract on the behavior of the equals and hashCode operations, allowing Set instances to be compared meaningfully, even if their implementation types differ. Two Set instances are equal if they contain the same elements.

The following is the Set interface:

```
public interface Set<E> extends Collection<E> {
    // Basic operations
    int size();
    boolean isEmpty();
    boolean contains(Object element);
    // optional
    boolean add(E element);
    // optional
    boolean remove(Object element);
    Iterator<E> iterator();

    // Bulk operations
    boolean containsAll(Collection<?> c);
    // optional
    boolean addAll(Collection<? extends E> c);
    // optional
    boolean removeAll(Collection<?> c);
    // optional
    boolean retainAll(Collection<?> c);
    // optional
    void clear();

    // Array Operations
    Object[] toArray();
    <T> T[] toArray(T[] a);
}
```

The Java platform contains three general-purpose Set implementations: Hash-Set, TreeSet, and LinkedHashSet. HashSet,[5] which stores its elements in a hash table, is the best-performing implementation; however, it makes no guarantees concerning the order of iteration. TreeSet,[6] which stores its elements in a red-black tree, orders its elements based on their values; it is substantially slower than

---

4. 7/docs/api/java/util/Set.html

5. 7/docs/api/java/util/HashSet.html

6. 7/docs/api/java/util/TreeSet.html

HashSet. LinkedHashSet,[7] which is implemented as a hash table with a linked list running through it, orders its elements based on the order in which they were inserted into the set (insertion order). LinkedHashSet spares its clients from the unspecified, generally chaotic ordering provided by HashSet at a cost that is only slightly higher.

Here's a simple but useful Set idiom: Suppose you have a Collection, c, and you want to create another Collection containing the same elements but with all duplicates eliminated. The following one-liner does the trick:

```
Collection<Type> noDups = new HashSet<Type>(c);
```

It works by creating a Set (which, by definition, cannot contain a duplicate), initially containing all the elements in c. It uses the standard conversion constructor described previously in "The Collection Interface" section.

Here is a minor variant of this idiom that preserves the order of the original collection while removing duplicate element:

```
Collection<Type> noDups = new LinkedHashSet<Type>(c);
```

The following is a generic method that encapsulates the preceding idiom, returning a Set of the same generic type as the one passed:

```
public static <E> Set<E> removeDups(Collection<E> c) {
    return new LinkedHashSet<E>(c);
}
```

11

Set Interface Basic Operations

The size operation returns the number of elements in the Set (its *cardinality*). The isEmpty method does exactly what you think it would. The add method adds the specified element to the Set if it's not already present and returns a boolean indicating whether the element was added. Similarly, the remove method removes the specified element from the Set if it's present and returns a boolean indicating whether the element was present. The iterator method returns an Iterator over the Set.

The following program takes the words in its argument list and prints out any duplicate words, the number of distinct words, and a list of the words with duplicates eliminated:

```
import java.util.*;

public class FindDups {
```

---

7.   7/docs/api/java/util/LinkedHashSet.html

```
    public static void main(String[] args) {
        Set<String> s = new HashSet<String>();
        for (String a : args)
            if (!s.add(a))
                System.out.println("Duplicate detected: " + a);

        System.out.println(s.size() + " distinct words: " + s);
    }
}
```

We can run the program:

```
java FindDups i came i saw i left
```

And the following output is produced:

```
Duplicate detected: i
Duplicate detected: i
4 distinct words: [i, left, saw, came]
```

Note that the code always refers to the `Collection` by its interface type (`Set`) rather than by its implementation type (`HashSet`). This is a *strongly* recommended programming practice because it gives you the flexibility to change implementations merely by changing the constructor. If either of the variables used to store a collection or the parameters used to pass it around are declared to be of the `Collection`'s implementation type rather than its interface type, *all* such variables and parameters must be changed in order to change the implementation type.

Furthermore, there's no guarantee that the resulting program will work. If the program uses any nonstandard operations present in the original implementation type but not in the new one, the program will fail. Referring to collections only by their interface prevents you from using any nonstandard operations.

The implementation type of the `Set` in the preceding example is `HashSet`, which makes no guarantees as to the order of the elements in the `Set`. If you want the program to print the word list in alphabetical order, merely change the `Set`'s implementation type from `HashSet` to `TreeSet`. Making this trivial one-line change causes the command line in the previous example to generate the following output:

```
java FindDups i came i saw i left
Duplicate detected: i
Duplicate detected: i
4 distinct words: [came, i, left, saw]
```

Set Interface Bulk Operations

Bulk operations are particularly well suited to Set objects; when applied, they perform standard set-algebraic operations. Suppose s1 and s2 are sets. Here's what bulk operations do:

- s1.containsAll(s2)—This returns true if s2 is a *subset* of s1; s2 is a subset of s1 if set s1 contains all of the elements in s2.
- s1.addAll(s2)—This transforms s1 into the *union* of s1 and s2. The union of two sets is the set containing all the elements contained in either set.
- s1.retainAll(s2)—This transforms s1 into the *intersection* of s1 and s2. The intersection of two sets is the set containing only the elements common to both sets.
- s1.removeAll(s2)—This transforms s1 into the *(asymmetric) set difference* of s1 and s2. For example, the set difference of s1 minus s2 is the set containing all the elements found in s1 but not in s2.

To calculate the union, intersection, or set difference of two sets *nondestructively* (without modifying either set), the caller must copy one set before calling the appropriate bulk operation. The following are the resulting idioms:

```
Set<Type> union = new HashSet<Type>(s1);
union.addAll(s2);

Set<Type> intersection = new HashSet<Type>(s1);
intersection.retainAll(s2);

Set<Type> difference = new HashSet<Type>(s1);
difference.removeAll(s2);
```

The implementation type of the result Set in the preceding idioms is Hash-Set, which, as mentioned previously, is the best all-around Set implementation in the Java platform. However, any general-purpose Set implementation could be substituted.

Let's revisit the FindDups program. Suppose you want to know which words in the argument list occur only once and which occur more than once, but you do not want any duplicates printed out repeatedly. This can be achieved by generating two sets—one containing every word in the argument list and the other containing only the duplicates. The words that occur only once are the set difference of these two sets, which we know how to compute. Here's how the resulting program looks:

```
import java.util.*;

public class FindDups2 {
```

```
        public static void main(String[] args) {
            Set<String> uniques = new HashSet<String>();
            Set<String> dups    = new HashSet<String>();

            for (String a : args)
                if (!uniques.add(a))
                    dups.add(a);

            // Destructive set-difference
            uniques.removeAll(dups);

            System.out.println("Unique words:    " + uniques);
            System.out.println("Duplicate words: " + dups);
        }
    }
```

When run with the same argument list used earlier (i came i saw i left), the program yields the following output:

```
Unique words:    [left, saw, came]
Duplicate words: [i]
```

A less common set-algebraic operation is the *symmetric set difference*—the set of elements contained in either of two specified sets but not in both. The following code calculates the symmetric set difference of two sets nondestructively:

```
Set<Type> symmetricDiff = new HashSet<Type>(s1);
symmetricDiff.addAll(s2);
Set<Type> tmp = new HashSet<Type>(s1);
tmp.retainAll(s2));
symmetricDiff.removeAll(tmp);
```

Set Interface Array Operations

The array operations don't do anything special for Sets beyond what they do for any other Collection. These operations are described in the previous section, "The Collection Interface."

The List Interface

A List[8] is an ordered Collection (sometimes called a *sequence*). A List may contain duplicate elements. In addition to the operations inherited from Collection, the List interface includes operations for the following:

- *Positional access.* Manipulates elements based on their numerical position in the list

---

8.   7/docs/api/java/util/List.html

- *Search.* Searches for a specified object in the list and returns its numerical position
- *Iteration.* Extends `Iterator` semantics to take advantage of the list's sequential nature
- *Range view.* Performs arbitrary *range operations* on the list

The `List` interface is as follows:

```java
public interface List<E> extends Collection<E> {
    // Positional access
    E get(int index);
    // optional
    E set(int index, E element);
    // optional
    boolean add(E element);
    // optional
    void add(int index, E element);
    // optional
    E remove(int index);
    // optional
    boolean addAll(int index, Collection<? extends E> c);

    // Search
    int indexOf(Object o);
    int lastIndexOf(Object o);

    // Iteration
    ListIterator<E> listIterator();
    ListIterator<E> listIterator(int index);

    // Range-view
    List<E> subList(int from, int to);
}
```

The Java platform contains two general-purpose `List` implementations: `ArrayList`,[9] which is usually the better-performing implementation, and `LinkedList`,[10] which offers better performance under certain circumstances. Also, `Vector` has been retrofitted to implement `List`.

Comparison to Vector

If you've used `Vector`,[11] you're already familiar with the general basics of `List`. (Of course, `List` is an interface, while `Vector` is a concrete implementation.) `List` fixes several minor API deficiencies in `Vector`. Commonly used `Vector` operations, such

9. 7/docs/api/java/util/ArrayList.html

10. 7/docs/api/java/util/LinkedList.html

11. 7/docs/api/java/util/Vector.html

as `elementAt` and `setElementAt`, have been given much shorter names. When you consider that these two operations are the `List` analog of square brackets for arrays, it becomes apparent that shorter names are highly desirable. Consider the following assignment statement:

```
a[i] = a[j].times(a[k]);
```

Here is the `Vector` equivalent:

```
v.setElementAt(v.elementAt(j).times(v.elementAt(k)), i);
```

And here is the `List` equivalent:

```
v.set(i, v.get(j).times(v.get(k)));
```

You may already have noticed that the `set` method, which replaces the `Vector` method `setElementAt`, reverses the order of the arguments so that they match the corresponding array operation. Consider the following assignment statement:

```
gift[5] = "golden rings";
```

Here is the `Vector` equivalent:

```
gift.setElementAt("golden rings", 5);
```

And here is the `List` equivalent:

```
gift.set(5, "golden rings");
```

For consistency, the method `add(int,  E)`, which replaces `insertElementAt (Object,  int)`, also reverses the order of the arguments.

The three range operations in `Vector` (`indexOf`, `lastIndexOf`, and `setSize`) have been replaced by a single range view operation (`subList`), which is far more powerful and consistent.

Collection Operations

The operations inherited from the `Collection` interface work pretty much as expected, assuming you're already familiar with them. If you're not familiar with them from `Collection`, now would be a good time to revisit "The Collection Interface" section. The `remove` operation always removes *the first* occurrence of the specified element from the list. The add and addAll operations always append the new element(s) to the *end* of the list. Thus the following idiom concatenates one list to another:

```
list1.addAll(list2);
```

Here's a nondestructive form of this idiom, which produces a third List consisting of the second list appended to the first:

```
List<Type> list3 = new ArrayList<Type>(list1);
list3.addAll(list2);
```

Note that the idiom, in its nondestructive form, takes advantage of ArrayList's standard conversion constructor.

Like the Set interface, List strengthens the requirements on the equals and hashCode methods so that two List objects can be compared for logical equality without regard to their implementation classes. Two List objects are equal if they contain the same elements in the same order.

Positional Access and Search Operations

The basic positional access operations (get, set, add, and remove) behave just like their longer-named counterparts in Vector (elementAt, setElementAt, insertElementAt, and removeElementAt), with one noteworthy exception: the set and remove operations return the old value that is being overwritten or removed; the Vector counterparts (setElementAt and removeElementAt) return nothing (void). The search operations indexOf and lastIndexOf behave exactly like the identically named operations in Vector.

The addAll operation inserts all the elements of the specified Collection, starting at the specified position. The elements are inserted in the order they are returned by the specified Collection's iterator. This call is the positional access analog of Collection's addAll operation.

Here's a little method to swap two indexed values in a List. It should look familiar from "Programming 101":

```
public static <E> void swap(List<E> a, int i, int j) {
    E tmp = a.get(i);
    a.set(i, a.get(j));
    a.set(j, tmp);
}
```

Of course, there's one big difference: this is a polymorphic algorithm. It swaps two elements in any `List`, regardless of its implementation type. Here's another polymorphic algorithm that uses the preceding `swap` method:

```
public static void shuffle(List<?> list, Random rnd) {
    for (int i = list.size(); i > 1; i--)
        swap(list, i - 1, rnd.nextInt(i));
}
```

This algorithm, which is included in the Java platform's `Collections`[12] class, randomly permutes the specified list using the specified source of randomness. It's a bit subtle: it runs up the list from the bottom, repeatedly swapping a randomly selected element into the current position. Unlike most naive attempts at shuffling, it's *fair* (with all permutations occurring with equal likelihood, assuming an unbiased source of randomness) and *fast* (requiring exactly `list.size()-1` swaps). The following program uses this algorithm to print the words in its argument list in random order:

```
import java.util.*;

public class Shuffle {
    public static void main(String[] args) {
        List<String> list = new ArrayList<String>();
        for (String a : args)
            list.add(a);
        Collections.shuffle(list, new Random());
        System.out.println(list);
    }
}
```

In fact, this program can be made even shorter and faster. The `Arrays`[13] class has a static factory method called `asList`, which allows an array to be viewed as a `List`. This method does not copy the array. Changes in the `List` write through to the array and vice versa. The resulting `List` is not a general-purpose `List` implementation because it doesn't implement the (optional) `add` and `remove` operations: arrays are not resizable. Taking advantage of `Arrays.asList` and calling the library version of `shuffle`, which uses a default source of randomness, you get the following shorter, faster program, whose behavior is identical to the previous program:

```
import java.util.*;

public class Shuffle {
    public static void main(String[] args) {
```

12. 7/docs/api/java/util/Collections.html
13. 7/docs/api/java/util/Arrays.html

```
                List<String> list = Arrays.asList(args);
                Collections.shuffle(list);
                System.out.println(list);
        }
    }
```

List Iterators

As you'd expect, the `Iterator` returned by `List`'s `iterator` operation returns the elements of the list in proper sequence. `List` also provides a richer iterator, called a `ListIterator`, which allows you to traverse the list in either direction, modify the list during iteration, and obtain the current position of the iterator. The `ListIterator` interface is as follows:

```
    public interface ListIterator<E> extends Iterator<E> {
        boolean hasNext();
        E next();
        boolean hasPrevious();
        E previous();
        int nextIndex();
        int previousIndex();
        void remove();   //optional
        void set(E e);   //optional
        void add(E e);   //optional
    }
```

The three methods that `ListIterator` inherits from `Iterator` (`hasNext`, `next`, and `remove`) do exactly the same thing in both interfaces. The `hasPrevious` and the `previous` operations are exact analogues of `hasNext` and `next`. The former operations refer to the element before the (implicit) cursor, whereas the latter refer to the element after the cursor. The `previous` operation moves the cursor backward, whereas `next` moves it forward.

Here's the standard idiom for iterating backward through a list:

```
    for (ListIterator<Type> it = list.listIterator(list.size());
         it.hasPrevious(); ) {
        Type t = it.previous();
            . . .
    }
```

Note the argument to `listIterator` in the preceding idiom. The `List` interface has two forms of the `listIterator` method. The form with no arguments returns a `ListIterator` positioned at the beginning of the list; the form with an `int` argument returns a `ListIterator` positioned at the specified index. The index refers to the element that would be returned by an initial call to `next`. An initial call to `previous` would return the element whose index was `index-1`. In a list of length n, there are n+1 valid values for `index`, from 0 to n, inclusive.

11

Index: 0   1   2   3   4

Figure 11.2 The Five Possible Cursor Positions

Intuitively speaking, the cursor is always between two elements—the one that would be returned by a call to `previous` and the one that would be returned by a call to `next`. The n+1 valid index values correspond to the n+1 gaps between elements, from the gap before the first element to the gap after the last one. Figure 11.2 shows the five possible cursor positions in a list containing four elements.

Calls to `next` and `previous` can be intermixed, but you need to be a bit careful. The first call to `previous` returns the same element as the last call to `next`. Similarly, the first call to `next` after a sequence of calls to `previous` returns the same element as the last call to `previous`.

It should come as no surprise that the `nextIndex` method returns the index of the element that would be returned by a subsequent call to `next`, and `previousIndex` returns the index of the element that would be returned by a subsequent call to `previous`. These calls are typically used to either report the position where something was found or record the position of the `ListIterator` so that another `ListIterator` with identical position can be created.

It should also come as no surprise that the number returned by `nextIndex` is always one greater than the number returned by `previousIndex`. This implies the behavior of the two boundary cases: one is a call to `previousIndex` when the cursor is before the initial element returns −1, and the other is a call to `nextIndex` when the cursor is after the final element returns `list.size()`. To make all this concrete, the following is a possible implementation of `List.indexOf`:

```
public int indexOf(E e) {
    for (ListIterator<E> it = listIterator(); it.hasNext(); )
        if (e == null ? it.next() == null : e.equals(it.next()))
            return it.previousIndex();
    // Element not found
    return -1;
}
```

Note that the `indexOf` method returns `it.previousIndex()` even though it is traversing the list in the forward direction. The reason is that `it.nextIndex()` would return the index of the element we are *about to* examine, and we want to return the index of the element we *just* examined.

The `Iterator` interface provides the `remove` operation to remove the last element returned by `next` from the `Collection`. For `ListIterator`, this operation removes the last element returned by `next` or `previous`. The `ListIterator` interface provides two additional operations to modify the list—`set` and `add`. The `set` method overwrites the last element returned by `next` or `previous` with the specified element. The following polymorphic algorithm uses `set` to replace all occurrences of one specified value with another:

```
public static <E> void replace(List<E> list, E val, E newVal) {
    for (ListIterator<E> it = list.listIterator(); it.hasNext(); )
        if (val == null ? it.next() == null : val.equals(it.next()))
            it.set(newVal);
}
```

The only tricky part of this example is the equality test between `val` and `it.next`. You need to special case a `val` value of `null` to prevent a `NullPointerException`.

The `add` method inserts a new element into the list immediately before the current cursor position. This method is illustrated in the following polymorphic algorithm to replace all occurrences of a specified value with the sequence of values contained in the specified list:

```
public static <E>
    void replace(List<E> list, E val, List<? extends E> newVals) {
    for (ListIterator<E> it = list.listIterator(); it.hasNext(); ){
        if (val == null ? it.next() == null : val.equals(it.next())) {
            it.remove();
            for (E e : newVals)
                it.add(e);
        }
    }
}
```

The Range View Operation: Lists

The range view operation, `subList(int fromIndex, int toIndex)`, returns a `List` view of the portion of this list whose indices range from `fromIndex` (inclusive) to `toIndex` (exclusive). This *half-open range* mirrors the typical `for` loop:

```
for (int i = fromIndex; i < toIndex; i++) {
    . . .
}
```

As the term *view* implies, the returned `List` is backed up by the `List` on which `subList` was called, so changes in the former are reflected in the latter.

This method eliminates the need for explicit range operations (of the sort that commonly exist for arrays). Any operation that expects a `List` can be used as a range operation by passing a subList view instead of a whole List. For example, the following idiom removes a range of elements from a List:

```
list.subList(fromIndex, toIndex).clear();
```

Similar idioms can be constructed to search for an element in a range:

```
int i = list.subList(fromIndex, toIndex).indexOf(o);
int j = list.subList(fromIndex, toIndex).lastIndexOf(o);
```

Note that the preceding idioms return the index of the found element in the sub-List, not the index in the backing List.

Any polymorphic algorithm that operates on a List, such as the replace and shuffle examples, works with the List returned by subList.

Here's a polymorphic algorithm whose implementation uses subList to deal a hand from a deck of cards. In other words, it returns a new List (the hand) containing the specified number of elements taken from the end of the specified List (the deck). The elements returned in the hand are removed from the deck:

```
public static <E> List<E> dealHand(List<E> deck, int n) {
    int deckSize = deck.size();
    List<E> handView = deck.subList(deckSize - n, deckSize);
    List<E> hand = new ArrayList<E>(handView);
    handView.clear();
    return hand;
}
```

Note that this algorithm removes the hand from the *end* of the deck. For many common List implementations, such as ArrayList, removing elements from the end of the list is substantially easier and faster than removing elements from the beginning.

The following is a program that uses the dealHand method in combination with Collections.shuffle to generate hands from a normal 52-card deck. The program takes two command-line arguments: (1) the number of hands to deal and (2) the number of cards in each hand.

```
import java.util.*;

public class Deal {
    public static void main(String[] args) {
        if (args.length < 2) {
            System.out.println("Usage: Deal hands cards");
            return;
        }
        int numHands = Integer.parseInt(args[0]);
        int cardsPerHand = Integer.parseInt(args[1]);
```

```
    // Make a normal 52-card deck.
    String[] suit = new String[] {
        "spades", "hearts",
        "diamonds", "clubs"
    };
    String[] rank = new String[] {
        "ace", "2", "3", "4",
        "5", "6", "7", "8", "9", "10",
        "jack", "queen", "king"
    };

    List<String> deck = new ArrayList<String>();
    for (int i = 0; i < suit.length; i++)
        for (int j = 0; j < rank.length; j++)
            deck.add(rank[j] + " of " + suit[i]);

    // Shuffle the deck.
    Collections.shuffle(deck);

    if (numHands * cardsPerHand > deck.size()) {
        System.out.println("Not enough cards.");
        return;
    }

    for (int i = 0; i < numHands; i++)
        System.out.println(dealHand(deck, cardsPerHand));
}

public static <E> List<E> dealHand(List<E> deck, int n) {
    int deckSize = deck.size();
    List<E> handView = deck.subList(deckSize - n, deckSize);
    List<E> hand = new ArrayList<E>(handView);
    handView.clear();
    return hand;
}
}
```

Here is an example of the output from this program:

```
% java Deal 4 5

[8 of hearts, jack of spades, 3 of spades, 4 of spades, king of diamonds]
[4 of diamonds, ace of clubs, 6 of clubs, jack of hearts, queen of hearts]
[7 of spades, 5 of spades, 2 of diamonds, queen of diamonds, 9 of clubs]
[8 of spades, 6 of diamonds, ace of spades, 3 of hearts, ace of hearts]
```

Although the subList operation is extremely powerful, some care must be exercised when using it. The semantics of the List returned by subList become undefined if elements are added to or removed from the backing List in any way other than via the returned List. Thus it's highly recommended that you use the List returned by subList only as a transient object—to perform one or a sequence of range operations on the backing List. The longer you use the subList instance, the greater the probability that you'll compromise it by modifying the backing List directly or through another subList object. Note that it is legal to modify a sublist of a sublist and to continue using the original sublist (though not concurrently).

List Algorithms

Most polymorphic algorithms in the Collections class apply specifically to List. Having all these algorithms at your disposal makes it very easy to manipulate lists. Here's a summary of these algorithms, which are described in more detail in the "Algorithms" section:

- sort—Sorts a List using a merge sort algorithm, which provides a fast, *stable sort* (i.e., one that does not reorder equal elements)
- shuffle—Randomly permutes the elements in a List
- reverse—Reverses the order of the elements in a List
- rotate—Rotates all the elements in a List by a specified distance
- swap—Swaps the elements at specified positions in a List
- replaceAll—Replaces all occurrences of one specified value with another
- fill—Overwrites every element in a List with the specified value
- copy—Copies the source List into the destination List
- binarySearch—Searches for an element in an ordered List using the binary search algorithm
- indexOfSubList—Returns the index of the first SubList of one List that is equal to another
- lastIndexOfSubList—Returns the index of the last SubList of one List that is equal to another

The Queue Interface

A Queue[14] is a collection for holding elements prior to processing. Besides basic Collection operations, queues provide additional insertion, removal, and inspection operations. The Queue interface is as follows:

```
public interface Queue<E> extends Collection<E> {
    E element();
    boolean offer(E e);
    E peek();
    E poll();
    E remove();
}
```

---

14. 7/docs/api/java/util/Queue.html

Table 11.1 Queue Interface Structure

Type of operation	Throws exception	Returns special value
Insert	add(e)	offer(e)
Remove	remove()	poll()
Examine	element()	peek()

Each `Queue` method exists in two forms: one throws an exception if the operation fails, and the other returns a special value if the operation fails (either `null` or `false`, depending on the operation). The regular structure of the interface is illustrated in Table 11.1.

Queues typically, but not necessarily, order elements in a FIFO manner. Among the exceptions are priority queues, which order elements according to their values. Whatever ordering is used, the head of the queue is the element that would be removed by a call to `remove` or `poll`. In a FIFO queue, all new elements are inserted at the tail of the queue. Other kinds of queues may use different placement rules. Every `Queue` implementation must specify its ordering properties.

It is possible for a `Queue` implementation to restrict the number of elements that it holds; such queues are referred to as *bounded*. Some `Queue` implementations in `java.util.concurrent` are bounded, but the implementations in `java.util` are not.

The `add` method, which `Queue` inherits from `Collection`, inserts an element unless it would violate the queue's capacity restrictions, in which case it throws `IllegalStateException`. The `offer` method, which is intended solely for use on bounded queues, differs from `add` only in that it indicates failure to insert an element by returning `false`.

The `remove` and `poll` methods both remove and return the head of the queue. Exactly which element gets removed is a function of the queue's ordering policy. The `remove` and `poll` methods differ in their behavior only when the queue is empty. Under these circumstances, `remove` throws `NoSuchElementException`, while `poll` returns `null`.

The `element` and `peek` methods return but do not remove the head of the queue. They differ from one another in precisely the same fashion as `remove` and `poll`: if the queue is empty, `element` throws `NoSuchElementException`, while `peek` returns `null`.

`Queue` implementations generally do not allow insertion of `null` elements. The `LinkedList` implementation, which was retrofitted to implement `Queue`, is an exception. For historical reasons, it permits `null` elements, but you should refrain from taking advantage of this because `null` is used as a special return value by the `poll` and `peek` methods.

11

Queue implementations generally do not define element-based versions of the equals and hashCode methods but instead inherit the identity-based versions from Object.

The Queue interface does not define the blocking queue methods, which are common in concurrent programming. These methods, which wait for elements to appear or for space to become available, are defined in the interface java.util.concurrent.BlockingQueue,[15] which extends Queue.

In the following example program, a queue is used to implement a countdown timer. The queue is preloaded with all the integer values from a number specified on the command line to zero, in descending order. Then the values are removed from the queue and printed at one-second intervals. The program is artificial in that it would be more natural to do the same thing without using a queue, but it illustrates the use of a queue to store elements prior to subsequent processing:

```
import java.util.*;

public class Countdown {
    public static void main(String[] args) throws InterruptedException {
        int time = Integer.parseInt(args[0]);
        Queue<Integer> queue = new LinkedList<Integer>();

        for (int i = time; i >= 0; i--)
            queue.add(i);

        while (!queue.isEmpty()) {
            System.out.println(queue.remove());
            Thread.sleep(1000);
        }
    }
}
```

In the following example, a priority queue is used to sort a collection of elements. Again, this program is artificial in that there is no reason to use it in favor of the sort method provided in Collections, but it illustrates the behavior of priority queues:

```
static <E> List<E> heapSort(Collection<E> c) {
    Queue<E> queue = new PriorityQueue<E>(c);
    List<E> result = new ArrayList<E>();

    while (!queue.isEmpty())
        result.add(queue.remove());

    return result;
}
```

15. 7/docs/api/java/util/concurrent/BlockingQueue.html

The Map Interface

A Map[16] is an object that maps keys to values. A Map instance cannot contain duplicate keys: Each key can map to at most one value. It models the mathematical *function* abstraction. The Map interface is as follows:

```
public interface Map<K,V> {
    // Basic operations
    V put(K key, V value);
    V get(Object key);
    V remove(Object key);
    boolean containsKey(Object key);
    boolean containsValue(Object value);
    int size();
    boolean isEmpty();

    // Bulk operations
    void putAll(Map<? extends K, ? extends V> m);
    void clear();

    // Collection Views
    public Set<K> keySet();
    public Collection<V> values();
    public Set<Map.Entry<K,V>> entrySet();

    // Interface for entrySet elements
    public interface Entry {
        K getKey();
        V getValue();
        V setValue(V value);
    }
}
```

The Java platform contains three general-purpose Map implementations: HashMap,[17] TreeMap,[18] and LinkedHashMap.[19] Their behavior and performance are precisely analogous to HashSet, TreeSet, and LinkedHashSet, as described previously in "The Set Interface" section. Also, Hashtable was retrofitted to implement Map.

Comparison to Hashtable

If you've used Hashtable, you're already familiar with the general basics of Map. (Of course, Map is an interface, while Hashtable is a concrete implementation.) The following are the major differences:

---

16. 7/docs/api/java/util/Map.html
17. 7/docs/api/java/util/HashMap.html
18. 7/docs/api/java/util/TreeMap.html
19. 7/docs/api/java/util/LinkedHashMap.html

- Map provides Collection views instead of direct support for iteration via Enumeration objects. Collection views greatly enhance the expressiveness of the interface, as discussed later in this section.
- Map allows you to iterate over keys, values, or key-value pairs; Hashtable does not provide the third option.
- Map provides a safe way to remove entries in the midst of iteration; Hashtable does not.

Note that Map fixes a minor deficiency in the Hashtable interface: Hashtable has a method called contains, which returns true if the Hashtable contains a given *value*. Given its name, you'd wrongly expect this method to return true if the Hashtable contains a given *key*, because the key is the primary access mechanism for a Hashtable. The Map interface eliminates this source of confusion by renaming the method containsValue. This also increases the interface's consistency—containsValue parallels containsKey.

Map Interface Basic Operations

The basic operations of Map (put, get, containsKey, containsValue, size, and isEmpty) behave exactly like their counterparts in Hashtable. The following program generates a frequency table of the words found in its argument list. The frequency table maps each word to the number of times it appears in the argument list:

```
import java.util.*;

public class Freq {
    public static void main(String[] args) {
        Map<String, Integer> m = new HashMap<String, Integer>();

        // Initialize frequency table from command line
        for (String a : args) {
            Integer freq = m.get(a);
            m.put(a, (freq == null) ? 1 : freq + 1);
        }

        System.out.println(m.size() + " distinct words:");
        System.out.println(m);
    }
}
```

The only tricky thing about this program is the second argument of the put statement. This argument is a conditional expression that can potentially set the frequency to one if the word has never been seen before or one more than its current value if the word has already been seen. Try running this program with the command:

```
java Freq if it is to be it is up to me to delegate
```

The program yields the following output:

```
8 distinct words:
{to=3, delegate=1, be=1, it=2, up=1, if=1, me=1, is=2}
```

Suppose you'd prefer to see the frequency table in alphabetical order. All you have to do is change the implementation type of the Map from HashMap to TreeMap. Making this four-character change causes the program to generate the following output from the same command line:

```
8 distinct words:
{be=1, delegate=1, if=1, is=2, it=2, me=1, to=3, up=1}
```

Similarly, you could make the program print the frequency table in the same order that the words first appear on the command line simply by changing the implementation type of the map to LinkedHashMap. Doing so results in the following output:

```
8 distinct words:
{if=1, it=2, is=2, to=3, be=1, up=1, me=1, delegate=1}
```

11

This flexibility provides a potent illustration of the power of an interface-based framework.

Like the Set and List[20] interfaces, Map strengthens the requirements on the equals and hashCode methods so that two Map objects can be compared for logical equality without regard to their implementation types. Two Map instances are equal if they represent the same key-value mappings.

By convention, all general-purpose Map implementations provide constructors that take a Map object and initialize the new Map to contain all the key-value mappings in the specified Map. This standard Map conversion constructor is very similar to the standard Collection constructor: it allows the caller to create a Map of a desired implementation type that initially contains all the mappings in another Map, regardless of the other Map's implementation type. For example, suppose you have a Map named m. The following one-liner creates a new HashMap initially containing all the same key-value mappings as m:

```
Map<K, V> copy = new HashMap<K, V>(m);
```

---

20. 7/docs/api/java/util/List.html

Map Interface Bulk Operations

The clear operation does exactly what you'd think: it removes all the mappings from the Map. The putAll operation is the Map analogue of the Collection interface's addAll operation. In addition to its obvious use of dumping one Map into another, it has a second, more subtle use. Suppose a Map is used to represent a collection of attribute-value pairs; the putAll operation, in combination with the Map conversion constructor, provides a neat way to implement attribute map creation with default values. The following is a static factory method that demonstrates this technique:

```
static <K, V> Map<K, V> newAttributeMap(Map<K, V>defaults,
    Map<K, V> overrides) {
    Map<K, V> result = new HashMap<K, V>(defaults);
    result.putAll(overrides);
    return result;
}
```

Collection Views

The Collection view methods allow a Map to be viewed as a Collection in these three ways:

- keySet—This refers to the Set of keys contained in the Map.
- values—This refers to the Collection of values contained in the Map. Note that this Collection is not a Set because multiple keys can map to the same value.
- entrySet—This refers to the Set of key-value pairs contained in the Map. Note that the Map interface provides a small nested interface called Map.Entry to show the types of elements in this Set.

The Collection views provide the *only* means to iterate over a Map. The following example illustrates the standard idiom for iterating over the keys in a Map with a for-each construct:

```
for (KeyType key : m.keySet())
    System.out.println(key);
```

Here is an example with an iterator:

```
// Filter a map based on some
// property of its keys.
for (Iterator<Type> it = m.keySet().iterator(); it.hasNext(); )
    if (it.next().isBogus())
        it.remove();
```

The idiom for iterating over values is similar. Here is the idiom for iterating over key-value pairs:

```
for (Map.Entry<KeyType, ValType> e : m.entrySet())
    System.out.println(e.getKey() + ": " + e.getValue());
```

At first, many people worry that these idioms may be slow because the `Map` has to create a new `Collection` instance each time a `Collection` view operation is called. However, there's no reason that a `Map` cannot always return the same object each time it is asked for a given `Collection` view. This is precisely what all the `Map` implementations in `java.util` do.

With all three `Collection` views, calling an `Iterator`'s remove operation removes the associated entry from the backing `Map`, assuming that the backing `Map` supports element removal to begin with. This is illustrated by the preceding filtering idiom.

With the `entrySet` view, it is also possible to change the value associated with a key by calling a `Map.Entry`'s `setValue` method during iteration (again, assuming the `Map` supports value modification to begin with). Note that these are the *only* safe ways to modify a `Map` during iteration; the behavior is unspecified if the underlying `Map` is modified in any other way while the iteration is in progress.

The `Collection` views support element removal in all its many forms—remove, `removeAll`, `retainAll`, and `clear` operations, as well as the `Iterator.remove` operation. (But, yet again, this assumes that the backing `Map` supports element removal.)

The `Collection` views *do not* support element addition under any circumstances. It would make no sense for the `keySet` and `values` views, and it's unnecessary for the `entrySet` view because the backing `Map`'s put and `putAll` methods provide the same functionality.

Fancy Uses of Collection Views: Map Algebra

When applied to the `Collection` views, bulk operations (`containsAll`, `removeAll`, and `retainAll`) are surprisingly potent tools. For starters, suppose you want to know whether one `Map` instance is a subset of another—that is, whether the first `Map` contains all the key-value mappings in the second. The following idiom does the trick:

```
if (m1.entrySet().containsAll(m2.entrySet())) {
    . . .
}
```

Along the same lines, suppose you want to know whether two `Map` objects contain mappings for all the same keys:

```
if (m1.keySet().equals(m2.keySet())) {
    . . .
}
```

Suppose you have a `Map` that represents a collection of attribute-value pairs and two `Set`s representing required attributes and permissible attributes. (The permissible attributes include the required attributes.) The following snippet determines if the attribute map conforms to these constraints and prints a detailed error message if it doesn't:

```
static <K, V> boolean validate(Map<K, V> attrMap, Set<K> requiredAttrs,
    Set<K>permittedAttrs) {
    boolean valid = true;
    Set<K> attrs = attrMap.keySet();

    if (! attrs.containsAll(requiredAttrs)) {
        Set<K> missing = new HashSet<K>(requiredAttrs);
        missing.removeAll(attrs);
        System.out.println("Missing attributes: " + missing);
        valid = false;
    }
    if (! permittedAttrs.containsAll(attrs)) {
        Set<K> illegal = new HashSet<K>(attrs);
        illegal.removeAll(permittedAttrs);
        System.out.println("Illegal attributes: " + illegal);
        valid = false;
    }
    return valid;
}
```

Suppose you want to know all the keys common to two `Map` objects. You would use the following:

```
Set<KeyType>commonKeys = new HashSet<KeyType>(m1.keySet());
commonKeys.retainAll(m2.keySet());
```

A similar idiom gets you the common values.

All the idioms presented thus far have been nondestructive—that is, they don't modify the backing `Map`. Here are a few that do. Suppose you want to remove all the key-value pairs that one `Map` has in common with another:

```
m1.entrySet().removeAll(m2.entrySet());
```

Or suppose you want to remove all the keys from one `Map` that have mappings in another:

```
m1.keySet().removeAll(m2.keySet());
```

What happens when you start mixing keys and values in the same bulk operation? Suppose you have a `Map`, `managers`, that maps each employee in a company to the employee's manager. We'll be deliberately vague about the types of the key and the value objects. It doesn't matter, as long as they're the same. Now suppose you want to know who all the `individualContributors` (or nonmanagers) are. The following snippet tells you exactly what you want to know:

```
Set<Employee> individualContributors = new HashSet<Employee>(managers.
    keySet());
individualContributors.removeAll(managers.values());
```

Suppose you want to fire all the employees who report directly to some manager, Simon:

```
Employee simon = . . . ;
managers.values().removeAll(Collections.singleton(simon));
```

Note that this idiom makes use of `Collections.singleton`—a static factory method that returns an immutable `Set` with the single, specified element.

Once you've done this, you may have a bunch of employees whose managers no longer work for the company (if any of Simon's team members were themselves managers). The following code will tell you which employees have managers who no longer works for the company:

```
Map<Employee, Employee> m = new HashMap<Employee, Employee>(managers);
m.values().removeAll(managers.keySet());
Set<Employee> slackers = m.keySet();
```

This example is a bit tricky. It makes a temporary copy of the `Map` and removes from the temporary copy all entries whose (manager) value is a key in the original `Map`. Remember that the original `Map` has an entry for each employee. Thus the remaining entries in the temporary `Map` are all the entries from the original `Map` whose (manager) values are no longer employees. The keys in the temporary copy then represent precisely the employees we're looking for.

There are many more idioms like the ones contained in this section, but it would be impractical and tedious to list them all. Once you get the hang of it, it's not that difficult to come up with the right one when you need it.

Multimaps

A *multimap* is like a `Map` but it can map each key to multiple values. The Java Collections Framework doesn't include an interface for multimaps because they aren't all that common. It's a fairly simple matter to use a `Map` whose values are `List` instances as a multimap. This technique is demonstrated in the next code example, which reads a word list containing one word per line (all lowercase) and prints out all the anagram groups that meet a specific size criterion. An *anagram group* is a bunch of words that contain exactly the same letters but in a different order. The program takes two arguments on the command line: (1) the name of the dictionary file and (2) the minimum size of anagram group to print out. Anagram groups containing fewer words than the specified minimum are not printed.

There is a standard trick for finding anagram groups: For each word in the dictionary (or the text in question), alphabetize the letters in the word (i.e., reorder the word's letters into alphabetical order) and put an entry into a multimap, mapping the alphabetized word to the original word. For example, the word *bad* causes an entry mapping *abd* into *bad* to be put into the multimap, and the word *dab* creates an entry mapping *abd* into *dab*. A moment's reflection will show that all the words (*bad*, *dab*) that map to the same given key (*abd*) form an anagram group. It's a simple matter to iterate over the keys in the multimap, printing out each anagram group that meets the size constraint.

The following program is a straightforward implementation of this technique:

```java
import java.util.*;
import java.io.*;

public class Anagrams {
    public static void main(String[] args) {
        int minGroupSize = Integer.parseInt(args[1]);

        // Read words from file and put into a simulated multimap
        Map<String, List<String>> m = new HashMap<String, List<String>>();

        try {
            Scanner s = new Scanner(new File(args[0]));
            while (s.hasNext()) {
                String word = s.next();
                String alpha = alphabetize(word);
                List<String> l = m.get(alpha);
                if (l == null)
                    m.put(alpha, l=new ArrayList<String>());
                l.add(word);
            }
        } catch (IOException e) {
            System.err.println(e);
            System.exit(1);
        }

        // Print all permutation groups above size threshold
        for (List<String> l : m.values())
            if (l.size() >= minGroupSize)
                System.out.println(l.size() + ": " + l);
    }

    private static String alphabetize(String s) {
        char[] a = s.toCharArray();
        Arrays.sort(a);
```

```
            return new String(a);
        }
    }
```

Running this program on a 173,000-word dictionary file with a minimum anagram group size of 8 produces the following output:

```
 9: [estrin, inerts, insert, inters, niters, nitres, sinter,
       triens, trines]
 8: [lapse, leaps, pales, peals, pleas, salep, sepal, spale]
 8: [aspers, parses, passer, prases, repass, spares, sparse,
       spears]
10: [least, setal, slate, stale, steal, stela, taels, tales,
       teals, tesla]
 8: [enters, nester, renest, rentes, resent, tenser, ternes,
       treens]
 8: [arles, earls, lares, laser, lears, rales, reals, seral]
 8: [earings, erasing, gainers, reagins, regains, reginas,
       searing, seringa]
 8: [peris, piers, pries, prise, ripes, speir, spier, spire]
12: [apers, apres, asper, pares, parse, pears, prase, presa,
       rapes, reaps, spare, spear]
11: [alerts, alters, artels, estral, laster, ratels, salter,
       slater, staler, stelar, talers]
 9: [capers, crapes, escarp, pacers, parsec, recaps, scrape,
       secpar, spacer]
 9: [palest, palets, pastel, petals, plates, pleats, septal,
       staple, tepals]
 9: [anestri, antsier, nastier, ratines, retains, retinas,
       retsina, stainer, stearin]
 8: [ates, east, eats, etas, sate, seat, seta, teas]
 8: [carets, cartes, caster, caters, crates, reacts, recast,
       traces]
```

Many of these words seem a bit bogus, but that's not the program's fault; they're
in the dictionary file.[21]

Object Ordering

A List1 can be sorted as follows:

```
Collections.sort(l);
```

If the List consists of String elements, it will be sorted into alphabetical order.
If it consists of Date elements, it will be sorted into chronological order. How does
this happen? String and Date both implement the Comparable[22] interface.

---

21. tutorial/collections/interfaces/examples/dictionary.txt

22. 7/docs/api/java/lang/Comparable.html

Table 11.2 Classes Implementing Comparable

Class	Natural ordering
Byte	Signed numerical
Character	Unsigned numerical
Long	Signed numerical
Integer	Signed numerical
Short	Signed numerical
Double	Signed numerical
Float	Signed numerical
BigInteger	Signed numerical
BigDecimal	Signed numerical
Boolean	Boolean.FALSE < Boolean.TRUE
File	System-dependent lexicographic on path name
String	Lexicographic
Date	Chronological
CollationKey	Locale-specific lexicographic

11

Comparable implementations provide a *natural ordering* for a class, which allows objects of that class to be sorted automatically. Table 11.2 summarizes some of the more important Java platform classes that implement Comparable.

If you try to sort a List whose elements do not implement Comparable, Collections.sort(list) will throw a ClassCastException.[23] Similarly, Collections.sort(list, comparator) will throw a ClassCastException if you try to sort a list whose elements cannot be compared to one another using the comparator. Elements that can be compared to one another are called *mutually comparable*. Although elements of different types may be mutually comparable, none of the classes listed here permit interclass comparison.

This is all you really need to know about the Comparable interface if you just want to sort lists of comparable elements or to create sorted collections of them. The next section will be of interest to you if you want to implement your own Comparable type.

Writing Your Own Comparable Types

The Comparable interface consists of the following method:

```
public interface Comparable<T> {
    public int compareTo(T o);
}
```

---

23. 7/docs/api/java/lang/ClassCastException.html

The `compareTo` method compares the receiving object with the specified object
and returns a negative integer, zero, or a positive integer, depending on whether
the receiving object is less than, equal to, or greater than the specified object. If the
specified object cannot be compared to the receiving object, the method throws a
`ClassCastException`.

The following class representing a person's name implements `Comparable`:

```java
import java.util.*;

public class Name implements Comparable<Name> {
    private final String firstName, lastName;

    public Name(String firstName, String lastName) {
        if (firstName == null || lastName == null)
            throw new NullPointerException();
        this.firstName = firstName;
        this.lastName = lastName;
    }

    public String firstName() { return firstName; }
    public String lastName()  { return lastName;  }

    public boolean equals(Object o) {
        if (!(o instanceof Name))
            return false;
        Name n = (Name) o;
        return n.firstName.equals(firstName) && n.lastName.equals(lastName);
    }

    public int hashCode() {
        return 31*firstName.hashCode() + lastName.hashCode();
    }

    public String toString() {
        return firstName + " " + lastName;
    }

    public int compareTo(Name n) {
        int lastCmp = lastName.compareTo(n.lastName);
        return (lastCmp != 0 ? lastCmp : firstName.compareTo(n.firstName));
    }
}
```

To keep the preceding example short, the class is somewhat limited: it doesn't
support middle names, it demands both a first and last name, and it is not inter-
nationalized in any way. Nonetheless, it illustrates the following important points:

- Name objects are *immutable*. All other things being equal, immutable types are
  the way to go, especially for objects that will be used as elements in Sets or as
  keys in Maps. These collections will break if you modify their elements or keys
  while they're in the collection.

- The constructor checks its arguments for `null`. This ensures that all `Name` objects are well formed so that none of the other methods will ever throw a `NullPointerException`.
- The `hashCode` method is redefined. This is essential for any class that redefines the `equals` method. (Equal objects must have equal hash codes.)
- The `equals` method returns `false` if the specified object is `null` or of an inappropriate type. The `compareTo` method throws a runtime exception under these circumstances. Both behaviors are required by the general contracts of the respective methods.
- The `toString` method has been redefined so it prints the `Name` in human-readable form. This is always a good idea, especially for objects that are going to be put into collections. The various collection types' `toString` methods depend on the `toString` methods of their elements, keys, and values.

Since this section is about element ordering, let's talk a bit more about `Name`'s `compareTo` method. It implements the standard name-ordering algorithm, where last names take precedence over first names. This is exactly what you want in a natural ordering. It would be very confusing indeed if the natural ordering were unnatural!

Take a look at how `compareTo` is implemented—it's quite typical. You begin by comparing the most significant part of the objects (in this case, the last name). Often, you can just use the natural ordering of the part's type. In this case, the part is a `String` and the natural (lexicographic) ordering is exactly what's called for. If the comparison results in anything other than zero, which represents equality, you're done: you just return the result. If the most significant parts are equal, you go on to compare the next most-significant parts. In this case, there are only two parts—first name and last name. If there were more parts, you'd proceed in the obvious fashion, comparing parts until you found two that weren't equal or you were comparing the least-significant parts, at which point you'd return the result of the comparison.

Just to show that it all works, here's a program that builds a list of names and sorts them:

```
import java.util.*;

public class NameSort {
    public static void main(String[] args) {
        Name nameArray[] = {
            new Name("John", "Smith"),
            new Name("Karl", "Ng"),
            new Name("Jeff", "Smith"),
            new Name("Tom", "Rich")
        };

        List<Name> names = Arrays.asList(nameArray);
```

```
        Collections.sort(names);
        System.out.println(names);
    ]
}
```

If you run this program, here's what it prints:

```
[Karl Ng, Tom Rich, Jeff Smith, John Smith]
```

There are four restrictions on the behavior of the compareTo method, which we won't go into now because they're fairly technical and boring and are better left in the API documentation. It's really important that all classes that implement Comparable obey these restrictions, so read the documentation for Comparable if you're writing a class that implements it. Attempting to sort a list of objects that violate the restrictions will result in undefined behavior. Technically speaking, these restrictions ensure that the natural ordering is a *total order* on the objects of a class that implements the Comparable interface; this is necessary to ensure that sorting is well defined.

Comparators

What if you want to sort some objects in an order other than their natural ordering? Or what if you want to sort some objects that don't implement Comparable? To do either of these things, you'll need to provide a Comparator[24]—an object that encapsulates an ordering. Like the Comparable interface, the Comparator interface consists of a single method:

```
public interface Comparator<T> {
    int compare(T o1, T o2);
}
```

The compare method compares its two arguments, returning a negative integer, zero, or a positive integer, depending on whether the first argument is less than, equal to, or greater than the second. If either of the arguments has an inappropriate type for the Comparator, the compare method throws a ClassCastException.

Much of what was said about Comparable applies to Comparator as well. Writing a compare method is nearly identical to writing a compareTo method, except that the former gets both objects passed in as arguments. The compare method has to obey the same four technical restrictions as Comparable's compareTo method for the same reason—a Comparator must induce a total order on the objects it compares.

---

24. 7/docs/api/java/util/Comparator.html

Suppose you have a class called `Employee`, as follows:

```
public class Employee implements Comparable<Employee> {
    public Name name()      { . . . }
    public int number()     { . . . }
    public Date hireDate() { . . . }
        . . .
}
```

Let's assume that the natural ordering of `Employee` instances is `Name` ordering (as defined in the previous example) on employee name. Unfortunately, the boss has asked for a list of employees in order of seniority. This means we have to do some work, but not much. The following program will produce the required list:

```
import java.util.*;
public class EmpSort {
    static final Comparator<Employee> SENIORITY_ORDER =
                                        new Comparator<Employee>() {
            public int compare(Employee e1, Employee e2) {
                return e2.hireDate().compareTo(e1.hireDate());
            }
    };

    // Employee database
    static final Collection<Employee> employees = . . . ;

    public static void main(String[] args) {
        List<Employee> e = new ArrayList<Employee>(employees);
        Collections.sort(e, SENIORITY_ORDER);
        System.out.println(e);
    }
}
```

The `Comparator` in the program is reasonably straightforward. It relies on the natural ordering of `Date` applied to the values returned by the `hireDate` accessor method. Note that the `Comparator` passes the hire date of its second argument to its first (rather than vice versa). The reason is that the employee who was hired most recently is the least senior; sorting in the order of hire date would organize the list beginning with the lowest (instead of the highest) seniority. Another technique people sometimes use to achieve this effect is to maintain the argument order but to negate the result of the comparison.

```
// Don't do this!!
return -r1.hireDate().compareTo(r2.hireDate());
```

You should always use the former technique in favor of the latter because the latter is not guaranteed to work. The reason is that the `compareTo` method can return any negative `int` if its argument is less than the object on which it is invoked. There is one negative `int` that remains negative when negated, strange as it may seem:

```
-Integer.MIN_VALUE == Integer.MIN_VALUE
```

The `Comparator` in the preceding program works fine for sorting a `List`, but it does have one deficiency: it cannot be used to order a sorted collection, such as `TreeSet`, because it generates an ordering that is *not compatible with* the `equals` method. This means that this `Comparator` equates objects that the `equals` method does not. In particular, any two employees who were hired on the same date will compare as equal. When you're sorting a `List`, this doesn't matter; but when you're using the `Comparator` to order a sorted collection, it's fatal. If you use this `Comparator` to insert multiple employees hired on the same date into a `TreeSet`, only the first one will be added to the set; the second will be seen as a duplicate element and will be ignored.

To fix this problem, simply tweak the `Comparator` so that it produces an ordering that *is* compatible with `equals`. In other words, tweak it so that the only elements seen as equal when using `compare` are those that are also seen as equal when compared using `equals`. The way to do this is to perform a two-part comparison (as we did with `Name`), where the first part is the one we're interested in (in this case, the hire date) and the second part is an attribute that uniquely identifies the object (in this case, the employee number). Here is the resulting `Comparator`:

```
static final Comparator<Employee> SENIORITY_ORDER =
                                    new Comparator<Employee>() {
    public int compare(Employee e1, Employee e2) {
        int dateCmp = e2.hireDate().compareTo(e1.hireDate());
        if (dateCmp != 0)
            return dateCmp;

        return (e1.number() < e2.number() ? -1 :
            (e1.number() == e2.number() ? 0 : 1));
    }
};
```

One last note: You might be tempted to replace the final `return` statement in the `Comparator` with something simpler, like this:

```
return e1.number() - e2.number();
```

Don't do it unless you're *absolutely sure* no one will ever have a negative employee number! Generally, this trick does not work because the signed integer type is not big enough to represent the difference of two arbitrary signed integers. If `i` is a large positive integer and `j` is a large negative integer, `i - j` will overflow and will return a negative integer. The resulting `comparator` violates one of the four technical restrictions we keep talking about (transitivity) and produces horrible, subtle bugs. This is not a purely theoretical concern; people get burned by it.

The SortedSet Interface

A SortedSet[25] is a Set that maintains its elements in ascending order, sorted according to the elements' natural ordering or according to a Comparator provided at SortedSet creation time. In addition to the normal Set operations, the SortedSet interface provides operations for the following:

- *Range view.* Allows arbitrary range operations on the sorted set
- *Endpoints.* Returns the first or last element in the sorted set
- *Comparator access.* Returns the Comparator, if any, used to sort the set

The code for the SortedSet interface is as follows:

```
public interface SortedSet<E> extends Set<E> {
    // Range-view
    SortedSet<E> subSet(E fromElement, E toElement);
    SortedSet<E> headSet(E toElement);
    SortedSet<E> tailSet(E fromElement);

    // Endpoints
    E first();
    E last();

    // Comparator access
    Comparator<? super E> comparator();
}
```

Set Operations

The operations that SortedSet inherits from Set behave identically on sorted sets and normal sets, with two exceptions:

- The Iterator returned by the iterator operation traverses the sorted set in order.
- The array returned by toArray contains the sorted set's elements in order.

Although the interface doesn't guarantee it, the toString method of the Java platform's SortedSet implementations returns a string containing all the elements of the sorted set, in order.

---

25. 7/docs/api/java/util/SortedSet.html

Standard Constructors

By convention, all general-purpose Collection implementations provide a standard conversion constructor that takes a Collection. SortedSet implementations are no exception. In TreeSet, this constructor creates an instance that sorts its elements according to their natural ordering. This was probably a mistake. It would have been better to check dynamically to see whether the specified collection was a SortedSet instance and, if so, sort the new TreeSet according to the same criterion (comparator or natural ordering). Because TreeSet took the approach that it did, it also provides a constructor that takes a SortedSet and returns a new TreeSet containing the same elements sorted according to the same criterion. Note that it is the compile-time type of the argument, not its runtime type, that determines which of these two constructors is invoked (and whether the sorting criterion is preserved).

SortedSet implementations also provide, by convention, a constructor that takes a Comparator and returns an empty set sorted according to the specified Comparator. If null is passed to this constructor, it returns a set that sorts its elements according to their natural ordering.

The Range View Operations: Sets

The range view operations are somewhat analogous to those provided by the List interface, but there is one big difference: range views of a sorted set remain valid even if the backing sorted set is modified directly. This is feasible because the endpoints of a range view of a sorted set are absolute points in the element space rather than specific elements in the backing collection, as is the case for lists. A range view of a sorted set is really just a window onto whatever portion of the set lies in the designated part of the element space. Changes to the range view write back to the backing sorted set and vice versa. Thus it's okay to use range views on sorted sets for long periods of time, unlike range views on lists.

Sorted sets provide three range view operations: subSet, headSet, and tailSet. The first, subSet, takes two endpoints, like subList. Rather than indices, the endpoints are objects and must be comparable to the elements in the sorted set, using the Set's Comparator or the natural ordering of its elements—whichever the Set uses to order itself. Like subList, the range is half open, including its low endpoint but excluding the high one.

Thus the following line of code tells you how many words between "doorbell" and "pickle" (including "doorbell" but excluding "pickle") are contained in a SortedSet of strings called dictionary:

```
int count = dictionary.subSet("doorbell", "pickle").size();
```

In a similar manner, the following one-liner removes all the elements beginning with the letter f:

```
dictionary.subSet("f", "g").clear();
```

A similar trick can be used to print a table telling you how many words begin with each letter:

```
for (char ch = 'a'; ch <= 'z'; ) {
    String from = String.valueOf(ch++);
    String to = String.valueOf(ch);
    System.out.println(from + ": " + dictionary.subSet(from, to).size());
}
```

Suppose you want to view a *closed interval*, which contains both of its endpoints, instead of an open interval. If the element type allows for the calculation of the successor of a given value in the element space, merely request the subSet from lowEndpoint to successor(highEndpoint). Although it isn't entirely obvious, the successor of a string s in String's natural ordering is s + "\0"—that is, s with a null character appended.

Thus the following one-liner tells you how many words between "doorbell" and "pickle" (including both "doorbell" and "pickle") are contained in the dictionary:

```
count = dictionary.subSet("doorbell", "pickle\0").size();
```

A similar technique can be used to view an *open interval*, which contains neither endpoint. The open-interval view from lowEndpoint to highEndpoint is the half-open interval from successor(lowEndpoint) to highEndpoint. Use the following line to calculate the number of words between "doorbell" and "pickle", excluding both:

```
count = dictionary.subSet("doorbell\0", "pickle").size();
```

The SortedSet interface contains two more range view operations—headSet and tailSet, both of which take a single Object argument. The former returns a view of the initial portion of the backing SortedSet, up to but not including the specified object. The latter returns a view of the final portion of the backing SortedSet, beginning with the specified object and continuing to the end of the backing SortedSet. Thus the following code allows you to view the dictionary as two disjoint volumes (a–m and n–z):

```
SortedSet<String> volume1 = dictionary.headSet("n");
SortedSet<String> volume2 = dictionary.tailSet("n");
```

Endpoint Operations

The SortedSet interface contains operations to return the first and last elements in the sorted set, not surprisingly called first and last. In addition to their obvious uses, `last` allows a workaround for a deficiency in the `SortedSet` interface. One thing you'd like to do with a `SortedSet` is to go into the interior of the `Set` and iterate forward or backward. It's easy enough to go forward from the interior: just get a `tailSet` and iterate over it. Unfortunately, there's no easy way to go backward.

The following idiom obtains the first element that is less than a specified object o in the element space:

```
Object predecessor = ss.headSet(o).last();
```

This is a fine way to go one element backward from a point in the interior of a sorted set. It could be applied repeatedly to iterate backward, but this is very inefficient, requiring a lookup for each element returned.

Comparator Accessor

The `SortedSet` interface contains an accessor method called `comparator` that returns the `Comparator` used to sort the set or `null` if the set is sorted according to the natural ordering of its elements. This method is provided so that sorted sets can be copied into new sorted sets with the same ordering. It is used by the `SortedSet` constructor described previously.

The SortedMap Interface

A `SortedMap`[26] is a `Map` that maintains its entries in ascending order, sorted according to the keys' natural ordering or according to a `Comparator` provided at the time of the `SortedMap` creation. Natural ordering and `Comparators` are discussed in the "Object Ordering" section. The `SortedMap` interface provides operations for normal `Map` operations and for the following:

- *Range view.* Performs arbitrary range operations on the sorted map
- *Endpoints.* Returns the first or the last key in the sorted map
- *Comparator access.* Returns the `Comparator`, if any, used to sort the map

The following interface is the `Map` analog of `SortedSet`:[27]

```
public interface SortedMap<K, V> extends Map<K, V>{
    Comparator<? super K> comparator();
    SortedMap<K, V> subMap(K fromKey, K toKey);
    SortedMap<K, V> headMap(K toKey);
    SortedMap<K, V> tailMap(K fromKey);
    K firstKey();
```

---

26. `7/docs/api/java/util/SortedMap.html`

27. `7/docs/api/java/util/SortedSet.html`

```
        K lastKey();
    }
```

Map Operations

The operations `SortedMap` inherits from `Map` behave identically on sorted maps and normal maps, with two exceptions:

- The `Iterator` returned by the `iterator` operation on any of the sorted map's `Collection` views traverse the collections in order.
- The arrays returned by the `Collection` views' `toArray` operations contain the keys, values, or entries in order.

Although it isn't guaranteed by the interface, the `toString` method of the `Collection` views in all the Java platform's `SortedMap` implementations returns a string containing all the elements of the view, in order.

Standard Constructors

By convention, all general-purpose `Map` implementations provide a standard conversion constructor that takes a `Map`. `SortedMap` implementations are no exception. In `TreeMap`, this constructor creates an instance that orders its entries according to their keys' natural ordering. As with `TreeSet`, this was probably a mistake. It would have been better to check dynamically to see whether the specified `Map` instance was a `SortedMap` and, if so, sort the new `Map` according to the same criterion (comparator or natural ordering). Because `TreeMap` took the approach it did, it also provides a constructor that takes a `SortedMap` and returns a new `TreeMap` containing the same mappings as the given `SortedMap`, sorted according to the same criterion. Note that it is the compile-time type of the argument, not its runtime type, that determines whether the `SortedMap` constructor is invoked instead of to the ordinary `Map` constructor.

`SortedMap` implementations also provide, by convention, a constructor that takes a `Comparator` and returns an empty `Map` sorted according to the specified `Comparator`. If `null` is passed to this constructor, it returns a `Map` that sorts its mappings according to their keys' natural ordering.

Comparison to SortedSet

Because this interface is a precise `Map` analog of `SortedSet`, all the idioms and code examples in "The SortedSet Interface" section apply to `SortedMap`, with only trivial modifications.

Summary of Interfaces

The core collection interfaces are the foundation of the Java Collections Framework. The Java Collections Framework hierarchy consists of two distinct interface trees.

The first tree starts with the `Collection` interface, which provides for the basic functionality used by all collections, such as `add` and `remove` methods. Its subinterfaces—`Set`, `List`, and `Queue`—provide for more specialized collections.

The `Set` interface does not allow duplicate elements. This can be useful for storing collections such as a deck of cards or student records. The `Set` interface has a subinterface, `SortedSet`, which sorts the elements in the set.

The `List` interface provides for an ordered collection, which is useful when you need precise control over where each element is inserted. You can retrieve elements from a `List` by their exact position.

The `Queue` interface enables additional insertion, extraction, and inspection operations. Elements in a `Queue` are typically ordered in on a FIFO basis.

The second tree starts with the `Map` interface, which maps keys and values similar to a `Hashtable`. `Map`'s subinterface, `SortedMap`, maintains its key-value pairs in ascending order or in an order specified by a `Comparator`.

These interfaces allow collections to be manipulated independently of the details of their representation.

Questions and Exercises: Interfaces

Questions

1. This chapter mentions three ways to traverse a `List`. Describe them, and note the limitations of each.

2. Consider the four core interfaces: `Set`, `List`, `Queue`, and `Map`. For each of the following four assignments, specify which of the four core interfaces is most appropriate, and explain how to use this core interface to implement the assignment.

   a. A company needs to record the names of all its employees. Every month, an employee will be chosen at random from these records to receive a free product.

   b. The company decides that each new product will be named after an employee. Only first names will be used, and each name will be used only once. Prepare a list of unique first names.

   c. The company decides that it only wants to use the most popular names for its products. Count the number of employees who have each first name.

d. The company acquires season tickets for the local football team, to be shared by employees. Create a waiting list for this popular sport.

3. The following program is supposed to print the string "Blue". Instead, it throws an error. Why?

```java
import java.util.*;

public class SortMe {
    public static void main(String args[]) {
        SortedSet<StringBuffer> s = new TreeSet<StringBuffer>();
        s.add(new StringBuffer("Red"));
        s.add(new StringBuffer("White"));
        s.add(new StringBuffer("Blue"));
        System.out.println(s.first());
    }
}
```

Exercises

1. Write a program that prints its arguments in random order. Do not make a copy of the argument array.

2. Take the FindDups example given previously and modify it to use a SortedSet instead of a Set. Specify a Comparator so that case is ignored when sorting and identifying set elements.

3. Write a method that takes a List<String> and applies String.trim[28] to each element. To do this, you'll need to pick one of the three iteration idioms that you described in question 1. Two of these will not give the result you want, so be sure to write a program to demonstrate that the method actually works!

Answers

You can find answers to these questions and exercises at http://docs.oracle.com/javase/tutorial/collections/interfaces/QandE/answers.html.

Implementations

Implementations are the data objects used to store collections, which implement the interfaces described previously in the "Interfaces" section. This section describes the following kinds of implementations:

- *General-purpose implementations* are the most commonly used implementations, designed for everyday use. They are summarized in Table 11.3.

---

28. 7/docs/api/java/lang/String.html#trim()

Table 11.3 General-Purpose Implementations

Interfaces	Implementations				
	Hash table	Resizable array	Tree	Linked list	Hash table and linked list
Set	HashSet		TreeSet		LinkedHashSet
List		ArrayList		LinkedList	
Queue					
Map	HashMap		TreeMap		LinkedHashMap

- *Special-purpose implementations* are designed for use in special situations and display nonstandard performance characteristics, usage restrictions, or behavior.

- *Concurrent implementations* are designed to support high concurrency, typically at the expense of single-threaded performance. These implementations are part of the `java.util.concurrent` package.

- *Wrapper implementations* are used in combination with other types of implementations, often the general-purpose ones, to provide added or restricted functionality.

- *Convenience implementations* are mini-implementations, typically made available via static factory methods, and provide convenient, efficient alternatives to general-purpose implementations for special collections (e.g., singleton sets).

- *Abstract implementations* are skeletal implementations that facilitate the construction of custom implementations.

As you can see from Table 11.3, the Java Collections Framework provides several general-purpose implementations of the `Set`, `List`, and `Map` interfaces. In each case, one respective implementation (`HashSet`, `ArrayList`,[29] and `HashMap`[30]) is clearly the one to use for most applications, all other things being equal. Note that the `SortedSet` and the `SortedMap` interfaces do not have rows in the table. Each of these interfaces has one implementation (`TreeSet` and `TreeMap`[31]) and is listed in the `Set` and the `Map` rows. There are two general-purpose `Queue` implementations—`LinkedList`,[32] which is also a `List` implementation, and `PriorityQueue`,[33] which

29. 7/docs/api/java/util/ArrayList.html

30. 7/docs/api/java/util/HashMap.html

31. 7/docs/api/java/util/TreeMap.html

32. 7/docs/api/java/util/LinkedList.html

33. 7/docs/api/java/util/PriorityQueue.html

is omitted from the table. These two implementations provide very different semantics: `LinkedList` provides FIFO semantics, while `PriorityQueue` orders its elements according to their values.

Each of the general-purpose implementations provides all optional operations contained in its interface. All permit `null` elements, keys, and values. None are synchronized (thread safe). All have *fail-fast iterators*, which detect illegal concurrent modification during iteration and fail quickly and cleanly rather than risking arbitrary, nondeterministic behavior at an undetermined time in the future. All are `Serializable` and all support a public `clone` method.

The fact that these implementations are unsynchronized represents a break with the past: the legacy collections `Vector` and `Hashtable` are synchronized. The present approach was taken because collections are frequently used when the synchronization is of no benefit. Such uses include single-threaded use, read-only use, and use as part of a larger data object that does its own synchronization. In general, it is good API design practice not to make users pay for a feature they don't use. Furthermore, unnecessary synchronization can result in deadlock under certain circumstances.

If you need thread-safe collections, the synchronization wrappers described later in the "Wrapper Implementations" section allow *any* collection to be transformed into a synchronized collection. Thus synchronization is optional for general-purpose implementations, whereas it is mandatory for legacy implementations. Moreover, the `java.util.concurrent` package provides concurrent implementations of the `BlockingQueue` interface, which extends `Queue`, and the `ConcurrentMap` interface, which extends `Map`. These implementations offer much higher concurrency than mere synchronized implementations.

As a rule, you should be thinking about the interfaces, *not* the implementations. That is why there are no programming examples in this section. For the most part, the choice of implementation only affects performance. The preferred style, as mentioned in the "Interfaces" section, is to choose an implementation when a `Collection` is created and immediately assign the new collection to a variable of the corresponding interface type (or pass the collection to a method expecting an argument of the interface type). This way, the program does not become dependent on any added methods in a given implementation, leaving the programmer free to change implementations anytime that it is warranted by performance concerns or behavioral details.

The sections that follow briefly discuss the implementations. The performance of the implementations is described using terms such as *constant time*, *log*, *linear*, *n log(n)*, and *quadratic* to refer to the asymptotic upper bound on the time complexity of performing the operation. All this is quite a mouthful, and it doesn't matter much if you don't know what it means. If you're interested in knowing more, refer to any good algorithms textbook. One thing to keep in mind is that this sort of performance metric has its limitations. Sometimes, the nominally slower implementation may be faster. When in doubt, measure the performance!

Set Implementations

The Set implementations are grouped into general-purpose and special-purpose implementations.

General-Purpose Set Implementations

There are three general-purpose Set implementations: HashSet, TreeSet, and LinkedHashSet. Choosing which of these three to use is generally straightforward. HashSet is much faster than TreeSet (constant time versus log time for most operations) but offers no ordering guarantees. If you need to use the operations in the SortedSet interface or if value-ordered iteration is required, use TreeSet; otherwise, use HashSet. It's a fair bet that you'll end up using HashSet most of the time.

LinkedHashSet is in some sense intermediate between HashSet and TreeSet. Implemented as a hash table with a linked list running through it, it provides *insertion-ordered* iteration (least recently inserted to most recently) and runs nearly as fast as HashSet. The LinkedHashSet implementation spares its clients from the unspecified, generally chaotic ordering provided by HashSet without incurring the increased cost associated with TreeSet.

One thing worth keeping in mind about HashSet is that iteration is linear in the sum of the number of entries and the number of buckets (the *capacity*). Thus choosing an initial capacity that's too high can waste both space and time. On the other hand, choosing an initial capacity that's too low wastes time by copying the data structure each time it's forced to increase its capacity. If you don't specify an initial capacity, the default is 16. In the past, there were some advantages to choosing a prime number as the initial capacity. This is no longer true. Internally, the capacity is always rounded up to a power of 2. The initial capacity is specified using the int constructor. The following line of code allocates a HashSet whose initial capacity is 64:

```
Set<String> s = new HashSet<String>(64);
```

The HashSet class has one other tuning parameter, called the *load factor*. If you care a lot about the space consumption of your HashSet, read the HashSet documentation for more information.[34] Otherwise, just accept the default; it's almost always the right thing to do.

---

34. 7/docs/api/java/util/HashSet.html

If you accept the default load factor but want to specify an initial capacity, pick a number that's about twice the size to which you expect the set to grow. If your guess is way off, you may waste a bit of space, time, or both, but it's unlikely to be a big problem.

LinkedHashSet has the same tuning parameters as HashSet, but iteration time is not affected by capacity. TreeSet has no tuning parameters.

Special-Purpose Set Implementations

There are two special-purpose Set implementations: EnumSet[35] and CopyOnWrite-ArraySet.[36]

EnumSet is a high-performance Set implementation for enum types. All of the members of an enum set must be of the same enum type. Internally, it is represented by a bit-vector, typically a single long. Enum sets support iteration over ranges of enum types. For example, given the enum declaration for the days of the week, you can iterate over the weekdays. The EnumSet class provides a static factory that makes it easy:

```
for (Day d : EnumSet.range(Day.MONDAY, Day.FRIDAY))
    System.out.println(d);
```

Enum sets also provide a rich, typesafe replacement for traditional bit flags.

```
EnumSet.of(Style.BOLD, Style.ITALIC)
```

CopyOnWriteArraySet is a Set implementation backed up by a *copy-on-write* array, a strategy that optimizes the use of a resource. All mutative operations, such as add, set, and remove, are implemented by making a new copy of the array; no locking is ever required. Even iteration may safely proceed concurrently with element insertion and deletion. Unlike most Set implementations, the add, remove, and contains methods require time proportional to the size of the set. This implementation is *only* appropriate for sets that are rarely modified but frequently iterated. It is well suited to maintaining event-handler lists that must prevent duplicates.

List Implementations

List implementations are grouped into general-purpose and special-purpose implementations.

---

35. 7/docs/api/java/util/EnumSet.html

36. 7/docs/api/java/util/concurrent/CopyOnWriteArraySet.html

General-Purpose List Implementations

There are two general-purpose List[37] implementations: ArrayList[38] and LinkedList.[39] Most of the time, you'll probably use ArrayList, which offers constant-time positional access and is just plain fast. It does not have to allocate a node object for each element in the List, and it can take advantage of System. arraycopy when it has to move multiple elements at the same time. Think of ArrayList as Vector without the synchronization overhead.

If you frequently add elements to the beginning of the List or iterate over the List to delete elements from its interior, you should consider using LinkedList. These operations require constant time in a LinkedList and linear time in an ArrayList, but you pay a big price in terms of performance. Positional access requires linear time in a LinkedList and constant time in an ArrayList. Furthermore, the constant factor for LinkedList is much worse. If you think you want to use a LinkedList, measure the performance of your application with both LinkedList and ArrayList before making your choice; ArrayList is usually faster.

ArrayList has one tuning parameter—the *initial capacity*, which refers to the number of elements the ArrayList can hold before it has to grow. LinkedList has no tuning parameters and seven optional operations, one of which is clone. The other six are addFirst, getFirst, removeFirst, addLast, getLast, and removeLast. LinkedList also implements the Queue interface.

11

Special-Purpose List Implementations

CopyOnWriteArrayList[40] is a List implementation backed up by a copy-on-write array. This implementation is similar in nature to CopyOnWriteArraySet. No synchronization is necessary, even during iteration, and iterators are guaranteed never to throw ConcurrentModificationException. This implementation is well suited to maintaining event-handler lists, in which change is infrequent and traversal is frequent and potentially time consuming.

If you need synchronization, a Vector will be slightly faster than an ArrayList synchronized with Collections.synchronizedList. But Vector has loads of legacy operations, so be careful to always manipulate the Vector with the List interface or else you won't be able to replace the implementation at a later time.

If your List is fixed in size (i.e., you'll never use remove, add, or any of the bulk operations other than containsAll), then you have a third option that's definitely

37. 7/docs/api/java/util/List.html
38. 7/docs/api/java/util/ArrayList.html
39. 7/docs/api/java/util/LinkedList.html
40. 7/docs/api/java/util/concurrent/CopyOnWriteArrayList.html

worth considering. See `Arrays.asList` in the "Convenience Implementations" section later in this chapter for more information.

Map Implementations

`Map` implementations are grouped into general-purpose, special-purpose, and concurrent implementations.

General-Purpose Map Implementations

The three general-purpose `Map` implementations are `HashMap`,[41] `TreeMap`,[42] and `LinkedHashMap`. If you need `SortedMap` operations or key-ordered `Collection`-view iteration, use `TreeMap`. If you want maximum speed and don't care about iteration order, use `HashMap`. If you want near-`HashMap` performance and insertion-order iteration, use `LinkedHashMap`. In this respect, the situation for `Map` is analogous to `Set`. Likewise, everything else in the "Set Implementations" section also applies to `Map` implementations.

`LinkedHashMap` provides two capabilities that are not available with `LinkedHashSet`. When you create a `LinkedHashMap`, you can order it based on key access rather than insertion. In other words, merely looking up the value associated with a key brings that key to the end of the map. Also, `LinkedHashMap` provides the `removeEldestEntry` method, which may be overridden to impose a policy for removing stale mappings automatically when new mappings are added to the map. This makes it very easy to implement a custom cache.

For example, this override will allow the map to grow up to as many as 100 entries, and then it will delete the eldest entry each time a new entry is added, maintaining a steady state of 100 entries:

```
private static final int MAX_ENTRIES = 100;

protected boolean removeEldestEntry(Map.Entry eldest) {
    return size() > MAX_ENTRIES;
}
```

Special-Purpose Map Implementations

There are three special-purpose `Map` implementations: `EnumMap`,[43] `WeakHashMap`,[44] and `IdentityHashMap`.[45] `EnumMap`, which is internally implemented as an `array`,

---

41. 7/docs/api/java/util/HashMap.html

42. 7/docs/api/java/util/TreeMap.html

43. 7/docs/api/java/util/EnumMap.html

44. 7/docs/api/java/util/WeakHashMap.html

45. 7/docs/api/java/util/IdentityHashMap.html

is a high-performance `Map` implementation for use with enum keys. This implementation combines the richness and safety of the `Map` interface with a speed approaching that of an array. If you want to map an enum to a value, you should always use an `EnumMap` instead of an array.

`WeakHashMap` is an implementation of the `Map` interface that stores only weak references to its keys. Storing only weak references allows a key-value pair to be garbage collected when its key is no longer referenced outside of the `WeakHashMap`. This class provides the easiest way to harness the power of weak references. It is useful for implementing "registry-like" data structures, where the utility of an entry vanishes when its key is no longer reachable by any thread.

`IdentityHashMap` is an identity-based `Map` implementation based on a hash table. This class is useful for topology-preserving object graph transformations, such as serialization or deep copying. To perform such transformations, you need to maintain an identity-based "node table" that keeps track of which objects have already been seen. Identity-based maps are also used to maintain object-to-metainformation mappings in dynamic debuggers and similar systems. Finally, identity-based maps are useful in thwarting "spoof attacks" that are a result of intentionally perverse `equals` methods because `IdentityHashMap` never invokes the `equals` method on its keys. An added benefit of this implementation is that it is fast.

Concurrent Map Implementations

The `java.util.concurrent`[46] package contains the `ConcurrentMap`[47] interface, which extends `Map` with atomic `putIfAbsent`, `remove`, and `replace` methods and the `ConcurrentHashMap`[48] implementation of that interface.

`ConcurrentHashMap` is a highly concurrent, high-performance implementation backed up by a hash table. This implementation never blocks when performing retrievals and allows the client to select the concurrency level for updates. It is intended as a drop-in replacement for `Hashtable`: in addition to implementing `ConcurrentMap`, it supports all the legacy methods peculiar to `Hashtable`. Again, if you don't need the legacy operations, be careful to manipulate it with the `ConcurrentMap` interface.

Queue Implementations

The `Queue` implementations are grouped into general-purpose and concurrent implementations.

---

46. 7/docs/api/java/util/concurrent/package-summary.html
47. 7/docs/api/java/util/concurrent/ConcurrentMap.html
48. 7/docs/api/java/util/concurrent/ConcurrentHashMap.html

General-Purpose Queue Implementations

As mentioned in the previous section, `LinkedList` implements the `Queue` interface, providing FIFO queue operations for `add`, `poll`, and so on.

The `PriorityQueue`[49] class is a priority queue based on the *heap* data structure. This queue orders elements according to the order specified at construction time, which can be the elements' natural ordering or the ordering imposed by an explicit `Comparator`.

The queue retrieval operations—`poll`, `remove`, `peek`, and `element`—access the element at the head of the queue. The *head of the queue* is the least element with respect to the specified ordering. If multiple elements are tied for least value, the head is one of those elements; ties are broken arbitrarily.

`PriorityQueue` and its iterator implement all the optional methods of the `Collection` and `Iterator` interfaces. The iterator provided in method `iterator` is not guaranteed to traverse the elements of the `PriorityQueue` in any particular order. For ordered traversal, consider using `Arrays.sort(pq.toArray())`.

Concurrent Queue Implementations

The `java.util.concurrent` package contains a set of synchronized `Queue` interfaces and classes. `BlockingQueue`[50] extends `Queue` with operations that wait for the queue to become nonempty when retrieving an element and for space to become available in the queue when storing an element. This interface is implemented by the following classes:

- `LinkedBlockingQueue`[51]—An optionally bounded FIFO blocking queue backed by linked nodes
- `ArrayBlockingQueue`[52]—A bounded FIFO blocking queue backed by an array
- `PriorityBlockingQueue`[53]—An unbounded blocking priority queue backed by a heap
- `DelayQueue`[54]—A time-based scheduling queue backed by a heap
- `SynchronousQueue`[55]—A simple rendezvous mechanism that uses the `BlockingQueue` interface

49. 7/docs/api/java/util/PriorityQueue.html
50. 7/docs/api/java/util/concurrent/BlockingQueue.html
51. 7/docs/api/java/util/concurrent/LinkedBlockingQueue.html
52. 7/docs/api/java/util/concurrent/ArrayBlockingQueue.html
53. 7/docs/api/java/util/concurrent/PriorityBlockingQueue.html
54. 7/docs/api/java/util/concurrent/DelayQueue.html
55. 7/docs/api/java/util/concurrent/SynchronousQueue.html

In JDK 7, `TransferQueue`[56] is a specialized `BlockingQueue` in which code that adds an element to the queue has the option of waiting (blocking) for code in another thread to retrieve the element. `TransferQueue` has a single implementation, `LinkedTransferQueue`,[57] which is an unbounded `TransferQueue` based on linked nodes.

Wrapper Implementations

Wrapper implementations delegate all their real work to a specified collection but add extra functionality on top of what this collection offers. For design pattern fans, this is an example of the *decorator* pattern. Although it may seem a bit exotic, it's really pretty straightforward.

These implementations are anonymous; rather than providing a public class, the library provides a static factory method. All these implementations are found in the `Collections` class, which consists solely of static methods.

Synchronization Wrappers

The synchronization wrappers add automatic synchronization (thread-safety) to an arbitrary collection. Each of the six core collection interfaces—`Collection`, `Set`, `List`,[58] `Map`, `SortedSet`,[59] and `SortedMap`[60]—has one static factory method:

```
public static <T> Collection<T> synchronizedCollection(Collection<T> c);
public static <T> Set<T> synchronizedSet(Set<T> s);
public static <T> List<T> synchronizedList(List<T> list);
public static <K,V> Map<K,V> synchronizedMap(Map<K,V> m);
public static <T> SortedSet<T> synchronizedSortedSet(SortedSet<T> s);
public static <K,V> SortedMap<K,V> synchronizedSortedMap(SortedMap<K,V> m);
```

Each of these methods returns a synchronized (thread-safe) `Collection` backed up by the specified collection. To guarantee serial access, *all* access to the backing collection must be accomplished through the returned collection. The easy way to guarantee this is not to keep a reference to the backing collection. Create the synchronized collection with the following trick:

```
List<Type> list = Collections.synchronizedList(new ArrayList<Type>());
```

---

56. `7/docs/api/java/util/concurrent/TransferQueue.html`

57. `7/docs/api/java/util/concurrent/LinkedTransferQueue.html`

58. `7/docs/api/java/util/List.html`

59. `7/docs/api/java/util/SortedSet.html`

60. `7/docs/api/java/util/SortedMap.html`

A collection created in this fashion is every bit as thread-safe as a normally synchronized collection, such as a `Vector`.[61]

In the face of concurrent access, it is imperative that the user manually synchronizes on the returned collection when iterating over it. This is because iteration is accomplished via multiple calls into the collection, which must be composed into a single atomic operation. The following is the idiom to iterate over a wrapper-synchronized collection:

```
Collection<Type> c = Collections.synchronizedCollection(myCollection);
synchronized(c) {
    for (Type e : c)
        foo(e);
}
```

If an explicit iterator is used, the `iterator` method must be called from within the `synchronized` block. Failure to follow this advice may result in nondeterministic behavior. The idiom for iterating over a `Collection` view of a synchronized `Map` is similar. It is imperative that the user synchronize on the synchronized `Map` when iterating over any of its `Collection` views, rather than synchronizing on the `Collection` view itself, as shown in the following example:

```
Map<KeyType, ValType> m = Collections.synchronizedMap(new HashMap<KeyType,
    ValType>());
        . . .
Set<KeyType> s = m.keySet();
        . . .
// Synchronizing on m, not s!
synchronized(m) {
    while (KeyType k : s)
        foo(k);
}
```

One minor downside of using wrapper implementations is that you do not have the ability to execute any *noninterface* operations of a wrapped implementation. So, for instance, in the preceding `List` example, you cannot call `ArrayList`'s `ensure-Capacity`[62] operation on the wrapped `ArrayList`.

Unmodifiable Wrappers

Unlike synchronization wrappers, which add functionality to the wrapped collection, the unmodifiable wrappers take functionality away. In particular, they take away the ability to modify the collection by intercepting all the operations that

---

61. 7/docs/api/java/util/Vector.html
62. 7/docs/api/java/util/ArrayList.html#ensureCapacity(int)

would modify the collection and throwing an `UnsupportedOperationException`. Unmodifiable wrappers have two main uses, as follows:

- They make a collection immutable once it has been built. In this case, it's good practice not to maintain a reference to the backing collection. This absolutely guarantees immutability.
- They allow certain clients read-only access to your data structures. You keep a reference to the backing collection but hand out a reference to the wrapper. In this way, clients can look but not modify, while you maintain full access.

Like synchronization wrappers, each of the six core `Collection` interfaces has one static factory method:

```
public static <T> Collection<T> unmodifiableCollection(Collection
    <? extends T> c);
public static <T> Set<T> unmodifiableSet(Set<? extends T> s);
public static <T> List<T> unmodifiableList(List<? extends T> list);
public static <K,V> Map<K, V> unmodifiableMap(Map<? extends K, ? extends V>
    m);
public static <T> SortedSet<T> unmodifiableSortedSet(SortedSet<? extends T>
    s);
public static <K,V> SortedMap<K, V> unmodifiableSortedMap(SortedMap<K, ?
    extends V> m);
```

Checked Interface Wrappers

The `Collections.checked` interface wrappers are provided for use with generic collections. These implementations return a *dynamically* type-safe view of the specified collection, which throws a `ClassCastException` if a client attempts to add an element of the wrong type. The generics mechanism in the language provides compile-time (static) type checking, but it is possible to defeat this mechanism. Dynamically type-safe views eliminate this possibility entirely.

Convenience Implementations

This section describes several mini-implementations that can be more convenient and more efficient than general-purpose implementations when you don't need their full power. All the implementations in this section are made available via static factory methods rather than `public` classes.

List View of an Array

The `Arrays.asList`[63] method returns a `List` view of its array argument. Changes to the `List` write through to the array and vice versa. The size of the collection is

---

63. 7/docs/api/java/util/Arrays.html#asList(T...)

that of the array and cannot be changed. If the add or the remove method is called on the List, an UnsupportedOperationException will result.

This implementation is normally used as a bridge between array-based and collection-based APIs. It allows you to pass an array to a method expecting a Collection or a List. However, this implementation also has another use. If you need a fixed-size List, it's more efficient than any general-purpose List implementation. Here is the idiom:

```
List<String> list = Arrays.asList(new String[size]);
```

Note that a reference to the backing array is not retained.

Immutable Multiple-Copy List

Occasionally you'll need an immutable List consisting of multiple copies of the same element. The Collections.nCopies[64] method returns such a list. This implementation has two main uses: The first is to initialize a newly created List; for example, suppose you want an ArrayList initially consisting of 1,000 null elements. The following incantation does the trick:

```
List<Type> list = new ArrayList<Type>(Collections.nCopies(1000, (Type)
    null);
```

Of course, the initial value of each element need not be null.

The second main use is to grow an existing List. For example, suppose you want to add 69 copies of the string "fruit bat" to the end of a List<String>. It's not clear why you'd want to do such a thing, but let's just suppose you did. Here's how you'd do it:

```
lovablePets.addAll(Collections.nCopies(69, "fruit bat"));
```

By using the form of addAll, which takes both an index and a Collection, you can add the new elements to the middle of a List instead of to the end of it.

Immutable Singleton Set

Sometimes you'll need an immutable *singleton set*, which consists of a single, specified element. The Collections.singleton[65] method returns such a Set. This implementation can be used to remove all occurrences of a specified element from a Collection:

---

64. 7/docs/api/java/util/Collections.html#nCopies(int,%20T)
65. 7/docs/api/java/util/Collections.html#singleton(T)

```
c.removeAll(Collections.singleton(e));
```

A related idiom removes all elements that map to a specified value from a Map. For example, suppose you have a Map—job—that maps people to their line of work, and suppose you want to eliminate all the lawyers. The following one-liner will do the deed:

```
job.values().removeAll(Collections.singleton(LAWYER));
```

This implementation can also provide a single input value to a method that is written to accept a collection of values.

Empty Set, List, and Map Constants

The Collections class provides methods to return the empty Set, List, and Map: emptySet,[66] emptyList,[67] and emptyMap.[68] These constants are mainly used as input to methods that take a Collection of values when you don't want to provide any values at all, as in this example:

```
tourist.declarePurchases(Collections.emptySet());
```

Summary of Implementations

Implementations are the data objects used to store collections, which implement the interfaces described in the "Interfaces" section. The Java Collections Framework provides several general-purpose implementations of the core interfaces:

- For the Set interface, HashSet is the most commonly used implementation.
- For the List interface, ArrayList is the most commonly used implementation.
- For the Map interface, HashMap is the most commonly used implementation.
- For the Queue interface, LinkedList is the most commonly used implementation.

Each of the general-purpose implementations provides all optional operations contained in its interface.

The Java Collections Framework also provides several special-purpose implementations for situations that require nonstandard performance, usage restrictions, or other unusual behavior.

The java.util.concurrent package contains several collections implementations, which are thread safe but not governed by a single exclusion lock.

---

66. 7/docs/api/java/util/Collections.html#emptySet()

67. 7/docs/api/java/util/Collections.html#emptyList()

68. 7/docs/api/java/util/Collections.html#emptyMap()

The `Collections` class (as opposed to the `Collection` interface) provides static methods that operate on or return collections, which are known as *wrapper implementations*.

Finally, there are several convenience implementations, which can be more efficient than general-purpose implementations when you don't need their full power. The convenience implementations are made available through static factory methods.

Questions and Exercises: Implementations

Questions

1. You plan to write a program that uses several basic collection interfaces: `Set`, `List`, `Queue`, and `Map`. You're not sure which implementations will work best, so you decide to use general-purpose implementations until you get a better idea how your program will work in the real world. Which implementations are these?

2. If you need a `Set` implementation that provides value-ordered iteration, which class should you use?

3. Which class do you use to access wrapper implementations?

Exercises

1. Write a program that reads a text file, specified by the first command line argument, into a `List`. The program should then print random lines from the file, with the number of lines printed to be specified by the second command line argument. Write the program so that a correctly sized collection is allocated all at once, instead of being gradually expanded as the file is read in. *Hint:* To determine the number of lines in the file, use `java.io.File.length`[69] to obtain the size of the file, then divide by an assumed size of an average line.

Answers

You can find answers to these questions and exercises at `http://docs.oracle.com/javase/tutorial/collections/implementations/QandE/answers.html`.

Algorithms

The *polymorphic algorithms* described here are pieces of reusable functionality provided by the Java platform. They all come from the `Collections` class and all take the form of static methods whose first argument is the collection on which the

---

69. `7/docs/api/java/io/File.html#length()`

operation is to be performed. A majority of the algorithms provided by the Java platform operate on List[70] instances, but a few of them operate on arbitrary Collection instances. This section briefly describes these algorithms.

Sorting

The sort algorithm reorders a List so that its elements are in ascending order according to an ordering relationship. Two forms of the operation are provided. The first form takes a List and sorts it according to its elements' *natural ordering*. If you're unfamiliar with the concept of natural ordering, revisit the "Object Ordering" section.

The sort operation uses a slightly optimized *merge sort* algorithm that is fast and stable:

- It is guaranteed to run in n log(n) time and runs substantially faster on nearly sorted lists. Empirical tests showed it to be as fast as a highly optimized quicksort. A quicksort is generally considered to be faster than a merge sort but isn't stable and doesn't guarantee n log(n) performance.

- It doesn't reorder equal elements. This is important if you sort the same list repeatedly on different attributes. If a user of a mail program sorts the inbox by mailing date and then sorts it by sender, the user naturally expects that the now-contiguous list of messages from a given sender will (still) be sorted by mailing date. This is guaranteed only if the second sort was stable.

The following trivial program prints out its arguments in lexicographic (alphabetical) order:

```
import java.util.*;

public class Sort {
    public static void main(String[] args) {
        List<String> list = Arrays.asList(args);
        Collections.sort(list);
        System.out.println(list);
    }
}
```

Let's run the program:

```
% java Sort i walk the line
```

---

70. 7/docs/api/java/util/List.html

The following output is produced:

```
[i, line, the, walk]
```

This program was included only to show you that algorithms really are as easy to use as they appear.

The second form of sort takes a Comparator[71] in addition to a List and sorts the elements with the Comparator. Suppose you want to print out the anagram groups from our earlier example in reverse order of size—largest anagram group first. The example that follows shows you how to achieve this with the help of the second form of the sort method.

Recall that the anagram groups are stored as values in a Map, in the form of List instances. The revised printing code iterates through the Map's values view, putting every List that passes the minimum-size test into a List of Lists. Then the code sorts this List, using a Comparator that expects List instances, and implements reverse size ordering. Finally, the code iterates through the sorted List, printing its elements (the anagram groups). The following code replaces the printing code at the end of the main method in the Anagrams example given previously:

```
// Make a List of all anagram groups above size threshold.
List<List<String>> winners = new ArrayList<List<String>>();
for (List<String> l : m.values())
    if (l.size() >= minGroupSize)
        winners.add(l);

// Sort anagram groups according to size
Collections.sort(winners, new Comparator<List<String>>() {
    public int compare(List<String> o1, List<String> o2) {
        return o2.size() - o1.size();
    }});

// Print anagram groups.
for (List<String> l : winners)
    System.out.println(l.size() + ": " + l);
```

Running the program on the same dictionary as in "The Map Interface" section, with the same minimum anagram group size (eight), produces the following output:

```
12: [apers, apres, asper, pares, parse, pears, prase,
        presa, rapes, reaps, spare, spear]
11: [alerts, alters, artels, estral, laster, ratels,
        salter, slater, staler, stelar, talers]
10: [least, setal, slate, stale, steal, stela, taels,
        tales, teals, tesla]
9: [estrin, inerts, insert, inters, niters, nitres,
        sinter, triens, trines]
```

---

71. 7/docs/api/java/util/Comparator.html

```
9: [capers, crapes, escarp, pacers, parsec, recaps,
      scrape, secpar, spacer]
9: [palest, palets, pastel, petals, plates, pleats,
      septal, staple, tepals]
9: [anestri, antsier, nastier, ratines, retains, retinas,
      retsina, stainer, stearin]
8: [lapse, leaps, pales, peals, pleas, salep, sepal, spale]
8: [aspers, parses, passer, prases, repass, spares,
      sparse, spears]
8: [enters, nester, renest, rentes, resent, tenser,
      ternes, treens]
8: [arles, earls, lares, laser, lears, rales, reals, seral]
8: [earings, erasing, gainers, reagins, regains, reginas,
      searing, seringa]
8: [peris, piers, pries, prise, ripes, speir, spier, spire]
8: [ates, east, eats, etas, sate, seat, seta, teas]
8: [carets, cartes, caster, caters, crates, reacts,
      recast, traces]
```

Shuffling

The shuffle algorithm does the opposite of what sort does, destroying any trace of order that may have been present in a List. In other words, this algorithm reorders the List based on input from a source of randomness, so that all possible permutations occur with equal likelihood, assuming a fair source of randomness. This algorithm is useful for implementing games of chance. For example, it could be used to shuffle a List of Card objects representing a deck. It's also useful for generating test cases.

This operation has two forms: one takes a List and uses a default source of randomness, and the other requires the caller to provide a Random[72] object to use as a source of randomness. The code for this algorithm was provided earlier in this chapter.[73]

Routine Data Manipulation

The Collections class provides five algorithms for doing routine data manipulation on List objects, all of which are pretty straightforward:

- reverse—This reverses the order of the elements in a List.
- fill—This overwrites every element in a List with the specified value. It is useful for reinitializing a List.
- copy—This takes two arguments, a destination List, and a source List, and copies the elements of the source into the destination, overwriting its contents.

---

72. 7/docs/api/java/util/Random.html
73. tutorial/collections/interfaces/list.html#shuffle

The destination `List` must be at least as long as the source. If it is longer, the remaining elements in the destination `List` are unaffected.

- `swap`—This swaps the elements at the specified positions in a `List`.
- `addAll`—This adds all the specified elements to a `Collection`. The elements to be added may be specified individually or as an array.

Searching

The `binarySearch` algorithm searches for a specified element in a sorted `List`. This algorithm has two forms: The first takes a `List` and an element to search for (the *search key*). This form assumes that the `List` is sorted in ascending order according to the natural ordering of its elements. The second form takes a `Comparator` in addition to the `List` and the search key and assumes that the `List` is sorted into ascending order according to the specified `Comparator`. The `sort` algorithm can be used to sort the `List` prior to calling `binarySearch`.

The return value is the same for both forms. If the `List` contains the search key, its index is returned. If not, the return value is `(-(insertion point) - 1)`, where the insertion point is the point at which the value would be inserted into the `List` or the index of the first element greater than the value or `list.size()` if all elements in the `List` are less than the specified value. This admittedly ugly formula guarantees that the return value will be `>= 0` if and only if the search key is found. It's basically a hack to combine a boolean (`found`) and an integer (`index`) into a single `int` return value.

The following idiom, usable with both forms of the `binarySearch` operation, looks for the specified search key and inserts it at the appropriate position if it's not already present:

```
int pos = Collections.binarySearch(list, key);
if (pos < 0)
    l.add(-pos-1);
```

Composition

The frequency and disjoint algorithms test some aspect of the composition of one or more `Collections`:

- `frequency`—Counts the number of times the specified element occurs in the specified collection
- `disjoint`—Determines whether two `Collections` are disjoint—that is, whether they contain no elements in common

Finding Extreme Values

The `min` and the `max` algorithms respectively return the minimum and maximum elements contained in a specified `Collection`. Both of these operations come in two forms. The simple form takes only a `Collection` and returns the minimum (or maximum) element according to the elements' natural ordering. The second form takes a `Comparator` in addition to the `Collection` and returns the minimum (or maximum) element according to the specified `Comparator`.

Custom Collection Implementations

Many programmers will never need to implement their own `Collections` classes. You can go pretty far using the implementations described in the preceding sections of this chapter. However, someday you might want to write your own implementation. It is fairly easy to do this with the aid of the abstract implementations provided by the Java platform. Before we discuss *how* to write an implementation, let's discuss why you might want to write one.

Reasons to Write an Implementation

The following list illustrates the sort of custom `Collections` you might want to implement. It is not intended to be exhaustive:

- *Persistent.* All the built-in `Collection` implementations reside in main memory and vanish when the program exits. If you want a collection that will still be present the next time the program starts, you can implement it by building a veneer over an external database. Such a collection might be concurrently accessible by multiple programs.
- *Application specific.* This is a very broad category. One example is an unmodifiable `Map` containing real-time telemetry data. The keys could represent locations, and the values could be read from sensors at these locations in response to the `get` operation.
- *High performance, special purpose.* Many data structures take advantage of restricted usage to offer better performance than is possible with general-purpose implementations. For instance, consider a `List` containing long runs of identical element values. Such lists, which occur frequently in text processing, can be *run-length encoded*—runs can be represented as a single object containing the repeated element and the number of consecutive repetitions. This example is interesting because it trades off two aspects of performance: it requires less space but more time than an `ArrayList`.

- *High performance, general purpose.* The Java Collections Framework's designers tried to provide the best general-purpose implementations for each interface, but many, many data structures could have been used, and new ones are invented every day. Maybe you can come up with something faster!
- *Enhanced functionality.* Suppose you need an efficient bag implementation (also known as a *multiset*)—a `Collection` that offers constant-time containment checks while allowing duplicate elements. It's reasonably straightforward to implement such a collection atop a `HashMap`.
- *Convenience.* You may want additional implementations that offer conveniences beyond those offered by the Java platform. For instance, you may frequently need `List` instances representing a contiguous range of `Integers`.
- *Adapter.* Suppose you are using a legacy API that has its own ad hoc collections API. You can write an adapter implementation that permits these collections to operate in the Java Collections Framework. An *adapter implementation* is a thin veneer that wraps objects of one type and makes them behave like objects of another type by translating operations on the latter type into operations on the former.

How to Write a Custom Implementation

Writing a custom implementation is surprisingly easy. The Java Collections Framework provides abstract implementations expressly designed to facilitate custom implementations. We'll start with the following example of an implementation of `Arrays.asList`:[74]

```
public static <T> List<T> asList(T[] a) {
    return new MyArrayList<T>(a);
}

private static class MyArrayList<T> extends AbstractList<T> {

    private final T[] a;

    MyArrayList(T[] array) {
        a = array;
    }

    public T get(int index) {
        return a[index];
    }

    public T set(int index, T element) {
        T oldValue = a[index];
        a[index] = element;
```

---

74. 7/docs/api/java/util/Arrays.html#asList(T...)

```
        return oldValue;
    }

    public int size() {
        return a.length;
    }
}
```

Believe it or not, this is very close to the implementation that is contained in `java.util.Arrays`. It's that simple! You provide a constructor and the `get`, `set`, and `size` methods, and `AbstractList` does all the rest. You get the `ListItera-tor`, bulk operations, search operations, hash code computation, comparison, and string representation for free.

Suppose you want to make the implementation a bit faster. The API documentation for abstract implementations describes precisely how each method is implemented, so you'll know which methods to override to get the performance you want. The preceding implementation's performance is fine, but it can be improved a bit. In particular, the `toArray` method iterates over the `List`, copying one element at a time. Given the internal representation, it's a lot faster and more sensible just to clone the array:

```
public Object[] toArray() {
    return (Object[]) a.clone();
}
```

With the addition of this override and a few more like it, this implementation is exactly the one found in `java.util.Arrays`. In the interest of full disclosure, it's a bit tougher to use the other abstract implementations because you will have to write your own iterator, but it's still not that difficult.

The following list summarizes the abstract implementations:

- `AbstractCollection`[75]—This is a `Collection` that is neither a `Set` nor a `List`. At a minimum, you must provide the `iterator` and the `size` methods.
- `AbstractSet`[76]—This is a `Set` whose use is identical to `AbstractCollection`.
- `AbstractList`[77]—This is a `List` backed up by a random-access data store, such as an array. At a minimum, you must provide the `positional access` methods (`get` and, optionally, `set`, `remove`, and `add`) and the `size` method. The abstract class takes care of `listIterator` (and `iterator`).

---

75. 7/docs/api/java/util/AbstractCollection.html

76. 7/docs/api/java/util/AbstractSet.html

77. 7/docs/api/java/util/AbstractList.html

- `AbstractSequentialList`[78]—This is a `List` backed up by a sequential-access data store, such as a linked list. At a minimum, you must provide the `listIterator` and `size` methods. The abstract class takes care of the positional access methods. (This is the opposite of `AbstractList`.)
- `AbstractQueue`[79]—At a minimum, you must provide the `offer`, `peek`, `poll`, and `size` methods and an `iterator` supporting `remove`.
- `AbstractMap`[80]—At a minimum you must provide the `entrySet` view. This is typically implemented with the `AbstractSet` class. If the `Map` is modifiable, you must also provide the `put` method.

The process of writing a custom implementation is as follows:

1. Choose the appropriate abstract implementation class from the preceding list.
2. Provide implementations for all the abstract methods of the class. If your custom collection is to be modifiable, you will have to override one or more of the concrete methods as well. The API documentation for the abstract implementation class will tell you which methods to override.
3. Test and, if necessary, debug the implementation. You now have a working custom collection implementation.
4. If you are concerned about performance, read the API documentation of the abstract implementation class for all the methods whose implementations you're inheriting. If any seem too slow, override them. If you override any methods, be sure to measure the performance of the method before and after the override. How much effort you put into tweaking performance should be a function of how much use the implementation will get and how critical to performance its use is. (Often this step is best omitted.)

Interoperability

In this section, you'll learn about the following two aspects of interoperability:

- *Compatibility*. This subsection describes how collections can be made to work with older APIs that predate the addition of `Collections` to the Java platform.
- *API design*. This subsection describes how to design new APIs so that they will interoperate seamlessly with one another.

78. 7/docs/api/java/util/AbstractSequentialList.html
79. 7/docs/api/java/util/AbstractQueue.html
80. 7/docs/api/java/util/AbstractMap.html

Compatibility

The Java Collections Framework was designed to ensure complete interoperability between the core collection interfaces and the types that were used to represent collections in the early versions of the Java platform: Vector,[81] Hashtable,[82] array, and Enumeration.[83] In this section, you'll learn how to transform old collections to the Java Collections Framework collections and vice versa.

Upward Compatibility

Suppose that you're using an API that returns legacy collections in tandem with another API that requires objects implementing the collection interfaces. To make the two APIs interoperate smoothly, you'll have to transform the legacy collections into modern collections. Luckily, the Java Collections Framework makes this easy.

Suppose the old API returns an array of objects and the new API requires a Collection. The collections framework has a convenience implementation that allows an array of objects to be viewed as a List. You use Arrays.asList[84] to pass an array to any method requiring a Collection or a List:

```
Foo[] result = oldMethod(arg);
newMethod(Arrays.asList(result));
```

If the old API returns a Vector or a Hashtable, you have no work to do at all because Vector was retrofitted to implement the List interface, and Hashtable was retrofitted to implement Map. Therefore, a Vector may be passed directly to any method calling for a Collection or a List:

```
Vector result = oldMethod(arg);
newMethod(result);
```

Similarly, a Hashtable may be passed directly to any method calling for a Map:

```
Hashtable result = oldMethod(arg);
newMethod(result);
```

Less frequently, an API may return an Enumeration that represents a collection of objects. The Collections.list method translates an Enumeration into a Collection:

---

81. 7/docs/api/java/util/Vector.html

81. 7/docs/api/java/util/Vector.html
82. 7/docs/api/java/util/Hashtable.html
83. 7/docs/api/java/util/Enumeration.html
84. 7/docs/api/java/util/Arrays.html#asList(T...)

```
Enumeration e = oldMethod(arg);
newMethod(Collections.list(e));
```

Backward Compatibility

Suppose you're using an API that returns modern collections in tandem with another API that requires you to pass in legacy collections. To make the two APIs interoperate smoothly, you have to transform modern collections into old collections. Again, the Java Collections Framework makes this easy.

Suppose the new API returns a `Collection`, and the old API requires an array of `Object`. As you're probably aware, the `Collection` interface contains a `toArray` method designed expressly for this situation:

```
Collection c = newMethod();
oldMethod(c.toArray());
```

What if the old API requires an array of `String` (or another type) instead of an array of `Object`? You just use the other form of `toArray`—the one that takes an array on input:

```
Collection c = newMethod();
oldMethod((String[]) c.toArray(new String[0]));
```

If the old API requires a `Vector`, the standard collection constructor comes in handy:

```
Collection c = newMethod();
oldMethod(new Vector(c));
```

The case where the old API requires a `Hashtable` is handled in a similar way:

```
Map m = newMethod();
oldMethod(new Hashtable(m));
```

Finally, what do you do if the old API requires an `Enumeration`? This case isn't common, but it does happen from time to time, and the `Collections.enumeration`[85] method was provided to handle it. This is a static factory method that takes a `Collection` and returns an `Enumeration` over the elements of the `Collection`:

```
Collection c = newMethod();
oldMethod(Collections.enumeration(c));
```

---

85. 7/docs/api/java/util/Collections.html#enumeration(java.util.
    Collection)

API Design

In this short but important section, you'll learn a few simple guidelines that will allow your API to interoperate seamlessly with all other APIs that follow these guidelines. In essence, these rules define what it takes to be a good "citizen" in the world of collections.

Parameters

If your API contains a method that requires a collection on input, it is of paramount importance that you declare the relevant parameter type to be one of the collection interface types. *Never* use an implementation type; this defeats the purpose of an interface-based collections framework, which should allow collections to be manipulated without regard to implementation details.

Further, you should always use the least-specific type that makes sense. For example, don't require a `List` or a `Set` if a `Collection` will suffice. It's not that you should never require a `List` or a `Set` on input; it is correct to do so if a method depends on a property of one of these interfaces. For example, many of the algorithms provided by the Java platform require a `List` on input because they depend on the fact that lists are ordered. As a general rule, however, the best types to use on input are the most general: `Collection` and `Map`.

> **Note**
>
> Never define your own ad hoc `Collection` class and require objects of this class on input. By doing this, you'll lose all the benefits provided by the Java Collections Framework.

11

Return Values

You can afford to be much more flexible with return values than with input parameters. It's fine to return an object of any type that implements or extends one of the collection interfaces. This can be one of the interfaces or a special-purpose type that extends or implements one of these interfaces.

For example, one could imagine an image-processing package, called `Image-List`, that returns objects of a new class that then implements `List`. In addition to the `List` operations, `ImageList` can support any application-specific operations that seem desirable. For example, it might provide an `indexImage` operation that returns an image containing thumbnails of each graphic in the `ImageList`. It's critical to note that even if the API furnishes `ImageList` instances on output, it should accept arbitrary `Collection` (or perhaps `List`) instances on input.

In one sense, return values should have the opposite behavior of input parameters: it's best to return the most specific applicable collection interface rather than the most general. For example, if you're sure that you'll always return a `SortedMap`, you should give the relevant method the return type of `SortedMap` rather than `Map`. `SortedMap` instances are more time consuming to build than ordinary `Map` instances and are also more powerful. Given that your module has already invested the time to build a `SortedMap`, it makes good sense to give the user access to its increased power. Furthermore, the user will be able to pass the returned object to methods that demand a `SortedMap`, as well as those that accept any `Map`.

Legacy APIs

There are currently plenty of APIs out there that define their own ad hoc collection types. While this is unfortunate, it's a fact of life, given that there was no collections framework in the first two major releases of the Java platform. Suppose you own one of these APIs; here's what you can do about it: If possible, retrofit your legacy collection type to implement one of the standard collection interfaces. Then all the collections you return will interoperate smoothly with other collection-based APIs. If this is impossible (e.g., because one or more of the preexisting type signatures conflict with the standard collection interfaces), define an `Adapter` class that wraps one of your legacy collections objects, allowing it to function as a standard collection. (The `Adapter` class is an example of a custom implementation.)

Retrofit your API with new calls that follow the input guidelines to accept objects of a standard collection interface, if possible. Such calls can coexist with the calls that take the legacy collection type. If this is impossible, provide a constructor or static factory for your legacy type that takes an object of one of the standard interfaces and returns a legacy collection containing the same elements (or mappings). Either of these approaches will allow users to pass arbitrary collections into your API.

12

Concurrency

Chapter Contents

Computer users take it for granted that their systems can do more than one thing at a time. They expect to be able to work in a word processor while other applications download files, manage the print queue, and stream audio. Even a single application is often expected to do more than one thing at a time. For example, that streaming audio application must simultaneously read the digital audio off the network, decompress it, manage playback, and update its display. Even the word processor is expected to respond to keyboard and mouse events, no matter how busy it is reformatting text or updating the display. Software that can do such things is known as *concurrent* software.

The Java platform is designed from the ground up to support concurrent programming, with basic concurrency support in the Java programming language and the Java class libraries. Since version 5.0, the Java platform has also included high-level concurrency Application Programming Interfaces (APIs). This chapter introduces the platform's basic concurrency support and summarizes some of the high-level APIs in the `java.util.concurrent` packages.

Processes and Threads

In concurrent programming, there are two basic units of execution: *processes* and *threads*. In the Java programming language, concurrent programming is mostly concerned with threads. However, processes are also important.

A computer system normally has many active processes and threads. This is true even in systems that only have a single execution core and thus only have one thread actually executing at any given moment. Processing time for a single core is shared among processes and threads through an open-source feature called *time slicing*.

It's becoming more and more common for computer systems to have multiple processors or processors with multiple execution cores. This greatly enhances a system's capacity for concurrent execution of processes and threads, but concurrency is possible even on simple systems, without multiple processors or execution cores.

Processes

A process has a self-contained execution environment. A process generally has a complete, private set of basic run-time resources; in particular, each process has its own memory space.

Processes are often seen as synonymous with programs or applications. However, what the user sees as a single application may in fact be a set of cooperating processes. To facilitate communication between processes, most operating systems support interprocess communication (IPC) resources, such as pipes and sockets. IPC is used for communication between processes on the same system and processes on different systems.

Most implementations of the Java Virtual Machine (Java VM) run as a single process. A Java application can create additional processes using a `ProcessBuilder`[1] object. Multiprocess applications are beyond the scope of this chapter.

Threads

Threads are sometimes called *lightweight processes*. Both processes and threads provide an execution environment, but creating a new thread requires fewer resources than creating a new process.

Threads exist within a process—every process has at least one. Threads share the process's resources, including memory and open files. This makes for efficient but potentially problematic communication.

---

1.   7/docs/api/java/lang/ProcessBuilder.html

Multithreaded execution is an essential feature of the Java platform. Every application has at least one thread—or several, if you count "system" threads that do things like memory management and signal handling. But from the application programmer's point of view, you start with just one thread, called the *main thread*. This thread has the ability to create additional threads, as we'll demonstrate in the next section.

Thread Objects

Each thread is associated with an instance of the class `Thread`.[2] There are two basic strategies for using `Thread` objects to create a concurrent application:

- To directly control thread creation and management, simply instantiate `Thread` each time the application needs to initiate an asynchronous task.
- To abstract thread management from the rest of your application, pass the application's tasks to an *executor*.

This section documents the use of `Thread` objects. Executors are discussed with other high-level concurrency objects.

Defining and Starting a Thread

An application that creates an instance of `Thread` must provide the code that will run in that thread. There are two ways to do this:

- *Provide a `Runnable` object.* The `Runnable`[3] interface defines a single method, `run`, meant to contain the code executed in the thread. The `Runnable` object is passed to the `Thread` constructor, as in the following example:

```
public class HelloRunnable implements Runnable {

    public void run() {
        System.out.println("Hello from a thread!");
    }

    public static void main(String args[]) {
        (new Thread(new HelloRunnable())).start();
    }

}
```

---

2. 7/docs/api/java/lang/Thread.html

3. 7/docs/api/java/lang/Runnable.html

- *Subclass* `Thread`. The `Thread` class itself implements `Runnable`, though its run method does nothing. An application can subclass `Thread`, providing its own implementation of `run`, as in the following example:

```
public class HelloThread extends Thread {

    public void run() {
        System.out.println("Hello from a thread!");
    }

    public static void main(String args[]) {
        (new HelloThread()).start();
    }

}
```

Notice that both examples invoke `Thread.start` in order to start the new thread.

Which of these idioms should you use? The first idiom, which employs a `Runnable` object, is more general because the `Runnable` object can subclass a class other than `Thread`. The second idiom is easier to use in simple applications but is limited by the fact that your task class must be a descendant of `Thread`. This section focuses on the first approach, which separates the `Runnable` task from the `Thread` object that executes the task. Not only is this approach more flexible; it is also applicable to the high-level thread management APIs covered later.

The `Thread` class defines a number of methods useful for thread management. These include `static` methods, which provide information about (or affect the status of) the thread invoking the method. The other methods are invoked from other threads involved in managing the thread and `Thread` object. We'll examine some of these methods in the following sections.

Pausing Execution with Sleep

`Thread.sleep` causes the current thread to suspend execution for a specified period. This is an efficient means of making processor time available to the other threads of an application or other applications that might be running on a computer system. The `sleep` method can also be used for pacing, as shown in the example that follows, and waiting for another thread with duties that are understood to have time requirements, as with the `SimpleThreads` example in a later section.

Two overloaded versions of `sleep` are provided: one that specifies the sleep time to the millisecond and one that specifies the sleep time to the nanosecond. However, these sleep times are not guaranteed to be precise because they are limited by the facilities provided by the underlying operating system. Also, the sleep period can be terminated by interrupts, as we'll see in a later section. In any case, you cannot assume that invoking `sleep` will suspend the thread for precisely the time period specified.

The following example uses `sleep` to print messages at four-second intervals:

```
public class SleepMessages {
    public static void main(String args[])
        throws InterruptedException {
        String importantInfo[] = {
            "Mares eat oats",
            "Does eat oats",
            "Little lambs eat ivy",
            "A kid will eat ivy too"
        };

        for (int i = 0;
            i < importantInfo.length;
            i++) {
            //Pause for 4 seconds
            Thread.sleep(4000);
            //Print a message
            System.out.println(importantInfo[i]);
        }
    }
}
```

Notice that `main` declares that it `throws InterruptedException`. This is an exception that `sleep` throws when another thread interrupts the current thread while `sleep` is active. Since this application has not defined another thread to cause the interrupt, it doesn't bother to catch `InterruptedException`.

Interrupts

An *interrupt* is an indication to a thread that it should stop what it is doing and do something else. It's up to the programmer to decide exactly how a thread responds to an interrupt, but it is very common for the thread to terminate (which is the usage emphasized in this chapter).

A thread sends an interrupt by invoking `interrupt`[4] on the `Thread` object. For the interrupt mechanism to work correctly, the interrupted thread must support its own interruption.

Supporting Interruption

How does a thread support its own interruption? This depends on what it's currently doing. If the thread is frequently invoking methods that throw `InterruptedException`, it simply returns from the run method after it catches that exception. For

---

4. `7/docs/api/java/lang/Thread.html#interrupt()`

example, suppose the central message loop in the `SleepMessages` example were in the run method of a thread's `Runnable` object. It might be modified as follows to support interrupts:

```
for (int i = 0; i < importantInfo.length; i++) {
    // Pause for 4 seconds
    try {
        Thread.sleep(4000);
    } catch (InterruptedException e) {
        // We've been interrupted: no more messages.
        return;
    }
    // Print a message
    System.out.println(importantInfo[i]);
}
```

Many methods that throw `InterruptedException`, such as `sleep`, are designed to cancel their current operation and return immediately when an interrupt is received.

What if a thread goes a long time without invoking a method that throws `InterruptedException`? Then it must periodically invoke `Thread.interrupted`, which returns `true` if an interrupt has been received. Here is an example:

```
for (int i = 0; i < inputs.length; i++) {
    heavyCrunch(inputs[i]);
    if (Thread.interrupted()) {
        // We've been interrupted: no more crunching.
        return;
    }
}
```

In this simple example, the code simply tests for the interrupt and exits the thread if one has been received. In more complex applications, it might make more sense to throw an `InterruptedException`:

```
if (Thread.interrupted()) {
    throw new InterruptedException();
}
```

This allows interrupt-handling code to be centralized in a `catch` clause.

The Interrupt Status Flag

The interrupt mechanism is implemented using an internal flag known as the *interrupt status*. Invoking `Thread.interrupt` sets this flag. When a thread checks for an interrupt by invoking the static method `Thread.interrupted`, interrupt status is cleared. The nonstatic `isInterrupted` method, which is used by one thread to query the interrupt status of another, does not change the interrupt status flag.

By convention, any method that exits by throwing an `InterruptedException` clears interrupt status when it does so. However, it's always possible that interrupt status will immediately be set again by another thread invoking `interrupt`.

Joins

The `join` method allows one thread to wait for the completion of another. If `t` is a `Thread` object whose thread is currently executing, consider the following example:

```
t.join();
```

This causes the current thread to pause execution until `t`'s thread terminates. Overloads of `join` allow the programmer to specify a waiting period. However, as with `sleep`, `join` is dependent on the operating system for timing, so you should not assume that `join` will wait exactly as long as specified. Like `sleep`, `join` responds to an interrupt by exiting with an `InterruptedException`.

The SimpleThreads Example

The following example brings together some of the concepts of this section. `SimpleThreads` consists of two threads. The first is the main thread that every Java application has. The main thread creates a new thread from the `Runnable` object, `MessageLoop`, and waits for it to finish. If the `MessageLoop` thread takes too long to finish, the main thread interrupts it.

The `MessageLoop` thread prints out a series of messages. If interrupted before it has printed all its messages, the `MessageLoop` thread prints a message and exits:

```java
public class SimpleThreads {

    // Display a message, preceded by
    // the name of the current thread
    static void threadMessage(String message) {
        String threadName =
            Thread.currentThread().getName();
        System.out.format("%s: %s%n",
                          threadName,
                          message);
    }

    private static class MessageLoop
        implements Runnable {
        public void run() {
            String importantInfo[] = {
                "Mares eat oats",
                "Does eat oats",
                "Little lambs eat ivy",
                "A kid will eat ivy too"
```

12

```
            };
            try {
                for (int i = 0;
                      i < importantInfo.length;
                      i++) {
                    // Pause for 4 seconds
                    Thread.sleep(4000);
                    // Print a message
                    threadMessage(importantInfo[i]);
                }
            } catch (InterruptedException e) {
                threadMessage("I wasn't done!");
            }
        }
    }

    public static void main(String args[])
        throws InterruptedException {

        // Delay, in milliseconds before
        // we interrupt MessageLoop
        // thread (default one hour).
        long patience = 1000 * 60 * 60;

        // If command line argument
        // present, gives patience
        // in seconds.
        if (args.length > 0) {
            try {
                patience = Long.parseLong(args[0]) * 1000;
            } catch (NumberFormatException e) {
                System.err.println("Argument must be an integer.");
                System.exit(1);
            }
        }

        threadMessage("Starting MessageLoop thread");
        long startTime = System.currentTimeMillis();
        Thread t = new Thread(new MessageLoop());
        t.start();

        threadMessage("Waiting for MessageLoop thread to finish");
        // loop until MessageLoop
        // thread exits
        while (t.isAlive()) {
            threadMessage("Still waiting . . . ");
            // Wait maximum of 1 second
            // for MessageLoop thread
            // to finish.
            t.join(1000);
            if (((System.currentTimeMillis() - startTime) > patience)
                    && t.isAlive()) {
                threadMessage("Tired of waiting!");
                t.interrupt();
                // Shouldn't be long now
                // -- wait indefinitely
                t.join();
            }
```

```
        }
        threadMessage("Finally!");
    }
}
```

Synchronization

Threads communicate primarily by sharing access to fields and the objects referenced by reference fields. This form of communication is extremely efficient but
makes two kinds of errors possible: *thread interference* and *memory consistency
errors*. The tool needed to prevent these errors is *synchronization*.

Thread Interference

This section describes how errors are introduced when multiple threads access
shared data. Consider a simple class called Counter:

```
class Counter {
    private int c = 0;

    public void increment() {
        c++;
    }

    public void decrement() {
        c--;
    }

    public int value() {
        return c;
    }

}
```

Counter is designed so that each invocation of increment will add 1 to c and
each invocation of decrement will subtract 1 from c. However, if a Counter object
is referenced from multiple threads, interference between threads may prevent this
from happening as expected.

Interference happens when two operations running in different threads but act-
ing on the same data *interleave*. This means that the two operations consist of multiple steps, and the sequences of steps overlap.

It might not seem possible for operations on instances of Counter to interleave,
since both operations on c are single, simple statements. However, even simple
statements can translate to multiple steps in the virtual machine. We won't examine the specific steps the virtual machine takes—it is enough to know that the single expression c++ can be decomposed into three steps:

1. Retrieve the current value of c.

2. Increment the retrieved value by 1.

3. Store the incremented value back in c.

The expression c-- can be decomposed the same way, except that the second step decrements instead of increments.

Suppose Thread A invokes increment at about the same time Thread B invokes decrement. If the initial value of c is 0, their interleaved actions might follow this sequence:

1. Thread A—Retrieve c.

2. Thread B—Retrieve c.

3. Thread A—Increment retrieved value; result is 1.

4. Thread B—Decrement retrieved value; result is −1.

5. Thread A—Store result in c; c is now 1.

6. Thread B—Store result in c; c is now −1.

Thread A's result is lost, overwritten by Thread B. This particular interleaving is only one possibility. Under different circumstances, it might be Thread B's result that gets lost, or there could be no error at all. Because they are unpredictable, thread-interference bugs can be difficult to detect and fix.

Memory Consistency Errors

Memory consistency errors occur when different threads have inconsistent views of what should be the same data. The causes of memory consistency errors are complex and beyond the scope of this book. Fortunately, the programmer does not need a detailed understanding of these causes. All that is needed is a strategy for avoiding them.

The key to avoiding memory consistency errors is understanding the *happens-before* relationship. This relationship is simply a guarantee that memory writes by one specific statement are visible to another specific statement. Consider the following example. Suppose a simple int field is defined and initialized:

```
int counter = 0;
```

The counter field is shared between two threads, A and B. Suppose Thread A increments counter:

```
counter++;
```

Then, shortly afterward, `Thread B` prints out `counter`:

```
System.out.println(counter);
```

If the two statements had been executed in the same thread, it would be safe to assume that the value printed out would be 1. But if the two statements are executed in separate threads, the value printed out might well be zero because there's no guarantee that `Thread A`'s change to `counter` will be visible to `Thread B`—unless the programmer has established a happens-before relationship between these two statements.

There are several actions that create happens-before relationships. One of them is synchronization, as we will see in the following sections.

We've already seen two actions that create happens-before relationships:

- When a statement invokes `Thread.start`, every statement that has a happens-before relationship with that statement also has a happens-before relationship with every statement executed by the new thread. The effects of the code that led up to the creation of the new thread are visible to the new thread.

- When a thread terminates and causes a `Thread.join` in another thread to return, all the statements executed by the terminated thread have a happens-before relationship with all the statements following the successful join. The effects of the code in the thread are now visible to the thread that performed the join.

For a list of actions that create happens-before relationships, refer to the Summary page of the `java.util.concurrent` package.[5]

Synchronized Methods

The Java programming language provides two basic synchronization idioms: *synchronized methods* and *synchronized statements*. The more complex of the two, synchronized statements, are described in the next section. This section focuses on synchronized methods.

To make a method synchronized, simply add the `synchronized` keyword to its declaration:

```
public class SynchronizedCounter {
    private int c = 0;

    public synchronized void increment() {
```

---

5. 7/docs/api/java/util/concurrent/package-summary.html#MemoryVisibility

```
        c++;
    }

    public synchronized void decrement() {
        c--;
    }

    public synchronized int value() {
        return c;
    }
}
```

If count is an instance of SynchronizedCounter, then making these methods synchronized has two effects:

- It is not possible for two invocations of synchronized methods on the same object to interleave. When one thread is executing a synchronized method for an object, all other threads that invoke synchronized methods for the same object block (suspend execution) until the first thread is done with the object.
- When a synchronized method exits, it automatically establishes a happens-before relationship with *any subsequent invocation* of a synchronized method for the same object. This guarantees that changes to the state of the object are visible to all threads.

Note that constructors cannot be synchronized; using the synchronized keyword with a constructor is a syntax error. Synchronizing constructors doesn't make sense because only the thread that creates an object should have access to it while it is being constructed.

> **Note**
>
> When constructing an object that will be shared between threads, be very careful that a reference to the object does not "leak" prematurely. For example, suppose you want to maintain a List called instances containing every instance of a class. You might be tempted to add the following line to your constructor:
>
>   instances.add(this);
>
> But if you do so, other threads can use instances to access the object before construction of the object is complete.

Synchronized methods enable a simple strategy for preventing thread interference and memory consistency errors: if an object is visible to more than one thread, all reads or writes to that object's variables are done through synchronized methods. (There is an important exception: final fields, which cannot be modified after the object is constructed, can be safely read through nonsynchronized methods once the object is constructed.) This strategy is effective but can present problems with liveness, as we'll see later in this chapter.

Intrinsic Locks and Synchronization

Synchronization is built around an internal entity known as the *intrinsic lock* or *monitor lock*. (The API specification often refers to this entity simply as a *monitor*.) Intrinsic locks play a role in both aspects of synchronization: enforcing exclusive access to an object's state and establishing happens-before relationships that are essential to visibility.

Every object has an intrinsic lock associated with it. By convention, a thread that needs exclusive and consistent access to an object's fields has to *acquire* the object's intrinsic lock before accessing them and then *release* the intrinsic lock when it's done with them. A thread is said to *own* the intrinsic lock between the time it has acquired the lock and released the lock. As long as a thread owns an intrinsic lock, no other thread can acquire the same lock. The other thread will block when it attempts to acquire the lock.

When a thread releases an intrinsic lock, a happens-before relationship is established between that action and any subsequent acquisition of the same lock.

Locks in Synchronized Methods

When a thread invokes a synchronized method, it automatically acquires the intrinsic lock for that method's object and releases it when the method returns. The lock release occurs even if the return was caused by an uncaught exception.

You might wonder what happens when a static synchronized method is invoked, since a static method is associated with a class, not an object. In this case, the thread acquires the intrinsic lock for the `Class` object associated with the class. Thus access to a class's static fields is controlled by a lock that's distinct from the lock for any instance of the class.

Synchronized Statements

Another way to create synchronized code is with *synchronized statements*. Unlike synchronized methods, synchronized statements must specify the object that provides the intrinsic lock:

```
public void addName(String name) {
    synchronized(this) {
        lastName = name;
        nameCount++;
    }
    nameList.add(name);
}
```

In this example, the addName method needs to synchronize changes to lastName and nameCount but also needs to avoid synchronizing invocations of other objects' methods. (Invoking other objects' methods from synchronized code can create problems that are described in the section on "Liveness" later in this chapter.) Without synchronized statements, there would have to be a separate, unsynchronized method for the sole purpose of invoking nameList.add.

Synchronized statements are also useful for improving concurrency with fine-grained synchronization. Suppose, for example, class MsLunch has two instance fields, c1 and c2, that are never used together. All updates of these fields must be synchronized, but there's no reason to prevent an update of c1 from being interleaved with an update of c2—and doing so reduces concurrency by creating unnecessary blocking. Instead of using synchronized methods or otherwise using the lock associated with this, we create two objects solely to provide locks:

```
public class MsLunch {
    private long c1 = 0;
    private long c2 = 0;
    private Object lock1 = new Object();
    private Object lock2 = new Object();

    public void inc1() {
        synchronized(lock1) {
            c1++;
        }
    }

    public void inc2() {
        synchronized(lock2) {
            c2++;
        }
    }
}
```

Use this idiom with extreme care. You must be absolutely sure that it really is safe to interleave access of the affected fields.

Reentrant Synchronization

Recall that a thread cannot acquire a lock owned by another thread. But a thread *can* acquire a lock that it already owns. Allowing a thread to acquire the same lock more than once enables *reentrant synchronization*. This describes a situation where synchronized code directly or indirectly invokes a method that also contains synchronized code, and both sets of code use the same lock. Without reentrant synchronization, synchronized code would have to take many additional precautions to avoid having a thread cause itself to block.

Atomic Access

In programming, an *atomic* action is one that effectively happens all at once. An atomic action cannot stop in the middle: it either happens completely or doesn't happen at all. No side effects of an atomic action are visible until the action is complete.

We have already seen that an increment expression, such as c++, does not describe an atomic action. Even very simple expressions can define complex actions that can decompose into other actions. However, there are actions you can specify that are atomic:

- Reads and writes are atomic for reference variables and for most primitive variables (all types except long and double).
- Reads and writes are atomic for *all* variables declared volatile (*including* long and double variables).

Atomic actions cannot be interleaved, so they can be used without fear of thread interference. However, this does not eliminate all need to synchronize atomic actions, because memory consistency errors are still possible. Using volatile variables reduces the risk of memory consistency errors because any write to a volatile variable establishes a happens-before relationship with subsequent reads of that same variable. This means that changes to a volatile variable are always visible to other threads. It also means that when a thread reads a volatile variable, it sees not just the latest change to the volatile but also the side effects of the code that led up the change.

Using simple atomic variable access is more efficient than accessing these variables through synchronized code but requires more care by the programmer to avoid memory consistency errors. Whether the extra effort is worthwhile depends on the size and complexity of the application.

Some of the classes in the java.util.concurrent[6] package provide atomic methods that do not rely on synchronization. We'll discuss them in the section on "High-Level Concurrency Objects" later in this chapter.

Liveness

A concurrent application's ability to execute in a timely manner is known as its *liveness*. This section describes the most common kind of liveness problem, *deadlock*, and goes on to briefly describe two other liveness problems, *starvation* and *livelock*.

---

6.   7/docs/api/java/util/concurrent/package-summary.html

Deadlock

Deadlock describes a situation where two or more threads are blocked forever, waiting for each other. Here's an example.

Alphonse and Gaston are friends and great believers in courtesy. A strict rule of courtesy is that when you bow to a friend, you must remain bowed until your friend has a chance to return the bow. Unfortunately, this rule does not account for the possibility that two friends might bow to each other at the same time. The following example application models this possibility:

```java
public class Deadlock {
    static class Friend {
        private final String name;
        public Friend(String name) {
            this.name = name;
        }
        public String getName() {
            return this.name;
        }
        public synchronized void bow(Friend bower) {
            System.out.format("%s: %s"
                + "  has bowed to me!%n",
                this.name, bower.getName());
            bower.bowBack(this);
        }
        public synchronized void bowBack(Friend bower) {
            System.out.format("%s: %s"
                + " has bowed back to me!%n",
                this.name, bower.getName());
        }
    }

    public static void main(String[] args) {
        final Friend alphonse =
            new Friend("Alphonse");
        final Friend gaston =
            new Friend("Gaston");
        new Thread(new Runnable() {
            public void run() { alphonse.bow(gaston); }
        }).start();
        new Thread(new Runnable() {
            public void run() { gaston.bow(alphonse); }
        }).start();
    }
}
```

When `Deadlock` runs, it's extremely likely that both threads will block when they attempt to invoke `bowBack`. Neither block will ever end because each thread is waiting for the other to exit `bow`.

Starvation and Livelock

Starvation and livelock are far less common than deadlock but are still problems that every designer of concurrent software is likely to encounter.

Starvation

Starvation describes a situation where a thread is unable to gain regular access to shared resources and is unable to make progress. This happens when shared resources are made unavailable for long periods by "greedy" threads. For example, suppose an object provides a synchronized method that often takes a long time to return. If one thread invokes this method frequently, other threads that also need frequent synchronized access to the same object will often be blocked.

Livelock

A thread often acts in response to the action of another thread. If the other thread's action is also a response to the action of another thread, then *livelock* may result. As with deadlock, livelocked threads are unable to make further progress. However, the threads are not blocked; they are simply too busy responding to each other to resume work. This is comparable to two people attempting to pass each other in a corridor: Alphonse moves to his left to let Gaston pass, while Gaston moves to his right to let Alphonse pass. Seeing that they are still blocking each other, Alphone moves to his right, while Gaston moves to his left. They're still blocking each other, so . . .

Guarded Blocks

Threads often have to coordinate their actions. The most common coordination idiom is the *guarded block*. Such a block begins by polling a condition that must be true before the block can proceed. There are a number of steps to follow in order to do this correctly.

Suppose, for example, guardedJoy is a method that must not proceed until a shared variable joy has been set by another thread. Such a method could, in theory, simply loop until the condition is satisfied, but that loop is wasteful, since it executes continuously while waiting:

```
public void guardedJoy() {
    // Simple loop guard. Wastes
    // processor time. Don't do this!
    while(!joy) {}
    System.out.println("Joy has been achieved!");
}
```

A more efficient guard invokes `Object.wait`[7] to suspend the current thread. The invocation of `wait` does not return until another thread has issued a notification that some special event may have occurred—though not necessarily the event this thread is waiting for:

```
public synchronized guardedJoy() {
    // This guard only loops once for each special event, which may not
    // be the event we're waiting for.
    while(!joy) {
        try {
            wait();
        } catch (InterruptedException e) {}
    }
    System.out.println("Joy and efficiency have been achieved!");
}
```

> **Note**
>
> Always invoke `wait` inside a loop that tests for the condition being waited for. Don't assume that the interrupt was for the particular condition you were waiting for or that the condition is still true.

Like many methods that suspend execution, `wait` can throw `Interrupted-Exception`. In this example, we can just ignore that exception; we only care about the value of `joy`.

Why is this version of `guardedJoy` synchronized? Suppose `d` is the object we're using to invoke `wait`. When a thread invokes `d.wait`, it must own the intrinsic lock for `d`; otherwise, an error is thrown. Invoking `wait` inside a synchronized method is a simple way to acquire the intrinsic lock.

When `wait` is invoked, the thread releases the lock and suspends execution. At some future time, another thread will acquire the same lock and invoke `Object.notifyAll`,[8] informing all threads waiting on that lock that something important has happened:

```
public synchronized notifyJoy() {
    joy = true;
    notifyAll();
}
```

Some time after the second thread has released the lock, the first thread reacquires the lock and resumes by returning from the invocation of `wait`.

---

7. 7/docs/api/java/lang/Object.html#wait()

8. 7/docs/api/java/lang/Object.html#notifyAll()

12

> **Note**
>
> There is a second notification method, `notify`, which wakes up a single thread. Because `notify` doesn't allow you to specify the thread that is woken up, it is useful only in massively parallel applications—that is, programs with a large number of threads, all doing similar chores. In such an application, you don't care which thread gets woken up.

Let's use guarded blocks to create a *producer–consumer* application. This kind of application shares data between two threads: the *producer* that creates the data and the *consumer* that does something with it. The two threads communicate using a shared object. Coordination is essential: the consumer thread must not attempt to retrieve the data before the producer thread has delivered the data, and the producer thread must not attempt to deliver new data if the consumer hasn't retrieved the old data.

In this example, the data is a series of text messages, which are shared through an object of type `Drop`:

```java
public class Drop {
    // Message sent from producer
    // to consumer.
    private String message;
    // True if consumer should wait
    // for producer to send message,
    // false if producer should wait for
    // consumer to retrieve message.
    private boolean empty = true;

    public synchronized String take() {
        // Wait until message is
        // available.
        while (empty) {
            try {
                wait();
            } catch (InterruptedException e) {}
        }
        // Toggle status.
        empty = true;
        // Notify producer that
        // status has changed.
        notifyAll();
        return message;
    }

    public synchronized void put(String message) {
        // Wait until message has
        // been retrieved.
        while (!empty) {
            try {
                wait();
```

```
            } catch (InterruptedException e) {}
        }
        // Toggle status.
        empty = false;
        // Store message.
        this.message = message;
        // Notify consumer that status
        // has changed.
        notifyAll();
    }
}
```

The producer thread defined in `Producer` sends a series of familiar messages.
The string `"DONE"` indicates that all messages have been sent. To simulate the
unpredictable nature of real-world applications, the producer thread pauses for random intervals between messages.

```
import java.util.Random;

public class Producer implements Runnable {
    private Drop drop;

    public Producer(Drop drop) {
        this.drop = drop;
    }

    public void run() {
        String importantInfo[] = {
            "Mares eat oats",
            "Does eat oats",
            "Little lambs eat ivy",
            "A kid will eat ivy too"
        };
        Random random = new Random();

        for (int i = 0;
             i < importantInfo.length;
             i++) {
            drop.put(importantInfo[i]);
            try {
                Thread.sleep(random.nextInt(5000));
            } catch (InterruptedException e) {}
        }
        drop.put("DONE");
    }
}
```

The consumer thread, defined in `Consumer`, simply retrieves the messages and
prints them out until it retrieves the `"DONE"` string. This thread also pauses for
random intervals:

```
import java.util.Random;

public class Consumer implements Runnable {
```

```
        private Drop drop;

        public Consumer(Drop drop) {
            this.drop = drop;
        }

        public void run() {
            Random random = new Random();
            for (String message = drop.take();
                ! message.equals("DONE");
                message = drop.take()) {
                System.out.format("MESSAGE RECEIVED: %s%n", message);
                try {
                    Thread.sleep(random.nextInt(5000));
                } catch (InterruptedException e) {}
            }
        }
    }
```

Finally, here is the main thread that launches the producer and consumer threads:

```
public class ProducerConsumerExample {
    public static void main(String[] args) {
        Drop drop = new Drop();
        (new Thread(new Producer(drop))).start();
        (new Thread(new Consumer(drop))).start();
    }
}
```

Note

The Drop class was written in order to demonstrate guarded blocks. To avoid reinventing the wheel, examine the existing data structures in the Java Collections Framework (Chapter 11) before trying to code your own data-sharing objects. For more information, refer to the questions and exercises at the end of the chapter.

Immutable Objects

An object is considered *immutable* if its state cannot change after it is constructed. Maximum reliance on immutable objects is widely accepted as a sound strategy for creating simple, reliable code.

Immutable objects are particularly useful in concurrent applications. Since they cannot change state, they cannot be corrupted by thread interference or observed in an inconsistent state.

Programmers are often reluctant to employ immutable objects because they worry about the cost of creating a new object as opposed to updating an object in place. The impact of object creation is often overestimated and can be offset by some of the efficiencies associated with immutable objects. These include decreased overhead due to garbage collection and the elimination of code needed to protect mutable objects from corruption.

The following subsections take a class whose instances are mutable and derives a class with immutable instances from it. In so doing, they give general rules for this kind of conversion and demonstrate some of the advantages of immutable objects.

A Synchronized Class Example

The class SynchronizedRGB defines objects that represent colors. Each object represents the color as three integers that stand for primary color values and a string that gives the name of the color:

```
public class SynchronizedRGB {

    // Values must be between 0 and 255.
    private int red;
    private int green;
    private int blue;
    private String name;

    private void check(int red,
                       int green,
                       int blue) {
        if (red < 0 || red > 255
            || green < 0 || green > 255
            || blue < 0 || blue > 255) {
            throw new IllegalArgumentException();
        }
    }

    public SynchronizedRGB(int red,
                           int green,
                           int blue,
                           String name) {
        check(red, green, blue);
        this.red = red;
        this.green = green;
        this.blue = blue;
        this.name = name;
    }

    public void set(int red,
                    int green,
                    int blue,
                    String name) {
        check(red, green, blue);
        synchronized (this) {
            this.red = red;
            this.green = green;
            this.blue = blue;
            this.name = name;
        }
    }
}
```

```
        public synchronized int getRGB() {
            return ((red << 16) | (green << 8) | blue);
        }

        public synchronized String getName() {
            return name;
        }

        public synchronized void invert() {
            red = 255 - red;
            green = 255 - green;
            blue = 255 - blue;
            name = "Inverse of " + name;
        }
    }
```

SynchronizedRGB must be used carefully to avoid being seen in an inconsistent state. Suppose, for example, a thread executes the following code:

```
SynchronizedRGB color =
    new SynchronizedRGB(0, 0, 0, "Pitch Black");
. . .
int myColorInt = color.getRGB();       //Statement 1
String myColorName = color.getName(); //Statement 2
```

If another thread invokes color.set after Statement 1 but before Statement 2, the value of myColorInt won't match the value of myColorName. To avoid this outcome, the two statements must be bound together:

```
synchronized (color) {
    int myColorInt = color.getRGB();
    String myColorName = color.getName();
}
```

This kind of inconsistency is only possible for mutable objects—it will not be an issue for the immutable version of SynchronizedRGB.

A Strategy for Defining Immutable Objects

The following rules define a simple strategy for creating immutable objects. Not all classes documented as *immutable* follow these rules. This does not necessarily mean the creators of these classes were sloppy—they may have good reason for believing that instances of their classes never change after construction. However, such strategies require sophisticated analysis and are not for beginners:

1. Don't provide *setter* methods—methods that modify fields or objects referred to by fields.
2. Make all fields final and private.

3. Don't allow subclasses to override methods. The simplest way to do this is to declare the class as final. A more sophisticated approach is to make the constructor private and construct instances in factory methods.

4. If the instance fields include references to mutable objects, don't allow those objects to be changed:

   ▪ Don't provide methods that modify the mutable objects.
   ▪ Don't share references to the mutable objects. Never store references to external, mutable objects passed to the constructor; if necessary, create copies and store references to the copies. Similarly, create copies of your internal mutable objects when necessary to avoid returning the originals in your methods.

Applying this strategy to SynchronizedRGB results in the following steps:

1. There are two setter methods in this class. The first one, set, arbitrarily transforms the object and has no place in an immutable version of the class. The second one, invert, can be adapted by having it create a new object instead of modifying the existing one.

2. All fields are already private; they are further qualified as final.

3. The class itself is declared final.

4. Only one field refers to an object, and that object is itself immutable. Therefore, no safeguards against changing the state of "contained" mutable objects are necessary.

After applying these changes, we have the following:

```
final public class ImmutableRGB {

    // Values must be between 0 and 255.
    final private int red;
    final private int green;
    final private int blue;
    final private String name;

    private void check(int red,
                       int green,
                       int blue) {
        if (red < 0 || red > 255
            || green < 0 || green > 255
            || blue < 0 || blue > 255) {
            throw new IllegalArgumentException();
        }
    }

    public ImmutableRGB(int red,
                        int green,
```

```
                              int blue,
                              String name) {
        check(red, green, blue);
        this.red = red;
        this.green = green;
        this.blue = blue;
        this.name = name;
    }

    public int getRGB() {
        return ((red << 16) | (green << 8) | blue);
    }

    public String getName() {
        return name;
    }

    public ImmutableRGB invert() {
        return new ImmutableRGB(255 - red,
                                255 - green,
                                255 - blue,
                                "Inverse of " + name);
    }
}
```

High-Level Concurrency Objects

So far, this chapter has focused on the low-level APIs that have been part of the Java platform from the very beginning. These APIs are adequate for very basic tasks, but higher-level building blocks are needed for more advanced tasks. This is especially true for massively concurrent applications that fully exploit today's multiprocessor and multicore systems.

In this section we'll look at some of the high-level concurrency features introduced in version 5.0 of the Java platform. Most of these features are implemented in the new java.util.concurrent packages. There are also new concurrent data structures in the Java Collections Framework:

- Lock objects support locking idioms that simplify many concurrent applications.
- Executors define a high-level API for launching and managing threads. Executor implementations provided by java.util.concurrent provide thread pool management suitable for large-scale applications.
- Concurrent collections make it easier to manage large collections of data and can greatly reduce the need for synchronization.
- Atomic variables have features that minimize synchronization and help avoid memory consistency errors.
- ThreadLocalRandom (in the Java SE Development Kit [JDK] 7) provides efficient generation of pseudorandom numbers from multiple threads.

12

Lock Objects

Synchronized code relies on a simple kind of reentrant lock. This kind of lock is easy to use but has many limitations. More sophisticated locking idioms are supported by the `java.util.concurrent.locks`[9] package. We won't examine this package in detail but instead will focus on its most basic interface, `Lock`.[10]

Lock objects work very much like the implicit locks used by synchronized code. As with implicit locks, only one thread can own a `Lock` object at a time. `Lock` objects also support a `wait/notify` mechanism through their associated `Condition`[11] objects.

The biggest advantage of `Lock` objects over implicit locks is their ability to back out of an attempt to acquire a lock. The `tryLock` method backs out if the lock is not available immediately or before a timeout expires (if specified). The `lockInterruptibly` method backs out if another thread sends an interrupt before the lock is acquired.

Let's use `Lock` objects to solve the deadlock problem we saw previously. Alphonse and Gaston have trained themselves to notice when a friend is about to bow. We model this improvement by requiring that our `Friend` objects must acquire locks for *both* participants before proceeding with the bow. Here is the source code for the improved model, `Safelock`. To demonstrate the versatility of this idiom, we assume that Alphonse and Gaston are so infatuated with their newfound ability to bow safely that they can't stop bowing to each other:

```java
import java.util.concurrent.locks.Lock;
import java.util.concurrent.locks.ReentrantLock;
import java.util.Random;

public class Safelock {
    static class Friend {
        private final String name;
        private final Lock lock = new ReentrantLock();

        public Friend(String name) {
            this.name = name;
        }

        public String getName() {
            return this.name;
        }

        public boolean impendingBow(Friend bower) {
            Boolean myLock = false;
            Boolean yourLock = false;
```

---

9. 7/docs/api/java/util/concurrent/locks/package-summary.html

10. 7/docs/api/java/util/concurrent/locks/Lock.html

11. 7/docs/api/java/util/concurrent/locks/Condition.html

```java
        try {
            myLock = lock.tryLock();
            yourLock = bower.lock.tryLock();
        } finally {
            if (! (myLock && yourLock)) {
                if (myLock) {
                    lock.unlock();
                }
                if (yourLock) {
                    bower.lock.unlock();
                }
            }
        }
        return myLock && yourLock;
    }

    public void bow(Friend bower) {
        if (impendingBow(bower)) {
            try {
                System.out.format("%s: %s has"
                    + " bowed to me!%n",
                    this.name, bower.getName());
                bower.bowBack(this);
            } finally {
                lock.unlock();
                bower.lock.unlock();
            }
        } else {
            System.out.format("%s: %s started"
                + " to bow to me, but saw that"
                + " I was already bowing to"
                + " him.%n",
                this.name, bower.getName());
        }
    }

    public void bowBack(Friend bower) {
        System.out.format("%s: %s has" +
            " bowed back to me!%n",
            this.name, bower.getName());
    }
}

static class BowLoop implements Runnable {
    private Friend bower;
    private Friend bowee;

    public BowLoop(Friend bower, Friend bowee) {
        this.bower = bower;
        this.bowee = bowee;
    }

    public void run() {
        Random random = new Random();
        for (;;) {
            try {
                Thread.sleep(random.nextInt(10));
            } catch (InterruptedException e) {}
```

12

```
                bowee.bow(bower);
            }
        }
    }

    public static void main(String[] args) {
        final Friend alphonse =
            new Friend("Alphonse");
        final Friend gaston =
            new Friend("Gaston");
        new Thread(new BowLoop(alphonse, gaston)).start();
        new Thread(new BowLoop(gaston, alphonse)).start();
    }
}
```

Executors

In the previous examples, there is a close connection between the task being done by a new thread (as defined by its `Runnable` object) and the thread itself (as defined by a `Thread` object). This works well for small applications, but in large-scale applications, it makes sense to separate thread management and creation from the rest of the application. Objects that encapsulate these functions are known as *executors*. The following subsections describe executors in detail.

Executor Interfaces

The `java.util.concurrent` package defines three executor interfaces:

- `Executor`, a simple interface that supports launching new tasks
- `ExecutorService`, a subinterface of `Executor` that adds features to help manage the life cycle, both of the individual tasks and of the executor itself
- `ScheduledExecutorService`, a subinterface of `ExecutorService` that supports future and/or periodic execution of tasks

Typically, variables that refer to executor objects are declared as one of these three interface types, without an executor class type.

The Executor Interface

The `Executor`[12] interface provides a single method, `execute`, designed to be a drop-in replacement for a common thread-creation idiom. Consider the following example:

```
(new Thread(r)).start();
```

---

12. 7/docs/api/java/util/concurrent/Executor.html

If r is a `Runnable` object and e is an `Executor` object, you can replace this with the following:

```
e.execute(r);
```

However, the definition of `execute` is less specific. The low-level idiom creates a new thread and launches it immediately. Depending on the `Executor` implementation, `execute` may do the same thing but is more likely to use an existing worker thread to run r or to place r in a queue to wait for a worker thread to become available. (We'll describe worker threads in the section "Thread Pools" later in this chapter.)

The executor implementations in `java.util.concurrent` are designed to make full use of the more advanced `ExecutorService` and `ScheduledExecutorService` interfaces, although they also work with the base `Executor` interface.

The ExecutorService Interface

The `ExecutorService`[13] interface supplements `execute` with a similar but more versatile `submit` method. Like `execute`, `submit` accepts `Runnable` objects, but it also accepts `Callable`[14] objects, which allow the task to return a value. The `submit` method returns a `Future`[15] object, which is used to retrieve the `Callable` return value and to manage the status of both `Callable` and `Runnable` tasks.

`ExecutorService` also provides methods for submitting large collections of `Callable` objects. Finally, `ExecutorService` provides a number of methods for managing the shutdown of the executor. To support immediate shutdown, tasks should handle interrupts correctly.

The ScheduledExecutorService Interface

The `ScheduledExecutorService`[16] interface supplements the methods of its parent `ExecutorService` with `schedule`, which executes a `Runnable` or `Callable` task after a specified delay. In addition, the interface defines `scheduleAtFixedRate` and `scheduleWithFixedDelay`, which executes specified tasks repeatedly at defined intervals.

---

13. 7/docs/api/java/util/concurrent/ExecutorService.html
14. 7/docs/api/java/util/concurrent/Callable.html
15. 7/docs/api/java/util/concurrent/Future.html
16. 7/docs/api/java/util/concurrent/ScheduledExecutorService.html

12

Thread Pools

Most of the executor implementations in `java.util.concurrent` use *thread pools*, which consist of *worker threads*. This kind of thread exists separately from the `Runnable` and `Callable` tasks it executes and is often used to execute multiple tasks.

Worker threads minimize the overhead due to thread creation. Thread objects use a significant amount of memory, and in a large-scale application, allocating and deallocating many thread objects creates a significant memory-management overhead.

One common type of thread pool is the *fixed thread pool*. This type of pool always has a specified number of threads running; if a thread is somehow terminated while it is still in use, it is automatically replaced with a new thread. Tasks are submitted to the pool via an internal queue, which holds extra tasks whenever there are more active tasks than threads.

An important advantage of the fixed thread pool is that applications using it *degrade gracefully*. To understand this, consider a web server application where each HTTP request is handled by a separate thread. If the application simply creates a new thread for every new HTTP request and the system receives more requests than it can handle immediately, then the application will suddenly stop responding to *all* requests when the overhead of all those threads exceed the capacity of the system. With a limit on the number of the threads that can be created, the application will no longer service HTTP requests as quickly as they come in; instead, it will service them as quickly as the system can sustain.

A simple way to create an executor that uses a fixed thread pool is to invoke the `newFixedThreadPool`[17] factory method in `java.util.concurrent.Executors`.[18] This class also provides the following factory methods:

- The `newCachedThreadPool`[19] method creates an executor with an expandable thread pool. This executor is suitable for applications that launch many short-lived tasks.

- The `newSingleThreadExecutor`[20] method creates an executor that executes a single task at a time.

- Several factory methods are `ScheduledExecutorService` versions of the previous executors.

---

17. `7/docs/api/java/util/concurrent/Executors.html#newFixedThreadPool(int)`
18. `7/docs/api/java/util/concurrent/Executors.html`
19. `7/docs/api/java/util/concurrent/Executors.html#newCachedThreadPool(int)`
20. `7/docs/api/java/util/concurrent/Executors`
    `.html#newSingleThreadExecutor(int)`

If none of the executors provided by these factory methods meet your needs, constructing instances of `java.util.concurrent.ThreadPoolExecutor`[21] or `java.util.concurrent.ScheduledThreadPoolExecutor`[22] will give you additional options.

Fork/Join

Introduced in the Java SE 7 release, the fork/join framework is an implementation of the `ExecutorService` interface that helps you take advantage of multiple processors. It is designed for work that can be broken into smaller pieces recursively. The goal is to use all the available processing power to enhance the performance of your application.

As with any `ExecutorService`, the fork/join framework distributes tasks to worker threads in a thread pool. The fork/join framework is distinct because it uses a *work-stealing* algorithm. Worker threads that run out of things to do can steal tasks from other threads that are still busy.

The center of the fork/join framework is the `ForkJoinPool`[23] class, an extension of `AbstractExecutorService`. `ForkJoinPool` implements the core work-stealing algorithm and can execute `ForkJoinTasks`.[24]

Basic Use

Using the fork/join framework is simple. The first step is to write some code that performs a segment of the work. Your code should look similar to this:

```
if (my portion of the work is small enough)
  do the work directly
else
  split my work into two pieces
  invoke the two pieces and wait for the results
```

Wrap this code as a `ForkJoinTask` subclass, typically as one of its more specialized types `RecursiveTask`[25] (which can return a result) or `RecursiveAction`.[26]

After your `ForkJoinTask` is ready, create one that represents all the work to be done and pass it to the `invoke()` method of a `ForkJoinPool` instance.

12

---

21. 7/docs/api/java/util/concurrent/ThreadPoolExecutor.html

22. 7/docs/api/java/util/concurrent/ScheduledThreadPoolExecutor.html

23. 7/docs/api/java/util/concurrent/ForkJoinPool.html

24. 7/docs/api/java/util/concurrent/ForkJoinTask.html

25. 7/docs/api/java/util/concurrent/RecursiveTask.html

26. 7/docs/api/java/util/concurrent/RecursiveAction.html

Blurring for Clarity

To help you understand how the fork/join framework works, consider a simple example. Suppose you want to perform a simple blur on an image. The original *source* image is represented by an array of integers, where each integer contains the color values for a single pixel. The blurred *destination* image is also represented by an integer array, with the same size as the source.

Performing the blur is accomplished by working through the source array one pixel at a time. Each pixel is averaged with its surrounding pixels (the red, green, and blue components are averaged), and the result is placed in the destination array. Here is one possible implementation:

```
public class ForkBlur extends RecursiveAction {
    private int[] mSource;
    private int mStart;
    private int mLength;
    private int[] mDestination;

    // Processing window size, should be odd.
    private int mBlurWidth = 15;

    public ForkBlur(int[] src, int start, int length, int[] dst) {
        mSource = src;
        mStart = start;
        mLength = length;
        mDestination = dst;
    }

    protected void computeDirectly() {
        int sidePixels = (mBlurWidth - 1) / 2;
        for (int index = mStart; index < mStart + mLength; index++) {
            // Calculate average.
            float rt = 0, gt = 0, bt = 0;
            for (int mi = -sidePixels; mi <= sidePixels; mi++) {
                int mindex = Math.min(Math.max(mi + index, 0),
                                      mSource.length - 1);
                int pixel = mSource[mindex];
                rt += (float)((pixel & 0x00ff0000) >> 16)
                    / mBlurWidth;
                gt += (float)((pixel & 0x0000ff00) >>  8)
                    / mBlurWidth;
                bt += (float)((pixel & 0x000000ff) >>  0)
                    / mBlurWidth;
            }

            // Re-assemble destination pixel.
            int dpixel = (0xff000000      ) |
                (((int)rt) << 16) |
                (((int)gt) <<  8) |
                (((int)bt) <<  0);
            mDestination[index] = dpixel;
        }
    }
}
```

. . .

Now you implement the abstract `compute()` method, which either performs the blur directly or splits it into two smaller tasks. A simple array length threshold helps determine whether the work is performed or split.

```
protected static int sThreshold = 100000;

protected void compute() {
    if (mLength < sThreshold) {
        computeDirectly();
        return;
    }

    int split = mLength / 2;

    invokeAll(new ForkBlur(mSource, mStart, split, mDestination),
              new ForkBlur(mSource, mStart + split, mLength - split,
                           mDestination));
}
```

If the previous methods are in a subclass of the `RecursiveAction` class, setting them up to run in a `ForkJoinPool` is straightforward.

Now, create a task that represents all the work to be done:

```
// source image pixels are in src
// destination image pixels are in dst
ForkBlur fb = new ForkBlur(src, 0, src.length, dst);
```

Create the `ForkJoinPool` that will run the task:

```
ForkJoinPool pool = new ForkJoinPool();
```

And, finally, run the task:

```
pool.invoke(fb);
```

For the full source code, including some extra code that shows the source and destination images in windows, see the `ForkBlur` class provided previously.

Concurrent Collections

The `java.util.concurrent` package includes a number of additions to the Java Collections Framework. These are most easily categorized by the following collection interfaces:

- BlockingQueue[27] defines a FIFO (first-in-first-out) data structure that blocks or times out when you attempt to add to a full queue or retrieve from an empty queue.

---

27. 7/docs/api/java/util/concurrent/BlockingQueue.html

- ConcurrentMap[28] is a subinterface of java.util.Map[29] that defines useful atomic operations. These operations remove or replace a key-value pair only if the key is present or add a key-value pair only if the key is absent. Making these operations atomic helps avoid synchronization. The standard general-purpose implementation of ConcurrentMap is ConcurrentHashMap,[30] which is a concurrent analog of HashMap.[31]
- ConcurrentNavigableMap[32] is a subinterface of ConcurrentMap that supports approximate matches. The standard general-purpose implementation of ConcurrentNavigableMap is ConcurrentSkipListMap,[33] which is a concurrent analog of TreeMap.[34]

These collections help avoid memory consistency errors by defining a happens-before relationship between an operation that adds an object to the collection with subsequent operations that access or remove that object.

Atomic Variables

The java.util.concurrent.atomic[35] package defines classes that support atomic operations on single variables. All classes have get and set methods that work like reads and writes on volatile variables. That is, a set has a happens-before relationship with any subsequent get on the same variable. The atomic compareAndSet method also has these memory consistency features, as do the simple atomic arithmetic methods that apply to integer atomic variables.

To see how this package might be used, let's return to the Counter class we originally used to demonstrate thread interference:

```
class Counter {
    private int c = 0;

    public void increment() {
        c++;
    }
```

---

28. 7/docs/api/java/util/concurrent/ConcurrentMap.html
29. 7/docs/api/java/util/Map.html
30. 7/docs/api/java/util/concurrent/ConcurrentHashMap.html
31. 7/docs/api/java/util/HashMap.html
32. 7/docs/api/java/util/concurrent/ConcurrentNavigableMap.html
33. 7/docs/api/java/util/concurrent/ConcurrentSkipListMap.html
34. 7/docs/api/java/util/TreeMap.html
35. 7/docs/api/java/util/concurrent/atomic/package-summary.html

```
public void decrement() {
    c--;
}

public int value() {
    return c;
}

}
```

One way to make `Counter` safe from thread interference is to make its methods synchronized, as in `SynchronizedCounter`:

```
class SynchronizedCounter {
    private int c = 0;

    public synchronized void increment() {
        c++;
    }

    public synchronized void decrement() {
        c--;
    }

    public synchronized int value() {
        return c;
    }

}
```

For this simple class, synchronization is an acceptable solution. But for a more complicated class, we might want to avoid the liveness impact of unnecessary synchronization. Replacing the `int` field with an `AtomicInteger` allows us to prevent thread interference without resorting to synchronization:

```
import java.util.concurrent.atomic.AtomicInteger;

class AtomicCounter {
    private AtomicInteger c = new AtomicInteger(0);

    public void increment() {
        c.incrementAndGet();
    }

    public void decrement() {
        c.decrementAndGet();
    }

    public int value() {
        return c.get();
    }

}
```

Concurrent Random Numbers

In JDK 7, `java.util.concurrent`[36] includes a convenience class, `ThreadLocal-Random`,[37] for applications that expect to use random numbers from multiple threads or `ForkJoinTasks`. For concurrent access, using `ThreadLocalRandom` instead of `Math.random()` results in less contention and, ultimately, better performance. All you need to do is call `ThreadLocalRandom.current()`; then call one of its methods to retrieve a random number. Here is an example:

```
int r = ThreadLocalRandom.current() .nextInt(4, 77);
```

Questions and Exercises: Concurrency

Question

1. Can you pass a `Thread` object to `Executor.execute`? Would such an invocation make sense?

Exercises

1. Compile and run `BadThreads.java`:

```
public class BadThreads {

    static String message;

    private static class CorrectorThread
        extends Thread {

        public void run() {
            try {
                sleep(1000);
            } catch (InterruptedException e) {}
            // Key statement 1:
            message = "Mares do eat oats.";
        }
    }

    public static void main(String args[])
        throws InterruptedException {

        (new CorrectorThread()).start();
        message = "Mares do not eat oats.";
        Thread.sleep(2000);
        // Key statement 2:
        System.out.println(message);
```

36. 7/docs/api/java/util/concurrent/package-summary.html
37. 7/docs/api/java/util/concurrent/ThreadLocalRandom.html

```
        }
    }
```

The application is supposed to print out "Mares do eat oats." Is it guaranteed to always do this? If not, why? Would it help to change the parameters of the two invocations of Sleep? How would you guarantee that all changes to message will be visible in the main thread?

2. Modify the producer–consumer example in the "Guarded Blocks" section to use a standard library class instead of the Drop class.

Answers

You can find answers to these questions and exercises at http://docs.oracle.com/ javase/tutorial/essential/concurrency/QandE/answers.html.

12

13

Regular Expressions

Chapter Contents

This chapter explains how to use the `java.util.regex`[1] Application Programming Interface (API) for pattern matching with regular expressions. Although the syntax accepted by this package is similar to the Perl[2] programming language, knowledge of Perl is not a prerequisite. This chapter starts with the basics and gradually builds to cover more advanced techniques.

The introductory section provides a general overview of regular expressions. It also introduces the core classes that comprise this API.

---

1. `7/docs/api/java/util/regex/package-summary.html`
2. `http://www.perl.com`

The other sections do the following:

- Define a simple application for testing pattern matching with regular expressions
- Introduce basic pattern matching, metacharacters, and quoting
- Describe simple character classes, negation, ranges, unions, intersections, and subtraction
- Describe the basic predefined character classes for white space, word, and digit characters
- Explain greedy, reluctant, and possessive quantifiers for matching a specified expression x number of times
- Explain how to treat multiple characters as a single unit
- Describe line, word, and input boundaries
- Examine other useful methods of the `Pattern` class and explore advanced features such as compiling with flags and using embedded flag expressions
- Describe the commonly used methods of the `Matcher` class
- Explain how to match a Unicode code point and how to search on a Unicode character property
- Describe how to examine a `PatternSyntaxException`

To learn more about regular expressions, consult the "Additional Resources" section and test your knowledge using the questions and exercises at the end of the chapter.

13

Introduction

What Are Regular Expressions?

Regular expressions are a way to describe a set of strings based on common characteristics shared by each string in the set. They can be used to search, edit, or manipulate text and data. You must learn a specific syntax to create regular expressions—one that goes beyond the normal syntax of the Java programming language. Regular expressions vary in complexity, but once you understand the basics of how they're constructed, you'll be able to decipher (or create) any regular expression.

This chapter teaches the regular expression syntax supported by the `java.util. regex` API and presents several working examples to illustrate how the various objects interact. In the world of regular expressions, there are many different flavors to choose from, such as grep, Perl, Tcl, Python, PHP, and awk. The regular expression syntax in the `java.util.regex` API is most similar to that found in Perl.

How Are Regular Expressions Represented in This Package?

The `java.util.regex` package primarily consists of three classes: `Pattern`,[3] `Matcher`,[4] and `PatternSyntaxException`.[5]

- A `Pattern` object is a compiled representation of a regular expression. The `Pattern` class provides no public constructors. To create a pattern, you must first invoke one of its `public static compile` methods, which will then return a `Pattern` object. These methods accept a regular expression as the first argument; the first few sections of this chapter will teach you the required syntax.

- A `Matcher` object is the engine that interprets the pattern and performs match operations against an input string. Like the `Pattern` class, `Matcher` defines no public constructors. You obtain a `Matcher` object by invoking the `matcher` method on a `Pattern` object.

- A `PatternSyntaxException` object is an unchecked exception that indicates a syntax error in a regular expression pattern.

The last few sections of this chapter explore each class in detail. But, first, you must understand how regular expressions are actually constructed. The next section introduces a simple test harness that will be used repeatedly to explore their syntax.

Test Harness

13

This section defines a reusable test harness, `RegexTestHarness.java`, for exploring the regular expression constructs supported by this API. The command to run this code is `java RegexTestHarness`; no command-line arguments are accepted. The application loops repeatedly, prompting the user for a regular expression and input string. Using this test harness is optional, but you may find it convenient for exploring the test cases discussed in the following pages.

```
import java.io.Console;
import java.util.regex.Pattern;
import java.util.regex.Matcher;

public class RegexTestHarness {
```

---

3. 7/docs/api/java/util/regex/Pattern.html

4. 7/docs/api/java/util/regex/Matcher.html

5. 7/docs/api/java/util/regex/PatternSyntaxException.html

```
public static void main(String[] args){
    Console console = System.console();
    if (console == null) {
        System.err.println("No console.");
        System.exit(1);
    }
    while (true) {

        Pattern pattern =
        Pattern.compile(console.readLine("%nEnter your regex: "));

        Matcher matcher =
        pattern.matcher(console.readLine("Enter input string to search: "));

        boolean found = false;
        while (matcher.find()) {
            console.format("I found the text" +
                " \"%s\" starting at " +
                "index %d and ending at index %d.%n",
                matcher.group(),
                matcher.start(),
                matcher.end());
            found = true;
        }
        if(!found){
            console.format("No match found.%n");
        }
    }
}
```

Before continuing to the next section, copy and compile this code[6] to ensure that your development environment supports the required packages.

String Literals

The most basic form of pattern matching supported by this API is the match of a string literal. For example, if the regular expression is foo and the input string is foo, the match will succeed because the strings are identical. Try this out with the test harness:

```
Enter your regex: foo
Enter input string to search: foo
I found the text foo starting at index 0 and ending at index 3.
```

This match was a success. Note that while the input string is 3 characters long, the start index is 0 and the end index is 3. By convention, ranges are inclusive of the beginning index and exclusive of the end index, as shown in Figure 13.1.

6. essential/regex/examples/RegexTestHarness.java

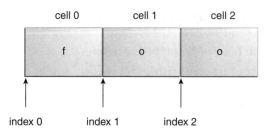

Figure 13.1 The String Literal Foo, with Numbered Cells and Index Values

Each character in the string resides in its own *cell*, with the index positions pointing between each cell. The string foo starts at index 0 and ends at index 3, even though the characters themselves only occupy cells 0, 1, and 2.

With subsequent matches, you'll notice some overlap; the start index for the next match is the same as the end index of the previous match:

```
Enter your regex: foo
Enter input string to search: foofoofoo
I found the text foo starting at index 0 and ending at index 3.
I found the text foo starting at index 3 and ending at index 6.
I found the text foo starting at index 6 and ending at index 9.
```

Metacharacters

This API also supports a number of special characters that affect the way a pattern is matched. Change the regular expression to cat. and the input string to cats. The output will appear as follows:

```
Enter your regex: cat.
Enter input string to search: cats
I found the text cats starting at index 0 and ending at index 4.
```

The match still succeeds, even though the dot (.) is not present in the input string. It succeeds because the dot is a *metacharacter*—a character with special meaning interpreted by the matcher. The dot metacharacter (.) means *any character*, which is why the match succeeds in this example. The metacharacters supported by this API are as follows: <([{\^-=$!|]})?*+.>

> **Note**
>
> In certain situations, the special characters listed here will *not* be treated as metacharacters. You'll encounter this as you learn more about how regular expressions are constructed. You can, however, use this list to check whether or not a specific character will ever be considered a metacharacter. For example, the characters @ and # never carry a special meaning.

There are two ways to force a metacharacter to be treated as an ordinary character:

- Place a backslash before the metacharacter.
- Enclose the metacharacter within \Q (which starts a quote) and \E (which ends it).

When using this technique, the \Q and \E can be placed at any location within the expression, provided that the \Q comes first.

Character Classes

If you browse through the `Pattern` class specification,[7] you'll see tables summarizing the supported regular expression constructs. Table 13.1 is an example of one of these tables.

The left-hand column specifies the regular expression constructs, while the right-hand column describes the conditions under which each construct will match.

> **Note**
>
> The word *class* in the phrase *character class* does not refer to a `.class` file. In the context of regular expressions, a *character class* is a set of characters enclosed within square brackets. It specifies the characters that will successfully match a single character from a given input string.

Simple Classes

The most basic form of a character class is to simply place a set of characters side-by-side within square brackets. For example, the regular expression [bcr]at will

Table 13.1. Regular Expression Constructs

Construct	Description
[abc]	a, b, or c (simple class)
[^abc]	Any character except a, b, or c (negation)
[a-zA-Z]	a through z, or A through Z, inclusive (range)
[a-d[m-p]]	a through d, or m through p (union)
[a-z&&[def]]	d, e, or f (intersection)
[a-z&&[^bc]]	a through z, except for b and c (subtraction)
[a-z&&[^m-p]]	a through z, but not m through p (subtraction)

---

7. 7/docs/api/java/util/regex/Pattern.html

match the words *bat*, *cat*, or *rat* because it defines a character class (accepting either
b, *c*, or *r*) as its first character.

```
Enter your regex: [bcr]at
Enter input string to search: bat
I found the text "bat" starting at index 0 and ending at index 3.

Enter your regex: [bcr]at
Enter input string to search: cat
I found the text "cat" starting at index 0 and ending at index 3.

Enter your regex: [bcr]at
Enter input string to search: rat
I found the text "rat" starting at index 0 and ending at index 3.

Enter your regex: [bcr]at
Enter input string to search: hat
No match found.
```

In these examples, the overall match succeeds only when the first letter matches
one of the characters defined by the character class.

Negation

To match all characters *except* those listed, insert the ^ metacharacter at the beginning of the character class. This technique is known as *negation*:

```
Enter your regex: [^bcr]at
Enter input string to search: bat
No match found.

Enter your regex: [^bcr]at
Enter input string to search: cat
No match found.

Enter your regex: [^bcr]at
Enter input string to search: rat
No match found.

Enter your regex: [^bcr]at
Enter input string to search: hat
I found the text "hat" starting at index 0 and ending at index 3.
```

The match is successful only if the first character of the input string does *not*
contain any of the characters defined by the character class.

Ranges

Sometimes you'll want to define a character class that includes a range of values,
such as the letters *a* through *h* or the numbers 1 through 5. To specify a range, simply insert the – metacharacter between the first and last character to be matched,

such as [1-5] or [a-h]. You can also place different ranges beside each other within the class to further expand the match possibilities. For example, [a-zA-Z] will match any letter of the alphabet: *a* to *z* (lowercase) or *A* to *Z* (uppercase).

Here are some examples of ranges and negation:

```
Enter your regex: [a-c]
Enter input string to search: a
I found the text "a" starting at index 0 and ending at index 1.

Enter your regex: [a-c]
Enter input string to search: b
I found the text "b" starting at index 0 and ending at index 1.

Enter your regex: [a-c]
Enter input string to search: c
I found the text "c" starting at index 0 and ending at index 1.

Enter your regex: [a-c]
Enter input string to search: d
No match found.

Enter your regex: foo[1-5]
Enter input string to search: foo1
I found the text "foo1" starting at index 0 and ending at index 4.

Enter your regex: foo[1-5]
Enter input string to search: foo5
I found the text "foo5" starting at index 0 and ending at index 4.

Enter your regex: foo[1-5]
Enter input string to search: foo6
No match found.

Enter your regex: foo[^1-5]
Enter input string to search: foo1
No match found.

Enter your regex: foo[^1-5]
Enter input string to search: foo6
I found the text "foo6" starting at index 0 and ending at index 4.
```

Unions

You can also use *unions* to create a single character class composed of two or more separate character classes. To create a union, simply nest one class inside the other, such as [0-4[6-8]]. This particular union creates a single character class that matches the numbers 0, 1, 2, 3, 4, 6, 7, and 8.

```
Enter your regex: [0-4[6-8]]
Enter input string to search: 0
I found the text "0" starting at index 0 and ending at index 1.

Enter your regex: [0-4[6-8]]
Enter input string to search: 5
No match found.
```

```
Enter your regex: [0-4[6-8]]
Enter input string to search: 6
I found the text "6" starting at index 0 and ending at index 1.

Enter your regex: [0-4[6-8]]
Enter input string to search: 8
I found the text "8" starting at index 0 and ending at index 1.

Enter your regex: [0-4[6-8]]
Enter input string to search: 9
No match found.
```

Intersections

To create a single character class matching only the characters common to all its nested classes, use &&, as in [0-9&&[345]]. This particular intersection creates a single character class matching only the numbers common to both character classes: 3, 4, and 5.

```
Enter your regex: [0-9&&[345]]
Enter input string to search: 3
I found the text "3" starting at index 0 and ending at index 1.

Enter your regex: [0-9&&[345]]
Enter input string to search: 4
I found the text "4" starting at index 0 and ending at index 1.

Enter your regex: [0-9&&[345]]
Enter input string to search: 5
I found the text "5" starting at index 0 and ending at index 1.

Enter your regex: [0-9&&[345]]
Enter input string to search: 2
No match found.

Enter your regex: [0-9&&[345]]
Enter input string to search: 6
No match found.
```

13

And here's an example that shows the intersection of two ranges:

```
Enter your regex: [2-8&&[4-6]]
Enter input string to search: 3
No match found.

Enter your regex: [2-8&&[4-6]]
Enter input string to search: 4
I found the text "4" starting at index 0 and ending at index 1.

Enter your regex: [2-8&&[4-6]]
Enter input string to search: 5
I found the text "5" starting at index 0 and ending at index 1.

Enter your regex: [2-8&&[4-6]]
Enter input string to search: 6
```

```
I found the text "6" starting at index 0 and ending at index 1.

Enter your regex: [2-8&&[4-6]]
Enter input string to search: 7
No match found.
```

Subtraction

Finally, you can use *subtraction* to negate one or more nested character classes, such as `[0-9&&[^345]]`. This example creates a single character class that matches everything from 0 to 9, *except* the numbers 3, 4, and 5:

```
Enter your regex: [0-9&&[^345]]
Enter input string to search: 2
I found the text "2" starting at index 0 and ending at index 1.

Enter your regex: [0-9&&[^345]]
Enter input string to search: 3
No match found.

Enter your regex: [0-9&&[^345]]
Enter input string to search: 4
No match found.

Enter your regex: [0-9&&[^345]]
Enter input string to search: 5
No match found.

Enter your regex: [0-9&&[^345]]
Enter input string to search: 6
I found the text "6" starting at index 0 and ending at index 1.

Enter your regex: [0-9&&[^345]]
Enter input string to search: 9
I found the text "9" starting at index 0 and ending at index 1.
```

Now that we've covered how character classes are created, you may want to revisit Table 13.1 before continuing to the next section.

Predefined Character Classes

The `Pattern` API[8] contains a number of useful *predefined character classes*, which offer convenient shorthands for commonly used regular expressions:

In Table 13.2, each construct in the left-hand column is shorthand for the character class in the right-hand column. For example, \d means a range of digits (0 through 9), and \w means a word character (any lowercase letter, any uppercase letter, the underscore character, or any digit). Use the predefined classes whenever

---

8. `7/docs/api/java/util/regex/Pattern.html`

Table 13.2 Character Constructs

Construct	Description
.	Any character (may or may not match line terminators)
\d	A digit: [0-9]
\D	A nondigit: [^0-9]
\s	A white-space character: [\t\n\x0B\f\r]
\S	A non-white-space character: [^\s]
\w	A word character: [a-zA-Z_0-9]
\W	A nonword character: [^\w]

possible. They make your code easier to read and eliminate errors introduced by malformed character classes.

Constructs beginning with a backslash are called *escaped constructs*. We previewed escaped constructs in the "String Literals" section, where we mentioned the use of backslash and \Q and \E for quotations. If you are using an escaped construct within a string literal, you must precede the backslash with another backslash for the string to compile. Here's an example:

```java
private final String REGEX = "\\d"; // a single digit
```

In this example, \d is the regular expression; the extra backslash is required for the code to compile. The test harness reads the expressions directly from the Console, however, so the extra backslash is unnecessary.

The following examples demonstrate the use of predefined character classes:

```
Enter your regex: .
Enter input string to search: @
I found the text "@" starting at index 0 and ending at index 1.

Enter your regex: .
Enter input string to search: 1
I found the text "1" starting at index 0 and ending at index 1.

Enter your regex: .
Enter input string to search: a
I found the text "a" starting at index 0 and ending at index 1.

Enter your regex: \d
Enter input string to search: 1
I found the text "1" starting at index 0 and ending at index 1.

Enter your regex: \d
Enter input string to search: a
No match found.

Enter your regex: \D
```

```
Enter input string to search: 1
No match found.

Enter your regex: \D
Enter input string to search: a
I found the text "a" starting at index 0 and ending at index 1.

Enter your regex: \s
Enter input string to search:
I found the text " " starting at index 0 and ending at index 1.

Enter your regex: \s
Enter input string to search: a
No match found.

Enter your regex: \S
Enter input string to search:
No match found.

Enter your regex: \S
Enter input string to search: a
I found the text "a" starting at index 0 and ending at index 1.

Enter your regex: \w
Enter input string to search: a
I found the text "a" starting at index 0 and ending at index 1.

Enter your regex: \w
Enter input string to search: !
No match found.

Enter your regex: \W
Enter input string to search: a
No match found.

Enter your regex: \W
Enter input string to search: !
I found the text "!" starting at index 0 and ending at index 1.
```

In the first three examples, the regular expression is simply the dot metacharacter (.), which indicates *any character*. Therefore, the match is successful in all three cases (a randomly selected @ character, a digit, and a letter). The remaining examples each use a single regular expression construct from Table 13.2. You can refer to this table to figure out the logic behind each match:

- \d matches all digits
- \s matches spaces
- \w matches word characters

Alternatively, a capital letter means the opposite:

- \D matches nondigits
- \S matches nonspaces
- \W matches nonword characters

Quantifiers

Quantifiers allow you to specify the number of occurrences to match against. For convenience, the three sections of the `Pattern` API specification describing greedy, reluctant, and possessive quantifiers are presented in Table 13.3. At first glance, it may appear that the quantifiers X?, X??, and X?+ do exactly the same thing, since they all promise to match "X, once or not at all." But there are subtle implementation differences that will be explained near the end of this section.

Let's look at greedy quantifiers by creating three different regular expressions: the letter *a* followed by either ?, *, or +. Let's see what happens when these expressions are tested against an empty input string " ":

```
Enter your regex: a?
Enter input string to search:
I found the text "" starting at index 0 and ending at index 0.

Enter your regex: a*
Enter input string to search:
I found the text "" starting at index 0 and ending at index 0.

Enter your regex: a+
Enter input string to search:
No match found.
```

Zero-Length Matches

In the previous example, the match is successful in the first two cases because the expressions a? and a* both allow for zero occurrences of the letter *a*. You'll also notice that the start and end indices are both zero, which is unlike any of the

Table 13.3 Quantifiers for Character Matching

Greedy	Reluctant	Possessive	Meaning
X?	X??	X?+	X, once or not at all
X*	X*?	X*+	X, zero or more times
X+	X+?	X++	X, one or more times
X{n}	X{n}?	X{n}+	X, exactly n times
X{n,}	X{n,}?	X{n,}+	X, at least n times
X{n,m}	X{n,m}?	X{n,m}+	X, at least n but not more than m times

examples we've seen so far. The empty input string " " has no length, so the test simply matches nothing at index 0. Matches of this sort are known as *zero-length matches*. A zero-length match can occur in several cases: in an empty input string, at the beginning of an input string, after the last character of an input string, or in between any two characters of an input string. Zero-length matches are easily identifiable because they always start and end at the same index position.

Let's explore zero-length matches with a few more examples. Change the input string to a single letter *a* and you'll notice something interesting:

```
Enter your regex: a?
Enter input string to search: a
I found the text "a" starting at index 0 and ending at index 1.
I found the text "" starting at index 1 and ending at index 1.

Enter your regex: a*
Enter input string to search: a
I found the text "a" starting at index 0 and ending at index 1.
I found the text "" starting at index 1 and ending at index 1.

Enter your regex: a+
Enter input string to search: a
I found the text "a" starting at index 0 and ending at index 1.
```

All three quantifiers found the letter *a*, but the first two also found a zero-length match at index 1—that is, after the last character of the input string. Remember, the matcher sees the character *a* as sitting in the cell between index 0 and index 1, and our test harness loops until it can no longer find a match. Depending on the quantifier used, the presence of "nothing" at the index after the last character may or may not trigger a match.

Now change the input string to the letter *a* five times in a row, and you'll get the following:

```
Enter your regex: a?
Enter input string to search: aaaaa
I found the text "a" starting at index 0 and ending at index 1.
I found the text "a" starting at index 1 and ending at index 2.
I found the text "a" starting at index 2 and ending at index 3.
I found the text "a" starting at index 3 and ending at index 4.
I found the text "a" starting at index 4 and ending at index 5.
I found the text "" starting at index 5 and ending at index 5.

Enter your regex: a*
Enter input string to search: aaaaa
I found the text "aaaaa" starting at index 0 and ending at index 5.
I found the text "" starting at index 5 and ending at index 5.

Enter your regex: a+
Enter input string to search: aaaaa
I found the text "aaaaa" starting at index 0 and ending at index 5.
```

The expression a? finds an individual match for each character, since it matches when *a* appears zero or one times. The expression a* finds two separate matches: all the letter *a*'s in the first match and the zero-length match after the last character at index 5. Finally, a+ matches all occurrences of the letter *a*, ignoring the presence of "nothing" at the last index.

At this point, you might be wondering what the results would be if the first two quantifiers encounter a letter other than *a*. For example, what happens if it encounters the letter *b*, as in *ababaaaab*? Let's find out:

```
Enter your regex: a?
Enter input string to search: ababaaaab
I found the text "a" starting at index 0 and ending at index 1.
I found the text "" starting at index 1 and ending at index 1.
I found the text "a" starting at index 2 and ending at index 3.
I found the text "" starting at index 3 and ending at index 3.
I found the text "a" starting at index 4 and ending at index 5.
I found the text "a" starting at index 5 and ending at index 6.
I found the text "a" starting at index 6 and ending at index 7.
I found the text "a" starting at index 7 and ending at index 8.
I found the text "" starting at index 8 and ending at index 8.
I found the text "" starting at index 9 and ending at index 9.

Enter your regex: a*
Enter input string to search: ababaaaab
I found the text "a" starting at index 0 and ending at index 1.
I found the text "" starting at index 1 and ending at index 1.
I found the text "a" starting at index 2 and ending at index 3.
I found the text "" starting at index 3 and ending at index 3.
I found the text "aaaa" starting at index 4 and ending at index 8.
I found the text "" starting at index 8 and ending at index 8.
I found the text "" starting at index 9 and ending at index 9.

Enter your regex: a+
Enter input string to search: ababaaaab
I found the text "a" starting at index 0 and ending at index 1.
I found the text "a" starting at index 2 and ending at index 3.
I found the text "aaaa" starting at index 4 and ending at index 8.
```

13

Even though the letter *b* appears in cells 1, 3, and 8, the output reports a zero-length match at those locations. The regular expression a? is not specifically looking for the letter *b*; it's merely looking for the presence (or lack thereof) of the letter *a*. If the quantifier allows for a match of *a* zero times, anything in the input string that's not an *a* will show up as a zero-length match. The remaining *a*'s are matched according to the rules discussed in the previous examples.

To match a pattern exactly *n* number of times, simply specify the number inside a set of braces:

```
Enter your regex: a{3}
Enter input string to search: aa
No match found.
```

```
Enter your regex: a{3}
Enter input string to search: aaa
I found the text "aaa" starting at index 0 and ending at index 3.

Enter your regex: a{3}
Enter input string to search: aaaa
I found the text "aaa" starting at index 0 and ending at index 3.
```

Here, the regular expression a{3} is searching for three occurrences of the letter *a* in a row. The first test fails because the input string does not have enough *a*'s to match against. The second test contains exactly three *a*'s in the input string, which triggers a match. The third test also triggers a match because there are exactly three *a*'s at the beginning of the input string. Anything following this is irrelevant to the first match. If the pattern should appear again after that point, it would trigger subsequent matches:

```
Enter your regex: a{3}
Enter input string to search: aaaaaaaaa
I found the text "aaa" starting at index 0 and ending at index 3.
I found the text "aaa" starting at index 3 and ending at index 6.
I found the text "aaa" starting at index 6 and ending at index 9.
```

To require a pattern to appear at least *n* times, add a comma after the number:

```
Enter your regex: a{3,}
Enter input string to search: aaaaaaaaa
I found the text "aaaaaaaaa" starting at index 0 and ending at index 9.
```

With the same input string, this test finds only one match, because the nine *a*'s in a row satisfy the need for "at least" three *a*'s. Finally, to specify an upper limit on the number of occurrences, add a second number inside the braces:

```
Enter your regex: a{3,6} // find at least 3 (but no more than 6) a's in a row
Enter input string to search: aaaaaaaaa
I found the text "aaaaaa" starting at index 0 and ending at index 6.
I found the text "aaa" starting at index 6 and ending at index 9.
```

Here, the first match is forced to stop at the upper limit of six characters. The second match includes whatever is leftover, which happens to be three *a*'s—the minimum number of characters allowed for this match. If the input string were one character shorter, there would not be a second match, since only two *a*'s would remain.

Capturing Groups and Character Classes with Quantifiers

Until now, we've only tested quantifiers on input strings containing one character. In fact, quantifiers can only attach to one character at a time, so the regular expression abc+ would mean *a*, followed by *b*, followed by *c* one or more times. It would not mean *abc* one or more times. However, quantifiers can also attach to character classes and capturing groups, such as [abc]+ (*a* or *b* or *c*, one or more times) or (abc)+ (the group *abc*, one or more times).

Let's illustrate by specifying the group (dog), three times in a row:

```
Enter your regex: (dog){3}
Enter input string to search: dogdogdogdogdogdog
I found the text "dogdogdog" starting at index 0 and ending at index 9.
I found the text "dogdogdog" starting at index 9 and ending at index 18.

Enter your regex: dog{3}
Enter input string to search: dogdogdogdogdogdog
No match found.
```

Here the first example finds three matches, since the quantifier applies to the entire capturing group. Remove the parentheses, however, and the match fails because the quantifier {3} now applies only to the letter *g*.

Similarly, we can apply a quantifier to an entire character class:

```
Enter your regex: [abc]{3}
Enter input string to search: abccabaaaccbbbc
I found the text "abc" starting at index 0 and ending at index 3.
I found the text "cab" starting at index 3 and ending at index 6.
I found the text "aaa" starting at index 6 and ending at index 9.
I found the text "ccb" starting at index 9 and ending at index 12.
I found the text "bbc" starting at index 12 and ending at index 15.

Enter your regex: abc{3}
Enter input string to search: abccabaaaccbbbc
No match found.
```

13

In the first example, the quantifier {3} applies to the entire character class, but in the second example, it only applies to the letter *c*.

Differences among Greedy, Reluctant, and Possessive Quantifiers

There are subtle differences among greedy, reluctant, and possessive quantifiers.

Greedy quantifiers are considered "greedy" because they force the matcher to read in, or *eat*, the entire input string prior to attempting the first match. If the first match attempt (the entire input string) fails, the matcher backs off the input string by one character and tries again, repeating the process until a match is found or there are no more characters left to back off from. Depending on the quantifier used in the expression, the last thing it will try matching against is 1 or 0 characters.

The reluctant quantifiers, however, take the opposite approach: they start at the beginning of the input string, then reluctantly eat one character at a time looking for a match. The last thing they try is the entire input string.

Finally, the possessive quantifiers always eat the entire input string, trying once (and only once) for a match. Unlike the greedy quantifiers, possessive quantifiers never back off, even if doing so would allow the overall match to succeed.

To illustrate, consider the input string xfooxxxxxxfoo:

```
Enter your regex: .*foo  // greedy quantifier
Enter input string to search: xfooxxxxxxfoo
I found the text "xfooxxxxxxfoo" starting at index 0 and ending at index 13.

Enter your regex: .*?foo  // reluctant quantifier
Enter input string to search: xfooxxxxxxfoo
I found the text "xfoo" starting at index 0 and ending at index 4.
I found the text "xxxxxxfoo" starting at index 4 and ending at index 13.

Enter your regex: .*+foo // possessive quantifier
Enter input string to search: xfooxxxxxxfoo
No match found.
```

The first example uses the greedy quantifier .* to find *anything* zero or more times, followed by *foo*. Because the quantifier is greedy, the .* portion of the expression first eats the entire input string. At this point, the overall expression cannot succeed because the last three letters (*foo*) have already been consumed. So the matcher slowly backs off one letter at a time until the rightmost occurrence of *foo* has been regurgitated, at which point the match succeeds and the search ends.

The second example, however, is reluctant, so it starts by first consuming *nothing*. Because *foo* doesn't appear at the beginning of the string, it's forced to swallow the first letter (*x*), which triggers the first match at 0 and 4. Our test harness continues the process until the input string is exhausted. It finds another match at 4 and 13.

The third example fails to find a match because the quantifier is possessive. In this case, the entire input string is consumed by .*+, leaving nothing leftover to satisfy the *foo* at the end of the expression. Use a possessive quantifier for situations where you want to seize every instance of something without ever backing off; it will outperform the equivalent greedy quantifier in cases where the match is not immediately found.

Capturing Groups

In the previous section, we saw how quantifiers attach to one character, character class, or capturing group at a time. But until now, we have not discussed the notion of capturing groups in any detail.

Capturing groups treat multiple characters as a single unit. They are created by placing the characters to be grouped inside a set of parentheses. For example, the regular expression (dog) creates a single group containing the letters *d*, *o*, and *g*. The portion of the input string that matches the capturing group will be saved in memory for later recall via backreferences (as will be discussed later in this chapter).

Numbering

As described in the `Pattern` API, capturing groups are numbered by counting their opening parentheses from left to right. In the expression `((A)(B(C)))`, for example, there are four such groups:

1. `((A)(B(C)))`
2. `(A)`
3. `(B(C))`
4. `(C)`

To find out how many groups are present in the expression, call the `groupCount` method on a matcher object. The `groupCount` method returns an `int` showing the number of capturing groups present in the matcher's pattern. In this example, `groupCount` would return the number 4, showing that the pattern contains 4 capturing groups.

There is also a special group, group 0, that always represents the entire expression. This group is not included in the total reported by `groupCount`. Groups beginning with `(?` are pure, *noncapturing groups* that do not capture text and do not count toward the group total. (You'll see examples of noncapturing groups later on in this chapter.)

It's important to understand how groups are numbered because some `Matcher` methods accept an `int`, specifying a particular group number as a parameter:

- `public int start(int group)`[9]—Returns the start index of the subsequence captured by the given group during the previous match operation
- `public int end (int group)`[10]—Returns the index of the last character, plus one, of the subsequence captured by the given group during the previous match operation
- `public String group (int group)`[11]—Returns the input subsequence captured by the given group during the previous match operation

---

9. `7/docs/api/java/util/regex/Matcher.html#start(int)`
10. `7/docs/api/java/util/regex/Matcher.html#end(int)`
11. `7/docs/api/java/util/regex/Matcher.html#group(int)`

Backreferences

The section of the input string matching the capturing group(s) is saved in memory for later recall via *backreference*. A backreference is specified in the regular expression as a backslash (\) followed by a digit indicating the number of the group to be recalled. For example, the expression (\d\d) defines one capturing group matching two digits in a row, which can be recalled later in the expression via the backreference \1.

To match any two digits followed by the exact same two digits, you would use (\d\d)\1 as the regular expression:

```
Enter your regex: (\d\d)\1
Enter input string to search: 1212
I found the text "1212" starting at index 0 and ending at index 4.
```

If you change the last two digits, the match will fail:

```
Enter your regex: (\d\d)\1
Enter input string to search: 1234
No match found.
```

For nested capturing groups, backreferencing works in exactly the same way: specify a backslash followed by the number of the group to be recalled.

Boundary Matchers

Until now, we've only been interested in whether or not a match is found *at some location* within a particular input string. We never cared about *where* in the string the match was taking place.

You can make your pattern matches more precise by specifying such information with *boundary matchers*. For example, maybe you're interested in finding a particular word but only if it appears at the beginning or end of a line. Or maybe you want to know if the match is taking place on a word boundary or at the end of the previous match. Table 13.4 lists and explains all the boundary matchers.

The following examples demonstrate the use of boundary matchers ^ and $. As noted previously, ^ matches the beginning of a line, and $ matches the end:

```
Enter your regex: ^dog$
Enter input string to search: dog
I found the text "dog" starting at index 0 and ending at index 3.

Enter your regex: ^dog$
Enter input string to search:        dog
No match found.
```

```
Enter your regex: \s*dog$
Enter input string to search:              dog
⊥ found the text "             dog" starting at index 0 and ending at index 15.

Enter your regex: ^dog\w*
Enter input string to search: dogblahblah
I found the text "dogblahblah" starting at index 0 and ending at index 11.
```

The first example is successful because the pattern occupies the entire input string. The second example fails because the input string contains extra white space at the beginning. The third example specifies an expression that allows for unlimited white space, followed by *dog* at the end of the line. The fourth example requires *dog* to be present at the beginning of a line, followed by an unlimited number of word characters.

To check if a pattern begins and ends on a word boundary (as opposed to a substring within a longer string), just use \b on either side (e.g., \bdog\b).

```
Enter your regex: \bdog\b
Enter input string to search: The dog plays in the yard.
I found the text "dog" starting at index 4 and ending at index 7.

Enter your regex: \bdog\b
Enter input string to search: The doggie plays in the yard.
No match found.
```

To match the expression on a nonword boundary, use \B instead:

```
Enter your regex: \bdog\B
Enter input string to search: The dog plays in the yard.
No match found.

Enter your regex: \bdog\B
Enter input string to search: The doggie plays in the yard.
I found the text "dog" starting at index 4 and ending at index 7.
```

Table 13.4 Constructs Used to Define Boundaries

Boundary construct	Description
^	The beginning of a line
$	The end of a line
\b	A word boundary
\B	A nonword boundary
\A	The beginning of the input
\G	The end of the previous match
\Z	The end of the input except for the final terminator, if any
\z	The end of the input

To require the match to occur only at the end of the previous match, use \G:

```
Enter your regex: dog
Enter input string to search: dog dog
I found the text "dog" starting at index 0 and ending at index 3.
I found the text "dog" starting at index 4 and ending at index 7.

Enter your regex: \Gdog
Enter input string to search: dog dog
I found the text "dog" starting at index 0 and ending at index 3.
```

Here, the second example finds only one match because the second occurrence of *dog* does not start at the end of the previous match.

Methods of the Pattern Class

Until now, we've only used the test harness to create `Pattern` objects in their most basic form. This section explores advanced techniques such as creating patterns with flags and using embedded flag expressions. It also explores some additional useful methods that we haven't yet discussed.

Creating a Pattern with Flags

The `Pattern` class defines an alternate `compile` method that accepts a set of flags affecting the way the pattern is matched. The flags parameter is a bit mask that may include any of the following public static fields:

- `Pattern.CANON_EQ`—This enables canonical equivalence. When this flag is specified, two characters will be considered to match if and only if their full canonical decompositions match. For example, the expression `"a\u030A"` will match the string `"\u00E5"` when this flag is specified. By default, matching does not take canonical equivalence into account. Specifying this flag may impose a performance penalty.

- `Pattern.CASE_INSENSITIVE`—This enables case-insensitive matching. By default, case-insensitive matching assumes that only characters in the US-ASCII character set are being matched. Unicode-aware, case-insensitive matching can be enabled by specifying the `UNICODE_CASE` flag in conjunction with this flag. Case-insensitive matching can also be enabled via the embedded flag expression `(?i)`. Specifying this flag may impose a slight performance penalty.

- `Pattern.COMMENTS`—This permits white space and comments in the pattern. In this mode, white space is ignored, and embedded comments starting with # are ignored until the end of a line. Comments mode can also be enabled via the embedded flag expression `(?x)`.

13

- `Pattern.DOTALL`—This enables dotall mode. In dotall mode, the expression `.` matches any character, including a line terminator. By default, this expression does not match line terminators. Dotall mode can also be enabled via the embedded flag expression `(?s)`. (The s is a mnemonic for *single-line* mode, which is what this is called in Perl.)
- `Pattern.LITERAL`—This enables literal parsing of the pattern. When this flag is specified, the input string that specifies the pattern is treated as a sequence of literal characters. Metacharacters or escape sequences in the input sequence will be given no special meaning. The flags `CASE_INSENSITIVE` and `UNICODE_CASE` retain their impact on matching when used in conjunction with this flag. The other flags become superfluous. There is no embedded flag character for enabling literal parsing.
- `Pattern.MULTILINE`—This enables multiline mode. In multiline mode, the expressions `^` and `$` respectively match just after or just before a line terminator or the end of the input sequence. By default, these expressions only match at the beginning and the end of the entire input sequence. Multiline mode can also be enabled via the embedded flag expression `(?m)`.
- `Pattern.UNICODE_CASE`—This enables Unicode-aware case folding. When this flag is specified, case-insensitive matching (enabled by the `CASE_INSEN-SITIVE` flag) is done in a manner consistent with the Unicode standard. By default, case-insensitive matching assumes that only characters in the US-ASCII character set are being matched. Unicode-aware case folding can also be enabled via the embedded flag expression `(?u)`. Specifying this flag may impose a performance penalty.
- `Pattern.UNIX_LINES`—This enables Unix lines mode. In this mode, only the `'\n'` line terminator is recognized in the behavior of `.`, `^`, and `$`. Unix lines mode can also be enabled via the embedded flag expression `(?d)`.

In the following steps, we will modify the test harness `RegexTestHarness.java` to create a pattern with case-insensitive matching. First, modify the code to invoke the alternate version of `compile`:

```
Pattern pattern =
Pattern.compile(console.readLine("%nEnter your regex: "),
Pattern.CASE_INSENSITIVE);
```

Then compile and run the test harness to get the following results:

```
Enter your regex: dog
Enter input string to search: DoGDOg
I found the text "DoG" starting at index 0 and ending at index 3.
I found the text "DOg" starting at index 3 and ending at index 6.
```

As you can see, the string literal *dog* matches both occurrences, regardless of case. To compile a pattern with multiple flags, separate the flags to be included using the bitwise "or" operator |. For clarity, the following code samples hardcode the regular expression instead of reading it from the `Console`:

```
pattern = Pattern.compile("[az]$", Pattern.MULTILINE | Pattern.UNIX_LINES);
```

You could also specify an `int` variable instead:

```
final int flags = Pattern.CASE_INSENSITIVE | Pattern.UNICODE_CASE;
Pattern pattern = Pattern.compile("aa", flags);
```

Embedded Flag Expressions

It's also possible to enable various flags using *embedded flag expressions*. Embedded flag expressions are an alternative to the two-argument version of `compile` and are specified in the regular expression itself. The following example uses the original test harness, `RegexTestHarness.java`, with the embedded flag expression (?i) to enable case-insensitive matching:

```
Enter your regex: (?i)foo
Enter input string to search: FOOfooFoOfoO
I found the text "FOO" starting at index 0 and ending at index 3.
I found the text "foo" starting at index 3 and ending at index 6.
I found the text "FoO" starting at index 6 and ending at index 9.
I found the text "foO" starting at index 9 and ending at index 12.
```

Once again, all matches succeed regardless of case. The embedded flag expressions that correspond to `Pattern`'s publicly accessible fields are presented in Table 13.5.

Table 13.5 Constants for Embedded Flag Expressions

Constant	Equivalent embedded flag expression
Pattern.CANON_EQ	None
Pattern.CASE_INSENSITIVE	(?i)
Pattern.COMMENTS	(?x)
Pattern.MULTILINE	(?m)
Pattern.DOTALL	(?s)
Pattern.LITERAL	None
Pattern.UNICODE_CASE	(?u)
Pattern.UNIX_LINES	(?d)

Using the matches(String,CharSequence) Method

The `Pattern` class defines a convenient `matches`[12] method that allows you to quickly check if a pattern is present in a given input string. As with all public static methods, you should invoke `matches` by its class name, such as `Pattern.matches("\\d","1");`. In this example, the method returns `true` because the digit 1 matches the regular expression `\d`.

Using the split(String) Method

The `split`[13] method is a great tool for gathering the text that lies on either side of the pattern that's been matched. As shown in the following example, the `split` method can extract the words "one two three four five" from the string "one:two:three:four:five":

```java
import java.util.regex.Pattern;
import java.util.regex.Matcher;

public class SplitDemo {

    private static final String REGEX = ":";
    private static final String INPUT =
        "one:two:three:four:five";

    public static void main(String[] args) {
        Pattern p = Pattern.compile(REGEX);
        String[] items = p.split(INPUT);
        for(String s : items) {
            System.out.println(s);
        }
    }
}

OUTPUT:

one
two
three
four
five
```

---

12. 7/docs/api/java/util/regex/Pattern.html#matches(java.lang.String, java.lang.CharSequence)

13. 7/docs/api/java/util/regex/Pattern.html#split(java.lang.CharSequence)

For simplicity, we've matched a string literal, the colon (:), instead of a complex regular expression. Since we're still using `Pattern` and `Matcher` objects, you can use `split` to get the text that falls on either side of any regular expression. Here's the same example, `SplitDemo2.java`, modified to split on digits instead:

```java
import java.util.regex.Pattern;
import java.util.regex.Matcher;

public class SplitDemo2 {

    private static final String REGEX = "\\d";
    private static final String INPUT =
        "one9two4three7four1five";

    public static void main(String[] args) {
        Pattern p = Pattern.compile(REGEX);
        String[] items = p.split(INPUT);
        for(String s : items) {
            System.out.println(s);
        }
    }
}

OUTPUT:

one
two
three
four
five
```

Other Utility Methods

You may find the following methods to be of some use as well:

- `public static String quote(String s)`[14]—This returns a literal pattern `String` for the specified `String`. This method produces a `String` that can be used to create a `Pattern` that would match `String` s as if it were a literal pattern. Metacharacters or escape sequences in the input sequence will be given no special meaning.

- `public String toString()`[15]—Returns the `String` representation of this pattern. This is the regular expression from which this pattern was compiled.

---

14. 7/docs/api/java/util/regex/Pattern.html#quote(java.lang.String)

15. 7/docs/api/java/util/regex/Pattern.html#toString()

Pattern Method Equivalents in java.lang.String

Regular expression support also exists in `java.lang.String`, through several methods that mimic the behavior of `java.util.regex.Pattern`. For convenience, here are some key excerpts from their API:

- `public boolean matches(String regex)`[16]—This tells whether or not the string matches the given regular expression. An invocation of this method of the form *str*.matches(*regex*) yields exactly the same result as the expression `Pattern.matches(`*regex*`, `*str*`)`.

- `public String[] split(String regex, int limit)`[17]—This splits the string around matches of the given regular expression. An invocation of this method of the form *str*.split(*regex*, *n*) yields the same result as the expression `Pattern.compile(`*regex*`).split(`*str*`, `*n*`)`.

- `public String[] split(String regex)`[18]—This splits the string around matches of the given regular expression. This method works the same as if you invoked the two-argument split method with the given expression and a limit argument of zero. Trailing empty strings are not included in the resulting array.

There is also a replace method that replaces one `CharSequence` with another:

- `public String replace(CharSequence target, CharSequence replacement)`[19]—This replaces each substring of the string that matches the literal target sequence with the specified literal replacement sequence. The replacement proceeds from the beginning of the string to the end. For example, replacing *aa* with *b* in the string *aaa* will result in *ba* rather than *ab*.

Methods of the Matcher Class

This section describes some additional useful methods of the `Matcher` class. For convenience, they are grouped according to functionality.

---

16. `7/docs/api/java/lang/String.html#matches(java.lang.String)`
17. `7/docs/api/java/lang/String.html#split(java.lang.String, int)`
18. `7/docs/api/java/lang/String.html#split(java.lang.String)`
19. `7/docs/api/java/lang/String.html#replace(java.lang.CharSequence, java.lang.CharSequence)`

Index Methods

Index methods provide useful index values that show precisely where the match was found in the input string:

- `public int start()`[20]—Returns the start index of the previous match
- `public int start(int group)`—Returns the start index of the subsequence captured by the given group during the previous match operation
- `public int end()`[21]—Returns the offset after the last character matched
- `public int end(int group)`—Returns the offset after the last character of the subsequence captured by the given group during the previous match operation

Study Methods

Study methods review the input string and return a boolean indicating whether or not the pattern is found:

- `public boolean lookingAt()`[22]—Attempts to match the input sequence, starting at the beginning of the region, against the pattern
- `public boolean find()`[23]—Attempts to find the next subsequence of the input sequence that matches the pattern
- `public boolean find(int start)`[24]—Resets this matcher and then attempts to find the next subsequence of the input sequence that matches the pattern, starting at the specified index
- `public boolean matches()`[25]—Attempts to match the entire region against the pattern

Replacement Methods

Replacement methods are useful methods for replacing text in an input string:

---

20. `7/docs/api/java/util/regex/Matcher.html#start()`
21. `7/docs/api/java/util/regex/Matcher.html#end()`
22. `7/docs/api/java/util/regex/Matcher.html#lookingAt()`
23. `7/docs/api/java/util/regex/Matcher.html#find()`
24. `7/docs/api/java/util/regex/Matcher.html#find(int)`
25. `7/docs/api/java/util/regex/Matcher.html#matches()`

- public Matcher appendReplacement(StringBuffer sb, String replacement)[26]—This implements a nonterminal append-and-replace step.
- public StringBuffer appendTail(StringBuffer sb)[27]—This implements a terminal append-and-replace step.
- public String replaceAll(String replacement)[28]—This replaces every subsequence of the input sequence that matches the pattern with the given replacement string.
- public String replaceFirst(String replacement)[29]—This replaces the first subsequence of the input sequence that matches the pattern with the given replacement string.
- public static String quoteReplacement(String s)[30]—This returns a literal replacement String for the specified String. This method produces a String that will work as a literal replacement s in the appendReplacement method of the Matcher class. The String produced will match the sequence of characters in s treated as a literal sequence. Slashes (\) and dollar signs ($) will be given no special meaning.

Using the start and end Methods

Here's an example that counts the number of times the word *dog* appears in the input string:

```
import java.util.regex.Pattern;
import java.util.regex.Matcher;

public class MatcherDemo {

    private static final String REGEX =
        "\\bdog\\b";
    private static final String INPUT =
```

13

---

26. 7/docs/api/java/util/regex/Matcher.html#appendReplacement(java .lang.StringBuffer, java.lang.String)
27. 7/docs/api/java/util/regex/Matcher.html#appendTail(java.lang .StringBuffer)
28. 7/docs/api/java/util/regex/Matcher.html#replaceAll(java.lang .String)
29. 7/docs/api/java/util/regex/Matcher.html#replaceFirst(java.lang .String)
30. 7/docs/api/java/util/regex/Matcher.html#quoteReplacement(java.lang .String)

```
                    "dog dog dog doggie dogg";

        public static void main(String[] args) {
            Pattern p = Pattern.compile(REGEX);
            //  get a matcher object
            Matcher m = p.matcher(INPUT);
            int count = 0;
            while(m.find()) {
                count++;
                System.out.println("Match number "
                                    + count);
                System.out.println("start(): "
                                    + m.start());
                System.out.println("end(): "
                                    + m.end());
            }
        }
    }
```

```
OUTPUT:

Match number 1
start(): 0
end(): 3
Match number 2
start(): 4
end(): 7
Match number 3
start(): 8
end(): 11
```

You can see that this example uses word boundaries to ensure that the letters *d*, *o*, *g* are not merely a substring in a longer word. It also gives some useful information about where in the input string the match has occurred. The `start` method returns the start index of the subsequence captured by the given group during the previous match operation, and `end` returns the index of the last character matched, plus one.

Using the matches and lookingAt Methods

The `matches` and `lookingAt` methods both attempt to match an input sequence against a pattern. The difference, however, is that `matches` requires the entire input sequence to be matched, while `lookingAt` does not. Both methods always start at the beginning of the input string. Here's the full code, `MatchesLooking.java`:

```
import java.util.regex.Pattern;
import java.util.regex.Matcher;

public class MatchesLooking {

    private static final String REGEX = "foo";
    private static final String INPUT =
        "fooooooooooooooooo";
```

```
        private static Pattern pattern;
        private static Matcher matcher;

        public static void main(String[] args) {

            // Initialize
            pattern = Pattern.compile(REGEX);
            matcher = pattern.matcher(INPUT);

            System.out.println("Current REGEX is: "
                            + REGEX);
            System.out.println("Current INPUT is: "
                            + INPUT);

            System.out.println("lookingAt(): "
                + matcher.lookingAt());
            System.out.println("matches(): "
                + matcher.matches());
        }
    }
```

```
Current REGEX is: foo
Current INPUT is: fooooooooooooooooooo
lookingAt(): true
matches(): false
```

Using replaceFirst(String) and replaceAll(String)

The `replaceFirst` and `replaceAll` methods replace text that matches a given regular expression. As their names indicate, `replaceFirst` replaces the first occurrence, and `replaceAll` replaces all occurrences. Here's the `ReplaceDemo.java` code:

```
import java.util.regex.Pattern;
import java.util.regex.Matcher;

public class ReplaceDemo {

    private static String REGEX = "dog";
    private static String INPUT =
        "The dog says meow. All dogs say meow.";
    private static String REPLACE = "cat";

    public static void main(String[] args) {
        Pattern p = Pattern.compile(REGEX);
        // get a matcher object
        Matcher m = p.matcher(INPUT);
        INPUT = m.replaceAll(REPLACE);
        System.out.println(INPUT);
    }
}
```

```
OUTPUT: The cat says meow. All cats say meow.
```

In this first version, all occurrences of dog are replaced with cat. But why stop here? Rather than replace a simple literal like dog, you can replace text that matches *any* regular expression. The API for this method states that "given the regular expression a*b, the input aabfooaabfooabfoob, and the replacement string -, an invocation of this method on a matcher for that expression would yield the string -foo-foo-foo-."

Here's the ReplaceDemo2.java code:

```java
import java.util.regex.Pattern;
import java.util.regex.Matcher;

public class ReplaceDemo2 {

    private static String REGEX = "a*b";
    private static String INPUT =
        "aabfooaabfooabfoob";
    private static String REPLACE = "-";

    public static void main(String[] args) {
        Pattern p = Pattern.compile(REGEX);
        // get a matcher object
        Matcher m = p.matcher(INPUT);
        INPUT = m.replaceAll(REPLACE);
        System.out.println(INPUT);
    }
}

OUTPUT: -foo-foo-foo-
```

To replace only the first occurrence of the pattern, simply call replaceFirst instead of replaceAll. It accepts the same parameter.

Using appendReplacement(StringBuffer,String) and appendTail(StringBuffer)

The Matcher class also provides appendReplacement and appendTail methods for text replacement. The following example uses these two methods to achieve the same effect as replaceAll:

```java
import java.util.regex.Pattern;
import java.util.regex.Matcher;

public class RegexDemo {

    private static String REGEX = "a*b";
    private static String INPUT = "aabfooaabfooabfoob";
    private static String REPLACE = "-";

    public static void main(String[] args) {
        Pattern p = Pattern.compile(REGEX);
```

```
            Matcher m = p.matcher(INPUT); // get a matcher object
            StringBuffer sb = new StringBuffer();
            while(m.find()){
                m.appendReplacement(sb,REPLACE);
            }
            m.appendTail(sb);
            System.out.println(sb.toString());
        }
    }
```

OUTPUT: -foo-foo-foo-

Matcher Method Equivalents in java.lang.String

For convenience, the String class mimics a couple of Matcher methods as well:

- public String replaceFirst(String regex, String replacement)[31]—
  This replaces the first substring of this String that matches the given regular expression with the given replacement. An invocation of this method of the form str.replaceFirst(regex, repl) yields exactly the same result as the expression Pattern.compile(regex).matcher(str).replaceFirst(repl).

- public String replaceAll(String regex, String replacement)[32]—
  This replaces each substring of this String that matches the given regular expression with the given replacement. An invocation of this method of the form str.replaceAll(regex, repl) yields exactly the same result as the expression Pattern.compile(regex).matcher(str).replaceAll(repl).

Methods of the PatternSyntaxException Class

A PatternSyntaxException[33] is an unchecked exception that indicates a syntax error in a regular expression pattern. The PatternSyntaxException class provides the following methods to help you determine what went wrong:

- public String getDescription()[34]—Retrieves the description of the error
- public int getIndex()[35]—Retrieves the error index

---

31. 7/docs/api/java/lang/String.html#replaceFirst(java.lang.String, java.lang.String)

32. 7/docs/api/java/lang/String.html#replaceAll(java.lang.String, java.lang.String)

33. 7/docs/api/java/util/regex/PatternSyntaxException.html

34. 7/docs/api/java/util/regex/PatternSyntaxException.html#getDescription()

35. 7/docs/api/java/util/regex/PatternSyntaxException.html#getIndex()

- `public String getPattern()`[36]—Retrieves the erroneous regular expression pattern
- `public String getMessage()`[37]—Returns a multiline string containing the description of the syntax error and its index, the erroneous regular expression pattern, and a visual indication of the error index within the pattern

The following source code, `RegexTestHarness2.java`, updates our test harness to check for malformed regular expressions:

```java
import java.io.Console;
import java.util.regex.Pattern;
import java.util.regex.Matcher;
import java.util.regex.PatternSyntaxException;

public class RegexTestHarness2 {

    public static void main(String[] args){
        Pattern pattern = null;
        Matcher matcher = null;

        Console console = System.console();
        if (console == null) {
            System.err.println("No console.");
            System.exit(1);
        }
        while (true) {
            try{
                pattern =
                Pattern.compile(console.readLine("%nEnter your regex: "));

                matcher =
                pattern.matcher(console.readLine("Enter input string to
                    search: "));
            }
            catch(PatternSyntaxException pse){
                console.format("There is a problem" +
                        " with the regular expression!%n");
                console.format("The pattern in question is: %s%n",
                        pse.getPattern());
                console.format("The description is: %s%n",
                        pse.getDescription());
                console.format("The message is: %s%n",
                        pse.getMessage());
                console.format("The index is: %s%n",
                        pse.getIndex());
                System.exit(0);
            }
            boolean found = false;
```

---

36. 7/docs/api/java/util/regex/PatternSyntaxException.html#getPattern()

37. 7/docs/api/java/util/regex/PatternSyntaxException.html#getMessage()

```
while (matcher.find()) {
    console.format("I found the text" +
        " \"%s\" starting at " +
        "index %d and ending at index %d.%n",
        matcher.group(),
        matcher.start(),
        matcher.end());
    found = true;
}
if(!found){
    console.format("No match found.%n");
}
        }
    }
}
```

To run this test, enter ?i)foo as the regular expression. This mistake is a common—the programmer forgets the opening parenthesis in the embedded flag expression (?i). Doing so produces the following results:

```
Enter your regex: ?i)
There is a problem with the regular expression!
The pattern in question is: ?i)
The description is: Dangling meta character '?'
The message is: Dangling meta character '?' near index 0
?i)
^
The index is: 0
```

From this output, we can see that the syntax error is a dangling metacharacter (?) at index 0. A missing opening parenthesis is the culprit.

13

Unicode Support

In the JDK 7 release, regular expression pattern matching expanded functionality to support Unicode 6.0.

Matching a Specific Code Point

You can match a specific Unicode code point using an escape sequence of the form \uFFFF, where FFFF is the hexidecimal value of the code point you want to match. For example, \u6771 matches the Han character for east.

Alternatively, you can specify a code point using Perl-style hex notation, \x{ . . . }. Here is an example:

```
String hexPattern = "\x{" + Integer.toHexString(codePoint) + "}";
```

Unicode Character Properties

In addition to its value, each Unicode character has certain attributes or properties. You can match a single character belonging to a particular category with the expression \p{*prop*}. You can match a single character *not* belonging to a particular category with the expression \P{*prop*}.

The three supported property types are scripts, blocks, and a "general" category.

Scripts

To determine if a code point belongs to a specific script, you can either use the script keyword or the sc short form: \p{script=Hiragana}. Alternatively, you can prefix the script name with the string Is, such as \p{IsHiragana}. Valid script names supported by Pattern are those accepted by UnicodeScript.forName.[38]

Blocks

A block can be specified using the block keyword or the blk short form: \p{block=Mongolian}. Alternatively, you can prefix the block name with the string In, such as \p{InMongolian}. Valid block names supported by Pattern are those accepted by UnicodeBlock.forName.

General Category

Categories can be specified with optional prefix Is. For example, IsL matches the category of Unicode letters. Categories can also be specified by using the general_category keyword or the short form gc. For example, an uppercase letter can be matched using general_category=Lu or gc=Lu. Supported categories are those of the Unicode standard[39] in the version specified by the Character[40] class.

Additional Resources

Now that you've completed this chapter on regular expressions, you'll probably find that your main references will be the API documentation for the following classes: Pattern,[41] Matcher,[42] and PatternSyntaxException.[43]

---

38. 7/docs/api/java/lang/Character.UnicodeScript.html#forName(java.lang.String)

39. http://www.unicode.org/unicode/standard/standard.html

40. 7/docs/api/java/lang/Character.html

41. 7/docs/api/java/util/regex/Pattern.html

42. 7/docs/api/java/util/regex/Matcher.html

43. 7/docs/api/java/util/regex/PatternSyntaxException.html

Questions and Exercises: Regular Expressions

Questions

1. What are the three public classes in the `java.util.regex` package? Describe the purpose of each.

2. Consider the string literal `"foo"`. What is the start index? What is the end index? Explain what these numbers mean.

3. What is the difference between an ordinary character and a metacharacter? Give an example of each.

4. How do you force a metacharacter to act like an ordinary character?

5. What do you call a set of characters enclosed in square brackets? What does this notation do?

6. Here are three predefined character classes: \d, \s, and \w. Describe each and rewrite it using square brackets.

7. For \d, \s, and \w, write *two* simple expressions that match the *opposite* set of characters.

8. Consider the regular expression `(dog){3}`. Identify the two subexpressions. What string does the expression match?

Exercise

1. Use a backreference to write an expression that will match a person's name only if that person's first name and last name are the same.

13

Answers

You can find answers to these questions and exercises at `http://docs.oracle.com/javase/tutorial/essential/regex/QandE/answers.html`.

14

The Platform Environment

An application runs in a *platform environment* defined by the underlying operating system, the Java Virtual Machine (Java VM), the class libraries, and various configuration data supplied when the application is launched. This chapter describes some of the Application Programming Interfaces (APIs) an application uses to examine and configure its platform environment.

The first section describes APIs used to access configuration data supplied when the application is deployed or data supplied by the application's user. The second section describes miscellaneous APIs defined in the `System` and `Runtime` classes. The third section describes environment variables used to configure Java SE Development Kit (JDK) tools and other applications. There are questions and exercises at the end of the chapter to test your understanding.

Configuration Utilities

This section describes some of the configuration utilities that help an application access its start-up context.

Properties

Properties are configuration values managed as *key/value pairs*. In each pair, the key and value are both String[1] values. The key identifies and is used to retrieve the value, much like a variable name is used to retrieve the variable's value. For example, an application capable of downloading files might use a property named download.lastDirectory to keep track of the directory used for the last download.

To manage properties, create instances of java.util.Properties.[2] This class provides methods for the following:

- Loading key/value pairs into a Properties object from a stream
- Retrieving a value from its key
- Listing the keys and their values
- Enumerating over the keys
- Saving the properties to a stream

For an introduction to streams, refer to Chapter 10, "I/O Streams."

Properties extends java.util.Hashtable.[3] Some of the methods inherited from Hashtable support the following actions:

- Testing to see if a particular key or value is in the Properties object
- Getting the current number of key/value pairs
- Removing a key and its value
- Adding a key/value pair to the Properties list
- Enumerating over the values or the keys
- Retrieving a value by its key
- Finding out if the Properties object is empty

14

> **Note**
>
> Access to properties is subject to approval by the current security manager. The example code segments in this section are assumed to be in standalone applications, which by default have no security manager. The same code in an applet may not work, depending on the browser in which it is running. See Chapter 17 (specifically "What Applets Can and Cannot Do") for information about security restrictions on applets.

---

1. 7/docs/api/java/lang/String.html
2. 7/docs/api/java/util/Properties.html
3. 7/docs/api/java/util/Hashtable.html

The `System` class maintains a `Properties` object that defines the configuration of the current working environment. For more about these properties, see the "System Properties" section in this chapter. The remainder of this section explains how to use properties to manage application configuration.

Properties in the Application Life Cycle

Figure 14.1 illustrates how a typical application might manage its configuration data with a `Properties` object over the course of its execution:

- *Starting up.* The actions given in the first three boxes occur when the application is starting up. First, the application loads the default properties from a well-known location into a `Properties` object. Normally, the default properties are stored in a file on disk along with the `.class` and other resource files for the application.

  Next, the application creates another `Properties` object and loads the properties that were saved from the last time the application was run. Many applications store properties on a per-user basis, so the properties loaded in this step are usually in a specific file in a particular directory maintained by this application in the user's home directory. Finally, the application uses the default and remembered properties to initialize itself.

  The key here is consistency. The application must always load and save properties to the same location so that it can find them the next time it's executed.

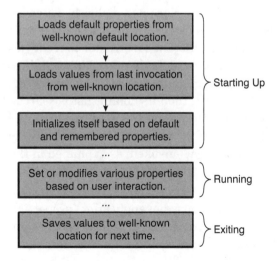

Figure 14.1 Managing Properties in an Application's Life Cycle

- *Running.* During the execution of the application, the user may change some settings, perhaps in a preferences window, and the `Properties` object is updated to reflect these changes. If the users changes are to be remembered in future sessions, they must be saved.

- *Exiting.* Upon exiting, the application saves the properties to its well-known location, to be loaded again when the application is next started up.

Setting Up the Properties Object

The following Java code performs the first two steps described in the previous section (loading the default properties and loading the remembered properties):

```
. . .
// create and load default properties
Properties defaultProps = new Properties();
FileInputStream in = new FileInputStream("defaultProperties");
defaultProps.load(in);
in.close();

// create application properties with default
Properties applicationProps = new Properties(defaultProps);

// now load properties
// from last invocation
in = new FileInputStream("appProperties");
applicationProps.load(in);
in.close();
. . .
```

First, the application sets up a default `Properties` object. This object contains the set of properties to use if values are not explicitly set elsewhere. Then the load method reads the default values from a file on disk named `defaultProperties`.

Next, the application uses a different constructor to create a second `Properties` object, `applicationProps`, whose default values are contained in `defaultProps`. The defaults come into play when a property is being retrieved. If the property can't be found in `applicationProps`, then its default list is searched.

Finally, the code loads a set of properties into `applicationProps` from a file named `appProperties`. The properties in this file are those that were saved from the application the last time it was invoked, as explained in the next section.

Saving Properties

The following example writes out the application properties from the previous example using `Properties.store`. The default properties don't need to be saved each time because they never change:

```
FileOutputStream out = new FileOutputStream("appProperties");
applicationProps.store(out, "---No Comment---");
out.close();
```

The store method needs a stream to write to, as well as a string that it uses as a comment at the top of the output.

Getting Property Information

Once the application has set up its Properties object, the application can query the object for information about various keys and values that it contains. An application gets information from a Properties object after start-up so that it can initialize itself based on choices made by the user. The Properties class has several methods for getting property information:

- contains(Object value) and containsKey(Object key)—These return true if the value or the key is in the Properties object. Properties inherits these methods from Hashtable. Thus they accept Object arguments, but only String values should be used.

- getProperty(String key) and getProperty(String key, String default)—These return the value for the specified property. The second version provides for a default value. If the key is not found, the default is returned.

- list(PrintStream s) and list(PrintWriter w)—These write all the properties to the specified stream or writer and are useful for debugging.

- elements(), keys(), and propertyNames()—These return an Enumeration containing the keys or values (as indicated by the method names) contained in the Properties object. The keys method only returns the keys for the object itself; the propertyNames method returns the keys for default properties as well.

- stringPropertyNames()—These are like propertyNames, but they return a Set<String> and only return names of properties where both key and value are strings. Note that the Set object is not backed by the Properties object, so changes in one do not affect the other.

- size()—This returns the current number of key/value pairs.

Setting Properties

A user's interaction with an application during its execution may impact property settings. These changes should be reflected in the Properties object so that they

14

are saved when the application exits (and calls the `store` method). The following methods change the properties in a `Properties` object:

- `setProperty(String key, String value)`—Puts the key/value pair in the `Properties` object
- `remove(Object key)`—Removes the key/value pair associated with key

Note

Some of the methods described here are defined in `Hashtable` and thus accept key and value argument types other than `String`. Always use `Strings` for keys and values, even if the method allows other types. Also do not invoke `Hashtable.set` or `Hastable.setAll` on `Properties` objects; always use `Properties.setProperty`.

Command-Line Arguments

A Java application can accept any number of arguments from the command line. This allows the user to specify configuration information when the application is launched.

The user enters command-line arguments when invoking the application and specifies them after the name of the class to be run. For example, suppose a Java application called `Sort` sorts lines in a file. To sort the data in a file named `friends.txt`, a user would enter the following:

```
java Sort friends.txt
```

When an application is launched, the runtime system passes the command-line arguments to the application's main method via an array of `Strings`. In the previous example, the command-line arguments passed to the `Sort` application in an array that contains a single `String`: `friends.txt`.

Echoing Command-Line Arguments

The `Echo` example displays each of its command-line arguments on a line by itself:

```
public class Echo {
    public static void main (String[] args) {
        for (String s: args) {
            System.out.println(s);
        }
    }
}
```

The following example shows how a user might run `Echo`. User input is in italics:

```
java Echo Drink Hot Java
Drink
```

```
Hot
Java
```

Note that the application displays each word—Drink, Hot, and Java—on a line by itself. This is because the space character separates command-line arguments. To have Drink, Hot, and Java interpreted as a single argument, the user would join them by enclosing them within quotation marks.

```
java Echo "Drink Hot Java"
Drink Hot Java
```

Parsing Numeric Command-Line Arguments

If an application needs to support a numeric command-line argument, it must convert a String argument that represents a number (such as 34) to a numeric value. Here is a code snippet that converts a command-line argument to an int:

```
int firstArg;
if (args.length > 0) {
    try {
        firstArg = Integer.parseInt(args[0]);
    } catch (NumberFormatException e) {
        System.err.println("Argument" + " must be an integer");
        System.exit(1);
    }
}
```

parseInt throws a NumberFormatException if the format of args[0] isn't valid. The Number classes—Integer, Float, Double, and so on—have parseXXX methods that convert a String representing a number to an object of their type.

Environment Variables

Many operating systems use *environment variables* to pass configuration information to applications. Like properties in the Java platform, environment variables are key/value pairs, where both the key and value are strings. The conventions for setting and using environment variables vary between operating systems and also between command-line interpreters. To learn how to pass environment variables to applications on your system, refer to your system documentation.

Querying Environment Variables

On the Java platform, an application uses System.getenv[4] to retrieve environment variable values. Without an argument, getenv returns a read-only instance of java.util.Map, where the map keys are the environment variable names and

---

4. 7/docs/api/java/lang/System.html#getenv()

the map values are the environment variable values. This is demonstrated in the following example:

```
import java.util.Map;

public class EnvMap {
    public static void main (String[] args) {
        Map<String, String> env = System.getenv();
        for (String envName : env.keySet()) {
            System.out.format("%s=%s%n",
                              envName,
                              env.get(envName));
        }
    }
}
```

With a `String` argument, `getenv` returns the value of the specified variable. If the variable is not defined, `getenv` returns `null`. The `Env` example uses `getenv` this way to query specific environment variables, specified on the command line:

```
public class Env {
    public static void main (String[] args) {
        for (String env: args) {
            String value = System.getenv(env);
            if (value != null) {
                System.out.format("%s=%s%n",
                                  env, value);
            } else {
                System.out.format("%s is"
                    + " not assigned.%n", env);
            }
        }
    }
}
```

Passing Environment Variables to New Processes

When a Java application uses a `ProcessBuilder`[5] object to create a new process, the default set of environment variables passed to the new process is the same set provided to the application's virtual machine process. The application can change this set using `ProcessBuilder.environment`.

Platform Dependency Issues

Environment variables are implemented in different ways on different systems. For example, Windows ignores case in environment variable names, while UNIX does not. The way environment variables are used also varies. For example, Windows

5.   7/docs/api/java/lang/ProcessBuilder.html

provides the user name in an environment variable called USERNAME, while UNIX implementations might provide the user name in USER, LOGNAME, or both.

To maximize portability, never refer to an environment variable when the same value is available in a system property. For example, if the operating system provides a user name, it will always be available in the system property user.name.

Other Configuration Utilities

Here is a summary of some other configuration utilities.

The *preferences API* allows applications to store and retrieve configuration data in an implementation-dependent backing store. Asynchronous updates are supported, and the same set of preferences can be safely updated by multiple threads and even multiple applications. For more information, refer to the Preferences API Guide.[6]

An application deployed in a *JAR archive* uses a *manifest* to describe the contents of the archive. For more information, see Chapter 15.

The configuration of a *Java Web Start application* is contained in a *JNLP file*. For more information, see Chapter 16.

The configuration of a *Java Plug-In applet* is partially determined by the HTML tags used to embed the applet in the web page. Depending on the applet and the browser, these tags can include <applet>, <object>, <embed>, and <param>. For more information, see Chapter 17

The class java.util.ServiceLoader[7] provides a simple *service provider* facility. A service provider is an implementation of a *service*—a well-known set of interfaces and (usually abstract) classes. The classes in a service provider typically implement the interfaces and subclass the classes defined in the service. Service providers can be installed as extensions. Providers can also be made available by adding them to the class path or by some other platform-specific means.

14

System Utilities

The System[8] class implements a number of system utilities. Some of these have already been covered in the previous section. This section covers some of the other system utilities.

---

6. 7/docs/technotes/guides/preferences/index.html

7. 7/docs/api/java/util/ServiceLoader.html

8. 7/docs/api/java/lang/System.html

Command-Line I/O Objects

`System` provides several predefined I/O objects that are useful in Java applications intended for launch from the command line. These implement the standard I/O streams provided by most operating systems and also a console object that is useful for entering passwords. For more information, refer to Chapter 10, "I/O from the Command Line."

System Properties

In the "Properties" section, we examined the way an application can use `Properties` objects to maintain its configuration. The Java platform itself uses a `Properties` object to maintain its own configuration. The `System` class maintains a `Properties` object that describes the configuration of the current working environment. System properties include information about the current user, the current version of the Java runtime, and the character used to separate components of a file path name. Table 14.1 describes some of the most important system properties.

Table 14.1 System Properties

Key	Meaning
`file.separator`	This is the character that separates components of a file path. This is a forward slash (/) on UNIX and a backslash (\) on Windows.
`java.class.path`	This is the path used to find directories and JAR archives containing class files. Elements of the `class` path are separated by platform-specific characters specified in the `path.separator` property.
`java.home`	This is the installation directory for Java Runtime Environment (JRE).
`java.vendor`	This is the JRE vendor name.
`java.vendor.url`	This is the JRE vendor URL.
`java.version`	This is the JRE version number.
`line.separator`	This is the sequence used by operating systems to separate lines in text files.
`os.arch`	This is the operating system architecture.
`os.name`	This is the operating system name.
`os.version`	This is the operating system version.
`path.separator`	This is the path separator character used in `java.class.path`.
`user.dir`	This is the user working directory.
`user.home`	This is the user home directory.
`user.name`	This is the user account name.

> **Note**
>
> Access to system properties can be restricted by the security manager. This is most often an issue in applets, which are prevented from reading some system properties writing *any* system properties. For more on accessing system properties in applets, refer to Chapter 18, "System Properties."

Reading System Properties

The System class has two methods used to read system properties: getProperty and getProperties. There are two different versions of getProperty. Both retrieve the value of the property named in the argument list. The simpler of the two getProperty methods takes a single argument—a property key. For example, to get the value of path.separator, use the following statement:

```
System.getProperty("path.separator");
```

The getProperty method returns a string containing the value of the property. If the property does not exist, this version of getProperty returns null.

The other version of getProperty requires two String arguments: the first argument is the key to look up and the second argument is a default value to return if the key cannot be found or if it has no value. For example, the following invocation of getProperty looks up the System property called subliminal. message. This is not a valid system property, so instead of returning null, this method returns the default value provided as a second argument: Buy StayPuft Marshmallows!

```
System.getProperty("subliminal.message", "Buy StayPuft Marshmallows!");
```

The last method provided by the System class to access property values is the getProperties method, which returns a Properties[9] object. This object contains a complete set of system property definitions.

Writing System Properties

To modify the existing set of system properties, use System.setProperties. This method takes a Properties object that has been initialized to contain the properties to be set. This method replaces the entire set of system properties with the new set represented by the Properties object.

---

9.   `7/docs/api/java/util/Properties.html`

The next example, `PropertiesTest`, creates a `Properties` object and initializes it from `myProperties.txt`:

```
subliminal.message=Buy StayPuft Marshmallows!
```

`PropertiesTest` then uses `System.setProperties` to install the new `Properties` objects as the current set of system properties:

```java
import java.io.FileInputStream;
import java.util.Properties;

public class PropertiesTest {
    public static void main(String[] args)
        throws Exception {

        // set up new properties object
        // from file "myProperties.txt"
        FileInputStream propFile =
            new FileInputStream( "myProperties.txt");
        Properties p =
            new Properties(System.getProperties());
        p.load(propFile);

        // set the system properties
        System.setProperties(p);
        // display new properties
        System.getProperties().list(System.out);
    }
}
```

Note how `PropertiesTest` creates the `Properties` object, p, which is used as the argument to `setProperties`:

```java
Properties p = new Properties(System.getProperties());
```

This statement initializes the new properties object p with the current set of system properties, which in the case of this small application is the set of properties initialized by the runtime system. Then the application loads additional properties into p from the file `myProperties.txt` and sets the system properties to p. This has the effect of adding the properties listed in `myProperties.txt` to the set of properties created by the runtime system at start-up. Note that an application can create p without any default Properties object, like this:

```
Properties p = new Properties();
```

Also note that the value of system properties can be overwritten! For example, if myProperties.txt contains the following line, the java.vendor system property will be overwritten:

```
java.vendor=Acme Software Company
```

In general, be careful not to overwrite system properties.

The setProperties method changes the set of system properties for the current running application. These changes are not persistent—that is, changing the system properties within an application will not affect future invocations of the Java interpreter for this or any other application. The runtime system reinitializes the system properties each time it starts up. If changes to system properties are to be persistent, then the application must write the values to some file before exiting and read them in again during start-up.

The Security Manager

A *security manager* is an object that defines a security policy for an application. This policy specifies actions that are unsafe or sensitive. Any actions not allowed by the security policy cause a SecurityException[10] to be thrown. An application can also query its security manager to discover which actions are allowed.

Typically, a web applet runs with a security manager provided by the browser or Java Web Start plugin. Other kinds of applications normally run without a security manager, unless the application itself defines one. If no security manager is present, the application has no security policy and acts without restrictions.

This section explains how an application interacts with an existing security manager. For more detailed information, including information on how to design a security manager, refer to the Security Guide.[11]

Interacting with the Security Manager

The security manager is an object of type SecurityManager.[12] To obtain a reference to this object, invoke System.getSecurityManager:

---

10. 7/docs/api/java/lang/SecurityException.html

11. 7/docs/technotes/guides/security/index.html

12. 7/docs/api/java/lang/SecurityManager.html

```
SecurityManager appsm = System.getSecurityManager();
```

If there is no security manager, this method returns `null`.

Once an application has a reference to the security manager object, it can request permission to do specific things. Many classes in the standard libraries do this. For example, `System.exit`, which terminates the Java VM with an exit status, invokes `SecurityManager.checkExit` to ensure that the current thread has permission to shut down the application.

The `SecurityManager` class defines many other methods used to verify other kinds of operations. For example, `SecurityManager.checkAccess` verifies thread accesses, and `SecurityManager.checkPropertyAccess` verifies access to the specified property. Each operation or group of operations has its own `checkXXX()` method.

In addition, the set of `checkXXX()` methods represents the set of operations that are already subject to the protection of the security manager. Typically, an application does not have to directly invoke any `checkXXX()` methods.

Recognizing a Security Violation

Many actions that are routine without a security manager can throw a `Security-Exception` when run with a security manager. This is true even when invoking a method that isn't documented as throwing `SecurityException`. For example, consider the following code used to read a file:

```
reader = new FileReader("xanadu.txt");
```

In the absence of a security manager, this statement executes without error, provided `xanadu.txt` exists and is readable. But suppose this statement is inserted in a web applet, which typically runs under a security manager that does not allow file input. The following error messages might result:

```
appletviewer fileApplet.html
Exception in thread "AWT-EventQueue-1" java.security.
AccessControlException: access denied (java.io.FilePermission
characteroutput.txt write)
        at java.security.AccessControlContext.checkPermission(AccessControl
            Context.java:323)
        at java.security.AccessController.checkPermission(AccessController.
            java:546)
        at java.lang.SecurityManager.checkPermission(SecurityManager.
            java:532)
        at java.lang.SecurityManager.checkWrite(SecurityManager.java:962)
        at java.io.FileOutputStream.<init>(FileOutputStream.java:169)
        at java.io.FileOutputStream.<init>(FileOutputStream.java:70)
        at java.io.FileWriter.<init>(FileWriter.java:46)
    . . .
```

Note that the specific exception thrown in this case, java.security. AccessControlException,[13] is a subclass of SecurityException.

Miscellaneous Methods in System

This section describes some of the methods in System that aren't covered in the previous sections.

The arrayCopy method efficiently copies data between arrays. For more information, refer to Chapter 3, "Arrays."

The currentTimeMillis[14] and nanoTime[15] methods are useful for measuring time intervals during the execution of an application. To measure a time interval in milliseconds, invoke currentTimeMillis twice, at the beginning and end of the interval, and subtract the first value returned from the second. Similarly, invoking nanoTime twice measures an interval in nanoseconds.

> **Note**
>
> The accuracy of both currentTimeMillis and nanoTime is limited by the time services provided by the operating system. Do not assume that currentTimeMillis is accurate to the nearest millisecond or that nanoTime is accurate to the nearest nanosecond. Also, neither currentTimeMillis nor nanoTime should be used to determine the current time. Use a high-level method, such as java.util.Calendar.getInstance.[16]

The exit[17] method causes the Java VM to shut down, with an integer exit status specified by the argument. The exit status is available to the process that launched the application. By convention, an exit status of zero indicates normal termination of the application, while any other value is an error code.

14

PATH and CLASSPATH

This section explains how to use the PATH and CLASSPATH environment variables on Microsoft Windows, Solaris, and Linux. Consult the installation instructions included with your installation of the JDK software bundle for current information. After installing the software, the JDK directory will have the structure shown in Figure 14.2. The bin directory contains both the compiler and the launcher.

---

13. 7/docs/api/java/security/AccessControlException.html

14. 7/docs/api/java/lang/System.html#currentTimeMillis()

15. 7/docs/api/java/lang/System.html#nanoTime()

16. 7/docs/api/java/util/Calendar.html#getInstance()

17. 7/docs/api/java/lang/System.html#exit(int)

jdk1.version.0

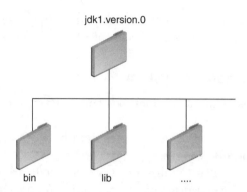

bin   lib   ....

Figure 14.2 Directory Structure after Installation of the JDK

Update the PATH Environment Variable (Microsoft Windows)

You can run Java applications just fine without setting the PATH environment variable, or you can optionally set it for convenience. Set the PATH environment variable if you want to be able to conveniently run the executables (javac.exe, java.exe, javadoc.exe, and so on) from any directory without having to type the full path of the command. If you do not set the PATH variable, you need to specify the full path to the executable every time you run it:

```
C:\Java\jdk1.7.0\bin\javac MyClass.java
```

The PATH environment variable is a series of directories separated by semicolons (;). Microsoft Windows looks for programs in the PATH directories in order, from left to right. You should have only one bin directory for the JDK in the path at a time (as those following the first are ignored), so if one is already present, you can update that particular entry.

The following is an example of a PATH environment variable:

```
C:\Java\jdk1.7.0\bin;C:\Windows\System32\;C:\Windows\;C:\Windows\System32\Wbem
```

It is useful to set the PATH environment variable permanently so it will persist after rebooting. To make a permanent change to the PATH variable, click the System icon in the Control Panel. The precise procedure varies depending on the version of Windows:

Windows XP

1. Select **Start**, select **Control Panel**. Double click **System**, and select the **Advanced** tab.
2. Click **Environment Variables**. In the section System Variables, find the PATH environment variable and select it. Click **Edit**. If the PATH environment variable does not exist, click **New**.

3. In the Edit System Variable (or New System Variable) window, specify the value of the PATH environment variable. Click **OK**. Close all remaining windows by clicking **OK**.

Windows Vista

1. From the desktop, right click the **My Computer** icon.
2. Choose **Properties** from the context menu.
3. Click the **Advanced** tab (**Advanced system settings** link in Vista).
4. Click **Environment Variables**. In the section System Variables, find the PATH environment variable and select it. Click **Edit**. If the PATH environment variable does not exist, click **New**.
5. In the Edit System Variable (or New System Variable) window, specify the value of the PATH environment variable. Click **OK**. Close all remaining windows by clicking **OK**.

Windows 7

1. On the desktop, right click the **Computer** icon.
2. Choose **Properties** from the context menu.
3. Click the **Advanced system settings** link.
4. Click **Environment Variables**. In the section System Variables, find the PATH environment variable and select it. Click **Edit**. If the PATH environment variable does not exist, click **New**.
5. In the Edit System Variable (or New System Variable) window, specify the value of the PATH environment variable. Click **OK**. Close all remaining windows by clicking **OK**.

14

Note

You may see a PATH environment variable similar to the following when editing it from the Control Panel:

```
%JAVA_HOME%\bin;%SystemRoot%\system32;%SystemRoot%;%SystemRoot%\
    System32\Wbem
```

Variables enclosed in percentage signs (%) are existing environment variables. If one of these variables is listed in the Environment Variables window from the Control Panel (such as JAVA_HOME), then you can edit its value. If it does not appear, then it is a special environment variable that the operating system has defined. For example, SystemRoot is the location of the Microsoft Windows system folder. To obtain the value of a environment variable, enter the following at a command prompt. This example obtains the value of the SystemRoot environment variable:

```
echo %SystemRoot%
```

Update the PATH Variable (Solaris and Linux)

Just as in Windows, you can run the JDK just fine without setting the PATH variable, or you can optionally set it for convenience. However, you should set the path variable if you want to be able to run the executables (javac, java, javadoc, and so on) from any directory without having to type the full path of the command. If you do not set the PATH variable, you need to specify the full path to the executable every time you run it:

```
% /usr/local/jdk1.7.0/bin/javac MyClass.java
```

To find out if the path is properly set, execute as follows:

```
% java -version
```

This will print the version of the java tool, if it can find it. If the version is old or you get the error java: Command not found, then the path is not properly set. To set the path permanently, set the path in your start-up file. For C shell (csh), edit the start-up file (~/.cshrc):

```
set path=(/usr/local/jdk1.7.0/bin )
```

For bash, edit the start-up file (~/.bashrc):

```
PATH=/usr/local/jdk1.7.0/bin:
export PATH
```

For ksh, the start-up file is named by the environment variable, ENV. Set the path as follows:

```
PATH=/usr/local/jdk1.7.0/bin:
export PATH
```

For sh, edit the profile file (~/.profile):

```
PATH=/usr/local/jdk1.7.0/bin:
export PATH
```

Then load the start-up file and verify that the path is set by repeating the java command. Enter the following for C shell (csh):

```
% source ~/.cshrc
% java -version
```

Enter the following for ksh, bash, or sh:

```
% . /.profile
% java -version
```

Checking the CLASSPATH Variable (All Platforms)

The CLASSPATH variable is one way to tell applications, including the JDK tools, where to look for user classes. (Classes that are part of the JRE, JDK platform, and extensions should be defined through other means, such as the bootstrap class path or the extensions directory.)

The preferred way to specify the class path is by using the -cp command-line switch. This allows the CLASSPATH to be set individually for each application without affecting other applications. Setting the CLASSPATH can be tricky and should be performed with care.

The default value of the class path is the dot operator (.), meaning that only the current directory is searched. Specifying either the CLASSPATH variable or the -cp command-line switch overrides this value.

To check whether CLASSPATH is set on Microsoft Windows, execute the following:

```
C:> echo %CLASSPATH%
```

On Solaris or Linux, execute the following:

```
% echo $CLASSPATH
```

14

If CLASSPATH is not set, you will get a CLASSPATH: Undefined variable error (Solaris or Linux) or simply %CLASSPATH% (Microsoft Windows). To modify the CLASSPATH, use the same procedure you used for the PATH variable.

Class path wildcards allow you to include an entire directory of JAR files in the class path without explicitly naming them individually. For more information, including an explanation of class path wildcards and a detailed description on how to clean up the CLASSPATH environment variable, see the Setting the Class Path[18] technical note.

---

18. 7/docs/technotes/tools/windows/classpath.html

Questions and Exercises: The Platform Environment

Question

1. A programmer installs a new library contained in a JAR file. In order to access the library from his code, he sets the CLASSPATH environment variable to point to the new JAR file. Now he finds that he gets an error message when he tries to launch simple applications:

   ```
   java Hello
   Exception in thread "main" java.lang.NoClassDefFoundError: Hello
   ```

   In this case, the Hello class is compiled into a .class file in the current directory—yet the java command can't seem to find it. What's going wrong?

Exercise

1. Write an application, PersistentEcho, with the following features:

   - If PersistentEcho is run with command-line arguments, it prints out those arguments. It also saves the string printed out to a property and saves the property to a file called PersistentEcho.txt.

   - If PersistentEcho is run with no command-line arguments, it looks for an environment variable called PERSISTENTECHO. If that variable exists, PersistentEcho prints out its value and also saves the value in the same way it does for command-line arguments.

   - If PersistentEcho is run with no command line arguments, and the PERSISTENTECHO environment variable is not defined, it retrieves the property value from PersistentEcho.txt and prints that out.

Answers

You can find answers to these questions and exercises at http://docs.oracle.com/javase/tutorial/essential/environment/QandE/answers.html.

Packaging Programs in JAR Files

Chapter Contents

The Java Archive (JAR) file format enables you to bundle multiple files into a single archive file. Typically a JAR file contains the class files and auxiliary resources associated with applets and applications.

The JAR file format provides many benefits:

- *Security*. You can digitally sign the contents of a JAR file. Users who recognize your signature can then optionally grant your software security privileges it wouldn't otherwise have.

- *Decreased download time*. If your applet is bundled in a JAR file, the applet's class files and associated resources can be downloaded to a browser in a single HTTP transaction without the need for opening a new connection for each file.

- *Compression*. The JAR format allows you to compress your files for efficient storage.

- *Packaging for extensions*. The extensions framework provides a means by which you can add functionality to the Java core platform, and the JAR file format defines the packaging for extensions. By using the JAR file format, you can turn your software into extensions as well.

- *Package sealing.* Packages stored in JAR files can be optionally sealed so that the package can enforce version consistency. Sealing a package within a JAR file means that all classes defined in that package must be found in the same JAR file.
- *Package versioning.* A JAR file can hold data about the files it contains, such as vendor and version information.
- *Portability.* The mechanism for handling JAR files is a standard part of the Java platform's core API.

This chapter has four sections: The first section shows you how to perform basic JAR file operations and how to run software that is bundled in JAR files. The second section explains manifest files and how to customize them so you can do such things as seal packages and set an application's entry point. The third section shows you how to digitally sign JAR files and verify the signatures of signed JAR files. The fourth section explains JAR-related APIs. The chapter ends with questions and exercises to test what you've learned about JAR files.

Using JAR Files: The Basics

JAR files are packaged with the ZIP file format, so you can use them for tasks such as lossless data compression, archiving, decompression, and archive unpacking. These tasks are among the most common uses of JAR files, and you can realize many JAR file benefits using only these basic features.

Even if you want to take advantage of advanced functionality provided by the JAR file format, such as electronic signing, you'll first need to become familiar with the fundamental operations.

To perform basic tasks with JAR files, you use the Java archive tool provided as part of the Java SE Development Kit (JDK). Because the Java archive tool is invoked by using the `jar` command, this book refers to it as *the JAR tool*. As a synopsis and preview of some of the topics to be covered in this section, Table 15.1 summarizes common JAR file operations.

This section shows you how to perform the most common JAR file operations, with examples for each of the basic features.

Creating a JAR File

The basic format of the command for creating a JAR file is as follows:

```
jar cf jar-file input-file(s)
```

Table 15.1 Common JAR File Operations

Operation	Command
Create a JAR file	`jar cf jar-file input-file(s)`
View the contents of a JAR file	`jar tf jar-file`
Extract the contents of a JAR file	`jar xf jar-file`
Extract specific files from a JAR file	`jar xf jar-file archived-file(s)`
Run an application packaged as a JAR file (which requires the `Main-Class` manifest header)	`java -jar app.jar`

Invoke an applet packaged as a JAR file	`<applet code=AppletClassName.class`
	`        archive="JarFileName.jar"`
	`        width=width height=height>`
	`</applet>`

Here are the options and arguments used in this command:

- The c option indicates that you want to *create* a JAR file.
- The f option indicates that you want the output to go to a *file* rather than standard output (`stdout`).
- `jar-file` is the name that you want the resulting JAR file to have. You can use any file name for a JAR file. By convention, JAR file names are given a `.jar` extension, though this is not required.
- The `input-file(s)` argument is a space-separated list of one or more files that you want to include in your JAR file. The `input-file(s)` argument can contain the wildcard * symbol. If any of the input files are directories, the contents of those directories are added to the JAR archive recursively.

The c and f options can appear in either order, but there must not be any space between them. This command will generate a compressed JAR file and place it in the current directory. The command will also generate a default manifest file for the JAR archive.

> **Note**
>
> The metadata in the JAR file, such as the entry names, comments, and contents of the manifest, must be encoded in UTF-8.

You can also add any of the options listed in Table 15.2 to the cf options of the basic command.

15

Table 15.2 jar Command Options

Option	Description
v	This produces *verbose* output on stdout while the JAR file is being built. The verbose output tells you the name of each file as it's added to the JAR file.
0 (zero)	This indicates that you don't want the JAR file to be compressed.
M	This indicates that the default manifest file should not be produced.
m	This is used to include manifest information from an existing manifest file. The format for using this option is jar cmf existing-manifest jar-file input-file(s). See the "Modifying a Manifest File" section in this chapter for more information about his option. Note that the manifest must end with a new line or carriage return. The last line will not be parsed properly if it does not end with a new line or carriage return.
-C	This changes directories during execution of the command. See the following section for an example.

> **Note**
>
> When you create a JAR file, the time of creation is stored in the JAR file. Therefore, even if the contents of the JAR file do not change, when you create a JAR file multiple times, the resulting files are not exactly identical. You should be aware of this when you are using JAR files in a build environment. It is recommended that you use versioning information in the manifest file, rather than creation time, to control versions of a JAR file. See the "Setting Package Version Information" section in this chapter.

An Example

Let's look at an example: a simple TicTacToe applet. You can see the source code of this applet at TicTacToe.java when you download the JDK Demos and Samples bundle from oracle.com.[1] This demo contains a class file, audio files, and images (Figure 15.1).

The audio and images subdirectories contain sound files and GIF images used by the applet. To package this demo into a single JAR file named TicTacToe.jar, you would run this command from inside the TicTacToe directory:

```
jar cvf TicTacToe.jar TicTacToe.class audio images
```

The audio and images arguments represent directories, so the JAR tool will recursively place them and their contents in the JAR file. The generated JAR file TicTacToe.jar will be placed in the current directory. Because the command used

---

1.   http://www.oracle.com/technetwork/java/javase/downloads/index.html

Figure 15.1 TicTacToe Folder Hierarchy

the v option for verbose output, you would see something similar to this output when you run the command:

```
adding: TicTacToe.class (in=3825) (out=2222) (deflated 41%)
adding: audio/ (in=0) (out=0) (stored 0%)
adding: audio/beep.au (in=4032) (out=3572) (deflated 11%)
adding: audio/ding.au (in=2566) (out=2055) (deflated 19%)
adding: audio/return.au (in=6558) (out=4401) (deflated 32%)
adding: audio/yahoo1.au (in=7834) (out=6985) (deflated 10%)
adding: audio/yahoo2.au (in=7463) (out=4607) (deflated 38%)
adding: images/ (in=0) (out=0) (stored 0%)
adding: images/cross.gif (in=157) (out=160) (deflated -1%)
adding: images/not.gif (in=158) (out=161) (deflated -1%)
```

You can see from this output that the JAR file `TicTacToe.jar` is compressed. The JAR tool compresses files by default. You can turn off the compression feature by using the 0 (zero) option, producing the following result:

```
jar cvf0 TicTacToe.jar TicTacToe.class audio images
```

You might want to avoid compression in some instances (e.g., to increase the speed of loading JAR files in a browser). Uncompressed JAR files can generally be loaded more quickly than compressed files because the need to decompress the files during loading is eliminated. However, there is a trade-off in that download time over a network may be longer for larger, uncompressed files.

The JAR tool will accept arguments that use the wildcard * symbol. As long as there weren't any unwanted files in the `TicTacToe` directory, you could have used this alternative command to construct the JAR file:

```
jar cvf TicTacToe.jar *
```

Though the verbose output doesn't indicate it, the JAR tool automatically adds a manifest file to the JAR archive with path name `META-INF/MANIFEST.MF`. The section "Working with Manifest Files: The Basics" later in this chapter provides more information about manifest files.

15

In the previous example, the files in the archive retain their relative path names and directory structure. The JAR tool provides the -C option that you can use to create a JAR file in which the relative paths of the archived files are not preserved. It's modeled after TAR's -C option.

As an example, suppose you wanted to put the audio files and GIF images used by the TicTacToe demo into a JAR file and wanted all the files to be on the top level, with no directory hierarchy. You could accomplish this by issuing this command from the parent directory of the images and audio directories:

```
jar cf ImageAudio.jar -C images . -C audio .
```

The -C images part of this command directs the JAR tool to go to the images directory, and the dot (.) following -C images directs the JAR tool to archive all the contents of that directory. The -C audio . part of the command then does the same with the audio directory. The resulting JAR file would have this table of contents:

```
META-INF/MANIFEST.MF
cross.gif
not.gif
beep.au
ding.au
return.au
yahoo1.au
yahoo2.au
```

By contrast, suppose that you used a command that did not employ the -C option:

```
jar cf ImageAudio.jar images audio
```

15

The resulting JAR file would have this table of contents:

```
META-INF/MANIFEST.MF
images/cross.gif
images/not.gif
audio/beep.au
audio/ding.au
audio/return.au
audio/yahoo1.au
audio/yahoo2.au
```

Viewing the Contents of a JAR File

The basic format of the command for viewing the contents of a JAR file is the following:

```
jar tf jar-file
```

Let's look at the options and argument used in this command:

- The t option indicates that you want to view the *table* of contents of the JAR file.
- The f option indicates that the JAR file whose contents are to be viewed is specified on the command line.
- The jar-file argument is the path and name of the JAR file whose contents you want to view.

The t and f options can appear in either order, but there must not be any space between them. This command will display the JAR file's table of contents to stdout. You can optionally add the verbose option, v, to produce additional information about file sizes and last-modified dates in the output.

An Example

Let's use the JAR tool to list the contents of the TicTacToe.jar file we created in the previous section:

```
jar tf TicTacToe.jar
```

This command displays the contents of the JAR file to stdout:

```
META-INF/MANIFEST.MF
TicTacToe$1.class
TicTacToe.class
audio/
audio/beep.au
audio/ding.au
audio/return.au
audio/yahoo1.au
audio/yahoo2.au
example1.html
images/
images/cross.gif
images/not.gif
```

The JAR file contains the TicTacToe class file and the audio and images directory, as expected. The output also shows that the JAR file contains a default manifest file, META-INF/MANIFEST.MF, which was automatically placed in the archive by the JAR tool. For more information, see the "Understanding the Default Manifest" section.

15

All path names are displayed with forward slashes, regardless of the platform or operating system you're using. Paths in JAR files are always relative; you'll never see a path beginning with C:, for example.

The JAR tool will display additional information if you use the v option:

```
jar tvf TicTacToe.jar
```

For example, the verbose output for the TicTacToe JAR file would look similar to this:

```
   0 Thu Nov 01 20:00:40 PDT 2012 META-INF/
  68 Thu Nov 01 20:00:40 PDT 2012 META-INF/MANIFEST.MF
 553 Mon Sep 24 21:57:48 PDT 2012 TicTacToe$1.class
3708 Mon Sep 24 21:57:48 PDT 2012 TicTacToe.class
9584 Mon Sep 24 21:57:48 PDT 2012 TicTacToe.java
   0 Mon Sep 24 21:57:48 PDT 2012 audio/
4032 Mon Sep 24 21:57:48 PDT 2012 audio/beep.au
2566 Mon Sep 24 21:57:48 PDT 2012 audio/ding.au
6558 Mon Sep 24 21:57:48 PDT 2012 audio/return.au
7834 Mon Sep 24 21:57:48 PDT 2012 audio/yahoo1.au
7463 Mon Sep 24 21:57:48 PDT 2012 audio/yahoo2.au
 424 Mon Sep 24 21:57:48 PDT 2012 example1.html
   0 Mon Sep 24 21:57:48 PDT 2012 images/
 157 Mon Sep 24 21:57:48 PDT 2012 images/cross.gif
 158 Mon Sep 24 21:57:48 PDT 2012 images/not.gif
```

Extracting the Contents of a JAR File

The basic command to use for extracting the contents of a JAR file is the following:

```
jar xf jar-file [archived-file(s)]
```

Let's look at the options and arguments in this command:

- The x option indicates that you want to *extract* files from the JAR archive.
- The f options indicates that the JAR *file* from which files are to be extracted is specified on the command line rather than through standard input (stdin).
- The jar-file argument is the file name (or path and file name) of the JAR file from which to extract files.
- archived-file(s) is an optional argument consisting of a space-separated list of the files to be extracted from the archive. If this argument is not present, the JAR tool will extract all the files in the archive.

As usual, the order in which the x and f options appear in the command doesn't matter, but there must not be a space between them.

When extracting files, the JAR tool makes copies of the desired files and writes them to the current directory, reproducing the directory structure that the files have in the archive. The original JAR file remains unchanged.

> **Note**
>
> When it extracts files, the JAR tool will overwrite any existing files having the same path name as the extracted files.

An Example

Let's extract some files from the `TicTacToe` JAR file from previous sections. Here are the contents of `TicTacToe.jar`:

```
META-INF/MANIFEST.MF

TicTacToe$1.class
TicTacToe.class
audio/
audio/beep.au
audio/ding.au
audio/return.au
audio/yahoo1.au
audio/yahoo2.au
example1.html
images/
images/cross.gif
images/not.gif
```

Suppose you want to extract the `TicTacToe` class file and the `cross.gif` image file. To do so, you can use this command:

```
jar xf TicTacToe.jar TicTacToe.class images/cross.gif
```

This command does two things:

- It places a copy of `TicTacToe.class` in the current directory.
- It creates the directory `images`, if it doesn't already exist, and places a copy of `cross.gif` within it.

The original `TicTacToe` JAR file remains unchanged.

As many files as desired can be extracted from the JAR file in the same way. When the command doesn't specify which files to extract, the JAR tool extracts all files in the archive. For example, you can extract all the files in the `TicTacToe` archive by using this command:

```
jar xf TicTacToe.jar
```

Updating a JAR File

The JAR tool provides a u option, which you can use to update the contents of an existing JAR file by modifying its manifest or by adding files.

The basic command for adding files has this format:

```
jar uf jar-file input-file(s)
```

Here are the options and arguments in this command:

- The u option indicates that you want to *update* an existing JAR file.
- The f option indicates that the JAR file to update is specified on the command line.
- jar-file is the existing JAR file that's to be updated.
- input-file(s) is a space-delimited list of one or more files that you want to add to the JAR file.

Any files already in the archive that have the same path name as a file being added will be overwritten. When creating a new JAR file, you can optionally use the -C option to indicate a change of directory. For more information, see the "Creating a JAR File" section in this chapter.

Examples

Recall that TicTacToe.jar has these contents:

```
META-INF/MANIFEST.MF

TicTacToe$1.class
TicTacToe.class
audio/
audio/beep.au
audio/ding.au
audio/return.au
audio/yahoo1.au
audio/yahoo2.au
example1.html
images/
images/cross.gif
images/not.gif
```

Suppose that you want to add the file `images/new.gif` to the JAR file. You could accomplish this by issuing the following command from the parent directory of the `images` directory:

```
jar uf TicTacToe.jar images/new.gif
```

The revised JAR file would have this table of contents:

```
META-INF/MANIFEST.MF

TicTacToe$1.class
TicTacToe.class
audio/
audio/beep.au
audio/ding.au
audio/return.au
audio/yahoo1.au
audio/yahoo2.au
example1.html
images/
images/cross.gif
images/not.gif
images/new.gif
```

You can use the −C option to "change directories" during execution of the command. Here is an example:

```
jar uf TicTacToe.jar -C images new.gif
```

This command would change to the `images` directory before adding `new.gif` to the JAR file. The `images` directory would not be included in the path name of `new.gif` when it's added to the archive, resulting in a table of contents that looks like this:

```
META-INF/MANIFEST.MF

TicTacToe$1.class
TicTacToe.class
audio/
audio/beep.au
audio/ding.au
audio/return.au
audio/yahoo1.au
audio/yahoo2.au
example1.html
images/
images/cross.gif
images/not.gif
new.gif
```

15

Running JAR Packaged Software

Now that you've learned how to create JAR files, how do you actually run the code that you've packaged? Consider these three scenarios:

- Your JAR file contains an applet that is to be run inside a browser.
- Your JAR file contains an application that is to be invoked from the command line.
- Your JAR file contains code that you want to use as an extension.

Applets Packaged in JAR Files

To invoke any applet from an HTML file for running inside a browser, you can use the `applet` tag. For more information about other ways to deploy applets, see Chapter 17. If the applet is bundled as a JAR file, the only thing you need to do differently is use the `archive` parameter to specify the relative path to the JAR file.

As an example, let's revisit the `TicTacToe` demo applet. The `applet` tag in the HTML file that displays the applet can be marked up like this:

```
<applet code=TicTacToe.class
        width="120" height="120">
</applet>
```

If the `TicTacToe` demo were packaged in a JAR file named `TicTacToe.jar`, you could modify the `applet` tag with the simple addition of an `archive` parameter:

```
<applet code=TicTacToe.class
        archive="TicTacToe.jar"
        width="120" height="120">
</applet>
```

The `archive` parameter specifies the relative path to the JAR file that contains `TicTacToe.class`. This example assumes that the JAR file and the HTML file are in the same directory. If they're not, you would need to include the JAR file's relative path in the `archive` parameter's value. For example, if the JAR file is one directory below the HTML file in a directory called `applets`, the `applet` tag would look like this:

```
<applet code=TicTacToe.class
        archive="applets/TicTacToe.jar"
        width="120" height="120">
</applet>
```

JAR Files as Applications

You can run JAR packaged applications with the Java launcher (java command). Here's the basic command:

```
java -jar jar-file
```

The -jar flag tells the launcher that the application is packaged in the JAR file format. You can only specify one JAR file, which must contain all the application-specific code.

Before you execute this command, make sure the runtime environment has information about which class within the JAR file is the application's entry point. To indicate which class is the application's entry point, you must add a Main-Class header to the JAR file's manifest. The header takes the following form:

```
Main-Class: classname
```

The header's value, classname, is the name of the class that is the application's entry point. For more information, see the "Setting an Application's Entry Point" section in this chapter.

When the Main-Class is set in the manifest file, you can run the application from the command line:

```
java -jar app.jar
```

To run the application from JAR file that is in other directory, we need to specify the path of that directory as follows, where path is the directory path at which this app.jar resides:

```
java -jar path/app.jar
```

15

Working with Manifest Files: The Basics

JAR files support a wide range of functionality, including electronic signing, version control, package sealing, and others. What gives a JAR file this versatility? The answer is the JAR file's *manifest*.

The manifest is a special file that can contain information about the files packaged in a JAR file. By tailoring this "metainformation" in the manifest, you enable the JAR file to serve a variety of purposes.

This section will explain the contents of the manifest file and show you how to work with it, with examples of the basic features.

Understanding the Default Manifest

When you create a JAR file, it automatically receives a default manifest file. There can be only one manifest file in an archive, and it always has the following path name:

```
META-INF/MANIFEST.MF
```

When you create a JAR file, the default manifest file simply contains the following:

```
Manifest-Version: 1.0
Created-By: 1.7.0_06 (Oracle Corporation)
```

These lines show that a manifest's entries take the form of "header: value" pairs. The name of a header is separated from its value by a colon. The default manifest conforms to version 1.0 of the manifest specification and was created by the 1.7.0_06 version of the JDK.

The manifest can also contain information about the other files that are packaged in the archive. Exactly what file information should be recorded in the manifest depends on how you intend to use the JAR file. The default manifest makes no assumptions about what information it should record about other files.

Digest information is not included in the default manifest. To learn more about digests and signing, see the "Signing and Verifying JAR Files" section in this chapter.

Modifying a Manifest File

You use the m command-line option to add custom information to the manifest during creation of a JAR file. This section describes the m option.

The JAR tool automatically puts a default manifest with the path name META-INF/MANIFEST.MF into any JAR file you create. You can enable special JAR file functionality, such as package sealing, by modifying the default manifest. Typically, modifying the default manifest involves adding special-purpose *headers* to the manifest that allow the JAR file to perform a particular desired function.

To modify the manifest, you must first prepare a text file containing the information you wish to add to the manifest. You then use the JAR tool's m option to add the information in your file to the manifest.

15

Note
The text file from which you are creating the manifest must end with a new line or carriage return. The last line will not be parsed properly if it does not end with a new line or carriage return.

The basic command has this format:

```
jar cfm jar-file manifest-addition input-file(s)
```

Let's look at the options and arguments used in this command:

- The c option indicates that you want to *create* a JAR file.
- The m option indicates that you want to merge information from an existing file with the manifest file of the JAR file you're creating.
- The f option indicates that you want the output to go to a *file* (the JAR file you're creating) rather than to stdout.
- *manifest-addition* is the name (or path and name) of the existing text file whose contents you want to add to the contents of JAR file's manifest.
- *jar-file* is the name that you want the resulting JAR file to have.
- The *input-file(s)* argument is a space-separated list of one or more files that you want to be placed in your JAR file.

The m and f options must be in the same order as the corresponding arguments.

Note
The contents of the manifest must be encoded in UTF-8.

The remaining sections of this chapter demonstrate specific modifications you may want to make to the manifest file.

Setting an Application's Entry Point

If you have an application bundled in a JAR file, you need some way to indicate which class within the JAR file is your application's entry point. You provide this information with the Main-Class header in the manifest, which has the general form:

```
Main-Class: classname
```

The value *classname* is the name of the class that is your application's entry point.

Recall that the entry point is a class having a method with signature public static void main(String[] args). After you set the Main-Class header in the manifest, run the JAR file using the following form of the java command:

```
java -jar JAR-name
```

The `main` method of the class specified in the `Main-Class` header is executed.

An Example

We want to execute the `main` method in the class `MyClass` in the package `MyPackage` when we run the JAR file. We first create a text file named `Manifest.txt` with the following contents:

```
Main-Class: MyPackage.MyClass
```

> **Note**
> The text file must end with a new line or carriage return. The last line will not be parsed properly if it does not end with a new line or carriage return.

We then create a JAR file named `MyJar.jar` by entering the following command:

```
jar cfm MyJar.jar Manifest.txt MyPackage/*.class
```

This creates the JAR file with a manifest with the following contents:

```
Manifest-Version: 1.0
Created-By: 1.7.0_06 (Oracle Corporation)
Main-Class: MyPackage.MyClass
```

When you run the JAR file with the following command, the `main` method of `MyClass` executes:

```
java -jar MyJar.jar
```

Setting an Entry Point with the JAR Tool

The e flag (for *entry point*) introduced in JDK 6 creates or overrides the manifest's `Main-Class` attribute. It can be used while creating or updating a JAR file. Use it to specify the application entry point without editing or creating the manifest file.

For example, this command creates `app.jar`, where the `Main-Class` attribute value in the manifest is set to `MyApp`:

```
jar cfe app.jar MyApp MyApp.class
```

You can directly invoke this application by running the following command:

```
java -jar app.jar
```

If the entry-point class name is in a package, it may use a dot character (.) as the delimiter. For example, if Main.class is in a package called foo, the entry point can be specified in the following way:

```
jar cfe Main.jar foo.Main foo/Main.class
```

Adding Classes to the JAR File's Class Path

You may need to reference classes in other JAR files from within a JAR file. For example, in a typical situation, an applet is bundled in a JAR file whose manifest references a different JAR file (or several different JAR files) that serve as utilities for the purposes of that applet.

You specify classes to include in the Class-Path header field in the manifest file of an applet or application. The Class-Path header takes the following form:

```
Class-Path: jar1-name jar2-name directory-name/jar3-name
```

By using the Class-Path header in the manifest, you can avoid having to specify a long –classpath flag when invoking Java to run the your application.

> **Note**
>
> The Class-Path header points to classes or JAR files on the local network, not JAR files within the JAR file or classes accessible over Internet protocols. To load classes in JAR files within a JAR file into the class path, you must write custom code to load those classes. For example, if MyJar.jar contains another JAR file called MyUtils.jar, you cannot use the Class-Path header in MyJar.jar's manifest to load classes in MyUtils.jar into the class path.

An Example

We want to load classes in MyUtils.jar into the class path for use in MyJar.jar. These two JAR files are in the same directory.

We first create a text file named Manifest.txt with the following contents:

```
Class-Path: MyUtils.jar
```

> **Note**
>
> The text file must end with a new line or carriage return. The last line will not be parsed properly if it does not end with a new line or carriage return.

15

We then create a JAR file named `MyJar.jar` by entering the following command:

```
jar cfm MyJar.jar Manifest.txt MyPackage/*.class
```

This creates the JAR file with a manifest with the following contents:

```
Manifest-Version: 1.0
Class-Path: MyUtils.jar
Created-By: 1.7.0_06 (Oracle Corporation)
```

The classes in `MyUtils.jar` are now loaded into the class path when you run `MyJar.jar`.

Setting Package Version Information

You may need to include package version information in a JAR file's manifest. You provide this information with the headers shown in Table 15.3.

One set of such headers can be assigned to each package. The versioning headers should appear directly beneath the `Name` header for the package. This example shows all the versioning headers:

```
Name: java/util/
Specification-Title: Java Utility Classes
Specification-Version: 1.2
Specification-Vendor: Example Tech, Inc.
Implementation-Title: java.util
Implementation-Version: build57
Implementation-Vendor: Example Tech, Inc.
```

For more information about package version headers, see the Package Versioning specification.[2]

An Example

We want to include the headers from the previous example in the manifest of `MyJar.jar`. We first create a text file named `Manifest.txt` with the following contents:

```
Name: java/util/
Specification-Title: Java Utility Classes
Specification-Version: 1.2
Specification-Vendor: Example Tech, Inc.
Implementation-Title: java.util
Implementation-Version: build57
Implementation-Vendor: Example Tech, Inc.
```

---

2.   7/docs/technotes/guides/versioning/spec/versioning2.html#wp89936

Table 15.3 Headers in a Manifest

Header	Definition
Name	The name of the specification
Specification-Title	The title of the specification
Specification-Version	The version of the specification
Specification-Vendor	The vendor of the specification
Implementation-Title	The title of the implementation
Implementation-Version	The build number of the implementation
Implementation-Vendor	The vendor of the implementation

Note

The text file must end with a new line or carriage return. The last line will not be parsed properly if it does not end with a new line or carriage return.

We then create a JAR file named `MyJar.jar` by entering the following command:

```
jar cfm MyJar.jar Manifest.txt MyPackage/*.class
```

This creates the JAR file with a manifest with the following contents:

```
Manifest-Version: 1.0
Created-By: 1.7.0_06 (Oracle Corporation)
Name: java/util/
Specification-Title: Java Utility Classes
Specification-Version: 1.2
Specification-Vendor: Example Tech, Inc.
Implementation-Title: java.util
Implementation-Version: build57
Implementation-Vendor: Example Tech, Inc.
```

15

Sealing Packages within a JAR File

Packages within JAR files can be optionally sealed, which means that all classes defined in that package must be archived in the same JAR file. For example, you might want to seal a package to ensure version consistency among the classes in your software.

You seal a package in a JAR file by adding the `Sealed` header in the manifest, which has the general form:

```
Name: myCompany/myPackage/
Sealed: true
```

The value `myCompany/myPackage/` is the name of the package to seal. Note that the package name must end with a slash (/).

An Example

We want to seal two packages, `firstPackage` and `secondPackage`, in the JAR file `MyJar.jar`. We first create a text file named `Manifest.txt` with the following contents:

```
Name: myCompany/firstPackage/
Sealed: true

Name: myCompany/secondPackage/
Sealed: true
```

> **Note**
>
> The text file must end with a new line or carriage return. The last line will not be parsed properly if it does not end with a new line or carriage return.

We then create a JAR file named `MyJar.jar` by entering the following command:

```
jar cmf MyJar.jar Manifest.txt MyPackage/*.class
```

This creates the JAR file with a manifest with the following contents:

```
Manifest-Version: 1.0
Created-By: 1.7.0_06 (Oracle Corporation)
Name: myCompany/firstPackage/
Sealed: true
Name: myCompany/secondPackage/
Sealed: true
```

Sealing JAR Files

If you want to guarantee that all classes in a package come from the same code source, use JAR sealing. A sealed JAR specifies that all packages defined by that JAR are sealed unless overridden on a per-package basis.

To seal a JAR file, use the `Sealed` manifest header with the value true. For example, `Sealed: true` specifies that all packages in this archive are sealed unless explicitly overridden for particular packages with the `Sealed` attribute in a manifest entry.

Signing and Verifying JAR Files

You can optionally sign a JAR file with your electronic "signature." Users who verify your signature can grant your JAR bundled software security privileges that it wouldn't ordinarily have. Conversely, you can verify the signatures of signed JAR files that you want to use. This section shows you how to use the tools provided in the JDK to sign and verify JAR files.

Understanding Signing and Verification

The Java platform enables you to digitally sign JAR files. You digitally sign a file for the same reason you might sign a paper document with pen and ink—to let readers know that you wrote the document or that the document has your approval.

When you sign a letter, for example, everyone who recognizes your signature can confirm that you wrote the letter. Similarly, when you digitally sign a file, anyone who "recognizes" your digital signature knows that the file came from you. The process of "recognizing" electronic signatures is called *verification*.

The ability to sign and verify files is an important part of the Java platform's security architecture. Security is controlled by the security *policy* that's in force at runtime. You can configure the policy to grant security privileges to applets and applications. For example, you could grant permission to an applet to perform normally forbidden operations such as reading and writing local files or running local executable programs. If you have downloaded some code that's signed by a trusted entity, you can use that fact as criteria for deciding which security permissions to assign to the code.

Once you (or your browser) have verified that an applet is from a trusted source, you can have the platform relax security restrictions to let the applet perform operations that would ordinarily be forbidden. A trusted applet can have freedoms, as specified by the *policy file*.

The Java platform enables signing and verification by using special numbers called public and private *keys*. Public keys and private keys come in pairs, and they play complementary roles.

The private key is the electronic "pen" with which you can sign a file. As its name implies, your private key is known only to you so that no one else can "forge" your signature. A file signed with your private key can only be verified by the corresponding public key.

Public and private keys alone, however, aren't enough to truly verify a signature. Even if you've verified that a signed file contains a matching key pair, you still need some way to confirm that the public key actually comes from the signer that it purports to come from.

One more element, therefore, is required to make signing and verification work. That additional element is the *certificate* that the signer includes in a signed JAR file. A certificate is a digitally signed statement from a recognized *certification authority* that indicates who owns a particular public key. Certification authorities are entities (typically firms specializing in digital security) that are trusted

15

2

throughout the industry to sign and issue certificates for keys and their owners. In the case of signed JAR files, the certificate indicates who owns the public key contained in the JAR file.

When you sign a JAR file, your public key is placed inside the archive along with an associated certificate so that it's easily available for use by anyone wanting to verify your signature.

Here is a quick recap of the digital signing process:

- The signer signs the JAR file using a private key.
- The corresponding public key is placed in the JAR file, together with its certificate, so that it is available for use by anyone who wants to verify the signature.

Digests and the Signature File

When you sign a JAR file, each file in the archive is given a digest entry in the archive's manifest. Here's an example of what such an entry might look like:

```
Name: test/classes/ClassOne.class
SHA1-Digest: TD1GZt8G11dXY2p4olSZPc5Rj64=
```

The digest values are *hashes*, or encoded representations of the contents of the files as they were at the time of signing. A file's digest will change if and only if the file itself changes.

When a JAR file is signed, a *signature* file is automatically generated and placed in the JAR file's META-INF directory—the same directory that contains the archive's manifest. Signature files have file names with an .SF extension. Here is an example of the contents of a signature file:

```
Signature-Version: 1.0
SHA1-Digest-Manifest: h1yS+K9T7DyHtZrtI+LxvgqaMYM=
Created-By: 1.7.0_06 (Oracle Corporation)

Name: test/classes/ClassOne.class
SHA1-Digest: fcav7ShIG6i86xPepmitOVo4vWY=

Name: test/classes/ClassTwo.class
SHA1-Digest: xrQem9snnPhLySDiZyclMlsFdtM=

Name: test/images/ImageOne.gif
SHA1-Digest: kdHbE7kL9ZHLgK7akHttYV4XIa0=

Name: test/images/ImageTwo.gif
SHA1-Digest: mFOD5zpk68R4oaxEqoS9Q7nhm60=
```

As you can see, the signature file contains digest entries for the archive's files that look similar to the digest-value entries in the manifest. However, while the digest values in the manifest are computed from the files themselves, the digest values in the signature file are computed from the corresponding entries in the manifest. Signature files also contain a digest value for the entire manifest (see the `SHA1-Digest-Manifest` header in the previous example).

When a signed JAR file is being verified, the digests of each of its files are recomputed and compared with the digests recorded in the manifest to ensure that the contents of the JAR file haven't changed since it was signed. As an additional check, digest values for the manifest file itself are recomputed and compared against the values recorded in the signature file.

You can read additional information about signature files on the Manifest Format[3] page of the JDK documentation.

The Signature Block File

In addition to the signature file, a *signature block* file is automatically placed in the `META-INF` directory when a JAR file is signed. Unlike the manifest file or the signature file, users can't read signature block files (because they are not "human readable").

The signature block file contains two elements essential for verification:

- The digital signature for the JAR file that was generated with the signer's private key
- The certificate containing the signer's public key, to be used by anyone wanting to verify the signed JAR file

Signature block file names typically have a `.DSA` extension, indicating that they were created by the default digital signature algorithm. Other file name extensions are possible if keys associated with some other standard algorithm are used for signing.

Related Documentation

For additional information about keys, certificates, and certification authorities, consult the following resources:

- The JDK Security Tools[4]
- X.509 Certificates[5]

---

3.   `7/docs/technotes/guides/jar/jar.html#JAR%20Manifest`

4.   `7/docs/technotes/tools/index.html#security`

5.   `7/docs/technotes/guides/security/cert3.html`

For more information about the Java platform's security architecture, consult the following related documentation:

- Security Features in Java SE[6]
- Java SE Security[7]

Signing JAR Files

You use the JAR signing and verification tool to sign JAR files. The JAR signing and verification tool is invoked by the `jarsigner` command, so we'll refer to it as "JAR signer" for short.

To sign a JAR file, you must first have a private key. Private keys and their associated public-key certificates are stored in password-protected databases called *keystores*. A keystore can hold the keys of many potential signers. Each key in the keystore can be identified by an alias, which is typically the name of the signer who owns the key. The key belonging to Rita Jones might have the alias *rita*, for example.

The basic form of the command for signing a JAR file is as follows:

```
jarsigner jar-file alias
```

Here are the details of this command:

- *jar-file* is the path name of the JAR file that's to be signed.
- *alias* is the alias identifying the private key that's to be used to sign the JAR file and the key's associated certificate.

The JAR signer tool will prompt you for the passwords for the keystore and alias.

This basic form of the command assumes that the keystore to be used is in a file named `.keystore` in your home directory. It will create signature and signature block files with names *x*.`SF` and *x*.`DSA`, respectively, where *x* is the first eight letters of the alias, all converted to uppercase. This basic command will *overwrite* the original JAR file with the signed JAR file.

In practice, you may want to use this command in conjunction with one or more of these options, which must precede the `jar-file` path name:

---

6. `tutorial/security/index.html`
7. `http://www.oracle.com/technetwork/java/javase/tech/index-jsp-136007`
    `.html`

Table 15.4 JAR Signer Command Options

Option	Description
-keystore *url*	This specifies a keystore to be used if you don't want to use the .keystore default database.
-storepass *password*	This allows you to enter the keystore's password on the command line rather than be prompted for it.
-keypass *password*	This allows you to enter your alias's password on the command line rather than be prompted for it.
-sigfile *file*	This specifies the base name for the .SF and .DSA files if you don't want the base name to be taken from your alias; *file* can only be composed of uppercase letters (A-Z), numerals (0-9), hyphens (-), and underscores (_).
-signedjar *file*	This specifies the name of the signed JAR file to be generated if you don't want the original unsigned file to be overwritten with the signed file.

Example

Let's look at a couple of examples of signing a JAR file with the JAR signer tool. In these examples we will assume the following:

- Your alias is johndoe.
- The keystore you want to use is in a file named mykeys in the current working directory.
- The keystore's password is abc123.

Under these assumptions, you could use this command to sign a JAR file named app.jar:

```
jarsigner -keystore mykeys -storepass abc123 app.jar johndoe
```

You will be prompted for the keystore password. Because this command doesn't make use of the -sigfile option, the .SF and .DSA files it creates are named JOHN-DOE.SF and JOHNDOE.DSA. Because the command doesn't use the -signedjar option, the resulting signed file will overwrite the original version of app.jar.

Let's look at what would happen if you used a different combination of options:

```
jarsigner -keystore mykeys -sigfile SIG
          -signedjar SignedApp.jar app.jar johndoe
```

15

This time, you would be prompted to enter the passwords for both the keystore and your alias because the passwords aren't specified on the command line. The signature and signature block files would be named `SIG.SF` and `SIG.DSA`, respectively, and the signed JAR file `SignedApp.jar` would be placed in the current directory. The original unsigned JAR file would remain unchanged.

Additional Information

Complete reference pages for the JAR signing and verification tool are available online; consult the Summary of Security Tools.[8]

> **Note**
> When a certificate is self-signed, unknown will be displayed as the publisher of the application.[9]

Verifying Signed JAR Files

Typically, verification of signed JAR files is the responsibility of your Java runtime environment. Your browser verifies signed applets that it downloads. Signed applications invoked with the `-jar` option of the interpreter are verified by the runtime environment.

However, you can verify signed JAR files yourself by using the JAR signer tool. For example, you might want to do this to test a signed JAR file that you've prepared.

Here is the basic command for verifying a signed JAR file:

```
jarsigner -verify jar-file
```

This command will verify the JAR file's signature and ensure that the files in the archive haven't changed since it was signed. You'll see the following message if the verification is successful:

```
jar verified.
```

If you try to verify an unsigned JAR file, the following message results:

```
jar is unsigned. (signatures missing or not parsable)
```

If the verification fails, an appropriate message is displayed. For example, if the contents of a JAR file have changed since the JAR file was signed, a message similar to the following will result if you try to verify the file:

---

8.   `7/docs/technotes/guides/security/SecurityToolsSummary.html`

9.   `http://www.java.com/en/download/faq/self_signed.xml`

```
jarsigner: java.lang.SecurityException: invalid SHA1
signature file digest for test/classes/Manifest.class
```

Using JAR-Related APIs

The Java platform contains several classes for use with JAR files. Here are some examples:

- The `java.util.jar` package[10]
- The `java.net.JarURLConnection` class[11]
- The `java.net.URLClassLoader` class[12]

To give you an idea of the possibilities that are opened up by these new APIs, this section guides you through the inner workings of a sample application called `JarRunner`.

An Example: The JarRunner Application

`JarRunner` enables you to run an application that's bundled in a JAR file by specifying the JAR file's URL on the command line. For example, if an application called `TargetApp` were bundled in a JAR file at `http://www.example.com/TargetApp.jar`, you could run the application using the following command:

```
java JarRunner http://www.example.com/TargetApp.jar
```

In order for `JarRunner` to work, it must be able to perform the following tasks, all of which are accomplished by using the new APIs:

- Access the remote JAR file and establish a communications link with it.
- Inspect the JAR file's manifest to see which of the classes in the archive is the main class.
- Load the classes in the JAR file.

The `JarRunner` application consists of two classes, `JarClassLoader` and `JarRunner`. `JarClassLoader` extends the `java.net.URLClassLoader` class. `JarRunner` delegates most of the JAR handling tasks to the `JarClassLoader` class.

15

---

10. 7/docs/api/java/util/jar/package-summary.html
11. 7/docs/api/java/net/JarURLConnection.html
12. 7/docs/api/java/net/URLClassLoader.html

You should browse the source code for the `JarClassLoader` and `JarRunner` classes before proceeding.[13]

The JarClassLoader Class

The `JarClassLoader` class extends `java.net.URLClassLoader`. As its name implies, `URLClassLoader` is designed for loading classes and resources that are accessed by searching a set of URLs. The URLs can refer to either directories or JAR files.

In addition to subclassing `URLClassLoader`, `JarClassLoader` also makes use of features in two other new JAR-related APIs: the `java.util.jar` package and the `java.net.JarURLConnection` class. In this section, we'll examine the constructor and two methods of `JarClassLoader`.

The JarClassLoader Constructor

The constructor takes an instance of `java.net.URL` as an argument. The URL passed to this constructor will be used elsewhere in `JarClassLoader` to find the JAR file from which classes are to be loaded:

```
public JarClassLoader(URL url) {
    super(new URL[] { url });
    this.url = url;
}
```

The `URL` object is passed to the constructor of the superclass, `URLClassLoader`, which takes a `URL[ ]` array, rather than a single `URL` instance, as an argument.

The getMainClassName Method

Once a `JarClassLoader` object is constructed with the URL of a JAR bundled application, it needs to determine which class in the JAR file is the application's entry point. That's the job of the `getMainClassName` method:

```
public String getMainClassName() throws IOException {
    URL u = new URL("jar", "", url + "!/");
    JarURLConnection uc = (JarURLConnection)u.openConnection();
    Attributes attr = uc.getMainAttributes();
    return attr != null
                    ? attr.getValue(Attributes.Name.MAIN_CLASS)
                    : null;
}
```

---

13. `tutorial/deployment/jar/examples/JarRunner.java`

You may recall that a JAR bundled application's entry point is specified by the Main-Class header of the JAR file's manifest. To understand how getMainClassName accesses the Main-Class header value, let's look at the method in detail, paying special attention to the new JAR handling features that it uses.

The JarURLConnection Class and JAR URLs

The getMainClassName method uses the JAR URL format specified by the java.net.JarURLConnection class. Here is the syntax for the URL of a JAR file:

```
jar:http://www.example.com/jarfile.jar!/
```

The terminating !/ separator indicates that the URL refers to an entire JAR file. Anything following the separator refers to specific JAR file contents, as in this example:

```
jar:http://www.example.com/jarfile.jar!/mypackage/myclass.class
```

Here is the first line in the getMainClassName method:

```
URL u = new URL("jar", "", url + "!/");
```

This statement constructs a new URL object representing a JAR URL, appending the !/ separator to the URL that was used to create the JarClassLoader instance.

The java.net.JarURLConnection Class

This class represents a communication link between an application and a JAR file. It has methods for accessing the JAR file's manifest. Here is the second line of getMainClassName:

```
JarURLConnection uc = (JarURLConnection)u.openConnection();
```

In this statement, the URL instance created in the first line opens a URLConnection. The URLConnection instance is then cast to JarURLConnection so it can take advantage of JarURLConnection's JAR handling features.

Fetching Manifest Attributes: java.util.jar.Attributes

With a JarURLConnection open to a JAR file, you can access the header information in the JAR file's manifest by using the getMainAttributes method of JarURL-Connection. This method returns an instance of java.util.jar.Attributes,

15

a class that maps header names in JAR file manifests with their associated string values. The third line in `getMainClassName` creates an `Attributes` object:

```
Attributes attr = uc.getMainAttributes();
```

To get the value of the manifest's `Main-Class` header, the fourth line of `getMain-ClassName` invokes the `Attributes.getValue` method:

```
return attr != null
            ? attr.getValue(Attributes.Name.MAIN_CLASS)
            : null;
```

The method's argument, `Attributes.Name.MAIN_CLASS`, specifies that what we want: the value of the `Main-Class` header. (The `Attributes.Name` class also provides static fields such as `MANIFEST_VERSION`, `CLASS_PATH`, and `SEALED` for specifying other standard manifest headers.)

The invokeClass Method

We've seen how `JarURLClassLoader` can identify the main class in a JAR bundled application. The last method to consider, `JarURLClassLoader.invokeClass`, enables that main class to be invoked to launch the JAR bundled application:

```
public void invokeClass(String name, String[] args)
    throws ClassNotFoundException,
           NoSuchMethodException,
           InvocationTargetException {
    Class c = loadClass(name);
    Method m = c.getMethod("main", new Class[] { args.getClass() });
    m.setAccessible(true);
    int mods = m.getModifiers();
    if (m.getReturnType() != void.class || !Modifier.isStatic(mods) ||
        !Modifier.isPublic(mods)) {
        throw new NoSuchMethodException("main");
    }
    try {
        m.invoke(null, new Object[] { args });
    } catch (IllegalAccessException e) {
        // This should not happen, as we have disabled access checks
    }
}
```

The `invokeClass` method takes two arguments: the name of the application's entry-point class and an array of string arguments to pass to the entry-point class's `main` method. First, the main class is loaded:

```
Class c = loadClass(name);
```

The `loadClass` method is inherited from `java.lang.ClassLoader`.

Once the main class is loaded, the reflection API of the `java.lang.reflect` package is used to pass the arguments to the class and launch it. For more information on *reflection,* consult the Reflection API Tutorial.[14]

The JarRunner Class

The `JarRunner` application is launched with the following command:

```
java JarRunner url [arguments]
```

The previous section shows us how `JarClassLoader` is able to identify and load the main class of a JAR bundled application from a given URL. Therefore, to complete the `JarRunner` application, we need to be able to take a URL and any arguments from the command line and pass them to an instance of `JarClassLoader`. These tasks belong to the `JarRunner` class, the entry point of the `JarRunner` application.

This begins by creating a `java.net.URL` object from the URL specified on the command line:

```
public static void main(String[] args) {
    if (args.length < 1) {
        usage();
    }
    URL url = null;
    try {
        url = new URL(args[0]);
    } catch (MalformedURLException e) {
        fatal("Invalid URL: " + args[0]);
    }
```

If `args.length < 1`, then no URL was specified on the command line, so a usage message is printed. If the first command-line argument is a good URL, a new URL object is created to represent it.

Next, `JarRunner` creates a new instance of `JarClassLoader`, passing the URL that was specified on the command-line to the constructor:

```
JarClassLoader cl = new JarClassLoader(url);
```

---

14. `tutorial/reflect/index.html`

As we saw in the previous section, it's through `JarClassLoader` that `JarRunner` taps into the JAR-handling APIs.

The URL that's passed to the `JarClassLoader` constructor is the URL of the JAR bundled application that you want to run. `JarRunner` next calls the class loader's `getMainClassName` method to identify the entry-point class for the application:

```
String name = null;
try {
    name = cl.getMainClassName();
} catch (IOException e) {
    System.err.println("I/O error while loading JAR file:");
    e.printStackTrace();
    System.exit(1);
}
if (name == null) {
    fatal("Specified jar file does not contain a 'Main-Class'" +
            " manifest attribute");
}
```

The key statement is highlighted in bold. The other statements are for error handling.

Once `JarRunner` has identified the application's entry-point class, only two steps remain: passing any arguments to the application and actually launching the application. `JarRunner` performs these steps with the following code:

```
// Get arguments for the application
String[] newArgs = new String[args.length - 1];
System.arraycopy(args, 1, newArgs, 0, newArgs.length);
// Invoke application's main class
try {
    cl.invokeClass(name, newArgs);
} catch (ClassNotFoundException e) {
    fatal("Class not found: " + name);
} catch (NoSuchMethodException e) {
    fatal("Class does not define a 'main' method: " + name);
} catch (InvocationTargetException e) {
    e.getTargetException().printStackTrace();
    System.exit(1);
}
```

Recall that the first command-line argument was the URL of the JAR bundled application. Any arguments to be passed to that application are therefore in element 1 and beyond in the `args` array. `JarRunner` takes those elements and creates a new array called `newArgs` to pass to the application (via the bold line in our example). `JarRunner` then passes the entry point's class name and the new argument list to the `invokeClass` method of `JarClassLoader`. As we saw in the previous section, `invokeClass` will load the application's entry-point class, pass it any arguments, and launch the application.

Questions: Packaging Programs in JAR Files

Questions

1. How do you invoke an applet that is packaged as a JAR file?
2. What is the purpose of the -e option in a `jar` command?
3. What is the significance of the manifest in a JAR file?
4. How do you modify a JAR's manifest file?

Answers

You can find answers to these questions at `http://docs.oracle.com/javase/tutorial/deployment/jar/QandE/answers.html`.

15

16

Java Web Start

Java Web Start software has the power to launch full-featured applications with a single click. Users can download and launch applications, such as a complete spreadsheet program or an Internet chat client, without going through lengthy installation procedures.

With Java Web Start software, users can launch a Java application by clicking a link on a web page. The link points to a Java Network Launch Protocol (JNLP) file, which instructs Java Web Start software to download, cache, and run the application.

Java Web Start software provides Java developers and users with many deployment advantages:

- With Java Web Start software, you can place a single Java application on a web server for deployment to a wide variety of platforms, including Windows, Linux, and Solaris.

- Java Web Start software supports multiple, simultaneous versions of the Java platform. An application can request a specific version of the Java Runtime Environment (JRE) software without conflicting with the needs of other applications. Java Web Start software automatically downloads and installs the correct version of the Java platform, based on the application's needs and the user's environment.

- Users can create a desktop shortcut to launch a Java Web Start application outside a browser.
- Java Web Start software takes advantage of the inherent security of the Java platform. By default, applications have restricted access to local disk and network resources. Users can safely run applications from sources that are not trusted.
- Applications launched with Java Web Start software are cached locally for improved performance.
- Updates to a Java Web Start application are automatically downloaded when the application is run standalone from the user's desktop.

Java Web Start software is installed as part of the JRE software. Users do not need to install Java Web Start software separately or perform additional tasks to use Java Web Start applications.

This chapter is intended to get you started with Java Web Start technology and does not include all available documentation. For more information about Java Web Start technology, see the following:

- Java Web Start Guide[1]
- Java Web Start FAQ[2]
- JNLP Specification[3]
- `javax.jnlp` API Documentation[4]
- Java Web Start Developers Site[5]

Developing a Java Web Start Application

Software designed by using component-based architecture can easily be developed and deployed as a Java Web Start application. Consider the example of a Java Web Start application with a Swing-based graphical user interface (GUI). With component-based design, the GUI can be built with smaller building blocks or components. The following general steps are used to create an application's GUI:

---

1. `7/docs/technotes/guides/javaws/developersguide/contents.html`
2. `7/docs/technotes/guides/javaws/developersguide/faq.html`
3. `http://jcp.org/en/jsr/detail?id=56`
4. `7/docs/jre/api/javaws/jnlp/index.html`
5. `http://www.oracle.com/technetwork/java/javase/javawebstart/index.html`

- Create a `MyTopJPanel` class that is a subclass of `JPanel`. Lay out your application's GUI components in the constructor of the `MyTopJPanel` class.
- Create a class called `MyApplication` that is a subclass of the `JFrame` class.
- In the `main` method of the `MyApplication` class, instantiate the `MyTopJPanel` class and set it as the content pane of the `JFrame`.

The following sections explore these steps in greater detail by using the Dynamic Tree Demo application.

Creating the Top JPanel Class

Create a class that is a subclass of `JPanel`. This top `JPanel` acts as a container for all your other user-interface components. In the following example, the `DynamicTreePanel` class is the topmost `JPanel`. The constructor of the `DynamicTreePanel` class invokes other methods to create and lay out the user interface controls properly.

```
public class DynamicTreePanel extends JPanel implements ActionListener {
    private int newNodeSuffix = 1;
    private static String ADD_COMMAND = "add";
    private static String REMOVE_COMMAND = "remove";
    private static String CLEAR_COMMAND = "clear";

    private DynamicTree treePanel;

    public DynamicTreePanel() {
        super(new BorderLayout());

        //Create the components.
        treePanel = new DynamicTree();
        populateTree(treePanel);

        JButton addButton = new JButton("Add");
        addButton.setActionCommand(ADD_COMMAND);
        addButton.addActionListener(this);

        JButton removeButton = new JButton("Remove");
        . . . .

        JButton clearButton = new JButton("Clear");
        . . .

        //Lay everything out.
        treePanel.setPreferredSize(
            new Dimension(300, 150));
        add(treePanel, BorderLayout.CENTER);

        JPanel panel = new JPanel(new GridLayout(0,3));
        panel.add(addButton);
        panel.add(removeButton);
        panel.add(clearButton);
        add(panel, BorderLayout.SOUTH);
```

```
        }
    // . . .
}
```

Creating the Application

For an application that has a Swing-based GUI, create a class that is a subclass of `javax.swing.JFrame`.

Instantiate your top `JPanel` class and set it as the content pane of the `JFrame` in the application's `main` method. The `main` method of the `DynamicTreeApplica-tion` class invokes the `createGUI` method in the Abstract Window Toolkit event dispatcher thread.[6]

```
package webstartComponentArch;

import javax.swing.JFrame;

public class DynamicTreeApplication extends JFrame {
    public static void main(String [] args) {
        DynamicTreeApplication app = new DynamicTreeApplication();
        app.createGUI();
    }

    private void createGUI() {
        //Create and set up the content pane.
        DynamicTreePanel newContentPane = new DynamicTreePanel();
        newContentPane.setOpaque(true);
        setContentPane(newContentPane);
        setDefaultCloseOperation(JFrame.EXIT_ON_CLOSE);
        pack();
        setVisible(true);
    }
}
```

The Benefits of Separating Core Functionality from the Final Deployment Mechanism

Another way to create an application is to just remove the layer of abstraction (use a separate top `JPanel`) and lay out all the controls in the application's `main` method itself. The downside to creating the GUI directly in the application's `main` method is that it will be more difficult to deploy your functionality as an applet if you choose to do so later.

In the Dynamic Tree Demo example, the core functionality is separated into the `DynamicTreePanel` class. It is now trivial to drop the `DynamicTreePanel` class into a `JApplet` and deploy it as an applet.

---

6. `tutorial/uiswing/events`

Hence, to preserve portability and keep deployment options open, follow component-based design, as described in this section.

Retrieving Resources

Use the `getResource` method to read resources from a JAR file. For example, the following code retrieves images from a JAR file:

```
// Get current classloader
ClassLoader cl = this.getClass().getClassLoader();
// Create icons
Icon saveIcon  = new ImageIcon(cl.getResource("images/save.gif"));
Icon cutIcon   = new ImageIcon(cl.getResource("images/cut.gif"));
```

This example assumes that the following entries exist in the application's JAR file:

```
images/save.gif
images/cut.gif
```

Deploying a Java Web Start Application

To deploy your Java Web Start application, first compile the source code and package it as a JAR file. Java Web Start applications are launched by using the JNLP. Hence, you must create a JNLP file to deploy your application. The Deployment Toolkit script contains useful JavaScript functions that can be used to deploy Java Web Start applications on a web page. If you are unfamiliar with these deployment technologies, see Chapter 19 before proceeding.

Here are some step-by-step instructions for packaging and deploying your application. The Dynamic Tree Demo application[7] is used to illustrate the deployment of Java Web Start applications. You might want to set up build scripts to execute some of the following steps:

1. Compile your application's Java code and make sure that all class files and resources (such as images) are in a separate directory. In the Dynamic Tree Demo application, the compiled classes are placed in the `build/classes/webstartComponentArch` directory.

2. Create a JAR file containing your application's class files and resources. See Chapter 15 to learn more about creating and using JAR files. For example, the following command creates a JAR file with the class files in the `build/classes/webstartComponentArch` directory:

---

7. `tutorial/deployment/webstart/examples/zipfiles/webstart_ComponentArch_DynamicTreeDemo.zip`

```
% cd build/classes
% jar cvf  DynamicTreeDemo.jar  webstartComponentArch
```

3. Create a JNLP file that describes how your application should be launched.
    Chapter 19, "Structure of the JNLP File," describes the JNLP file syntax and
    options. Here is the JNLP file that is used to launch the Dynamic Tree Demo
    application. The source for `dynamictree-webstart.jnlp` follows:

```
<?xml version="1.0" encoding="UTF-8"?>
<jnlp spec="1.0+" codebase=
"http://docs.oracle.com/javase/tutorialJWS/deployment/webstart/
ex6/webstart_ComponentArch_DynamicTreeDemo"
    href="dynamictree-webstart.jnlp">
    <information>
        <title>Dynamic Tree Demo</title>
        <vendor>Dynamic Team</vendor>
    </information>
    <resources>
        <!-- Application Resources -->
        <j2se version="1.6+"
            href="http://java.sun.com/products/autodl/j2se"/>
        <jar href="DynamicTreeDemo.jar"
            main="true" />

    </resources>
    <application-desc
        name="Dynamic Tree Demo Application"
        main-class=
          "webstartComponentArch.DynamicTreeApplication"
        width="300"
        height="300">
    </application-desc>
    <update check="background"/>
</jnlp>
```

> **Note**
>
> The `codebase` and `href` attributes are optional when deploying Java Web Start applica-
> tions that will run on the JDK 6 update 18 release or later. You must specify the `codebase`
> and `href` attributes when deploying Java Web Start applications that will run with previ-
> ous releases of the JRE software.

16

4. Create the HTML page from which your application will be launched. Invoke
    Deployment Toolkit functions to deploy the Java Web Start application. In the
    example, the Dynamic Tree Demo application is deployed in `JavaWebStar-
    tAppPage.html`:

```
<body>
    <!-- . . . -->
    <script src=
      "http://www.java.com/js/deployJava.js"></script>
    <script>
```

```
                    // using JavaScript to get location of JNLP
                    // file relative to HTML page
                    var dir = location.href.substring(0,
                        location.href.lastIndexOf('/')+1);
                    var url = dir + "dynamictree-webstart.jnlp";
                    deployJava.createWebStartLaunchButton(url, '1.6.0');
                </script>
                <!-- . . . -->
            </body>
```

If you are not sure whether your end users will have the JavaScript interpreter enabled in their browsers, you can deploy the Java Web Start application directly by creating a link to the JNLP file as follows:

```
<a href="/absolute path to JNLP file/dynamictree-webstart.
jnlp">Launch Notepad Application</a>
```

If you deploy the Java Web Start application with a direct link, you cannot take advantage of the additional checks that the Deployment Toolkit functions provide. See Chapter 19, "Deploying a Java Web Start Application," for details.

5. Place the application's JAR file, JNLP file, and HTML page in the appropriate folders. For this example, place `DynamicTreeDemo.jar`, `dynamictree-webstart.jnlp`, and `JavaWebStartAppPage.html` in the same directory on the local machine or a web server. A web server is not required to test the Java Web Start application.

6. Open the application's HTML page in a browser to view the application. Check the Java console log for error and debugging messages.

Setting Up a Web Server

You might need to configure your web server to handle JNLP files. If the web server is not set up properly, the Java Web Start application will not launch when you click on the link to the JNLP file. Configure the web server so that files with the `.jnlp` extension are set to the `application/x-java-jnlp-file` MIME type. The specific steps to set up the JNLP MIME type will vary depending on the web server. As an example, to configure an Apache web server, you should add the following line to the `mime.types` file:

```
application/x-java-jnlp-file JNLP
```

Displaying a Customized Loading Progress Indicator

A Java Web Start application can display a customized loading progress indicator that shows the progress of download of the application's resources. Consider the following example to understand how to implement a customized loading progress

16

indicator for a Java Web Start application. For the purpose of demonstrating a large
and prolonged download, the example Java Web Start application's JAR file has
been artificially inflated and the customprogress-webstart.jnlp file specifies
additional JAR files as resources.

Developing a Customized Loading Progress Indicator

To develop a customized loading progress indicator for your Java Web Start application, create a class that implements the DownloadServiceListener[8] interface. The
constructor of the loading progress indicator class should not have any parameters:

```
import javax.jnlp.DownloadServiceListener;
import java.awt.Container;
import java.applet.AppletStub;
import netscape.javascript.*;
// . . .
public class CustomProgress
        implements DownloadServiceListener {
    JFrame frame = null;
    JProgressBar progressBar = null;
    boolean uiCreated = false;

    public CustomProgress() {
    }
    . . .
}
```

The following code snippet shows how to build the user interface for the loading
progress indicator:

```
private void create() {
    JPanel top = createComponents();
    frame = new JFrame(); // top level custom progress
                          // indicator UI
    frame.getContentPane().add(top,
                              BorderLayout.CENTER);
    frame.setBounds(300,300,400,300);
    frame.pack();
    updateProgressUI(0);
}

private JPanel createComponents() {
    JPanel top = new JPanel();
    top.setBackground(Color.WHITE);
    top.setLayout(new BorderLayout(20, 20));

    String lblText =
        "<html><font color=green size=+2" +
        ">JDK Documentation</font><br/> " +
```

8.   7/docs/jre/api/javaws/jnlp/javax/jnlp/DownloadServiceListener.html

```
            "The one-stop shop for Java enlightenment! <br/></html>";
        JLabel lbl = new JLabel(lblText);
        top.add(lbl, BorderLayout.NORTH);
            . . .
        progressBar = new JProgressBar(0, 100);
        progressBar.setValue(0);
        progressBar.setStringPainted(true);
        top.add(progressBar, BorderLayout.SOUTH);

        return top;
    }
```

Create and update the loading progress indicator in the following methods based on the overallPercent argument. These methods are invoked regularly by the Java Web Start software to show the progress of the application's download. Java Web Start software will always send a message when download and validation of resources is 100 percent complete:

```
public void progress(URL url, String version, long readSoFar,
                     long total, int overallPercent) {
    updateProgressUI(overallPercent);

}

public void upgradingArchive(java.net.URL url,
                java.lang.String version,
                int patchPercent,
                int overallPercent) {
    updateProgressUI(overallPercent);
}

public void validating(java.net.URL url,
            java.lang.String version,
            long entry,
            long total,
            int overallPercent) {
    updateProgressUI(overallPercent);
}

private void updateProgressUI(int overallPercent) {
    if (overallPercent > 0 && overallPercent < 99) {
        if (!uiCreated) {
            uiCreated = true;
            // create custom progress indicator's
            // UI only if there is more work to do,
            // meaning overallPercent > 0 and
            // < 100 this prevents flashing when
            // RIA is loaded from cache
            create();
        }
        progressBar.setValue(overallPercent);
        SwingUtilities.invokeLater(new Runnable() {
            public void run() {
                frame.setVisible(true);
            }
```

16

```
                });
            } else {
                // hide frame when overallPercent is
                // above 99
                SwingUtilities.invokeLater(new Runnable() {
                    public void run() {
                        frame.setVisible(false);
                        frame.dispose();
                    }
                });
            }
        }
    }
```

Compile the loading progress indicator class and build a JAR file with all the resources needed to display the loading progress indicator. Include the <your JRE directory>/lib/javaws.jar file in your classpath to enable compilation.

The loading progress indicator class is now ready for use. The next step is to specify this loading progress indicator JAR file as your Java Web Start application's progress indicator.

Specifying a Customized Loading Progress Indicator for a Java Web Start Application

To specify a customized loading progress indicator for a Java Web Start application, include the following information in the application's JNLP file:

- jar tag with the download="progress" attribute
- progress-class attribute with the fully qualified name of the customized loading progress class

The following code snippet from the customprogress-webstart.jnlp file displays the usage of the download="progress" and progress-class attributes:

```
<jnlp spec="1.0+" codebase=
    "http://docs.oracle.com/javase/tutorialJWS/deployment/webstart/ex6"
    href=
    "webstart_AppWithCustomProgressIndicator/customprogress-webstart.jnlp">
    <!-- . . . -->
    <resources>
        <j2se version="1.6+"/>
        <jar href=
            "webstart_AppWithCustomProgressIndicator/webstart_
AppWithCustomProgressIndicator.jar" />
        <jar href=
            "webstart_CustomProgressIndicator/webstart_CustomProgressIndicator.jar"
            download="progress" />
        <jar href=
            "webstart_AppWithCustomProgressIndicator/lib/IconDemo.jar" />
        <jar href=
            "webstart_AppWithCustomProgressIndicator/lib/SplitPaneDemo.jar" />
```

16

```
      <jar href=
        "webstart_AppWithCustomProgressIndicator/lib/SplitPaneDemo2.jar" />
      <jar href=
        "webstart_AppWithCustomProgressIndicator/lib/TextBatchPrintingDemo.jar" />
      <jar href=
        "webstart_AppWithCustomProgressIndicator/lib/ToolBarDemo.jar" />
      <jar href=
        "webstart_AppWithCustomProgressIndicator/lib/ToolBarDemo2.jar" />
      <jar href=
        "webstart_AppWithCustomProgressIndicator/lib/SwingSet2.jar" />
   </resources>
   <application-desc
      main-class="customprogressindicatordemo.Main"
      progress-class="customprogressindicator.CustomProgress"
   />
   <!-- . . . -->
</jnlp>
```

See Chapter 18, "Customizing the Loading Experience," for more information about customizing the rich Internet application (RIA) loading experience.

Running a Java Web Start Application

Users can run Java Web Start applications in a number of ways, as described in the sections that follow.

> **Note**
>
> To run applications deployed with Java Web Start technology, you must have a compatible version of the JRE software. The complete Java SE Development Kit (JDK) is not required.

Running a Java Web Start Application from a Browser

You can run a Java Web Start application from a browser by clicking a link to the application's JNLP file. Here is an example of a link to a JNLP file:

```
<a href="/some/path/Notepad.jnlp">Launch Notepad Application</a>
```

16

Java Web Start software loads and runs the application based on instructions in the JNLP file.

Running a Java Web Start Application from the Java Cache Viewer

If you are using JDK 6 or later, you can run a Java Web Start application through the Java Cache Viewer. When Java Web Start software first loads an application, information from the application's JNLP file is stored in the local Java Cache Viewer. To launch the application again, you do not need to return to the web page where

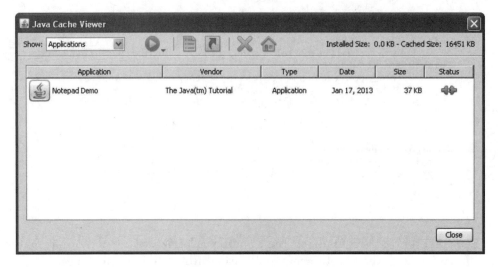

Figure 16.1 Java Cache Viewer Application

you first launched it; you can launch it from the Java Cache Viewer. You can open the Java Cache Viewer by the following steps:

1. Open the Control Panel.
2. Double click on the Java icon. The Java Control Panel opens.
3. Select the General tab.
4. Click **View**. The Java Cache Viewer opens.

The application is then listed on the Java Cache Viewer screen. To run the application, select it and click the Run button or double click the application. The application starts just as it did from the web page (Figure 16.1).

Running a Java Web Start Application from the Desktop

You can add a desktop shortcut to a Java Web Start application. Select the application in the Java Cache Viewer. Right click and select **Install Shortcuts** or click the Install button. A shortcut is added to the desktop. You can then launch the Java Web Start application just as you would any native application.

Java Web Start and Security

This section describes the basics of security for applications deployed through Java Web Start. Applications launched with Java Web Start are, by default, run in a restricted environment, known as a *sandbox*. In this sandbox, Java Web Start does the following:

- Protects users against malicious code that could affect local files
- Protects enterprises against code that could attempt to access or destroy data on networks

Unsigned JAR files launched by Java Web Start remain in this sandbox, meaning they cannot access local files or the network. See Chapter 18, "Security in Rich Internet Applications," for information.

Dynamic Downloading of HTTPS Certificates

Java Web Start dynamically imports certificates like browsers typically do. To do this, Java Web Start sets its own `https` handler, using the `java.protocol.handler.pkgs` system properties, to initialize defaults for the `SSLSocketFactory`[9] and `HostnameVerifier`.[10] It sets the defaults with the methods `HttpsURLConnection.setDefaultSSLSocketFactory`[11] and `HttpsURLConnection.setDefaultHostnameVerifier`.[12]

If your application uses these two methods, ensure that they are invoked after the Java Web Start initializes the `https` handler; otherwise, your custom handler will be replaced by the Java Web Start default handler.

You can ensure that your own customized `SSLSocketFactory` and `HostnameVerifiter` are used by taking one of the following steps:

- Install your own `https` handler to replace the Java Web Start `https` handler.
- In your application, invoke `HttpsURLConnection.setDefaultSSLSocketFactory` or `HttpsURLConnection.setDefaultHostnameVerifier` only after the first `https URL` object is created, which executes the Java Web Start `https` handler initialization code first.

Common Java Web Start Problems

16

This section covers some common problems that you might encounter when developing and deploying Java Web Start applications. After each problem is a list of possible reasons and solutions.

---

9. `7/docs/api/javax/net/ssl/SSLSocketFactory.html`

10. `7/docs/api/javax/net/ssl/HostnameVerifier.html`

11. `7/docs/api/javax/net/ssl/HttpsURLConnection.html#setDefaultSSLSocket`
`Factory(javax.net.ssl.SSLSocketFactory)`

12. `7/docs/api/javax/net/ssl/HttpsURLConnection.html#setDefaultHostname`
`Verifier(javax.net.ssl.HostnameVerifier)`

"My Browser Shows the JNLP File for My Application as Plain Text"

Most likely, your web server is not aware of the proper MIME type for JNLP files. See the "Setting Up the Web Server" section in this chapter for more information.

Furthermore, if you are using a proxy server, ensure that the updated versions of the files are returned by updating the time stamp of the resources on the web server so that the proxies update their caches.

"When I Try to Launch My JNLP File, I Get an Error"

Here is the error:

```
MissingFieldException[ The following required field is missing from the
launch
    file: (<application-desc>|<applet-desc>|<installer-desc>|
      <component-desc>)]
        at com.sun.javaws.jnl.XMLFormat.parse(Unknown Source)
        at com.sun.javaws.jnl.LaunchDescFactory.buildDescriptor
          (Unknown Source)
        at com.sun.javaws.jnl.LaunchDescFactory.buildDescriptor
          (Unknown Source)
        at com.sun.javaws.jnl.LaunchDescFactory.buildDescriptor
          (Unknown Source)
        at com.sun.javaws.Main.launchApp(Unknown Source)
        at com.sun.javaws.Main.continueInSecureThread(Unknown Source)
        at com.sun.javaws.Main.run(Unknown Source)
        at java.lang.Thread.run(Unknown Source)
```

This often occurs when your XML is malformed. You can stare at the code until you figure it out, but it is easier to run an XML syntax checker over the file. (NetBeans IDE and jEdit both provide XML syntax checkers.)

This error can also occur in a other situations; here, it was caused by the following line in an otherwise well-formed XML file:

```
<description kind="short">Demonstrates choosing the drop location in the
    target <code>TransferHandler</code></description>
```

The line contains illegally embedded code tags.

Questions and Exercises: Java Web Start

Questions

1. In a link that is to run a Java Web Start application, which file is specified as the a tag's href attribute?

2. Which MIME type must a web server recognize in order for it to host Java Web Start applications?

3. In an application's JNLP file, which two elements must be specified within the resources element?

4. Which interface provides the ability to control how the Java Web Start application's resources are cached?

    a. BasicService

    b. DownloadService

    c. PersistenceService

    d. ExtendedService

5. True or false: Java Web Start applications run in a secure sandbox by default.

6. True or false: If a Java Web Start application is running in a secure sandbox, JAR files for the application can reside on different servers.

7. For a Java Web Start application to support operations outside of the secure sandbox, what must you do with its JAR files?

Exercises

1. Write the XML code you would add to a JNLP file in order to request that the application have complete access to the client system.

2. For a Java Web Start application, you have two icons, one.gif and two.gif, in the images directory in a JAR file. Write the application code you would use to access these images.

Answers

You can find answers to these questions and exercises at http://docs.oracle.com/javase/tutorial/deployment/webstart/QandE/answers.html.

16

17

Applets

Chapter Contents

This chapter discusses the basics of Java applets, how to develop applets that interact richly with their environment, and how to deploy applets. A Java applet is a special kind of Java program that a browser enabled with Java technology can download from the Internet and run. An applet is typically embedded inside a web page and runs in the context of a browser. It must be a subclass of the `java.applet.Applet` class. The `Applet` class provides the standard interface between the applet and the browser environment.

Swing provides a special subclass of the `Applet` class called `javax.swing.JApplet`. The `JApplet` class should be used for all applets that use Swing components to construct their graphical user interfaces (GUIs). The browser's Java Plug-In software manages the life cycle of an applet.

Getting Started with Applets

The `HelloWorld` applet is a Java class that displays the string "Hello World". Here is the source code for the `HelloWorld` applet:

Note

Some features of Java applets may not work as described on Mac. This is because of the way the Java Plug-In software interfaces with browsers on Mac.

To properly view the example applets provided in this chapter, you need to install at least the Java SE Development Kit (JDK) 6 update 21.[1] If you have viewed an applet before, clear your cache by using the Java Control Panel before viewing the applet again. You will not be able to see a progress indicator for a previously cached applet. And if you don't see the example running, you might need to enable the JavaScript interpreter in your browser so that the Deployment Toolkit script can function properly.

```java
import javax.swing.JApplet;
import javax.swing.SwingUtilities;
import javax.swing.JLabel;

public class HelloWorld extends JApplet {
    //Called when this applet is loaded into the browser.
    public void init() {
        //Execute a job on the event-dispatching thread; creating this
          applet's GUI.
        try {
            SwingUtilities.invokeAndWait(new Runnable() {
                public void run() {
                    JLabel lbl = new JLabel("Hello World");
                    add(lbl);
                }
            });
        } catch (Exception e) {
            System.err.println("createGUI didn't complete successfully");
        }
    }
}
```

An applet such as this is typically managed and run by the Java Plug-In software in the browser.

Defining an Applet Subclass

Every Java applet must define a subclass of the `Applet` or `JApplet` class. In the `HelloWorld` applet, this subclass is called `HelloWorld`. Here is the source for the `HelloWorld` class:

```java
import javax.swing.JApplet;
import javax.swing.SwingUtilities;
import javax.swing.JLabel;
```

---

1. http://www.oracle.com/technetwork/java/javase/downloads/index.html

```
public class HelloWorld extends JApplet {
    //Called when this applet is loaded into the browser.
    public void init() {
        //Execute a job on the event-dispatching thread; creating this
          applet's GUI.
        try {
            SwingUtilities.invokeAndWait(new Runnable() {
                public void run() {
                    JLabel lbl = new JLabel("Hello World");
                    add(lbl);
                }
            });
        } catch (Exception e) {
            System.err.println("createGUI didn't complete successfully");
        }
    }
}
```

Java applets inherit significant functionality from the `Applet` or `JApplet` class, including the capabilities to communicate with the browser and present a GUI to the user. An applet that uses GUI components from Swing (Java's GUI toolkit) should extend the `javax.swing.JApplet`[2] base class, which provides the best integration with Swing's GUI facilities. `JApplet` provides a root pane, which is the same top-level component structure as Swing's `JFrame` and `JDialog` components, whereas `Applet` provides just a basic panel. An applet can extend the `java.applet.Applet`[3] class when it does not use Swing's GUI components.

Methods for Milestones

The `Applet`[4] class provides a framework for applet execution, defining methods that the system calls when milestones occur. *Milestones* are major events in an applet's life cycle. Most applets override some or all of these methods to respond appropriately to milestones.

init Method

The `init` method is useful for one-time initialization that doesn't take very long. The `init` method typically contains the code that you would normally put into a constructor. The reason applets don't usually have constructors is that they aren't guaranteed to have a full environment until their `init` method is called. Keep the `init` method short so that your applet can load quickly.

---

2.   7/docs/api/javax/swing/JApplet.html
3.   7/docs/api/java/applet/Applet.html
4.   7/docs/api/java/applet/Applet.html

17

start Method

Every applet that performs tasks after initialization (except in direct response to user actions) must override the `start` method. The `start` method starts the execution of the applet. It is good practice to return quickly from the `start` method. If you need to perform computationally intensive operations, it might be better to start a new thread for this purpose.

stop Method

Most applets that override the `start` should also override the `stop` method. The `stop` method should suspend the applet's execution so that it doesn't take up system resources when the user isn't viewing the applet's page. For example, an applet that displays an animation should stop trying to draw the animation when the user isn't viewing it.

destroy Method

Many applets don't need to override the `destroy` method because their `stop` method (which is called before `destroy`) performs all tasks necessary to shut down the applet's execution. However, the `destroy` method is available for applets that need to release additional resources.

> **Note**
>
> Keep implementations of the `destroy` method as short as possible because there is no guarantee that this method will be completely executed. The Java Virtual Machine (Java VM) might exit before a long `destroy` method has completed.

Life Cycle of an Applet

An applet can react to major events in the following ways:

- It can *initialize* itself.
- It can *start* running.
- It can *stop* running.
- It can perform a *final cleanup* in preparation for being unloaded.

This section introduces a new applet, `Simple`, that uses all these methods. Unlike Java applications, applets do *not* need to implement a `main` method.

The following is the source code for the `Simple` applet.[5] This applet displays a descriptive string whenever it encounters a major milestone in its life, such as when the user first visits the page the applet is on:

---

5. `tutorial/deployment/applet/examples/applet_Simple/src/Simple.java`

```java
import java.applet.Applet;
import java.awt.Graphics;

//No need to extend JApplet, since we don't add any components;
//we just paint.
public class Simple extends Applet {

    StringBuffer buffer;

    public void init() {
        buffer = new StringBuffer();
        addItem("initializing . . . ");
    }

    public void start() {
        addItem("starting . . . ");
    }

    public void stop() {
        addItem("stopping . . . ");
    }

    public void destroy() {
        addItem("preparing for unloading . . . ");
    }

    private void addItem(String newWord) {
        System.out.println(newWord);
        buffer.append(newWord);
        repaint();
    }

    public void paint(Graphics g) {
//Draw a Rectangle around the applet's display area.
        g.drawRect(0, 0,
      getWidth() - 1,
      getHeight() - 1);

//Draw the current string inside the rectangle.
        g.drawString(buffer.toString(), 5, 15);
    }
}
```

Note

In this example, the `Applet` class is extended, not the Swing `JApplet` class, because Swing components do not need to be added to this applet.

17

Loading the Applet

As a result of the applet being loaded, you should see the text "initializing . . . starting . . .". When an applet is loaded, here's what happens:

- An instance of the applet's controlling class (an `Applet` subclass) is created.
- The applet initializes itself.

- The applet starts running.

Leaving and Returning to the Applet's Page

When the user leaves the page (e.g., to go to another page), the browser stops and destroys the applet. The state of the applet is not preserved. When the user returns to the page, the browser initializes and starts a new instance of the applet.

Reloading the Applet

When you refresh or reload a browser page, the current instance of the applet is stopped and destroyed and a new instance is created.

Quitting the Browser

When the user quits the browser, the applet has the opportunity to stop itself and perform a final cleanup before the browser exits. Download source code for the `Sim-ple` Applet example to experiment further.

Applet's Execution Environment

A Java applet runs in the context of a browser. The Java Plug-In software in the browser controls the launch and execution of Java applets. The browser also has a JavaScript interpreter, which runs the JavaScript code on a web page. This topic describes the behavior of the Java Plug-In software released in Java Platform SE 6 update 10.

Java Plug-In

The Java Plug-In software creates a worker thread for every Java applet. It launches an applet in an instance of the Java Runtime Environment (JRE) software. Normally, all applets run in the same instance of the JRE. The Java Plug-In software starts a new instance of the JRE in the following cases:

- An applet requests to be executed in a specific version of the JRE.
- An applet specifies its own JRE start-up parameters (e.g., the heap size). A new applet uses an existing JRE if its requirements are a subset of an existing JRE. Otherwise, a new JRE instance is started.

An applet will run in an existing JRE if the following conditions are met:

- The JRE version required by the applet matches an existing JRE.
- The JRE's start-up parameters satisfy the applet's requirements.

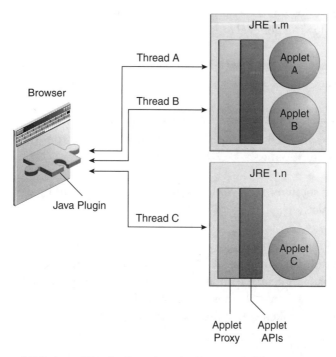

Figure 17.1 Java Plug-In Running Applets on Different JRE Versions

Figure 17.1 shows how applets are executed in the JRE.

Java Plug-In and JavaScript Interpreter Interaction

Java applets can invoke JavaScript functions present in the web page. JavaScript functions are also allowed to invoke methods of an applet embedded on the same web page. The Java Plug-In software and the JavaScript interpreter orchestrate calls from Java code to JavaScript code and calls from JavaScript code to Java code.

The Java Plug-In software is multithreaded, while the JavaScript interpreter runs on a single thread. Hence, to avoid thread-related issues, especially when multiple applets are running simultaneously, keep the calls between Java code and JavaScript code short and avoid round trips, if possible. See the "Invoking JavaScript Code from an Applet" and "Invoking Applet Methods from JavaScript Code" sections in this chapter for more information.

Developing an Applet

An application designed using component-based architecture can be developed into a Java applet. Consider the example of a Java applet with a Swing-based GUI. With

17

component-based design, the GUI can be built with smaller building blocks or components. The following general steps are used to create an applet GUI:

- Create a class `MyTopJPanel` that is a subclass of `javax.swing.JPanel`. Lay out your applet's GUI components in the constructor of the `MyTopJPanel` class.
- Create a class called `MyApplet` that is a subclass of `javax.swing.JApplet`.
- In the `init` method of `MyApplet`, instantiate `MyTopJPanel` and set it as the applet's content pane.

The following sections explore these steps in greater detail by using the `Dynamic Tree Demo` applet.

Creating the Top JPanel Class

Create a class that is a subclass of `JPanel`. This top `JPanel` acts as a container for all your other user-interface components. In the following example, the `DynamicTreePanel` class is the topmost `JPanel`. The constructor of the `DynamicTreePanel` class invokes other methods to create and lay out the user interface controls properly:

```
public class DynamicTreePanel extends JPanel implements ActionListener {
    private int newNodeSuffix = 1;
    private static String ADD_COMMAND = "add";
    private static String REMOVE_COMMAND = "remove";
    private static String CLEAR_COMMAND = "clear";

    private DynamicTree treePanel;

    public DynamicTreePanel() {
        super(new BorderLayout());

        //Create the components.
        treePanel = new DynamicTree();
        populateTree(treePanel);

        JButton addButton = new JButton("Add");
        addButton.setActionCommand(ADD_COMMAND);
        addButton.addActionListener(this);

        JButton removeButton = new JButton("Remove");

        // . . .

        JButton clearButton = new JButton("Clear");

        // . . .

        //Lay everything out.
        treePanel.setPreferredSize(
```

```
              new Dimension(300, 150));
          add(treePanel, BorderLayout.CENTER);

          JPanel panel = new JPanel(new GridLayout(0,3));
          panel.add(addButton);
          panel.add(removeButton);
          panel.add(clearButton);
          add(panel, BorderLayout.SOUTH);
      }
      // . . .
  }
```

Creating the Applet

For a Java applet that has a Swing-based GUI, create a class that is a subclass of
`javax.swing.JApplet`. An applet that does not contain a Swing-based GUI can
extend the `java.applet.Applet` class.

Override the applet's `init` method to instantiate your top `JPanel` class and create the applet's GUI. The `init` method of the `DynamicTreeApplet` class invokes
the `createGUI` method in the Abstract Window Toolkit (AWT) Event Dispatcher
thread:

```
package appletComponentArch;

import javax.swing.JApplet;
import javax.swing.SwingUtilities;

public class DynamicTreeApplet extends JApplet {
    //Called when this applet is loaded into the browser.
    public void init() {
        //Execute a job on the event-dispatching thread; creating this
        //applet's GUI.
        try {
            SwingUtilities.invokeAndWait(new Runnable() {
                public void run() {
                    createGUI();
                }
            });
        } catch (Exception e) {
            System.err.println("createGUI didn't complete successfully");
        }
    }

    private void createGUI() {
        //Create and set up the content pane.
        DynamicTreePanel newContentPane = new DynamicTreePanel();
        newContentPane.setOpaque(true);
        setContentPane(newContentPane);
    }
}
```

17

Benefits of Separating Core Functionality from the Final Deployment Mechanism

Another way to create an applet is to just remove the layer of abstraction (separate top `JPanel`) and lay out all the controls in the applet's `init` method itself. The downside to creating the GUI directly in the applet is that it will make it more difficult to deploy your functionality as a Java Web Start application, if you choose to do so later.

In the `Dynamic Tree Demo` example, the core functionality resides in the `DynamicTreePanel` class. It is now trivial to drop the `DynamicTreePanel` class into a `JFrame` and deploy it as a Java Web Start application.

Hence, to preserve portability and keep deployment options open, follow the component-based design as described in this chapter.

Deploying an Applet

To deploy your Java applet, first compile the source code and package it as a JAR file. Java applets can be launched in two ways:

- You can launch an applet by specifying the applet's launch properties directly in the applet tag. This old way of deploying applets imposes severe security restrictions on the applet.
- Alternatively, you can launch your applet by using Java Network Launch Protocol (JNLP). Applets launched by using JNLP have access to powerful JNLP Application Programming Interfaces (APIs) and extensions.

The Deployment Toolkit script contains useful JavaScript functions that can be used to deploy applets in a web page. If you are unfamiliar with these deployment technologies, review Chapter 19 before proceeding further.

Here are some step-by-step instructions to package and deploy your applet. The `Dynamic Tree Demo` applet is used to illustrate applet deployment. You might want to set up build scripts to execute some of the following steps:

1. Compile your applet's Java code and make sure all class files and resources such as images are in a separate directory. In the case of the `Dynamic Tree Demo` applet, the compiled classes are placed in the `build/classes/applet-ComponentArch` directory.

2. Create a JAR file containing your applet's class files and resources. See Chapter 15 to learn more about creating and using JAR files. For example, the following command creates a JAR file with the class files in the `build/classes/appletComponentArch` directory:

```
% cd build/classes
% jar cvf DynamicTreeDemo.jar appletComponentArch
```

17

3. Create a JNLP file that describes how your applet should be launched. Here is
    the JNLP file used to launch the `Dynamic Tree Demo` applet. (Note that Chap-
    ter 19, "Structure of the JNLP File," describes JNLP file syntax and options.)

```
<?xml version="1.0" encoding="UTF-8"?>
<jnlp spec="1.0+" codebase="" href="">
    <information>
        <title>Dynamic Tree Demo</title>
        <vendor>Dynamic Team</vendor>
    </information>
    <resources>
        <!-- Application Resources -->
        <j2se version="1.6+"
            href="http://java.sun.com/products/autodl/j2se" />
        <jar href="DynamicTreeDemo.jar" main="true" />

    </resources>
    <applet-desc
        name="Dynamic Tree Demo Applet"
        main-class="components.DynamicTreeApplet"
        width="300"
        height="300">
    </applet-desc>
    <update check="background"/>
</jnlp>
```

4. Create the HTML page that will display the applet. Invoke Deployment Tool-
    kit functions to deploy the applet. In our example, the `Dynamic Tree Demo`
    applet is deployed in `AppletPage.html`:

```
<body>
    <!-- . . . -->
    <script src="http://www.java.com/js/deployJava.js"></script>
    <script>
        var attributes = {
            code:'components.DynamicTreeApplet', width:300,
            height:300} ;
        var parameters = {jnlp_href: 'dynamictree-applet.jnlp'} ;
        deployJava.runApplet(attributes, parameters, '1.6');
    </script>
    <!-- . . . -->
</body>
```

5. Place the applet's JAR file, JNLP file, and HTML page in the appropriate
    folder(s). For our example, place `DynamicTreeDemo.jar`, `dynamictree-`
    `applet.jnlp`, and `AppletPage.html` in the same directory on the local
    machine or a web server. A web server is not required for testing this applet.

6. Open the applet's HTML page in a browser to view the applet. Check the Java
    Console log for error and debugging messages.

Deploying with the Applet Tag

If you are not sure if your end users' browsers will have the JavaScript interpreter
enabled, you can deploy your Java applet by manually coding the `<applet>` HTML

tag instead of using the Deployment Toolkit functions. Depending on the browsers you need to support, you may need to deploy your Java applet using the `<object>` or `<embed>` HTML tag. Check the W3C HTML Specification[6] for details on the usage of these tags. You can launch your applet using JNLP or specify the launch attributes directly in the `<applet>` tag.

Preparing for Deployment

Follow the steps described in the "Deploying an Applet" section to compile your source code, and create a JAR file or JNLP file if necessary. The overall steps for deployment are still relevant. Only the contents of your HTML page containing the applet will change.

Manually Coding the Applet Tag and Launching Using JNLP

The `AppletPage_WithAppletTag.html` page deploys the `Dynamic Tree Demo` applet with an `<applet>` tag that has been manually coded (i.e., the applet is not deployed using the Deployment Toolkit, which automatically generates the required HTML). The applet is still launched using JNLP. The JNLP file is specified in the `jnlp_href` attribute:

```
<applet code = 'appletComponentArch.DynamicTreeApplet'
        jnlp_href = 'dynamictree-applet.jnlp'
        width = 300
        height = 300 />
```

Manually Coding the Applet Tag and Launching without JNLP

If your applet does not need special permissions to perform certain sensitive operations, you can also deploy your applet without a JNLP file. The `AppletPage_WithAppletTagNoJNLP.html` deploys the `Dynamic Tree Demo` applet, as shown in the following code snippet:

```
<applet code = 'appletComponentArch.DynamicTreeApplet'
        archive = 'DynamicTreeDemo.jar'
        width = 300
        height = 300 />
```

In this code snippet, the following is true:

- `code` is the name of the applet class.
- `archive` is the name of the JAR file containing the applet and its resources.
- `width` is the width of the applet.
- `height` is the height of the applet.

6. http://www.w3.org/TR/1999/REC-html401-19991224

Doing More with Applets

The Java applet API enables you to take advantage of the close relationship that applets have with browsers. The API is provided by the `javax.swing.JApplet` class and the `java.applet.AppletContext` interface. The applet execution architecture enables applets to interact with their environment to produce a rich user experience. An applet can manipulate its parent web page, interact with JavaScript code in the web page, find other applets running in the same web page, and much more.

The advanced capabilities of Java applets are explored in the sections that follow. See Chapter 18 for further information on advanced topics that are common to applets and Java Web Start applications (such as setting arguments and properties using JNLP API).

Finding and Loading Data Files

Whenever a Java applet needs to load data from a file that is specified with a relative URL (i.e., a URL that doesn't completely specify the file's location), the applet usually uses either the code base or the document base to form the complete URL.

The code base, returned by the `JAppletgetCodeBase` method, is a URL that specifies the directory from which the applet's classes were loaded. The document base, returned by the `JAppletgetDocumentBase` method, specifies the directory of the HTML page that contains the applet. Unless the `<applet>` tag specifies a code base, both the code base and document base refer to the same directory on the same server.

Data that the applet might need or data that the applet needs to rely on as a backup is usually specified relative to the code base. Data that the applet developer specifies, often by using parameters, is usually specified relative to the document base.

> **Note**
>
> For security reasons, browsers limit the URLs from which untrusted applets can read. For example, most browsers don't allow untrusted applets to use `..` to access directories above the code base or document base. Also, because untrusted applets cannot read files except for those files on the applet's originating host, the document base is generally not useful if the document and the untrusted applet reside on different servers.

17

The `JApplet` class defines convenient forms of image-loading and sound-loading methods that enable you to specify images and sounds relative to a base URL. For example, assume an applet is set up with one of the directory structures shown in Figure 17.2. To create an `Image` object that uses the `a.gif` image file under `imgDir`, the applet can use the following code:

```
Image image = getImage(getCodeBase(), "imgDir/a.gif");
```

No Package Statements
in Applet Code

package com.myco.myproject

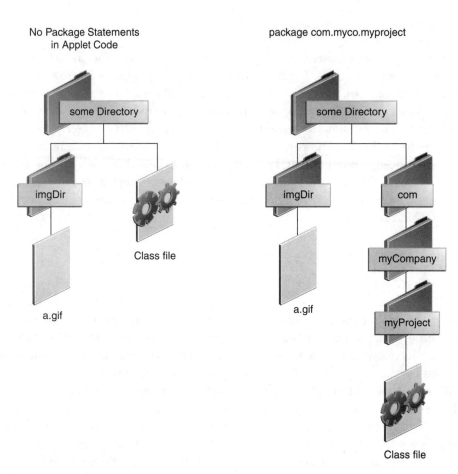

Figure 17.2 Code Directory Structures with and without Package Statements

Defining and Using Applet Parameters

Parameters are to Java applets what command-line arguments are to applications. They enable the user to customize the applet's operation. By defining parameters, you can increase your applet's flexibility, making your applet work in multiple situations without recoding and recompiling it.

Specifying an Applet's Input Parameters

You can specify an applet's input parameters in the applet's JNLP file or in the `<parameter>` element of the `<applet>` tag. It is usually better to specify the parameters in the applet's JNLP file so that the parameters can be supplied consistently, even if the applet is deployed on multiple web pages. If the applet's parameters will vary by web page, then you should specify the parameters in the `<parameter>` element of the `<applet>` tag. If you are unfamiliar with JNLP, see Chapter 19, "Java Network Launch Protocol," for more information.

Consider an applet that takes three parameters. The `paramStr` and `paramInt` parameters are specified in the applet's JNLP file, `applettakesparams.jnlp`:

```
<?xml version="1.0" encoding="UTF-8"?>
<jnlp spec="1.0+" codebase="" href="">
    <!-- . . . -->
    <applet-desc
        name="Applet Takes Params"
        main-class="AppletTakesParams"
        width="800"
        height="50">
            <param name="paramStr"
                value="someString"/>
            <param name="paramInt" value="22"/>
    </applet-desc>
    <!-- . . . -->
</jnlp>
```

The `paramOutsideJNLPFile` parameter is specified in the `parameters` variable passed to the Deployment Toolkit script's `runApplet` function in `AppletPage.html`:

```
<html>
  <head>
    <title>Applet Takes Params</title>
    <meta http-equiv="Content-Type" content="text/html;
        charset=windows-1252">
  </head>
  <body>
    <h1>Applet Takes Params</h1>

    <script
      src="http://www.java.com/js/deployJava.js"></script>
    <script>
        var attributes = { code:'AppletTakesParams.class',
            archive:'applet_AppletWithParameters.jar',
            width:800, height:50} ;
        var parameters = {jnlp_href: 'applettakesparams.jnlp',
            paramOutsideJNLPFile: 'fooOutsideJNLP'} ;
        deployJava.runApplet(attributes, parameters, '1.4');
    </script>

  </body>
</html>
```

See Chapter 19, "Deploying an Applet," for more information about the runApplet function.

Retrieving the Applet's Input Parameters

You can retrieve the applet's input parameters by using the getParameter[7] method of the Applet class. The AppletTakesParams.java applet retrieves and displays all its input parameters (paramStr, paramInt, and paramOutsideJNLPFile):

```java
import javax.swing.JApplet;
import javax.swing.SwingUtilities;
import javax.swing.JLabel;

public class AppletTakesParams extends JApplet {
    public void init() {
        final String  inputStr = getParameter("paramStr");
        final int inputInt = Integer.parseInt(getParameter("paramInt"));
        final String inputOutsideJNLPFile =
            getParameter("paramOutsideJNLPFile");

        try {
            SwingUtilities.invokeAndWait(new Runnable() {
                public void run() {
                    createGUI(inputStr, inputInt, inputOutsideJNLPFile);
                }
            });
        } catch (Exception e) {
            System.err.println("createGUI didn't successfully complete");
        }
    }
    private void createGUI(String inputStr, int inputInt,
        String inputOutsideJNLPFile) {
        String text = "Applet's parameters are -- inputStr: " + inputStr +
                      ",  inputInt: " + inputInt +
                      ",  paramOutsideJNLPFile: " + inputOutsideJNLPFile;
        JLabel lbl = new JLabel(text);
        add(lbl);
    }
}
```

Displaying Short Status Strings

All browsers allow Java applets to display a short status string. All Java applets on the page, as well as the browser itself, share the same status line.

Never put crucial information in the status line. If many users might need the information, display that information within the applet area. If only a few, sophisticated users might need the information, consider sending the information to standard output. (See the "Writing Diagnostics to Standard Output and Error Streams" section in this chapter.)

The status line is not usually very prominent, and it can be overwritten by other applets or by the browser. For these reasons, it is best used for incidental, transitory

---

7. 7/docs/api/java/applet/Applet.html#getParameter(java.lang.String)

information. For example, an applet that loads several image files might display the name of the image file it is currently loading.

Applets display status lines with the `showStatus`[8] method, inherited in the `JApplet` class from the `Applet` class. Here is an example of its use:

```
showStatus("MyApplet: Loading image file " + file);
```

> **Note**
> Don't put scrolling text in the status line. Browser users find such behavior highly annoying.

Displaying Documents in the Browser

A Java applet can load a web page in a browser window using the `showDocument` methods in the `java.applet.AppletContext`[9] class.

Here are the two forms of `showDocument`:

```
public void showDocument(java.net.URL url)
public void showDocument(java.net.URL url, String targetWindow)
```

The one-argument form of `showDocument` simply instructs the browser to display the document at the specified URL without specifying the window in which to display the document. The two-argument form of `showDocument` lets you specify the window or HTML frame in which to display the document. The second argument can have one of the following values:

- `"_blank"`—This displays the document in a new, nameless window.
- `"windowName"`—This displays the document in a window named *windowName*. This window is created if necessary.
- `"_self"`—This displays the document in the window and frame that contain the applet.
- `"_parent"`—This displays the document in the parent frame of the applet's frame. If the applet frame has no parent frame, this acts the same as `"_self"`.
- `"_top"`—This displays the document in the top-level frame. If the applet's frame is the top-level frame, this acts the same as `"_self"`.

17

---

8. `7/docs/api/java/applet/Applet.html#showStatus(java.lang.String)`
9. `7/docs/api/java/applet/AppletContext.html`

> **Note**
>
> In this discussion, *frame* doesn't refer to a Swing `JFrame` but to an HTML frame within a browser window.

The `ShowDocument` applet enables you to try every argument of both forms of showDocument. The applet opens a window that lets you type in a URL and choose an option for the `targetWindow` argument. When you press **Return** or click the **Show Document** button, the applet calls showDocument:

```
        . . . //In an Applet subclass:
      urlWindow = new URLWindow(getAppletContext());
        . . .

class URLWindow extends Frame {
    . . .
    public URLWindow(AppletContext appletContext) {
        . . .
        this.appletContext = appletContext;
        . . .
    }
    . . .
    public boolean action(Event event, Object o) {
        . . .
        String urlString =
            /* user-entered string */;
        URL url = null;
        try {
            url = new URL(urlString);
        } catch (MalformedURLException e) {
            . . . //Inform the user and return . . .
        }

        if (url != null) {
            if (/* user doesn't want to specify
                    the window */) {
                appletContext.showDocument(url);
            } else {
                appletContext.showDocument(url,
                    /* user-specified window */);
            }
        }
    }
    . . .
```

17

Invoking JavaScript Code from an Applet

Java applets can invoke JavaScript functions present in the same web page as the applet. The LiveConnect Specification[10] describes details about how JavaScript code communicates with Java code.

---

10. `http://www.oracle.com/technetwork/java/javase/plugin2-142482.html`
   `#LIVECONNECT`

The `netscape.javascript.JSObject` class enables Java applets to retrieve a reference to JavaScript objects and interact with the web page. The `Data Summary` applet described next invokes JavaScript code to retrieve information from the web page and writes a data summary back to the web page.

Assume you have a web page with a few JavaScript functions. The example `AppletPage.html` has JavaScript functions to retrieve age, address, and phone numbers. There is also a variable called `userName` that has no value at the outset:

```
<head>
<title>Data Summary Applet Page - Java to JavaScript LiveConnect</title>
<meta http-equiv="Content-Type" content="text/html; charset=windows-1252"/>
<script language="javascript">
    var userName = "";

    // returns number
    function getAge() {
        return 25;
    }
    // returns an object
    function address() {
        this.street = "1 Example Lane";
        this.city = "Santa Clara";
        this.state = "CA";
    }
    // returns an array
    function getPhoneNums() {
        return ["408-555-0100", "408-555-0102"];
    }
    function writeSummary(summary) {
        summaryElem =
            document.getElementById("summary");
        summaryElem.innerHTML = summary;
    }
</script>

<!-- . . . -->
</head>
<body>
    <script src =
      "http://www.java.com/js/deployJava.js"></script>
    <script>
        <!-- . . . -->
        deployJava.runApplet(attributes,
            parameters, '1.6');
    </script>
    <!-- . . . -->
    <p id="summary"/>  // this HTML element contains
                               // the summary
    <!-- . . . -->
</body>
```

Next, consider an applet class called `DataSummaryApplet`. The `DataSummary-Applet` class performs the following operations:

- Invoke the `JSObject`'s `setMember` method to set the `userName` variable to "John Doe."
- Retrieve the age, address, and phone numbers, and build a string containing a summary of this data.
- Invoke the `writeSummary` JavaScript function to write the summary back to the web page.

This applet first needs to retrieve a reference to `JSObject`, as follows:

```
. . .
JSObject window = JSObject.getWindow(this);
. . .
```

Put the preceding statement in a `try . . . catch` block to handle `netscape. javascript.JSException`. Now that the applet has a reference to `JSObject`, it can invoke the relevant JavaScript functions by using the `eval` and `call` methods of `JSObject`:

```java
package javatojs;

import java.applet.Applet;
import netscape.javascript.*; // add plugin.jar to classpath during
compilation

public class DataSummaryApplet extends Applet {
    public void start() {
        try {
            JSObject window = JSObject.getWindow(this);

            String userName = "John Doe";

            // set JavaScript variable
            window.setMember("userName", userName);

            // invoke JavaScript function
            Number age = (Number) window.eval("getAge()");

            // get a JavaScript object and retrieve its contents
            JSObject address = (JSObject) window.eval("new address();");
            String addressStr = (String) address.getMember("street")
                + ", " +
                    (String) address.getMember("city") + ", " +
                    (String) address.getMember("state");

            // get an array from JavaScript and retrieve its contents
            JSObject phoneNums = (JSObject) window.eval("getPhoneNums()");
            String phoneNumStr = (String) phoneNums.getSlot(0) + ", " +
                    (String) phoneNums.getSlot(1);

            // dynamically change HTML in page; write data summary
            String summary = userName + " : " + age + " : " +
```

```
                        addressStr + " : " + phoneNumStr;
            window.call("writeSummary", new Object[] {summary})   ;
        } catch (JSException jse) {
            jse.printStackTrace();
        }
    }
}
```

To compile Java code that has a reference to classes in the `netscape.javascript` package, include `<your JDK path>/jre/lib/plugin.jar` in your class path. At runtime, the Java Plug-In software automatically makes these classes available to applets.

The `Data Summary` applet displays the following result on the web page:

```
Result of applet's Java calls to JavaScript on this page
John Doe : 25 : 1 Example Lane, Santa Clara, CA : 408-555-0100,
408-555-0102
```

Invoking Applet Methods from JavaScript Code

JavaScript code on a web page can interact with Java applets embedded on the page. JavaScript code can perform operations such as the following:

- Invoke methods on Java objects.
- Get and set fields in Java objects.
- Get and set Java array elements.
- Create new instances of Java objects.

The LiveConnect Specification[11] describes details about how JavaScript code communicates with Java code.

This section explores JavaScript code to Java applet communication using the `Math Applet` example. The `MathApplet` class and supporting `Calculator` class provide a set of public methods and variables. The JavaScript code on the web page invokes and evaluates these public members to pass data and retrieve calculated results.

Math Applet and Related Classes

Here is the source code for the `MathApplet` class. The `getCalculator` method returns a reference to the `Calculator` helper class:

```
package jstojava;
import java.applet.Applet;
```

17

---

11. http://www.oracle.com/technetwork/java/javase/plugin2-142482.html #LIVECONNECT

```
public class MathApplet extends Applet{

    public String userName = null;

    public String getGreeting() {
        return "Hello " + userName;
    }

    public Calculator getCalculator() {
        return new Calculator();
    }
}
```

The methods in the `Calculator` class let the user set two values, add numbers, and retrieve the numbers in a range:

```
package jstojava;

public class Calculator {
    private int a = 0;
    private int b = 0; // assume b > a

    public void setNums(int numA, int numB) {
        a = numA;
        b = numB;
    }

    public int add() {
        return a + b;
    }

    public int [] getNumInRange() {
        int x = a;
        int len = (b - a) + 1;
        int [] range = new int [len];
        for (int i = 0; i < len; i++) {
            range[i]= x++;
            System.out.println("i: " + i + " ; range[i]: " + range[i]);
        }
        return range;
    }
}
```

The `getDate` method of the `DateHelper` class returns the current date:

```
package jstojava;
import java.util.Date;
import java.text.SimpleDateFormat;

public class DateHelper {

    public static String label = null;

    public String getDate() {
```

```
            return label + " " + new SimpleDateFormat().format(new Date());
    }

}
```

Deploying the Applet

Deploy the applet in a web page, `AppletPage.html`. When deploying the applet, be sure to specify an `id` for the applet. The applet `id` is used later to obtain a reference to the applet object:

```
<script src=
  "http://www.java.com/js/deployJava.js"></script>
<script>
    <!-- applet id can be used to get a reference to
    the applet object -->
    var attributes = { id:'mathApplet',
        code:'jstojava.MathApplet', width:1, height:1} ;
    var parameters = {jnlp_href: 'math-applet.jnlp'} ;
    deployJava.runApplet(attributes, parameters, '1.6');
</script>
```

Next, add some JavaScript code to the `AppletPage.html` web page. The JavaScript code can use the applet `id` as a reference to the applet object and invoke the applet's methods. In the following example, the JavaScript code sets the applet's public member variables, invokes public methods, and retrieves a reference to another object referenced by the applet (`Calculator`). The JavaScript code is able to handle primitive, array, and object return types. The JavaScript code can also invoke methods from classes or objects in other packages using the `Packages` keyword:

```
<script language="javascript">
    function enterNums(){
        var numA = prompt('Enter number \'a\'?','0');
        var numB = prompt(
            'Enter number \'b\' (should be greater than number \'a\' ?','1');
        // set applet's public variable
        mathApplet.userName = "John Doe";

        // invoke public applet method
        var greeting = mathApplet.getGreeting();

        // get another class referenced by applet and
        // invoke its methods
        var calculator = mathApplet.getCalculator();
        calculator.setNums(numA, numB);

        // primitive datatype returned by applet
        var sum = calculator.add();

        // array returned by applet
        var numRange = calculator.getNumInRange();
```

17

```
        // "Packages" keyword; check Java console log
        // for this message
        mathApplet.Packages.java.lang.System.out.
            println("Testing printing to System.out");

        // Set static field using "Packages" keyword;
        // static methods may be similarly invoked
        mathApplet.Packages.jstojava.DateHelper.label =
            "Today\'s date is: ";

        // Create an instance of a class and invoke
        // method using "Packages" keyword
        var dateHelper =
            new mathApplet.Packages.jstojava.DateHelper();
        var dateStr = dateHelper.getDate();
        <!-- . . . -->
    </script>
```

The Math applet displays the following results on the web page when the number a = 0 and b = 5:

```
Results of JavaScript to Java Communication

Hello John Doe

a = 0 ; b = 5

Sum: 5

Numbers in range array: [ 0, 1, 2, 3, 4, 5 ]

Today's date is: 11/13/12 10:12 AM //shows current date
```

Open `AppletPage.html` in a browser to view the Math applet. Check security restrictions placed on applets invoked by JavaScript code.

> **Note**
>
> If you don't see the applet running, you need to install at least JDK 6 update 10.[12] You might need to enable the JavaScript interpreter in your browser so that the Deployment Toolkit script can function properly.

Handling Initialization Status with Event Handlers

An applet cannot handle requests from JavaScript code in the web page until the applet has been initialized. A call to an applet method or access to an applet variable from JavaScript code will be blocked until the applet's `init()` method is complete

---

12. http://www.oracle.com/technetwork/java/javase/downloads/index.html

or the applet first invokes JavaScript code from the web page in which it is deployed. As the JavaScript implementation is single-threaded in many browsers, the web page may appear to be frozen during applet start-up.

Beginning in the JDK 7 release, you can check the `status` variable of the applet while it is loading to determine if the applet is ready to handle requests from JavaScript code. You can also register event handlers that will automatically be invoked during various stages of applet initialization. To leverage this functionality, the applet should be deployed with the `java_status_events` parameter set to `"true"`.

In the following status and event handler example, JavaScript code registers an `onLoad` handler with the applet. The `onLoad` handler is automatically invoked by the Java Plug-In software when the applet has been initialized. The `onLoad` handler invokes other methods of the applet to draw the graph on the web page. The `init` method of the `DrawingApplet` class sleeps for two seconds to simulate a long applet initialization period.

The following steps describe how to register event handlers and check an applet's status. See Applet Status and Event Handlers[13] for a complete list of applet status values and applet events for which event handlers can be registered.

1. Create a JavaScript function to register event handlers. The following code snippet shows the `registerAppletStateHandler` function that registers an `onLoad` event handler if the applet has not already loaded:

```
<script>
<!-- . . . -->
    var READY = 2;
    function registerAppletStateHandler() {
        // register onLoad handler if applet has
        // not loaded yet
        if (drawApplet.status < READY) {
            drawApplet.onLoad = onLoadHandler;
        } else if (drawApplet.status >= READY) {
            // applet has already loaded or there
            // was an error
            document.getElementById("mydiv").innerHTML =
              "Applet event handler not registered because applet
                 status is: "
              + drawApplet.status;
        }
    }

    function onLoadHandler() {
        // event handler for ready state
        document.getElementById("mydiv").innerHTML =
           "Applet has loaded";
        draw();
```

17

13. 7/docs/technotes/guides/jweb/applet/appletStatus.html

```
    }
<!-- . . . -->
</script>
```

2. Invoke the previously created `registerAppletStateHandler` function in the body tag's onLoad method. This ensures that the HTML tag for the applet has been created in the Document Object Model (DOM) tree of the web page before the applet's event handlers are registered:

    ```
    <body onload="registerAppletStateHandler()">
    ```

3. Deploy the applet with the `java_status_events` parameter set to "true":

    ```
    <script src=
      "http://www.java.com/js/deployJava.js"></script>
    <script>
        // set java_status_events parameter to true
        var attributes = { id:'drawApplet',
            code:'DrawingApplet.class',
            archive: 'applet_StatusAndCallback.jar',
            width:600, height:400} ;
        var parameters = {java_status_events: 'true'} ;
        deployJava.runApplet(attributes, parameters, '1.7');
    </script>
    ```

Manipulating DOM of an Applet's Web Page

Every web page is composed of a series of nested objects. These objects make up the DOM. A Java applet can traverse and modify objects of its parent web page using the Common DOM API.[14]

Consider an example of a Java applet that dumps the contents of its parent web page. In order to traverse and manipulate the DOM tree, you must first obtain a reference to the Document object for the web page. You can do so by using the getDocument method in the com.sun.java.browser.plugin2.DOM class. Here is a code snippet that retrieves a reference to a Document object in the DOMDump applet's start method. See in-line comments in the code:

```
public void start() {
    try {
        // use reflection to get document
        Class c =
          Class.forName("com.sun.java.browser.plugin2.DOM");
        Method m = c.getMethod("getDocument",
          new Class[] { java.applet.Applet.class });

        // cast object returned as HTMLDocument;
        // then traverse or modify DOM
        HTMLDocument doc = (HTMLDocument) m.invoke(null,
            new Object[] { this });
        HTMLBodyElement body =
```

---

14. 7/docs/jre/api/plugin/dom/index.html

```
                    (HTMLBodyElement) doc.getBody();
                dump(body, INDENT);
            } catch (Exception e) {
                System.out.println("New Java Plug-In not available");
                // In this case, you could fallback to the old
                // bootstrapping mechanism available in the
                // com.sun.java.browser.plugin.dom package
            }
        }
    }
```

Now that you have a reference to the Document object, you can traverse and modify the DOM tree using the Common DOM API. The DOMDump applet traverses the DOM tree and writes its contents to the Java Console log:

```
private void dump(Node root, String prefix) {
    if (root instanceof Element) {
        System.out.println(prefix +
            ((Element) root).getTagName() +
            " / " + root.getClass().getName());
    } else if (root instanceof CharacterData) {
        String data =
            ((CharacterData) root).getData().trim();
        if (!data.equals("")) {
            System.out.println(prefix +
                "CharacterData: " + data);
        }
    } else {
        System.out.println(prefix +
            root.getClass().getName());
    }
    NamedNodeMap attrs = root.getAttributes();
    if (attrs != null) {
        int len = attrs.getLength();
        for (int i = 0; i < len; i++) {
            Node attr = attrs.item(i);
            System.out.print(prefix + HALF_INDENT +
                "attribute " + i + ": " +
                attr.getNodeName());
            if (attr instanceof Attr) {
                System.out.print(" = " +
                    ((Attr) attr).getValue());
            }
            System.out.println();
        }
    }

    if (root.hasChildNodes()) {
        NodeList children = root.getChildNodes();
        if (children != null) {
            int len = children.getLength();
            for (int i = 0; i < len; i++) {
                dump(children.item(i), prefix +
                    INDENT);
            }
        }
    }
}
```

17

Displaying a Customized Loading Progress Indicator

A Java applet can display a customized loading progress indicator that shows the progress of the download of the applet's resources as well as other applet specific data.

Consider the `Weather` applet and the `CustomProgress` class described in this section to understand how to implement a customized loading progress indicator for a Java applet.[15] For the purpose of demonstrating a large and prolonged download, this applet's JAR file has been artificially inflated and the `customprogress-applet.jnlp` file specifies additional JAR files as resources.

Developing a Customized Loading Progress Indicator

To develop a customized loading progress indicator for your applet, create a class that implements the `DownloadServiceListener`[16] interface. The constructor of the loading progress indicator class will vary depending on how the user interface should be displayed and the capabilities needed by the class. The following guidelines should be applied:

- To display the loading progress indicator in a separate top-level window, create a constructor that does not have any parameters.
- To display the loading progress indicator for an applet in the applet's container, create a constructor that takes an `Object` as a parameter. The `Object` argument can be typecast to an instance of the `java.awt.Container`[17] class.
- If the loading progress indicator class needs to access the applet's parameters, create two constructors:
  - ⌐ Create a constructor that takes an `Object` as a parameter (as described previously).
  - ⌐ Create a constructor that takes two parameters of type `Object`. The first argument can be typecast to an instance of the `java.awt.Container`[18] class, and the second argument can be typecast to an instance of the `java.applet.AppletStub`[19] class.

The Java Plug-In software will invoke the appropriate constructor depending on the capabilities of the JRE software on the client machine.

---

15. `tutorial/deployment/applet/examples/zipfiles/applet_CustomProgress`
    `Indicator.zip`
16. `7/docs/jre/api/javaws/jnlp/javax/jnlp/DownloadServiceListener.html`
17. `7/docs/api/java/awt/Container.html`
18. `7/docs/api/java/awt/Container.html`
19. `7/docs/api/java/applet/AppletStub.html`

Here is the class that implements the `DownloadServiceListener` interface:

```
import javax.jnlp.DownloadServiceListener;
import java.awt.Container;
import java.applet.AppletStub;
import netscape.javascript.*;

// . . .

public class CustomProgress implements DownloadServiceListener {
    Container surfaceContainer = null;
    AppletStub appletStub = null;
    JProgressBar progressBar = null;
    JLabel statusLabel = null;
    boolean uiCreated = false;

    public CustomProgress(Object surface) {
        init(surface, null);
    }

    public CustomProgress(Object surface, Object stub) {
        init(surface, stub);
    }

    public void init(Object surface, Object stub) {
        try {
            surfaceContainer = (Container) surface;
            appletStub = (AppletStub) stub;
        } catch (ClassCastException cce) {
            // . . .
        }
    }
}
// . . .
}
```

The following code snippet shows how to build the user interface for the loading progress indicator. Use the instance of the `java.applet.AppletStub`[20] class to retrieve the applet's parameters. Invoke the `JSObject.getWindow(null)` method to obtain a reference to the applet's parent web page and invoke JavaScript code on that page:

```
private void create() {
    JPanel top = createComponents();
    if (surfaceContainer != null) {
        // lay out loading progress UI in the given
        // Container
        surfaceContainer.add(top, BorderLayout.NORTH);
        surfaceContainer.invalidate();
        surfaceContainer.validate();
    }
}
private JPanel createComponents() {
```

17

---

20. 7/docs/api/java/applet/AppletStub.html

```
        JPanel top = new JPanel();
        // . . .
        // get applet parameter using an instance of the
        // AppletStub class "tagLine" parameter specified
        // in applet's JNLP file
        String tagLine = "";
        if (appletStub != null) {
            tagLine = appletStub.getParameter("tagLine");
        }
        String lblText = "<html><font color=red size=+2>JDK
            Documentation</font><br/>" +
            tagLine + " <br/></html>";
        JLabel lbl = new JLabel(lblText);
        top.add(lbl, BorderLayout.NORTH);

        // use JSObject.getWindow(null) method to retrieve
        // a reference to the web page and make JavaScript
        // calls. Duke logo displayed if displayLogo variable
        // set to "true" in the web page
        String displayLogo = "false";
        JSObject window = JSObject.getWindow(null);
        if (window != null) {
            displayLogo = (String)window.getMember("displayLogo");
        }
        if (displayLogo.equals("true")) {
            lbl = new JLabel();
            ImageIcon logo = createImageIcon("images/DukeWave.gif", "logo");
            lbl.setIcon(logo);
            top.add(lbl, BorderLayout.EAST);
        }

        statusLabel = new JLabel(
            "html><font color=green size=-2>" +
            "Loading applet . . . </font></html>");
        top.add(statusLabel, BorderLayout.CENTER);

        // progress bar displays progress
        progressBar = new JProgressBar(0, 100);
        progressBar.setValue(0);
        progressBar.setStringPainted(true);
        top.add(progressBar, BorderLayout.SOUTH);

        return top;
    }
```

Create and update the progress indicator in the following methods based on the `overallPercent` argument. The Java Plug-In software invokes these methods regularly to communicate the progress of the applet's download. Java Plug-In software will always send a message when download and validation of resources is 100 percent complete.

```
    public void progress(URL url, String version,
                         long readSoFar, long total,
                         int overallPercent) {
        // check progress of download and update display
        updateProgressUI(overallPercent);
```

```
    }
    public void upgradingArchive(java.net.URL url,
                    java.lang.String version,
                    int patchPercent,
                    int overallPercent) {
        updateProgressUI(overallPercent);
    }
    public void validating(java.net.URL url,
            java.lang.String version,
            long entry,
            long total,
            int overallPercent) {
        updateProgressUI(overallPercent);
    }
    private void updateProgressUI(int overallPercent) {
        if (!uiCreated && overallPercent > 0
            && overallPercent < 100) {
            // create custom progress indicator's
            // UI only if there is more work to do,
            // meaning overallPercent > 0 and
            // < 100 this prevents flashing when
            // RIA is loaded from cache
            create();
            uiCreated = true;
        }
        if (uiCreated) {
            progressBar.setValue(overallPercent);
        }
    }
}
```

Compile the loading progress indicator class and build a JAR file with all the resources needed to display the loading progress indicator. Include the following JAR files in your `classpath` to enable compilation:

- `<your JRE directory>/lib/javaws.jar`
- `<your JRE directory>/lib/plugin.jar`

Note that the second JAR file is required only if your loading progress indicator class uses the `JSObject.getWindow` method to invoke JavaScript code in the applet's parent web page.

The loading progress indicator class is now ready for use. The next step is to specify this loading progress indicator JAR file as your applet's loading progress indicator.

Specifying a Loading Progress Indicator for an Applet

To specify a customized loading progress indicator for an applet, include the following information in the applet's JNLP file:

- jar tag with the download="progress" attribute
- progress-class attribute with the fully qualified name of the loading progress class

The following code snippet from the customprogress-applet.jnlp[21] file displays the usage of the download="progress" and progress-class attributes:

```
<jnlp spec="1.0+"
  codebase="http://docs.oracle.com/javase/tutorial/deployment"
  href="">
  <!-- . . . -->
  <resources>
    <!-- . . . -->
    <jar
      href="applet/examples/dist/applet_AppletWithCustomProgressIndicator"
      main="true" />
    <jar href=
"applet/examples/dist/applet_CustomProgressIndicator/applet_CustomProgressIndicator.jar"
      download="progress" />
  </resources>
  <applet-desc
    name="customprogressindicatordemo.WeatherApplet"
    main-class="customprogressindicatordemo.WeatherApplet"
    progress-class="customprogressindicator.CustomProgress"
    width="600"
    height="200">
    <param
      name="tagLine"
      value="Information straight from the horse's mouth!"/>
  </applet-desc>
<!-- . . . -->
</jnlp>
```

Deploy the applet in a web page. Open AppletPage.html[22] in a web browser to view the loading progress indicator for the Weather applet.

Integrating the Loading Progress Indicator with an Applet's User Interface

You can also integrate the loading progress indicator into the applet's user interface. Open AppletPage.html[23] in a web browser to view the loading progress indicator

---

21. tutorial/deployment/applet/examples/applet_AppletWithCustomProgress Indicator/src/customprogress-applet.jnlp
22. tutorial/deployment/applet/examples/dist/applet_AppletWithCustom ProgressIndicator/AppletPage.html
23. tutorial/deployment/applet/examples/dist/applet_AppletWithIntegrated ProgressIndicator/AppletPage.html

integrated into the Weather applet's user interface. View the `IntegratedPro-gressIndicator.java`[24] class and the in-line comments for more information.

See Chapter 18, "Customizing the Loading Experience," for more information about customizing the rich Internet application (RIA) loading experience.

Writing Diagnostics to Standard Output and Error Streams

A Java applet can write messages to the standard output and standard error streams. Writing diagnostics to standard output can be an invaluable tool when you are debugging a Java applet. The following code snippet writes messages to the standard output stream and the standard error stream:

```
// Where instance variables are declared:
boolean DEBUG = true;
// . . .
// Later, when we want to print some status:
if (DEBUG) {
    try {
        // . . .
        //some code that throws an exception
        System.out.println("Called someMethod(" + x + "," + y + ")");
    } catch (Exception e) {
        e.printStackTrace()
    }
}
```

Check the Java Console log for messages written to the standard output stream or standard error stream. To store messages in a log file, enable logging in the Java Control Panel. Messages will be written to a log file in the user's home directory (e.g., on Windows, the log file might be in `C:\Documents and Settings\someuser\ Application Data\Sun\Java\Deployment\log`).

> **Note**
> Be sure to disable all debugging output before you release your applet.

17

Developing Draggable Applets

A Java applet that is deployed by specifying the `draggable` parameter can be dragged outside the browser and dynamically transformed into a Java Web Start

---

24. `tutorial/deployment/applet/examples/applet_AppletWithIntegrated ProgressIndicator/src/integratedprogressdemo/IntegratedProgress Indicator.java`

application. Drag the Java applet by pressing the **Alt** key and the left mouse button and dragging the mouse. When the drag operation begins, the applet is removed from its parent container (`Applet` or `JApplet`) and placed in a new undecorated top-level window (`Frame` or `JFrame`). A small floating Close button is displayed next to the dragged applet. When the floating Close button is clicked, the applet is placed back in the browser. Java applets that can be dragged out of the browser are sometimes referred to as *draggable applets*.

You can customize the behavior of a draggable applet in the following ways:

- You can change the keystroke and mouse button sequence that is used to drag the applet outside the browser.
- You can add a desktop shortcut that can be used to launch your application outside the browser.
- You can define how the applet should be closed after it has been dragged outside the browser.

The following sections describe how to implement and customize a draggable applet. The `MenuChooserApplet` class is used to demonstrate the development and deployment of draggable applets. Open `AppletPage.html` in a browser to view the Menu Chooser applet on a new page.

Enabling the Capability to Drag an Applet

You can enable the capability to drag an applet by setting the `draggable` parameter to `true` when deploying the applet, as shown in the following code snippet:

```
<script src="http://www.java.com/js/deployJava.js"></script>
<script>
    var attributes = { code:'MenuChooserApplet', width:900, height:300 };
    var parameters = {jnlp_href: 'draggableapplet.jnlp', draggable: 'true'} ;
    deployJava.runApplet(attributes, parameters, '1.6');
</script>
```

Changing the Keystroke and Mouse Button Sequence That Is Used to Drag an Applet

You can change the keystroke and mouse button sequence that is used to drag an applet by implementing the `isAppletDragStart` method. In the following code snippet, the applet can be dragged by pressing the left mouse button and dragging the mouse:

```
public boolean isAppletDragStart(MouseEvent e) {
        if(e.getID() == MouseEvent.MOUSE_DRAGGED) {
            return true;
        } else {
```

```
            return false;
        }
    }
```

Enabling the Addition of a Desktop Shortcut When the Applet Is Disconnected from the Browser

If the user closes the browser window or navigates away from the page after dragging an applet outside of the page, the applet is said to be *disconnected* from the browser. You can create a desktop shortcut for the applet when the applet is disconnected from the browser. The desktop shortcut can be used to launch the application outside the browser. To enable the creation of a desktop shortcut, add the `offline-allowed` and `shortcut` tags to the applet's JNLP file:

```
<information>
    <!-- . . . -->
    <offline-allowed />
    <shortcut online="false">
        <desktop />
    </shortcut>
</information>
```

> **Note**
> Depending on the setting for Shortcut Creation in the user's Java Control Panel, the user might be prompted for confirmation before the shortcut is created.

Defining How the Applet Should Be Closed

You can define how your applet can be closed. For example, your Swing applet could have a `JButton` to close the applet instead of relying on the default floating Close button.

The Java Plug-In software gives the applet an instance of the `ActionListener` class. This instance of the `ActionListener` class, also referred to as the *close listener*, can be used to modify the default close behavior of the applet.

To define how the applet should be closed, implement the `setAppletCloseListener` and `appletRestored` methods in your applet. In the following code snippet, the `MenuChooserApplet` class receives the close listener and passes it on to the instance of the `MenuItemChooser` class:

```
MenuItemChooser display = null;
// . . .
display = new MenuItemChooser();
// . . .
public void setAppletCloseListener(ActionListener cl) {
    display.setCloseListener(cl);
}
```

17

```
public void appletRestored() {
    display.setCloseListener(null);
}
```

The `MenuItemChooser` class is responsible for controlling the applet's user interface. The `MenuItemChooser` class defines a `JButton` labeled *Close*. The following code is executed when the user clicks this Close button:

```
private void close() {
    // invoke actionPerformed of closeListener received
    // from the Java Plug-in software.
    if (closeListener != null) {
        closeListener.actionPerformed(null);
    }
}
```

Requesting and Customizing Applet Decoration

Beginning in the JDK 7 release, when deploying an applet, you can specify that the window of the dragged applet should be decorated with the default or customized window title.

To enable window decoration of a dragged applet, specify the `java_decorated_frame` parameter with a value of `"true"`. To enable a customized window title, specify the `java_applet_title` parameter also. The value of this parameter should be the text of the window title.

```
<script src="http://www.java.com/js/deployJava.js"></script>
<script>
    var attributes =
      { code:'SomeDraggableApplet', width:100, height:100 };
    var parameters =
      {jnlp_href: 'somedraggableapplet.jnlp',
          java_decorated_frame: 'true',
          java_applet_title: 'A Custom Title'
      };
    deployJava.runApplet(attributes, parameters, '1.7');
</script>
```

The `java_decorated_frame` and `java_applet_title` parameters can also be specified in the applet's JNLP file as shown in the following code snippet:

```
<applet-desc main-class="SayHello" name="main test" height="150"
    width="300">
    <param name="java_decorated_frame" value="true" />
    <param name="java_applet_title" value="" />
</applet-desc>
```

Communicating with Other Applets

A Java applet can communicate with other Java applets by using JavaScript functions in the parent web page. JavaScript functions enable communication between applets by receiving messages from one applet and invoking methods from other applets. See the "Invoking JavaScript Code from an Applet" and "Invoking Applet Methods from JavaScript Code" sections in this chapter for more information about the interaction between Java code and JavaScript code.

You should avoid using certain mechanisms to find other applets and share data between applets:

- Avoid using static variables to share data between applets.
- Do not use the `getApplet` and `getApplets` methods of the `AppletContext`[25] class to find other applets. These methods only find applets that are running in the same instance of the JRE software.

Applets must originate from the same directory on the server in order to communicate with each other. The `Sender` and `Receiver` applets are discussed next. When a user clicks the button to increment the counter, the `Sender` applet invokes a JavaScript function to send a request to the `Receiver` applet. Upon receiving the request, the `Receiver` applet increments a counter variable and displays the value of the variable.

To enable communication with another applet, obtain a reference to an instance of the `netscape.javascript.JSObject` class. Use this instance to invoke JavaScript functions. The `Sender` applet uses an instance of the `netscape.javascript.JSObject` class to invoke a JavaScript function called `sendMsgToIncrementCounter`:

```
try {
    JSObject window = JSObject.getWindow(this);
    window.eval("sendMsgToIncrementCounter()");
} catch (JSException jse) {
    // . . .
}
```

Note

To compile Java code that has a reference to classes in the `netscape.javascript` package, include `<your JDK path>/jre/lib/plugin.jar` in your class path. At runtime, the Java Plug-In software automatically makes these classes available to applets.

17

Write the JavaScript function that will receive requests from one applet and invoke methods of another applet on the web page. The `sendMsgToIncrementCounter` JavaScript function invokes the `Receiver` applet's `incrementCounter` method.

---

25. `7/docs/api/java/applet/AppletContext.html`

```
<script>
    function sendMsgToIncrementCounter() {
        receiver.incrementCounter();
    }
<script>
```

Note that the JavaScript code uses the name `receiver` to obtain a reference to the `Receiver` applet on the web page. This name should match the value of the `id` attribute that is specified when you deploy the `Receiver` applet.

The `Receiver` applet's `incrementCounter` method is as follows:

```
public void incrementCounter() {
    ctr++;
    String text = " Current Value Of Counter: "
        + (new Integer(ctr)).toString();
    ctrLbl.setText(text);
}
```

Deploy the applets on the web page as shown in the following code snippet. You can view the `Sender` and `Receiver` applets and associated JavaScript code in `AppletPage.html`:

```
<!-- Sender Applet -->
<script src="http://www.java.com/js/deployJava.js"></script>
<script>
    var attributes = { code:'Sender.class',
        archive:'examples/dist/applet_SenderReceiver/applet_SenderReceiver.jar',
        width:300, height:50} ;
    var parameters = {};
    deployJava.runApplet(attributes, parameters, '1.6');
</script>

<!-- Receiver Applet -->
<script>
    var attributes = { id:'receiver', code:'Receiver.class',
        archive:'examples/dist/applet_SenderReceiver/applet_SenderReceiver.jar',
        width:300, height:50} ;
    var parameters = {};
    deployJava.runApplet(attributes, parameters, '1.6');
</script>
```

Working with a Server-Side Application

Java applets, like other Java programs, can use the API defined in the `java.net` package to communicate across the network. A Java applet can communicate with server applications that run on the same host as the applet. This communication does not require any special setup on the server.

> **Note**
>
> Depending on the networking environment that an applet is loaded into and depending on the browser that runs the applet, an applet might be unable to communicate with its originating host. For example, browsers running on hosts inside firewalls often cannot obtain much information about the world outside the firewall. As a result, some browsers might not allow applet communication to hosts outside the firewall.

To determine which host an applet came from, use the `AppletgetCodeBase` method and the `java.net.URLgetHost` method, as follows:

```
String host = getCodeBase().getHost();
```

> **Note**
>
> Not all browsers support all networking code flawlessly. For example, one widely used browser compatible with Java technology doesn't support posting to a URL.

The next section provides an example of implementing an applet that is a network client.

Network Client Applet Example

The `QuoteClientApplet` class allows you to fetch quotations from a server-side application that runs on the same host as this applet. This class also displays the quotation received from the server.

The `QuoteServer.java` and `QuoteServerThread.java` classes make up the server-side application that returns quotations. Here's a text file (`one-liners.txt`) that contains a number of quotations.

Perform the following steps to test `QuoteClientApplet`:

1. Download and save the following files to your local machine:

   - `QuoteClientApplet`
   - `QuoteServer.java`
   - `QuoteServerThread.java`
   - `one-liners.txt`
   - `quoteApplet.html`

2. Include the following HTML code in a web page to deploy `QuoteClientApplet`:

17

```
<script src=
  "http://www.java.com/js/deployJava.js"></script>
<script>
    var attributes =
      { code:'QuoteClientApplet.class',  width:500, height:100} ;
    var parameters =
      {codebase_lookup:'true'};
    deployJava.runApplet(attributes, parameters, '1.6');
</script>
```

Alternatively, you can use the `quoteApplet.html` page that already contains this HTML code.

3. Compile the `QuoteClientApplet.java` class. Copy the generated class files to the same directory where you saved your web page.

4. Compile the classes for the server-side application, `QuoteServer.java` and `QuoteServerThread.java`.

5. Copy the file `one-liners.txt` to the directory that has the class files for the server-side application (generated in the previous step).

6. Start the server-side application:

    ```
    java QuoteServer
    ```

    You should see a message with the port number, as follows (and note the port number):

    ```
    QuoteServer listening on port:3862
    ```

7. Open the web page containing your applet in a browser by entering the URL of the web page. The host name in the URL should be the same as the name of the host on which the server-side application is running. For example, if the server-side application is running on a machine named `JohnDoeMachine`, you should enter a similar URL. The exact port number and path will vary depending on your web server setup:

    ```
    http://JohnDoeMachine:8080/quoteApplet/quoteApplet.html
    ```

    The `QuoteClientApplet` will be displayed on the web page.

8. Enter the port number of your server-side application in the applet's text field and click **OK**. A quotation is displayed.

What Applets Can and Cannot Do

Java applets are loaded on a client when the user visits a page containing an applet. The security model behind Java applets has been designed with the goal of protecting the user from malicious applets.

Applets that are not signed using a security certificate are untrusted and referred to as *unsigned applets*. When running on a client, unsigned applets operate within a security sandbox that allows only a set of safe operations.

Applets can be signed using a security certificate to indicate that they come from a trusted source. Signed applets operate outside the security sandbox and have extensive capabilities to access the client. A signed applet will run outside the security sandbox only if the user accepts the applet's security certificate. If the user refuses to accept the certificate, the applet will run within the security sandbox, similar to an unsigned applet.

With recent improvements to the Java Plug-In software, unsigned applets launched using JNLP can safely access the client *with the user's permission*. It is recommended that you launch your applet using JNLP to leverage expanded capabilities and improve user experience. See the "Deploying an Applet" section in this chapter for step-by-step instructions on applet deployment. In this section we will discuss the security restrictions and capabilities of applets.

Unsigned Applets

Unsigned applets can perform the following operations:

- They can make network connections to the host they came from.
- They can easily display HTML documents using the `showDocument` method of the `java.applet.AppletContext` class.
- They can invoke public methods of other applets on the same page.
- They can read secure system properties. See Chapter 18, "System Properties," for a list of secure system properties.
- When launched by using JNLP, unsigned applets can also perform the following operations:
  - They can open, read, and save files on the client.
  - They can access the shared system-wide clipboard.
  - They can access printing functions.
  - They can store data on the client, decide how applets should be downloaded and cached, and much more. See Chapter 18, "JNLP API," for more information about developing applets by using the JNLP API.

Unsigned applets cannot perform the following operations:

- They cannot access client resources such as the local file system, executable files, system clipboard, and printers.

17

- They cannot connect to or retrieve resources from any third party server (i.e., any server other than the server the applet originated from).
- They cannot load native libraries.
- They cannot change the `SecurityManager`.
- They cannot create a `ClassLoader`.
- They cannot read certain system properties. See Chapter 18, "System Properties," for a list of forbidden system properties.

Note that applets that are loaded from the local file system (from a directory in the user's `CLASSPATH`) have none of the restrictions that apply to applets loaded over the network.

Signed Applets

Signed applets do not have the security restrictions that are imposed on unsigned applets and can run outside the security sandbox. See Chapter 18, "Security in Rich Internet Applications," for information on how to work with signed and unsigned code.

> **Note**
>
> JavaScript code is treated like unsigned code. When a signed applet is accessed from JavaScript code in an HTML page, the applet is executed *within* the security sandbox. This implies that the signed applet essentially behaves likes an unsigned applet.

Additional Information

For more information about applet security dialog boxes, see the `oracle.com` article Exploring Security Warning Functionality.[26]

Solving Common Applet Problems

This section covers some common problems that you might encounter when writing Java applets. After each problem is a list of possible reasons and solutions.

"My Applet Does Not Display"

- Check the Java Console log for errors.
- Check the syntax of the applet's JNLP file. Incorrect JNLP files are the most common reason for failures without obvious errors.

---

26. `http://www.oracle.com/technetwork/articles/javase/appletwarning`
    `-135102.html`

- Check the JavaScript syntax if deploying using the `runApplet` function of the Deployment Toolkit. See Chapter 19, "Deploying an Applet," for details.

"The Java Console Log Displays java.lang.ClassNotFoundException"

- Make sure your Java source files compiled correctly.
- If deploying using the `<applet>` tag, check that the path to the applet JAR file is specified accurately in the `archive` attribute.
- If launching using a JNLP file, check the path in the `jar` tag in the JNLP file.
- Make sure the applet's JAR file, JNLP file, and web page are located in the correct directory and reference each other accurately.

"I Was Able to Build the Code Once, but Now the Build Fails Even Though There Are No Compilation Errors"

- Close your browser and run the build again. The browser most likely has a lock on the JAR file, and because of this, the build process is unable to regenerate the JAR file.

"When I Try to Load a Web Page That Has an Applet, My Browser Redirects Me to www.java.com without Any Warning"

- The applet on the web page is most likely deployed using the Deployment Toolkit script. The applet may require a later version of the JRE software than the version that currently exists on the client. Check the `minimumVersion` parameter of the `runApplet` function in the applet's web page. See Chapter 19, "Deploying an Applet," for details.

"I Fixed Some Bugs and Rebuilt My Applet's Source Code, but When I Reload the Applet's Web Page, My Fixes Are Not Showing Up"

- You may be viewing a previously cached version of the applet. Close the browser. Open the Java Control Panel and delete temporary Internet files. This will remove your applet from cache. Try viewing your applet again.

17

Questions and Exercises: Applets

Questions

1. Which classes can an applet extend?

2. When should you use the `start()` method?

3. True or false: An applet can make network connections to any host on the Internet.

4. How do you get the value of a parameter specified in the JNLP file from within the applet's code?

5. Which class enables applets to interact with JavaScript code in the applet's web page?

6. True or false: Applets can modify the contents of the parent web page.

Exercises

1. The `Exercise` applet's parent web page has a JavaScript variable called `memberId`. Write the code to set the value of the `memberId` equal to `123489` in the applet's `start` method.

2. Try an `oracle.com` quiz[27] about Java applets.

Answers

You can find answers to these questions and exercises at `http://docs.oracle.com/javase/tutorial/deployment/applet/QandE/answers.html`.

---

27. `tutorial/JWS/flash/AppletQuiz/AppletQuiz.html`

18

Doing More with Java Rich Internet Applications

Chapter Contents

Applets launched by using the JNLP have capabilities similar to those of Java Web Start applications. This chapter contains topics common to the development and deployment of applets and Java Web Start applications (together known as *rich Internet applications*, or *RIAs*). If you are unfamiliar with applets or Java Web Start applications, you can learn more in the following chapters:

- To learn more about applet development and deployment, see Chapter 17.
- To learn more about the development and deployment of Java Web Start applications, see Chapter 16.

Setting Trusted Arguments and Secure Properties

You can set certain Java Virtual Machine (Java VM) arguments and secure properties for your RIA in the JNLP file. For applets, you can also set arguments in the `java_arguments` parameter of the `<applet>` tag. Although there is a predefined set of secure properties, you can also define new secure properties by prefixing the property name with `jnlp.` or `javaws.`. Properties can be retrieved in your RIA by using the `System.getProperty` method.

Consider the `Properties and Arguments Demo` applet. The following Java VM arguments and properties are set in the applet's JNLP file, `appletpropsargs.jnlp`:

- `-Xmx`—A secure argument set equal to "256M"
- `sun.java2d.noddraw`—A predefined secure property set equal to "true"
- `jnlp.myProperty`—A user-defined secure property set equal to "a user-defined property"

Here is the applet:

```
<?xml version="1.0" encoding="UTF-8"?>
<jnlp spec="1.0+" codebase="" href="">
    <information>
        <title>Properties and Arguments Demo Applet</title>
        <vendor>Dynamic Team</vendor>
    </information>
    <resources>
        <!-- Application Resources -->
        <j2se version="1.6+"
            href="http://java.sun.com/products/autodl/j2se"
            <!-- secure java vm argument -->
            java-vm-args="-Xmx256M"/>
        <jar href="applet_PropertiesAndVMArgs.jar"
            main="true" />
            <!-- secure properties -->
        <property name="sun.java2d.noddraw"
            value="true"/>
        <property name="jnlp.myProperty"
            value="a user-defined property"/>
    </resources>
    <applet-desc
        name="Properties and Arguments Demo Applet"
        main-class="PropertiesArgsDemoApplet"
        width="800"
        height="50">
    </applet-desc>
    <update check="background"/>
</jnlp>
```

The `PropertiesArgsDemoApplet` class uses the `System.getProperty` method to retrieve the `java.version` property and other properties that are set in the JNLP file. The `PropertiesArgsDemoApplet` class also displays the properties:

```
import javax.swing.JApplet;
import javax.swing.SwingUtilities;
import javax.swing.JLabel;

public class PropertiesArgsDemoApplet extends JApplet {
    public void init() {
        final String javaVersion = System.getProperty("java.version");
        final String  swing2dNoDrawProperty =
            System.getProperty("sun.java2d.noddraw");
```

18

```
            final String  jnlpMyProperty =
                System.getProperty("jnlp.myProperty");

            try {
                SwingUtilities.invokeAndWait(new Runnable() {
                    public void run() {
                        createGUI(javaVersion, swing2dNoDrawProperty,
                            jnlpMyProperty);
                    }
                });
            } catch (Exception e) {
                System.err.println("createGUI didn't successfully complete");
            }
        }
        private void createGUI(String javaVersion,
            String swing2dNoDrawProperty, String jnlpMyProperty) {
            String text = "Properties: java.version = " + javaVersion +
                    ",  sun.java2d.noddraw = " + swing2dNoDrawProperty +
                    ",  jnlp.myProperty = " + jnlpMyProperty;
            JLabel lbl = new JLabel(text);
            add(lbl);
        }
    }
```

The section that follows provides a complete set of system properties that can be accessed by RIAs.

System Properties

This topic lists system properties that can be accessed by *unsigned* RIAs that are launched with or without the JNLP. Some system properties cannot be accessed by unsigned RIAs.

Secure System Properties Accessible by All RIAs

All RIAs can retrieve the following secure system properties:

- `java.class.version`
- `java.vendor`
- `java.vendor.url`
- `java.version`
- `os.name`
- `os.arch`
- `os.version`
- `file.separator`
- `path.separator`
- `line.separator`

18

Secure System Properties Accessible by RIAs Launched by Using JNLP

RIAs launched by using JNLP can set and retrieve the following secure properties:

- `awt.useSystemAAFontSettings`
- `http.agent`
- `http.keepAlive`
- `java.awt.syncLWRequests`
- `java.awt.Window.locationByPlatform`
- `javaws.cfg.jauthenticator`
- `javax.swing.defaultlf`
- `sun.awt.noerasebackground`
- `sun.awt.erasebackgroundonresize`
- `sun.java2d.d3d`
- `sun.java2d.dpiaware`
- `sun.java2d.noddraw`
- `sun.java2d.opengl`
- `swing.boldMetal`
- `swing.metalTheme`
- `swing.noxp`
- `swing.useSystemFontSettings`

Forbidden System Properties

Unsigned RIAs cannot access the following system properties:

- `java.class.path`
- `java.home`
- `user.dir`
- `user.home`
- `user.name`

18

JNLP API

RIAs can use the JNLP Application Programming Interface (API) to perform extensive operations on the user's environment. When launched by using JNLP, even unsigned RIAs can perform the following operations with the user's permission:

- They can use the `FileOpenService`[1] and `FileSaveService`[2] API to access the user's file system.
- They can use the `ClipboardService`[3] API to access the shared system-wide clipboard.
- They can use the `PrintService`[4] API to access printing functions.
- They can use the `PersistenceService`[5] API to access persistence storage.
- They can use the `DownloadService`[6] API to control how the RIA is downloaded and cached.
- They can use the `DownloadServiceListener`[7] API to determine progress of the RIA's download.
- They can use the `SingleInstanceService`[8] API to decide how to handle arguments when multiple instances of the RIA are launched.
- They can use the `ExtendedService`[9] API to request permission to open certain files that have not been opened before.

Check the JNLP API documentation[10] to see the complete list of the functionality available to RIAs that are launched by using JNLP.

Accessing the Client Using JNLP API

When launched by using the JNLP, RIAs can access the client with the user's permission. Consider the applet example `TextEditor`[11] to understand how to use JNLP API based services. `TextEditor` has a text area and buttons labeled *Open*, *Save*, and *Save As*. `TextEditor` can be used to open an existing text file, edit it, and save it back to disk.

---

1. 7/docs/jre/api/javaws/jnlp/javax/jnlp/FileOpenService.html
2. 7/docs/jre/api/javaws/jnlp/javax/jnlp/FileSaveService.html
3. 7/docs/jre/api/javaws/jnlp/javax/jnlp/ClipboardService.html
4. 7/docs/jre/api/javaws/jnlp/javax/jnlp/PrintService.html
5. 7/docs/jre/api/javaws/jnlp/javax/jnlp/PersistenceService.html
6. 7/docs/jre/api/javaws/jnlp/javax/jnlp/DownloadService.html
7. 7/docs/jre/api/javaws/jnlp/javax/jnlp/DownloadServiceListener.html
8. 7/docs/jre/api/javaws/jnlp/javax/jnlp/SingleInstanceService.html
9. 7/docs/jre/api/javaws/jnlp/javax/jnlp/ExtendedService.html
10. 7/docs/jre/api/javaws/jnlp/javax/jnlp/package-summary.html
11. tutorial/deployment/doingMoreWithRIA/examples/applet_JNLP_API/src/
    TextEditor.java

The `TextEditor` and `TextEditorApplet` classes lay out the user interface and display it as an applet. The `FileHandler` class contains the core functionality with respect to using JNLP API based services. Remember, the techniques described in this topic apply to Java Web Start applications as well.

To make use of a JNLP service, first retrieve a reference to the service. The `initialize` method of the `FileHandler` class retrieves references to JNLP services as shown in the following code snippet:

```
private static synchronized void initialize() {
    . . .
    try {
        fos = (FileOpenService)
            ServiceManager.lookup("javax.jnlp.FileOpenService");
        fss = (FileSaveService)
            ServiceManager.lookup("javax.jnlp.FileSaveService");
    } catch (UnavailableServiceException e) {
        . . .
    }
}
```

After you have a reference to the required services, invoke methods on the service to perform the necessary operations. The `open` method of the `FileHandler` class invokes the `openFileDialog` method of the `FileOpenService` class to display a file chooser. The `open` method returns the contents of the selected file:

```
public static String open() {
    initialize();
    try {
        fc = fos.openFileDialog(null, null);
        return readFromFile(fc);
    } catch (IOException ioe) {
        ioe.printStackTrace(System.out);
        return null;
    }
}
```

Similarly, the `save` and `saveAs` methods of the `FileHandler` class invoke corresponding methods of the `FileSaveService`[12] class to enable the user to select a file name and save the contents of the text area to disk:

```
public static void saveAs(String txt) {
    initialize();
    try {
        if (fc == null) {
            // If not already saved.
            // Save-as is like save
            save(txt);
```

---

12. `7/docs/jre/api/javaws/jnlp/javax/jnlp/FileSaveService.html`

```
            } else {
                fc = fss.saveAsFileDialog(null, null, fc);
                save(txt);
            }
        } catch (IOException ioe) {
            ioe.printStackTrace(System.out);
        }
    }
```

At runtime, when the RIA attempts to open or save a file, users see a security dialog asking them if they want to allow the action. The operation will proceed only if users allow the RIA to access their environment.

Here is the complete source of the FileHandler class:[13]

```
// add javaws.jar to the classpath during compilation
import javax.jnlp.FileOpenService;
import javax.jnlp.FileSaveService;
import javax.jnlp.FileContents;
import javax.jnlp.ServiceManager;
import javax.jnlp.UnavailableServiceException;
import java.io.*;

public class FileHandler {

    static private FileOpenService fos = null;
    static private FileSaveService fss = null;
    static private FileContents fc = null;

    // retrieves a reference to the JNLP services
    private static synchronized void initialize() {
        if (fss != null) {
            return;
        }
        try {
            fos = (FileOpenService)
                ServiceManager.lookup("javax.jnlp.FileOpenService");
            fss = (FileSaveService)
                ServiceManager.lookup("javax.jnlp.FileSaveService");
        } catch (UnavailableServiceException e) {
            fos = null;
            fss = null;
        }
    }

    // displays open file dialog and reads selected file using
    // FileOpenService
    public static String open() {
        initialize();
        try {
            fc = fos.openFileDialog(null, null);
```

---

13. tutorial/deployment/doingMoreWithRIA/examples/applet_JNLP_API/src/
    FileHandler.java

```
            return readFromFile(fc);
        } catch (IOException ioe) {
            ioe.printStackTrace(System.out);
            return null;
        }
    }

    // displays saveFileDialog and saves file using FileSaveService
    public static void save(String txt) {
        initialize();
        try {
            // Show save dialog if no name is already given
            if (fc == null) {
                fc = fss.saveFileDialog(null, null,
                        new ByteArrayInputStream(txt.getBytes()), null);
                // file saved, done
                return;
            }
            // use this only when filename is known
            if (fc != null) {
                writeToFile(txt, fc);
            }
        } catch (IOException ioe) {
            ioe.printStackTrace(System.out);
        }
    }

    // displays saveAsFileDialog and saves file using FileSaveService
    public static void saveAs(String txt) {
        initialize();
        try {
            if (fc == null) {
                // If not already saved. Save-as is like save
                save(txt);
            } else {
                fc = fss.saveAsFileDialog(null, null, fc);
                save(txt);
            }
        } catch (IOException ioe) {
            ioe.printStackTrace(System.out);
        }
    }

    private static void writeToFile(String txt, FileContents fc) throws
        IOException {
        int sizeNeeded = txt.length() * 2;
        if (sizeNeeded > fc.getMaxLength()) {
            fc.setMaxLength(sizeNeeded);
        }
        BufferedWriter os = new BufferedWriter(new OutputStreamWriter(fc.
            getOutputStream(true)));
        os.write(txt);
        os.close();
    }

    private static String readFromFile(FileContents fc) throws IOException {
        if (fc == null) {
            return null;
        }
```

```
        BufferedReader br = new BufferedReader(new InputStreamReader
            (fc.getInputStream()));
        StringBuffer sb = new StringBuffer((int) fc.getLength());
        String line = br.readLine();
        while (line != null) {
            sb.append(line);
            sb.append("\n");
            line = br.readLine();
        }
        br.close();
        return sb.toString();
    }
}
```

> **Note**
>
> To compile Java code that has a reference to classes in the `javax.jnlp` package, include `<your JDK path>/jre/lib/javaws.jar` in your class path. At runtime, the Java Runtime Environment (JRE) software automatically makes these classes available to RIAs.

Cookies

Web applications are typically a series of HTTP requests and responses. Because HTTP is a stateless protocol, information is not automatically saved between HTTP requests. Web applications use cookies to store state information on the client. Cookies can be used to store information about the user, the user's shopping cart, and so on.

Types of Cookies

There are two types of cookies:

- *Session cookies*. These are stored in memory and are accessible as long as the user is using the web application. Session cookies are lost when the user exits the web application. Such cookies are identified by a session ID and are most commonly used to store details of a shopping cart.
- *Permanent cookies*. These are used to store long-term information such as user preferences and user identification information. Permanent cookies are stored in persistent storage and are not lost when the user exits the application. Permanent cookies are only lost when they expire.

Cookie Support in RIAs

RIAs (applets and Java Web Start applications) support session and permanent cookies. The underlying cookie store depends on the browser and the operating system on the client.

To learn more about cookies, see the following:

- The Working with Cookies[14] lesson in the online version of the Java Tutorial
- The API Documentation for CookieManager[15] and related classes

Accessing Cookies

You can set and retrieve cookies in your RIA. Cookies can enhance the capabilities of your RIA. For example, consider the scenario where you have applets on various web pages. An applet on a web page cannot directly access or share information with an applet on another web page. In this scenario, cookies provide an important connection between applets and help one applet pass information to another applet on a different web page. Java Web Start applications can also use cookies to store information on the client.

The `Cookie` applet example discussed in the following sections has a `CookieAccessor`[16] class that retrieves and sets cookies.

Retrieving Cookies

The following code snippet shows the `getCookieUsingCookieHandler` method of the `CookieAccessor` class:

```
public void getCookieUsingCookieHandler() {
    try {
        // Instantiate CookieManager;
        // make sure to set CookiePolicy
        CookieManager manager = new CookieManager();
        manager.setCookiePolicy(CookiePolicy.ACCEPT_ALL);
        CookieHandler.setDefault(manager);

        // get content from URLConnection;
        // cookies are set by web site
        URL url = new URL("http://www.example.com");
        URLConnection connection = url.openConnection();
        connection.getContent();

        // get cookies from underlying
        // CookieStore
        CookieStore cookieJar =  manager.getCookieStore();
        List <HttpCookie> cookies =
            cookieJar.getCookies();
        for (HttpCookie cookie: cookies) {
          System.out.println("CookieHandler retrieved cookie: " + cookie);
```

18

---

14. `tutorial/networking/cookies/index.html`

15. `7/docs/api/java/net/CookieManager.html`

16. `tutorial/deployment/doingMoreWithRIA/examples/applet_AccessingCookies/`
    `src/CookieAccessor.java`

```
                }
            } catch(Exception e) {
                System.out.println("Unable to get cookie using CookieHandler");
                e.printStackTrace();
            }
        }
```

The `CookieManager` class is the main entry point for cookie management. Create an instance of the `CookieManager` class and set its `CookiePolicy`.[17] Set this instance of the `CookieManager` as the default `CookieHandler`.[18]

Open a `URLConnection`[19] to the web site of your choice. In the example, the cookies that are set by the web site `www.example.com` are retrieved.

Next, retrieve cookies from the underlying `CookieStore`[20] by using the get-Cookies method.

Setting Cookies

The following code snippet shows the `setCookieUsingCookieHandler` method of the `CookieAccessor` class:

```
public void setCookieUsingCookieHandler() {
    try {
        // instantiate CookieManager
        CookieManager manager = new CookieManager();
        CookieHandler.setDefault(manager);
        CookieStore cookieJar =  manager.getCookieStore();

        // create cookie
        HttpCookie cookie = new HttpCookie("UserName", "John Doe");

        // add cookie to CookieStore for a
        // particular URL
        URL url = new URL("http://www.example.com");
        cookieJar.add(url.toURI(), cookie);
        System.out.println("Added cookie using cookie handler");
    } catch(Exception e) {
        System.out.println("Unable to set cookie using CookieHandler");
        e.printStackTrace();
    }
}
```

As shown in the "Retrieving Cookies" section of this chapter, the `CookieManager` class is the main entry point for cookie management. Create an instance of the `CookieManager` class and set the instance as the default `CookieHandler`.

18

17. 7/docs/api/java/net/CookiePolicy.html

18. 7/docs/api/java/net/CookieHandler.html

19. 7/docs/api/java/net/URLConnection.html

20. 7/docs/api/java/net/CookieStore.html

Create the desired HttpCookie[21] with the necessary information. In our example, we have created a new HttpCookie that sets the UserName as John Doe.
Next, add the cookie to the underlying cookie store.

> **Note**
> You must sign your RIA JAR file in order to access cookies. See the documentation for the jarsigner[22] tool to learn how to sign JAR files.

Customizing the Loading Experience

RIAs may take a few seconds to load depending on factors such as network speed and resources required by the RIA. Customize the RIA loading experience by providing a splash screen or a customized loading progress indicator to engage the end user during the loading process and to communicate measurable progress information.

While the overall mechanisms to customize the loading experience for applets and Java Web Start applications are similar, there are subtle differences in syntax and implementation. See the following sections for step-by-step instructions and conceptual information about customizing the RIA loading experience:

- Chapter 16, "Displaying a Customized Loading Progress Indicator" (for a Java Web Start application)
- Chapter 17, "Displaying a Customized Loading Progress Indicator" (for an applet)
- Chapter 19, "Customizing the Loading Screen"

Security in RIAs

The security model behind RIAs ensures that the user is protected from malicious Internet applications. This topic discusses security aspects that are common to applets and Java Web Start applications. See the following sections for more information:

- Chapter 16, "Java Web Start and Security"
- Chapter 17, "What Applets Can and Cannot Do"

Unsigned RIAs run in a restricted environment known as a security sandbox. Apply the following guidelines to enable RIAs to run outside the security sandbox:

---

21. 7/docs/api/java/net/HttpCookie.html

22. 7/docs/technotes/tools/index.html#security

- Sign the JAR file of a RIA if code in the JAR file needs additional permissions to perform operations outside the sandbox, such as accessing the local file system or network resources. Specify the `all-permissions` element in the JNLP file for the RIA. For more information, see Chapter 15, "Signing and Verifying JAR Files." The following code snippet shows the `all-permissions` element in the RIA's JNLP file:

```
<security>
    <all-permissions/>
</security>
```

  If the certificate used to sign the RIA has not been previously approved, the JRE software opens a dialog box displaying the RIA's origin based on the signer's certificate. The user can then make an informed decision about running the application.

- A JNLP file can only include JAR files signed by the same certificate. If you have JAR files that are signed using different certificates, specify them in separate JNLP files. Create a separate JNLP file for unsigned JAR files. In the RIA's main JNLP file, specify the `component-desc` element to include the other JNLP files as component extensions. See Chapter 19, "Structure of the JNLP File," for information.

- The security model for RIAs does not allow code from an unsigned JAR file or JavaScript code from a web page to invoke security-sensitive code in a signed JAR file unless you explicitly enable this. In the signed JAR file, wrap the section of code that you want unsigned code to be able to invoke in a `AccessController.doPrivileged`[23] block. This allows the unsigned code to run with elevated permissions when executing the code in the `doPrivileged` code block.

- Avoid mixing signed and unsigned JARs in a RIA, if possible, as they can raise security warnings about mixed code. See Mixing Signed and Unsigned Code[24] for more information.

Questions and Exercises:
Doing More with Java Rich Internet Applications

Questions

1. True or false: Rich Internet applications (RIAs) can set secure properties by prefixing the property name with `jnlp.`

---

23. `7/docs/api/java/security/AccessController.html`
24. `7/docs/technotes/guides/jweb/mixed_code.html`

2. True or false: Only signed RIAs can use JNLP API to access files on the client.

Exercise

1. To the following JNLP file, add a secure property called `jnlp.foo` and set its value to `true`:

```
<?xml version="1.0" encoding="UTF-8"?>
<jnlp spec="1.0+" codebase="" href="">
    <information>
        <title>Dynamic Tree Demo</title>
        <vendor>Dynamic Team</vendor>

    </information>
    <resources>
        <!-- Application Resources -->
        <j2se version="1.6+" href=
            "http://java.sun.com/products/autodl/j2se" />
        <jar href="DynamicTreeDemo.jar" main="true" />
    </resources>
    <applet-desc
        name="Dynamic Tree Demo Applet"
        main-class="components.DynamicTreeApplet"
        width="300"
        height="300">
     </applet-desc>
     <update check="background"/>
</jnlp>
```

Answers

You can find answers to these questions and exercises at `http://docs.oracle.com/javase/tutorial/deployment/doingMoreWithRIA/QandE/answers.html`.

18

19

Deployment in Depth

Chapter Contents

Rich Internet application (RIA) deployment involves various technologies and tools such as the Java Network Launch Protocol (JNLP), Deployment Toolkit, pack200, jarsigner, and so on. This chapter explores how these technologies and tools help developers deploy RIAs (applets and Java Web Start applications).

The main components that are involved in RIA deployment are the following:

- The HTML page in which the RIA will be deployed
- The JNLP file for the RIA
- The JAR file containing the class files and resources of the RIA

These components are discussed in more detail throughout the chapter.

Deployment Toolkit

The Deployment Toolkit script is a set of JavaScript functions that can help developers deploy rich Internet applications (RIAs) consistently across various browser and operating system configurations. The Deployment Toolkit script evaluates the underlying browser and operating system and deploys the RIA with the correct HTML. This script can also ensure that the required version of the Java Runtime

Environment (JRE) software is present on the client machine. The Deployment Toolkit script was introduced in the Java Platform SE 6 update 10 release.

Location of Deployment Toolkit Script

The Deployment Toolkit script exists at the following web addresses:

- `http://www.java.com/js/deployJava.js`
- `https://www.java.com/js/deployJava.js`—When deploying your applet on a secure page, use the Deployment Toolkit script from this secure location to avoid mixed content warnings when the page is loaded.

The JavaScript code in these locations has been minimized so that it can load quickly. There is also a human readable version of the JavaScript code available online.[1]

> **Note**
>
> The JavaScript interpreter should be enabled in the client's browser so that the Deployment Toolkit script can run and deploy your RIA properly.

Deploying an Applet

You can deploy applets by using the `runApplet` function of the Deployment Toolkit script. The `runApplet` function ensures that the required minimum version of the JRE software exists on the client and then runs the applet. The `runApplet` function generates an HTML `<applet>` tag with the information provided.

> **Note**
>
> Depending on the type of browser, you might be unable to view the HTML generated by the Deployment Toolkit script when you try to view the source for the web page. To view the generated HTML, try saving the HTML page after it has been loaded or use a tool such as Firebug (a Mozilla Firefox add-on).

You can deploy applets by specifying the deployment options as attributes and parameters of the `<applet>` tag. You can also specify deployment options in a JNLP file to take advantage of advanced features. See the "Java Network Launch Protocol" section in this chapter for more information about this protocol.

---

1. `http://www.java.com/js/deployJava.txt`

> **Note**
> If the client does not have the required minimum version of the JRE software, the Deployment Toolkit script redirects the browser to www.java.com to allow users to download the latest JRE software. On some platforms, users might be redirected before they can view the web page containing the applet.

The parameters to the `runApplet` function vary depending on if you are using JNLP. Applets deployed by using JNLP can run only if the next generation Java Plug-In software exists on the client machine. (The next generation Java Plug-In software was introduced in Java Platform SE 6 update 10.)

The remainder of this section shows how to use the `runApplet` function in the HTML page that will display the applet. Here is the first function: `runApplet: function(attributes, parameters, minimumVersion)`.

Here are the *parameters*:

- `attributes`—The names and values of the attributes of the generated `<applet>` tag
- `parameters`—The names and values of the `<param>` tags in the generated `<applet>` tag
- `minimumVersion`—The minimum version of the JRE software that is required to run this applet

Here are some *usage scenarios*:

- *Specify deployment options as attribute and parameter name-value pairs.* The attributes and parameters passed as name-value pairs are written out as attributes and nested `<param>` tags in the generated `<applet>` tag. Applets deployed in this manner can be run by the old Java Plug-In software.

```
// launch the Java 2D applet on JRE version 1.6.0
// or higher with one parameter (fontSize)
<script src=
    "http://www.java.com/js/deployJava.js"></script>
<script>
    var attributes = {code:'java2d.Java2DemoApplet.class',
        archive:'http://java.sun.com/products/plugin/1.5.0/demos/
            plugin/jfc/Java2D/Java2Demo.jar',
        width:710, height:540} ;
    var parameters = {fontSize:16} ;
    var version = '1.6' ;
    deployJava.runApplet(attributes, parameters, version);
</script>
```

19

- *Use the `jnlp_href` parameter to specify deployment options in a JNLP file.*
  The attributes and parameters (`jnlp_href` in this case) passed as name-value pairs are written out as attributes and nested `<param>` tags in the generated `<applet>` tag. Applets deployed in this manner can be run by the next generation Java Plug-In software only. It is better to specify the applet's width and height as attributes:

```
<script src="http://www.java.com/js/deployJava.js"></script>
<script>
    var attributes = {code:'java2d.Java2DemoApplet', width:710,
                      height:540} ;
    var parameters = {jnlp_href: 'java2d.jnlp'} ;
    deployJava.runApplet(attributes, parameters, '1.6');
</script>
```

- *Specify attribute and parameter name-value pairs as well as a JNLP file.*
  Applets deployed by using JNLP will run only if end users have the next generation Java Plug-In software running on their browsers. If you would like your applet to also run on the old Java Plug-In software, specify deployment options using attribute and parameter name-value pairs as well as a JNLP file:

```
<script src="http://www.java.com/js/deployJava.js"></script>
<script>
    var attributes = {code:'java2d.Java2DemoApplet.class',
            archive:'http://java.sun.com/products/plugin/1.5.0/
                    demos/plugin/jfc/Java2D/Java2Demo.jar',
            width:710, height:540} ;
    var parameters = {fontSize:16, jnlp_href:'java2d.jnlp'} ;
    var version = '1.6' ;
    deployJava.runApplet(attributes, parameters, version);
</script>
```

The following guidelines are helpful if some deployment options have different values in the attribute name-value pairs and in the JNLP file:

- Specify `width` and `height` as attribute name-value pairs (not in the JNLP file).
- Specify parameters such as `image` and `boxbgcolor` as parameter name-value pairs (not in the JNLP file). These parameters are needed early on in the applet start-up process.
- In the JNLP file, leave the `codebase` attribute empty or specify an absolute URL. When the `codebase` attribute is left empty, it defaults to the directory containing the JNLP file.
- If the applet is launched using a JNLP file, the values for the `code`, `codebase`, and `archive` attributes are taken from the JNLP file. If these attributes are also specified separately as attribute name-value pairs, the attribute name-value pairs are ignored.

Customizing the Loading Screen

A default loading screen is displayed when an applet is being loaded in the web page. You can display a customized splash screen by specifying the following parameters when you deploy the applet:

- `image`—The image to be displayed in the splash screen
- `boxbgcolor`—The background color of the area in which the applet will be displayed
- `boxborder`—Defines whether the applet should have a border (defaults to `true`)
- `centerimage`—The position of the image (defaults to `false`)

The splash screen can display a static image or an animated gif.

The code snippet from `AppletPage.html`[2] shows how to customize the splash screen to display an animation of the Duke, the Java mascot:

```
<script src="http://www.java.com/js/deployJava.js"></script>
<script>
  var attributes = {code:'SwingSet2Applet.class',
      archive:'SwingSet2.jar', width:695, height:525} ;
    <!-- customize splash screen display options -->
  var parameters = {jnlp_href: 'SwingSet2.jnlp',
                    image: 'dukeanimated.gif',
                    boxbgcolor: 'cyan',
                    boxborder: 'true',
                    centerimage: 'true'
                    } ;
  deployJava.runApplet(attributes, parameters, '1.6');
</script>
```

See Chapter 17, "Displaying a Customized Loading Progress Indicator," for information about displaying a customized loading progress indicator when the applet's resources are being downloaded.

Embedding a JNLP File in an Applet Tag

When applets are deployed via the JNLP, the Java Plug-In software launches the applet after downloading the JNLP file from the network. Beginning in the JDK 7 release, you can reduce the time it takes for applets to launch by embedding the JNLP file in the web page itself so that an additional network request can be avoided the first time the applet is loaded. This will result in applets launching quickly on the web browser.

19

---

2. `tutorial/deployment/deploymentInDepth/examples/dist/depltoolkit`
    `_CustomizingSplashScreen/AppletPage.html`

A Base64 encoded JNLP file can be embedded in the `jnlp_embedded` parameter when deploying an applet in a web page. The attributes of the `<jnlp>` element should meet the following restrictions:

- The `href` attribute should contain a relative path.
- The `codebase` attribute should not be specified. This implies that the code base will be derived from the URL of the web page in which the applet is loaded.

The following steps describe how to embed a JNLP file in a web page to deploy an applet.

1. Create a JNLP file for your applet. Here is an example file:

```
<?xml version="1.0" encoding="UTF-8"?>
<!-- href attribute contains relative path;
     codebase attribute not specified -->
<jnlp href="dynamictree-applet.jnlp">
    <information>
        <title>Dynamic Tree Demo</title>
        <vendor>Dynamic Team</vendor>
    </information>
    <resources>
        <!-- Application Resources -->
        <j2se version="1.6+" />
        <jar href=
            "dist/applet_ComponentArch_DynamicTreeDemo/
                DynamicTreeDemo.jar"
             main="true" />
    </resources>
    <applet-desc
        name="Dynamic Tree Demo Applet"
        main-class="appletComponentArch.DynamicTreeApplet"
        width="300"
        height="300">
    </applet-desc>
    <update check="background"/>
</jnlp>
```

2. Encode the contents of the JNLP file using the Base64 scheme. You can use any Base64 encoding tool to encode the JNLP file. Check the usage of the tool to create a string with Base64 encoding. Some examples of tools and web sites that may be used are as follows:

   - Unix commands—base64, uuencode
   - Web sites—Base64 Encode and Decode,[3] Base64 Encoder[4]

3. When deploying the applet in a web page, specify the `jnlp_embedded` parameter with its value set to the Base64 encoded JNLP string. Make sure to include

3. `http://base64encode.org`

4. `http://www.opinionatedgeek.com/dotnet/tools/base64encode`

only the actual Base64 bytes without any encoding tool specific headers or footers.

```
<script src="http://www.java.com/js/deployJava.js"></script>
<script>
    var attributes = {} ;
    <!-- Base64 encoded string truncated below for readability -->
    var parameters = {jnlp_href: 'dynamictree-applet.jnlp',
        jnlp_embedded: 'PCEtLSAKLyoKICogQ29weX . . . HA+Cg=='
    } ;
    deployJava.runApplet(attributes, parameters, '1.6');
</script>
```

Some encoding tools may wrap the encoded string into several 76-column lines. To use this multiline attribute value in JavaScript code, specify the attribute value as a set of concatenated strings. You can include the multiline attribute value as is if the applet is deployed directly with the `<applet>` HTML tag.

Deploying a Java Web Start Application

You can deploy Java Web Start applications by using the `createWebStart-LaunchButton` function of the Deployment Toolkit script. Java Web Start applications are launched using JNLP. The `createWebStartLaunchButton` function generates a link (using the HTML anchor tag, `<a>`) to the Java Web Start application's JNLP file.

This generated anchor tag is the Java Web Start application's Launch button. When the end user clicks the Launch button, the Deployment Toolkit script ensures that the appropriate JRE software is installed and then launches the Java Web Start application.

> **Note**
>
> Depending on the type of browser, you might be unable to view the HTML generated by the Deployment Toolkit script when you try to view the source for the web page (as mentioned previously). To view the generated HTML, try saving the HTML page after it has been loaded, or use a tool such as Firebug (a Mozilla Firefox add-on). Also, if the client does not have the required minimum version of the JRE software, the Deployment Toolkit script redirects the browser to www.java.com to allow users to download the latest JRE software.

Here are the functions: `createWebStartLaunchButton: function(jnlp)` or `createWebStartLaunchButton: function(jnlp, minimumVersion)`.

Here are the *parameters*:

- `jnlp`—The URL of the JNLP file containing deployment information for the Java Web Start application (which should be an absolute path)

19

- `minimumVersion`—The minimum version of JRE software required to run this application

Here are some *usage scenarios*:

- *Specify a minimum version of JRE software that is required to run the application:*

```
<script src="http://www.java.com/js/deployJava.js"></script>
<script>
    var url = "http://java.sun.com/javase/technologies/desktop/
                javawebstart/apps/notepad.jnlp";
    deployJava.createWebStartLaunchButton(url, '1.6.0');
</script>
```

- *Enable a Java Web Start application to run on any JRE software version.* Use the `createWebStartLaunchButton: function(jnlp)` function if your application does not have a minimum JRE software version requirement.

> **Note**
>
> When deploying by using any of the previously described `createWebStartLaunchButton`
> functions, you must specify an absolute code base in the Java Web Start application's JNLP
> file. This enables the Java Web Start application to be launched from the command line
> with the `javaws <path/to/local JNLP file>` command.

Changing the Launch Button

You can change your Java Web Start application's Launch button image if you don't like the default Launch button or if you have another standardized image. Use the `deployJava.launchButtonPNG` variable to point to the location of your Launch button's image via the alternate image's URL.

The following example changes a Notepad application's Launch button to an image of Duke waving:

```
<script src="http://www.java.com/js/deployJava.js"></script>
<script>
    deployJava.launchButtonPNG='http://docs.oracle.com/javase/tutorial/
                images/DukeWave.gif';
    var url = "http://docs.oracle.com/javase/tutorialJWS/deployment/
                webstart/examples/Notepad.jnlp";
    deployJava.createWebStartLaunchButton(url, '1.6.0');
</script>
```

Deploying without Codebase

Beginning in the JDK 7 release, you do not have to specify an absolute path for the codebase attribute in the Java Web Start application's JNLP file. You can develop and test your applications in different environments without having to modify the path in the codebase attribute. If no code base is specified, the Java Web Start software assumes that the code base is relative to the web page from which the Java Web Start application is launched.

The following functions of the Deployment Toolkit script can be used to deploy Java Web Start applications in a web page when the JNLP file does not contain the codebase attribute:

- `launchWebStartApplication`—Use this function in an HTML link to deploy your Java Web Start application.
- `createWebStartLaunchButtonEx`—Use this function to create a Launch button for your Java Web Start application.

> **Note**
>
> To run, Java Web Start applications deployed by using the previously specified functions require at least the JDK 7 release. If the client does not have at least the JDK 7 release, the functions instruct the user to install the required JRE software before launching the Java Web Start application.

Here is the first function: `launchWebStartApplication: function(jnlp)`. Here is the *parameter*:

- `jnlp`—The path to the JNLP file containing deployment information for the Java Web Start application, which can be relative to the web page where the Java Web Start application is deployed

Here is a *usage scenario*: In the following example, the `launchWebStartApplication` function is invoked in the `href` attribute of an HTML anchor (a) tag. The `dynamictree-webstart-no-codebase.jnlp` JNLP file is used to deploy the `Dynamic Tree Demo` application:

```
<script src="http://www.java.com/js/deployJava.js"></script>
<a href="javascript:deployJava.launchWebStartApplication('dynamictree-
webstart-no-codebase.jnlp');">Launch</a>
```

The Java Web Start application is launched when the user clicks the resulting HTML link.

Here is the second function: `createWebStartLaunchButtonEx:function(jnlp)`. Here is the *parameter*:

- `jnlp`—The path to the JNLP file containing deployment information for the Java Web Start application, which can be relative to the web page where the Java Web Start application is deployed

19

Here is a *usage scenario*: The following example shows the usage of the `createWebStartLaunchButtonEx` function. The `dynamictree-webstart-no-codebase.jnlp` JNLP file is used to deploy the `Dynamic Tree Demo` application:

```
<script src="http://www.java.com/js/deployJava.js"></script>
<script>
    var jnlpFile = "dynamictree-webstart-no-codebase.jnlp";
    deployJava.createWebStartLaunchButtonEx(jnlpFile);
</script>
```

The Java Web Start application is launched when the user clicks the resulting Launch button.

Checking the Client JRE Software Version

There are many reasons to check if a particular version of the JRE software is available on a client machine. For example, you might want to launch a different version of your RIA or redirect the user to a different page depending on the client's JRE software version.

Use the Deployment Toolkit script's `versionCheck` function to check if a particular version or range of JRE versions is installed on the client.

Here is the function: `versionCheck:function(versionPattern)`.

Here is the *parameter*:

- `versionPattern`—String specifying the version or range of versions to check for, such as such as `1.4`, `1.5.0*` (`1.5.` and family), and `1.6.0_02+` (any version greater than or equal to 1.6.0_02)

Here is a *usage scenario*: In this example, we create a different user experience depending on the client's JRE software version. Here, a Launch button is created for the Notepad application only if the version of JRE software on the client is greater than or equal to 1.6. If not, the browser redirects the user to `oracle.com`:

```
<script src="http://www.java.com/js/deployJava.js"></script>
<script>
    if (deployJava.versionCheck('1.6+')) {
        var url = "http://docs.oracle.com/javase/tutorialJWS/deployment/
                    webstart/examples/Notepad.jnlp";

        <!-- you can also invoke deployJava.runApplet here -->
        deployJava.createWebStartLaunchButton(url, '1.6.0');
    } else {
        document.location.href="http://oracle.com";
    }
</script>
```

> **Note**
>
> Depending on the client's operating system and version of the Java platform, you might be able to verify version information for JRE software at the major version level (e.g., 1.6) or at a finer update level (e.g., 1.6.0_10).

Java Network Launch Protocol

The Java Network Launch Protocol (JNLP) enables an application to be launched on a client desktop by using resources that are hosted on a remote web server. Java Plug-In software and Java Web Start software are considered JNLP clients because they can launch remotely hosted applets and applications on a client desktop. See the Java Network Launching Protocol and API Specification[5] for details.

Recent improvements in deployment technologies enable us to launch RIAs by using JNLP. Both applets and Java Web Start applications can be launched by using this protocol. RIAs that are launched by using JNLP also have access to JNLP APIs. These JNLP APIs allow the RIAs to access the client desktop with the user's permission.

JNLP is enabled by a RIA's JNLP file. The JNLP file describes the RIA. The JNLP file specifies the name of the main JAR file, the version of JRE software that is required to run the RIA, name and display information, optional packages, runtime parameters, system properties, and so on.

You can find more information about deploying RIAs by using JNLP in the following sections:

- Chapter 16, "Deploying a Java Web Start Application"
- Chapter 17, "Deploying an Applet"
- Chapter 18, "JNLP API"
- "Structure of the JNLP File" in this chapter

Structure of the JNLP File

This section describes the syntax of the JNLP file for RIAs. The following code snippet shows a sample JNLP file for a Java Web Start application:

```
<?xml version="1.0" encoding="UTF-8"?>
<jnlp spec="1.0+" codebase="" href="">
    <information>
```

19

---

5. http://www.oracle.com/technetwork/java/javase/downloads/download
   -spec-142476.html

```
            <title>Dynamic Tree Demo</title>
            <vendor>Dynamic Team</vendor>
            <icon href="sometree-icon.jpg"/>
            <offline-allowed/>
        </information>
        <resources>
            <!-- Application Resources -->
            <j2se version="1.6+" href=
                "http://java.sun.com/products/autodl/j2se"/>
            <jar href="DynamicTreeDemo.jar"
                main="true" />

        </resources>
        <application-desc
            name="Dynamic Tree Demo Application"
            main-class="webstartComponentArch.DynamicTreeApplication"
            width="300"
            height="300">
        </application-desc>
        <update check="background"/>
    </jnlp>
```

Table 19.1 describes the elements and attributes commonly used in JNLP files.

Note

Table 19.1 does not include all possible contents of the JNLP file. For more information, see the Java Network Launching Protocol and API Specification.

Encoding JNLP Files

Java Web Start software supports encoding of JNLP files in any character encoding supported by the Java platform. For more information about character encoding in the Java platform, see the Supported Encodings Guide.[6] To encode a JNLP file, specify an encoding in the XML prolog of that file. For example, the following line indicates that the JNLP file is encoded in UTF-16:

```
<?xml version="1.0" encoding="utf-16"?>
```

Note

The XML prolog itself must be UTF-8-encoded.

6. 7/docs/technotes/guides/intl/encoding.doc.html

Table 19.1 Commonly Used Elements and Attributes in a JNLP file

Element	Attributes	Description	Since	Required
jnlp		The topmost xml element for a JNLP file	1.0	Yes
	spec	Value of the attribute can be 1.0, 1.5, or 6.0, or can use wildcards such as 1.0+. It denotes the minimum version of the JNLP specification that this JNLP file can work with.	1.0	
	codebase	The base location for all relative URLs specified in href attributes in the JNLP file	1.0	
	href	The URL of the JNLP file itself	1.0	
	version	The version of the RIA being launched, as well as the version of the JNLP file itself	1.0	
information		Contains other elements that describe the RIA and its source	1.0	Yes
	os	The operating system for which this information element should be considered	1.5.0	
	arch	The architecture for which this information element should be considered	1.5.0	
	platform	The platform for which this information element should be considered	1.5.0	
	locale	The locale for which this information element should be considered	1.5.0	
title		The title of the RIA	1.0	Yes
vendor		The provider of the RIA	1.0	Yes
homepage		The homepage of the RIA	1.0	
	href	A URL pointing to where more information about this RIA can be found	1.0	Yes
description		A short statement describing the RIA	1.0	
	kind	An indicator as to the type of description. Legal values are one-line, short, and tooltip.	1.0	

(continued)

19

Table 19.1 Commonly Used Elements and Attributes in a JNLP file (continued)

Element	Attributes	Description	Since	Required
icon		An icon that can be used to identify the RIA to the user	1.0	
	href	A URL pointing to the icon file. This can be in one of the following formats: gif, jpg, png, ico.	1.0	Yes
	kind	Indicates the suggested use of the icon. This can be default, selected, disabled, rollover, splash, or shortcut.	1.0	
	width	Can be used to indicate the resolution of the image	1.0	
	height	Can be used to indicate the resolution of the image	1.0	
	depth	Can be used to indicate the resolution of the image	1.0	
offline-allowed		Indicates that this RIA can operate when the client system is disconnected from the network	1.0	
shortcut		Can be used to indicate the RIA's preferences for desktop integration	1.5.0	
	online	Can be used to describe the RIA's preference for creating a shortcut to run online or offline	1.5.0	
desktop		Can be used to indicate the RIA's preference for putting a shortcut on the user's desktop	1.5.0	
menu		Can be used to indicate the RIA's preference for putting a menu item in the user's start menus	1.5.0	
	sub-menu	Can be used to indicate the RIA's preference for where to place the menu item	1.5.0	
association		Can be used to hint to the JNLP client that the RIA wants to be registered with the operating system as the primary handler of certain extensions and a certain MIME type	1.5.0	
	extensions	A list of file extensions (separated by spaces) that the RIA requests it be registered to handle	1.5.0	
	mimetype	The MIME type that the RIA requests it be registered to handle	1.5.0	

19

Element	Description	Version	Required
related-content	An additional piece of related content that can be integrated with the RIA	1.5.0	
href	A URL pointing to the related content	1.5.0	Yes
update	The preferences for how RIA updates should be handled by the JNLP client	1.6.0	
check	The preference for when the JNLP client should check for updates. Value can be always, timeout, or background.	1.6.0	
policy	The preference for how the JNLP client should handle a RIA update when a new version is available before the RIA is launched. Values can be always, prompt-update, or prompt-run.	1.6.0	
security	Can be used to request enhanced permissions	1.0	
all-permissions	Requests that the RIA be run with all permissions	1.0	
j2ee-application-client-permissions	Requests that the RIA be run with a permission set that meets the security specifications of the J2EE application client environment	1.0	
resources	Describes all the resources that are needed for the RIA	1.0	Yes
os	The operating system for which the resources element should be considered	1.0	
arch	The architecture for which the resources element should be considered	1.0	
locale	The locales for which the resources element should be considered	1.0	
java or j2se	Versions of Java software to run the RIA with	1.6.0 (java)	
version	Ordered list of version ranges to use	1.0	Yes
href	The URL denoting the supplier of this version of Java software and from where it can be downloaded	1.0	

(continued)

19

Table 19.1 Commonly Used Elements and Attributes in a JNLP file (continued)

Element	Attributes	Description	Since	Required
	java-vm-args	An additional set of standard and nonstandard virtual machine arguments that the RIA would prefer the JNLP client use when launching the JRE software	1.0	
	initial-heap-size	The initial size of the Java heap	1.0	
	max-heap-size	The maximum size of the Java heap	1.0	
jar		A JAR file that is part of the RIA's class path	1.0	Yes
	href	The URL of the JAR file	1.0	Yes
	version	The requested version of the JAR file. This requires using the version-based download protocol.	1.0	
	main	Indicates if this JAR file contains the class containing the main method of the RIA	1.0	
	download	Indicates that this JAR file can be downloaded lazily or when needed	1.0	
	size	The downloadable size of the JAR file in bytes	1.0	
	part	Can be used to group resources together so that they are downloaded at the same time	1.0	
nativelib		A JAR file that contains native libraries in its root directory	1.0	
	href	The URL of the JAR file	1.0	Yes
	version	The requested version of the JAR file. Requires using the version-based download protocol.	1.0	
	download	Can be used to indicate this JAR file can be downloaded lazily	1.0	
	size	The downloadable size of the JAR file in bytes	1.0	
	part	Can be used to group resources together so they will be downloaded at the same time	1.0	

Element	Attribute	Description	Version	Required
extension		A pointer to an additional component-desc or installer-desc to be used with this RIA	1.0	
	href	The URL to the additional extension JNLP file	1.0	Yes
	version	The version of the additional extension JNLP file	1.0	
	name	The name of the additional extension JNLP file	1.0	
ext-download		Can be used in an extension element to denote the parts contained in a component-extension	1.0	
	ext-part	The name of a part that can be expected in the extension	1.0	Yes
	download	Can be used to indicate this extension and downloaded eagerly or lazily	1.0	
	part	Denotes the name of a part in this JNLP file in which to include the extension	1.0	Yes
package		Can be used to indicate to the JNLP client which packages are implemented in which JAR files	1.0	
	name	Package name contained in the JAR files of the given part	1.0	Yes
	part	Part name containing the JAR files that include the given package name	1.0	Yes
	recursive	Can be used to indicate that all package names, beginning with the given name, can be found in the given part	1.0	
property		Defines a system property that will be available through the System.getProperty and System.getProperties methods	1.0	
	name	Name of the system property	1.0	Yes
	value	Value of the system property	1.0	Yes
		Note: A JNLP file must contain one of the following: application-desc, applet-desc, component-desc, or installer-desc.	1.0	Yes

(continued)

19

Table 19.1 Commonly Used Elements and Attributes in a JNLP file (continued)

Element	Attributes	Description	Since	Required
`application-desc`		Denotes this is the JNLP file for an application	1.0	
	`main-class`	The name of the class containing the `public static void main(String[])` method of the application	1.0	Yes
`argument`		Each argument contains (in order) an additional argument to be passed to the `main` method.	1.0	
`applet-desc`		Denotes this is the JNLP file for an applet	1.0	
	`main-class`	The name of the main applet class	1.0	Yes
	`document-base`	The document base for the applet as a URL	1.0	
	`name`	Name of the applet	1.0	Yes
	`width`	The width of the applet in pixels	1.0	Yes
	`height`	The height of the applet in pixels	1.0	Yes
`param`		A set of parameters that can be passed to the applet	1.0	
	`name`	The name of this parameter	1.0	Yes
	`value`	The value of this parameter	1.0	Yes
`component-desc`		Denotes this is the JNLP file for a component extension	1.0	
`installer-desc`		Denotes this is the JNLP file for an installed extension	1.0	
	`main-class`	The name of the class containing the `public static void main(String[])` method of the installer	1.0	Yes

19

Deployment Best Practices

You can improve the user experience of your RIA using the following best practices:

- Optimize the size of JAR files and related resources so that your RIA can load quickly. See the "Reducing the Download Time" section for optimization techniques.

- Enable the version download protocol and use background update checks to enable your RIA to start quickly. See the "Avoiding Unnecessary Update Checks" section to learn more about the version download protocol and update checks.

- Sign JAR files only when absolutely necessary. See the "Signing JAR Files Only When Necessary" section to learn when to sign your RIA.

- Make sure that the client has the required version of the JRE software. See the "Ensuring the Presence of the JRE Software" section for details on how the Deployment Toolkit script can be used for this purpose.

- Embed the contents of your applet's JNLP file in the <applet> tag to avoid loading the JNLP file from the network. This feature was introduced in the JDK 7 release. See the "Embedding JNLP File in Applet Tag" section to learn how to embed the contents of the applet's JNLP file in the web page.

- Preload your Java Web Start application, if possible. If you plan to deploy your RIA as a Java Web Start application in an enterprise where you have some administrative control, you can preload your application to various clients so that it is cached and ready to use. Use the following command to preload your Java Web Start application:

```
javaws -import -silent <jnlp url>
```

Reducing the Download Time

RIAs are downloaded from a web site when the user tries to access them. (RIAs can be cached after the initial download to improve performance.) The time taken to download a RIA depends on the size of the RIA's JAR file. Larger JAR files take longer to download.

You can reduce the download time of your RIA by applying the following techniques:

- Compress your RIA's JAR file by using the pack200[7] tool.

19

---

7. 7/docs/technotes/tools/share/pack200.html

- Remove unnecessary white space from the JNLP file and the JavaScript files.
- Optimize images and animation.

The following sections discuss pack200 compression for signed and unsigned RIAs.

Compressing the JAR File for an Unsigned RIA

The following steps describe how to create and deploy a compressed JAR file for an unsigned RIA:

1. Compress the JAR file of your RIA:

   ```
   // compresses DynamicTreeDemo.jar to produce DynamicTreeDemo.jar.
   pack.gz
   pack200 DynamicTreeDemo.jar.pack.gz DynamicTreeDemo.jar
   ```

2. Set the `jnlp.packEnabled` property to `true` in the RIA's JNLP file:

   ```
   <resources>
       <j2se version="1.6+"
           href="http://java.sun.com/products/autodl/j2se"
                 max-heap-size="128m" />
       <jar href="DynamicTreeDemo.jar"
           main="true"/>
       <property name="jnlp.packEnabled"
           value="true"/>
       <!-- . . . -->
   </resources>
   ```

Compressing and Signing RIA JAR File

The following steps describe how to create and deploy a compressed JAR file for a signed RIA. See the "Signing JAR Files Only When Necessary" section in this chapter to understand the impact of signing JAR files:

1. Normalize the JAR file using the `--repack` option. This step ensures that the security certificate and JAR file will pass verification checks when the RIA is launched:

   ```
   pack200 --repack DynamicTreeDemo.jar
   ```

2. Sign the normalized JAR file. Here, `myKeyStore` is the name of the keystore and `me` is the alias for the keystore:

   ```
   jarsigner -keystore myKeyStore DynamicTreeDemo.jar me
   ```

3. Pack the signed JAR file:

   ```
   pack200 DynamicTreeDemo.jar.pack.gz DynamicTreeDemo.jar
   ```

4. Set the `jnlp.packEnabled` property to `true` in the RIA's JNLP file:

```
<resources>
    <j2se version="1.6+"
        href="http://java.sun.com/products/autodl/j2se"
            max-heap-size="128m" />
    <jar href="DynamicTreeDemo.jar"
        main="true"/>
    <property name="jnlp.packEnabled"
        value="true"/>
    <!-- . . . -->
</resources>
```

When the `jnlp.packEnabled` property is set in the JNLP file, the Java Plug-In software looks for the compressed JAR file with the `.pack.gz` extension (e.g., `DynamicTreeDemo.jar.pack.gz`). If found, the Java Plug-In software automatically unpacks and loads the JAR file. If a file with the `.pack.gz` extension is not found, then the Java Plug-In software attempts to load the regular JAR file (e.g., `DynamicTreeDemo.jar`).

> **Note**
>
> You need to deploy your RIA on a web server to test the `jnlp.packEnabled` property.

Avoiding Unnecessary Update Checks

RIAs are cached locally to improve start-up time. However, before launching a RIA, the launch software checks to make sure that every JAR file referenced in the RIA's JNLP file is up to date. In other words, the launch software makes sure that you are running the latest version of the RIA and not an older cached copy. These update checks can take up to a few hundred milliseconds depending on the number of JAR files and network speed. Use the techniques described in this topic to avoid unnecessary update checks and to enhance the start-up time of your RIA.

> **Note**
>
> The phrase "launch software" is used here to collectively refer to the Java Plug-In software and the Java Web Start software. The Java Plug-In software launches applets while the Java Web Start software launches Java Web Start applications.

19

Leveraging the Version Download Protocol

You can leverage the *version download protocol* to eliminate unnecessary version checks. See the following steps to enable this protocol:

1. Rename the JAR files to include a version number suffix with the following naming convention:

   ```
   <JAR file name>__V<version number>.jar
   ```

   For example, rename `DynamicTreeDemo.jar` to `DynamicTreeDemo__V1.0.jar`.

2. In the JNLP file, specify a version for every JAR file, and set the `jnlp.versionEnabled` property to `true`:

   ```
   <resources>
       <!-- Application Resources -->
       <j2se version="1.6+"
           href="http://java.sun.com/products/autodl/j2se"
               max-heap-size="128m" />
       <jar href="DynamicTreeDemo.jar"
           main="true" version="1.0"/>
       <jar href="SomeOther.jar" version="2.0"/>
       <property name="jnlp.versionEnabled"
           value="true"/>
       <!-- . . . -->
   </resources>
   ```

When the `jnlp.versionEnabled` property is enabled, the launch software performs only *one* update check to make sure that the JNLP file is up to date. The software compares the version numbers that are specified in the JNLP file with the corresponding JAR file versions (according to the naming convention mentioned in step 1) and updates only the outdated JAR files. This approach is efficient because only the update check for the JNLP file occurs over the network. All other version checks occur locally. If a file with the correct version number is not found, the launch software attempts to load the default JAR file (e.g., `DynamicTreeDemo.jar`).

Performing Update Checks in the Background

If it is not critical for the user to immediately run the latest version of your RIA, you can specify that all update checks should occur in the background. In this case, the launch software launches the locally cached copy for immediate usage and downloads a newer version of the RIA in the background. The newer version of the RIA will be launched the next time the user attempts to use your RIA. To enable background update checks, add the following line to your JNLP file:

```
<update check='background'/>
```

The following code snippet shows a sample JNLP file with the background update check enabled:

```
<?xml version="1.0" encoding="UTF-8"?>
<jnlp spec="1.0+" codebase="" href="">
    <information>
        <title>Applet Takes Params</title>
        <vendor>Dynamic Team</vendor>
    </information>
    <resources>
        <!-- Application Resources -->
        <j2se version="1.6+" href=
            "http://java.sun.com/products/autodl/j2se"/>
        <jar href="applet_AppletWithParameters.jar"
            main="true" />
    </resources>
    <applet-desc
        name="Applet Takes Params"
        main-class="AppletTakesParams"
        width="800"
        height="50">
            <param name="paramStr" value="someString"/>
            <param name="paramInt" value="22"/>
    </applet-desc>
    <update check="background"/>
</jnlp>
```

Signing JAR Files Only When Necessary

Signed RIAs display security warnings when the user tries to launch and use the RIA. When users are trying to access a simple RIA, security dialog boxes might unnerve them and turn them away from the application. Thus you should only sign your RIA when it's necessary (e.g., when accessing native libraries).

Recent enhancements to the RIA technology eliminate the need to sign your RIA in the following cases:

- *Accessing services on web sites other than the RIA's own domain.* In the past, RIAs could only communicate with the server from which they were launched. The Java Plug-In software and the Java Web Start software now support cross-domain policy files. If a third-party site has set up cross-domain policies and allows access from other domains, your unsigned RIAs can invoke services from this site.

- *Setting trusted Java Virtual Machine arguments and secure properties.* You do not need to sign your RIA to set trusted Java Virtual Machine arguments or secure properties. You can set secure arguments and properties in the JNLP file. See Chapter 18, "System Properties," for more information.

19

- *Accessing certain client resources.* RIAs that are launched by using JNLP can access the client's resources with the user's permission. See Chapter 18, "JNLP API," for details on how to use the JNLP API to access the client.

See the following sections for more security related information about RIAs:

- Chapter 16, "Java Web Start and Security"
- Chapter 17, "What Applets Can and Cannot Do"

Ensuring the Presence of the JRE Software

RIAs usually need a minimum version of the JRE software to be present on the client machine. When deploying a RIA, you need to ensure that client machines have the required version of the JRE software so that your RIA can function well. With the Deployment Toolkit script, you have at least two ways to handle this requirement:

- You can check the version of client JRE software as soon as users access your web site and install the latest version if necessary.
- You can let users navigate the web site and check and install the latest JRE only when they attempt to use your RIA.

Checking and Installing the Latest JRE Software When the User Accesses Your Web Site

The following example checks if a user has at least version 1.6.0_13 of the JRE software installed. If not, the code installs the latest JRE software. See in-line comments in the code.

```
<script src="http://www.java.com/js/deployJava.js"></script>
<script>

    // check if current JRE version is greater than 1.6.0
    alert("versioncheck " + deployJava.versionCheck('1.6.0_10+'));
    if (deployJava.versionCheck('1.6.0_10+') == false) {
        userInput = confirm(
            "You need the latest Java(TM) Runtime Environment. " +
            "Would you like to update now?");
        if (userInput == true) {

            // Set deployJava.returnPage to make sure user comes back to
            // your web site after installing the JRE
            deployJava.returnPage = location.href;

            // Install latest JRE or redirect user to another page to get JRE
            deployJava.installLatestJRE();
        }
    }
</script>
```

Installing the Correct JRE Software Only When the User Attempts to Use Your RIA

When you specify the minimum version of the JRE software in the `runApplet` or `createWebStartLaunchButton` function, the Deployment Toolkit script makes sure that the required version of the JRE software exists on the client before running your RIA.

Use the `runApplet` function to deploy an applet, as shown in the following example. The last parameter of the `runApplet` function is the minimum version that is required to the run your applet (version 1.6).

```
<script src="http://www.java.com/js/deployJava.js"></script>
<script>
    var attributes = { code:'components.DynamicTreeApplet',
        width:300, height:300};
    var parameters = {jnlp_href: 'dynamictree-applet.jnlp'};
    deployJava.runApplet(attributes, parameters, '1.6');
</script>
```

To deploy a Java Web Start application, use the `createWebStartLaunchButton` function with the correct minimum version parameter (version 1.6).

```
<script src="http://www.java.com/js/deployJava.js"></script>
<script>
    var url = "dynamictree-applet.jnlp";
    deployJava.createWebStartLaunchButton(url, '1.6.0');
</script>
```

The `runApplet` and `createWebStartLaunchButton` functions check the client's version of the JRE software. If the minimum version is not installed, the functions install the latest version of the JRE software.

Questions and Exercises: Deployment In Depth

Questions

1. What script contains functions to deploy applets and Java Web Start applications?
2. True or false: You should always sign your RIA just to be sure it will always work.

Exercise

1. Write the JavaScript code to deploy the `Exercise` applet using the `ex.jnlp` file.

Answers

You can find answers to these questions and exercises at `http://docs.oracle.com/javase/tutorial/deployment/deploymentInDepth/QandE/answers.html`.

Appendix

Preparing for
Java Programming
Language Certification

Chapter Contents

Oracle provides three certification examinations and two certificates for Java SE 7 programmers. This book can be a valuable resource to help you prepare for the certification exams.

For more information on Oracle Java Certification and Oracle Java Training, including information on classes, exams, and prerequisites, go to oracle.com and click the Training tab. This appendix describes the three exams; it lists the sections of this book and external resources that contain pertinent and valuable information to use when preparing for these exams.

Programmer Level I Exam

This section discusses topics covered in the Java SE 7 Programmer I exam. This exam is associated with the "Oracle Certified Associate, Java SE 7 Programmer" certificate and includes eight topics.

Section 1: Java Basics

Item 1: Define the scope of variables.

- Chapter 3: Variables

Item 2: Define the structure of a Java class.

- Chapter 1: A Closer Look at the "Hello World!" Application
- Chapter 4: Classes

Item 3: Create executable Java applications with a main method.

- Chapter 1: "Hello World!" for the NetBeans IDE
- Chapter 1: "Hello World!" for Microsoft Windows
- Chapter 1: "Hello World!" for Solaris OS and Linux
- Chapter 1: A Closer Look at the "Hello World!" Application

Item 4: Import other Java packages to make them accessible in your code.

- Chapter 7: Creating and Using Packages
- Chapter 7: Using Package Members

Section 2: Working with Java Data Types

Item 1: Declare and initialize variables.

- Chapter 3: Variables
- Chapter 4: Initializing Fields

Item 2: Differentiate between object reference variables and primitive variables.

- Chapter 3: Primitive Data Types
- Chapter 8: The Numbers Classes

Item 3: Read or write to object fields.

- Chapter 5: Inheritance
- Chapter 4: Declaring Member Variables
- Chapter 4: Creating Objects
- Chapter 4: Using Objects

Item 4: Explain an object's life cycle.

- Chapter 4: Objects
- Chapter 4: Creating Objects
- Chapter 4: Using Objects

A

Item 5: Call methods on objects.

- Chapter 4: Using Objects

Item 6: Manipulate data using the `StringBuilder` class and its methods.

- Chapter 8: The StringBuilder Class
- Chapter 8: Summary of Characters and Strings

Item 7: Create and manipulate strings.

- Chapter 8: Strings
- Chapter 8: Converting between Numbers and Strings
- Chapter 8: Comparing Strings and Portions of Strings
- Chapter 8: Manipulating Characters in a String

Section 3: Using Operators and Decision Constructs

Item 1: Use Java operators.

- Chapter 3: Operators
- Chapter 3: Assignment, Arithmetic, and Unary Operators
- Chapter 3: Equality, Relational, and Conditional Operators
- Chapter 3: Bitwise and Bit Shift Operators

Item 2: Use parentheses to override operator precedence.

- Chapter 3: Expressions, Statements, and Blocks

Item 3: Test equality between strings and other objects using `==` and `equals()`.

- Chapter 5: Object as a Superclass

Item 4: Create and use `if-else` constructs.

- Chapter 3: The `if-then` and `if-then-else` Statements

Item 5: Use a `switch` statement.

- Chapter 3: The `switch` Statement

A

Section 4: Creating and Using Arrays

Item 1: Declare, instantiate, initialize, and use a one-dimensional array.

- Chapter 3: Arrays

Item 2: Declare, instantiate, initialize, and use a multidimensional array.

- Chapter 3: Arrays

Item 3: Declare and use an `ArrayList`.

- Chapter 11: The List Interface
- Chapter 11: List Implementations

Section 5: Using Loop Constructs

Item 1: Create and use `while` loops.

- Chapter 3: The while and do-while Statements

Item 2: Create and use `for` loops including the enhanced `for` loop.

- Chapter 3: The for Statement

Item 3: Create and use `do-while` loops.

- Chapter 3: The while and do-while Statements

Item 4: Compare loop constructs.

- Chapter 3: Summary of Control Flow Statements

Item 5: Use `break` and `continue`.
- Chapter 3: Branching Statements

Section 6: Working with Methods and Encapsulation

Item 1: Create methods with arguments and return values.

- Chapter 4: Returning a Value from a Method

Item 2: Apply the `static` keyword to methods and fields.

- Chapter 3: Variables
- Chapter 4: Understanding Instance and Class Members

Item 3: Create an overloaded method.

- Chapter 4: Defining Methods

Item 4: Differentiate between default and user-defined constructors.

- Chapter 4: Providing Constructors for Your Classes

Item 5: Apply access modifiers.

- Chapter 4: Controlling Access to Members of a Class

Item 6: Apply encapsulation principles to a class.

- Chapter 5: Inheritance
- Chapter 4: Inner Class Example
- Chapter 4: Nested Classes

Item 7: Determine the effect upon object references and primitive values when they are passed into methods that change the values.

- Chapter 4: Passing Information to a Method or a Constructor

Section 7: Working with Inheritance

Item 1: Implement inheritance.

- Chapter 5: Inheritance
- Chapter 5: Overriding and Hiding Methods

Item 2: Develop code that demonstrates the use of polymorphism.

- Chapter 5: Polymorphism

Item 3: Differentiate between the type of a reference and the type of an object.

- Chapter 4: Creating Objects
- Chapter 4: Using Objects

Item 4: Determine when casting is necessary.

- Chapter 5: Inheritance

A

Item 5: Use `super` and `this` to access objects and constructors.

- Chapter 5: Using the Keyword super
- Chapter 4: Using the this Keyword

Item 6: Use abstract classes and interfaces.

- Chapter 5: Abstract Methods and Classes
- Chapter 5: Defining an Interface
- Chapter 5: Implementing an Interface

Section 8: Handling Exceptions

Item 1: Differentiate among checked exceptions, `RuntimeException`, and `Error`.

- Chapter 9: The Catch or Specify Requirement

Item 2: Create a `try-catch` block and determine how exceptions alter normal program flow.

- Chapter 9: Catching and Handling Exceptions
- Chapter 9: The try Block
- Chapter 9: The catch Blocks

Item 3: Describe what exceptions are used for in Java.

- Chapter 9: What Is an Exception?
- Chapter 9: Advantages of Exceptions

Item 4: Invoke a method that throws an exception.

- Chapter 10: Catching Exceptions

Item 5: Recognize common exception classes and categories.

Programmer Level II Exam

This section discusses topics covered in the Java SE 7 Programmer II exam. This exam is associated with the "Oracle Certified Professional, Java SE 7 Programmer" certificate and includes twelve topics.

Section 1: Java Class Design

Item 1: Use access modifiers: `private`, `protected`, `public`.

- Chapter 4: Controlling Access to Members of a Class

Item 2: Override methods.

- Chapter 5: Overriding and Hiding Methods
- Chapter 4: Defining Methods
- Chapter 5: Using the Keyword super

Item 3: Overload constructors and other methods appropriately.

- Chapter 4: Defining Methods

Item 4: Use the `instanceof` operator and casting.

- Chapter 5: Inheritance

Item 5: Use virtual method invocation.

- Chapter 5: Polymorphism

Item 6: Override methods from the `Object` class to improve the functionality of your class.

- Chapter 5: Overriding and Hiding Methods

Item 7: Use `package` and `import` statements.

- Chapter 7: Creating and Using Packages
- Chapter 7: Using Package Members

Section 2: Advanced Class Design

Item 1: Identify when and how to apply abstract classes.

- Chapter 5: Abstract Methods and Classes

Item 2: Construct abstract Java classes and subclasses.

- Chapter 5: Abstract Methods and Classes

A

Item 3: Use the `static` and `final` keywords.

- Chapter 3: Variables
- Chapter 4: Understanding Instance and Class Members

Item 4: Create top-level and nested classes.

- Chapter 4: Declaring Classes
- Chapter 4: Nested Classes

Item 5: Use enumerated types.

- Chapter 4: Enum Types

Section 3: Object-Oriented Design Principles

This book does not cover design patterns. The following references cover design patterns using the Java programming language:

- *Head First Design Patterns* by Elizabeth Freeman et al.
- *Java Design Pattern Essentials* by Tony Bevis

Item 1: Write code that declares, implements, and/or extends interfaces.

- Chapter 5: Defining an Interface
- Chapter 5: Interfaces
- Chapter 5: Implementing an Interface

Item 2: Choose between interface inheritance and class inheritance.
Item 3: Develop code that implements "is-a" and/or "has-a" relationships.
Item 4: Apply object composition principles.
Item 5: Design a class using the `singleton` design pattern.
Item 6: Write code to implement the Data Across Object (DAO) pattern.
Item 7: Design and create objects using a factory, and use factories from the API.

Section 4: Generics and Collections

Chapters 6 and 11 contain the most information on generics and collections, but consult the following sections in particular.
Item 1: Create a generic class.

- Chapter 6: Generic Types

A

Item 2: Use the diamond syntax to create a collection.

- Chapter 6: The Diamond

Item 3: Analyze the interoperability of collections that use raw types and generic types.

- Chapter 6: Raw Types
- Chapter 6: Type Inference and Instantiation of Generic Classes

Item 4: Use wrapper classes and autoboxing.

- Chapter 8: Autoboxing and Unboxing
- Chapter 11: Wrapper Implementations

Item 5: Create and use a `List`, a `Set`, and a `Deque`.

- Chapter 11: The List Interface
- Chapter 11: List Implementations
- Chapter 11: The Set Interface
- Chapter 11: List Implementations
- Chapter 11: The Queue Interface
- Chapter 11: Queue Implementations

Item 6: Create and use a `Map`.

- Chapter 11: The Map Interface
- Chapter 11: Map Implementations

Item 7: Use `java.util.Comparator` and `java.lang.Comparable`.

- Chapter 11: Object Ordering
- Chapter 11: The SortedMap Interface
- Chapter 11: The SortedSet Interface

Item 8: Sort and search arrays and lists.

- Chapter 11: Algorithms
- Chapter 11: The List Interface
- Chapter 11: Object Ordering
- Chapter 11: The SortedSet Interface
- Chapter 11: The SortedMap Interface

A

Section 5: String Processing

Item 1: Search, parse, and build strings.

- Chapter 8: Strings
- Chapter 8: Converting between Numbers and Strings
- Chapter 8: Comparing Strings and Portions of Strings
- Chapter 8: Manipulating Characters in a String

Item 2: Search, parse, and replace strings by using regular expressions.

- Chapter 13: Methods of the Pattern Class
- Chapter 13: Methods of the Matcher Class

Item 3: Use string formatting.

- Chapter 8: Strings
- Chapter 8: Formatting Numeric Print Output

Section 6: Exceptions and Assertions

Item 1: Use `throw` and `throws` statements.

- Chapter 9: Specifying the Exceptions Thrown by a Method
- Chapter 9: How to Throw Exceptions

Item 2: Use the `try` statement with multicatch and `finally` clauses.

- Chapter 9: Catching and Handling Exceptions
- Chapter 9: The try Block
- Chapter 9: The catch Blocks
- Chapter 9: The finally Block
- Chapter 9: Putting It All Together

Item 3: Autoclose resources with a `try-with-resources` statement.

- Chapter 9: The try-with-resources Statement

Item 4: Create custom exceptions.

- Chapter 9: Creating Exception Classes

Item 5: Test invariants by using assertions.

- Chapter 4: Questions and Exercises: Classes

Section 7: Java I/O Fundamentals

Item 1: Read and write data from the console.

- Chapter 10: I/O Streams
- Chapter 10: Byte Streams
- Chapter 10: I/O from the Command Line

Item 2: Use streams to read and write files.

- Chapter 10: File I/O (Featuring NIO.2)
- Chapter 10: Reading, Writing, and Creating Files
- Chapter 10: Creating and Reading Directories
- Chapter 10: Random Access Files

Section 8: Java File I/O (NIO.2)

Item 1: Use the Path class to operate on file and directory paths.

- Chapter 10: What Is a Path? (And Other File System Facts)
- Chapter 10: Path Operations

Item 2: Use the Files class to check, delete, copy, or move a file or directory.

- Chapter 10: File Operations
- Chapter 10: Checking a File or Directory
- Chapter 10: Deleting a File or Directory
- Chapter 10: Copying a File or Directory
- Chapter 10: Moving a File or Directory

Item 3: Read and change file and directory attributes.

- Chapter 10: Managing Metadata (File and File Store Attributes)

Item 4: Recursively access a directory tree.

- Chapter 10: Walking the File Tree

Item 5: Find a file by using the PathMatcher class.

- Chapter 10: Finding Files
- Chapter 10: What Is a Glob?

A

Item 6: Watch a directory for changes by using `WatchService`.

- Chapter 10: Watching a Directory for Changes

Section 9: Building Database Applications with JDBC

Item 1: Define the layout of the JDBC API.

- JDBC Basics—Getting Started: `http://docs.oracle.com/javase/tutorial/jdbc/basics/gettingstarted.html`

Item 2: Connect to a database by using a JDBC driver.

- Establishing a Connection: `http://docs.oracle.com/javase/tutorial/jdbc/basics/connecting.html`
- Connecting with `DataSource` Objects: `http://docs.oracle.com/javase/tutorial/jdbc/basics/sqldatasources.html`

Item 3: Update and query a database.

- Processing SQL Statements with JDBC: `http://docs.oracle.com/javase/tutorial/jdbc/basics/processingsqlstatements.html`

Item 4: Customize the transaction behavior of JDBC and commit transactions.

- Using Transactions: `http://docs.oracle.com/javase/tutorial/jdbc/basics/transactions.html`

Item 5: Use the JDBC 4.1 `RowSetProvider`, `RowSetFactory`, and `RowSet` interfaces.

- Using `RowSet` Objects: `http://docs.oracle.com/javase/tutorial/jdbc/basics/rowset.html`
- Using `JdbcRowSet` Objects: `http://docs.oracle.com/javase/tutorial/jdbc/basics/jdbcrowset.html`

Section 10: Threads

Item 1: Create and use the `Thread` class and the `Runtime` interface.

- Chapter 12: Defining and Starting a Thread

A

Item 2: Manage and control thread life cycle.

- Chapter 12: Pausing Execution with Sleep
- Chapter 12: Interrupts
- Chapter 12: Joins

Item 3: Synchronize thread access to shared data.

- Chapter 12: Synchronization
- Chapter 12: Thread Interference
- Chapter 12: Synchronized Methods
- Chapter 12: Intrinsic Locks and Synchronization

Item 4: Identify potential threading problems.

- Chapter 12: Memory Consistency Errors
- Chapter 12: Deadlock

Section 11: Concurrency

Item 1: Use `java.util.concurrent` collections.

- Chapter 12: Concurrent Collections

Item 2: Apply atomic variables and looks.

- Chapter 12: Atomic Variables

Item 3: Use `Executors` and `ThreadPools`.

- Chapter 12: Executors
- Chapter 12: Executor Interfaces
- Chapter 12: Thread Pools

Item 4: Use the parallel `Fork/Join` Framework.

- Chapter 12: Fork/Join

Section 12: Localization

Item 1: Read and set the locale by using the `Locale` object.

A

- Setting the Locale: `http://docs.oracle.com/javase/tutorial/i18n/locale/index.html`
- Creating a Locale: `http://docs.oracle.com/javase/tutorial/i18n/locale/create.html`

Item 2: Build a resource bundle for each locale.

- About the `ResourceBundle` Class: `http://docs.oracle.com/javase/tutorial/i18n/resbundle/concept.html`
- Backing a `ResourceBundle` with Properties Files: `http://docs.oracle.com/javase/tutorial/i18n/resbundle/propfile.html`

Item 3: Load a resource bundle in an application.

- Customizing Resource Bundle Loading: `http://docs.oracle.com/javase/tutorial/i18n/resbundle/control.html`

Item 4: Format text for localization by using `NumberFormat` and `DateFormat`.

- Customizing Resource Bundle Loading: `http://docs.oracle.com/javase/tutorial/i18n/format/numberintro.html`
- Dates and Times: `http://docs.oracle.com/javase/tutorial/i18n/format/dateintro.html`

Java SE 7 Upgrade Exam

This section discusses topics covered in the Update to Java SE 7 Programmer exam. This exam is associated with the "Oracle Certified Professional, Java SE 7 Programmer" certificate and includes six topics.

Section 1: Language Enhancements

Item 1: Use `String` in switch statement.

- Chapter 3: The switch Statement

Item 2: Use binary literals and numeric literals with underscores.

- Chapter 3: Primitive Data Types

Item 3: Use `try-with-resources`.

- Chapter 9: The try-with-resources Statement

A

Item 4: Use multicatch in exception statements.

- Chapter 9: The catch Blocks

Item 5: Use diamond syntax with generic declarations.

- Chapter 6: The Diamond

Item 6: Use more precise rethrow in exceptions.

- Rethrowing Exceptions with More Inclusive Type Checking (Java Guides): `http://docs.oracle.com/javase/7/docs/technotes/guides/language/catch-multiple.html`

Section 2: Design Patterns

The Java Tutorials do not cover Design Patterns topics. The following references cover design patterns using the Java programming language:

- *Head First Design Patterns* by Elizabeth Freeman et al.
- *Java Design Pattern Essentials* by Tony Bevis

Item 1: Design a class using the `singleton` design pattern.
Item 2: Identify when and how to use composition to solve business problems.
Item 3: Write code to implement the DAO pattern.
Item 4: Design a class that uses the `factory` design pattern.

Section 3: Database Applications with JDBC

Item 1: Describe the JDBC API.

- JDBC Basics—Getting Started: `http://docs.oracle.com/javase/tutorial/jdbc/basics/gettingstarted.html`

Item 2: Identify the Java statements required to connect to a database using JDBC.

- Establishing a Connection: `http://docs.oracle.com/javase/tutorial/jdbc/basics/connecting.html`
- Connecting with `DataSource` Objects: `http://docs.oracle.com/javase/tutorial/jdbc/basics/sqldatasources.html`

Item 3: Use the JDBC 4.1 `RowSetProvider`, `RowSetFactory`, and new `RowSet` interfaces.

- Using RowSet Objects: http://docs.oracle.com/javase/tutorial/ jdbc/basics/rowset.html
- Using JdbcRowSet Objects: http://docs.oracle.com/javase/ tutorial/jdbc/basics/jdbcrowset.html

Item 4: Use JDBC transactions.

- Using Transactions: http://docs.oracle.com/javase/tutorial/ jdbc/basics/transactions.html

Item 5: Use the proper JDBC API to submit queries and read results from the database.

- Processing SQL Statements with JDBC: http://docs.oracle.com/ javase/tutorial/jdbc/basics/processingsqlstatements.html

Item 6: Use JDBC `PreparedStatement` and `CallableStatement`.

- Using Advanced Data Types: http://docs.oracle.com/javase/ tutorial/jdbc/basics/sqltypes.html
- Using Stored Procedures: http://docs.oracle.com/javase/tutorial/ jdbc/basics/storedprocedures.html

Section 4: Concurrency

Item 1: Identify potential threading problems.

- Chapter 12: Memory Consistency Errors
- Chapter 12: Deadlock

Item 2: Use `java.util.concurrent` collections.

- Chapter 12: Concurrent Collections

Item 3: Use atomic variables and locks.

- Chapter 12: Atomic Variables

Item 4: Use `Executors` and `ThreadPools`.

- Chapter 12: Executors
- Chapter 12: Executor Interfaces
- Chapter 12: Thread Pools

A

Item 5: Use the parallel fork/join framework.

- Chapter 12: Fork/Join

Section 5: Localization

Item 1: Describe the advantages of localizing an application.

- Internationlization—Introduction: `http://docs.oracle.com/javase/tutorial/i18n/intro/index.html`

Item 2: Define what a locale represents.

- Setting the Locale: `http://docs.oracle.com/javase/tutorial/i18n/locale/index.html`

Item 3: Read and set the locale by using the `Locale` object.

- Setting the Locale: `http://docs.oracle.com/javase/tutorial/i18n/locale/index.html`
- Creating a Locale: `http://docs.oracle.com/javase/tutorial/i18n/locale/create.html`

Item 4: Build a resource bundle for each locale.

- About the `ResourceBundle` Class: `http://docs.oracle.com/javase/tutorial/i18n/resbundle/concept.html`
- Backing a `ResourceBundle` with Properties Files: `http://docs.oracle.com/javase/tutorial/i18n/resbundle/propfile.html`

Item 5: Call a resource bundle from an application.

- Customizing Resource Bundle Loading: `http://docs.oracle.com/javase/tutorial/i18n/resbundle/control.html`

Item 6: Select a resource bundle based on locale.

- About the `ResourceBundle` Class: `http://docs.oracle.com/javase/tutorial/i18n/resbundle/concept.html`

Item 7: Format text for localization by using `NumberFormat` and `DateFormat`.

- Numbers and Currencies: `http://docs.oracle.com/javase/tutorial/i18n/format/numberintro.html`

A

- Dates and Times: `http://docs.oracle.com/javase/tutorial/i18n/format/dateintro.html`

Section 6: Java File I/O (NIO.2)

Item 1: Use the `Path` class to operate on file and directory paths.

- Chapter 10: What Is a Path? (And Other File System Facts)
- Chapter 10: Path Operations

Item 2: Use the `Files` class to check, delete, copy, or move a file or directory.

- Chapter 10: File Operations
- Chapter 10: Checking a File or Directory
- Chapter 10: Deleting a File or Directory
- Chapter 10: Copying a File or Directory
- Chapter 10: Moving a File or Directory

Item 3: Read and change file and directory attributes.

- Chapter 10: Managing Metadata (File and File Store Attributes)

Item 4: Recursively access a directory tree.

- Chapter 10: Walking the File Tree

Item 5: Find a file by using the `PathMatcher` class.

- Chapter 10: Finding Files
- Chapter 10: What Is a Glob?

Item 6: Watch a directory for changes by using `WatchService`.

- Chapter 10: Watching a Directory for Changes

A

Index

The Java Tutorial
A Short Course on the Basics
Fifth Edition

ORACLE

FREE
Online Edition

Safari
Books Online

Your purchase of *The Java® Tutorial, Fifth Edition,* includes access to a free online edition for 45 days through the **Safari Books Online** subscription service. Nearly every Addison-Wesley Professional book is available online through **Safari Books Online**, along with thousands of books and videos from publishers such as Cisco Press, Exam Cram, IBM Press, O'Reilly Media, Prentice Hall, Que, Sams, and VMware Press.

Safari Books Online is a digital library providing searchable, on-demand access to thousands of technology, digital media, and professional development books and videos from leading publishers. With one monthly or yearly subscription price, you get unlimited access to learning tools and information on topics including mobile app and software development, tips and tricks on using your favorite gadgets, networking, project management, graphic design, and much more.

Activate your FREE Online Edition at
informit.com/safarifree

STEP 1:   Enter the coupon code: QUPUHFH.

STEP 2:   New Safari users, complete the brief registration form.
Safari subscribers, just log in.

If you have difficulty registering on Safari or accessing the online edition,
please e-mail customer-service@safaribooksonline.com